Pro SQL Server 2008
Service Broker

■■■

Klaus Aschenbrenner

Pro SQL Server 2008 Service Broker

Copyright © 2008 by Klaus Aschenbrenner

ISBN-13 : 978-1-4842-2039-9

ISBN-10 (pbk): 1-4842-2039-0

ISBN-13 : 978-1-4302-0865-5 (eBook)

DOI 10.1007/978-1-4302-0865-5

Lead Editor: Jonathan Gennick

Technical Reviewer: Fabio Ferracchiati

Editorial Board: Clay Andres, Steve Anglin, Ewan Buckingham, Tony Campbell, Gary Cornell,
   Jonathan Gennick, Kevin Goff, Matthew Moodie, Joseph Ottinger, Jeffrey Pepper, Frank Pohlmann,
   Ben Renow-Clarke, Dominic Shakeshaft, Matt Wade, Tom Welsh

Project Manager: Tracy Brown Collins

Copy Editor: Liz Welch

Associate Production Director: Kari Brooks-Copony

Production Editor: Katie Stence

Compositor: Patrick Cunningham

Proofreader: Lisa Hamilton

Indexer: Carol Burbo

Artist: April Milne

Cover Designer: Kurt Krames

Manufacturing Director: Tom Debolski

Distributed to the book trade worldwide by Springer-Verlag New York, Inc., 233 Spring Street, 6th Floor, New York, NY 10013. Phone 1-800-SPRINGER, fax 201-348-4505, e-mail orders-ny@springer-sbm.com, or visit http://www.springeronline.com.

For information on translations, please contact Apress directly at 2855 Telegraph Avenue, Suite 600, Berkeley, CA 94705. Phone 510-549-5930, fax 510-549-5939, e-mail info@apress.com, or visit http://www.apress.com.

Apress and friends of ED books may be purchased in bulk for academic, corporate, or promotional use. eBook versions and licenses are also available for most titles. For more information, reference our Special Bulk Sales—eBook Licensing web page at http://www.apress.com/info/bulksales.

The source code for this book is available to readers at http://www.apress.com.

For Karin. Every day that starts with you turns out to be a great day.
I will always love you.

Contents at a Glance

About the Author xv

About the Technical Reviewer xvii

Acknowledgments xix

Introduction xxi

PART 1 ■■■ The Service Broker Programming Model

■CHAPTER 1   Fundamentals of Message-Based Processing.................... 3

■CHAPTER 2   Introducing Service Broker.................................. 17

■CHAPTER 3   Service Broker in Action 33

■CHAPTER 4   Service Broker Activation 73

■CHAPTER 5   Service Broker with Managed Code 127

■CHAPTER 6   Locking and Transaction Management 163

■CHAPTER 7   Distributed Service Broker Applications 239

PART 2 ■■■ Advanced Service Broker Programming

■CHAPTER 8   Advanced Distributed Service Broker Progamming 271

■CHAPTER 9   Service-Oriented Database Architecture 305

■CHAPTER 10   Real-World Application Scenarios 351

■CHAPTER 11   High Availability and Scalability 461

■CHAPTER 12   Administration 513

■INDEX 551

Contents

About the Author xv

About the Technical Reviewer xvii

Acknowledgments xix

Introduction xxi

PART 1 ■■■ The Service Broker Programming Model

■CHAPTER 1   **Fundamentals of Message-Based Processing** 3

Message Concepts 4

    Message Anatomy 4

    Messaging in Daily Life 5

Why Messaging? 6

    Asynchronous Message Processing 6

    Deferred Message Processing 7

    Fault Tolerance 7

    Distributed Systems 8

Messaging Problems 9

    Performance 9

    Queue Reader Management 10

    Transaction Management 10

    Message Sequencing and Correlation 11

    Maintenance 12

Messaging Architectures 12

    SOA 12

    SODA 13

Available Messaging Technologies 14

    MSMQ 14

    Queued Components 15

    BizTalk Server 15

    XML Web Services 15

    WCF 15

Summary 16

■**CHAPTER 2**   **Introducing Service Broker**............................... 17

    Conversations.. 17

        Dialogs... 18

        Dialog Lifetime 18

        Conversation Groups 19

        Message Sequencing 20

        Reliable Delivery 21

        Error Handling.. 22

    Anatomy of a Service 22

        Message Types 23

        Contracts... 24

        Queues... 25

        Service Programs..................................... 26

        Routes 26

    Security.. 26

        Transport Security.................................... 27

        Dialog Security 27

    Message Processing... 28

    Performance.. 29

    Benefits.. 31

    Summary... 31

■**CHAPTER 3**   **Service Broker in Action**................................. 33

    Defining Service Broker Applications........................... 33

    Message Types 34

    Contracts.. 37

    Queue 41

    Service.. 43

    Sending Messages 47

    Retrieving and Processing Messages 53

    Retrieving Messages.. 54

    Processing Messages....................................... 57

    Error Handling 62

        Error Handling in Service Programs 62

        Poison-Message Handling 66

        Ending Conversations with Errors 69

    Summary 72

█CHAPTER 4 **Service Broker Activation** 73

Activation Basics 73
    Startup Strategies 74
    When Is Activation Needed? 75
Internal Activation 77
    Controlling Message Throughput 84
    Stored Procedure Signing 87
    Calling a Stored Procedure in Another Database 95
    Using a Single Stored Procedure to Process Many Queues 99
External Activation 103
    Using the Event Notification 104
    Enabling External Activation 105
    Implementing the External Console Application 107
    Activating the External Console Application 110
    Configuring ExternalActivator 112
    Several Activated External Console Applications 116
Parallel Activation 119
Troubleshooting Activation 124
    When the Activated Stored Procedure Doesn't Run 125
    When Messages Remain on the Queue 125
Summary 126

█CHAPTER 5 **Service Broker with Managed Code** 127

The Managed Assembly 128
Architecture and Design of the Managed Assembly 131
Building a Managed Service Broker Client 137
Building a Managed Service Program 143
    Deriving Your Service Class 143
    Implementing an Entry Point 143
    Implementing Message Type Handling 145
    Deploying the Assembly 145
    Registering the Managed Stored Procedure 147
    Configuring the Service Broker Activation 148
    Using the Service Program 148
A Practical Example 151
Summary 161

▌**CHAPTER 6** **Locking and Transaction Management** 163

Conversation Groups and Locks 163
State Handling 170
    GET CONVERSATION GROUP 171
    The Receive Loop with State Handling. 172
    State Handling with a Managed Stored Procedure 177
    A Practical Example. 183
    Compensation Logic with Service Broker 215
Transaction Management 222
    Basic Receive Loop 222
    Measuring Performance 223
    Batched Commits 225
    Cursor-Based Processing. 228
    Set-Based Processing. 231
    Binary Payload 235
Summary. 238

▌**CHAPTER 7** **Distributed Service Broker Applications** 239

Communication 239
    Service Broker Protocols 240
    Sending a Message. 240
Routing 242
    Routing Algorithm 244
    Managing Routes. 244
Distributed Applications 246
    The Application. 246
    Setting Up Routes 247
    Establishing a Communication Channel. 250
    Setting Up Security 253
Summary. 267

PART 2 ■ ■ ■ Advanced Service Broker Programming

▌**CHAPTER 8** **Advanced Distributed Service Broker Programming** 271

Transport Security. 272
    LOCAL Route. 272
    TRANSPORT Route. 273

Dialog Security. 275
    Service Broker Security Protocol. 275
    Configuration 278
Encryption. 287
    Transport Encryption. 287
    Dialog Encryption. 288
    Recommendation. 289
Transport Protocol. 290
    Setting Up Tracing. 290
    The Captured Service Broker Message 291
    Replaying Service Broker Messages 294
Replacing Certificates. 294
    Transport Security. 294
    Dialog Security. 295
Service Listing Manager. 296
    Exporting a Service Listing. 297
    Importing a Service Listing. 300
Summary. 304

CHAPTER 9   **Service-Oriented Database Architecture** 305

Service-Oriented Database Architecture. 305
    SOA 306
    Reasons for SODA Architectures. 307
    Requirements for a SODA Service Provider. 308
Data in SODA 308
    Outside Data. 309
    Inside Data 310
SODA Features in SQL Server 2008. 311
    XML Support. 312
    Native Web Services 315
    SQLCLR 326
    Query Notifications 337
Summary. 350

CHAPTER 10   **Real-World Application Scenarios** 351

Reliable Web Service Requests. 352
    Service Broker Infrastructure. 352
    Implementation of the Web Proxy. 357
    Using the Web Proxy in a Smart Client. 371

Asynchronous Triggers. 376

Defining the Problem. 376

Implementing the Trigger. 377

Creating the Service Broker Infrastructure 380

Writing the Service Program 383

Workflow-Driven Service Broker Solutions. 386

Combining Service Broker and WF. 387

Implementing the Local Service 390

Implementing the TargetService. 393

Implementing the InitiatorService. 401

Implementing a More Complex TargetService 407

Batch Frameworks 408

Creating the Service Broker Infrastructure 409

The Implementation of the Batch Framework. 410

Extending the Batch Framework. 417

Publish-Subscribe Frameworks 420

Defining the Infrastructure. 421

Applying Publisher Logic 423

Publishing Information 428

Workload Throttling Through Service Broker 430

Implementing the Service Broker Infrastructure 431

Writing the Stored Procedure. 432

Configuring Internal Activation 436

Queuing Up Some Synchronous Work. 436

Enabling Conversation Priorities 438

Priority-Based Message Processing. 445

Implementing Priority-Based Messaging. 446

Summary. 459

▇CHAPTER 11   **High Availability and Scalability** 461

Database Mirroring. 462

Implementation Details. 462

Setting Up Database Mirroring 463

Using Service Broker with Database Mirroring. 468

Load Balancing 470

Service Deployment 471

Initiator Configuration 472

Message Forwarding 474

    Reliable Delivery 475

    Security 475

    Network Topology Abstraction. 475

    Centralized Routing Instance 477

    Work Distribution 477

    Using Message Forwarding 478

    Monitoring Message Forwarding. 482

Configuration Notice Service 483

    Implementing Dynamic Routing 484

    Implementing the Configuration Notice Service 484

Data-Dependent Routing 490

    Data-Dependent Forwarding 491

    Data-Dependent Redirection 504

Summary. 511

CHAPTER 12   Administration 513

SQL Server Management Studio. 513

    Object Explorer. 514

    Template Explorer 514

    Broker Statistics Report 515

    Using SQL Profiler 520

System Monitor 525

SQL Server Management Objects. 530

    Creating Service Broker Objects 531

    Retrieving Information. 533

Troubleshooting. 534

    Conversation Problems. 534

    Connection Problems 537

    Internal Activation Problems 538

    Service Broker Diagnostics Tool 540

    Configuration Mode. 540

    Runtime Mode 542

    Service Broker Diagnostics Tool Output 544

Summary. 549

INDEX 551

About the Author

■**KLAUS ASCHENBRENNER** works as a software architect for ANECON (a Microsoft Gold Certified Partner for Data Management and ISV/Software Solutions) in Vienna, Austria. Klaus has worked with the .NET Framework and especially with SQL Server 2008 from the very beginning. In 2004 and 2005, Klaus was honored with Microsoft Most Valuable Professional (MVP) awards for his tremendous support of the .NET community. He currently travels around the world teaching clients the core concepts of SQL Server 2008 and distributed application programming based on the .NET Framework 3.5. Klaus is also a regular speaker at international developer conferences like SQLPASS, DevTeach, DevWeek, and SQLdays. For further information on Klaus, see his home page at http://www.csharp.at and on his weblog at http://www.csharp.at/blog.

About the Technical Reviewer

■**FABIO CLAUDIO FERRACCHIATI** is a senior consultant and a senior analyst/developer using Microsoft technologies. He works for Brain Force (www.brainforce.com) in its Italian branch (www.brainforce.it). He is a Microsoft Certified Solution Developer for .NET, a Microsoft Certified Application Developer for .NET, and a Microsoft Certified Professional, and a prolific author and technical reviewer. Over the past ten years he's written articles for Italian and international magazines and coauthored more than ten books on a variety of computer topics. You can read his LINQ blog at www.ferracchiati.com.

Acknowledgments

It's 9:00 p.m., and I'm sitting here in our new house in Vienna on a rainy evening writing this introduction. When I think back to when I wrote the introduction for the 2005 edition of this book, it was around 8:30 p.m., and I was sitting in a train between Vienna and Linz traveling to a customer. Since then, so many personal things have changed. First of all, we (Karin and I) became engaged and we have successfully completed the construction of our own house, which we started in March 2007 after I submitted the last reviewed chapters of my book *Pro SQL Server 2005 Service Broker*. We moved into the house in October last year, after a construction period of just seven months—this was a real challenge, but we've mastered it without big problems!

In the meantime, I've also presented so many sessions about SQL Server– and .NET-related development topics at many international conferences around the world that I lost count of them all. I've attended great conferences like the annual SQLPASS conference in the United States, the DevTeach conference in Canada, and the DevWeek conference in London, as a speaker. It's always great to speak to an international audience, tell them some stories about Austria, and teach them the insights of SQL Server 2008 and of the .NET Framework 3.5. I've also met so many new friends around the globe like Itzik Ben-Gan, Peter DeBetta, Adam Machanic, Fernando Guerrero, Dejan Sarka, Paul Nielsen, Rick Heiges, Joe Webb, Roman Rehak, Jean Rene Roy—the list could go on indefinitely!

Writing *Pro SQL Server 2008 Service Broker* was on the one hand very time-intensive work, because I had to use CTP versions of SQL Server 2008, and I think you know about the quality of CTP versions… But on the other hand it was also great work, because I had the chance to include so many new real-world examples in this book, examples that I've worked on during the last 18 months while consulting for several clients on SQL Server and Service Broker.

Since November 2007 when I started writing this book, a lot of time has passed, and many people have supported me in writing this book. I want to mention and thank the people around the world who helped me with their passion to put together this book on Service Broker. First of all, I want to thank my acquisition editor, Jonathan Gennick, for his support and input on this great book project.

As in the previous edition, Fabio Ferracchiati acted as my technical reviewer. Fabio, thanks for your detailed and great technical reviews of each chapter. I know I've made your life very hard during this time, but we finally produced the greatest book about Service Broker. Thanks for your help on this!

During the writing, I also got great support from Remus Rusanu, who has formerly worked on the Service Broker team in Redmond. Remus also acted as a guest author for this book. I invited Remus to write Chapter 12, where he talks about Service Broker Administration. Remus, thanks for your support and your excellent chapter on Service Broker Administration. Nobody else in the world could have written about this topic in a better way than you—thanks for this! Furthermore, I also want to mention Rick Negrin from the Service Broker team, who also provided me with additional information about Service Broker. Rick also introduced me to the other Service Broker team members. And it's great to see that new Service Broker team members are working through my book to get started with Service Broker.

A great book can't be made without a great publisher. The team at Apress helped me a lot to put everything together to write the best available book on Service Broker. First of all, there is my project manager, Tracy Brown Collins. Tracy, thanks for your help, for your direction, and for your easy-going project plan. I've enjoyed working for you.

A big thank-you also goes to Liz Welch for her help on the copy edits, and to Katie Stence, who acted as my production editor. Thanks for all your help, and I've enjoyed the time with both of you.

Last but not least, I have to thank my family. A big thank-you goes to my parents, Herbert and Dagmar. You were the driving factor in the last 15 years behind my passion for computers, computers, and computers. You supported me in every direction to move my career forward to the point where I'm standing now. Thanks for everything!

Finally, there's Karin, my girlfriend and the most important person in my life. Karin, I'm very, very amazed at how easy it is for you when I'm working on such time-intensive things like this book. There were so many evenings, weekends, and even weeks when I had no time, because my work drove my life. But you handled those days so easily, so that I could concentrate on the book. Thanks for your love, your support, your passion, and your easy understanding of the endless nights spent working on this book. Thanks for everything and especially for your love. I dedicate this book to you. I will always love you.

Introduction

SQL Server 2008 Service Broker is an asynchronous messaging framework directly built into SQL Server 2008. In this book I show how you can use the power of Service Broker to program asynchronous, message-based, distributed, secure, reliable, and scalable database applications.

Who This Book Is For

This book is for database developers and application developers who want to learn about Service Broker and programming message-based applications with SQL Server 2008.

How This Book Is Structured

The book is divided into two parts:

Part 1: The Service Broker Programming Model: The first part of this book introduces you to the general concepts and programming the APIs of Service Broker. After reading through this part, you'll be able to implement asynchronous, distributed, reliable, and secure Service Broker applications.

Part 2: Advanced Service Broker Programming: The second part of the book explores the more advanced Service Broker features, including the internals of Service Broker and how to scale out Service Broker applications to any required size. I also discuss Service-Oriented Database Architecture (SODA), where Service Broker acts as one of the key pillars.

The first part of the book is composed of the following chapters:

Chapter 1: Fundamentals of Message-Based Processing: This chapter introduces you to the core concepts of message-based programming, as well as to some of the fundamental issues you'll encounter in this programming approach. Once you understand the theory, you'll examine how to work through issues with Service Broker in the next chapter.

Chapter 2: Introducing Service Broker: This chapter introduces Service Broker from an architectural point of view and explains how Service Broker solves the problems discussed in Chapter 1.

Chapter 3: Service Broker in Action: This chapter teaches you how to program your first message-based application with Service Broker.

Chapter 4: Service Broker Activation: Now that you know the fundamentals of Service Broker, this chapter introduces you to the activation feature of Service Broker, which allows you to process incoming Service Broker messages automatically.

Chapter 5: Service Broker with Managed Code: This chapter shows you how you can use the advantages of the SQLCLR to implement Service Broker applications directly with managed code.

Chapter 6: Locking and Transaction Management: As soon as you want to implement asynchronous, scalable, message-based applications, you must take care of locking strategies. This chapter introduces the Service Broker locking functionalities and also shows you how to write highly efficient Service Broker applications through different transaction-management strategies.

Chapter 7: Distributed Service Broker Applications: This chapter, which closes the first part of this book, teaches you how to distribute Service Broker applications to physically different machines.

The second part of the book is composed of the following chapters:

Chapter 8: Advanced Distributed Service Broker Programming: This chapter goes into the more technical details of distributed Service Broker applications and shows which options are available for your applications.

Chapter 9: Service-Oriented Database Architecture: Service-Oriented Database Architecture (SODA) is a new concept propagated by Microsoft where the database server—in this case, SQL Server 2008—acts as a full-blown application server. SODA consists of several pillars, and as you'll see, Service Broker is one of those key pillars.

Chapter 10: Real-World Application Scenarios: This chapter details different real-world application scenarios where Service Broker can offer huge benefits and lead to better scalability. This chapter will also introduce conversation priorities to you, a new feature of SQL Service Broker 2008. Finally I've also added an application scenario that shows you how to combine the Windows Workflow Foundation programming model with Service Broker.

Chapter 11: High Availability and Scalability: SQL Server 2008 is all about high availability and scalability. One of the best things about Service Broker is that you can use SQL Server's high-availability and scalability features directly for your Service Broker applications without any effort. In this chapter you'll also find a section about data-dependent routing, which is another scale-out technology available with Service Broker.

Chapter 12: Administration: In this final chapter Remus Rusanu teaches you how you can administer your Service Broker applications and which features are provided by Service Broker in this area.

Prerequisites

You will need SQL Server 2008 Standard Edition/Developer Edition and Visual Studio 2008 Standard Edition.

Downloading the Code

The source code for this book is available to readers at www.apress.com in the Source Code/ Download section of this book's home page. Please feel free to visit the Apress website and download all the code there. You can also check for errata and find related titles from Apress.

Contacting the Author

You can reach Klaus at his website, http://www.csharp.at, or at his weblog, http:// www.csharp.at/blog. Further questions can be sent to Klaus.Aschenbrenner@csharp.at.

PART 1

The Service Broker Programming Model

■■■

## CHAPTER 1

Fundamentals of Message-Based Processing

Love is the message and the message is love.

This lyric from Arthur Baker's song "The Message Is Love" has been with me over the past few years, as I've worked and consulted with many clients around the world on .NET and SQL Server. Many of my clients have implemented large projects that incorporate message technologies in various forms, including Microsoft Message Queuing (MSMQ), XML web services, Microsoft BizTalk Server, and, of course, Microsoft SQL Server 2005/2008 Service Broker. But what does Arthur Baker's song have to do with IT technology and even with technologies that provide frameworks for message-based applications? The answer is easy: the core concept behind message systems is a message, so the message is the central point and the most important part of such a system.

In this first chapter, I'll introduce you to message-based processing, show you why messaging is suitable for scalable solutions, and discuss what problems can occur in distributed messaging architectures. Furthermore, I'll also show how Service Broker solves the messaging problems described throughout this chapter. I'll answer the following questions:

- *Why do you need messaging in your application?* You've probably written successful synchronous applications, so why do you need asynchronous messaging? I'll explain the advantages and benefits of this dramatic change in your software architectures.

- *What problems can a messaging infrastructure solve?* When you use a new technology, such as Service Broker, you might not see the underlying issues that it solves. Infrastructure services for message-based programming offer many different options that encapsulate and solve problems behind the scenes.

- *How do you achieve effective message processing?* You can take several approaches, each of which has its own advantages and disadvantages.

- *Which application architectures are suitable for message-based software systems?* With message-based architectures, you aren't restricted to only client/server or three-tier architectures; more options are available to you.

- *Why use Service Broker as your messaging technology when so many alternatives are available on the Windows platform?* For example, you have your choice between MSMQ, COM+ Queued Components, BizTalk Server, XML web services, and .NET Framework 3.0's Windows Communication Foundation (WCF).

As you can see, you can't just say to yourself or to your project manager, "Hey, there's Service Broker. Let's use it in our next project." So let's have a look at your options and start to answer the fundamental question of why modern software architectures need messaging.

Message Concepts

Message-based programming allows you to implement more flexible and scalable software architectures that other programming paradigms, such as classic client/server applications, cannot provide. If you want to implement scalable applications that are able to handle thousands of concurrent users, you must take a message-based approach. Otherwise, you'll struggle with performance issues and massive scalability problems. But before diving into the details, let's have a look at the central point of a messaging application—the message itself.

Message Anatomy

When you take a look at a message from a 1,000-foot level, you'll see that it's composed of three parts:

- Envelope

- Header

- Body

The message envelope is the wrapping in which the message header and the message body are transferred. The message header contains routing information, such as existing intermediaries on the route, the final destination, the sender, the priority, and so on. One important thing you should know is that the header is normally extensible—just think of a user-defined Simple Object Access Protocol (SOAP) header in a web services scenario. The body of the message stores the payload, which is transferred from the sender to the receiver. The body can be in any format, such as binary data, XML data, or even textual data (like in an email message). Figure 1-1 illustrates the structure of a message.

However, messages aren't used only in software systems. Messages are used all day long throughout daily life. The messages in your life provide you with the flexibility to do several things in parallel and asynchronously. You can map these concepts directly into message-based software solutions.

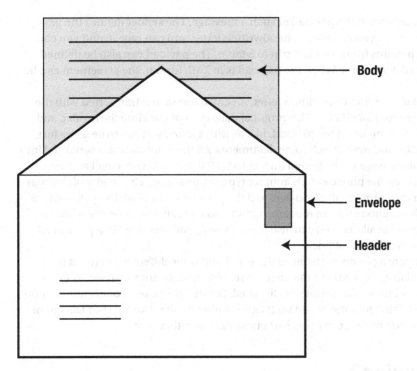

Figure 1-1. *The structure of a message*

Messaging in Daily Life

Before I cover messaging from a technical perspective, let's first discuss the various ways we all use messaging in daily life:

- Sending and receiving traditional mail

- Sending email

- Calling someone on the phone

When you send a letter, you perform an asynchronous process using a message. Such a message always contains three elements: an envelope, a header, and a body. Figure 1-1 illustrates this concept. The header contains some routing information (the address where the letter must be sent, or the *target*) and some information about the sender (the address of the *initiator*). The header also contains a stamp with the appropriate value. Using this information, the post office can route your letter to its final destination through some intermediaries. Intermediaries could be other post offices along the route to the receiver. For example, when I order books from an online store, the books are routed to a distribution center in Vienna. The local post office then takes the parcel and delivers it directly to my house. The distribution center is a kind of intermediary.

Let's concentrate now on the payload of such a message. The sender defines the payload (body). For example, you can write a handwritten letter, you can type it, and you can also enclose some pictures from your last trip to Seattle. The payload can also be defined through a formalized agreement. When the payload is in XML format, the agreement can be an XML schema.

Sending an email is similar to sending a letter. An email message is transferred with the Simple Mail Transfer Protocol (SMTP). This protocol defines what goes into the header, and the sender defines the contents of the payload. Just as with a letter, you can write some text, embed some graphics, and even attach some documents. All this information is serialized into the payload, and the message is transferred through SMTP to the receiver's email address.

Calling someone on the phone entails another type of messaging. The header of this message contains the phone number that you dial, and the payload consists of the spoken words you deliver through the phone line. In the same manner as you can send an email when the receiver is currently not available, you can also leave a voice-mail message. So, a phone call also works when the receiver is "offline."

When you compare a phone call to an email, you'll find some differences. First, a phone call is not always reliable. You can't assume that the receiver understands your words exactly, because the transmission can sometimes be distorted. Second, the phone connection may be cut off when you're talking to someone. In such cases, a phone call is like the User Datagram Protocol (UDP), because message delivery isn't guaranteed in either case.

Why Messaging?

When you want to use a new technology in a project, you must be able to argue its merits. Nobody can just go to a project leader and insist that messaging technology be used simply because it's available. Let's see how messaging solutions can have a positive impact on your application architecture.

Asynchronous Message Processing

Asynchronous message processing means that the sender can continue working while waiting for the receiver to process and eventually reply to the message. Asynchronous message processing is useful when long-duration business processes should be decoupled from a client application. The client application only captures the necessary input from the user, transforms the input into a message, and sends it to the destination, which does the real work asynchronously. The benefits of this design are that client applications are more responsive and users can immediately do other things within the application. This design may include several destinations to achieve a load-balancing scenario, so that the workload can be distributed and messages can be processed in parallel.

Sending a letter is a form of asynchronous message processing, because you don't have to wait at the post office until your letter arrives at its final destination. Likewise with email: you just click the Send button, and the email is transferred. In the meantime, you can continue with your other work.

When you implement message-based solutions, you work with an asynchronous processing paradigm. When you send a message, the message is sent asynchronously to the receiver, where it may be processed accordingly. I say "may be" here because asynchronous messaging does not define when the message is processed (the next section talks more about deferred message processing). One of the benefits of this asynchronous approach is that users can continue with their work while a message is being processed on an application server. This leads to more scalable applications, because clients only have to put messages into a queue. Most other things are done at some later time without further user interaction.

Deferred Message Processing

There's an important difference between asynchronous and deferred message processing: asynchronous message processing defines that the work is done later, and deferred message processing defines when the work is actually done on the application server. The message can be processed immediately, in a few hours, or in a few days—it depends on the message system configuration. Deferred message processing in an asynchronous scenario has the following advantages:

- The receiver controls when messages are processed.

- Load balancing occurs between several servers and during peak times.

- Fault tolerance exists on the receiving side.

Let's assume you run a messaging system based on Service Broker in a company where a high message load occurs during normal work hours. With deferred message processing, you can configure Service Broker so that messages are only put into the queue during the day and are processed overnight when more resources are available. This means that user requests can be processed more quickly, and applications are more responsive under high loads. This is similar to doing automatic database backups at night—another case where demand is less, and more resources are available at night.

With load balancing, you can define on which server a message should be processed. This is useful when you have a high load of messages that must be processed quickly. You can deploy several instances of a Service Broker service and have clients connect to one of them. If you must take an instance offline, perhaps to perform some maintenance work on the server, your messaging system will continue to work without any problems or changes in configuration, because new requests from clients will be distributed among the other available Service Broker instances.

Fault Tolerance

Messaging technologies can also help you provide fault-tolerant systems. You can achieve fault tolerance through the following ways in a message-based system:

- Reliable messaging

- Load balancing

- Dynamic rerouting

Reliable messaging means that the sender can ensure that a message will arrive at the target. This reliability is completely independent of whether the target is currently available. If the target is offline, the messaging infrastructure on the client will try to resend the message to the target as long as the target is offline or otherwise not reachable through the network. This approach has several advantages: maintenance work can be done more easily, sent messages cannot be lost, and offline scenarios are supported.

A big benefit of reliable messaging is that the target can send a response message back to the sender in a reliable fashion. So, reliable messaging works in both directions on a communication channel. Therefore, reliable messaging is also an important consideration when you design and implement smart client solutions. One characteristic of a smart client is that the application still functions in offline scenarios. Microsoft Office Outlook, for example, is an intelligent smart client because it allows you to work through your emails and even compose replies when you're on the road and not connected to the Internet. When you get back to your office, Outlook synchronizes its local data store with an Exchange Server in the background and sends all unsent emails to their receivers.

You can provide the same flexibility in your own smart client applications when you use a message-based approach. When users want to do some work offline, you can store their requests as messages locally on their notebooks and send the messages to the application server as soon as the notebook goes online and an Internet/intranet connection is established. Reliable messaging makes this possible without any programming.

Load balancing offers the same benefit for fault-tolerant systems that it does for deferred message processing. By distributing message-processing power between several servers, you can implement a scale-out scenario (scaling horizontally) for your messaging system. As you'll see in forthcoming chapters, you can do this easily with Service Broker.

Dynamic rerouting means that you can reconfigure a Service Broker service during the processing without making any changes on the client and without any further interruption. As soon as the endpoint of a Service Broker service is reconfigured and points to a new address, the clients send messages transparently to the new location, without any intervention from an administrator. This could be helpful when you need to take a service offline during maintenance work.

Distributed Systems

If you must implement or support a distributed topology for your application, a message-based approach can help you achieve the necessary functionality. Architectures are referred to as distributed when software components are running on different servers on the network. For example, you can implement an application server where business logic executes in a central location. This provides you the advantages of asynchronous and deferred message processing, and these architectures are also very scalable.

Some messaging technologies support scale-out scenarios without any change in the implementation of the message-based services. Service Broker supports this through a concept called *routes*. A route defines the endpoint on the network where a service is hosted. You'll find more information about routes in Chapter 7.

When you distribute software components across process boundaries, you must also give careful thought to the following questions about security:

- How are clients authenticated and authorized when they call services?

- How are messages transferred between the sender and the receiver? Is encryption necessary?

- Should you use symmetric or asymmetric encryption?

- How do you react to threats from the outside world?

As you can see, there are many aspects to consider when implementing distributed message-based scenarios. In Chapters 7 and 8, you'll get an in-depth look at how to set up distributed scenarios with Service Broker and how you can secure communication between sender and receiver.

Messaging Problems

You've seen why a messaging technology such as Service Broker makes sense for some scenarios. However, using a messaging technology just because it's available isn't necessarily a good idea. In fact, it can have an enormous negative impact on your application architecture. You must decide carefully if a messaging architecture provides benefits for your required scenarios. If you do decide you want to use messaging technology and you don't want the problems of message systems, Service Broker can help because it already includes functionality that solves the messaging problems described in this section. Let's take a detailed look at which messaging problems Service Broker tries to solve.

Performance

Performance is always an issue. When you ask developers what problems they have with their databases and applications, they'll almost always mention performance. Therefore, one of Microsoft's goals with Service Broker was to have it offer better performance than any other messaging technology can currently provide. For example, if you compare Service Broker to MSMQ, you'll see that the biggest difference is in the transaction handling. With Service Broker, you don't need distributed transactions.

Service Broker solves the transaction-handling problem completely differently. In the Service Broker world, queues, like tables, are native database objects, so distributed transactions are not needed when a message is processed and finally removed from the queue. Service Broker can handle all the different tasks in the context of a local SQL Server transaction—and this provides enormous performance benefits over MSMQ and other message systems. You can find out more about this topic in Chapter 6, which discusses transaction management in Service Broker.

TRANSACTION HANDLING IN MSMQ

With MSMQ, your data-processing logic is typically implemented in a database. The problem is that MSMQ messages are stored in the file system, but the data-processing logic is in a database. Because of this separation, you must coordinate two different resources during message processing.

You can't remove a message from an MSMQ queue when a database transaction fails, and you can't commit a database transaction when you can't remove a message from the queue. In both cases, you get inconsistent data between the MSMQ queue and the database.

In MSMQ, you use a distributed transaction when you must coordinate more than one resource in the context of a transaction. However, distributed transactions are relatively expensive in terms of execution time because of the coordination overhead. This can be a major problem in itself, so you must always carefully decide if you can afford this extra overhead.

Queue Reader Management

In every message system, a message is retrieved from a queue. This process is called *queue reader management*. There are two possible options: you can have several queues, where incoming messages are distributed among the queues, or you can have one queue that receives all the messages. Let's look at both solutions.

Several queues might seem at first to be the better option, because multiple components listening on the different queues can process the messages. You can compare this approach to a supermarket, where you must wait in one of several checkout lines (queues) to get to a cashier.

But what happens when a new line opens? Many move to the new line, and, of course, they all want to be the first there. It can become even more complicated. What if you're the second person in the newly opened line? It often seems like the person in front of you takes too much time, and it would have been better for you to have stayed in your original line. As you can see, more than one queue isn't always the best option, for supermarkets or for message systems.

Note The rebalancing of queues always has a cost, and that cost can negatively affect performance.

But can things work efficiently with just one queue? Think of the check-in process at an airport. Here you have one queue with several check-in stations. When a new station opens, does this lead to the same problem as with the supermarket checkouts? No, because the people in line are always distributed among the current available stations without being able to make the choice on their own. So no rebalancing is necessary among queues.

The second approach is the one that Service Broker takes. In Service Broker, there is only one queue, but you can configure the number of queue readers listening on the queue to process incoming messages. In fact, you have multiple concurrent queue readers processing the incoming messages. In a message system, this is a lot more efficient than multiple queues.

Transaction Management

An effective message system must also support transaction management. Transaction management defines how several instances of queue readers are coordinated against one queue. To make this clearer, let's assume a scenario where an order-entry application sends order request messages to a queue. Two kinds of request messages are involved:

- A message with the order header

- Several messages with the order line items

As soon as the first message arrives at the queue, a queue reader is instantiated, which takes the new order header message from the queue and processes it. The queue reader inserts a new row in an order table and commits the transaction. Then, a reader processes the line-item messages and also inserts new rows in the database. Everything seems OK, but what happens when an administrator configures more than one queue reader to listen for new messages? In this case, the order header and the line-item messages can be processed in parallel, with the possibility that an attempt could be made to insert a line item before the order header. This will raise an exception, because it violates referential integrity between an order header and its line items.

One possible way around this is to process messages in the correct order. Service Broker solves this problem through a feature called conversation group locking. Conversation group locking groups related messages for reading by multiple readers to prevent data integrity problems caused by processing related messages simultaneously on different threads. During the design of your Service Broker application, you must make sure that related messages are placed into the same conversation group.

When you use conversation group locking, Service Broker ensures that the same queue reader processes messages from the same conversation group, eliminating the need to explicitly synchronize message processing among several threads. Chapter 6 takes a more in-depth look at transactions, locking, and conversation groups.

■**Note** Conversation groups are similar to a dialog where several messages are exchanged between the sender and the receiver.

Message Sequencing and Correlation

Another issue in message systems is correctly sequencing and maintaining the right correlation among messages. Sequencing means that messages arrive in the same order as they're sent, as Figure 1-2 illustrates.

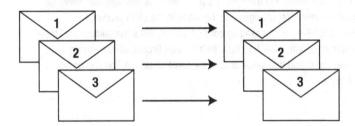

Figure 1-2. *Message sequencing*

Sequencing is always important when a receiver gets several messages, each of which depends on a previous message. In the order-header example, the message with the order header needs to be processed before the messages with line items. Therefore, you can again ensure the referential integrity of your data in the database. To preserve order, Service Broker includes a sequence number in every message it sends and forces the receiving application to accept the messages in the same order as they were sent. Some other messaging systems (such as MSMQ) allow messages to be received in any order, but Service Broker enforces the strict sequencing of messages. In SQL Server 2008, Service Broker now includes built-in support for conversation priorities. Chapter 10 shows you how you can use this feature and how you can resolve priority message ordering by yourself.

Message correlation is another problem. When a client sends several messages to a central service queue, the queue readers process the messages and send back response messages. But how can the client decide which response is for which request? Service Broker solves this problem easily, because each message is associated with a *conversation ID*. This unique identifier identifies the communication channel between the sender and the receiver in a unique fashion. The client application can then associate each response with the correct request.

Maintenance

Maintenance is an important issue for all applications, including message applications, and Microsoft addressed this issue when designing Service Broker. Compared to MSMQ, Service Broker is much easier to administer and maintain because its queues are native database objects. When you back up the database, you also back up both the data created by the messages and the queues holding messages that are not yet processed. This is possible because all Service Broker objects, like queues, are tied to a database.

In MSMQ, messages are always stored in the file system. When you do backups, the database and the messages in the file system can be out of sync (see the "Maintenance in MSMQ" sidebar). Another big advantage of Service Broker is that administration and maintenance are done with tools that database administrators already know. The best and only tool they need is SQL Server Management Studio, but they can use SQLCMD if they prefer to. You don't have to introduce a new management tool for your messaging solution.

MAINTENANCE IN MSMQ

With MSMQ, messages are stored in the file system, and data is stored in a database such as SQL Server. You must back up both the messages in the file system and the data in SQL Server. Your backups can easily get out of sync, because while you update one resource, changes may be made to the other resource.

The only solution to this problem is to take your messaging solution offline, make the backup, and then put it back online. However, this doesn't work with a 24/7 system. With Service Broker, synchronizing backups is not a problem, because both messages and data are stored in the same database. You can do one backup, on the whole database, and that's it.

Messaging Architectures

Implementing messaging solutions also leads to new application architectures that you can't achieve with traditional approaches such as client/server or three-tier architectures. Let's have a look at two other possible types of architecture for message-based software systems: Service-Oriented Architecture (SOA) and Service-Oriented Database Architecture (SODA).

SOA

SOA is a collection of several architectural patterns with the goal of combining heterogeneous application silos (such as mainframe applications). A quick search on Google may lead you to believe that SOA is only possible with XML web services, but that's not true.

You can use SOA with other technologies, such as Service Broker. SOA defines the following four core principles:

- Explicit service boundaries

- Autonomous services

- Explicit data contracts

- Interoperability

As you'll see throughout this book, you can satisfy these principles better and with more reliability with Service Broker. Explicit service boundaries mean that a SOA service must define a service contract that exposes the operations available to other client applications. This is important when a client uses discovery technologies to find an appropriate service on a network.

An autonomous service is one that a client can use to process a complete business request. Email, for example, is an autonomous service, because a user request can be completed with one service interaction. If you want to send an email with an attachment, you can do it in one step instead of two separate steps. The big challenge when you design your services is to find the right granularity and make them as autonomous as possible.

In SOA, the contract defines the contents of the messages sent in both directions. In the context of Service Broker, you can define the structure of the message body. You have no control over the structure of message headers. XML messages support interoperability, because any computer system can exchange and process them.

SQL Server 2008 allows you to expose Service Broker services to other clients through open standards, such as XML web services. This makes it possible for clients on other platforms, such as Java, to interact with your Service Broker services. You can adhere to all four SOA principles with Service Broker, making it an ideal platform for implementing SOA.

SODA

SQL Server 2005 offered at first a number of new features, including the following:

- Integration into .NET (SQLCLR)

- Query notifications

- Service Broker

- XML support

- Web services support

Many customers often ask why these features are now integrated directly into the database. There are several good reasons for each feature that I won't go into right now because that's not my purpose. My point is that you can only achieve real benefits from these features when you use them in conjunction. The correct use of these features leads to SODA, the concepts of which are explained in a white paper by David Campbell called "Service Oriented Database Architecture: App Server-Lite?"[1]

---

1. David Campbell, "Service Oriented Database Architecture: App Server-Lite?" Microsoft Research (September 2005), http://research.microsoft.com/research/pubs/view.aspx?tr_id=983.

In SODA, you implement business functionality as SQLCLR stored procedures in the database, and you use Service Broker as a reliable message bus to make your components available to other clients. To publish services, you use native web services support in combination with the new XML features available since SQL Server 2005. When you look at this new architecture, you can see that SQL Server 2008 is an important application server in such scenarios. Chapter 9 discusses implementing SODA applications with Service Broker.

Available Messaging Technologies

Service Broker is not the one and only messaging technology available for the Windows platform. You can use several technologies to implement a message-based system, but Service Broker offers some advantages over all the other messaging technologies described in this section. For example, one important aspect of Service Broker is its distributed programming paradigm. When you develop a Service Broker application dedicated for one SQL Server and you later decide to spread the Service Broker application out to several physical SQL Servers (maybe because of scalability problems), then you just have to configure your application to support a distributed scenario. You don't have to change the internal implementation details of your Service Broker application.

Likewise, with load balancing, if you see in a later phase of your project that you must support load balancing because of several thousands of concurrent users, you just have to deploy your Service Broker application to an additional SQL Server and make some configuration changes. Service Broker will handle the load-balancing mechanism for you in the background. Chapter 11 talks more about these scenarios.

Despite these advantages of Service Broker, let's now take a look at one of the most important and familiar messaging technologies available today.

MSMQ

MSMQ has been available as part of Windows since the first version of Windows NT. MSMQ was the first messaging technology from Microsoft used to provide messaging capabilities for a wide range of business applications. One of the biggest advantages of MSMQ is that it is licensed and distributed with Windows, so you don't have any additional licensing costs when you use it in your own applications. In addition, it's not bound to any specific database product. If you want to use Oracle with MSMQ, you can do it without any problems. However, as with every product and technology, there are also some drawbacks, including the following:

- Message size is limited to 4MB.

- MSMQ is not installed by default. Furthermore, you need the Windows installation disk to install MSMQ.

- You need distributed transactions if you want to run the message processing and data-processing logic in one Atomic, Consistent, Isolated, and Durable (ACID) transaction. This requires installation of the Microsoft Distributed Transaction Coordinator (MS DTC).

- Message ordering is not guaranteed.

- Message correlation is not supported out of the box.

- You must implement queue readers manually.

- You must conduct synchronization and locking between several queue readers manually.

- Backup and restoration can be a challenge, because message data and transactional data are stored in different places.

Queued Components

Queued Components are a part of the Component Object Model (COM+) infrastructure. With Queued Components, you have the possibility to enqueue a user request to a COM+ application and execute it asynchronously. Internally, a message is created and sent to a dedicated MSMQ queue. On the server side, a component referred to as a *Listener* is used to dequeue the message from the queue and make the needed method calls on the specified COM+ object. For replay of these method calls, a component referred to as a *Player* is used. Queued Components are attractive for a project that already uses the COM+ infrastructure and requires doing some functions asynchronously and decoupled from client applications.

BizTalk Server

BizTalk Server is a business process management (BPM) server that enables companies to automate, orchestrate, and optimize business processes. It includes powerful, familiar tools to design, develop, deploy, and manage those processes successfully. BizTalk Server also uses messaging technology for enterprise application integration (EAI). One drawback is its licensing costs, which are very high if you need to support larger scenarios where scale-out is an issue.

XML Web Services

XML web services is a messaging technology based on open standards such as SOAP and Web Services Description Language (WSDL), and it's suitable for interoperability scenarios. .NET 1.0 was the first technology from Microsoft that included full support for creating applications based on web services technologies.

Over the past few years, Microsoft has made several improvements in the communication stack and has made it even easier to design, implement, publish, and reuse web services.

WCF

The goal of WCF, which was introduced with .NET 3.0, is to provide a unique application programming interface (API) across all communication technologies currently available on Windows. This includes the technologies already mentioned, as well as some others, such as .NET Remoting. With a unique communication API, you can write distributed applications in a communication-independent way. During deployment, an administrator can configure which communication technology the application should use. Microsoft's Service Broker team might also include a WCF channel to Service Broker in an upcoming version of SQL Server, so that you can talk with Service Broker applications directly from WCF-based applications.

Summary

In this first chapter, I provided an overview of the fundamentals of message-based programming. I talked about the benefits of using messaging and how to achieve scalability for your applications. I then discussed several problems that can occur when using messaging technology, and I showed you how Service Broker solves these problems so that you don't need to bother with them and can simply concentrate on the implementation details of your distributed applications.

I then described possible application architectures based on messaging architectures such as SOA and SODA. Finally, I briefly described other messaging technologies available on Windows and presented the pros and cons for each. With this information, you have all the necessary knowledge for understanding the concepts behind Service Broker. In the next chapter, I'll introduce Service Broker itself.

CHAPTER 2

∎∎∎

Introducing Service Broker

This chapter will describe the Service Broker architecture, including the following components:

- *Conversations*: In Service Broker programming, everything revolves around a conversation. I'll explain exactly what a conversation is and what features it offers.

- *Anatomy of a service*: The core concept behind a Service Broker application is a service. A service is composed of several elements, such as message types, contracts, a queue, and a service program.

- *Security*: Service Broker is all about communication between services. It also provides several security models that you can apply to your Service Broker application.

- *Message processing*: Service Broker exchanges messages between services. I'll outline the steps you need to successfully send a message from one service to another, and I'll explain reliable messaging.

- *Performance*: Service Broker provides different performance benefits, including the transaction model and multiple queue readers.

Conversations

A conversation is a reliable, ordered exchange of messages between two Service Broker services. The Service Broker architecture defines two kinds of conversations:

- *Dialog*: A dialog is a two-way conversation between exactly two Service Broker services. Services exist on both the sending and receiving ends of a dialog. The one on the sending side is referred to as the *initiator service*, and the one on the receiving side is referred to as the *target service*. The initiator service starts a new dialog and sends the first message to the target service. Both services can then exchange messages in either direction.

- *Monologue*: A monologue is a one-way conversation between a single *publisher* service and several *subscriber* services. This is a reliable version of the popular publish-subscribe paradigm. Currently, monologues are not supported in Service Broker, but they may be included in a future version of Service Broker.

Dialogs

Dialogs are bidirectional conversations between two Service Broker services. Dialogs allow Service Broker to provide exactly-once-in-order message delivery. Each dialog follows a specific contract. A Service Broker dialog solves all the messaging problems discussed in Chapter 1, in addition to the following features:

- *Guaranteed delivery*: Service Broker is a reliable messaging system. Therefore, the sender of a message can be sure that the receiving side will receive the sent message safely—even if the receiving side is currently offline.

- *Long-lived*: Dialogs can live for only a few seconds, but they can also span several years for long-running business processes.

- *Exactly once*: Message delivery in Service Broker dialogs is guaranteed to occur exactly once. If the initiator service must resend a message because the previous message didn't arrive at the sending side, then both messages will be received on the other side, but only one message will be processed. The other duplicated message will be dropped automatically from the receiving queue.

- *In-order delivery*: Service Broker ensures that messages are received in the same order as they are sent from the initiator service. This addresses the message sequencing and ordering problem discussed in Chapter 1.

- *Persistence*: A Service Broker dialog survives the restart of the whole database server, because messages and dialogs are persisted directly in the database. This makes it easy to perform maintenance on the database, because when you shut down the database engine, all open dialogs and even unprocessed messages are persisted automatically and become available as soon as you take the database engine online again.

Figure 2-1 illustrates a Service Broker dialog.

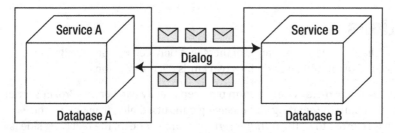

Figure 2-1. *A Service Broker dialog*

Dialog Lifetime

Applications can exchange messages during the lifetime of a dialog. The lifetime of a dialog lasts from the time a dialog is created until another Service Broker service ends the dialog. Each participant is responsible for explicitly ending the conversation when it receives a message that indicates an error or the end of the conversation. In general, one participant is responsible for indicating that the conversation is complete and successful by ending the conversation without an error.

Dialogs can also guarantee that the lifetime of a conversation doesn't exceed a specific limit. The initiating service can optionally specify a maximum lifetime for the dialog. Both services of a conversation keep track of this lifetime. When a dialog remains active at the maximum lifetime, the Service Broker infrastructure places a time-out error message on the service queue on each side of the conversation and refuses new messages for the dialog. Conversations never live beyond the maximum lifetime that is established when a new dialog begins.

Conversation Groups

A conversation group identifies one or more related conversations and allows a Service Broker application to easily coordinate conversations involved in a specific business task. Every conversation belongs to one conversation group, and every conversation group is associated with several conversations from different services. A conversation group can contain one or more conversations.

When an application sends or receives a message, SQL Service locks the conversation group to which the message belongs. This is called *conversation group locking*. Thus, only one session at a time can receive messages for the conversation group. Conversation group locking guarantees that a Service Broker application can process messages on each conversation exactly-once-in-order and keep state on a per-conversation group basis. Because a conversation group can contain more than one conversation, a Service Broker application can use conversation groups to identify messages related to the same business task and process those messages together.

This concept is important for business processes of long duration. For example, when you order books online, the order-entry service sends messages to several other services and starts a business process of reasonably long duration. The other called services could be any or all of the following:

- Credit-card validation service

- Inventory service

- Accounting service

- Shipping service

Say the order-entry service starts four different dialogs to each of these individual services. Service Broker groups these four dialogs together in a conversation group. These four services may all respond at nearly the same time, so it's possible that response messages for the same order may be processed on different threads simultaneously without being aware of each other. To solve this problem, Service Broker locks conversation groups—not conversations. By default, a conversation group contains a single conversation—the conversation started by the initiator service with the target service, the order-entry service. Figure 2-2 illustrates this concept.

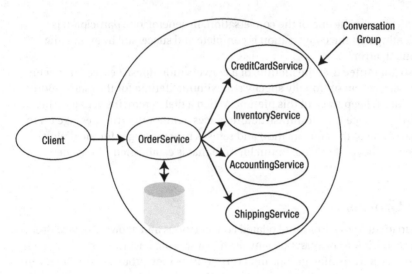

Figure 2-2. *Conversation groups*

The tasks of the four background services that are started by the order-entry service are normally done in the context of separate local SQL Server transactions. The message exchange between the individual services takes place in the form of reliable messaging through the Service Broker infrastructure. As soon as the order entry service receives replies from all of the background services, it can reply with a response message back to the client and the business process ends. When this event occurs, Service Broker closes the conversation group. Chapter 6 takes a detailed look at conversation groups and shows you how to achieve effective conversation group locking.

Message Sequencing

In Service Broker, message sequencing and ordering are ensured in the context of the complete lifetime of a conversation. Sequencing and ordering are maintained through *sequence numbers*, which are incremented for each sent message. If you send six messages, each message gets a sequence number starting with 1. As soon as a message is sent from the initiator service to the target service, Service Broker assigns the current sequence number to the outgoing message. When the messages are dequeued on the receiving side, Service Broker first tries to get the message with the sequence number 1, then the message with the sequence number 2, and so on. When a message gets lost during the sending process, the receiving side waits until the message is successfully resent—the receiving side can't skip a message that isn't delivered successfully from the sender. The message retry send period starts with four seconds and doubles up to 64 seconds. After this maximum of 64 seconds, the message is resent again once every 64 seconds—forever. Figure 2-3 illustrates this process.

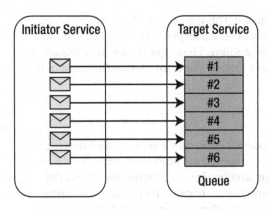

Figure 2-3. *Message ordering in Service Broker*

Reliable Delivery

Service Broker also ensures the reliable delivery of messages within the context of a dialog. Service Broker cannot ensure that messages are received in order unless it also ensures that they are all received. When messages are lost during the sending process, the messaging sequence contains gaps, which are not suitable in a dialog. Service Broker makes reliable messaging possible, because the sender resends missed messages periodically until it receives an acknowledgment from the receiver about the delivered message.

The resending and acknowledgment protocol is directly built into the infrastructure of Service Broker, so it is completely transparent to application developers. In Figure 2-4, you can see that messages that are sent across the network are placed in a temporary queue called the *transmission queue*. Service Broker sends messages over the network and marks them as waiting for an acknowledgment in this transmission queue. When a message is received at the destination service and stored in the target queue for further processing, the receiver sends an acknowledgment back to the sender—the initiating service. When the sender receives this acknowledgment message, it deletes the message from the transmission queue.

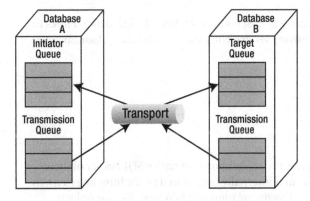

Figure 2-4. *Reliable messaging in Service Broker*

The initiator service must always define a queue. This queue is used for two purposes. The first purpose is when the target service wants to send a response message back to the initiator service. The second purpose is for error handling. The target service must always be able to send an error message back to the initiator service. The error message is stored in the initiator queue.

Error Handling

Asynchronous applications are often hard to code. When an application sends a message to a service, the application cannot ensure that the message is processed immediately. For example, the sending application and the processing service may not be executed at the same time. This makes error handling more complicated, because it's possible that one service might go offline due to an error without having the chance to inform the other service about the problem.

Because of this problem, a Service Broker dialog always has two services, each associated with a queue. This means that Service Broker always knows how to inform both ends of a dialog when an error occurs. This is called *symmetric error handling*.

Anatomy of a Service

A Service Broker service is a named endpoint to which messages from other services are sent. A Service Broker service has the following characteristics:

- The interface is defined through the messages it can receive and send.

- Services embody both application logic (code) and state (data).

- Services are living in the scope of a database.

- Services communicate through formal, reliable sessions known as *conversations* with each other.

- Services are mapped to queues. Messages sent to a service are stored in their associated queues.

A Service Broker service itself is a native SQL Server object, but it has also direct links to other Service Broker objects. A Service Broker service consists of the following four objects:

- Message types

- Contracts

- Queue

- Service program

Message types, contracts, and a queue are implemented as native SQL Server objects, while a service program can be implemented internally (as a stored procedure) or externally (as a separate application). Figure 2-5 depicts the relationship between the four objects.

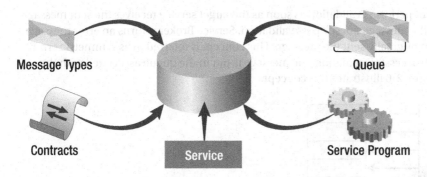

Message Types

Queue

Contracts

Service

Service Program

Figure 2-5. *The four objects that make up a Service Broker service*

When you create a new Service Broker service, you must create and configure all of these objects properly and link them together. A Service Broker service is always defined in the context of a SQL Server database, but Service Broker doesn't restrict where these services are deployed. Service Broker supports the following deployment scenarios:

- Both services are deployed in the same SQL Server database.

- Each service is deployed in a separate SQL Server database located on the same SQL Server instance.

- Each service is deployed in a separate SQL Server database located on another SQL Server instance on a different SQL Server.

The good thing about the Service Broker programming model is that you don't have to know during the development how your Service Broker services are deployed across your company. To the programming model, it is completely transparent. It doesn't matter if the service is running in the same SQL Server database or on a SQL Server running in another country connected through the Internet. Chapters 7 and 8 talk more about distributed scenarios with Service Broker. Now, let's take a detailed look at each of these components.

Message Types

A message type defines the type of data that a message contains, and its name is associated with that message type. You must create message types in each database that participates in a conversation. Message types can also use the [DEFAULT] message type or any other built-in message type. Each message type specifies the validation that Service Broker performs for messages of that type. Currently, Service Broker supports the following validations:

- XML validated against an XML schema

- Well-formed XML

- No validation (e.g., for binary data)

- Empty (the message body must be empty)

Service Broker performs validation as soon as the target service receives the sent message. If the content of the message doesn't pass validation, Service Broker returns an error message to the service that originally sent the message. This concept is referred to as symmetric error messaging. After successful validation, the message is put in the queue associated with the target service. Figure 2-6 illustrates this concept.

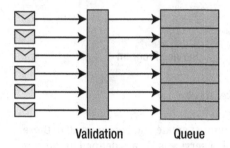

Validation   Queue

Figure 2-6. *Message validation in Service Broker programming*

Message validation has an impact on overall performance. The two XML validation types load every sent message into an XML parser when a message is received. If you receive messages from nontrusted sources and the message volume isn't high, validation makes sense. When you receive messages from trusted sources, it makes more sense for the sending application to validate the XML message and handle any validation errors. This improves the performance on the server side, but you must decide carefully if you can trust the source.

Contracts

A contract defines which message types a Service Broker service uses to accomplish a particular task. A contract is an agreement between two Service Broker services about which messages each service sends to the other service. You must create a contract in each database that participates in a conversation. When you look at a contract definition, you can determine easily which message types can be received and sent on a particular conversation.

Service Broker also ensures that only message types that are defined in a contract are handled and processed. When a service sends another message type, the sent message is rejected and an error message is returned to the sending service. The contract also determines whether a message type is sent strictly by the initiator of the conversation, strictly by the target of the conversation, or by either the initiator or the target of the conversation. Service Broker defines the following three sending directions:

- SENT BY INITIATOR: The initiator sends the message.

- SENT BY TARGET: The target sends the message.

- SENT BY ANY: Either the initiator or the target sends the message.

Figure 2-7 shows how message types are assembled together into a contract.

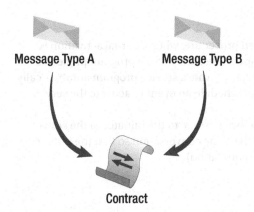

Figure 2-7. *Contracts in Service Broker programming*

Queues

In Service Broker, a queue is a storage provider for received messages (either from the target service or the initiator service) that must be processed. A queue must be defined for the initiator service and the target service. When Service Broker receives a message from a service, it inserts the message after a successful validation into the queue that is associated with the target service. A queue is a lot like a table in SQL Server, but with a few minor differences, as you'll see throughout the book. Each message is represented by a row in a queue. The row contains the payload of the message and some other information, such as the associated message type, the receiving date, and the contract.

When a message is processed inside a Service Broker service, the service reads the message directly from the queue and performs the necessary work with the payload of the message. When the work is done, the associated local SQL Server transaction is committed, and the processed message is removed from the queue.

Service Broker implements queues with a feature called *hidden tables* introduced in SQL Server 2005. Queues look like ordinary tables to the storage engine, but you can't use the usual Transact-SQL (T-SQL) commands (such as INSERT, DELETE, and UPDATE) to manipulate the data in a queue. You're also not allowed to define a trigger on a queue. A read-only view is associated with each queue, so you can use a SELECT statement to see what messages are currently stored inside a queue. This is much easier than many other messaging systems, which require you to peek at the messages one at a time to see what's in the queue.

Because queues are implemented as hidden database tables, messages share all the high-availability features that safeguard SQL Server data. All the features that you use to ensure that your SQL Server data isn't lost or damaged—such as transactions, logging, backup, mirroring, clustering, and so on—also apply to Service Broker messages.

Service Programs

In Service Broker, a service program can be a stored procedure, when internal activation is used, or a separate program, when external activation is used. A service program processes incoming messages from a queue. Service Broker can activate a service program automatically when a new message arrives. Alternatively, you can schedule an event to activate the service program, or you can execute it manually.

A service program often needs to send a response message to the initiator of the conversation to complete a task. This response is part of the same conversation so that the initiator can receive the right response (known as message correlation).

Routes

A route is a SQL Server object that specifies on which network address a Service Broker service is located. Because of this indirection, you can deploy your services to separate machines without changing any implementation details. During the development process, you can start with services in a local database, and in deployment, you can install each service on a different machine. In this case, you must configure the network addresses of both services with routes. Just think of a route as a piece of configuration information stored in the database. For more information about routes, refer to Chapter 7, which covers distributed Service Broker scenarios.

Security

Service Broker allows services hosted by different SQL Server instances to communicate securely, even when the instances are on different machines that have no other trust relationship or when the source and destination machines are not connected to the same network.

Service Broker provides two different types of security: transport security and dialog security. Understanding these two types of security and how they work together will help you design, deploy, and administer Service Broker applications:

- *Transport security*: This prevents unauthorized SQL Server instances from sending Service Broker messages to Service Broker services defined in another SQL Server instance. Transport security establishes an authenticated network connection between two SQL Server instances.

- *Dialog security*: This encrypts messages in an individual dialog conversation and verifies the identities of participants across the dialog. Dialog security also provides remote authorization and message integrity checking. Dialog security establishes authenticated and encrypted communication between two Service Broker services.

Transport Security

When you distribute Service Broker services to different SQL Server instances, you must establish an authenticated network connection between those instances. Furthermore, you must exchange messages often in a secure manner. For that reason, Service Broker provides transport security. With transport security, you're able to create a secure and authenticated communication channel between two SQL Server instances. Service Broker provides two authentication options:

- *Windows-based authentication*: This provides authentication to Service Broker services by using Windows authentication protocols such as NTLM or Kerberos. You can use Windows-based authentication only if both SQL Server instances that are hosting the different Service Broker services belong to the same Windows domain, or if they belong to two different Windows domains that are trusted between each other.

- *Certificate-based authentication*: This provides authentication by using certificates to establish authentication between two Service Broker services. You usually use certificate-based authentication when you have to work with systems on different physical networks on distrusted domains. You can also use certificate-based authentication when the two Service Broker services don't belong to the same Windows domain. Certificate-based authentication is a lot faster than Windows-based authentication. You establish authentication by exchanging a designated public key certificate of the opposite SQL Server instance.

You'll learn more about transport security in Chapter 7, where I talk about distributed Service Broker programming.

Dialog Security

Transport security only establishes authentication and protects messages through encryption between two SQL Server instances. This works fine in easy network topologies where the initiator service sends a message directly to the target service. However, Service Broker supports more complex network topologies through a concept referred to as a *Service Broker forwarder*.

A Service Broker forwarder is a SQL Server instance that accepts Service Broker messages and forwards them to the next hop on the route to the target service. In these network topologies, it's difficult to rely only on transport security, because each message must be decrypted at a passing Service Broker forwarder and finally encrypted when forwarded to the next hop along the route to the target service. The encryption and decryption of the messages slow down the overall performance of your Service Broker application. You'll learn more about Service Broker forwarders in Chapter 11, where I talk about scale-out scenarios with Service Broker.

Because you can't rely only on transport security in some scenarios, Service Broker provides dialog security. By using dialog security, you can establish a secure and authenticated communication channel between two Service Broker services, regardless of how many Service Broker forwarders are configured on the route from the initiator service to the target service. Figure 2-8 shows the difference between transport and dialog security.

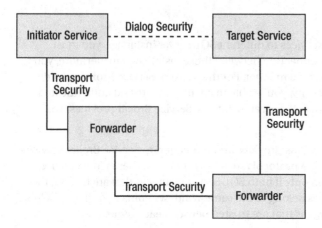

Figure 2-8. *Transport and dialog security in Service Broker*

Message Processing

Let's take a detailed look at the message flow from one service to another service in order to understand how messages are exchanged within a Service Broker conversation. Figure 2-9 shows all the tasks that the implemented Service Broker application must do when a message exchange occurs between two Service Broker services.

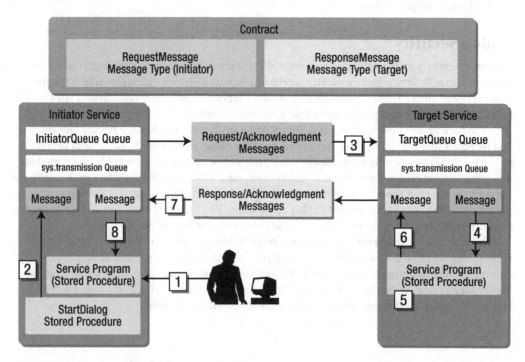

Figure 2-9. *Message exchange in Service Broker*

Let's take a look at the Service Broker objects created for this scenario. A contract is defined that includes two message types called RequestMessage and ResponseMessage. The contract and both message types must be deployed in each SQL Server database anticipating the Service Broker conversation. On the sender's side, a service named InitiatorService is created, and the InitiatorQueue is assigned to this service. Likewise, on the target's side, a service named TargetService is created, and the TargetQueue is assigned to this service. Let's focus now on the steps you need to take to send a message from the InitiatorService to the TargetService.

In the first step of this scenario, it is assumed that a user has some kind of application (such as a Windows Forms or Web Forms application) and calls a stored procedure named StartDialog in the database where InitiatorService is defined. This stored procedure is responsible for opening a new conversation between the InitiatorService and the TargetService.

The second step consists of putting a message with the message type RequestMessage in the local InitiatorQueue of the InitiatorService. Because of the reliable messaging features of Service Broker, the message isn't sent directly to the TargetService when both Service Broker services are running on different databases or different instances. Instead, the created message is moved in a queue called a *transmission queue*. From this queue, Service Broker tries to send the message over the network and marks the message in the transmission queue as waiting for an acknowledgment from the TargetService. Refer to Figure 2-4 earlier in this chapter for details about reliable messaging.

As the third step illustrates, as soon as the message arrives on the TargetService, the message is put in the TargetQueue where the message waits for further processing. In the meantime, an acknowledge message is sent back to the InitiatorService, so that the sent message can be deleted from the transmission queue on the sender's side.

In the fourth step, a service program—normally implemented as a stored procedure or an external application—is started that reads the message from the queue and processes it accordingly. You can start the service program manually or automatically as soon as a new message arrives at the queue. This process, shown in the fifth step, is referred to as *service program activation*. When the received message is processed, a response message is typically created, which must be sent back to the initiating service. As the sixth step illustrates, Service Broker again stores the message in the transmission queue on the target side.

In the seventh step, the response message is transferred from the transmission queue on the target side to the initiating service, where it is stored in the InitiatorQueue. As soon as the message arrives in the queue, a service program is needed to process the message. You can configure this service program so that it starts automatically as soon as a new message arrives in that queue. The service program can be implemented either as a stored procedure (through internal activation) or an external application (through external activation). As the eighth step illustrates, the service program processes the response message from the target service and can inform the client application about the outcome of the service request.

Performance

Performance is always a key requirement in a software system. When you implement message-based applications, you must consider performance. Service Broker provides performance benefits in several areas:

- *Message-processing logic*: You can implement the message-processing logic of your service programs in different ways. In a high-load production system where perform-ance is a key requirement, you need other message-processing approaches. This is in contrast with a Service Broker system, where only a few messages are exchanged within the whole day. Chapter 6 describes more message-processing techniques you can use to get the best message throughput out of your Service Broker application.

- *Multiple queue readers*: When you use Service Broker activation (whether internally or externally), you can define how many service programs are processing messages concurrently. Therefore, it's easy to control the message throughput and adjust it to your requirements.

- *Transaction management*: Other messaging systems such as MSMQ need distributed transactions to ensure the consistency of data over different resource managers that are incorporated in the message-processing logic. Distributed transactions make life easier when you work with different resource managers, but they're terrible in terms of performance. Service Broker takes another approach and uses local SQL Server transactions instead of distributed transactions. This is possible because messages and the message processing logic (service programs) are stored within the same database.

- *Single log writes*: Because Service Broker uses local SQL Server transactions, perform-ance is also better, since no transaction coordinator is needed. Furthermore, only one log write is needed when a local SQL Server transaction is committed.

Figure 2-10 shows the performance overhead introduced with distributed transactions.

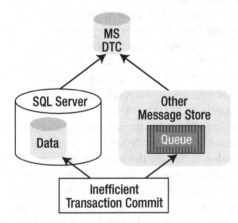

Figure 2-10. *Performance problems with distributed transactions*

Finally, Figure 2-11 shows how Service Broker handles the problems with local SQL Server transactions.

Compared to other messaging technologies, Service Broker provides better performance, as well as transactional reliability directly out of the box.

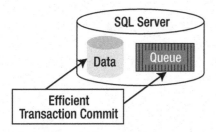

Figure 2-11. *Transaction management in Service Broker*

Benefits

As you've seen throughout this chapter, Service Broker provides several unique features that make it a powerful messaging platform:

- *One API*: Service Broker provides one API for both message and data-processing logic. With MSMQ, you must program with the System.Messaging and System.Data namespaces of the .NET Framework. Service Broker simplifies this, because it includes the messaging support directly in T-SQL instead of providing an additional API.

- *Centralized administration tools*: Whether you want to administer a SQL Server database with or without Service Broker functionality, you use the same tool: SQL Server Management Studio. If you want to back up or restore your Service Broker application, you can use the same process as you would for an online transaction processing (OLTP) database. Your administrators don't have to learn new tools.

- *Reliable messaging*: Reliability is one of the key features of Service Broker. The nice thing about reliability is that Service Broker provides it for you out of box. When you use Service Broker, you use reliable messaging automatically.

- *Scale-out scenarios*: From the programming perspective, it makes no difference if you implement a Service Broker application that is hosted on one SQL Server instance or if you implement a solution that is distributed to different SQL Server instances. All necessary aspects of physical service distribution are done through configuration steps during the deployment of a Service Broker application.

Summary

This chapter covered the architecture and the core concepts of Service Broker. You learned about conversations, dialogs, and conversation groups. You also looked at the components of a service, including objects such as message types, contracts, and queues. Because you can use Service Broker in distributed scenarios, you learned about transport and dialog security.

In the next chapter, you'll see how to implement a messaging application with Service Broker, and you'll learn the necessary steps to build one from scratch.

CHAPTER 3

■ ■ ■

Service Broker in Action

Now that you've learned the theoretical concepts about messaging and Service Broker architecture, it's time to talk about the actual implementation of Service Broker applications. In this chapter, you'll learn how to write your own Service Broker services and how these services can communicate with each other. I'll cover the following topics in detail:

- *Defining Service Broker applications*: A Service Broker application consists of several Service Broker objects, including message types, contracts, a queue, and a service. You'll learn how these objects are related to each other and how you can program them.

- *Sending messages*: Once you define your Service Broker application, you're able to send messages between your Service Broker services. You'll learn how to exchange messages successfully.

- *Retrieving and processing messages*: As soon as you send messages to another Service Broker service, you must retrieve and process the messages. You'll learn how to retrieve and process the messages and how to react to different message types.

- *Error handling*: Every robust software application needs error handling; the same is true with Service Broker. Service Broker provides error-handling possibilities that are directly integrated into the infrastructure provided by Service Broker. You'll learn how to use error handling and how to handle poison messages.

Let's start with how to define a Service Broker application.

Defining Service Broker Applications

Let's start with a simple "Hello World" Service Broker application in which you define both the initiator service and the target service in the same database. Because of this, you don't have to bother with security and distributed messaging complications.

One limitation of SQL Server 2008 is that you can't manage Service Broker objects through SQL Server Management Studio. There are no wizards for managing message types, contracts, a queue, and a service. You can manage these objects through the T-SQL statements described in this chapter. The only things that SQL Server 2008 provides you with in this area are template scripts that you can use as a beginning point for your Service Broker applications. In addition, you can manage them through SQL Server Management Objects (SMOs), which my coauthor, Remus, will cover in Chapter 12 when he discusses administration.

> ■**Note** Service Broker objects are always case-sensitive. This allows Service Broker to avoid spending time resolving the collation of the dialog initiator and target. The only exception to this is the queue object, which follows the collation of the database. This is acceptable because a queue is never referenced directly from an outside service.

Message Types

The simple sample application used in this chapter follows this messaging sequence:

- The initiator service sends a message to the target service containing some important information, such as a name.

- The target service receives the message and processes it.

- The target service creates a response message and sends it back to the initiator service.

Figure 3-1 illustrates this message flow.

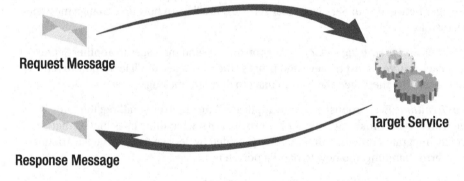

Figure 3-1. *A simple message flow*

As with every Service Broker application, you must first define the interface for your Service Broker services, which includes the exchanged message types and the contracts supported by your Service Broker services. As you can see in Figure 3-1, you need a request message (sent by the initiator service) and a response message (sent by the target service). Both message types are grouped together in a contract.

Now let's look at how you define a message type in the context of a Service Broker application. SQL Server 2008 offers some Data Definition Language (DDL) enhancements to T-SQL for creating Service Broker objects. When you want to create a new message type, you use the CREATE MESSAGE TYPE statement. Listing 3-1 shows the syntax for this statement.

Listing 3-1. *Syntax for* CREATE MESSAGE TYPE

```
CREATE MESSAGE TYPE message_type_name
   [ AUTHORIZATION owner_name ]
   [ VALIDATION =
      {
         NONE |
         EMPTY |
         WELL_FORMED_XML |
         VALID_XML WITH SCHEMA COLLECTION schema_collection_name
      }
   ]
```

Table 3-1 describes the several arguments of the CREATE MESSAGE TYPE statement.

Table 3-1. *Arguments for* CREATE MESSAGE TYPE

Argument	Description
message_type_name	The name of the message type to create. The new message type is created within the current database and is owned by the principal specified in the AUTHORIZATION clause. You can't put a message type into a schema.
AUTHORIZATION owner_name	Specifies the owner of the message type. You can specify a database user or a database role.
VALIDATION	Specifies the validation of incoming messages used by Service Broker. If no validation is specified, the NONE validation is used.
NONE	Used when the incoming message isn't validated. In this case, the message body can contain any data or even NULL.
EMPTY	Used when the body of the incoming message must contain NULL.
WELL_FORMED_XML	Used when the body of the incoming message must contain valid XML data.
VALID_XML WITH SCHEMA COLLECTION	Used when the body of the incoming message must contain XML data that can be validated against the specified XML schema collection. See the accompanying sidebar for more information.

XML SCHEMA COLLECTION

An XML schema collection stores one or more XML Schema Definition (XSD) schemas in a SQL Server 2008 database. When you create an instance of the xml data type, you can assign an XML schema collection to the data type. Therefore, any change in the xml data type must conform to the associated XML schema collection.

When you define Service Broker message types, you can also assign an XML schema collection to an XML message. In this case, Service Broker automatically validates the XML contained in the message and checks if the XML data conforms to the XSD schema stored in the XML schema collection. Be cautious, because the XML validation takes a lot of time and can hurt your message-processing performance. I suggest using XML validation only during development and just using WELL_FORMED_XML for your production system.

You can now create message types for both the request and the response messages used by your Service Broker application. It's important that you give each message type (and also each contract) a unique name. This is necessary because you must define message types and contracts in each database where a Service Broker service is running. Therefore, you can get naming conflicts with other Service Broker services that define the same name for message types that have other meanings. It's conventional to prefix each message type and each contract with your own Internet domain. Listing 3-2 shows you how you can define both message types needed for the sample Service Broker conversation. (I create two message types: RequestMessage and ResponseMessage.)

■Note Please be sure to create a new database in which you execute the following listings in this chapter.

Listing 3-2. *Defining Message Types*

```
CREATE MESSAGE TYPE [http://ssb.csharp.at/SSB_Book/c03/RequestMessage]
    VALIDATION = NONE


CREATE MESSAGE TYPE [http://ssb.csharp.at/SSB_Book/c03/ResponseMessage]
    VALIDATION = NONE
```

As soon as you define the message types, you can also view them in SQL Server Management Studio, as shown in Figure 3-2.

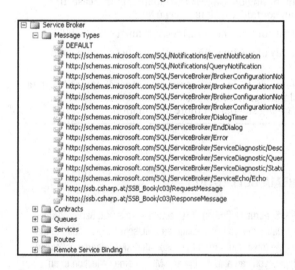

Figure 3-2. *Viewing defined message types*

You can also see the registered message types through the sys.service_message_types catalog view. This view is handy when you must determine programmatically which message types are defined in your database. Table 3-2 lists the columns in this view.

Table 3-2. *Columns in the* `sys.service_message_types` *Catalog View*

Column	Data Type	Description
name	SYSNAME	The name of the message type. It must be unique within the database.
message_type_id	INT	The internal identifier of the message type. It must be unique within the database.
principal_id	INT	The identifier for the database principal that owns this message type.
validation	CHAR(2)	The message type validation done by Service Broker when receiving a message of this type: N = None X = XML E = Empty.
validation_desc	NVARCHAR(60)	The description of the validation done by Service Broker when receiving a message of this type: NONE XML EMPTY.
xml_collection_id	INT	The identifier of the XML schema collection used to validate a message of this type when XML schema validation is used.

When you want to change the validation of an already registered message type, you can use the ALTER MESSAGE TYPE T-SQL statement. You can change the owner of a message type through the ALTER AUTHORIZATION T-SQL statement. Listing 3-3 shows how you can change the validation of the registered message types to WELL_FORMED_XML.

Listing 3-3. *Changing a Message Type*

```
ALTER MESSAGE TYPE [http://ssb.csharp.at/SSB_Book/c03/RequestMessage]
    VALIDATION = WELL_FORMED_XML

ALTER MESSAGE TYPE [http://ssb.csharp.at/SSB_Book/c03/ResponseMessage]
    VALIDATION = WELL_FORMED_XML
```

You can delete existing message types with the DROP MESSAGE TYPE T-SQL statement. Additionally, each SQL Server database contains the predefined message type [DEFAULT]. This message type is equivalent to each message type that you created explicitly. The validation of this message type is set to NONE, which means that this message type can contain any information you need. This message type is handy when you want to quickly set up a Service Broker application and you don't want to concentrate on message type definitions. However, I don't suggest using this message type in production, because then you can't control the format of the message body.

Contracts

Once you've defined the message types for your Service Broker application, you can create the needed contract. The contract defines the message types used in a Service Broker conversation

and also determines which side of the conversation can send messages of which type.
In other words, the contract defines the sending direction of each message. You can create
contracts with the CREATE CONTRACT T-SQL statement. Listing 3-4 shows the complete syntax
of this statement.

Listing 3-4. *Syntax for* CREATE CONTRACT

```
CREATE CONTRACT contract_name
   [ AUTHORIZATION owner_name ]
   (
      {
         message_type_name SENT BY { INITIATOR | TARGET | ANY }
      | [ DEFAULT ] } [ ,...n ]
   )
```

Table 3-3 describes the several arguments of the CREATE CONTRACT statement.

Table 3-3. *Arguments for* CREATE CONTRACT

Argument	Description
contract_name	Specifies the name of the contract created inside the database.
AUTHORIZATION owner_name	Specifies the owner of the contract. You can specify a database user or a database role.
message_type_name	Specifies the message type included in this contract.
SENT BY	Specifies in which direction a Service Broker service can send a message of the specified message type.
INITIATOR	Specifies that the initiator of the conversation can send the specified message type. A service that begins a conversation is referred to as the initiator of the conversation.
TARGET	Specifies that the target of the conversation can send the specified message type. A service that accepts a conversation that was started by another service is referred to as the target of the conversation.
ANY	Specifies that either the initiator or the target service can send the message type.
[DEFAULT]	Specifies that this contract supports the [DEFAULT] message type. This option is equivalent to specifying [DEFAULT] SENT BY ANY. By default, all databases contain a message type named [DEFAULT]. This message type uses a validation of NONE. In the context of this clause, [DEFAULT] is not a keyword and must be delimited as an identifier. Service Broker also provides the [DEFAULT] contract, which specifies the [DEFAULT] message type.

As you can see in Listing 3-4, you can provide several message types for a contract. In the sample, you need a contract that specifies that the initiator service can send the request message type and that the target service can send the response message type. Listing 3-5 shows the necessary code fragment.

Listing 3-5. *Defining the Contract*

```
CREATE CONTRACT [http://ssb.csharp.at/SSB_Book/c03/HelloWorldContract]
(
    [http://ssb.csharp.at/SSB_Book/c03/RequestMessage] SENT BY INITIATOR,
    [http://ssb.csharp.at/SSB_Book/c03/ResponseMessage] SENT BY TARGET
)
GO
```

As soon as you define the contract in your database, you can view it through the SQL Server Management Studio, as shown in Figure 3-3.

Figure 3-3. *Viewing the defined contract*

The registered contracts are also available through the sys.service_contracts and sys.service_contract_message_usages catalog views. The first catalog view retrieves all registered contracts. The second one retrieves the message types associated with a specified contract. Table 3-4 describes the columns in the sys.service_contracts catalog view.

Table 3-4. *Columns in the* sys.service_contracts *Catalog View*

Column	Data Type	Description
name	SYSNAME	Contains the name of the registered contract.
service_contract_id	INT	Contains the internal identifier of the contract. This identifier is used to join with other catalog views.
principal_id	INT	Contains the identifier for the database principal that owns this contract.

Table 3-5 describes the columns in the sys.service_contract_message_usages catalog view.

Table 3-5. *Columns in the* sys.service_contract_message_usages *Catalog View*

Column	Data Type	Description
service_contract_id	INT	Contains the internal identifier of the contract
message_type_id	INT	Contains the identifier of the message type used by the contract
is_sent_by_initiator	BIT	Indicates that the message type can be sent by the initiator
is_sent_by_target	BIT	Indicates that the message type can be sent by the target

With the three catalog views, you can write a query that returns all associated message types of a contract. Listing 3-6 shows the query, and Figure 3-4 shows its results.

Listing 3-6. *Getting Contract Information Through the Catalog Views*

```
SELECT
    sc.name AS 'Contract',
    mt.name AS 'Message type',
    cm.is_sent_by_initiator,
    cm.is_sent_by_target,
    mt.validation
FROM sys.service_contract_message_usages cm
    INNER JOIN sys.service_message_types mt ON cm.message_type_id =
        mt.message_type_id
    INNER JOIN sys.service_contracts sc ON sc.service_contract_id =
        cm.service_contract_id
GO
```

	Contract	Message type	is_sent_by_initiator	is_sent_by_target	validation
1	DEFAULT	DEFAULT	1	1	N
2	http://schemas.microsoft.com/SQL/Notifications/Pos...	http://schemas.microsoft.com/SQL/Notifications/Even...	1	0	X
3	http://schemas.microsoft.com/SQL/Notifications/Pos...	http://schemas.microsoft.com/SQL/Notifications/Quer...	1	0	X
4	http://schemas.microsoft.com/SQL/ServiceBroker/Br...	http://schemas.microsoft.com/SQL/ServiceBroker/Bro...	1	0	X
5	http://schemas.microsoft.com/SQL/ServiceBroker/Br...	http://schemas.microsoft.com/SQL/ServiceBroker/Bro...	1	0	X
6	http://schemas.microsoft.com/SQL/ServiceBroker/Br...	http://schemas.microsoft.com/SQL/ServiceBroker/Bro...	1	0	X
7	http://schemas.microsoft.com/SQL/ServiceBroker/Br...	http://schemas.microsoft.com/SQL/ServiceBroker/Bro...	1	0	X
8	http://schemas.microsoft.com/SQL/ServiceBroker/S...	http://schemas.microsoft.com/SQL/ServiceBroker/Ser...	1	0	X
9	http://schemas.microsoft.com/SQL/ServiceBroker/S...	http://schemas.microsoft.com/SQL/ServiceBroker/Ser...	0	1	X
10	http://schemas.microsoft.com/SQL/ServiceBroker/S...	http://schemas.microsoft.com/SQL/ServiceBroker/Ser...	0	1	N
11	http://schemas.microsoft.com/SQL/ServiceBroker/S...	http://schemas.microsoft.com/SQL/ServiceBroker/Ser...	1	1	N
12	http://ssb.csharp.at/SSB_Book/c03/HelloWorldCont...	http://ssb.csharp.at/SSB_Book/c03/RequestMessage	1	0	N
13	http://ssb.csharp.at/SSB_Book/c03/HelloWorldCont...	http://ssb.csharp.at/SSB_Book/c03/ResponseMessage	0	1	N

Figure 3-4. *The registered contracts*

Sometimes customers ask how they can alter a Service Broker contract, because there is no corresponding ALTER CONTRACT T-SQL statement. The short answer is that they can't alter an existing contract. You can compare a contract with an interface description in COM. Also, a rule exists that says you can't change published interfaces; the same is true with a Service Broker contract. So, when you need to change a Service Broker contract, you have to implement some kind of versioning.

You can delete existing contracts with the DROP CONTRACT T-SQL statement. If the contract is associated with a Service Broker service, then you can't drop the contract, and SQL Server returns an error message. If there is an open conversation based on the dropped contract, the conversation closes and an error message returns to both Service Broker services.

As with message types, Service Broker provides a contract named [DEFAULT]. The [DEFAULT] contract indicates that ALL can send the [DEFAULT] message type (but no other message type). However, there are some confusing things about the [DEFAULT] contract, which I cover in the "Service" section.

Queue

After you define the appropriate message types and contracts, each service side must define a queue where received messages are stored for further processing through a service program. In the sample, you need two queues in the same database, because the services are not distributed between several SQL Server instances. You create queues with the CREATE QUEUE T-SQL statement. Listing 3-7 shows the complete syntax for this statement.

Listing 3-7. *Syntax for* CREATE QUEUE

```
CREATE QUEUE queue_name
    [WITH
        [STATUS = { ON | OFF },
        [RETENTION = { ON | OFF },
        [ACTIVATION
        (
            [STATUS = { ON | OFF },
            PROCEDURE_NAME = procedure_name,
            MAX_QUEUE_READERS = max_queue_readers
            EXECUTE AS { SELF | 'user_name' | OWNER }
        )]
    ]
    [ ON { filegroup | [ DEFAULT ] } ]
    ]
```

Table 3-6 describes the most important arguments of the CREATE QUEUE statement.

Table 3-6. *Arguments for* CREATE QUEUE

Argument	Description
queue_name	Specifies the name of the queue created inside the database.
STATUS	Specifies the status of the queue. It can be online (ON) or offline (OFF). When the queue is offline, no messages can be added to the queue or processed from the queue. This would make sense when you must turn off a service for maintenance work.
RETENTION	Specifies if retention is used for this queue. If set to ON, all messages sent or received on conversation groups using this queue are stored in the queue until the conversation has ended. This allows you to store messages for auditing purposes, or to perform compensating transactions if an error occurred.
ACTIVATION	Specifies the information needed to activate a stored procedure when a new message arrives at the queue.
STATUS	Indicates if activation is used for this queue. It can be ON or OFF.
PROCEDURE_NAME	Specifies the name of the stored procedure to activate when a new message arrives at the queue.
MAX_QUEUE_READERS	Specifies the maximum number of instances of the activation stored procedure that the queue starts at the same time to process the incoming messages.
EXECUTE AS	Specifies the SQL Server database user account under which the activation stored procedure runs.
ON filegroup [DEFAULT]	Specifies the SQL Server filegroup on which you want to create this queue. You can use the DEFAULT identifier to create the queue on the default filegroup, or you can specify another filegroup.

Note from these descriptions that you can also control the activation mechanism of the queue. I cover this more in Chapter 4, where I discuss the activation scenarios available in Service Broker. Listing 3-8 shows how you can create the sending and receiving queues.

Listing 3-8. *Creating the Needed Queues*

```
CREATE QUEUE InitiatorQueue
WITH STATUS = ON

CREATE QUEUE TargetQueue
WITH STATUS = ON
```

As soon as you create your queues, they're visible in SQL Server Management Studio, as shown in Figure 3-5. The created queues are also available through the sys.service_queues catalog view. Each row in this view represents a queue defined in the current database. Table 3-7 lists the columns in this catalog view.

Figure 3-5. *The created queues*

Table 3-7. *Columns in the* sys.service_queues *Catalog View*

Column	Data Type	Description
max_readers	SMALLINT	Specifies the maximum number of parallel queue readers used for this queue
activation_procedure	NVARCHAR(776)	The name of the activated stored procedure in the three-part syntax
execute_as_principal_id	INT	ID of the EXECUTE AS database principal; NULL by default, or if EXECUTE AS CALLER, –2 = EXECUTE AS OWNER
is_activation_enabled	BIT	Indicates if activation is enabled
is_receive_enabled	BIT	Indicates if the queue is currently able to receive messages
is_enqueue_enabled	BIT	Indicates if the queue is currently able to enqueue new messages
is_retention_enabled	BIT	Indicates if retention is enabled

Service

After defining message types, contracts, and a queue, you must finally define your Service Broker service in each database participating in the conversation. In the example, you must define two services in the same database because you don't use Service Broker's distributed message-processing capabilities. You create services through the CREATE SERVICE T-SQL statement. Service Broker uses the name of the created service to route messages, deliver messages to the correct queue within a database, and enforce the contract for a conversation. Listing 3-9 shows the complete syntax for the CREATE SERVICE T-SQL statement.

Listing 3-9. *Syntax for* CREATE SERVICE

```
CREATE SERVICE service_name
   [ AUTHORIZATION owner_name ]
   ON QUEUE [ schema_name. ]queue_name
   [
   (contract_name | [DEFAULT] [ , ...n ])
   ]
```

Table 3-8 describes the arguments of the CREATE SERVICE statement.

Table 3-8. *Arguments for* CREATE SERVICE

Argument	Description
service_name	Specifies the name of the service to create. The service is created in the current database, and the owner of the service is specified through the AUTHORIZATION clause.
AUTHORIZATION owner_name	Specifies the owner of the service to the specified database user or role.
ON QUEUE queue_name	Specifies the queue that is associated with this service.
contract_name	Specifies the contract that is supported by this service. If you specify no contract, the service can only initiate conversations with a target service.
[DEFAULT]	Specifies that the service may be a target for conversations using the [DEFAULT] contract. [DEFAULT] is not a keyword, so you must delimit it as an identifier.

Listing 3-10 shows how to define both the Service Broker services needed for the sample application.

Listing 3-10. *Creating the Necessary Service Broker Services*

```
CREATE SERVICE InitiatorService
ON QUEUE InitiatorQueue
(
    [http://ssb.csharp.at/SSB_Book/c03/HelloWorldContract]
)
GO

CREATE SERVICE TargetService
ON QUEUE TargetQueue
(
    [http://ssb.csharp.at/SSB_Book/c03/HelloWorldContract]
)
GO
```

As soon as you create the needed Service Broker services, they become available in the SQL Server Management Studio, as shown in Figure 3-6.

Figure 3-6. *The created services*

The created services are also available through the sys.services catalog view. Table 3-9 lists the columns available in the sys.services catalog view.

Table 3-9. *Columns in the* sys.services *Catalog View*

Column	Data Type	Description
name	SYSNAME	The name of the service; must be unique within the current database
service_id	INT	The internal identifier of the new service
principal_id	INT	The identifier for the database principal that owns this service
service_queue_id	INT	The object ID for the queue that is associated with this service

Listing 3-11 shows how you can join the sys.services, sys.service_contract_usages, and sys.service_contracts catalog views to retrieve the contracts that a service supports.

Listing 3-11. *Getting the Contracts of the Defined Services*

```
SELECT
    sv.name AS 'Service',
    sc.name AS 'Contract'
FROM sys.services sv
    INNER JOIN sys.service_contract_usages scu ON scu.service_id =
        sv.service_id
    INNER JOIN sys.service_contracts sc ON sc.service_contract_id =
        scu.service_contract_id
GO
```

Figure 3-7 shows the result of the T-SQL query from Listing 3-11.

	Service	Contract
1	InitiatorService	http://ssb.csharp.at/SSB_Book/c03/HelloWorldCont...
2	TargetService	http://ssb.csharp.at/SSB_Book/c03/HelloWorldCont...
3	http://schemas.microsoft.com/SQL/ServiceBroker/S...	http://schemas.microsoft.com/SQL/ServiceBroker/S...
4	http://schemas.microsoft.com/SQL/ServiceBroker/S...	http://schemas.microsoft.com/SQL/ServiceBroker/S...

Figure 3-7. *The services with the associated contracts*

You can alter an existing service with the ALTER SERVICE T-SQL statement. There are three possible aspects you can change for a service:

- *The queue associated with the service*: You can specify a new queue for the service. Service Broker moves all messages for this service from the current queue to the new queue.

- *Adding a contract*: You can specify a contract that is added to the service definition.

- *Dropping a contract*: You can specify a contract that is dropped from the service definition.

Listing 3-12 shows the usage of this T-SQL statement.

Listing 3-12. *Altering a Service Definition*

```
ALTER SERVICE TargetService
ON QUEUE MyNewTargetQueue
(
    ADD CONTRACT [MyNewContract]
    DROP CONTRACT [http://ssb.csharp.at/SSB_Book/c03/HelloWorldContract]
)
```

If you want to delete a Service Broker service, you can use the DROP SERVICE T-SQL statement. You must supply as a parameter the name of the service to be dropped.

I want to mention a few important things about the [DEFAULT] contract. When you want to use the [DEFAULT] contract, you must explicitly specify it at the target service, as Listing 3-13 demonstrates.

Listing 3-13. *Using the* [DEFAULT] *Contract on the Target Service*

```
CREATE SERVICE TargetService
    ON QUEUE TargetQueue
(
    [DEFAULT]
)
```

This is confusing, because you don't have to specify the [DEFAULT] contract at the initiating service, since you also define the contract when you start a new conversation with another Service Broker service. Listing 3-14 shows a valid service definition when you also want to use the [DEFAULT] contract.

Listing 3-14. *Using the* [DEFAULT] *Contract on the Initiator Service*

```
CREATE SERVICE InitiatorService
    ON QUEUE InitiatorQueue
```

INITIATOR SERVICES AND CONTRACTS

By now, you've learned that each service must specify the supported contracts. That's true for target services, but it's not completely true for initiator services. Initiator services aren't bound to a contract, because they can initiate conversations with many different targets.

This also prevents them from ever being targeted. That's an important concept, because when an initiating service isn't bound to a specified contract, the target service isn't able to send response messages back to this service.

Sending Messages

By now, you've set up all the infrastructure objects that Service Broker needs. The next logical step is to send a message from the InitiatorService to the TargetService. To accomplish this task, you must perform the following two steps:

1. Create a new conversation between the two Service Broker services.

2. Send a message of the message type
   [http://ssb.csharp.at/SSB_Book/c03/RequestMessage] to the TargetService.

For both steps, Service Broker offers you special T-SQL statements: BEGIN DIALOG CONVERSATION and SEND ON CONVERSATION. Listing 3-15 shows you the syntax of the BEGIN DIALOG CONVERSATION statement.

Listing 3-15. *Syntax for* BEGIN DIALOG CONVERSATION

```
BEGIN DIALOG [ CONVERSATION ] @dialog_handle
   FROM SERVICE initiator_service_name
   TO SERVICE 'target_service_name'
      [ , { 'service_broker_guid' | 'CURRENT DATABASE' } ]
   [ ON CONTRACT contract_name ]
   [ WITH
   {
      RELATED_CONVERSATION = related_conversation_handle |
      RELATED_CONVERSATION_GROUP = related_conversation_group_id
   } ]
   [ LIFETIME = dialog_lifetime ]
   [ ENCRYPTION = { ON | OFF } ]
```

Table 3-10 describes the arguments of this T-SQL statement.

Table 3-10. *Arguments for* BEGIN DIALOG CONVERSATION

Argument	Description
@dialog_handle	This variable stores the conversation dialog handle returned by this T-SQL statement. The conversation dialog handle uniquely identifies the conversation started with this statement.
FROM SERVICE initiator_service_name	Specifies the service that starts the conversation. The name specified must be the name of a service in the current database.
TO SERVICE 'target_service_name'	Specifies the target service of the initiated conversation.
service_broker_guid	The ID of the Service Broker instance that hosts the target service. If you host a Service Broker service in more than one database, you can use the service_broker_guid argument to identify in a unique way the target of your new conversation.
ON CONTRACT contract_name	Specifies the contract used by this conversation. The contract must exist in the current database.

Continued

Table 3-10. *Continued*

Argument	Description
RELATED_CONVERSATION related_conversation_handle	Specifies an existing conversation group that the new conversation is added to. When this clause is present, the new conversation belongs to the same conversation group as the dialog specified by related_conversation_handle. The statement fails if the related_conversation_handle doesn't reference an existing dialog.
RELATED_CONVERSATION_GROUP related_conversation_group_id	Specifies the existing conversation group that the new conversation is added to. When this clause is present, the new conversation is added to the conversation group specified by related_conversation_group_id. If related_conversation_ group_id doesn't reference an existing conversation group, Service Broker will create a new conversation group with the specified related_conversation_group_id and relate the new conversation to that conversation group.
LIFETIME	Specifies the maximum amount of time the conversation will be active. To complete the dialog successfully, each Service Broker service must explicitly end the dialog before the lifetime expires.
ENCRYPTION	Specifies if encryption is used for the message sending.

As soon as you start a new conversation between both Service Broker services, you can send a message from the initiator to the target. For this purpose, you use the SEND ON CONVERSATION T-SQL statement. Listing 3-16 shows the syntax for the SEND ON CONVERSATION T-SQL statement.

Listing 3-16. *Syntax for* SEND ON CONVERSATION

```
SEND ON CONVERSATION conversation_handle
    [ MESSAGE TYPE message_type_name ]
    [ (message_body) ]
```

Table 3-11 describes the arguments of this T-SQL statement.

Table 3-11. *Arguments for* SEND ON CONVERSATION

Argument	Description
conversation_handle	Specifies the conversation under which the message should be sent.
message_type_name	The message type used for the sent message. You must define this message type in the service contract used by this conversation. The contract must allow the message type to be sent from this side of the conversation.
message_body	The message body of the message sent to the other Service Broker service.

Listing 3-17 shows you how to send a message from the InitiatorService to the TargetService.

Listing 3-17. *Sending a Message*

```
BEGIN TRY
   BEGIN TRANSACTION;
      DECLARE @ch UNIQUEIDENTIFIER
      DECLARE @msg NVARCHAR(MAX);

      BEGIN DIALOG CONVERSATION @ch
         FROM SERVICE [InitiatorService]
         TO SERVICE 'TargetService'
         ON CONTRACT [http://ssb.csharp.at/SSB_Book/c03/HelloWorldContract]
         WITH ENCRYPTION = OFF;

      SET @msg =
         '<HelloWorldRequest>
            Klaus Aschenbrenner
         </HelloWorldRequest>';

      SEND ON CONVERSATION @ch MESSAGE TYPE
         [http://ssb.csharp.at/SSB_Book/c03/RequestMessage]
      (
         @msg
      );
   COMMIT;
END TRY
BEGIN CATCH
   ROLLBACK TRANSACTION
END CATCH
GO
```

Let's step through this T-SQL batch line by line:

```
BEGIN TRANSACTION;
   DECLARE @ch UNIQUEIDENTIFIER
   DECLARE @msg NVARCHAR(MAX);
```

In the first three lines, a new local SQL Server transaction is created and two variables are declared. The first variable, @ch, stores the unique identifier of the new conversation, referred to as conversation dialog handle. The variable @msg stores the message body sent to the other Service Broker service.

Within these next five lines, a new conversation between the two services is created:

```
BEGIN DIALOG CONVERSATION @ch
   FROM SERVICE [InitiatorService]
   TO SERVICE 'TargetService'
   ON CONTRACT [http://ssb.csharp.at/SSB_Book/c03/HelloWorldContract]
   WITH ENCRYPTION = OFF;
```

You must specify both service names, as well as the contract on which the conversation is based. Note carefully that the service name specified in the TO SERVICE clause must be specified as a string literal, because the target service can live on another SQL Server instance. When you want to distribute your Service Broker application across several SQL Server instances, you don't need to update this code because you can create a route for the service name specified in the TO SERVICE clause.

During the development of this T-SQL batch, you can't even know if the target service runs in the same database (as in this case) or on a SQL Server instance several thousand miles away from you. Because you specified the target service name as a string literal, no changes must be applied to this T-SQL batch when an administrator moves the target service to another SQL Server instance. For simplification, message encryption is turned off for this conversation.

In these next few lines, you create the body of your message:

```
SET @msg =
    '<HelloWorldRequest>
        Klaus Aschenbrenner
    </HelloWorldRequest>';
```

Because the validation of the message type [http://ssb.csharp.at/SSB_Book/c03/RequestMessage] is defined as WELL_FORMED_XML, you can send any valid XML document as a payload for this message. When you turn on XML schema validation for this message type, you must successfully validate the XML data assigned here to the variable @msg against an XML schema collection that you specify in the CREATE MESSAGE TYPE T-SQL statement.

Finally, you send the message over the previously created conversation, and you commit the transaction:

```
SEND ON CONVERSATION @ch
    MESSAGE TYPE [http://ssb.csharp.at/SSB_Book/c03/RequestMessage]
(
    @msg
);
COMMIT;
```

When you send the message through SEND ON CONVERSATION, you must supply the conversation dialog handle that was initialized with a unique identifier from the call to BEGIN DIALOG CONVERSATION. Furthermore, you must also supply the message type of the message you want to send to the target service.

When you want to use the [DEFAULT] contract, you must not specify it in the BEGIN DIALOG CONVERSATION statement. The two statements in Listing 3-18 are equivalent.

Listing 3-18. *Sending a Message on the* [DEFAULT] *Contract*

```
SEND ON CONVERSATION @handle
(
    'Hello World'
)
```

```
-- or

SEND ON CONVERSATION @handle
MESSAGE TYPE [DEFAULT]
(
    'Hello World'
)
```

As you can see from these descriptions about the [DEFAULT] contract, the whole thing can be a bit complicated.

As soon as you initiate a new conversation between two services through BEGIN DIALOG CONVERSATION, a conversation endpoint is created for the initiating service. The conversation endpoint for the target service is created when you send the first message. A conversation endpoint represents the ongoing conversation for the associated service. From the sys. conversation_endpoints catalog view, you can obtain more information about the conversation. Table 3-12 describes the columns that are available through the sys.conversation_ endpoints catalog view.

Table 3-12. *Columns in the* sys.conversation_endpoints *Catalog View*

Column	Data Type	Description
conversation_handle	UNIQUEIDENTIFIER	The identifier used for this conversation endpoint
conversation_id	UNIQUEIDENTIFIER	The identifier shared by both Service Broker services of the ongoing conversation
is_initiator	TINYINT	Specifies if this conversation is the initiator or the target of the conversation
service_contract_id	INT	The identifier of the contract that this conversation follows
conversation_group_id	UNIQUEIDENTIFIER	The identifier of the conversation group that this conversation belongs to
service_id	INT	The identifier of the Service Broker service of this side of the conversation
lifetime	DATETIME	The expiration date/time of this conversation
state	CHAR(2)	The current state of the conversation (see Table 3-14 for the possible values)
state_desc	NVARCHAR(60)	The description of the current state of the conversation (see Table 3-13 for the possible values)
far_service	NVARCHAR(256)	The name of the service on the remote side of the conversation

Continued

Table 3-12. *Continued*

Column	Data Type	Description
far_broker_instance	NVARCHAR(128)	The identifier of the broker instance on the remote side of the conversation
principal_id	INT	The identifier of the principal whose certificate is used by the local side of this conversation
far_principal_id	INT	The identifier of the principal whose certificate is used by the remote side of this conversation
outbound_session_key_identifier	UNIQUEIDENTIFIER	The identifier for the outbound encryption key for this conversation
inbound_session_key_identifier	UNIQUEIDENTIFIER	The identifier for the inbound encryption key for this conversation
security_timestamp	DATETIME	The time when the local session key was created
dialog_timer	DATETIME	The time at which the conversation timer for this conversation sends a DialogTimer message
send_sequence	BIGINT	The next message number in the send sequence
last_send_tran_id	BINARY(6)	The internal transaction ID of the last transaction to send a message
end_dialog_sequence	BIGINT	The sequence number of the EndDialog message
receive_sequence	BIGINT	The next message number expected in the message receive sequence
receive_sequence_flag	INT	The next message fragment number expected in the message receive sequence
system_sequence	BIGINT	The sequence number of the last system message for this dialog
first_out_of_order_sequence	BIGINT	The sequence number of the first message in the out-of-order messages for this conversation
last_out_of_order_sequence	BIGINT	The sequence number of the last message in the out-of-order messages for this conversation
last_out_of_order_frag	INT	The sequence number of the last message in the out-of-order fragments for this dialog
is_system	BIT	1 if this is a system dialog
priority	TINYINT	The assigned conversation priority for this conversation

Table 3-13 shows the possible states for a conversation that are stored in the column state_desc of the sys.conversation_endpoints catalog view.

Table 3-13. *Possible States for a Conversation*

state	state_desc	Description
SO	STARTED_OUTBOUND	Indicates that Service Broker processed a BEGIN CONVERSATION for this conversation, but no messages have been sent yet.
SI	STARTED_INBOUND	Indicates that another instance started a new conversation with Service Broker, but Service Broker has not yet completely received the first message.
CO	CONVERSING	Indicates that the conversation is established, and both sides of the conversation send messages.
DI	DISCONNECTED_INBOUND	Indicates that the remote side of the conversation has issued an END CONVERSATION. The conversation remains in this state until the local side of the conversation issues an END CONVERSATION.
DO	DISCONNECTED_OUTBOUND	Indicates that the local side of the conversation has issued an END CONVERSATION. The conversation remains in this state until the remote side of the conversation issues an END CONVERSATION.
CD	CLOSED	Indicates that the conversation endpoint is no longer in use.
ER	ERROR	Indicates that an error has occurred on this endpoint.

When you execute the query SELECT * FROM sys.conversation_endpoints, two rows are returned, as you can see in Figure 3-8.

	conversation_handle	conversation_id	is_initiator	state	state_desc	service_contract_id
1	2ED49C37-8C79-DB11-A30E-0080C81899BB	0D59EF6D-C75D-4734-B832-6A8CDC9E810F	1	CO	CONVERSING	65536
2	31D49C37-8C79-DB11-A30E-0080C81899BB	0D59EF6D-C75D-4734-B832-6A8CDC9E810F	0	CO	CONVERSING	65536

Figure 3-8. *The created conversation endpoints for both services*

Retrieving and Processing Messages

If you've followed the steps so far, you should have sent your first message from one Service Broker service to another Service Broker service located in the same database. If everything went fine, your sent message was stored in the TargetQueue associated with the TargetService. When you execute the query SELECT * FROM TargetQueue on the queue, you should see the output shown in Figure 3-9.

	status	priority	queuing_order	conversation_group_id	conversation_handle	message_sequence_number	service_name
1	1	0	0	30D49C37-8C79-DB11-A30E-0080C81899BB	31D49C37-8C79-DB11-A30E-0080C81899BB	0	TargetService

Figure 3-9. *The received message in the target queue*

As you can see in Figure 3-9, a queue is implemented as a table. Each message stored in a queue is represented as a row. However, you can't manipulate the contents of a queue with INSERT, DELETE, and UPDATE T-SQL statements. You've already seen that you can insert new messages into a queue with the SEND ON CONVERSATION statement. Table 3-14 lists the columns available for a queue.

Table 3-14. *Columns Available for a Queue*

Column	Data Type	Description
status	TINYINT	The status of the message. Messages in the queue contain one of the following values: 0 = Ready 1 = Received 2 = Not yet complete 3 = Retained sent message.
priority	INT	The assigned conversation priority for this message.
queuing_order	BIGINT	The message order number within the queue.
conversation_group_id	UNIQUEIDENTIFIER	The identifier of the conversation group that this message belongs to.
conversation_handle	UNIQUEIDENTIFIER	The handle for the conversation that this message is a part of.
message_sequence_number	BIGINT	The sequence number of the message within the conversation.
service_name	NVARCHAR(512)	The name of the service to which the message is sent.
service_id	INT	The service identifier to which the message is sent.
service_contract_name	NVARCHAR(256)	The name of the contract that the conversation follows.
service_contract_id	INT	The contract identifier that the conversation follows.
message_type_name	NVARCHAR(256)	The name of the message type that describes the message.
message_type_id	INT	The message type identifier that describes the message.
validation	NCHAR(2)	The validation used by the message. The possible values are E = Empty N = None X = XML.
message_body	VARBINARY(MAX)	The content of the message.

Retrieving Messages

Let's now concentrate on how you can process a message from a queue and how you can send a response message back to the initiating service. Service Broker offers the RECEIVE T-SQL statement so you can process pending messages from a queue. The RECEIVE T-SQL statement pulls one or more messages from a queue and removes them physically from the queue. The syntax is similar to a SELECT statement, as shown in Listing 3-19.

Listing 3-19. *Syntax for* RECEIVE

```
[ WAITFOR ( ]
   RECEIVE [ TOP (n) ]
      column_name [ ,...n ]
   FROM queue_name
   [ INTO table_variable ]
   [ WHERE { conversation_handle = conversation_handle |
      conversation_group_id = conversation_group_id } ]
[ ) ] [ , TIMEOUT timeout ]
```

Table 3-15 describes the arguments of this T-SQL statement.

Table 3-15. *Arguments for* RECEIVE

Argument	Description
WAITFOR	Indicates that the RECEIVE statement waits for a message to arrive on the queue, if no messages are currently present.
TOP (n)	Indicates the maximum number of message to be returned. If this clause is not specified, all messages are returned that meet the statement criteria.
column_name	Specifies the names of the columns to include in the result set.
queue_name	Specifies the name of the queue from where the messages are received.
INTO table_variable	Specifies the table variable into which the received messages are stored.
conversation_handle	Specifies the conversation handle for the conversation where messages are received.
conversation_group_id	Specifies the conversation group ID or the conversation group where messages are received.
TIMEOUT timeout	Specifies the amount of time, in milliseconds, for the WAITFOR T-SQL statement to wait for a new message.

Even though the statement looks a lot like a SELECT statement, the RECEIVE statement is a bit different in that a given message can only be received once and is then deleted from the queue. Once a successful RECEIVE is committed, the message can't be received again. The RECEIVE statement doesn't retrieve all the messages on the queue. It locks the first available conversation group that has messages available and is not locked by another RECEIVE statement. Listing 3-20 shows how you can use this statement to retrieve sent messages from the queue. This listing assumes that the sent messages contain valid XML data, because the message body is cast to the SQL Server 2008 XML data type.

Listing 3-20. *Receiving Messages from a Queue*

```
DECLARE @cg UNIQUEIDENTIFIER
DECLARE @ch UNIQUEIDENTIFIER
DECLARE @messagetypename NVARCHAR(256)
DECLARE @messagebody XML;

BEGIN TRY
   BEGIN TRANSACTION;

      RECEIVE TOP(1)
         @cg = conversation_group_id,
         @ch = conversation_handle,
         @messagetypename = message_type_name,
         @messagebody = CAST(message_body AS XML)
      FROM TargetQueue

      PRINT 'Conversation group: ' + CAST(@cg AS NVARCHAR(MAX))
      PRINT 'Conversation handle: ' + CAST(@ch AS NVARCHAR(MAX))
      PRINT 'Message type: ' + @messagetypename
      PRINT 'Message body: ' + CAST(@messagebody AS NVARCHAR(MAX))
   COMMIT
END TRY
BEGIN CATCH
   ROLLBACK TRANSACTION
END CATCH
GO
```

Note The WHERE clause in the RECEIVE statement is slightly different from the one in the SELECT statement. You can only make a restriction for the columns conversation_handle and conversation_group_id. If you try to apply a restriction on another column, you'll get an error from SQL Server.

One drawback of the code in Listing 3-20 is that a message must already be in the queue when you execute the T-SQL batch. One solution to this problem is to use the RECEIVE statement in combination with the WAITFOR statement. You can use the WAITFOR T-SQL statement to force the RECEIVE statement to wait for a message if the queue is empty. The TIMEOUT clause specifies how many milliseconds the RECEIVE statement will wait for a message to appear on the queue before returning. A WAITFOR without a timeout means that the RECEIVE statement will wait for a message no matter how long it takes. Waiting for a message to appear in a queue is generally more efficient than periodically polling the queue with RECEIVE. The RECEIVE statement also has a TOP clause to control the number of messages returned.

Listing 3-21 uses the WAITFOR T-SQL statement in combination with the RECEIVE T-SQL statement. To demonstrate the behavior of the WAITFOR T-SQL statement, you can execute this

T-SQL batch in a separate query window inside SQL Server Management Studio and send messages to the target service in a separate query window.

Listing 3-21. *Using the* WAITFOR *Statement with the* RECEIVE *Statement*

```
DECLARE @cg UNIQUEIDENTIFIER
DECLARE @ch UNIQUEIDENTIFIER
DECLARE @messagetypename NVARCHAR(256)
DECLARE @messagebody XML;

BEGIN TRY
    BEGIN TRANSACTION;

        WAITFOR (
            RECEIVE TOP (1)
                @cg = conversation_group_id,
                @ch = conversation_handle,
                @messagetypename = message_type_name,
                @messagebody = CAST(message_body AS XML)
            FROM TargetQueue
        ), TIMEOUT 60000

        IF (@@ROWCOUNT > 0)
        BEGIN
            PRINT 'Conversation group: ' + CAST(@cg AS NVARCHAR(MAX))
            PRINT 'Conversation handle: ' + CAST(@ch AS NVARCHAR(MAX))
            PRINT 'Message type: ' + @messagetypename
            PRINT 'Message body: ' + CAST(@messagebody AS NVARCHAR(MAX))
        END

    COMMIT
END TRY
BEGIN CATCH
    ROLLBACK TRANSACTION
END CATCH
GO
```

Processing Messages

Now that you've seen how to retrieve a received message from a queue, let's explore how to process a retrieved message and send a response message back to the initiator service. You need to implement the following steps:

1. Process the message and create a response message.

2. Send the response message on the same conversation back to the initiating service.

Let's look in detail at processing the incoming message. As you saw in Listings 3-20 and 3-21, you can easily store the XML message body in a variable. As soon as you have the whole XML message in a variable, you can use the XML features of SQL Server 2008 to easily select the needed data out of the XML document and process it accordingly.

In this case, let's store the message payload in a table called ProcessedMessages. Listing 3-22 shows the CREATE TABLE T-SQL statement needed to create this table.

Listing 3-22. *Definition of the* ProcessedMessages *Table*

```
CREATE TABLE ProcessedMessages
(
    ID UNIQUEIDENTIFIER NOT NULL,
    MessageBody XML NOT NULL,
    ServiceName NVARCHAR(MAX) NOT NULL
)
GO
```

XML FEATURES IN SQL SERVER 2008

Since the 2005 version, SQL Server provides you with a lot of new XML features. The biggest improvement is the implementation of a native XML data type. With this data type, you have the ability to store XML documents directly in your tables. You can also associate this data type with an XML schema collection to enforce a specific XML schema when inserting and updating the XML data.

The xml data type also offers methods with which you can manipulate the XML data. These methods are value(), exist(), query(), nodes(), and modify(). With modify(), you can even change the XML documents stored in a table, directly inside SQL Server. You don't have to load the XML data into a middle-tier component, do the necessary updates on the XML data, and write the XML data back to SQL Server.

In Listing 3-24 in a moment, you can also see that you can encapsulate the data-processing logic and message-processing logic in a local SQL Server transaction. How you process messages in a production system is up to your business requirements. As soon as the message is processed, you can compose a response message and send it back to the initiating service through the SEND ON CONVERSATION T-SQL statement. At this point, you can close the conversation between both services, because you don't have anything else to do. You use END CONVERSATION, and Service Broker sends a message of the message type [http://schemas.microsoft.com/SQL/ServiceBroker/EndDialog] to the initiating service. The initiating service must then receive this message and also use END CONVERSATION on its side. Note carefully that you must explicitly end Service Broker conversations on both service sides.

■Caution If you forget to end a conversation on one side, the conversation will remain open forever!

Listing 3-23 shows the syntax for the END CONVERSATION T-SQL statement.

Listing 3-23. *Syntax for* END CONVERSATION

```
END CONVERSATION conversation_handle
    [ [ WITH ERROR = failure_code DESCRIPTION = 'failure_text' ]
    [ WITH CLEANUP ] ]
```

Table 3-16 describes the arguments of this T-SQL statement.

Table 3-16. *Arguments for* END CONVERSATION

Argument	Description
conversation_handle	Specifies the conversation handle for the conversation to end.
WITH ERROR = failure_code	Specifies the failure code that is included in the error message sent to the other side of the conversation. The failure code must be greater than 0.
DESCRIPTION = failure_text	Specifies the failure text that is included in the error message sent to the other side of the conversation.
WITH CLEANUP	Removes all messages and catalog view entries for this side of the conversation without notifying the other side of the conversation. Service Broker drops the conversation endpoint, all messages for the conversation in the transmission queue, and all messages for the conversation in the service queue. Use this option to remove conversations that cannot complete normally. For example, if the remote service has been permanently removed, you can use WITH CLEANUP to remove open conversations to that service.

You can now extend the code in Listing 3-21 with all the needed tasks. Listing 3-24 shows the complete T-SQL batch, which performs the following tasks:

- Message receiving

- Message processing

- Storing the message body in a table

- Sending a response message back to the initiating service

- Ending the open conversation on the target service side

Listing 3-24. *The Whole Message-Processing Logic on the Target Side*

```
DECLARE @ch UNIQUEIDENTIFIER
DECLARE @messagetypename NVARCHAR(256)
DECLARE @messagebody XML
DECLARE @responsemessage XML;

BEGIN TRY
   BEGIN TRANSACTION
      WAITFOR (
         RECEIVE TOP (1)
            @ch = conversation_handle,
            @messagetypename = message_type_name,
            @messagebody = CAST(message_body AS XML)
         FROM TargetQueue
      ), TIMEOUT 60000

      IF (@@ROWCOUNT > 0)
      BEGIN
         IF (@messagetypename = 'http://ssb.csharp.at/SSB_Book/c03/RequestMessage')
         BEGIN
            -- Store the received request message in a table
            INSERT INTO ProcessedMessages (ID, MessageBody, ServiceName)
            VALUES (NEWID(), @messagebody, 'TargetService')

            -- Construct the response message
            SET @responsemessage = '<HelloWorldResponse>' +
               @messagebody.value('/HelloWorldRequest[1]', 'NVARCHAR(MAX)') +
               '</HelloWorldResponse>';

            -- Send the response message back to the initiating service
            SEND ON CONVERSATION @ch MESSAGE TYPE
            [http://ssb.csharp.at/SSB_Book/c03/ResponseMessage]
            (
               @responsemessage
            );

            -- End the conversation on the target's side
            END CONVERSATION @ch;
         END
      END
   COMMIT
END TRY
BEGIN CATCH
   ROLLBACK TRANSACTION
END CATCH
GO
```

Now you can send a message from the initiating service to the target service. As soon as you execute the batch, the message is stored in the table ProcessedMessages, and a response message and an EndDialog message are sent back to the initiating service. When you query the InitiatorQueue, you see the two messages shown in Figure 3-10.

	status	queuing_order	conversation_group_id	conversation_handle	message_type_name	message_sequence_number	service_name
1	1	0	630D8560-318D-DB11-B9BE-0013D3C2A015	620D8560-318D-DB11-B9BE-0013D3C2A015	http://ssb.csharp.at/SSB_Book/c03/ResponseMessage	0	InitiatorService
2	1	1	630D8560-318D-DB11-B9BE-0013D3C2A015	620D8560-318D-DB11-B9BE-0013D3C2A015	http://schemas.microsoft.com/SQL/ServiceBroker/En...	1	InitiatorService

Figure 3-10. *The received messages in the initiating queue*

As you can see in Figure 3-10, each received message on the initiating service has a different message type. This distinction is important for the message-processing logic, because you must handle different message types. The code in Listing 3-24 isn't 100 percent correct, because you also must be able to handle error messages and end-dialog messages sent by Service Broker. You now develop the service program for the InitiatorService, which processes these two messages to handle this. You can then apply the same strategy to the service program you used to process the messages sent from the target service back to the initiator service. Listing 3-25 shows the complete T-SQL batch, which does the message processing for the InitiatorService service.

Listing 3-25. *The Whole Message-Processing Logic on the Initiator Side*

```
DECLARE @ch UNIQUEIDENTIFIER
DECLARE @messagetypename NVARCHAR(256)
DECLARE @messagebody XML;

BEGIN TRY
    BEGIN TRANSACTION
        WAITFOR (
            RECEIVE TOP (1)
                @ch = conversation_handle,
                @messagetypename = message_type_name,
                @messagebody = CAST(message_body AS XML)
            FROM InitiatorQueue
        ), TIMEOUT 60000

        IF (@@ROWCOUNT > 0)
        BEGIN
            IF (@messagetypename = 'http://ssb.csharp.at/SSB_Book/c03/ResponseMessage')
            BEGIN
                -- Store the received response message in a table
                INSERT INTO ProcessedMessages (ID, MessageBody, ServiceName)
                VALUES (NEWID(), @messagebody, 'InitiatorService')
            END

            IF (@messagetypename =
                'http://schemas.microsoft.com/SQL/ServiceBroker/EndDialog')
```

```
            BEGIN
                -- End the conversation on the initiator's side
                END CONVERSATION @ch;
            END
        END
    COMMIT
END TRY
BEGIN CATCH
    ROLLBACK TRANSACTION
END CATCH
GO
```

As you can see from the code in Listing 3-25, the RECEIVE statement returns only one row. So you must execute the previous T-SQL batch two times to process both messages. Another option would be to store all retrieved messages in a table variable and process them from there accordingly. In Chapter 6, where I talk about writing effective service programs, you'll see several patterns for processing messages. As soon as you process the EndDialog message on the initiator side, the conversation will end on both sides and then be discarded from memory. However, for security reasons, it takes about 30 minutes until the initiator's conversation endpoint is deleted from the sys.conversation_endpoints catalog view.

Congratulations, you've now successfully implemented your first Service Broker messaging application! In the next section, I show you how to deal with error handling and poison messages.

Error Handling

In this last section of the chapter, I talk a little bit about error handling in Service Broker applications. Error handling can often be complex in distributed messaging applications, because the sender and the receiver aren't running in parallel. As you know, the receiver's side of a Service Broker application can run on a remote server anywhere in the world and process incoming messages at any time—maybe now, maybe a few days later. Debugging and troubleshooting such applications can be an interesting and time-intensive task.

Error Handling in Service Programs

All work done by Service Broker occurs asynchronously, deferred in a background process. Therefore, you have no chance to inform users directly about problems during message processing. A good practice is to handle each different message type in separate TRY/CATCH statements. Transactions make error handling straightforward by allowing you to roll back all the work done in processing a message—including all sent and received messages. The key to making this work correctly is to roll back transactions only when reprocessing the message is likely to succeed.

For example, you should retry a deadlock error, because it will eventually succeed. However, a primary key violation caused by trying to insert a record that already exists will retry forever. A message that raises, for example, a primary key violation is called a *poison message*, because no matter how often you repeat the message processing, it will always fail.

If you decide to roll back a transaction, remember that everything is rolled back. Therefore, if you want to log the error, you have to do it after the rollback is complete. If you choose not to roll back the current transaction, you have the following two options:

- *End the conversation with an error and commit the transaction*: This is the normal way to handle permanent errors, such as poison messages. In most cases, if one message in a conversation can't be processed, the whole conversation can't be completed successfully.

- *Commit the* RECEIVE *statement to remove the message from the queue, but continue the ongoing conversation*: This is only appropriate if the conversation can complete successfully without processing this message. A typical example might be an error that must be resolved manually but doesn't prevent the business transaction represented by the dialog from completing successfully. In this case, you must roll back the work that was done without rolling back the RECEIVE part of the transaction. You can achieve this with a *savepoint*. You can create a savepoint with the SAVE TRANSACTION T-SQL statement. After receiving the message, a savepoint is established in the current transaction so that you can roll back the following work without rolling back the RECEIVE statement. If the error is a permanent error, such as a primary key constraint violation, the message is saved in a log table, the message processing is rolled back to the savepoint of the transaction, and the RECEIVE statement is committed to the database.

Listing 3-26 shows you how you can implement error handling with a savepoint in your service program.

Listing 3-26. *Error Handling with a Savepoint*

```
DECLARE @ch UNIQUEIDENTIFIER
DECLARE @messagetypename NVARCHAR(256)
DECLARE @messagebody XML
DECLARE @responsemessage XML;

WHILE (1=1)
BEGIN
   BEGIN TRANSACTION

   WAITFOR (
      RECEIVE TOP (1)
         @ch = conversation_handle,
         @messagetypename = message_type_name,
         @messagebody = CAST(message_body AS XML)
      FROM TargetQueue
   ), TIMEOUT 60000

   IF (@@ROWCOUNT = 0)
   BEGIN
      ROLLBACK TRANSACTION
      BREAK
   END
```

```
        SAVE TRANSACTION MessageReceivedSavepoint

IF (@messagetypename = 'http://ssb.csharp.at/SSB_Book/c03/RequestMessage')
BEGIN
    BEGIN TRY
        -- Store the received request message in a table
        INSERT INTO ProcessedMessages (ID, MessageBody, ServiceName)
        VALUES (NEWID(), @messagebody, 'TargetService')

        -- Construct the response message
        SET @responsemessage = '<HelloWorldResponse>' +
            @messagebody.value('/HelloWorldRequest[1]', 'nvarchar(max)') +
            '</HelloWorldResponse>';

        -- Send the response message back to the initiating service
        SEND ON CONVERSATION @ch
            MESSAGE TYPE [http://ssb.csharp.at/SSB_Book/c03/ResponseMessage]
            (
                @responsemessage
            );

        -- End the conversation on the target's side
        END CONVERSATION @ch;
    END TRY
    BEGIN CATCH
        IF (ERROR_NUMBER() = 1205)
        BEGIN
            -- A deadlock occurred.
            -- We can try it again...
            ROLLBACK TRANSACTION
            CONTINUE
        END
        ELSE
        BEGIN
            -- Another error occurred.
            -- The message can't be processed successfully
            ROLLBACK TRANSACTION MessageReceivedSavepoint
            PRINT 'Error occurred: ' + CAST(@messagebody AS NVARCHAR(MAX))
        END
    END CATCH
END
```

```
IF (@messagetypename =
   'http://schemas.microsoft.com/SQL/ServiceBroker/EndDialog')
BEGIN
   -- End the conversation
   END CONVERSATION @ch;
END

COMMIT TRANSACTION
END
GO
```

Let's step through Listing 3-26. The first step consists of the message retrieving logic using the `RECEIVE` T-SQL statement, which you already know from previous listings. After a new message is retrieved successfully from the `TargetQueue`, a savepoint is established through the T-SQL statement `SAVE TRANSACTION`. This savepoint is given the name `MessageReceivedSavepoint`:

```
-- Message retrieving through the RECEIVE T-SQL statement
-- ...

IF (@@ROWCOUNT = 0)
BEGIN
  ROLLBACK TRANSATION
  BREAK
END

SAVE TRANSACTION MessageReceivedSavepoint
```

After the savepoint is established, you try to process the message type [http://ssb.csharp.at/ SSB_Book/c03/RequestMessage]. If an error occurs during the process of this message type, the execution goes directly into the `CATCH` block. Inside the `CATCH` block, you check to see if a permanent error occurred. If this is the case, you roll back the transaction to the established savepoint named `MessageReceivedSavepoint`. If it is not a permanent error (like a deadlock), you roll back the whole transaction and try it again:

```
BEGIN CATCH
   IF (ERROR_NUMBER() = 1205)
   BEGIN
      -- A deadlock occurred.
      -- We can try it again...
      ROLLLBACK TRANSACTION
      CONTINUE
   END
   ELSE
   BEGIN
      -- Another error occurred.
      -- The message can't be processed successfully, because it's a poison message
      ROLLBACK TRANSACTION MessageReceivedSavepoint
      PRINT 'Error occurred: ' + CAST(@messagebody AS NVARCHAR(MAX))
   END
END CATCH
```

Poison-Message Handling

Careful coding is always the best approach to handling poison messages, because only the application knows whether it makes sense to roll back a transaction and try the RECEIVE statement again. Service Broker includes a mechanism for detecting and dealing with poison messages. When a queue experiences five rollbacks in a row, Service Broker disables the queue and raises a SQL Server event. An application that subscribes to the poison message event notification with the CREATE EVENT NOTIFICATION T-SQL statement can either try to resolve the poison message automatically or notify an administrator who can manually resolve the poison message and reenable the queue.

Service Broker's poison-message handling is different from most other messaging systems. Other messaging systems move poison messages to a "dead-letter" queue and go on to process the rest of the messages in the queue. This approach won't work for Service Broker dialogs, because dialog messages must be processed in order. Skipping a poison message violates the dialog semantics. While Service Broker effectively detects poison messages, disabling the queue temporarily halts all processing for applications associated with this queue. For this reason, you should use good defensive coding techniques to prevent poison messages in the first place.

To show you how Service Broker handles poison messages, let's create two T-SQL batches. The first one sends a message, and the second one retrieves the message and just rolls back the current transaction. After the service program has tried to process the message from the queue five times, the message will become a poison message and Service Broker will disable the queue automatically, as shown in Listing 3-27.

Listing 3-27. *Handling Poison Messages in Service Broker*

```
DECLARE @ch UNIQUEIDENTIFIER
DECLARE @messagetypename NVARCHAR(256)
DECLARE @messagebody XML

WHILE (1=1)
BEGIN
   BEGIN TRANSACTION

   WAITFOR (
      RECEIVE TOP (1)
         @ch = conversation_handle,
         @messagetypename = message_type_name,
         @messagebody = CAST(message_body AS XML)
      FROM TargetQueue
   ), TIMEOUT 60000

   IF (@@ROWCOUNT = 0)
   BEGIN
      ROLLBACK TRANSACTION
      BREAK
   END
```

```
-- Rolling back the current transaction
PRINT 'Rollback the current transaction - simulating a poison message...'
ROLLBACK TRANSACTION
END
GO
```

Now, when you place a message into the TargetQueue and execute the service program shown in Listing 3-27, you'll see that Service Broker deactivates the queue automatically, and you'll get an error message, as shown in Figure 3-11.

```
(1 row(s) affected)
Rollback the current transaction - simulating a poison message...

(1 row(s) affected)
Rollback the current transaction - simulating a poison message...

(1 row(s) affected)
Rollback the current transaction - simulating a poison message...

(1 row(s) affected)
Rollback the current transaction - simulating a poison message...

(1 row(s) affected)
Rollback the current transaction - simulating a poison message...

(1 row(s) affected)
Rollback the current transaction - simulating a poison message...
Msg 9617, Level 16, State 1, Line 9
The service queue "TargetQueue" is currently disabled.
```

Figure 3-11. *Poison messages in Service Broker*

When you want to reenable the queue, you must execute the following T-SQL statement:

```
ALTER QUEUE TargetQueue WITH STATUS = ON
```

Note that Service Broker creates an event notification only when a Service Broker queue is disabled because of a poison message. When you disable a queue manually, no event notification message is created. Because of this, an application has the possibility to subscribe to this event notification and react accordingly in this error situation. You can use the CREATE EVENT NOTIFICATION T-SQL statement to set up an event notification. Listing 3-28 shows the syntax for this statement.

Listing 3-28. *Syntax for* CREATE EVENT NOTIFICATION

```
CREATE EVENT NOTIFICATION event_notification_name
ON { SERVER | DATABASE | QUEUE queue_name }
[ WITH FAN_IN ]
FOR { event_type | event_group } [ ,...n ]
TO SERVICE 'broker_service', { 'broker_instance_specifier' | 'current database' }
```

Table 3-17 describes the arguments for this statement.

Table 3-17. *Arguments for* CREATE EVENT NOTIFICATION

Argument	Description
event_notification_name	Specifies the name of the event notification to be created
SERVER	Creates the event notification for the current instance of SQL Server
DATABASE	Creates the event notification for the current SQL Server database
queue_name	Specifies the name of the queue to which the event notification applies
WITH FAN_IN	Instructs SQL Server to send only one message per event to any specified service for all event notifications that are created on the same event, are created by the same principal, and specify the same service and broker_instance_specifier
event_type	Specifies the name of the event type that causes the event notification to occur
event_group	Specifies the name of a predefined group of T-SQL or SQL Trace event types
broker_service	Specifies the target service that receives the event notification message that occurred
broker_instance_specifier	Specifies a Service Broker instance against which broker_service is resolved

Listing 3-29 shows how you can set up the event notification and create the T-SQL batch that handles the event notification.

Listing 3-29. *Using Event Notification of Poison Messages*

```
-- Create the queue that stores the event notification messages
CREATE QUEUE PoisonMessageNotifyQueue
GO

-- Create the service that accepts the event notification messages
CREATE SERVICE PoisonMessageNotifyService ON QUEUE PoisonMessageNotifyQueue
(
    [http://schemas.microsoft.com/SQL/Notifications/PostEventNotification]
);
GO

-- Create the event notification itself
CREATE EVENT NOTIFICATION PoisonMessageNotification ON QUEUE TargetQueue
FOR Broker_Queue_Disabled
TO SERVICE 'PoisonMessageNotifyService', 'current database'
GO

-- Select the received event notification message
SELECT * FROM PoisonMessageNotifyQueue
GO
```

Listing 3-30 shows the message body for the event notification message.

Listing 3-30. *The Body of the Event Notification Message*

```
<EVENT_INSTANCE>
    <EventType>BROKER_QUEUE_DISABLED>
    <PostTime>2006-09-15T23:56:19.187</PostTime>
    <SPID>21</SPID>
    <ServerName>WINXP_KLAUS</ServerName>
    <LoginName>sa</LoginName>
    <UserName>dbo</UserName>
    <DatabaseName>Chapter3_HelloWorldSvc</DatabaseName>
    <SchemaName>dbo</SchemaName>
    <ObjectName>TargetQueue</ObjectName>
    <ObjectType>QUEUE</ObjectType>
</EVENT_INSTANCE>
```

Ending Conversations with Errors

You must be aware that Service Broker can send error messages along with the ongoing conversation (the user also has this ability through END CONVERSATION conversation_handle WITH ERROR). This means that your service programs must be able to handle the message type [http://schemas.microsoft.com/SQL/ServiceBroker/Error] that indicates an error. Once an error is sent to one side of the conversation, neither side can do a SEND. However, the error receiver can still receive messages already in the queue. The content of this message type is well-formed XML. A message of this type is also delivered to the initiator service if the target service ends a dialog with an error message. Listing 3-31 shows the code needed for a target service to end a conversation with an error.

Listing 3-31. *Ending a Conversation with an Error*

```
DECLARE @ch UNIQUEIDENTIFIER
DECLARE @messagetypename NVARCHAR(256)
DECLARE @messagebody XML

BEGIN TRY
    BEGIN TRANSACTION
        WAITFOR (
            RECEIVE TOP (1)
                @ch = conversation_handle,
                @messagetypename = message_type_name,
                @messagebody = CAST(message_body AS XML)
            FROM TargetQueue
        ), TIMEOUT 60000
```

```
      IF (@messagetypename = 'http://ssb.csharp.at/SSB_Book/c03/RequestMessage')
      BEGIN
         -- End the conversation with an error
         END CONVERSATION @ch
            WITH ERROR = 4242
            DESCRIPTION = 'My custom error message'

      END
   COMMIT
END TRY
BEGIN CATCH
   ROLLBACK TRANSACTION
END CATCH
GO
```

As soon as a service has ended its side of the conversation with an error, an error message is sent to the other endpoint of the conversation. The other side still must call END CONVERSATION. The message body contains the error code and the error message specified by the other service. Listing 3-32 shows the XML error message.

Listing 3-32. *The XML Error Message*

```
<Error xmlns="http://schemas.microsoft.com/SQL/ServiceBroker/Error">
   <Code>4242</Code>
   <Description>My custom error message</Description>
</Error>
```

With the XML features in SQL Server 2008, you can extract the necessary error information easily out of the message and store it in a table, for example. Listing 3-33 shows an example of a service program that handles error messages accordingly.

Listing 3-33. *Handling Error Messages*

```
DECLARE @ch UNIQUEIDENTIFIER
DECLARE @messagetypename NVARCHAR(256)
DECLARE @messagebody XML
DECLARE @errorcode INT
DECLARE @errormessage NVARCHAR(3000);

BEGIN TRY
   BEGIN TRANSACTION
      WAITFOR (
         RECEIVE TOP(1)
            @ch = conversation_handle,
            @messagetypename = message_type_name,
            @messagebody = CAST(message_body AS XML)
         FROM InitiatorQueue
      ), TIMEOUT 60000
```

```
    IF (@@ROWCOUNT > 0)
    BEGIN
        IF (@messagetypename = 'http://ssb.csharp.at/SSB_Book/c03/ResponseMessage')
        BEGIN
            -- Store the received response) message in a table
            INSERT INTO ProcessedMessages (ID, MessageBody, ServiceName)
            VALUES (NEWID(), @messagebody, 'InitiatorService')
        END


        IF (@messagetypename =
            'http://schemas.microsoft.com/SQL/ServiceBroker/EndDialog')
        BEGIN
            -- End the conversation on the initiator's side
            END CONVERSATION @ch;
        END


        IF (@messagetypename =
            'http://schemas.microsoft.com/SQL/ServiceBroker/Error')
        BEGIN
            -- Extract the error information from the sent message
            SET @errorcode = (SELECT @messagebody.value(
                N'declare namespace
                brokerns="http://schemas.microsoft.com/SQL/ServiceBroker/Error";
                (/brokerns:Error/brokerns:Code)[1]', 'int'));
            SET @errormessage = (SELECT @messagebody.value(
                'declare namespace
                brokerns="http://schemas.microsoft.com/SQL/ServiceBroker/Error";
                (/brokerns:Error/brokerns:Description)[1]', 'nvarchar(3000)'));

            -- Log the error
            INSERT INTO ErrorLog(ID, ErrorCode, ErrorMessage)
            VALUES (NEWID(), @errorcode, @errormessage)

            -- End the conversation on the initiator's side
            END CONVERSATION @ch;
        END
    END
    COMMIT
END TRY
BEGIN CATCH
    ROLLBACK TRANSACTION
END CATCH
GO
```

Summary

In this chapter, you've seen how Service Broker applications are developed. You started by defining message types, contracts, queues, and services. You then moved on to sending and receiving messages, where you learned the usage of the T-SQL statements SEND and RECEIVE. In the last section of this chapter, you learned about troubleshooting, and you saw how Service Broker handles poison messages. Finally, you learned about Service Broker error messages and how you can process them in your own service programs.

In the next chapter, I cover Service Broker activation, with which you can automatically start a stored procedure when a new message arrives at a Service Broker queue. Stay tuned.

Service Broker Activation

With activation, you can specify that Service Broker starts a service program automatically as soon as a new message arrives at a queue. In this chapter, I'll present activation in detail and show you how you can use it to implement great Service Broker solutions. I'll cover the following:

- *Activation basics*: Activation allows you to start a service program as soon as a new message arrives in a service queue. With activation, you can process received messages automatically without any additional coding efforts.

- *Internal activation*: With internal activation, you have the ability to activate a stored procedure as soon as a new message arrives. As you'll see, there are several options, as well as some issues you must be careful of.

- *External activation*: External activation allows you to start an external application when a message arrives in a service queue. You can move long-running processing logic away from SQL Server and put it into separate processes for better performance and scalability.

- *Parallel activation*: Normally, activated stored procedures are only started when Service Broker encounters receiving new messages. However, there are some tricks to starting more than one stored procedure simultaneously for message processing.

- *Troubleshooting activation*: If you're not careful during activation setup, you could encounter several problems. You'll learn about common configuration issues introduced with Service Broker activation.

Activation Basics

Traditionally, a messaging application handled a queue by continuously polling the queue to see if any messages had arrived or by using a trigger on the queue that would start the receiving application every time a message arrived on the queue. The first approach wastes a lot of resources when few messages are arriving on the queue, and the second approach wastes a lot of resources upon starting the application if messages are arriving at a high rate. Service Broker activation takes the best features of both approaches. When a message arrives on a queue, a stored procedure starts to process if a stored procedure isn't already running to process it.

When a stored procedure starts, it keeps receiving messages until the queue is empty. This means that resources aren't wasted by polling an empty queue, and resources aren't wasted by starting an application to process each message that arrives. Therefore, activation addresses two issues:

- Having to start service programs manually when a new message arrives on a queue

- Terminating service programs when all messages on the queue are processed

Service Broker activation is a unique way to ensure that the right resources are available to process messages as they arrive on a queue. Service Broker supports two different kinds of activation:

- Internal activation

- External activation

When you use internal activation, a specified stored procedure starts as soon as a new message arrives on a queue. The stored procedure must receive and process messages from the queue it is associated with. You use external activation when you want to process incoming messages in an external application such as a Windows service. When you use external activation, you must register for a notification of an event that fires when an external activation should occur. The receiving application completely defines the way messages are processed in the external application.

Before going into the details about internal and external activation, let's look at when to use which type of activation and when activation occurs in a database.

Startup Strategies

The strategies for starting an application fall into four different categories:

- Internal activation

- External activation

- Scheduled tasks

- Startup tasks

Each activation strategy has different pros and cons. A Service Broker application can also combine some of these strategies. For example, an application can use internal activation with a small number of queue readers most of the time and then start more queue readers automatically at certain peak times during the day. Let's take a brief look at each of these startup strategies.

Internal Activation

With Service Broker internal activation, a Service Broker queue monitor directly activates a stored procedure when necessary. This is often the most straightforward approach. With the internal activation of a stored procedure, you don't need to write additional code in the application to manage the activation. However, internal activation requires that you write the application as a stored procedure, either as T-SQL or Common Language Runtime (CLR) code. When you use internal activation, you write your service program in a fashion that it terminates if no messages are available on the associated queue.

External Activation

Some applications run in response to a specific event. For example, you can run a monitoring application when the CPU usage on the computer falls below a specific level, or you can run a logging application when a new table is created. External activation is a special case of this event-based activation.

For events that event notifications can trigger, event-based activation can be combined with Service Broker activation. In this case, you can use internal activation on the queue that receives the event notification. The activation stored procedure receives the notification message and starts an external application. The problem with this solution is that you can't control which things the application does with the received messages. Therefore, this approach could lead to several security risks when external applications are involved.

Scheduled Tasks

With a scheduled task, an application is activated on a configured schedule. This strategy is convenient for batch-processing applications. An application that runs as a scheduled task can exit when there are no more messages to process, or the application can exit at a certain time. For example, an application that processes orders to a supplier can store messages during the day and then process the messages overnight to produce a single order to the supplier. In this case, the application can use a SQL Server Agent job to start the application at a specific time each night.

Startup Tasks

Some applications start once, typically when the computer starts or when SQL Server starts. Examples of these tasks are a startup stored procedure in SQL Server, an application in the Windows startup group, or a Windows service. In this case, the application remains running and processes messages as they arrive. An application that runs continuously doesn't require startup time when a message arrives on the queue. However, because the application doesn't exit when there are no messages, the program consumes resources even when there is no work for the program to do.

When Is Activation Needed?

Activation is necessary whenever a queue has useful work to perform. Queue monitors determine whether activation is necessary. Service Broker creates a queue monitor for each queue with activation STATUS = ON or for which a QUEUE_ACTIVATION event notification has been registered. The sys.dm_broker_queue_monitors dynamic management view (DMV) lists the queue monitors active in the SQL Server instance. Each queue monitor tracks whether the queue contains messages that are ready to be received, how recently a RECEIVE T-SQL statement on the queue returned an empty result set, and how many activated stored procedures are currently running for the queue.

A queue monitor checks whether activation is necessary every few seconds and when any of the following events occur:

- A new message arrives at the queue.

- SQL Server executes a RECEIVE T-SQL statement for the queue.

- A transaction containing a RECEIVE T-SQL statement rolls back.

- All stored procedures started by the queue monitor exit.

- SQL Server executes an ALTER T-SQL statement for the queue.

Activation is necessary if one of the following things is true:

- A new message arrives on a queue that contains no unread messages, and there are no activated stored procedures running for the queue.

- The queue contains unread messages, there is no session waiting in a GET CONVERSATION GROUP T-SQL statement or a RECEIVE T-SQL statement without a WHERE clause, and no GET CONVERSATION GROUP T-SQL statement or RECEIVE T-SQL statement without a WHERE clause has returned an empty result set for a few seconds. In other words, when messages are accumulating on the queue, the activated stored procedures aren't able to read them fast enough. You can find more details on the GET CONVERSATION GROUP T-SQL statement in Chapter 6.

In effect, this activation approach allows the queue monitor to tell whether the queue readers processing the queue are keeping up with the incoming message traffic. Notice that this approach takes conversation group locking into account. Because only one queue reader at a time can process messages for a conversation group, starting queue readers in response to a simpler approach, such as the number of unread messages in the queue, might waste resources. Instead, Service Broker activation considers whether a new queue reader will have useful work to do.

For example, a queue may contain a large number of unprocessed messages on a single conversation. In this case, only one queue reader can process the messages. The queue monitor activates another queue reader. The second queue reader waits in the RECEIVE T-SQL statement, since all of the messages belong to the same conversation group. As long as all the messages in the queue belong to the same conversation group and the second queue reader remains running, the queue monitor doesn't start another queue reader.

Once Service Broker determines that activation is necessary, Service Broker must decide whether activation occurs. For internal activation, the queue monitor activates a new instance of the activated stored procedure when the existing ones can't keep up with processing the current messages in the queue. If the number of running programs is equal to or greater than the MAX_QUEUE_READERS value, the queue monitor won't start a new instance of the stored procedure. The sys.dm_broker_activated_tasks DMV contains information on stored procedures started by Service Broker.

For external activation, Service Broker has no information on the number of distinct queue readers that may be working with the queue. Further, some startup time may be required between the time that the activation event is raised and the time that a reader begins reading the queue. Therefore, Service Broker provides a time-out for an external application to respond. Once an application calls RECEIVE on the queue or the time-out expires, Service Broker will create another event notification if activation is required. An external application monitors the EVENT NOTIFICATION while the program is running to determine whether more queue readers are required to read messages. Let's now have a look at both internal and external activation.

Internal Activation

When you want to use internal activation, you must configure a service queue according to your requirements. The first thing you need when you set up internal activation is a stored procedure that contains the service programs that process incoming messages on the associated service queue. All the service programs you've seen in the previous chapters can be used in a stored procedure for internal activation. Listing 4-1 shows a stored procedure that processes incoming request messages on the associated queue.

Listing 4-1. *A Stored Procedure Used for Internal Activation on the Target Side*

```
CREATE PROCEDURE ProcessRequestMessages
AS
    DECLARE @ch UNIQUEIDENTIFIER
    DECLARE @messagetypename NVARCHAR(256)
    DECLARE @messagebody XML
    DECLARE @responsemessage XML;

    WHILE (1=1)
    BEGIN
        BEGIN TRY
            BEGIN TRANSACTION

            WAITFOR (
                RECEIVE TOP(1)
                    @ch = conversation_handle,
                    @messagetypename = message_type_name,
                    @messagebody = CAST(message_body AS XML)
                FROM TargetQueue
            ), TIMEOUT 60000

            IF (@@ROWCOUNT = 0)
            BEGIN
                ROLLBACK TRANSACTION
                BREAK
            END

            IF (@messagetypename = 'http://ssb.csharp.at/SSB_Book/c04/RequestMessage')
            BEGIN
                -- Store the received request message in a table
                INSERT INTO ProcessedMessages (ID, MessageBody, ServiceName)
                VALUES (NEWID(), @messagebody, 'TargetService')

                -- Construct the response message
                SET @responsemessage = '<HelloWorldResponse>' +
                    @messagebody.value('/HelloWorldRequest[1]', 'NVARCHAR(MAX)') +
                    '</HelloWorldResponse>';
```

```
            -- Send the response message back to the initiating service
            SEND ON CONVERSATION @ch
                MESSAGE TYPE [http://ssb.csharp.at/SSB_Book/c04/ResponseMessage]
                (
                    @responsemessage
                );

            -- End the conversation on the target's side
            END CONVERSATION @ch;
        END

        IF (@messagetypename =
            'http://schemas.microsoft.com/SQL/ServiceBroker/EndDialog')
        BEGIN
            -- End the conversation
            END CONVERSATION @ch;
        END

            COMMIT TRANSACTION
        END TRY
        BEGIN CATCH
            ROLLBACK TRANSACTION
        END CATCH
    END
GO
```

As soon as you create the needed stored procedure, you can enable the internal activation mechanism on a service queue. You can do this during the creation of the queue with the CREATE QUEUE T-SQL statement or later through the ALTER QUEUE T-SQL statement. Listing 4-2 demonstrates both techniques.

Listing 4-2. *Setting Up a Queue for Internal Activation*

```
CREATE QUEUE [TargetQueue]
WITH ACTIVATION
(
    STATUS = ON,
    PROCEDURE_NAME = [ProcessRequestMessages],
    MAX_QUEUE_READERS = 1,
    EXECUTE AS SELF
)

-- or
```

```
ALTER QUEUE [TargetQueue]
WITH ACTIVATION
(
    STATUS = ON,
    PROCEDURE_NAME = [ProcessRequestMessages],
    MAX_QUEUE_READERS = 1,
    EXECUTE AS SELF
)
```

Table 4-1 shows the arguments you need to specify in the CREATE QUEUE/ALTER QUEUE T-SQL statement, when you want to configure internal activation for a service queue.

Table 4-1. *The Needed Arguments for Internal Activation*

Argument	Description
STATUS	Indicates if the activation feature of Service Broker is used. If STATUS = ON, Service Broker will start the specified stored procedure (indicated with PROCEDURE_NAME) when the number of procedures currently running is less than MAX_QUEUE_READERS and when messages arrive on the queue faster than the stored procedure receives messages. When STATUS = OFF, the queue doesn't activate the stored procedure. If this clause is not specified, the default is ON.
PROCEDURE_NAME	Specifies the name of the stored procedure you need to activate to process messages in this queue.
MAX_QUEUE_READERS	Specifies the maximum number of instances of the activated stored procedure that the queue starts at the same time. The value of MAX_QUEUE_READERS must be a number between 0 and 32,767.
EXECUTE AS	Specifies the SQL Server database user account under which the activated stored procedure runs. SQL Server must be able to check the permissions for this user at the time that the queue activates the stored procedure. For a Windows domain user, the server must be connected to the domain when the procedure is activated or when activation fails. For a SQL Server user, Service Broker always checks the permissions. EXECUTE AS SELF means that the stored procedure executes as the current user.

As soon as you configure the internal activation on the TargetQueue, you can use the sys.service_queues catalog view to show if the configuration of the internal activation completed successfully (see Figure 4-1). If a stored procedure is registered for activation, the activation_procedure column will show the name of this procedure.

	name	object_id	principal_id	schema_id	parent_object_id	activation_procedure	type	type_desc
1	QueryNotificationErrorsQueue	1977058079	NULL	1	0	NULL	SQ	SERVICE_QUEUE
2	EventNotificationErrorsQueue	2009058193	NULL	1	0	NULL	SQ	SERVICE_QUEUE
3	ServiceBrokerQueue	2041058307	NULL	1	0	NULL	SQ	SERVICE_QUEUE
4	InitiatorQueue	2105058535	NULL	1	0	NULL	SQ	SERVICE_QUEUE
5	TargetQueue	2137058649	NULL	1	0	[dbo].[ProcessRequestMessages]	SQ	SERVICE_QUEUE

Figure 4-1. sys.service_queues *for an activated stored procedure*

As soon as you set up internal activation on a service queue, you can use the sys.dm_broker_queue_monitors DMV to view the currently available queue monitors that manage the activation of your queues. This DMV returns a row for each available queue monitor. Table 4-2 describes the columns in the sys.dm_broker_queue_monitors DMV.

Table 4-2. *Columns in* sys.dm_broker_queue_monitors

Column	Data Type	Description
database_id	INT	The identifier for the database that contains the queue that the queue monitor watches.
queue_id	INT	The identifier for the queue that the queue monitor watches.
state	NVARCHAR(64)	Represents the state of the queue monitor. The state can be one of the following possible values: INACTIVE, NOTIFIED, RECEIVES_OCCURING.
last_empty_rowset_time	DATETIME	The last time that a RECEIVE T-SQL statement from the queue returned an empty result set.
last_activated_time	DATETIME	The last time that this queue monitor activated a stored procedure.
tasks_waiting	INT	The number of sessions that are currently waiting within a RECEIVE T-SQL statement for this queue.

Listing 4-3 shows how you can use the information provided by this DMV to retrieve the current status of all message queues available in the current database.

Listing 4-3. *Retrieving the Status of the Message Queues*

```
SELECT
    t1.name AS [Service Name],
    t3.name AS [Schema Name],
    t2.name AS [Queue Name],
    CASE WHEN t4.state IS NULL
        THEN 'Not available'
        ELSE t4.state
        END AS [Queue State],

    CASE WHEN t4.tasks_waiting IS NULL THEN '--'
        ELSE CONVERT(VARCHAR, t4.tasks_waiting)
        END AS [Tasks Waiting],
    CASE WHEN t4.last_activated_time IS NULL THEN '--'
        ELSE CONVERT(VARCHAR, t4.last_activated_time)
        END AS [Last Activated Time],
    CASE WHEN t4.last_empty_rowset_time IS NULL THEN '--'
        ELSE CONVERT(VARCHAR, t4.last_empty_rowset_time)
        END AS [Last Empty Rowset Time],
```

```
(
   SELECT
      COUNT(*)
   FROM sys.transmission_queue t6
   WHERE (t6.from_service_name = t1.name)
   AND (t5.service_broker_guid = t6.to_broker_instance)
)
AS [Message Count]
FROM sys.services t1
   INNER JOIN sys.service_queues t2 ON t1.service_queue_id = t2.object_id
   INNER JOIN sys.schemas t3 ON t2.schema_id = t3.schema_id
   LEFT OUTER JOIN sys.dm_broker_queue_monitors t4 ON t2.object_id = t4.queue_id
      AND t4.database_id = DB_ID()
   INNER JOIN sys.databases t5 ON t5.database_id = DB_ID()
GO
```

By now, you've configured the internal activation on the TargetQueue, so now you can send a request message to the TargetService. In this case, the configured stored procedure is activated, receives the message, processes it, and returns a response message back to the InitiatorService. Listing 4-4 shows the code needed to send a request message to the TargetService.

■**Note** Be sure to create a new database in which you create all the necessary Service Broker objects (message types, contracts, queues, and services) needed for this chapter. Refer to the code samples for this chapter in the Source Code/Download area of the Apress website (http://www.apress.com) for more details.

Listing 4-4. *Sending a Message to an Internal Activated Queue*

```
BEGIN TRY;
   BEGIN TRANSACTION
      DECLARE @ch UNIQUEIDENTIFIER
      DECLARE @msg NVARCHAR(MAX);

      BEGIN DIALOG CONVERSATION @ch
         FROM SERVICE [InitiatorService]
         TO SERVICE 'TargetService'
         ON CONTRACT [http://ssb.csharp.at/SSB_Book/c04/HelloWorldContract]
         WITH ENCRYPTION = OFF;
```

```
    SET @msg =
       '<HelloWorldRequest>
          Klaus Aschenbrenner
       </HelloWorldRequest>';

    SEND ON CONVERSATION @ch
       MESSAGE TYPE [http://ssb.csharp.at/SSB_Book/c04/RequestMessage] (@msg);

  COMMIT;
END TRY
BEGIN CATCH
  ROLLBACK TRANSACTION
END CATCH
```

As you can see in Listing 4-4, there are no differences in the sending code from the samples shown in Chapter 3, where you use activation on the receiving side. It is completely transparent to a sending service whether the target queue is activated internally. As soon as the stored procedure is activated on the receiving side, you can also query the sys.dm_broker_activated_tasks DMV to determine if the activation of the stored procedure was successful. However, you must investigate this view quickly after sending a message, because otherwise, the stored procedure will have processed the message already and won't be activated anymore. In this case, the stored procedure won't be listed anymore in the sys.dm_broker_activated_tasks DMV. Table 4-3 describes the columns available through this view.

Table 4-3. *Columns Available for the* sys.dm_broker_activated_tasks *DMV*

Column	Data Type	Description
spid	INT	The session ID of the activated stored procedure
database_id	INT	The database ID in which the queue is defined
queue_id	INT	The object ID of the queue for which the stored procedure is activated
procedure_name	NVARCHAR(650)	The name of the activated stored procedure
execute_as	INT	The user ID that the stored procedure runs as

Figure 4-2 shows the output of the sys.dm_broker_activated_tasks DMV.

	spid	database_id	queue_id	procedure_name	execute_as
1	55	27	2137058649	[dbo].[ProcessRequestMessages]	1

Figure 4-2. *Output of the* sys.dm_broker_activated_tasks *DMV*

By now, you've configured internal activation on the TargetQueue on the receiving side. You can also apply the same technique on the sending side where the InitiatorQueue lives. Listing 4-5 shows a stored procedure for processing incoming response messages on the InitiatorQueue.

Listing 4-5. *A Stored Procedure Used for Internal Activation on the Initiator Side*

```
CREATE PROCEDURE ProcessResponseMessages
AS
    DECLARE @ch UNIQUEIDENTIFIER
    DECLARE @messagetypename NVARCHAR(256)
    DECLARE @messagebody XML;

    WHILE (1=1)
    BEGIN
        BEGIN TRY
            BEGIN TRANSACTION

            WAITFOR (
                RECEIVE TOP (1)
                    @ch = conversation_handle,
                    @messagetypename = message_type_name,
                    @messagebody = CAST(message_body AS XML)
                FROM InitiatorQueue
            ), TIMEOUT 60000

            IF (@@ROWCOUNT = 0)
            BEGIN
                ROLLBACK TRANSACTION
                BREAK
            END

            IF (@messagetypename = 'http://ssb.csharp.at/SSB_Book/c04/ResponseMessage')
            BEGIN
                INSERT INTO ProcessedMessages (ID, MessageBody, ServiceName)
                VALUES(NEWID(), @messagebody, 'InitiatorService')
            END

            IF (@messagetypename =
                'http://schemas.microsoft.com/SQL/ServiceBroker/EndDialog')
            BEGIN
                END CONVERSATION @ch;
            END

        COMMIT TRANSACTION
    END TRY
    BEGIN CATCH
        ROLLBACK TRANSACTION
    END CATCH
        END
```

Finally, you need to configure the stored procedure ProcessResponseMessages as an activated stored procedure for the InitiatorQueue, as shown in Listing 4-6.

Listing 4-6. *Internal Activation Configuration on the Initiator Side*

```
ALTER QUEUE [InitiatorQueue]
WITH ACTIVATION
(
    STATUS = ON,
    PROCEDURE_NAME = [ProcessResponseMessages],
    MAX_QUEUE_READERS = 1,
    EXECUTE AS SELF
)
```

As soon as you enable internal activation on the queue, Service Broker starts the stored procedure and processes all available messages in the queue sent by the stored procedure ProcessRequestMessages used on the other side of this conversation.

Controlling Message Throughput

The most interesting thing about activation is that it helps you control the message throughput of your Service Broker application through the parameters STATUS and MAX_QUEUE_READERS in the CREATE QUEUE and ALTER QUEUE T-SQL statements.

Let's assume that you have a Service Broker application that receives several thousand messages per hour during the whole day. Processing each message takes a lot of time, because you must interact with some other Service Broker services spread across the country. Because of this high workload, you're unable to process the messages immediately through a service program when they arrive at the service queue. Activation allows you to disable the activation mechanism or set the MAX_QUEUE_READERS parameters to 0.

When you disable the activation mechanism, new messages are stored in the service queue but aren't processed by the service program immediately. Therefore, you need no additional processing power, but you're able to support a high workload scenario. As soon as you have more processing power available (e.g., during the night, when no one works with the system), you can activate the activation mechanism so that the retrieved messages of the whole day get processed automatically and consume the available processing power. Listing 4-7 demonstrates this.

Listing 4-7. *Disabling Activation for a Service Queue*

```
ALTER QUEUE [TargetQueue]
WITH ACTIVATION
(
    STATUS = OFF
)

-- or

ALTER QUEUE [TargetQueue]
WITH ACTIVATION
(
    MAX_QUEUE_READERS = 0
)
```

With the code in Listing 4-8, you can generate a high workload for your Service Broker application. In this case, the messages are stored in the service queue and aren't processed by the activated stored procedure.

Listing 4-8. *Generating a High Message Workload for the Target Queue*

```
DECLARE @i INT
SET @i = 1

WHILE (@i <= 10000)
BEGIN
    BEGIN TRANSACTION;
        DECLARE @ch UNIQUEIDENTIFIER
        DECLARE @msg NVARCHAR(MAX);

        BEGIN DIALOG CONVERSATION @ch
            FROM SERVICE [InitiatorService]
            TO SERVICE 'TargetService'
            ON CONTRACT [http://ssb.csharp.at/SSB_Book/c04/HelloWorldContract]
            WITH ENCRYPTION = OFF;

        SET @msg =
            '<HelloWorldRequest>
                Klaus Aschenbrenner
            </HelloWorldRequest>';

        SEND ON CONVERSATION @ch
            MESSAGE TYPE [http://ssb.csharp.at/SSB_Book/c04/RequestMessage]
            (
                @msg
            );

    COMMIT TRANSACTION;
    SET @i = @i + 1
END
```

This T-SQL batch generates 10,000 request messages for you that are sent to the TargetService. Because MAX_QUEUE_READERS is set to 0, the messages are stored in the target queue and aren't processed further, as you can see in Figure 4-3.

When you enable the internal activation on the target queue or when you set the parameter MAX_QUEUE_READERS to a value greater than 0, Service Broker starts processing the stored messages automatically, as Listing 4-9 demonstrates.

	status	priority	queuing_order	conversation_group_id	conversation_handle	message_sequence_number	service_name	service_id	service_contract_name
1	1	0	993	280DE73B-8F79-DB11-A30E-0080C81899BB	290DE73B-8F79-DB11-A30E-0080C81899BB	0	TargetService	65537	http://ssb.csharp.at/SSB_Book/c04/HelloWc
2	1	0	994	2C0DE73B-8F79-DB11-A30E-0080C81899BB	2D0DE73B-8F79-DB11-A30E-0080C81899BB	0	TargetService	65537	http://ssb.csharp.at/SSB_Book/c04/HelloWc
3	1	0	995	300DE73B-8F79-DB11-A30E-0080C81899BB	310DE73B-8F79-DB11-A30E-0080C81899BB	0	TargetService	65537	http://ssb.csharp.at/SSB_Book/c04/HelloWc
4	1	0	996	340DE73B-8F79-DB11-A30E-0080C81899BB	350DE73B-8F79-DB11-A30E-0080C81899BB	0	TargetService	65537	http://ssb.csharp.at/SSB_Book/c04/HelloWc
5	1	0	997	380DE73B-8F79-DB11-A30E-0080C81899BB	390DE73B-8F79-DB11-A30E-0080C81899BB	0	TargetService	65537	http://ssb.csharp.at/SSB_Book/c04/HelloWc
6	1	0	998	3C0DE73B-8F79-DB11-A30E-0080C81899BB	3D0DE73B-8F79-DB11-A30E-0080C81899BB	0	TargetService	65537	http://ssb.csharp.at/SSB_Book/c04/HelloWc
7	1	0	999	400DE73B-8F79-DB11-A30E-0080C81899BB	410DE73B-8F79-DB11-A30E-0080C81899BB	0	TargetService	65537	http://ssb.csharp.at/SSB_Book/c04/HelloWc
8	1	0	1000	440DE73B-8F79-DB11-A30E-0080C81899BB	450DE73B-8F79-DB11-A30E-0080C81899BB	0	TargetService	65537	http://ssb.csharp.at/SSB_Book/c04/HelloWc
9	1	0	1001	480DE73B-8F79-DB11-A30E-0080C81899BB	490DE73B-8F79-DB11-A30E-0080C81899BB	0	TargetService	65537	http://ssb.csharp.at/SSB_Book/c04/HelloWc
10	1	0	1002	4C0DE73B-8F79-DB11-A30E-0080C81899BB	4D0DE73B-8F79-DB11-A30E-0080C81899BB	0	TargetService	65537	http://ssb.csharp.at/SSB_Book/c04/HelloWc
11	1	0	1003	500DE73B-8F79-DB11-A30E-0080C81899BB	510DE73B-8F79-DB11-A30E-0080C81899BB	0	TargetService	65537	http://ssb.csharp.at/SSB_Book/c04/HelloWc
12	1	0	1004	540DE73B-8F79-DB11-A30E-0080C81899BB	550DE73B-8F79-DB11-A30E-0080C81899BB	0	TargetService	65537	http://ssb.csharp.at/SSB_Book/c04/HelloWc
13	1	0	1005	580DE73B-8F79-DB11-A30E-0080C81899BB	590DE73B-8F79-DB11-A30E-0080C81899BB	0	TargetService	65537	http://ssb.csharp.at/SSB_Book/c04/HelloWc
14	1	0	1006	5C0DE73B-8F79-DB11-A30E-0080C81899BB	5D0DE73B-8F79-DB11-A30E-0080C81899BB	0	TargetService	65537	http://ssb.csharp.at/SSB_Book/c04/HelloWc
15	1	0	1007	600DE73B-8F79-DB11-A30E-0080C81899BB	610DE73B-8F79-DB11-A30E-0080C81899BB	0	TargetService	65537	http://ssb.csharp.at/SSB_Book/c04/HelloWc
16	1	0	1008	640DE73B-8F79-DB11-A30E-0080C81899BB	650DE73B-8F79-DB11-A30E-0080C81899BB	0	TargetService	65537	http://ssb.csharp.at/SSB_Book/c04/HelloWc
17	1	0	1009	680DE73B-8F79-DB11-A30E-0080C81899BB	690DE73B-8F79-DB11-A30E-0080C81899BB	0	TargetService	65537	http://ssb.csharp.at/SSB_Book/c04/HelloWc
18	1	0	1010	6C0DE73B-8F79-DB11-A30E-0080C81899BB	6D0DE73B-8F79-DB11-A30E-0080C81899BB	0	TargetService	65537	http://ssb.csharp.at/SSB_Book/c04/HelloWc

Figure 4-3. *The unprocessed messages stored in the target queue*

Listing 4-9. *Configuration of* MAX_QUEUE_READERS

```
ALTER QUEUE [TargetQueue]
WITH ACTIVATION
(
    MAX_QUEUE_READERS = 20
)
```

With the MAX_QUEUE_READERS parameter, you can control how many conversation groups can be processed in parallel. You can put a throttle on your queue, depending on the configured value of MAX_QUEUE_READERS. For example, if you set MAX_QUEUE_READERS to 20, the sys.dm_broker_activated_tasks DMV will show 20 stored procedures running in parallel and processing the stored messages, as you can see in Figure 4-4.

	spid	database_id	queue_id	procedure_name	execute_as
1	64	27	2105058535	[dbo].[ProcessResponseMessages]	1
2	65	27	2105058535	[dbo].[ProcessResponseMessages]	1
3	68	27	2105058535	[dbo].[ProcessResponseMessages]	1
4	60	27	2105058535	[dbo].[ProcessResponseMessages]	1
5	62	27	2105058535	[dbo].[ProcessResponseMessages]	1
6	66	27	2137058649	[dbo].[ProcessRequestMessages]	1
7	67	27	2137058649	[dbo].[ProcessRequestMessages]	1
8	69	27	2137058649	[dbo].[ProcessRequestMessages]	1
9	70	27	2137058649	[dbo].[ProcessRequestMessages]	1
10	71	27	2137058649	[dbo].[ProcessRequestMessages]	1
11	72	27	2137058649	[dbo].[ProcessRequestMessages]	1
12	73	27	2137058649	[dbo].[ProcessRequestMessages]	1
13	74	27	2137058649	[dbo].[ProcessRequestMessages]	1
14	75	27	2137058649	[dbo].[ProcessRequestMessages]	1
15	76	27	2137058649	[dbo].[ProcessRequestMessages]	1
16	77	27	2137058649	[dbo].[ProcessRequestMessages]	1
17	78	27	2137058649	[dbo].[ProcessRequestMessages]	1
18	59	27	2137058649	[dbo].[ProcessRequestMessages]	1
19	61	27	2137058649	[dbo].[ProcessRequestMessages]	1
20	63	27	2137058649	[dbo].[ProcessRequestMessages]	1

Figure 4-4. *The current activated stored procedures*

Note that an activated stored procedure can only handle messages from one conversation group concurrently. For example, if you have a conversation group with several hundred messages, and you set MAX_QUEUE_READERS to a higher number, then Service Broker only starts one stored procedure that processes all messages from this conversation group sequentially. This is because messages from one conversation group can only be executed sequentially due to the synchronization issues. Think back to Chapter 1, where I talked about the synchronization problems introduced with several concurrent queue readers.

Stored Procedure Signing

When you work with activated stored procedures in Service Broker, you may encounter strange behavior, because a number of features behave differently when you use them in the context of an activated stored procedure. This often happens because the activated stored procedure is executed in a security context that is different from the user you're currently working with. Therefore, you can encounter strange behavior when you do the following in your activated stored procedure:

- *Querying server-level views*: Querying server-level views requires special permissions that standard users don't have. Therefore, your activated stored procedure will return fewer rows than you have tested it for under a higher-privileged user account.

- *Querying DMVs*: DMVs return only rows to which the user of the current used security context has permissions. When you query DMVs with your current user account, you may get more rows back from a DMV than when you use a lower-privileged security context in your activated stored procedure.

When you execute the same stored procedure from a user session, everything seems to work as you'd expect because of the higher-privileged security context. A typical example is when a stored procedure does a lookup in a DMV such as sys.dm_exec_sessions. This DMV returns one row per authenticated session on SQL Server. When you execute this stored procedure in the context of internal activation, you get fewer rows back, as expected. Let's demonstrate this in a practical example.

■**Note** You must create a new database, because the objects you'll use here were already used in the previous sample.

Listing 4-10 shows the complete Service Broker code needed to set up a Service Broker application that returns the current active sessions from the sys.dm_exec_sessions DMV.

Listing 4-10. *Service Broker Service for Retrieving Session Information*

```
CREATE MESSAGE TYPE [http://ssb.csharp.at/SSB_Book/c04/RequestSessions]
   VALIDATION = EMPTY
GO

CREATE MESSAGE TYPE [http://ssb.csharp.at/SSB_Book/c04/Sessions]
   VALIDATION = WELL_FORMED_XML
GO


CREATE CONTRACT [http://ssb.csharp.at/SSB_Book/c04/SessionsContract]
(
   [http://ssb.csharp.at/SSB_Book/c04/RequestSessions] SENT BY INITIATOR,
   [http://ssb.csharp.at/SSB_Book/c04/Sessions] SENT BY TARGET
)
GO

CREATE QUEUE [TargetQueue]
GO

CREATE SERVICE [TargetService]
ON QUEUE [TargetQueue]
(
   [http://ssb.csharp.at/SSB_Book/c04/SessionsContract]
)
GO

CREATE QUEUE [InitiatorQueue]
GO

CREATE SERVICE [InitiatorService]
ON QUEUE [InitiatorQueue]
GO

CREATE PROCEDURE SessionsServiceProcedure
AS
BEGIN
   DECLARE @ch UNIQUEIDENTIFIER
   DECLARE @messagetypename SYSNAME;

   BEGIN TRY
      BEGIN TRANSACTION
      WAITFOR (
         RECEIVE TOP (1)
            @ch = conversation_handle,
            @messagetypename = message_type_name
         FROM TargetQueue
      ), TIMEOUT 60000;
```

```
        IF (@@ROWCOUNT > 0)
        BEGIN
            IF (@messagetypename = 'http://ssb.csharp.at/SSB_Book/c04/RequestSessions')
            BEGIN
                DECLARE @response XML;


                SELECT @response =
                (
                    SELECT * FROM sys.dm_exec_sessions
                    FOR XML PATH ('session'), TYPE
                );

                SEND ON CONVERSATION @ch
                MESSAGE TYPE [http://ssb.csharp.at/SSB_Book/c04/Sessions]
                (
                    @response
                );

                END CONVERSATION @ch;
            END
        END

        COMMIT TRANSACTION
    END TRY
    BEGIN CATCH
        ROLLBACK TRANSACTION
    END CATCH
END
GO
```

As you can see in Listing 4-10, you use the FOR XML PATH feature of SQL Server to transform the returned rows of the sys.dm_exec_sessions DMV directly into an XML document stored in an XML data type. The retrieved XML document is finally sent back to the initiator service with this code:

```
DECLARE @response XML;

SELECT @response =
(
    SELECT * FROM sys.dm_exec_sessions
    FOR XML PATH ('session'), TYPE
);

SEND ON CONVERSATION @ch
MESSAGE TYPE [http://ssb.csharp.at/SSB_Book/c04/Sessions]
(
    @response
);
```

Now, when you send a message to the TargetService and you execute the SessionServiceProcedure stored procedure manually, you get several sessions back in the response message, as you can see in Figure 4-5.

```
⊞ <session>...
⊞ <session>...
⊞ <session>...
⊞ <session>...
⊞ <session>...
⊟ <session>
    <session_id>8</session_id>
    <login_time>2006-11-21T11:07:50.590</login_time>
    <security_id>AQ==</security_id>
    <login_name>sa</login_name>
    <status>sleeping</status>
    <context_info />
    <cpu_time>0</cpu_time>
    <memory_usage>0</memory_usage>
    <total_scheduled_time>0</total_scheduled_time>
    <total_elapsed_time>0</total_elapsed_time>
    <endpoint_id>0</endpoint_id>
    <last_request_start_time>2006-11-21T11:07:50.590</last_request_start_time>
    <reads>0</reads>
    <writes>0</writes>
    <logical_reads>0</logical_reads>
    <is_user_process>0</is_user_process>
    <text_size>4096</text_size>
    <language>us_english</language>
    <date_format>mdy</date_format>
    <date_first>7</date_first>
    <quoted_identifier>0</quoted_identifier>
    <arithabort>0</arithabort>
    <ansi_null_dflt_on>0</ansi_null_dflt_on>
    <ansi_defaults>0</ansi_defaults>
    <ansi_warnings>0</ansi_warnings>
    <ansi_padding>0</ansi_padding>
    <ansi_nulls>0</ansi_nulls>
    <concat_null_yields_null>0</concat_null_yields_null>
    <transaction_isolation_level>2</transaction_isolation_level>
    <lock_timeout>-1</lock_timeout>
    <deadlock_priority>0</deadlock_priority>
    <row_count>0</row_count>
    <prev_error>0</prev_error>
  </session>
```

Figure 4-5. *The current sessions returned by the Service Broker service*

Let's now enable internal activation for the TargetQueue. See Listing 4-11.

Listing 4-11. *Enabling Internal Activation*

```
ALTER QUEUE [TargetQueue]
WITH ACTIVATION
(
    STATUS = ON,
    MAX_QUEUE_READERS = 1,
    PROCEDURE_NAME = SessionServiceProcedure,
    EXECUTE AS OWNER
)
GO
```

When you execute the query SELECT CAST(message_body) FROM InitiatorQueue, the returned response message from the TargetService is different, as you can see in Figure 4-6.

```
⊟ <session>
    <session_id>53</session_id>
    <login_time>2006-11-21T11:07:50.590</login_time>
    <security_id>AQ==</security_id>
    <login_name>sa</login_name>
    <status>sleeping</status>
    <context_info />
    <cpu_time>0</cpu_time>
    <memory_usage>0</memory_usage>
    <total_scheduled_time>0</total_scheduled_time>
    <total_elapsed_time>0</total_elapsed_time>
    <endpoint_id>0</endpoint_id>
    <last_request_start_time>2006-11-21T11:07:50.590</last_request_start_time>
    <reads>0</reads>
    <writes>0</writes>
    <logical_reads>0</logical_reads>
    <is_user_process>0</is_user_process>
    <text_size>4096</text_size>
    <language>us_english</language>
    <date_format>mdy</date_format>
    <date_first>7</date_first>
    <quoted_identifier>1</quoted_identifier>
    <arithabort>0</arithabort>
    <ansi_null_dflt_on>1</ansi_null_dflt_on>
    <ansi_defaults>0</ansi_defaults>
    <ansi_warnings>1</ansi_warnings>
    <ansi_padding>1</ansi_padding>
    <ansi_nulls>1</ansi_nulls>
    <concat_null_yields_null>1</concat_null_yields_null>
    <transaction_isolation_level>2</transaction_isolation_level>
    <lock_timeout>-1</lock_timeout>
    <deadlock_priority>0</deadlock_priority>
    <row_count>0</row_count>
    <prev_error>0</prev_error>
  └ </session>
```

Figure 4-6. *The one and only session returned by the Service Broker service*

As you can see, the Service Broker service now returns only one session. But what causes this difference? The activated stored procedure is executing in an EXECUTE AS context. A great article in SQL Server 2005 Books Online (BOL)[1] explains the behavior of EXECUTE AS. It is not activation that causes the different behavior, but rather the fact that activation always uses an EXECUTE AS context. The activation execution context is trusted only in the database, not the whole server. Anything related to the whole server, such as a linked server or a DMV, acts if you're logged in as [Public]. When activated, the stored procedure loses the necessary privileges and can only see its own sessions.

The recommended way to fix this issue is to sign the SessionServiceProcedure stored procedure with a server-level certificate that has the proper rights (in this case, the VIEW SERVER STATE privilege) needed to execute a SELECT on the proper DMV. You must perform the following steps to sign this stored procedure:

---

1. "Extending Database Impersonation by Using EXECUTE AS," SQL Server 2005 Books Online, http:// msdn2.microsoft.com/en-us/library/ms188304.aspx.

1. Change the procedure to have an EXECUTE AS OWNER clause. EXECUTE AS OWNER speci-fies that the stored procedure will execute in the context of the owner of the stored procedure.

2. Create a certificate with a private key in the database.

3. Sign the procedure with the private key of the certificate created.

4. Drop the private key of the certificate.

5. Copy the certificate into the master database.

6. Create a login from this certificate.

7. Grant AUTHENTICATE SERVER to the certificate-derived login.

8. Grant any additional privileges required by the procedure (such as VIEW SERVER STATE).

Let's take a detailed look at each of these steps.

Changing the Execution Context

In the first step, you must modify the stored procedure that is executed in the execution context of the owner. You can use the WITH EXECUTE clause in the CREATE PROCEDURE T-SQL statement. Listing 4-12 demonstrates this.

Listing 4-12. *Changing the Execution Context of the Stored Procedure*

```
CREATE PROCEDURE SessionsServiceProcedure
WITH EXECUTE AS OWNER
AS
BEGIN
    DECLARE @ch UNIQUEIDENTIFIER
    DECLARE @messagetypename SYSNAME;

    BEGIN TRY
        BEGIN TRANSACTION
        WAITFOR (
            RECEIVE TOP (1)
                @ch = conversation_handle,
                @messagetypename = message_type_name
            FROM TargetQueue
        ), TIMEOUT 60000;

        IF (@@ROWCOUNT > 0)
        BEGIN
            IF (@messagetypename = 'http://ssb.csharp.at/SSB_Book/c04/RequestSessions')
            BEGIN
                DECLARE @response XML;
```

```
        SELECT @response =
        (
            SELECT * FROM sys.dm_exec_sessions
            FOR XML PATH ('session'), TYPE
        );

        SEND ON CONVERSATION @ch
        MESSAGE TYPE [http://ssb.csharp.at/SSB_Book/c04/Sessions] (@response);

        END CONVERSATION @ch;
      END
    END

    COMMIT TRANSACTION
  END TRY
  BEGIN CATCH
    ROLLBACK TRANSACTION
  END CATCH
END
GO
```

Certificate Creation

In the next step (see Listing 4-13), you must create a certificate in the current database. You later use this certificate to sign the SessionsServiceProcedure stored procedure and map it to a login to which the needed permissions are granted.

Listing 4-13. *Create a Certificate That Is Needed for Code Signing*

```
CREATE CERTIFICATE SessionsServiceProcedureCertificate
  ENCRYPTION BY PASSWORD = 'Password123'
  WITH SUBJECT = 'SessionsServiceProcedure signing certificate'
GO
```

As you can see in Listing 4-13, you encrypt the SessionsServiceProcedureCertificate with a password and assign a subject to it.

Code Signing

As soon as you create the certificate, you can sign the stored procedure SessionsServiceProcedure with the SessionsServiceProcedureCertificate. You can use the ADD SIGNATURE T-SQL statement, as Listing 4-14 shows.

Listing 4-14. *Signing the Stored Procedure*

```
ADD SIGNATURE TO OBJECT::[SessionsServiceProcedure]
  BY CERTIFICATE [SessionsServiceProcedureCertificate]
  WITH PASSWORD = 'Password123'
GO
```

When you sign the SessionsServiceProcedure stored procedure, you must supply the password that you used to decrypt the certificate.

Removing the Private Key

After signing the stored procedure, it's always a good practice to remove the private key from the certificate used to sign the stored procedure. This way, you can guarantee that the certificate is not used again to sign any other stored procedure; see Listing 4-15.

Listing 4-15. *Removing the Private Key from the Certificate*

```
ALTER CERTIFICATE [SessionsServiceProcedureCertificate]
   REMOVE PRIVATE KEY
GO
```

Copying the Certificate into the master Database and Creating the Login

In the next step, you must create a login for the SessionsServiceProcedureCertificate. To do this, you must first copy the certificate into the master database. You can use simple BACKUP CERTIFICATE and CREATE CERTIFICATE T-SQL statements, as shown in Listing 4-16.

■**Caution** Make sure that the user account with which you execute Listing 4-16 has write permissions to the given path.

Listing 4-16. *Copying the Certificate into the* master *Database*

```
BACKUP CERTIFICATE [SessionsServiceProcedureCertificate]
   TO FILE = 'c:\SessionsServiceProcedureCertificate.cert'
GO

USE master
GO

CREATE CERTIFICATE [SessionsServiceProcedureCertificate]
   FROM FILE = 'c:\SessionsServiceProcedureCertificate.cert'
GO
```

Granting Permissions

In the final step, you can create a login in the master database for the certificate and grant it the necessary permissions needed to execute the activated SessionsServiceProcedure stored procedure, as shown in Listing 4-17.

Listing 4-17. *Creating a Login for the Certificate*

```
CREATE LOGIN [SessionsServiceProcedureLogin]
   FROM CERTIFICATE [SessionsServiceProcedureCertificate]
GO

GRANT AUTHENTICATE SERVER TO [SessionsServiceProcedureLogin]
GRANT VIEW SERVER STATE TO [SessionsServiceProcedureLogin]
GO
```

When you want to query the sys.dm_exec_sessions DMV, the
SessionServiceProcedureLogin needs the permissions AUTHENTICATE SERVER and VIEW
SERVER STATE.

Executing the Stored Procedure with Higher Privileges

When you've successfully done all these steps, you can send a new request message to the
TargetService. You'll receive a response message containing all the current sessions. As you
can see from this example, you must think carefully of the needed permissions when you use
an activated stored procedure in Service Broker, because otherwise you'll lose the execution
context and your service will return data other than what you originally expected.

If you think that signing a stored procedure is too much work for you during the development phase of your Service Broker application, then you might be interested to know that
there's a shortcut. You can activate the TRUSTWORTHY flag on the database, and everything will
work fine. Listing 4-18 shows how you can activate the TRUSTWORTHY flag for a database.

Listing 4-18. *Activating the* TRUSTWORTHY *Flag*

```
ALTER DATABASE MyDatabaseName
   SET TRUSTWORTHY ON
```

■**Caution** You should do this only if you completely trust the database administrator of the database in
question. I recommend this setting only when you're on a development server. If you're in production, please
use the code-signing approach.

Calling a Stored Procedure in Another Database

You might be asking when it would make sense in a Service Broker application to call a stored
procedure in another database. Let's say you've implemented a logging framework in a database, and you want to use it inside your Service Broker application. In this case, calling a
stored procedure in another database is a requirement for you.

The interesting thing about an activated stored procedure in Service Broker is that you
can't call a stored procedure in a database other than the activated one. In this case, there is a
transition in the execution context, so the activated stored procedure doesn't have the neces-

sary permissions to call another stored procedure in another database. Let's assume from the example in Listing 4-12 that you're now calling inside the activated stored procedure SessionsServiceProcedure a stored procedure located inside another database.

Creating the Logging Functionality

First, you want to create the database that hosts a simple logging functionality; see Listing 4-19.

Listing 4-19. *Creating the Logging Functionality*

```
CREATE DATABASE Chapter4_LoggingDatabase
GO

USE Chapter4_LoggingDatabase
GO

CREATE TABLE LoggingTable
(
   ID UNIQUEIDENTIFIER NOT NULL PRIMARY KEY,
   [Message] NVARCHAR(MAX) NOT NULL
)
GO

CREATE PROCEDURE LoggingProcedure
@Message NVARCHAR(MAX)
AS
   INSERT INTO LoggingTable (ID, [Message])
   VALUES (NEWID(), @Message)
GO
```

Listing 4-20 shows how the stored procedure from the logging database can be called from the activated stored procedure. Keep in mind, however, that this won't work, because there is a transition in the execution context.

Listing 4-20. *The Wrong Way to Call a Stored Procedure Located in Another Database*

```
IF (@messagetypename = 'http://ssb.csharp.at/SSB_Book/c04/RequestSessions')
BEGIN
   DECLARE @response XML;

   SELECT @response =
   (
      SELECT * FROM sys.dm_exec_sessions
      FOR XML PATH ('session'), TYPE
   );
```

```
-- Calling a stored procedure in another database
EXEC Chapter4_LoggingDatabase.dbo.LoggingProcedure
    'This is a test message for the logging database';

SEND ON CONVERSATION @ch
MESSAGE TYPE [http://ssb.csharp.at/SSB_Book/c04/Sessions]
(
    @response
);

END CONVERSATION @ch;
END
```

Listing 4-20 produces an error because the activated stored procedure doesn't have the necessary permissions to do the cross-database stored procedure call. You can find the error in the event log of Windows, as shown in Figure 4-7, when you use this stored procedure as an activated stored procedure for the service queue.

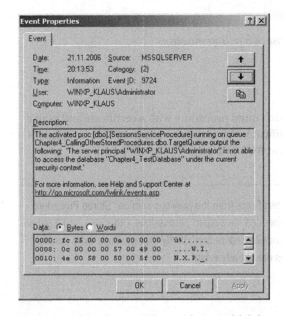

Figure 4-7. *The other stored procedure couldn't be executed.*

Because of the transactional reliability features of Service Broker, the current transaction is rolled back, and the received message is put back into the TargetQueue. The activation will kick in again, causing the same error and causing the request to roll back again. Then activation will kick in again, and so on. After five consecutive rollbacks, Service Broker *poison-message support* will detect this situation and will disable the queue; see Figure 4-8.

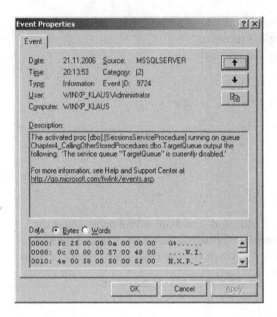

Figure 4-8. *The queue is now deactivated because of a poison message.*

Code Signing

To fix this problem, you must sign the activated stored procedure with a certificate and map a user with the needed permissions to this certificate. This is the same approach as Listing 4-14 demonstrates. Listing 4-21 shows the complete code to achieve this goal.

■**Caution** Make sure that you delete the backup certificate from the previous section "Stored Procedure Signing" from the file system and that you have the needed file system permissions. Otherwise, you'll get an error such as "Cannot write into file 'C:\SessionsServiceProcedure.cert'. Verify that you have write permissions, that the file path is valid, and that the file does not already exist."

Listing 4-21. *The Right Way to Call a Stored Procedure Located in Another Database*

```
CREATE PROCEDURE SessionsServiceProcedure
WITH EXECUTE AS OWNER
AS
BEGIN
    -- The same code as before...
    -- ...
END
GO
```

```
CREATE CERTIFICATE SessionsServiceProcedureCertificate
   ENCRYPTION BY PASSWORD = 'Password123'
   WITH SUBJECT = 'SessionsServiceProcedure Signing certificate'
GO

ADD SIGNATURE TO OBJECT::[SessionsServiceProcedure]
   BY CERTIFICATE [SessionsServiceProcedureCertificate]
   WITH PASSWORD = 'Password123'
GO

ALTER CERTIFICATE [SessionsServiceProcedureCertificate]
   REMOVE PRIVATE KEY
GO

BACKUP CERTIFICATE [SessionsServiceProcedureCertificate]
   TO FILE = 'c:\SessionsServiceProcedure.cert'
GO

USE Chapter4_TestDatabase
GO

CREATE CERTIFICATE [SessionsServiceProcedureCertificate]
   FROM FILE = 'c:\SessionsServiceProcedure.cert'
GO

CREATE USER [SessionsServiceProcedureUser]
   FROM CERTIFICATE [SessionsServiceProcedureCertificate]
GO


GRANT AUTHENTICATE TO [SessionsServiceProcedureUser]
GRANT EXECUTE ON [TestProcedure] TO [SessionsServiceProcedureUser]

USE Chapter4_CallingOtherStoredProcedures
GO

ALTER QUEUE TargetQueue
WITH STATUS = ON
GO
```

As soon as you complete these steps, you can send a new request message to the TargetService. A response message will be returned, while the stored procedure in the other database will also execute successfully.

Using a Single Stored Procedure to Process Many Queues

As you've seen throughout this chapter, you need one activated stored procedure for each queue you've created. Let's assume a scenario where you have several more queues. In this case, you must create an associated activated stored procedure for each queue. Wouldn't it be nice if you could have one stored procedure that handles all the messages automatically on all the available queues? You need to perform the following steps if you want to implement such a scenario:

1. Create the necessary queues with the associated services.

2. Set up internal activation on each queue and point to the same stored procedure.

3. Write a stored procedure that determines which queue you'll use to query for the messages to process.

You can accomplish the first two steps easily, because you just have to use the T-SQL statements shown in Chapter 3.

Writing the Activated Stored Procedure

During the creation of the queues, each queue must point to the same stored procedure that is activated when a new message arrives. The most interesting thing in this puzzle is how the stored procedure knows from which queue messages must be processed. Fortunately, Service Broker provides you with this information through the dynamic management views.

Your first place of refuge is the sys.dm_broker_activated_tasks DMV. This DMV returns all activated stored procedures that are currently running, as well as the stored procedure from which you issue a SELECT on this view.

■**Note** Because you're querying a DMV, you have to make sure to sign your activated stored procedure, as you've learned in the previous two sections.

You can find your own stored procedure when you use the WHERE clause on the spid column, and you can provide the current spid of the running stored procedure through the @@SPID variable. The interesting column in the returned result set is the queue_id column, which represents the internal object ID of the queue for which the stored procedure was activated. You can use this information to query the sys.service_queues catalog view and use a WHERE clause on the object_id column where you provide the content of the queue_id column from the previous DMV. Listing 4-22 shows the needed queries.

Listing 4-22. *Getting the Associated Queue for the Current Running Stored Procedure*

```
DECLARE @queue_id INT
DECLARE @queue_name NVARCHAR(MAX)

SELECT @queue_id = queue_id FROM sys.dm_broker_activated_tasks
WHERE spid = @@SPID

SELECT @queue_name = [name] FROM sys.service_queue
WHERE object_id = @queue_id
```

As soon as you determine the queue name, you can easily build a dynamic RECEIVE T-SQL statement that uses the correct queue. You can use the sp_executesql built-in procedure with a parameter substitution so that you can store the result of your RECEIVE T-SQL statement in T-SQL variables for further processing. Listing 4-23 shows the most important part of the ProcessRequestMessages stored procedure.

Listing 4-23. *An Activated Stored Procedure That Handles Multiple Queues*

```
CREATE PROCEDURE ProcessRequestMessages
AS
    DECLARE @ch UNIQUEIDENTIFIER -- conversation handle
    DECLARE @messagetypename NVARCHAR(256)
    DECLARE @messagebody XML
    DECLARE @responsemessage XML
    DECLARE @queue_id INT
    DECLARE @queue_name NVARCHAR(MAX)
    DECLARE @sql NVARCHAR(MAX)
    DECLARE @param_def NVARCHAR(MAX);

    -- Determining the queue for which the stored procedure was activated
    SELECT @queue_id = queue_id FROM sys.dm_broker_activated_tasks
    WHERE spid = @@SPID

    SELECT @queue_name = [name] FROM sys.service_queues
    WHERE object_id = @queue_id

    -- Creating the parameter substitution
    SET @param_def = '
        @ch UNIQUEIDENTIFIER OUTPUT,
        @messagetypename NVARCHAR(MAX) OUTPUT,
        @messagebody XML OUTPUT'

    -- Creating the dynamic T-SQL statement, which does a query on the actual queue
    SET @sql = '
        WAITFOR (
            RECEIVE TOP(1)
                @ch = conversation_handle,
                @messagetypename = message_type_name,
                @messagebody = CAST(message_body AS XML)
            FROM '
                + QUOTENAME(@queue_name) + '
        ), TIMEOUT 60000'


    WHILE (1=1)
    BEGIN
        BEGIN TRY
            BEGIN TRANSACTION
```

```sql
        -- Executing the dynamic T-SQL statement that contains the actual queue
        EXEC sp_executesql
            @sql,
            @param_def,
            @ch = @ch OUTPUT,
            @messagetypename = @messagetypename OUTPUT,
            @messagebody = @messagebody OUTPUT

        IF (@@ROWCOUNT = 0)
        BEGIN
            ROLLBACK TRANSACTION
            BREAK
        END

        IF (@messagetypename = 'http://ssb.csharp.at/SSB_Book/c04/RequestMessage')
        BEGIN
            -- Construct the response message
            SET @responsemessage = '<HelloWorldResponse>' +
                @messagebody.value('/HelloWorldRequest[1]', 'nvarchar(max)') +', ' +
                @queue_name + '</HelloWorldResponse>';

            -- Send the response message back to the initiating service
            SEND ON CONVERSATION @ch
                MESSAGE TYPE [http://ssb.csharp.at/SSB_Book/c04/ResponseMessage]
                (
                    @responsemessage
                );

            -- End the conversation on the target's side
            END CONVERSATION @ch;
        END

        IF (@messagetypename =
            'http://schemas.microsoft.com/SQL/ServiceBroker/EndDialog')
        BEGIN
            -- End the conversation
            END CONVERSATION @ch;
        END

        COMMIT TRANSACTION
    END TRY
    BEGIN CATCH
        ROLLBACK TRANSACTION
    END CATCH
    END
GO
```

Parameter Substitution

Let's take a detailed look at the ProcessRequestMessages stored procedure from Listing 4-23. After you determine the correct queue name (see Listing 4-22), you create the dynamic T-SQL statement that does the query on the actual queue. Note that you need to create a parameter substitution, because the dynamic T-SQL statement uses parameters; see Listing 4-24.

Listing 4-24. *Creating the Parameter Substitution*

```
-- Creating the parameter substitution
SET @param_def =
    '@ch UNIQUEIDENTIFIER OUTPUT,
    @messagetypename NVARCHAR(MAX) OUTPUT,
    @messagebody XML OUTPUT'

-- Creating the dynamic T-SQL statement, which does a query on the actual queue
SET @sql =
    'WAITFOR (
        RECEIVE TOP(1)
            @ch = conversation_handle,
            @messagetypename = message_type_name,
            @messagebody = CAST(message_body AS XML)
        FROM '
        + QUOTENAME(@queue_name) + '
    ), TIMEOUT 60000'
```

After you build the dynamic T-SQL statement that contains the actual queue name, you execute the T-SQL statement through a call to sp_executesql. After you execute the T-SQL statement, you'll see that the message-processing logic is the same as you've seen throughout the book; see Listing 4-25.

Listing 4-25. *Executing the Dynamically Built T-SQL Statement*

```
-- Executing the dynamic T-SQL statement that contains the actual queue
EXEC sp_executesql
    @sql,
    @param_def,
    @ch = @ch OUTPUT,
    @messagetypename = @messagetypename OUTPUT,
    @messagebody = @messagebody OUTPUT
```

Note that you must also sign the stored procedure; otherwise, you'll have no access to the sys.dm_broker_activated_tasks DMV. Alternatively, you can activate the TRUSTWORTHY flag on the database.

External Activation

When you use internal activation, you must always keep in mind that the activated stored procedure is executed in a background thread inside the process space of SQL Server. Therefore, internal activation is useful when you have to do a few short tasks inside your activated stored procedure. However, sometimes you might need to do some long-duration work inside the stored procedure. For example, you might need to perform one of the following tasks:

- Invoke web services.

- Call other stored procedures that take a long time to execute.

- Call services that are only available through a slow connection.

In these cases, you're tying a long-running SQL Server thread to your activated stored procedure. This can lead to scalability problems in your Service Broker application, because important database resources (such as threads) aren't available to other requests. For these scenarios, Service Broker offers external activation.

With external activation, you can process a Service Broker message outside of SQL Server. You can perform the message processing in different kinds of applications available for the Windows platform, including traditional Windows applications, console applications, and Windows services. These applications are referred to as *external activators*.

Using the Event Notification

The current Service Broker release doesn't include an external activator, but it does include hooks that an external activator can use and an example implementation that you can use to build your own external activator. You implement the hooks for external activation as a SQL Server event notification. With SQL Server event notification, you have the ability to receive an event when some events occur inside the SQL Server engine. The event-notification mechanism of SQL Server offers an event that fires every time Service Broker activation starts a new copy of an activated stored procedure. The event notification fired by SQL Server is implemented as a Service Broker message, which follows the internal Service Broker contract [http://schemas.microsoft.com/SQL/ Notifications/PostEventNotification].

The sent message can be handled by any other external application that can start the correct message-processing logic (indicated through the message type) in an external process that is completely isolated from SQL Server. When a service queue must be activated, Service Broker fires the QUEUE_ACTIVATION event notification. You can subscribe to this event notification for each Service Broker queue defined in the database.

When you want to set up the external activation for a Service Broker queue, you must perform the following steps:

1. If necessary, deactivate the internal activation on the queue.

2. Create a new queue, which receives the QUEUE_ACTIVATION event-notification messages.

3. Create a Service Broker service for the event notification on the new queue.

4. Create an event notification for the QUEUE_ACTIVATION event on the necessary queue.

You can create a new event notification with the CREATE EVENT NOTIFICATION T-SQL statement. Listing 4-26 shows the syntax for this statement.

Listing 4-26. *Syntax for* CREATE EVENT NOTIFICATION

```
CREATE EVENT NOTIFICATION event_notification_name
ON { SERVER | DATABASE | QUEUE queue_name }
[ WITH FAN_IN ]
FOR { event_type | event_group } [ ,...n ]
TO SERVICE 'broker_service', { 'broker_instance_specifier' | 'current database' }
```

Table 4-4 describes the arguments for this statement.

Table 4-4. *Arguments for the* CREATE EVENT NOTIFICATION *T-SQL Statement*

Argument	Description
event_notification_name	Specifies the name of the event notification.
SERVER	Indicates that the event notification is applied to the current instance of SQL Server. If specified, the event notification fires whenever the specified event in the FOR clause occurs anywhere in the instance of SQL Server.
DATABASE	Indicates that the event notification is applied to the current database of SQL Server. If specified, the event notification fires whenever the specified event in the FOR clause occurs in the current database.
QUEUE	Indicates that the event notification is applied to the specified queue in the current database. QUEUE can be specified only if FOR QUEUE_ACTIVATION or FOR BROKER_QUEUE_DISABLED are also specified.
queue_name	Specifies the name of the queue to which the event notification applies. queue_name can be specified only if QUEUE is specified.
WITH FAN_IN	Instructs SQL Server to send only one message per event to any specified service for all event notifications that are created on the same event, are created by the same principal, specify the same service and broker_instance_specifier, and specify WITH FAN_IN.
event_type	The name of an event type that causes the event notification to execute. event_type can be a T-SQL DDL event type, a SQL Trace event type, or a Service Broker event type.
event_group	The name of a predefined group of T-SQL or SQL Trace event types.
broker_service	Specifies the target service that receives the event instance data. SQL Server opens one or more conversations to the target service for the event notification. This service must honor the same SQL Server Events message type and contract that is used to send the message.
broker_instance_specifier	Specifies a Service Broker instance against which broker_service is resolved. You can acquire the value for a specific Service Broker instance by querying the service_broker_guid column of the sys.databases catalog view. Use 'current database' to specify the Service Broker instance in the current database. 'current database' is a case-sensitive string literal.

Enabling External Activation

Listing 4-27 shows the necessary steps to enable external activation for the TargetQueue that you use with the TargetService.

Listing 4-27. *Setting Up External Activation on* TargetQueue

```
-- Deactivate internal activation on the queue if necessary
ALTER QUEUE TargetQueue
   WITH ACTIVATION (DROP)
GO


-- Create the event-notification queue
CREATE QUEUE ExternalActivatorQueue
GO


-- Create the event-notification service
CREATE SERVICE ExternalActivatorService
ON QUEUE ExternalActivatorQueue
(
   [http://schemas.microsoft.com/SQL/Notifications/PostEventNotification]
)
GO


-- Subscribe to the QUEUE_ACTIVATION event on the queue TargetQueue
CREATE EVENT NOTIFICATION EventNotificationTargetQueue
   ON QUEUE TargetQueue
   FOR QUEUE_ACTIVATION
   TO SERVICE 'ExternalActivatorService', 'current database'
GO
```

As you can see in Listing 4-27, you can easily set up event notification for a Service Broker queue. When you send a message to the TargetService (refer to Listing 4-4), the sent message is put into the TargetQueue, and an event-notification message is put into the EventNotificationTargetQueue. When you cast the column message_body to the XML data type, you'll see the XML document shown in Listing 4-28.

Listing 4-28. *The Content of the Event-Notification Message*

```
<EVENT_INSTANCE>
   <EventType>QUEUE_ACTIVATION</EventType>
   <PostTime>2006-09-26T19:09:21.860</PostTime>
   <SPID>23</SPID>
   <ServerName>WINDOWSVISTA</ServerName>
   <LoginName>sa</LoginName>
   <UserName>dbo</UserName>
   <DatabaseName>Chapter4_ExternalActivation</DatabaseName>
   <SchemaName>dbo</SchemaName>
   <ObjectName>TargetQueue</ObjectName>
   <ObjectType>QUEUE</ObjectType>
</EVENT_INSTANCE>
```

This event-notification message provides an external application with all the information it needs to determine in which queue a message is waiting for processing. After you successfully set up the external activation, you need an application that waits for an event-notification message and then processes the messages available in the queue determined by the event-notification message.

Implementing the External Console Application

To demonstrate the behavior of the external activation mechanism, let's write a simple C# program that waits until an event-notification message arrives at the ExternalActivatorQueue, as configured in Listing 4-27. As soon as the event-notification message is sent, the C# application starts the processing logic, which performs a RECEIVE on the TargetQueue and sends a response message back to the InitiatorService. To simplify this sample, I've written a class named Broker that encapsulates the necessary T-SQL statements for a Service Broker conversation. Table 4-5 describes the available methods.

Table 4-5. *Available Methods of the* Broker *Class*

Method	Description
Send	Sends a message (parameter msg) on the specified conversation (parameter dialogHandle)
Receive	Receives a message from a queue (parameter queueName) and returns all necessary information about the message (output parameters msgType, msg, ConversationGroup, and dialogHandle)
EndDialog	Ends the dialog for the specified conversation (parameter dialogHandle)

Listing 4-29 shows the main logic for the external console application.

Listing 4-29. *The* Main *Method of the External Application*

```
public static void Main(string [] args)
{
    Broker broker = new Broker();

    while (true)
    {
        string msg;
        string msgType;
        Guid dialogHandle;
        Guid serviceInstance;

        broker.tran = broker.cnn.BeginTransaction();
        broker.Receive("ExternalActivatorQueue",
            out msgType,
            out msg,
            out serviceInstance,
            out dialogHandle);
```

```
      if (msg != null)
      {
          Console.WriteLine("External activation occurred...");
          new TargetService().ProcessMessages();
      }

      broker.tran.Commit();
   }
}
```

As you can see from Listing 4-29, the main program contains an endless loop, which checks periodically if a new event-notification message is available on the ExternalActivatorQueue. If a new message is available on that queue, the program calls the ProcessMessages method of the TargetService class, which does further processing. Listing 4-30 shows the concrete usage of this method.

Listing 4-30. *The* ProcessMessages *Method of the* TargetService *Class*

```
public void ProcessMessages
{
   Broker broker = new Broker();

   while (true)
   {
      string msg;
      string msgType;
      Guid dialogHandle;
      Guid serviceInstance;

      broker.tran = broker.cnn.BeginTransaction();
      broker.Receive("TargetQueue",
         out msgType,
         out msg,
         out serviceInstance,
         out dialogHandle);

      if (msg == null)
      {
         broker.tran.Commit();
         break;
      }
```

```
    switch (msgType)
    {
        case "http://ssb.csharp.at/SSB_Book/c04/RequestMessage":
        {
            broker.Send(dialogHandle, "<Response />");
            break;
        }
        case "http://schemas.microsoft.com/SQL/ServiceBroker/EndDialog":
        {
            broker.EndDialog(dialogHandle);
            break;
        }
        case "http://schemas.microsoft.com/SQL/ServiceBroker/Error":
        {
            // You don't have to call broker.tran.Rollback() here, because then
            // the current message would become a poison message after 5 retries.
            broker.EndDialog(dialogHandle);
            break;
        }
    }

    broker.tran.Commit();
  }
}
```

The interesting part of Listing 4-30 is that you retrieve the message from the TargetQueue. Listing 4-31 shows how you use the Receive method of the Broker class.

Listing 4-31. *Retrieving a Sent Message*

```
broker.tran = broker.cnn.BeginTransaction();
broker.Receive("TargetQueue",
    out msgType,
    out msg,
    out serviceInstance,
    out dialogHandle);
```

Figure 4-9 shows the output of the external console application.

Figure 4-9. *Output of the external console application*

Activating the External Console Application

When you look carefully at Listing 4-30, you might decide that it wouldn't make much sense to use external activation, because the C# application can also do a RECEIVE on the TargetQueue periodically. This assumption is correct for this simple example, but let's assume that you have several different queues that need external activation. In that case, you can redirect the event-notification messages to one queue—the ExternalActivatorQueue (used in this example). Now you can write an external application that either checks on that queue periodically or uses a WAITFOR statement until new event-notification messages appear. The application starts the correct external application for the current external event-notification message. Figure 4-10 illustrates this technique.

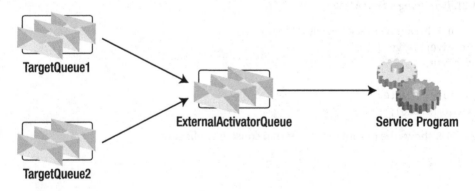

Figure 4-10. *External activation for several queues*

If you use this technique for the external activation mechanism, then a separate queue for the event-notification messages makes much more sense. Microsoft provides a ready-to-use external application sample that periodically checks if new event-notification messages are available on a configured queue. This sample is named ExternalActivator and is available through the CodePlex site[2] in the code gallery. If an event-notification message is detected on the specified queue, then ExternalActivator looks into the configuration file. The configuration file is used to determine which external processing application it must launch to process the incoming message on the original queue that triggered the external activation event inside Service Broker. Figure 4-11 shows ExternalActivator when running in the console.

```
d:\Klaus\Work\Private\Apress\Pro SQL 2005 Service Broker\Chapter 4\Samples\02 ExternalProcessi...  _ □ ×
--- Output logging has started ---
External Activator is initializing...
Running recovery using 'd:\Klaus\Work\Private\Apress\Pro SQL 2005 Service Broker
\Chapter 4\Samples\02 ExternalProcessingApplication\ExternalActivator\ExternalAc
tivator.exe.RecoveryLog' ...
Recovery completed.
Initializing configuration manager...
Debug information will be reported in the output log.
External Activator initialization completed.
Commands
Help|?     - displays this list
Status     - displays the current status of each configured application
Config     - displays the current configuration for this activator (in memory)
Activator  - reports the overall status for the activator itself
Recycle    - recycles the output log file
Debug      - displays if debug information is reported in the output log
Debug on|off - controls the report of debug information in the output log
Quit       - shuts down this activator
Entering command mode.

External Activator> ▄
```

Figure 4-11. ExternalActivator

From the ExternalActivator command prompt, you can choose from the following commands:

- *Help*: Displays the list of available commands.

- *Status*: Displays the current status of each configured application. You can also see how many activated external applications are currently running and how many applications already started successfully.

- *Config*: Displays the current configuration for the activator. You can check whether each configuration application was initialized successfully.

- *Activator*: Reports the overall status for the activator itself. You can check whether the activator was connected successfully to the database.

- *Recycle*: Recycles the output log file.

- *Debug*: Displays whether debug information is reported in the output log.

- *Debug on|off*: Controls the report of debug information in the output log.

- *Quit*: Shuts down the activator.

---

2. http://www.codeplex.com/SQLSrvSrvcBrkr

Configuring ExternalActivator

Let's have a look now at how you can configure ExternalActivator. The configuration is stored in the ExternalActivator.exe.xml XML file. Listing 4-32 shows the basic configuration used in this example.

Listing 4-32. *Configuration of* ExternalActivator

```
<Activator>
  <Setup>
    <!-- define the notification service that we will listen on -->
    <NotificationSQLServer>localhost</NotificationSQLServer>
    <NotificationDatabase>Chapter4_ExternalActivation</NotificationDatabase>
    <NotificationService>ExternalActivatorService</NotificationService>

    <!-- optional elements -->
    <!-- default false -->
    <EnableDebugTrace>true</EnableDebugTrace>
  </Setup>
</Activator>
```

Table 4-6 describes the available configuration options.

Table 4-6. *Configuration Options for* ExternalActivator

Option	Description
<NotificationSQLServer>	Specifies the SQL Server instance where the external activation service was created and is receiving event-notification messages about an external activation request
<NotificationDatabase>	Specifies the database in which the external activation service was created
<NotificationService>	Specifies the name of the external activation service
<EnableDebugTrace>	Specifies whether the debug trace of ExternalActivator is enabled

As soon as you specify the needed information about the external activation service, you must configure each external application and its associated queue. Listing 4-33 shows the additional configuration needed for an external application.

Listing 4-33. *Configuration for an External Application*

```
<Activator>
  <Setup>
    ...
  </Setup>
```

```
<ConfigurationRecord Enabled ="true">
    <ApplicationName>c:\ProcessingApplication.exe</ApplicationName>
    <SQLServer>WINDOWSVISTA</SQLServer>
    <Database>Chapter4_ExternalActivation</Database>
    <Schema>dbo</Schema>
    <Queue>TargetQueue</Queue>
    <CommandLineArgs/>
    <Min>0</Min>
    <Max>10</Max>
    <HasConsole>true</HasConsole>
    <StandardOut/>
    <StandardIn/>
    <StandardErr/>
  </ConfigurationRecord>
</Activator
```

Table 4-7 describes the configuration options for an external application.

Table 4-7. *Configuration Options for an External Application*

Option	Description
`<ApplicationName>`	Specifies the path and the name of the executable to launch
`<SQLServer>`	Specifies the SQL Server instance on which the queue of the original incoming message is hosted
`<Database>`	Specifies the name of the database in which the queue of the original incoming message is hosted
`<Schema>`	Specifies the schema associated with the queue
`<Queue>`	Specifies the name of the queue to which the original message was sent
`<CommandLineArgs>`	Specifies the command-line arguments passing to the external application when launched
`<Min>`	Specifies how many instances of the external application should run at minimum
`<Max>`	Specifies how many instances of the external application should run at maximum

When you configure ExternalActivator with the settings specified in Table 4-7, you can start it again. You can then send a new message to the TargetService. As soon as the message is sent, an event-notification message is sent to the ExternalActivatorService. ExternalActivator receives this message and retrieves the message_body column from the associated queue (which was described in Listing 4-28).

Then ExternalActivator tries to find a <ConfigurationRecord> element where the configured options match the content of the message_body from the event-notification message. The following options are matched:

- `<ConfigurationRecord><SQLServer>` is matched with `<EVENT_INSTANCE><ServerName>`.

- `<ConfigurationRecord><Database>` is matched with `<EVENT_INSTANCE><DatabaseName>`.

- `<ConfigurationRecord><Schema>` is matched with `<EVENT_INSTANCE><SchemaName>`.

- `<ConfigurationRecord><Queue>` is matched with `<EVENT_INSTANCE><ObjectName>`.

When a matched configuration record is found in the configuration file, the specified executable starts.

Note You must always specify in `<ConfigurationRecord><SQLServer>` the Network Basic Input/Output System (NetBIOS) name of the SQL Server instance, because the event-notification message also contains the NetBIOS name. If you're working locally during development, this implies that you also can't use the shortcut `localhost`. You must also specify the NetBIOS name of your local computer on which SQL Server runs.

The executable's responsibility is now to do a RECEIVE T-SQL statement on the original queue and to process the received message according to the message-processing logic. Listing 4-34 shows an updated version of the C# program, which now only does a RECEIVE T-SQL statement on the original queue and processes the received message.

Listing 4-34. *The External Activated Application*

```
public static void Main(string [] args)
{
    Broker broker = new Broker();

    while (true)
    {
        string msg;
        string msgType;
        Guid dialogHandle;
        Guid serviceInstance;

        broker.tran = broker.cnn.BeginTransaction();
        broker.Receive("TargetQueue",
            out msgType,
            out msg,
            out ServiceInstance,
            out dialogHandle);
```

```
        if (msg == null)
        {
            broker.tran.Commit();
            break;
        }

        switch (msgType)
        {
            case "http://ssb.csharp.at/SSB_Book/c04/RequestMessage":
            {
                broker.Send(dialogHandle, "<Response>Response from C#...</Response>");
                break;
            }
            case "http://schemas.microsoft.com/SQL/ServiceBroker/EndDialog":
            {
                broker.EndDialog(dialogHandle);
                break;
            }
            case "http://schemas.microsoft.com/SQL/ServiceBroker/Error":
            {
                broker.EndDialog(dialogHandle);
                break;
            }
        }
    }

    broker.tran.Commit();
}
```

The external console application starts as soon as you send a message to the TargetService. In this case, ExternalActivator retrieves the event-notification message and starts your external console application. Figure 4-12 shows the output of the external console application.

Figure 4-12. *Output of the external console application*

Several Activated External Console Applications

Let's extend this example with an additional Service Broker service that also activates
another external application through the ExternalActivator. For this scenario, let's create the
InitiatorService and two target services named TargetService1 and TargetService2. For
each target service, you enable the external-activation mechanism and send both event-
notification messages to the ExternalActivatorService. ExternalActivator then activates
the external applications ProcessingApplication1.exe and ProcessingApplication2.exe
according to the received event-notification message. Figure 4-13 shows the overall architecture
for this scenario.

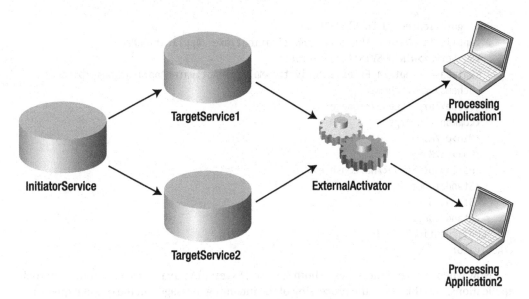

Figure 4-13. *Architecture for multiple external activated applications*

Listing 4-35 shows the configuration file for the ExternalActivator application.

Listing 4-35. *Configuration for Two Externally Activated Applications*

```
<Activator>
   <Setup>
   ...
   </Setup>

   <ConfigurationRecord Enabled="true">
      <ApplicationName>c:\ProcessingApplication1.exe</ApplicationName>
      <SQLServer>WINDOWSVISTA</SQLServer>
      <Database>Chapter4_ExternalActivationMultipleActivatedApplications</Database>
      <Schema>dbo</Schema>
      <Queue>TargetQueue1</Queue>
      <CommandLineArgs />
      <Min>0</Min>
      <Max>5</Max>
      <HasConsole>true</HasConsole>
      <StandardOut />
      <StandardIn />
      <StandardErr />
   </ConfigurationRecord>
```

```
    <ConfigurationRecord Enabled="true">
        <ApplicationName>c:\ProcessingApplication2.exe</ApplicationName>
        <SQLServer>WINDOWSVISTA</SQLServer>
        <Database>Chapter4_ExternalActivationMultipleActivatedApplications</Database>
        <Schema>dbo</Schema>
        <Queue>TargetQueue2</Queue>
        <CommandLineArgs />
        <Min>0</Min>
        <Max>5</Max>
        <HasConsole>true</HasConsole>
        <StandardOut />
        <StandardIn />
        <StandardErr />
    </ConfigurationRecord>
</Activator>
```

Now when you send messages to both services, ExternalActivator executes both external
applications, and this starts the processing of the incoming messages on the original queues
(TargetQueue1, TargetQueue2). As soon as there are no available messages, both external applications are shut down. Figure 4-14 shows both activated console applications.

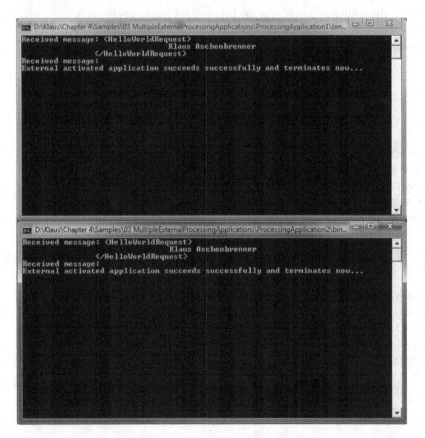

Figure 4-14. *Output of both external console applications*

Another nice feature of the `ExternalActivator` application is that you can install it as a Windows service. Then it can start automatically as soon as the computer is booted. If you want to install the application as a Windows service, you can use the `/Install` option from the command line. You must also supply the name of the Windows service; otherwise, the registration of `ExternalActivator` as a Windows service fails:

```
ExternalActivator.exe /Install:External_Activator
```

Figure 4-15 shows `ExternalActivator` registered as a Windows service.

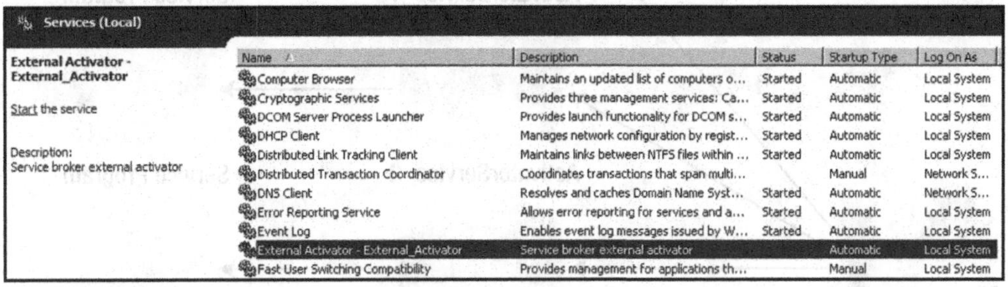

Name	Description	Status	Startup Type	Log On As
Computer Browser	Maintains an updated list of computers o...	Started	Automatic	Local System
Cryptographic Services	Provides three management services: Ca...	Started	Automatic	Local System
DCOM Server Process Launcher	Provides launch functionality for DCOM s...	Started	Automatic	Local System
DHCP Client	Manages network configuration by regist...	Started	Automatic	Local System
Distributed Link Tracking Client	Maintains links between NTFS files within ...	Started	Automatic	Local System
Distributed Transaction Coordinator	Coordinates transactions that span multi...		Manual	Network S...
DNS Client	Resolves and caches Domain Name Syst...	Started	Automatic	Network S...
Error Reporting Service	Allows error reporting for services and a...	Started	Automatic	Local System
Event Log	Enables event log messages issued by W...	Started	Automatic	Local System
External Activator - External_Activator	Service broker external activator		Automatic	Local System
Fast User Switching Compatibility	Provides management for applications th...		Manual	Local System

Figure 4-15. `ExternalActivator` *installed as a Windows service*

As soon as `ExternalActivator` is registered and running, you can send messages to the queues, and everything will work the same as before. When an error occurs, `ExternalActivator` writes an entry to the event log. If something is not working as expected, the event log should be your first source of information. If you want to uninstall the `ExternalActivator` Windows service, you can do it from the command line:

```
ExternalActivator.exe /Uninstall:External_Activator
```

Parallel Activation

A frequent question in newsgroups and from customers is how to start all configured queue readers (set through `MAX_QUEUE_READERS`) simultaneously, so that they process messages in parallel. The basic answer to this question is that you can't do it, because Service Broker provides no support for this scenario. However, there is a trick for achieving the same result with the external-activation mechanism.

Normally, the activation mechanism monitors the queues and the `RECEIVE` T-SQL statements and decides when it's appropriate to launch a new instance of the activated stored procedure. However, there is also the `QUEUE_ACTIVATION` event notification, which you used earlier to set up external activation and which the external-activation sample also uses. In this case, a notification is sent to the subscribed service. The point here is that there is no restriction on how many different notification subscriptions you can create for the same `QUEUE_ACTIVATION` event. When it's time to activate, all the subscribed Service Broker services are alerted to the notification.

These subscribed Service Broker services run on queues that can have attached stored procedures to be activated. So, you can use the subscribed service's queue activation to launch a separate procedure per subscribed service for each original queue-activation notification.

For example, if you create five QUEUE_ACTIVATION subscriptions from five separate Service Broker services, you will launch five stored procedures nearly simultaneously. Figure 4-16 illustrates this.

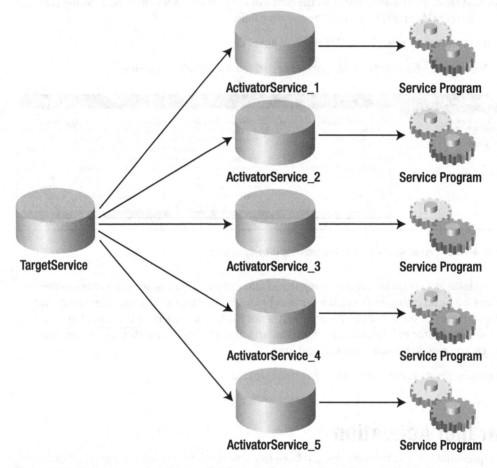

Figure 4-16. *Using external activation for the parallel activation of internal stored procedures*

▪Note Be sure to execute the scripts in the following listings in a new database.

The code in Listing 4-36 sets up the needed infrastructure.

Listing 4-36. *Setting Up the Infrastructure for Parallel Activation*

```
CREATE QUEUE [TargetQueue]
GO

CREATE SERVICE [TargetService]
ON QUEUE [TargetQueue]
(
   [DEFAULT]
)
GO

CREATE QUEUE [ActivatorQueue_1];
CREATE QUEUE [ActivatorQueue_2];
CREATE QUEUE [ActivatorQueue_3];
CREATE QUEUE [ActivatorQueue_4];
CREATE QUEUE [ActivatorQueue_5];
GO

CREATE SERVICE [ActivatorService_1]
ON QUEUE [ActivatorQueue_1]
(
   [http://schemas.microsoft.com/SQL/Notifications/PostEventNotification]
)
GO

CREATE SERVICE [ActivatorService_2]
ON QUEUE [ActivatorQueue_2]
(
   [http://schemas.microsoft.com/SQL/Notifications/PostEventNotification]
)
GO

CREATE SERVICE [ActivatorService_3]
ON QUEUE [ActivatorQueue_3]
(
   [http://schemas.microsoft.com/SQL/Notifications/PostEventNotification]
)
GO

CREATE SERVICE [ActivatorService_4]
ON QUEUE [ActivatorQueue_4]
(
   [http://schemas.microsoft.com/SQL/Notifications/PostEventNotification]
)
GO
```

```
CREATE SERVICE [ActivatorService_5]
ON QUEUE [ActivatorQueue_5]
(
    [http://schemas.microsoft.com/SQL/Notifications/PostEventNotification]
)
GO
```

As you can see in Listing 4-36, you create the "real" Service Broker service with its queue (TargetQueue) and the services and queues to which a post-event-notification message is sent (ActivatorQueue_1 – ActivatorQueue_5). By now, you've set up the whole infrastructure needed to use parallel activation. The only thing you need is a service program for the queues ActivatorQueue_1 – ActivatorQueue_5 to be activated automatically as soon as a post-event-notification message is received on those queues. One very important point to note here is that the service programs must first receive the original sent message from the TargetQueue. Otherwise, this approach won't work. Take a look at Listing 4-37, which shows the implementation of the service program.

Listing 4-37. *Service Program for Parallel Activation*

```
CREATE PROCEDURE [ApplicationServiceProgram_1]
AS
BEGIN
    DECLARE @conversationHandle UNIQUEIDENTIFIER;
    DECLARE @messageTypeName SYSNAME;
    DECLARE @notification XML;
    DECLARE @applicationMessage VARBINARY(MAX);

    BEGIN TRY
        BEGIN TRANSACTION;

        RECEIVE TOP (1)
            @conversationHandle = conversation_handle,
            @messageTypeName = message_type_name,
            @notification = CAST(message_body AS XML)
        FROM [ActivatorQueue_1];

        IF (@messageTypeName =
            'http://schemas.microsoft.com/SQL/ServiceBroker/EndDialog')
        BEGIN
            END CONVERSATION @conversationHandle;
        END

        IF (@messageTypeName =
            'http://schemas.microsoft.com/SQL/ServiceBroker/Error')
        BEGIN
            END CONVERSATION @conversationHandle;
        END
```

```
    WHILE (1 = 1)
    BEGIN
      WAITFOR (
        RECEIVE
          @conversationHandle = conversation_handle,
          @messageTypeName = message_type_name,
          @applicationMessage = message_body
        FROM [TargetQueue]
      ), TIMEOUT 1000;

      IF (@@ROWCOUNT = 0)
      BEGIN
        -- Do not rollback here!
        BREAK;
      END

      IF (@messageTypeName =
        'http://schemas.microsoft.com/SQL/ServiceBroker/EndDialog')
      BEGIN
        END CONVERSATION @conversationHandle;
      END

      IF (@messageTypeName =
        'http://schemas.microsoft.com/SQL/ServiceBroker/Error')
      BEGIN
        END CONVERSATION @conversationHandle;
      END


      IF (@messageTypeName = 'DEFAULT')
      BEGIN
        -- Here's the place where you implement your application logic
        SEND ON CONVERSATION @conversationHandle (@applicationMessage);
        END CONVERSATION @conversationHandle;
      END

      COMMIT TRANSACTION;
      BEGIN TRANSACTION;
    END

    COMMIT TRANSACTION;
  END TRY
  BEGIN CATCH
    ROLLBACK TRANSACTION
  END CATCH
END
```

As you can see in Listing 4-37, this stored procedure is very straightforward. The only thing you must remember is that you need to first retrieve the post-event notification before you do a RECEIVE on the original TargetQueue. The only problem now is that five different stored procedures must be dedicated to each activated queue. The only difference in these stored procedures is the queue from which they are receiving the post-event-notification message.

You can also write a stored procedure that several different queues can use. Listing 4-23 already demonstrated this approach. But in this case, you must sign your stored procedure, because reading from the sys.dm_broker_activated_tasks DMV requires server-level access. Refer back to the "Stored Procedure Signing" section, which covered this in more detail. Finally, Listing 4-38 shows how to set up the post-event notification and configure the internal activation of the ApplicationServiceProgram_1 stored procedure. Repeat this step for each defined Service Broker service.

Listing 4-38. *Setting Up the Post-Event Notification*

```
CREATE EVENT NOTIFICATION [ActivatorEvent_1]
   ON QUEUE [TargetQueue]
   FOR QUEUE_ACTIVATION
   TO SERVICE 'ActivatorService_1', 'current database';
GO

ALTER QUEUE [ActivatorQueue_1]
WITH ACTIVATION
(
   STATUS = ON,
   MAX_QUEUE_READERS = 1,
   PROCEDURE_NAME = [ApplicationServiceProgram_1],
   EXECUTE AS OWNER
)
GO
```

Now when you send a bunch of messages to the TargetService, the TargetQueue gets activated and sends a post-event-notification message to the ActivatorService_1 – ActivatorService_5 services. As soon as the post-event-notification messages are sent, the configured service programs are launched. These do the actual processing of the received message from the TargetQueue.

Troubleshooting Activation

Activated stored procedures run on a background thread in SQL Server 2005. Therefore, the techniques for troubleshooting an activated stored procedure differ slightly from the techniques used for troubleshooting stored procedures that are part of an interactive session.

The database engine writes output from an activated stored procedure to the SQL Server error log. If the activated stored procedure produces incorrect results or fails to read from the queue, you should check the SQL Server error log for output from the stored procedure. Statements such as the PRINT T-SQL statement also output to the error log when they're executed in the context of an activated stored procedure.

One of the best ways to troubleshoot an activated stored procedure is to turn off activation on the queue and then run the stored procedure from SQL Server Management Studio. Running the stored procedure from an interactive session allows you to see any errors that the stored procedure returns. However, when the database engine activates the stored procedure, the database settings and security context may be different. Before running the procedure, use the EXECUTE AS clause to set the user for the session to the user specified for activation, and set the options for the session to the database defaults.

The following sections provide more information and troubleshooting techniques when Service Broker activation doesn't work the way it should.

When the Activated Stored Procedure Doesn't Run

There are two common causes for the activated stored procedure not running:

- *The settings for the queue may have been changed*: In this case, use the sys.service_queues catalog view to confirm the settings for the queue. In particular, check to ensure that activation for the queue is enabled, that the queue specifies the correct stored procedure, and that the queue specifies the correct security principal. Confirm that the security principal has EXECUTE permissions on the specified stored procedure.

- *The stored procedure may have failed to start or may have exited immediately after starting*: In this case, check the SQL Server log for errors from the stored procedure. You can also run the stored procedure from SQL Server Management Studio and check the results.

When Messages Remain on the Queue

When messages remain on the queue, make sure that the activated stored procedures were correctly started by performing the following steps:

1. *Check the sys.dm_broker_queue_monitors DMV to ensure that a queue monitor is active for the queue*: If it isn't, then the activation is not ON for the queue. Use the ALTER QUEUE T-SQL statement to turn activation ON.

2. *Check the state of the queue monitor for the queue*: It should be RECEIVES_OCCURRING. If the queue monitor is not in this state, check the sys.dm_broker_activated_tasks DMV to ensure that activated tasks for the queue are currently running. If no activated tasks are running, then activation is failing.

If activated tasks are running, but messages remain on the queue, then the task is either failing to RECEIVE or failing to commit transactions. Check the SQL Server error log for errors from the stored procedure. Stopping activation and running the stored procedure by hand may help to troubleshoot the problem.

Summary

This chapter looked at the activation feature in Service Broker. You saw how to start a stored procedure automatically as soon as a message arrives on a queue. This process is referred to as internal activation.

As you've seen throughout this chapter, Service Broker activation is a powerful technique, but its security requirements make it complex. You must always keep in mind that an activated stored procedure executes in a different security context. Therefore, the stored procedure may return other results, as you'd expect when you run the stored procedure in an interactive session inside SQL Server Management Studio. To solve this problem, sign your stored procedure so you can execute it with the needed SQL Server permissions.

In the last section, you also saw how to activate an external application when a message arrives. This process is referred to as external activation. Microsoft provides the ExternalActivator sample application, where you can configure tasks that should be activated when a new message arrives on a queue.

In the next chapter, you'll learn how to program Service Broker applications in the .NET language of your choice, such as C# or Visual Basic (VB).

CHAPTER 5

■■■

Service Broker with Managed Code

A Service Broker application always consists of Service Broker objects (such as message types, contracts, queues, and services) and maybe an associated service program in the form of a stored procedure or an external application. The drawback to this approach is that you must implement everything with T-SQL code. When you build a Service Broker client in the .NET language of your choice, you must also use T-SQL code to communicate with Service Broker in the database.

Microsoft ships a managed assembly with SQL Server 2008 that implements an object model around Service Broker. Therefore, you can build Service Broker clients in managed code (such as C# or VB), and you also have the ability to write stored procedures for a service program in a .NET language. This managed assembly provides you with several classes that encapsulate Service Broker objects, such as message types, contracts, queues, service programs, and conversations. Methods of these classes generate the needed T-SQL statements you saw in Chapter 3. This chapter will cover the following topics:

- *The managed assembly*: I'll give you an overview about the managed assembly and which classes are available.

- *Architecture and design*: To get the most power out of the managed assembly, you must have a basic understanding of the architecture and the internal design of the managed assembly.

- *Building a managed Service Broker client*: With the managed assembly, you can write a managed Service Broker client that uses functionality of the managed assembly.

- *Building a managed service program*: The managed assembly also provides you with functionality to easily write programs for Service Broker services.

- *Practical example*: I'll wrap everything up by providing you with a practical example of the managed assembly.

The Managed Assembly

The managed assembly for Service Broker objects is implemented in a C# Visual Studio 2008 solution called ServiceBrokerInterface, which you can find in the Samples directory within the SQL Server 2008 installation path. Figure 5-1 shows the solution in Visual Studio 2008.

Figure 5-1. *The Service Broker managed assembly inside Visual Studio 2008*

As you can see in Figure 5-1, several classes are available in this solution. Table 5-1 describes the general purpose of each class.

Table 5-1. *The Classes in the Service Broker Managed Assembly*

Class	Description
BrokerMethodAttribute	This class implements a .NET attribute with which you can decorate a method with a Service Broker message type. When a message of the specified message type is received in the managed service program, the associated method is called.
Conversation	This class encapsulates all the aspects and behaviors of a Service Broker conversation. This class provides methods such as Receive, Send, End, and EndWithError.
Message	This class encapsulates a Service Broker message. With this class, you have direct access to the body of the message, the associated validation, and so on.
Service	This class encapsulates a Service Broker service. This class provides you with methods such as BeginDialog, GetConversation, LoadState, SaveState, and Run.
ServiceException	This class wraps the exceptions thrown in the Run method of the Service class.

Let's take a detailed look at each of these classes and how they're implemented internally. I'll start with the Service class. This class represents a Service Broker service on either the initiator or the target side. Table 5-2 describes the most important methods of this class.

Table 5-2. *Methods for the* Service *Class*

Method	Description
Service(string name, SqlConnection connection, SqlTransaction transaction)	This constructor initializes a new service object by querying the appropriate database management view for the associated queue name.
Run(bool autoCommit, SqlConnection connection, SqlTransaction transaction)	Implements the message loop for the Service Broker service. It fetches the next conversation from the message queue, reads one message at a time from the conversation, translates the message using the current application object, and fires the corresponding event to the application. Application state is saved automatically whenever a new batch of messages is fetched. The autoCommit parameter indicates if you'd like the message loop to commit automatically at the end of each fetched batch.
BeginDialog(string toServiceName, string brokerInstance, string contractName, TimeSpan lifetime, bool encryption, Guid groupId, SqlConnection connection, SqlTransaction transaction)	This method begins a new dialog with a remote service by invoking the corresponding database commands. It associates the dialog with the specified conversation group (parameter groupId).
GetConversation(Conversation conversation, SqlConnection connection, SqlTransaction transaction	This method blocks (or times out) until the specified conversation is available on the message queue.
LoadState(SqlDataReader reader, SqlConnection connection, SqlTransaction transaction)	This method is invoked inside the message loop for loading the application state associated with the conversation group being processed into the current context. You must override this method in your own service class to perform application-specific database operations.
SaveState(SqlConnection connection, SqlTransaction transaction)	This method is invoked inside the message loop when the service program has finished processing a conversation group and wishes to save the state to the database.

When you start a new dialog between two Service Broker services with BeginDialog, an object of the type Conversation is returned. Table 5-3 shows the available Conversation methods.

Table 5-3. *Methods for the* Conversation *Class*

Method	Description
Cleanup(SqlConnection connection, SqlTransaction transaction)	Ends the conversation with a cleanup. Changes are not reflected until the transaction commits.
Conversation(Service service, Guid handle)	This constructor doesn't create a new conversation by running the BEGIN DIALOG T-SQL command. Instead, you use it to create conversation objects from a conversation handle and an associated service object. To create a new conversation with a remote service, use the method Service.BeginDialog.
End(SqlConnection connection, SqlTransaction transaction)	Ends the conversation by invoking the END T-SQL command. Changes are not reflected until the transaction commits.
EndWithError(int errorCode, string errorDescription, SqlConnection connection, SqlTransaction transaction)	Ends the conversation with an error. Changes are not reflected until the transaction commits.
MoveToGroup(Guid newGroupId, SqlConnection connection, SqlTransaction transaction)	Moves the conversation to a new group by invoking the MOVE CONVERSATION T-SQL command. Changes are not reflected until the transaction commits.
Receive()	Receives a new message from the fetched batch of messages from the queue.
Send(Message message, SqlConnection connection, SqlTransaction transaction)	Sends the message on this conversation to the remote service. The message is not actually sent until the transaction is committed.

Table 5-4 shows the last important class of the managed assembly, the Message class.

Table 5-4. *Methods/Properties for the* Message *Class*

Method/Property	Description
Message(string type, Stream body)	This constructor creates a new message object with the given message type and with the given stream as the message payload.
Guid ConversationGroupId	This property represents the conversation group of the conversation from which the message was received.
long SequenceNumber	This property represents the sequence number of the message in the queue.
string ServiceName	This property represents the service to which this message is sent.
string Type	This property represents the message type of this message.
string Validation	This property represents the associated validation with the message type of this message. E means empty, N means none, and X means well-formed XML.

Architecture and Design of the Managed Assembly

Before I show you how to use the managed assembly, I want you to have a better understanding about the architecture and the internal design. The most important class of the managed assembly is the Service class. Refer back to Table 5-2, which shows the available methods in this class.

When you derive your own service class from the Service base class, you have to call the base class constructor in your own constructor. This is a necessary step, because the base constructor determines the associated queue with that service and stores its name in the m_queueName instance variable. Finally, the method callback map is built with a call to the BuildCallbackMap method, which I'll cover soon. Listing 5-1 shows the implementation of the base class constructor.

Listing 5-1. *Implementation of the Base Class Constructor of the* Service *Class*

```
public Service(string name, SqlConnection connection, SqlTransaction transaction)
{
    if (connection.State != ConnectionState.Open)
        throw new ArgumentException("Database connection is not open");

    m_name = name;

    SqlCommand cmd = connection.CreateCommand();
    cmd.CommandText = "SELECT q.name " +
        "FROM sys.service_queues q JOIN sys.services as s " +
        "ON s.service_queue_id = q.object_id " +
        "WHERE s.name = @sname";
    cmd.Transaction = transaction;

    SqlParameter param;
    param = cmd.Parameters.Add("@sname", SqlDbType.NChar, 255);
    param.Value = m_name;

    m_queueName = (string)cmd.ExecuteScalar();

    if (m_queueName == null)
        throw new ArgumentException("Could not find any service with the name '" +
            name + "' in this database.");

    m_appLoaderProcName = null;
    m_fetchSize = 0;
    m_reader = new MessageReader(this);
    BuildCallbackMap();
}
```

As soon as you create a class implementation that represents your own Service Broker service, you must implement methods for the message types you want to process inside the managed stored procedure. Because of the design of the managed assembly, you must write a

separate method for each message type you want to handle and decorate each of these methods with the [BrokerMethod] attribute. This attribute associates a message type with a method.
In other words, this ensures that the method is called when the message type—defined with
the [BrokerMethod] attribute—is received on the service queue. Listing 5-2 demonstrates this.

Listing 5-2. *Associating Message Types with Method Implementations*

```
public class TargetService : Service
{
   [BrokerMethod("http://ssb.csharp.at/SSB_Book/c05/RequestMessage")]
   public void ProcessRequestMessage(
      Message ReceivedMessage,
      SqlConnection Connection,
      SqlTransaction Transaction)
   {
      // Create the response message
      MemoryStream body = new MemoryStream(Encoding.ASCII.GetBytes(
         "<HelloWorldResponse>Hello world from a managed stored procedure " +
         "activated by Service Broker!</HelloWorldResponse>"));
      Message msgSend = new Message(
         "http://ssb.csharp.at/SSB_Book/c05/ResponseMessage, body);

      // Send the response message back to the initiator of the conversation
      ReceivedMessage.Conversation.Send(msgSend, Connection, Transaction);
   }

   [BrokerMethod(Message.EndDialogType)]
   public void EndConversation(
      Message ReceivedMessage,
      SqlConnection Connection,
      SqlTransaction Transaction)
   {
      // Ends the current Service Broker conversation
      ReceivedMessage.Conversation.End(Connection, Transaction);
   }

   [BrokerMethod(Message.ErrorType)]
   public void ProcessErrorMessages(
      Message ReceivedMessage,
      SqlConnection Connection,
      SqlTransaction Transaction)
   {
      // Ends the current Service Broker conversation due to an error
      ReceivedMessage.Conversation.End(Connection, Transaction);
   }
}
```

As soon as the managed service receives a new message on its service queue, it looks into the callback map for the method to execute for the received message-type name. The base class constructor builds the callback method through a call to BuildCallbackMap (as you saw in Listing 5-1). Listing 5-3 shows the implementation of the BuildCallbackMap method, which is part of the managed assembly.

Listing 5-3. *Implementation of the* BuildCallbackMap *Method*

```
private void BuildCallbackMap()
{
   Type t = this.GetType();
   m_dispatchMap = new Dictionary<BrokerMethodAttribute, MethodInfo>();
   MethodInfo [] methodInfoArray = t.GetMethods(
      BindingFlags.Public | BindingFlags.Instance);

   foreach (MethodInfo methodInfo in methodInfoArray)
   {
      object [] attributes = methodInfo.GetCustomAttributes(
         typeof(BrokerMethodAttribute), true);

      foreach (BrokerMethodAttribute statefulTransition in attributes)
      {
         BrokerMethodAttribute statelessTransition =
            new BrokerMethodAttribute(statefulTransition.Contract,
               statefulTransition.MessageType);

         if (m_dispatchMap.ContainsKey(statefulTransition) ||
            (m_dispatchMap.ContainsKey(statelessTransition))
         {
            string exceptionMessage = "Method '" + methodInfo.Name +
               "' redefines a handler for message type '" +
               statefulTransition.MessageType + "'";

            if (statefulTransition.State != -1)
               exceptionMessage += " in state " + statefulTransition.State;

            throw new NotSupportedException(exceptionMessage);
         }

         m_dispatchMap[statefulTransition] = methodInfo;
      }
   }
}
```

BuildCallbackMap builds a dictionary that stores for each [BrokerMethod] attribute the corresponding method (methodInfo variable) that must be called as soon as a new message is received on that service. It also includes some error handling to check that no message type is associated with more than one callback method.

Now let's look at how a message is received from the corresponding queue and how that message is dispatched to the configured callback method. To accomplish this behavior, the managed assembly executes several methods from the Service, Conversation, and Message classes. Figure 5-2 shows the UML sequence diagram that executes when the managed assembly reads a new message from a queue.

■**Note** A sequence diagram is one of the available diagram types in Unified Modeling Language (UML). You can find more information about UML at http://en.wikipedia.org/wiki/ Unified_Modeling_Language.

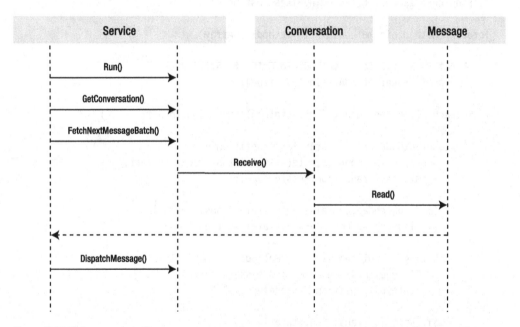

Figure 5-2. *This sequence diagram executes when a new message is received and processed.*

Now let's look at each of these methods, which are called during the message receiving and processing. Listing 5-4 shows the GetConversation method, which is executed inside the Run method that is called when SQL Server starts the managed stored procedure.

Listing 5-4. *Implementation of the* GetConversation *Method*

```
public Conversation GetConversation(
   SqlConnection connection,
   SqlTransaction transaction)
{
   if (!m_reader.IsOpen)
      FetchNextMessageBatch(null, connection, transaction);

   return m_reader.GetNextConversation();
}
```

GetConversation calls FetchNextMessageBatch. The purpose of this method is to fetch a new set of messages from the associated service queue. Listing 5-5 shows the implementation of FetchNextMessageBatch.

Listing 5-5. *Implementation of the* FetchNextMessageBatch *Method*

```
private void FetchNextMessageBatch(
   Conversation conversation,
   SqlConnection connection,
   SqlTransaction transaction)
{
   SqlCommand cmd;

   if (conversation != null || m_appLoaderProcName == null)
   {
      cmd = BuildReceiveCommand(conversation, connection, transaction);

      SqlDataReader dataReader = cmd.ExecuteReader();
      m_reader.Open(dataReader);
   }
   else if (m_appLoaderProcName != null)
   {
      cmd = BuildGcgrCommand(connection, transaction);

      SqlDataReader dataReader = cmd.ExecuteReader();

      if (!LoadState(dataReader, connection, transaction))
      {
         dataReader.Close();
         return;
      }

      m_reader.Open(dataReader);
   }
}
```

FetchNextMessageBatch builds the needed T-SQL statements for retrieving messages from the associated queue. When state information is also retrieved for the current conversation group, FetchNextMessageBatch calls either BuildGcgrCommand or BuildReceiveCommand. Chapter 6 provides more information about state handling within Service Broker applications. As soon as the messages are retrieved into an instance of a SqlDataReader, the SqlDataReader is passed to the Open method of the MessageReader class. The main purpose of this class is to create instances of the Message class out of the messages read from the queue.

As soon as GetConversation returns a conversation, the Receive method is called on that conversation. Receive calls Read of the MessageReader class. Listing 5-6 shows the implementation of the Read method.

Listing 5-6. *Implementation of the* Read *Method*

```
public Message Read(Conversation conversation)
{
    if (m_curMsg == null || m_curMsg.Conversation.Handle != conversation.Handle)
        return null;

    Message result = m_curMsg;
    AdvanceCursor();

    return result;
}
```

When Receive retrieves the received message, it dispatches the message to the corresponding callback method, which the base constructor of the service class defined. The dispatching mechanism is implemented in Service's DispatchMessage method, as shown in Listing 5-7.

Listing 5-7. *Implementation of the* DispatchMessage *Method*

```
public virtual void DispatchMessage(
    Message message,
    SqlConnection connection,
    SqlTransaction transaction)
{
    if (message.Type == Message.EchoType && message.ContractName = EchoContractName)
    {
        EchoHandler(message, connection, transaction);
        return;
    }

    MethodInfo mi;
    BrokerMethodAttribute statefulTransition = new BrokerMethodAttribute(
        State, message.ContractName, message.Type);
    BrokerMethodAttribute statefulMessageTypeTransition = new BrokerMethodAttribute(
        State, message.Type);
```

```
BrokerMethodAttribute statelessTransition = new BrokerMethodAttribute(
    message.ContractName, message.Type);
BrokerMethodAttribute statelessMessageTypeTransition = new BrokerMethodAttribute(
    message.Type);

if (m_dispatchMap.ContainsKey(statefulTransition))
    mi = m_dispatchMap[statefulTransition];
else if (m_dispatchMap.ContainsKey(statefulMessageTypeTransition))
    mi = m_dispatchMap[statefulMessageTypeTransition];
else if (m_dispatchMap.ContainsKey(statelessTransition))
    mi = m_dispatchMap[statelessTransition];
else if (m_dispatchMap.ContainsKey(statelessMessageTypeTransition))
    mi = m_dispatchMap[statelessMessageTypeTransition];
else
{
    string exceptionMessage = "No broker method defined for message type '" +
        message.Type + "' on contract '" + message.ContractName + "'";

    if (State != -1)
        exceptionMessage += " in state " + State;

    throw new InvalidOperationException(exceptionMessage);
}

  mi.Invoke(this, new object[3] { message, connection, transaction });

if (connection.State != ConnectionState.Open)
    throw new ObjectDisposeException("Connection", "Method '" + mi.Name +
        "' closed the database connection.");
}
```

As you can see from Listing 5-7, the corresponding MethodInfo object is retrieved from the dictionary, and the method is called through .NET reflection.

Building a Managed Service Broker Client

Let's see now how to write a managed Service Broker client with a .NET language of your choice that sends messages through the Service Broker infrastructure to another Service Broker service on the network. I assume that you've already set up your Service Broker infrastructure that includes the following objects. The creation of these objects is also provided as an external T-SQL script in the Source Code/Download area of the Apress website (http://www.apress.com) for this chapter.

- *Message types*: [http://ssb.csharp.at/SSB_Book/c05/RequestMessage] and [http://ssb.csharp.at/SSB_Book/c05/ResponseMessage]

- *Contract*: [http://ssb.csharp.at/SSB_Book/c05/HelloWorldContract]

- *Queues*: InitiatorQueue and TargetQueue

- *Services*: InitiatorService and TargetService

To send a new message from a managed Service Broker client, follow these steps:

1. Create and open a new SqlConnection to the database hosting the client side of the Service Broker application.

2. Begin a new transaction.

3. Create a new Service class object.

4. Begin a new dialog with another Service Broker service.

5. Send a message over the created dialog.

6. Close the connection to the database.

Listing 5-8 shows how you can accomplish these steps with the features provided by the managed assembly.

Listing 5-8. *Implementing the Managed Service Broker Client*

```
public static void Main()
{
    SqlConnection cnn = null;
    SqlTransaction tran = null;
    TextReader reader = null;

    try
    {
        // Open a new database connection
        cnn = new SqlConnection("Initial Catalog=Chapter5_ManagedServiceBroker;
            Data Source=localhost;Integrated Security=SSPI;");
        cnn.Open();

        // Start a new database transaction
        tran = cnn.BeginTransaction();


        // Create a new service object
        Service initiatorService = new Service("InitiatorService", cnn, tran);
        initiatorService.FetchSize = 1;
```

```csharp
        // Begin a new dialog with the service TargetService
        Conversation dialog = initiatorService.BeginDialog(
            "TargetService",
            null,
            "http://ssb.csharp.at/SSB_Book/c05/HelloWorldContract",
            TimeSpan.FromMinutes(1),
            false,
            cnn,
            tran);

        // Create a new request message
        Message request = new Message(
            "http://ssb.csharp.at/SSB_Book/c05/RequestMessage",
            null);

        // Send the message over the new dialog
        dialog.Send(request, cnn, tran);

        // Commit the transaction, so that the message is really sent to the
        // other Service Broker service
        tran.Commit();

        Console.WriteLine("Press Enter to Exit");
        Console.ReadLine();
    }
    catch (ServiceException ex)
    {
        Console.WriteLine("An exception occurred - {0}\n", ex.ToString());

        if (tran != null)
            tran.Rollback();
    }
    finally
    {
        if (reader != null)
            reader.Close();

        if (cnn != null)
            cnn.Close();
    }
}
```

Figure 5-3 shows the output of this simple Service Broker client.

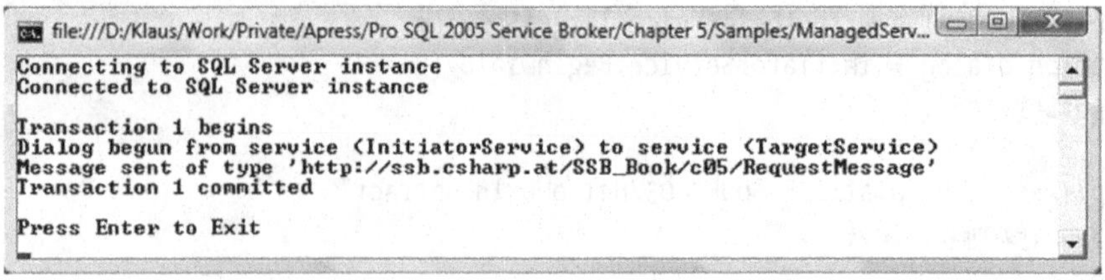

Figure 5-3. *The managed Service Broker client built with the managed assembly*

If you take a look at the `TargetQueue` in the SQL Server database (with a T-SQL statement such as `SELECT * FROM TargetQueue`), you'll see that the client application sent the message successfully (see Figure 5-4).

	status	priority	queuing_order	conversation_group_id	conversation_handle	message_sequence_number	service_name
1	1	0	2	229ED8B9-9979-DB11-A30E-0080C81899BB	239ED8B9-9979-DB11-A30E-0080C81899BB	0	TargetService

Figure 5-4. *The sent message on the* `TargetQueue`

After the client application sends the message successfully, you can implement an activated stored procedure that processes the message and sends a response back to the client. Have a look at Listing 5-9.

Listing 5-9. *Message-Processing Stored Procedure for the* `TargetQueue`

```
CREATE PROCEDURE ProcessRequestMessages
AS
   DECLARE @ch UNIQUEIDENTIFIER
   DECLARE @messagetypename NVARCHAR(256)
   DECLARE @messagebody XML
   DECLARE @responsemessage XML;

   WHILE (1=1)
   BEGIN
      BEGIN TRANSACTION

      WAITFOR (
         RECEIVE TOP (1)
            @ch = conversation_handle,
            @messagetypename = message_type_name,
            @messagebody = CAST(message_body AS XML)
         FROM TargetQueue
      ), TIMEOUT 1000

      IF (@@ROWCOUNT = 0)
      BEGIN
         ROLLBACK TRANSACTION
         BREAK
      END
```

```
    IF (@messagetypename = 'http://ssb.csharp.at/SSB_Book/c05/RequestMessage')
    BEGIN
        SET @responsemessage = '<HelloWorldResponse>' +
            @messagebody.value('/HelloWorldRequest[1]', 'nvarchar(max)') +
            '</HelloWorldResponse>';

        SEND ON CONVERSATION @ch
            MESSAGE TYPE [http://ssb.csharp.at/SSB_Book/c05/ResponseMessage]
            (@responsemessage);

        END CONVERSATION @ch;
    END

    IF (@messagetypename =
        'http://schemas.microsoft.com/SQL/ServiceBroker/EndDialog')
    BEGIN
        END CONVERSATION @ch;
    END
    END
GO

ALTER QUEUE TargetQueue
WITH ACTIVATION
(
    STATUS = ON,
    PROCEDURE_NAME = ProcessRequestMessages,
    MAX_QUEUE_READERS = 5,
    EXECUTE AS SELF
)
GO
```

You can now extend the client application to wait for the sent response message and handle it correctly (see Listing 5-10).

Listing 5-10. *Waiting for Response Messages in the Client Application*

```
// Here comes the code from Listing 5-8...
// ...

// Begin a new transaction for receiving messages
tran = cnn.BeginTransaction();

// Wait for 5 seconds
initiatorService.WaitforTimeout = TimeSpan.FromSeconds(5);
```

```
// Check if there is a message from a conversation available on the queue
if (initiatorService.GetConversation(dialog, cnn, tran) == null)
{
    dialog.EndWithError(1, "No response within 5 seconds.");
    tran.Commit();


    cnn.Close();
    return;
}

// Read the sent message
Message response = dialog.Receive();

if (response.Body != null)
{
    reader = new StreamReader(response.Body);
    Console.WriteLine(reader.ReadToEnd());
}

// End the dialog
dialog.End(cnn, tran);

// Committing the transaction
tran.Commit();
cnn.Close();
```

Figure 5-5 shows the output of the managed Service Broker client.

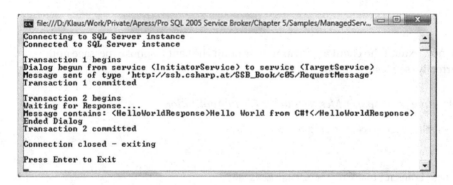

Figure 5-5. *The managed Service Broker client built with the managed assembly*

The activated T-SQL stored procedure starts automatically as soon as the client application sends a request message and sends a response message back to the client, which is received with the code shown in Listing 5-10.

Building a Managed Service Program

Another nice feature of the managed assembly for Service Broker is that it lets you write an activated managed stored procedure for Service Broker. You must deploy the managed stored procedure to SQL Server 2008. It executes automatically when a new message arrives in the specified queue through the SQLCLR mechanism available since SQL Server 2008. When you implement an activated stored procedure with the managed assembly, follow these steps:

1. Derive your own service class from the Service base class.

2. Implement the entry point for your managed stored procedure.

3. Implement all necessary methods and associate them—through the .NET attribute [BrokerMethod]—with your custom message types and with the error message type and the end dialog message type provided by Service Broker.

4. Deploy the assembly into SQL Server 2008.

5. Register the managed stored procedure.

6. Configure the managed stored procedure for Service Broker activation.

Deriving Your Service Class

First, you must define the TargetService in a class derived from the Service base class. Listing 5-11 shows this definition.

Listing 5-11. *Deriving a Service Class from the* Service *Base Class*

```
public class TargetService : Service
{
   public TargetService(SqlConnection Connection)
      : base("TargetService", Connection)
   {
      WaitforTimeout = TimeSpan.FromSeconds(1);
   }
}
```

As you can see in Listing 5-11, you must call the base constructor in the class constructor and pass the service name as an argument. Refer back to Listing 5-1 for more information about the internal implementation of the base constructor and why you have to call it.

Implementing an Entry Point

After you create your derived service class, you're able to implement the entry point of your managed stored procedure. Listing 5-12 shows the basic skeleton of an entry point that you can use in every managed stored procedure written with the managed assembly.

Listing 5-12. *Implementing the Entry Point for the* TargetService

```
public class TargetService : Service
{
    public static void ServiceProcedure()
    {
        Service service = null;
        SqlConnection cnn = null;


        try
        {
            // Open the database connection
            cnn = new SqlConnection("context connection=true;");
            cnn.Open();

            // Instantiate the Service Broker service "TargetService"
            service = new TargetService(cnn);
            service.FetchSize = 1;

            // Run the message loop of the service
            service.Run(true, cnn, null);
        }
        catch (ServiceException ex)
        {
            if (ex.Transaction != null)
                ex.Transaction.Rollback();
        }
        finally
        {
            if (cnn != null)
                cnn.Close();
        }
    }
}
```

As you can see in Listing 5-12, you have to open a new context connection to SQL Server 2008. After you acquire the context connection, you must create a new instance of your service class—in this case, the TargetService class. After you set the properties of the service class (which properties you set is completely up to your requirements), you call the Run method of the service class to start the message-processing logic.

CONTEXT CONNECTIONS IN SQL SERVER 2008

Since SQL Server 2008, the database engine supports the concept of a context connection. When you're implementing a managed stored procedure and you need a connection inside the managed stored procedure to the database that hosts the managed stored procedure, you can use the context connection. The context connection is the database connection under which the managed stored procedure is actually executed. Therefore, you don't have to open an additional connection to the SQL Server database.

However, keep in mind that you can't open more than one context connection inside a managed stored procedure. You must pass the context connection to each method that wants to use the context connection. As you can see in Listing 5-12, you create the context connection inside the entry point of the managed stored procedure and then hand it over to the Run method of the service class.

Implementing Message Type Handling

After you implement the entry point for your managed stored procedure, you have to write the methods that process your different supported message types. Please refer back to Listing 5-2, which demonstrated how you can use the [BrokerMethod] attribute to associate a message type with a method.

As you can see in Listing 5-2, you have to handle the message types [http://ssb.csharp.at/ SSB_Book/c05/RequestMessage], [http://schemas.microsoft.com/SQL/ServiceBroker/ EndDialog], and [http://schemas.microsoft.com/SQL/ServiceBroker/Error] in this example.

Deploying the Assembly

After you implement all the needed methods, you can deploy the assembly to your SQL Server 2008 database. You can start this task automatically from Visual Studio 2008 or start the deployment directly from Microsoft SQL Server Management Studio with the T-SQL statement CREATE ASSEMBLY. Listing 5-13 shows the syntax for this statement.

Listing 5-13. *Syntax for the* CREATE ASSEMBLY *T-SQL Statement*

```
CREATE ASSEMBLY assembly_name
[ AUTHORIZATION owner_name ]
FROM { <client_assembly_specifier> | <assembly_bits> [ ,...n] }
[ WITH PERMISSION_SET = { SAFE | EXTERNAL_ACCESS | UNSAFE } ]
[ ; ]
```

Table 5-5 describes the arguments for this statement.

Table 5-5. *Arguments for the* CREATE ASSEMBLY *T-SQL Statement*

Argument	Description
assembly_name	The name of the assembly used to reference it within the database. The name must be unique within the database and a valid identifier.
AUTHORIZATION	Specifies the owner of the assembly. You can specify a database user or a database role. If you don't specify anything, ownership is given to the current user.
<client_assembly_specifier>	Indicates the local path or network location where the assembly that is being registered is located, and also indicates the manifest file name that corresponds to the assembly. SQL Server also looks for any dependent assemblies of this assembly in the same location and registers them with the same owner as the root-level assembly.
<assembly_bits>	Represents the list of binary values that make up the assembly and its dependent assemblies. The first value in this list is considered the root-level assembly. The values corresponding to the dependent assemblies can be supplied in any order.
PERMISSION_SET	Specifies a set of code access permissions that are granted to the assembly when it is accessed by SQL Server. If not specified, SAFE is applied as the default. SAFE is the most restrictive permission set. The code executed by an assembly with SAFE permission cannot access external system resources such as files, the network, environment variables, or the registry. EXTERNAL_ACCESS enables assemblies to access certain external system resources such as files, networks, environment variables, and the registry. UNSAFE enables unrestricted access to resources, both within and outside an instance of SQL Server. Code running from within an UNSAFE assembly can also call unmanaged code.

Listing 5-14 shows how to use the CREATE ASSEMBLY T-SQL statement to register the created assembly in the database you've built in this section for the target service. Please be sure to point to the correct path where you've built the assembly.

Listing 5-14. *Registering the Service Broker Assembly in the Database*

```
-- Add the assembly file to the database
CREATE ASSEMBLY BackendServiceAssembly
FROM 'c:\BackendService.dll'
GO

-- Add the debug information to the assembly
ALTER ASSEMBLY BackendServiceAssembly
ADD FILE FROM 'c:\BackendService.pdb'
GO
```

PERMISSION SETS IN THE SQLCLR

The SQLCLR supports the permission sets SAFE, EXTERNAL_ACCESS, and UNSAFE. Whenever you deploy assemblies to a SQL Server database, you should use the permission set SAFE for security reasons. However, sometimes you need access to resources such as files and networks, and Web services. In these scenarios, you can use the permission set EXTERNAL_ACCESS.

UNSAFE is the permission set where the assembly can do everything in the database. You can call unmanaged code or instantiate COM objects. You should not use this permission set for your assemblies, because then your code will be completely unsafe and could do everything that is possible with extended stored procedures.

Registering the Managed Stored Procedure

As soon as you register the managed assembly in your database, you can register the managed stored procedure. Listing 5-15 shows the required T-SQL code.

Listing 5-15. *Registration of the Managed Stored Procedure*

```
-- Register the stored procedure written in managed code
CREATE PROCEDURE ProcessRequestMessagesManaged
AS
EXTERNAL NAME BackendServiceAssembly.BackendService.TargetService.ServiceProcedure
GO
```

If you want to make sure that the registration of the assembly is successful, you can use the sys.assemblies catalog view. This catalog view returns for each registered assembly in the database a row with more information about the registered assembly. Table 5-6 describes the columns available in this catalog view.

Table 5-6. *Columns in the* sys.assemblies *Catalog View*

Column	Data Type	Description
name	SYSNAME	Represents the name of the registered assembly. The name is unique within the database.
principal_id	INT	The ID of the principal that owns the assembly.
assembly_id	INT	The ID of the assembly. The assembly ID is unique within the database.
permission_set	TINYINT	Specifies the used permission set for the assembly: 1 = SAFE 2 = EXTERNAL_ACCESS 3 = UNSAFE.
permission_set_desc	NVARCHAR(60)	Specifies the description of the permission set for the registered assembly.
is_visible	BIT	1 = Assembly is visible to register T-SQL entry points. 2 = Assembly is intended only for managed callers.

Continued

Table 5-6. *Continued*

Column	Data Type	Description
clr_name	NVARCHAR(4000)	String that encodes the simple name, version number, culture, public key, and CPU architecture of the assembly.
create_date	DATETIME	Specifies the date on which the assembly was created or registered.
modify_date	DATETIME	Specifies the date on which the assembly was modified.

Figure 5-6 shows the content of the sys.assemblies catalog view after the managed assembly is deployed to the database.

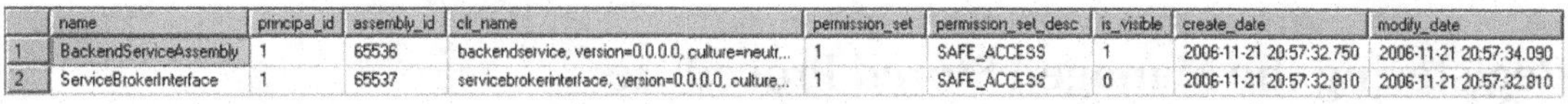

	name	principal_id	assembly_id	clr_name	permission_set	permission_set_desc	is_visible	create_date	modify_date
1	BackendServiceAssembly	1	65536	backendservice, version=0.0.0.0, culture=neutr...	1	SAFE_ACCESS	1	2006-11-21 20:57:32.750	2006-11-21 20:57:34.090
2	ServiceBrokerInterface	1	65537	servicebrokerinterface, version=0.0.0.0, culture...	1	SAFE_ACCESS	0	2006-11-21 20:57:32.810	2006-11-21 20:57:32.810

Figure 5-6. *The content of the* sys.assemblies *catalog view*

As you can see in Figure 5-6, the referenced ServiceBrokerInterface assembly is also deployed to the database automatically.

Configuring the Service Broker Activation

As soon as you register the assembly in the database, you can change the activation for the TargetQueue to use the managed stored procedure for message processing. Listing 5-16 shows the required T-SQL code.

Listing 5-16. *Configuration of Service Broker Activation*

```
-- Use the managed stored procedure for activation
ALTER QUEUE TargetQueue
WITH ACTIVATION
(
    STATUS = ON,
    PROCEDURE_NAME = ProcessRequestMessagesManaged,
    MAX_QUEUE_READERS = 5,
    EXECUTE AS SELF
)
GO
```

Using the Service Program

Now when you call the managed client you developed earlier in this chapter, the managed stored procedure processes the incoming messages and returns the corresponding return message back to the client. Figure 5-7 shows the response from the managed stored procedure.

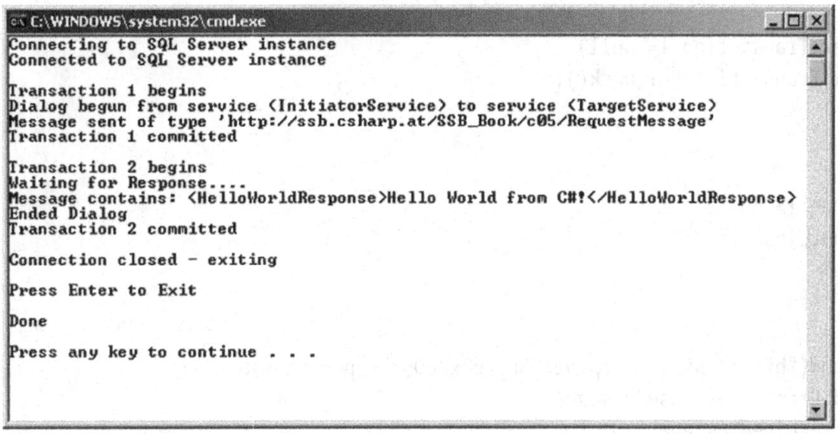

```
C:\WINDOWS\system32\cmd.exe                                    _|□|×|
Connecting to SQL Server instance
Connected to SQL Server instance

Transaction 1 begins
Dialog begun from service <InitiatorService> to service <TargetService>
Message sent of type 'http://ssb.csharp.at/SSB_Book/c05/RequestMessage'
Transaction 1 committed

Transaction 2 begins
Waiting for Response....
Message contains: <HelloWorldResponse>Hello World from C#!</HelloWorldResponse>
Ended Dialog
Transaction 2 committed

Connection closed - exiting

Press Enter to Exit

Done

Press any key to continue . . .
```

Figure 5-7. *Processing Service Broker messages by a managed stored procedure*

With this information in hand, you can now write an additional managed stored procedure that does the message processing on the InitiatorQueue. This managed stored procedure handles the messages sent from TargetService back to the InitiatorService. You can then send Service Broker messages from either T-SQL or managed code, and the message processing is done in managed code. Listing 5-17 shows the needed code for the InitiatorService.

Listing 5-17. *Implementing the* InitiatorService

```csharp
public class InitiatorService : Service
{
    public InitiatorService(SqlConnection Connection)
        : base("InitiatorService", Connection)
    {
        WaitforTimeout = TimeSpan.FromSeconds(1);
    }

    public static void ServiceProcedure()
    {
        Service service = null;
        SqlConnection cnn = null;

        try
        {
            cnn = new SqlConnection("context connection=true;");
            cnn.Open();

            service = new InitiatorService(cnn);
            service.FetchSize = 1;
            service.Run(true, cnn, null);
        }
        catch (ServiceException ex)
```

```csharp
        {
            if (ex.Transaction != null)
                ex.Transaction.Rollback();
        }
        finally
        {
            if (cnn != null)
                cnn.Close();
        }
    }

    [BrokerMethod("http://ssb.csharp.at/SSB_Book/c05/ResponseMessage")]
    public void ProcessResponseMessage(
        Message ReceivedMessage,
        SqlConnection Connection,
        SqlTransaction Transaction)
    {
        ReceivedMessage.Conversation.End(Connection, Transaction);
    }

    [BrokerMethod(Message.EndDialogType)]
    public void EndConversation(
        Message ReceivedMessage,
        SqlConnection Connection,
        SqlTransaction Transaction)
    {
        ReceivedMessage.Conversation.End(Connection, Transaction);
    }

    public void ProcessErrorMessage(
        Message ReceivedMessage,
        SqlConnection Connection,
        SqlTransaction Transaction)
    {
        ReceivedMessage.Conversation.End(Connection, Transaction);
    }
}
```

As soon as you develop the InitiatorService class, you can deploy the assembly again in your database and activate the internal activation on the InitiatorQueue, as shown in Listing 5-18. Please be sure to point to the correct path where you've built the assembly.

Listing 5-18. *Deployment of the Managed Assembly*

```
-- Add the assembly file to the database
CREATE ASSEMBLY InitiatorServiceAssembly
FROM 'c:\InitiatorService.dll'
GO

-- Add the debug information to the assembly
ALTER ASSEMBLY InitiatorServiceAssembly
ADD FILE FROM 'c:\InitiatorService.pdb'
GO

-- Register the stored procedure written in managed code
CREATE PROCEDURE ProcessRequestMessagesManaged
AS
EXTERNAL NAME
InitiatorServiceAssembly.InitiatorService.InitiatorService.
ServiceProcedure
GO

-- Use the managed stored procedure for activation
ALTER QUEUE InitiatorQueue
WITH ACTIVATION
(
   STATUS = ON,
   PROCEDURE_NAME = ProcessResponseMessagesManaged,
   MAX_QUEUE_READERS = 5,
   EXECUTE AS SELF
)
GO
```

When you register the managed stored procedure for internal activation, you can use
the code from Listing 5-8 to send a message to the Service Broker service. In this case, the
ProcessRequestMessagesManaged managed stored procedure starts and processes the messages
arriving in the TargetQueue. This stored procedure sends a response message back to the
InitiatorService, where the ProcessResponseMessages managed stored procedure starts
and finally ends the dialog between the two services.

A Practical Example

Now that you've seen how to use managed code to implement Service Broker solutions, let's
look at a more complex sample where you'll see how easy it is to implement Service Broker
applications with managed code. I'll show you how to implement an inventory application
where a client can submit two different types of messages:

- InventoryUpdate: Updates the inventory in the database.

- InventoryRequest: Checks if the specified quantity of the inventory is in stock. If it is,
  the requested quantity is removed from the inventory.

Listing 5-19 shows the T-SQL code for creating the necessary Service Broker infrastructure objects.

Listing 5-19. *Creating the Service Broker Infrastructure for the Inventory Application*

```
-- Message type and contract for updating the inventory
CREATE MESSAGE TYPE
[http://ssb.csharp.at/SSB_Book/c05/InventoryUpdateMessage]
VALIDATION = WELL_FORMED_XML
GO

CREATE CONTRACT
[http://ssb.csharp.at/SSB_Book/c05/InventoryUpdateContract]
(
    [http://ssb.csharp.at/SSB_Book/c05/InventoryUpdateMessage]
    SENT BY INITIATOR
)
GO


-- Message types and contract for removing items from the inventory
CREATE MESSAGE TYPE
[http://ssb.csharp.at/SSB_Book/c05/InventoryQueryRequestMessage]
VALIDATION = WELL_FORMED_XML
GO

CREATE MESSAGE TYPE
[http://ssb.csharp.at/SSB_Book/c05/InventoryQueryResponseMessage]
VALIDATION = WELL_FORMED_XML
GO

CREATE CONTRACT
[http://ssb.csharp.at/SSB_Book/c05/InventoryQueryContract]
(
    [http://ssb.csharp.at/SSB_Book/c05/InventoryQueryRequestMessage]
    SENT BY INITIATOR,
    [http://ssb.csharp.at/SSB_Book/c05/InventoryQueryResponseMessage]
    SENT BY TARGET
)
GO


-- Create the target service
CREATE QUEUE [InventoryTargetQueue]
GO
```

```
CREATE SERVICE [InventoryTargetService]
ON QUEUE [InventoryTargetQueue]
(
    [http://ssb.csharp.at/SSB_Book/c05/InventoryUpdateContract],
    [http://ssb.csharp.at/SSB_Book/c05/InventoryQueryContract]
)
GO

-- Create the initiator service
CREATE QUEUE [InventoryInitiatorQueue]
GO

CREATE SERVICE [InventoryInitiatorService]
ON QUEUE [InventoryInitiatorQueue]
(
    [http://ssb.csharp.at/SSB_Book/c05/InventoryUpdateContract],
    [http://ssb.csharp.at/SSB_Book/c05/InventoryQueryContract]
)
GO
```

Note two differences between the code in Listing 5-19 and all the other samples up to this point in this book. The first is that the contract [http://ssb.csharp.at/SSB_Book/c05/InventoryUpdateContract] consists of only one message type, [http://ssb.csharp.at/SSB_Book/c05/InventoryUpdateMessage], which is sent by the initiator of the conversation. It's a one-way messaging scenario. The second is that both queues accept more than one contract, so messages of both contracts can be sent to and retrieved from the queues and are processed accordingly.

The last thing you need for this sample is to populate the Inventory table with several items. The T-SQL code in Listing 5-20 creates and populates this table.

Listing 5-20. *Creating and Populating the* Inventory *Table*

```
-- Create the inventory table
CREATE TABLE Inventory
(
    InventoryId NVARCHAR(10) NOT NULL,
    Quantity INT NOT NULL,
    PRIMARY KEY (InventoryId)
)
GO


-- Populate the inventory table
INSERT Inventory VALUES ('PS1372', 200)
INSERT Inventory VALUES ('PC1035', 200)
INSERT Inventory VALUES ('BU1111', 200)
-- and the rest comes here...
```

With this Service Broker infrastructure, you can now create the managed stored procedure that processes the incoming messages on the InventoryTargetService. The entry point
for this managed stored procedure is the same code as in Listings 5-11 and 5-12. The first use
case for this example is the requirement to update the inventory. To accomplish this task,
a client sends a message of the type [http://ssb.csharp.at/SSB_Book/c05/
InventoryUpdateMessage] bound to the Service Broker contract [http://ssb.csharp.at/
SSB_Book/c05/InventoryUpdateContract]. Listing 5-21 shows the ProcessInventoryUpdate
method that processes this message type.

Listing 5-21. *Updating the* Inventory *Table*

```
[BrokerMethod("http://ssb.csharp.at/SSB_Book/c05/InventoryUpdateMessage")]
public void ProcessInventoryUpdate(
    Message ReceivedMessage,
    SqlConnection Connection,
    SqlTransaction Transaction)
{
    try
    {
        XmlDocument doc = new XmlDocument();
        doc.LoadXml(ReceivedMessage.BodyAsString);

        XmlNodeList list = doc.GetElementsByTagName("InventoryId");
        string inventoryId = list.Items(0).InnerXml;

        list = doc.GetElementsByTagName("Quantity");
        int quantity = Convert.ToInt32(list.Items(0).InnerXml);

        // Updating the inventory
        UpdateInventory(Connection, Transaction, inventoryId, quantity);

        // End the conversation between the two services
        ReceivedMessage.Conversation.End(Connection, Transaction);
    }
    catch (Exception ex)
    {
        ReceivedMessage.Conversation.EndWithError(
            1, ex.Message, Connection, Transaction);
    }
}

private void UpdateInventory(
    SqlConnection Connection,
    SqlTransaction Transaction,
    string InventoryId,
    int Quantity)
```

```
{
   // Creating the SqlCommand
   SqlCommand cmd = new SqlCommand("UPDATE Inventory " +
      "SET Quantity = Quantity + @Quantity " +
      "WHERE InventoryId = @InventoryId", Connection);
   cmd.Transaction = Transaction;


   // Add InventoryId parameter
   SqlParameter paramInventoryId = new SqlParameter("@InventoryId",
      SqlDbType.NVarChar, 10);
   paramInventoryId.Value = InventoryId;
   cmd.Parameters.Add(paramInventory);

   // Add Quantity parameter
   SqlParameter paramQuantity = new SqlParameter("@Quantity", SqlDbType.Int);
   paramQuantity.Value = Quantity;
   cmd.Parameters.Add(paramQuantity);

   // Execute the SqlCommand
   cmd.ExecuteNonQuery();
}
```

Once you write the necessary methods in the managed stored procedure, you must deploy the stored procedure to the database. You do this through the CREATE ASSEMBLY T-SQL statement already described in Listing 5-13 and Table 5-5. Listing 5-22 shows the needed T-SQL.

Listing 5-22. *Registering the Managed Stored Procedure*

```
CREATE ASSEMBLY [InventoryTargetServiceAssembly]
FROM 'c:\InventoryTargetService.dll'
GO


ALTER ASSEMBLY [InventoryTargetServiceAssembly]
ADD FILE FROM 'c:\InventoryTargetService.pdb'
GO


CREATE PROCEDURE InventoryTargetProcedure
AS
EXTERNAL NAME
[InventoryTargetServiceAssembly].
[InventoryTargetService.TargetService].
   ServiceProcedure
GO
```

```
ALTER QUEUE [InventoryTargetQueue]
WITH ACTIVATION
(
    STATUS = ON,
    PROCEDURE_NAME = InventoryTargetProcedure,
    MAX_QUEUE_READERS = 5,
    EXECUTE AS SELF
)
GO
```

As soon as you set up the internal activation with the managed stored procedure, a client can send a message to the service. Listing 5-23 shows how to update the inventory with a message of type [http://ssb.csharp.at/SSB_Book/c05/InventoryUpdateMessage].

Listing 5-23. *Updating the* Inventory *Table Through a Service Broker Message*

```
BEGIN TRANSACTION;
    DECLARE @dh UNIQUEIDENTIFIER;
    DECLARE @msg NVARCHAR(MAX);
    DECLARE @count INT;
    DECLARE @MAX INT;

    BEGIN DIALOG @dh
        FROM SERVICE [InventoryInitiatorService]
        TO SERVICE 'InventoryTargetService'
        ON CONTRACT [http://ssb.csharp.at/SSB_Book/c05/InventoryUpdateContract]
        WITH ENCRYPTION = OFF;

    SET @msg =
        '<InventoryUpdate>
            <InventoryId>BU1032</InventoryId>
            <Quantity>30</Quantity>
        </InventoryUpdate>';

    SEND ON CONVERSATION @dh MESSAGE TYPE
        [http://ssb.csharp.at/SSB_Book/c05/InventoryUpdateMessage] (@msg);
COMMIT;
```

Figure 5-8 shows the updated Inventory table in the SQL Server database.

	InventoryId	Quantity
1	BU1032	170
2	BU1111	200
3	BU2075	200
4	BU7832	200
5	MC2222	200
6	MC3021	200
7	MC3026	200

Figure 5-8. *The updated* Inventory *table*

The second functionality of this sample application is to order items through a message of type [http://ssb.csharp.at/SSB_Book/c05/InventoryQueryRequestMessage]. When this message type arrives at the InventoryTargetQueue, the associated managed stored procedure performs the following actions:

- Checks if the needed quantity is available in the inventory

- Calculates the new items count in the inventory

- Sends a response message back to the sender with the result

Listing 5-24 shows the ProcessInventoryQueryRequest method that handles all three tasks.

Listing 5-24. ProcessInventoryQueryRequest *Method*

```
[BrokerMethod("http://ssb.csharp.at/SSB_Book/c05/InventoryQueryRequestMessage")]
public void ProcessInventoryQueryRequest
    Message ReceivedMessage,
    SqlConnection Connection,
    SqlTransaction Transaction)
{
    try
    {
        XmlDocument doc = new XmlDocument();
        doc.LoadXml(ReceivedMessage.BodyAsString);

        XmlNodeList list = doc.GetElementsByTagName("InventoryId");
        string inventoryId = list.Item(0).InnerXml;

        list = doc.GetElementsByTagName("Quantity");
        int quantity = Convert.ToInt32(list.Item(0).InnerXml);

        // Remove the items from the inventory, if available
        bool rc = CheckInventory(Connection, Transaction, inventoryId, quantity);

        // Send a response message back to the initiator of the conversation
        SendCustomerReply(ReceivedMessage.Conversation, Connection, Transaction, rc);
    }
    catch (Exception ex)
    {
        ReceivedMessage.Conversation.EndWithError(
            1, ex.Message, Connection, Transaction);
    }
}

private bool CheckInventory(
    SqlConnection Connection,
    SqlTransaction Transaction,
    string InventoryId,
    int Quantity)
```

```
{
    int realQuantity;

    SqlCommand cmd = new SqlCommand("SELECT Quantity FROM Inventory " +
        "WHERE InventoryId = @InventoryId", Connection);
    cmd.Transaction = Transaction;

    // Add InventoryId parameter
    SqlParameter paramInventoryId = new SqlParameter("@InventoryId",
        SqlDbType.NVarChar, 10);
    paramInventoryId.Value = InventoryId;
    cmd.Parameters.Add(paramInventoryId);


    SqlDataReader reader = cmd.ExecuteReader();

    if (reader.Read())
    {
        realQuantity = reader.GetInt32(0);
        reader.Close();

        if (Quantity <= realQuantity)
        {
            SubtractFromInventory(Connection, Transaction, InventoryId, Quantity);
            return true;
        }
        else return false;
    }
    else
    {
        reader.Close();
        return false;
    }
}

private void SubtractFromInventory(
    SqlConnection Connection,
    SqlTransaction Transaction,
    string InventoryId,
    int Quantity)
{
    SqlCommand cmd = new SqlCommand("UPDATE Inventory SET Quantity = Quantity - " +
        "@Quantity WHERE InventoryId = @InventoryId", Connection);
    cmd.Transaction = Transaction;
```

```csharp
    // Add InventoryId parameter
    SqlParameter paramInventoryId = new SqlParameter("@InventoryId",
        SqlDbType.NVarChar, 10);
    paramInventoryId.Value = InventoryId;
    cmd.Parameters.Add(paramInventoryId);

    // Add Quantity parameter
    SqlParameter paramQuantity = new SqlParameter("@Quantity", SqlDbType.Int);
    paramQuantity.Value = Quantity;
    cmd.Parameters.Add(Quantity);

    // Execute the command
    cmd.ExecuteNonQuery();
}

private void SendCustomerReply(
    Conversation Conversation,
    SqlConnection Connection,
    SqlTransaction Transaction,
    bool InStockFlag)

{

    XmlDocument doc = new XmlDocument();
    XmlElement root = doc.CreateElement("InventoryResponse");
    doc.AppendChild(root);

    XmlElement response = doc.CreateElement("Response");

    if (InStockFlag)
        response.InnerText = "In stock";
    else
        response.InnerText = "Out of stock";

    root.AppendChild(response);

    // Send the message
    Message msg = new Message(
        "http://ssb.csharp.at/SSB_Book/c05/InventoryQueryResponseMessage",
        new MemoryStream(Encoding.ASCII.GetBytes(doc.InnerXml)));
    Conversation.Send(msg, Connection, Transaction);

    // End the dialog
    Conversation.End(Connection, Transaction);
}
```

After you've successfully redeployed the changed managed stored procedure to the database, you can use the T-SQL code in Listing 5-25 to send a Service Broker message to order items from the inventory.

Listing 5-25. *Ordering Items from the Inventory*

```
BEGIN TRANSACTION;
    DECLARE @dh UNIQUEIDENTIFIER;
    DECLARE @msg NVARCHAR(MAX);
    DECLARE @count INT;
    DECLARE @MAX INT;

    BEGIN DIALOG @dh
        FROM SERVICE [InventoryInitiatorService]
        TO SERVICE 'InventoryTargetService'
        ON CONTRACT [http://ssb.csharp.at/SSB_Book/c05/InventoryQueryContract]
        WITH ENCRYPTION = OFF;

    SET @msg =
        '<InventoryUpdate>
            <InventoryId>BU1032</InventoryId>
            <Quantity>30</Quantity>
        </InventoryUpdate>';

    SEND ON CONVERSATION @dh MESSAGE TYPE
        [http://ssb.csharp.at/SSB_Book/c05/InventoryQueryRequestMessage] (@msg);
COMMIT;
```

As soon as this T-SQL batch executes, the InventoryTargetService processes your request and returns a response message back to the initiator of the conversation. Figure 5-9 shows the returned response message in the InventoryTargetQueue.

	[No column name]	status	priority	queuing_order	conversation_group_id	conversation_handle
1	NULL	1	0	0	794012C0-9B79-DB11-A30E-0080C81899BB	784012C0-9B79-DB11-A30E-0080C81899BB
2	<InventoryResponse><Response>In stock</Response>...	1	0	1	7D4012C0-9B79-DB11-A30E-0080C81899BB	7C4012C0-9B79-DB11-A30E-0080C81899BB
3	NULL	1	0	2	7D4012C0-9B79-DB11-A30E-0080C81899BB	7C4012C0-9B79-DB11-A30E-0080C81899BB
4	<InventoryResponse><Response>In stock</Response>...	1	0	3	614C15E2-9B79-DB11-A30E-0080C81899BB	604C15E2-9B79-DB11-A30E-0080C81899BB
5	NULL	1	0	4	614C15E2-9B79-DB11-A30E-0080C81899BB	604C15E2-9B79-DB11-A30E-0080C81899BB

Figure 5-9. *The returned response message*

The only thing left to do now is to write an activated stored procedure (managed code or T-SQL code) that processes the response message and the end dialog messages received from the target service.

Summary

In this chapter, I moved a bit away from T-SQL code and discussed how to implement Service Broker applications with managed code in SQL Server 2008. I showed how you can build a simple managed client for Service Broker applications and how messages are sent to Service Broker services.

I described how you can use managed stored procedures to implement service programs for Service Broker. I introduced the ServiceBrokerInterface managed assembly, which is a sample that ships with SQL Server 2008. The managed assembly provides several classes that encapsulate the necessary T-SQL statements needed for Service Broker. Then I showed in detail how to combine what you learned in previous chapters to write a complete Service Broker application with managed code. In the next chapter, I'll explain transaction management and locking strategies in Service Broker applications.

Summary

CHAPTER 6

■ ■ ■

Locking and Transaction Management

A Service Broker application must always use some kind of locking logic to process messages from a service queue. Service Broker provides a concept referred to as *conversation groups* for this reason. As soon as you begin working with locking, you must also have a look at transaction management with Service Broker, because transaction management affects the overall performance of your Service Broker application. This chapter will discuss the following two techniques:

- *Conversation groups and locks*: Service Broker puts messages of related conversations into a so-called conversation group. Within a conversation group, Service Broker ensures things such as ordered message processing, reliable delivery, and synchronization support for multiple queue readers.

- *Transaction management*: You can design and build scalable Service Broker applications through different approaches in the transaction management. This chapter will look at several approaches and show you how they affect performance.

Conversation Groups and Locks

Conversation groups ensure that messages are processed in order. While it is reasonably straightforward to ensure that messages are received in order, it is more difficult to ensure that they are processed in order. To see why this is a problem, just think of a large, multithreaded application that receives and processes order-entry messages. One thread receives the order-header message and starts processing it. In the meantime, other threads may receive order-line-item messages that are related to the order-header message. Because line items are processed quicker than the order-header message, the order-line-item message transaction commits sooner than the order-header message and fails. Why? Because no corresponding order header is available in the table.

Even though messages are received in order, a multithreaded application may not process them in order. Writing an application that works correctly with messages that are processed out of order and processed on multiple threads simultaneously can be difficult to implement. For this reason, many message-processing applications are single-threaded. While this solves the ordering problem, it has an impact on the scalability of the application.

The great thing about Service Broker is that it gets around this issue by using a special kind of lock to ensure that only one task can read messages from a particular conversation at a time. This ensures that a multithreaded application that receives messages in order will also process them in order. This special kind of lock is called a *conversation group lock*.

As described in Chapter 2, a conversation group identifies one or more related conversations and allows a Service Broker application to easily coordinate conversations involved in a specific business task. Every conversation belongs to exactly one conversation group. Every conversation group is associated with several conversations from different services. A conversation group can contain one or more conversations.

It's easy to see the value of locking a conversation during message processing, but there are some cases where this isn't enough. For example, imagine again an order-entry application that sends messages to credit card validation, inventory adjustment, shipping, and accounting services on four different dialogs. These services may all respond roughly at the same time, so it's possible that response messages from these four services for the same order may be processed on different threads simultaneously. This can cause problems: if two different services update the order status simultaneously without being aware of each other, status information could get lost.

To solve this problem, Service Broker locks conversation groups, not conversations. By default, a conversation group contains a single conversation—the conversation that was started from the initiator's service. In this case, conversation group locking is the same thing as conversation locking. The conversation group lock guarantees that a Service Broker application can process messages on each conversation exactly once in order and keep state on a per-conversation-group basis. Because a conversation group can contain more than one conversation, a Service Broker application can use conversation groups to identify messages related to the same business task and process those messages together. If your Service Broker application can benefit from locking more than one conversation at a time, you may expand the conversation group by adding more conversations to it. Figure 6-1 shows how conversations are grouped together with a conversation group.

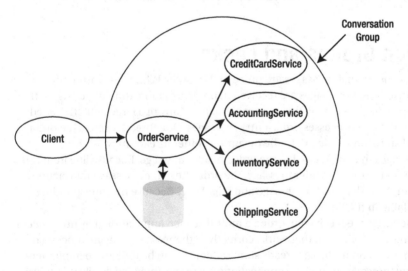

Figure 6-1. *Conversations grouped by a conversation group*

There are several ways to group dialogs into the same conversation group. Any time you create a new dialog with the BEGIN DIALOG T-SQL statement, Service Broker will automatically create a conversation group for you and assign the new dialog to this conversation group. You can retrieve more information about the current opened conversation groups through the sys.conversation_groups catalog view. Listing 6-1 shows you how to implicitly create a new conversation group.

Listing 6-1. *Creating a New Conversation Group*

```
DECLARE @ch UNIQUEIDENTIFIER;

BEGIN DIALOG @ch
    FROM SERVICE [InitiatorService]
    TO SERVICE 'TargetService'
    WITH ENCRYPTION = OFF;
GO

SELECT * FROM sys.conversation_groups
GO
```

Figure 6-2 shows the result of the sys.conversation_groups catalog view.

	conversation_group_id	service_id	is_system
1	6741F4BF-9D79-DB11-A30E-0080C81899BB	65536	0

Figure 6-2. *The* sys.conversation_groups *catalog view*

Table 6-1 describes the columns available in this catalog view.

Table 6-1. *Available Columns in the* sys.conversation_groups *Catalog View*

Column	Data Type	Description
conversation_group_id	UNIQUEIDENTIFIER	The identifier for the conversation group
service_id	INT	The identifier of the service for this conversation group
is_system	BIT	Specifies whether this is a system instance of a conversation group

In Figure 6-2, you saw a row in the sys.conversation_groups catalog view that matches the corresponding row in the sys.conversation_endpoints table for the conversation just created. This is the row that Service Broker locks when it receives messages from any of the conversations in the conversation group. Notice that Service Broker locks the row in the sys.conversation_groups catalog view, not in the sys.conversation_endpoints catalog view or directly in the queue. This means that if more messages are received for the conversation, they can be added to the conversation while the conversation group is locked. The sys.conversation_endpoints row isn't locked, so it can be changed while the conversation group is locked. Figure 6-3 illustrates this important concept. The dark gray rows represent the locked rows.

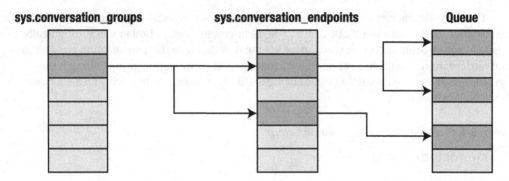

sys.conversation_groups   **sys.conversation_endpoints**   **Queue**

Figure 6-3. *Locking of the* sys.conversation_groups *catalog view*

To initiate multiple conversations in the same conversation group, you first begin one dialog that creates a new conversation group automatically. You then expand the conversation group by adding dialogs related to the first one, as shown in Listing 6-2.

■**Note** Please create a new database for the samples used in this chapter.

Listing 6-2. *Expanding a Conversation Group with Additional Conversations*

```
DECLARE @ch1 UNIQUEIDENTIFIER;
DECLARE @ch2 UNIQUEIDENTIFIER;

BEGIN TRANSACTION;

BEGIN DIALOG @ch1
    FROM SERVICE [InitiatorService]
    TO SERVICE 'TargetService1'
    WITH ENCRYPTION = OFF;

BEGIN DIALOG @ch2
    FROM SERVICE [InitiatorService]
    TO SERVICE 'TargetService2'
    WITH RELATED_CONVERSATION = @ch1,
    ENCRYPTION = OFF;

SEND ON CONVERSATION @ch1
    (CAST('<Request></Request>' AS XML));
SEND ON CONVERSATION @ch2
    (CAST('<Request></Request>' AS XML));
```

```
COMMIT TRANSACTION;
GO

SELECT * FROM sys.conversation_groups cg
INNER JOIN sys.services svc on cg.service_id = svc.service_id
GO
```

The difference in Listing 6-2 from all the other listings you've already seen is that you use the WITH RELATED_CONVERSATION clause in the second BEGIN DIALOG T-SQL statement to join the second dialog to the conversation group of the first conversation. When you use this clause, you must provide the conversation handle from the conversation to which you want to join the current beginning conversation. Now, when you do a SELECT to the sys.conversation_groups catalog view, you would expect that each conversation would belong to the same conversation group. Figure 6-4 shows the output from this catalog view.

	conversation_group_id	service_id	is_system	name	service_id	principal_id	service_queue_id
1	C54E3621-9E79-DB11-A30E-0080C81899BB	65536	0	InitiatorService	65536	1	2073058421
2	C74E3621-9E79-DB11-A30E-0080C81899BB	65538	0	TargetService1	65538	1	2137058649
3	C94E3621-9E79-DB11-A30E-0080C81899BB	65539	0	TargetService2	65539	1	21575115

Figure 6-4. *The conversations don't belong to the same conversation group.*

Figure 6-5 shows the output from both target queues, where you can also see that each message belongs to another conversation group.

	status	priority	queuing_order	conversation_group_id	conversation_handle	message_sequence_number	service_name	service_id	service_contract_name
1	1	0	0	C74E3621-9E79-DB11-A30E-0080C81899BB	C84E3621-9E79-DB11-A30E-0080C81899BB	0	TargetService1	65538	DEFAULT

	status	priority	queuing_order	conversation_group_id	conversation_handle	message_sequence_number	service_name	service_id	service_contract_name
1	1	0	0	C94E3621-9E79-DB11-A30E-0080C81899BB	CA4E3621-9E79-DB11-A30E-0080C81899BB	0	TargetService2	65539	DEFAULT

Figure 6-5. *The received messages on the queues don't belong to the same conversation group.*

I assume that you now might be asking, "What the heck is going on here? Why did Service Broker put all conversations in different conversation groups although I placed them into the same conversation group with the WITH RELATED_CONVERSATION clause?"

The conversation group is a locking primitive. Conversations in the same group are locked together, so that any transaction is guaranteed to be the only transaction that processes messages on the current group. As such, conversation groups are pertinent only for the side declaring the conversation group—the sender's side. The conversation group information doesn't travel with the message to the other side—the target service. The two conversations are related, but only on the sender's side. If you actually send back a reply on each dialog, the replies will have the same conversation_group_id.

Conversation groups can apply to either the initiator or the target or both. The issue here is that a conversation group is limited to a single queue. This means you can put conversations into a group on the initiator, but the conversation group ID isn't sent over the network to the target. You can also put conversations into a group on the target queue, but this is independent of any conversation groups that you may have set up on the initiator. The conversation group is primarily used for a locking context for Service Broker commands.

SEND and RECEIVE commands can't span queues in a single command, so a lock that locks conversations on two different queues doesn't make sense.

Conversation groups aren't sent along with messages from the initiator to the target, because there is no way for the sender of the message to know whether the targets of the conversations in the group are in the same queue. In fact, developers can change around the destination queues, so in general, the conversation initiator has no knowledge of the queue configuration of the target.

When you want to prove that both messages are sent on the same conversation group, you must process the sent messages on both targets and send a response message back to the initiator of both conversations. These response messages are then in the same conversation group on the initiator's side. To accomplish this, you can create the ProcessTargetQueue1 and ProcessTargetQueue2 stored procedures that process incoming messages on both queues. Listing 6-3 shows the implementation of one of these stored procedures.

Listing 6-3. *Retrieving Messages on the Target Queue*

```
CREATE PROCEDURE ProcessTargetQueue1
AS
BEGIN
    DECLARE @ch UNIQUEIDENTIFIER
    DECLARE @messagetypename NVARCHAR(256)
    DECLARE @messagebody XML

    WHILE (1=1)
    BEGIN
        BEGIN TRANSACTION

        WAITFOR (
            RECEIVE TOP (1)
                @ch = conversation_handle,
                @messagetypename = message_type_name,
                @messagebody = CAST(message_body AS XML)
            FROM TargetQueue1
        ), TIMEOUT 1000

        IF (@@ROWCOUNT = 0)
        BEGIN
            ROLLBACK TRANSACTION
            BREAK
        END

        IF (@messagetypename = 'DEFAULT')
        BEGIN
            END CONVERSATION @ch;
        END
```

```
     IF (@messagetypename =
       'http://schemas.microsoft.com/SQL/ServiceBroker/EndDialog')
     BEGIN
        -- End the conversation
        END CONVERSATION @ch;
     END

     COMMIT TRANSACTION
  END
END
GO
```

Now when you send both messages with the code in Listing 6-2, you can execute both stored procedures on the target side to process the received messages and send an END DIALOG message back to the initiator of the conversation. As soon as the request messages are processed on the target side, you can do a SELECT on the InitiatorQueue. Now, as you can see in Figure 6-6, both END DIALOG messages are grouped together in the same conversation group.

	status	priority	queuing_order	conversation_group_id	conversation_handle	message_sequence_number	service_name	service_id	service_contract_name
1	1	0	0	C54E3621-9E79-DB11-A30E-0080C81899BB	C44E3621-9E79-DB11-A30E-0080C81899BB	0	InitiatorService	65536	DEFAULT
2	1	0	1	C54E3621-9E79-DB11-A30E-0080C81899BB	C64E3621-9E79-DB11-A30E-0080C81899BB	0	InitiatorService	65536	DEFAULT

Figure 6-6. *Both* END DIALOG *messages are grouped together in the same conversation group.*

To get a feeling for how the conversation group lock works, you can try to process messages from InitiatorQueue on two different threads—just use two SQL Server connections inside Microsoft SQL Server Management Studio. Inside the first connection, begin a new transaction and try to receive a message from InitiatorQueue (see Listing 6-4).

Listing 6-4. *Processing Messages on the First Thread*

```
BEGIN TRANSACTION;
  RECEIVE TOP (1) * FROM InitiatorQueue
```

The interesting thing about Listing 6-4 is that a new transaction is opened but not committed. Therefore, you can guarantee that the conversation group lock is held when you execute the code from Listing 6-5 in a new connection inside Microsoft SQL Server Management Studio.

Listing 6-5. *Processing Messages on the Second Thread*

```
BEGIN TRANSACTION;
  RECEIVE TOP (1) * FROM InitiatorQueue
COMMIT TRANSACTION;
```

As you can see from the output, nothing is returned in this query. This is because just one other message is in the queue, and this message belongs to the conversation group where the conversation group lock is held. Therefore, the query returns no more messages that are ready to process. You can also have a look at the Activity Monitor of SQL Server 2008, where you can see the conversation group lock. Refer to Figure 6-7 for further details.

When you do a `COMMIT` on the opened transaction from Listing 6-4, the conversation group lock is released and the T-SQL batch from Listing 6-5 can return the one and only message available for processing in the `InitiatorQueue`.

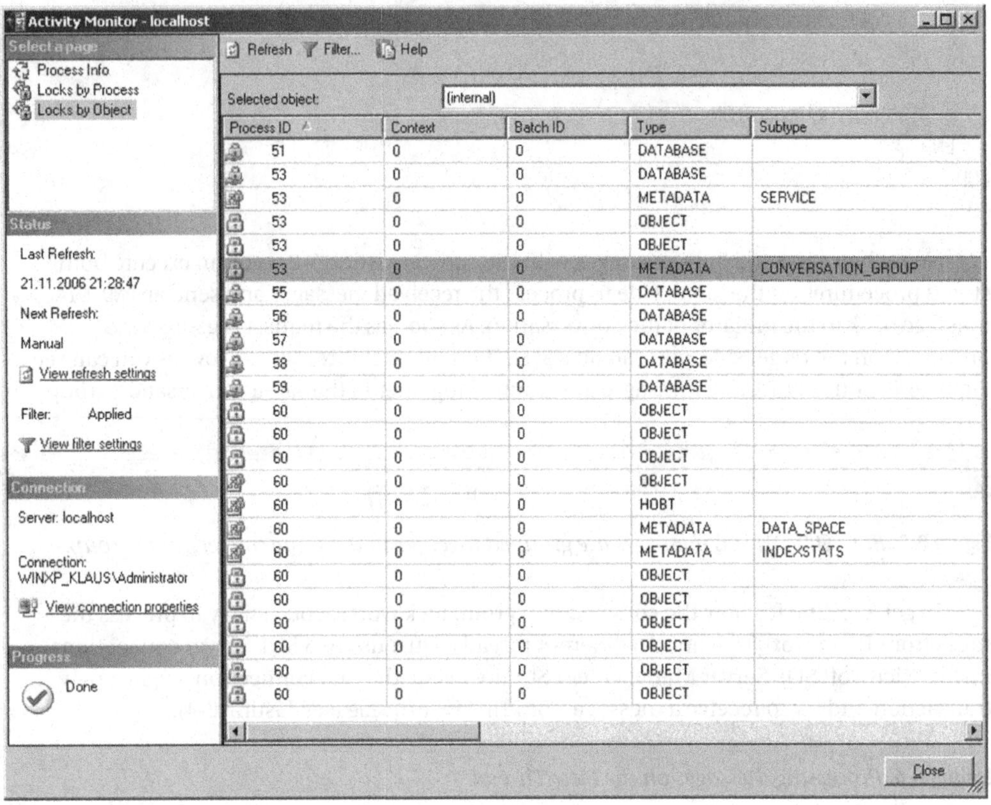

Figure 6-7. *The conversation group lock in the Activity Monitor of SQL Server 2008*

State Handling

As you know, Service Broker conversations can be long-running dialogs that last for days or even months or years. It would obviously be incredibly inefficient and probably impossible to keep a copy of the application active for every active conversation. Service Broker applications, like most highly scalable applications, solve this problem by maintaining a persistent state between messages.

The state of an application contains enough information to pick up processing when the next message arrives. For example, the state for an order-entry application might track the status of each order and the schedule of that order, so that the application knows what's going on for a specific order when you ask about it. As soon as the order gets processed through a message, the status of the order is modified and the state is saved to reflect the changes that processing the message caused.

Maintaining too much state in web applications or in web services leads to huge scalability problems in your application. However, if your application is running in the database, storing the application state doesn't impact scalability that much. The messaging operations, database updates, and state updates are all part of a simple single-phase transaction and are committed with the same log write.

You might wonder how you can identify the state of your current business transaction inside the database. Because you can group together all dialogs used for a business transaction to a conversation group, you can use the conversation group ID as your key for storing the needed state of the conversation group. Each message contains the key for the state tables, which makes it simple to retrieve and restore the state inside your message-processing logic. As an added feature, there is a lock associated with the conversation group, so if the state only updates while processing messages, you don't have to worry about concurrent updates to your state table. The rows in the state table aren't actually locked, but if the application only updates the state while it holds the conversation group lock, only one application thread at a time can do inserts or updates to the state tables.

GET CONVERSATION GROUP

If you implement your message-processing logic in a stored procedure, you can retrieve state information whenever you need it. Service Broker includes the GET CONVERSATION GROUP T-SQL statement to make state-retrieval operations easier for you. This statement locks the first conversation group with associated messages on the queue and returns the conversation group ID as a result. You can then select the state from your state tables and receive and process your messages associated with the previous associated conversation group retrieved by the GET CONVERSATION GROUP T-SQL statement. Listing 6-6 shows the syntax for this T-SQL statement.

Listing 6-6. *Syntax for the* GET CONVERSATION GROUP *T-SQL Statement*

```
[ WAITFOR ( ]
   GET CONVERSATION GROUP @conversation_group_id
   FROM queue
[ ) ] [, TIMEOUT timeout ]
```

Table 6-2 describes the parameters for this statement.

Table 6-2. *Parameters for the* GET CONVERSATION GROUP *T-SQL Statement*

Parameter	Description
WAITFOR	Indicates that the GET CONVERSATION GROUP T-SQL statement waits for a message to arrive on the queue if no messages are currently available.
@conversation_group_id	This variable stores the conversation group ID returned by the GET CONVERSATION GROUP T-SQL statement. If no conversation groups are available, the variable is set to NULL.
queue	Specifies the queue name to get the conversation group from.
timeout	Specifies the length of time (in milliseconds) that Service Broker waits for a message to arrive on the queue. This clause may only be used with the WAITFOR clause. If a statement that uses WAITFOR doesn't include this clause or the time-out is -1, the wait time is unlimited. If the time-out expires, GET CONVERSATION GROUP sets the @conversation_group_id to NULL.

Listing 6-7 shows how you use the GET CONVERSATION GROUP T-SQL statement in practice.

Listing 6-7. *Using the* GET CONVERSATION GROUP *T-SQL Statement*

```
DECLARE @conversationGroup UNIQUEIDENTIFIER;
DECLARE @messageTypeName NVARCHAR(256);
DECLARE @messageBody XML;

WAITFOR (
    GET CONVERSATION GROUP @conversationGroup FROM TargetQueue
), TIMEOUT 1000

IF (@conversationGroup IS NOT NULL)
BEGIN
    RECEIVE TOP (1)
        @messageTypeName = message_type_name,
        @messageBody = CAST(message_body AS XML)
    FROM TargetQueue
    WHERE conversation_group_id = @conversationGroup;

    PRINT 'Message body: ' + CAST(@messageBody AS NVARCHAR(MAX));
END
```

As you can see in Listing 6-7, you use GET CONVERSATION GROUP in combination with the WAITFOR statement to wait for one second until a new message arrives on the TargetQueue. Then you check if you got a message IF (@conversationGroup IS NOT NULL). When GET CONVERSATION GROUP returns a conversation group ID, this conversation group is locked. Therefore, you finally retrieve the sent message through the RECEIVE statement. An important point to mention here is that you must use the WHERE clause and make a constraint on the conversation_group_id column with the value you got from the GET CONVERSATION GROUP statement. This way, you can ensure that you're only processing messages from the conversation group where you acquired a lock through the GET CONVERSATION GROUP statement. Otherwise, you may retrieve messages for a different conversation group where you haven't acquired a conversation group lock before.

The Receive Loop with State Handling

Retrieving messages with GET CONVERSATION GROUP only makes sense when you also retrieve application state from a state table before you retrieve a message from a queue. Retrieving and updating state changes the receive loop pattern you've already encountered and used throughout this book. Now I want to show you a receive loop pattern where you can also retrieve and save state information in a state table. The receive loop now contains two nested loops:

- *The outer loop*: This loop starts a new transaction, uses the GET CONVERSATION GROUP statement to lock a conversation group, and retrieves the application state from a state table.

- *The inner loop*: This loop receives all messages available in the conversation group one at a time. The inner loop also ensures that all the messages on the queue are associated with the application state and are processed before the outer loop retrieves another application state for another conversation group.

Once all the messages in the queue from that conversation group are processed, the state is updated with any data that has changed while processing the messages. Finally, the transaction commits. This works well if a limited number of messages from the conversation group are on the queue. In applications where a continuous stream of messages arrives on a conversation group, you should consider committing the transaction after a number of messages so that the transactions don't get too big. You'll find more about this topic in the "Transaction Management" section, where I talk about transaction management with Service Broker. Listing 6-8 shows the basic receive loop pattern. The code in Listing 6-8 assumes that you've already created a table called ApplicationState with the structure shown in Figure 6-8.

Column Name	Data Type	Allow Nulls
ConversationGroupID	uniqueidentifier	☐
CreditCardValidation	bit	☐
InventoryAdjustment	bit	☐
Shipping	bit	☐
Accounting	bit	☐
		☐

Figure 6-8. *The* ApplicationState *table*

Let's have a look at the code.

Listing 6-8. *The Receive Loop with State Handling*

```
CREATE PROCEDURE ProcessOrderMessages
AS
BEGIN
   DECLARE @conversationGroup UNIQUEIDENTIFIER;
   DECLARE @CreditCardValidationStatus BIT;
   DECLARE @InventoryAdjustmentStatus BIT;
   DECLARE @ShippingStatus BIT;
   DECLARE @AccountingStatus BIT;

   -- Outer Loop (State Handling)
   WHILE (1 = 1)
   BEGIN
      BEGIN TRANSACTION;

      WAITFOR (
         GET CONVERSATION GROUP @conversationGroup FROM [ProductOrderQueue]
      ), TIMEOUT 1000

      IF (@@ROWCOUNT = 0)
      BEGIN
         ROLLBACK TRANSACTION
         BREAK
      END
```

```
-- Retrieving the application state for the current conversation group
SELECT
    @CreditCardValidationStatus = CreditCardValidation,
    @InventoryAdjustmentStatus = InventoryAdjustment,
    @ShippingStatus = Shipping,
    @AccountingStatus = Accounting
FROM ApplicationState
WHERE ConversationGroupId = @conversationGroup;


IF (@@ROWCOUNT = 0)
BEGIN
    -- There is currently no application state available,
    -- so we insert the application state into the state table
    SET @CreditCardValidationStatus = 0;
    SET @InventoryAdjustmentStatus = 0;
    SET @ShippingStatus = 0;
    SET @AccountingStatus = 0;

    -- Insert the state record
    INSERT INTO ApplicationState
    (
        ConversationGroupId,
        CreditCardValidation,
        InventoryAdjustment,
        Shipping,
        Accounting
    )
    VALUES
    (
        @conversationGroup,
        @CreditCardValidationStatus,
        @InventoryAdjustmentStatus,
        @ShippingStatus,
        @AccountingStatus
    )
END

DECLARE @messageTypeName NVARCHAR(256);
DECLARE @ch UNIQUEIDENTIFIER;
DECLARE @messageBody XML;
```

```
-- Inner Loop (Message Processing)
WHILE (1 = 1)
BEGIN
    WAITFOR (
        RECEIVE TOP (1)
            @messageTypeName = message_type_name,
            @messageBody = CAST(message_body AS XML),
            @ch = conversation_handle
        FROM [ProductOrderQueue]
        WHERE conversation_group_id = @conversationGroup
    ), TIMEOUT 1000

    IF (@@ROWCOUNT = 0)
    BEGIN
        BREAK
    END


    IF (@messageTypeName =
        'http://schemas.microsoft.com/SQL/ServiceBroker/EndDialog')
    BEGIN
        END CONVERSATION @ch;
    END

    IF (@messageTypeName =
        'http://schemas.microsoft.com/SQL/ServiceBroker/Error')
    BEGIN
        -- Handle errors
        END CONVERSATION @ch;
    END

    IF (@messageTypeName =
        'http://ssb.csharp.at/SSB_Book/c06/ProductOrderMessage')
    BEGIN
        -- Process the message
        SELECT @messageBody;

        SET @CreditCardValidationStatus = 1;
        END CONVERSATION @ch;
    END
END
```

```
    -- Update the application state
    UPDATE ApplicationState SET
       CreditCardValidation = @CreditCardValidationStatus,
       InventoryAdjustment = @InventoryAdjustmentStatus,
       Shipping = @ShippingStatus,
       Accounting = @AccountingStatus
    WHERE ConversationGroupId = @conversationGroup;

    COMMIT TRANSACTION;
  END
END
```

Let's walk through this stored procedure step by step. In the first step, you use the GET CONVERSATION GROUP T-SQL statement to acquire a conversation group lock on an available conversation group:

```
WAITFOR (
   GET CONVERSATION GROUP @conversationGroup FROM [ProductOrderQueue]
), TIMEOUT 1000
```

In the second step, you use the returned conversation group identifier to retrieve the application state for the current locked conversation group:

```
SELECT
   @CreditCardValidationStatus = CreditCardValidation,
   @InventoryAdjustmentStatus = InventoryAdjustment,
   @ShippingStatus = Shipping,
   @AccountingStatus = Accounting
FROM ApplicationState
WHERE ConversationGroupId = @conversationGroup;
```

If the ProcessOrderMessages stored procedure finds no application state for the current locked conversation group, then the stored procedure inserts an initial state into the ApplicationState table. By now, the state-retrieval process is finished, and you start retrieving messages from the current locked conversation group inside a nested loop in the stored procedure. You use the RECEIVE T-SQL statement, and then you use the WHERE clause to restrict the returned result set only to messages of the current locked conversation group:

```
WAITFOR (
   RECEIVE TOP (1)
      @messageTypeName = message_type_name,
      @messageBody = CAST(message_body AS XML),
      @ch = conversation_handle
   FROM [ProductOrderQueue]
   WHERE conversation_group_id = @conversationGroup
), TIMEOUT 1000
```

After the RECEIVE T-SQL statement, you have all required message data stored in local T-SQL variables, so you can process the message through the specified message type as you've already seen in the previous chapters. After all messages of the current conversation group are processed, the stored procedure updates the application state in the state table and commits the pending transaction:

```
UPDATE ApplicationState SET
   CreditCardValidation = @CreditCardValidationStatus,
   InventoryAdjustment = @InventoryAdjustmentStatus,
   Shipping = @ShippingStatus,
   Accounting = @AccountingStatus
WHERE ConversationGroupId = @conversationGroup;

COMMIT TRANSACTION;
```

As long as messages from other conversation groups are available, the outer loop continues to run and processes the associated messages inside the inner loop of the stored procedure. You can start the ProcessOrderMessages stored procedure and view the content of the ApplicationState table with the following two T-SQL statements:

```
EXEC ProcessOrderMessages
GO

SELECT * FROM ApplicationState
GO
```

Figure 6-9 shows the content of the ApplicationState table.

	ConversationGroupID	CreditCardValidation	InventoryAdjustment	Shipping	Accounting
1	6FA070D1-2EBD-DB11-9933-0014C2E615AA	1	0	0	0

Figure 6-9. *The content of the* ApplicationState *table*

State Handling with a Managed Stored Procedure

In Chapter 5, I introduced the ServiceBrokerInterface managed assembly. With this assembly, you can write Service Broker applications with managed code. One nice thing about this managed assembly is that it also supports message processing with state handling. In this section, I will show you step by step how you can port the T-SQL processing logic from Listing 6-8 to a managed stored procedure that incorporates functionality from the ServiceBrokerInterface managed assembly.

First, you have to create a new managed class library that implements the managed stored procedure. For this sample, I have called this library TargetService. Inside this class library, you create a new class called ProductOrderService that represents the server-side managed stored procedure that processes request messages from other Service Broker services. Listing 6-9 shows the skeleton of the managed stored procedure.

Listing 6-9. *The Skeleton of a Managed Stored Procedure*

```
public class ProductOrderService : Service
{
    private Guid _conversationGroupId;
    private bool _creditCardValidationStatus;
    private bool _inventoryAdjustmentStatus;
    private bool _shippingStatus;
    private bool _accountingStatus;

    public ProductOrderService(SqlConnection Connection)
        : base("ProductOrderService", Connection)
    {
        WaitforTimeout = TimeSpan.FromSeconds(1);
        AppLoaderProcName = "LoadApplicationState";
    }

    public static void ServiceProcedure()
    {
        Service service = null;
        SqlConnection cnn = null;

        try
        {
            cnn = new SqlConnection("context connection=true;");
            cnn.Open();

            service = new ProductOrderService(cnn);
            service.FetchSize = 1;
            service.Run(true, cnn, null);
        }
        catch (ServiceException ex)
        {
            if (ex.Transaction != null)
                ex.Transaction.Rollback();
        }
        finally
        {
            if (cnn != null)
                cnn.Close();
        }
    }
}
```

The only difference in this skeleton is that you initialize the AppLoaderProcName property with the name of another stored procedure implemented in T-SQL. This stored procedure loads the application state for the conversation group that is currently processed. For this reason, the managed assembly provides the virtual LoadState method that you can override in your derived service class. The LoadState method is called inside the private FetchNextMessageBatch method in the Service base class when the managed stored procedure wants to retrieve new messages from the service queue. Listing 6-10 shows the implementation of the FetchNextMessageBatch method, which also calls the overridden LoadState method.

Listing 6-10. *The* FetchNextMessageBatch *Method*

```
private void FetchNextMessageBatch(
   Conversation conversation,
   SqlConnection connection,
   SqlTransaction transaction)
{
   SqlCommand cmd;

   if (conversation != null || m_appLoaderProcName == null)
   {
      cmd = BuildReceiveCommand(conversation, connection, transaction);

      SqlDataReader dataReader = cmd.ExecuteReader();
      m_reader.Open(dataReader);
   }
   else if (m_appLoaderProcName != null)
   {
      cmd = BuildGcgrCommand(connection, transaction);
      SqlDataReader dataReader = cmd.ExecuteReader();

      if (!LoadState(dataReader, connection, transaction))
      {
         dataReader.Close();
         return;
      }

      m_reader.Open(dataReader);
   }
}
```

As you can see in Listing 6-10, the LoadState method is called automatically when the AppLoaderProcName property is set accordingly. The interesting thing about this is that your specified stored procedure was already executed when your implementation of the LoadState method was called in the derived class. Therefore, you only get as a parameter an instance of a SqlDataReader class that contains the application state that your specified stored procedure has returned as a result. Before I show you the actual implementation of the LoadState method, I'll show you (in Listing 6-11) the T-SQL statements that the BuildGcgrCommand method creates for SqlCommand execution.

Listing 6-11. *Message Receiving and State Handling in One T-SQL Batch*

```
DECLARE @cgid UNIQUEIDENTIFIER;

WAITFOR (
   GET CONVERSATION GROUP @cgid FROM ProductOrderQueue
), TIMEOUT @to;


IF (@cgid IS NOT NULL)
BEGIN
   EXEC LoadApplicationState @cgid;

   RECEIVE TOP (1)
      conversation_group_id,
      conversation_handle,
      message_sequence_number,
      service_name,
      service_contract_name,
      message_type_name,
      validation,
      message_body
   FROM ProductOrderQueue
   WHERE conversation_group_id = @cgid;
END
```

In Listing 6-11, the T-SQL batch first tries to find a conversation group where messages are available to process (through the call to GET CONVERSATION GROUP). When the T-SQL batch successfully acquires the conversation group lock, it calls your specified stored procedure (in this case, LoadApplicationState), which loads the current state for the given conversation group. Finally, the RECEIVE statement that selects the needed messages from the given queue is executed.

As you can see, it's important to know that each stored procedure used for state loading must accept a parameter of the UNIQUEIDENTIFIER data type that represents the conversation group ID of the current processed conversation group. Listing 6-12 shows the implementation of the LoadApplicationState stored procedure that loads the application state from the ApplicationState state table.

Listing 6-12. *The* LoadApplicationState *Stored Procedure Used for State Loading*

```
CREATE PROCEDURE LoadApplicationState
@ConversationGroupID UNIQUEIDENTIFIER
AS
BEGIN
   DECLARE @CreditCardValidationStatus BIT;
   DECLARE @InventoryAdjustmentStatus BIT;
   DECLARE @ShippingStatus BIT;
   DECLARE @AccountingStatus BIT;

   SELECT
      @CreditCardValidationStatus = CreditCardValidation,
      @InventoryAdjustmentStatus = InventoryAdjustment,
      @ShippingStatus = Shipping,
      @AccountingStatus = Accounting
   FROM ApplicationState
   WHERE @ConversationGroupId = @ConversationGroupID;

   IF (@@ROWCOUNT = 0)
   BEGIN
      SET @CreditCardValidationStatus = 0;
      SET @InventoryAdjustmentStatus = 0;
      SET @ShippingStatus = 0;
      SET @AccountingStatus = 0;

      INSERT INTO ApplicationState (ConversationGroupId, CreditCardValidation,
         InventoryAdjustment, Shipping, Accounting)
      VALUES
      (
         @ConversationGroupID,
         @CreditCardValidationStatus,
         @InventoryAdjustmentStatus,
         @ShippingStatus,
         @AccountingStatus
      )
   END

   SELECT
      ConversationGroupId,
      CreditCardValidation,
      InventoryAdjustment,
      Shipping,
      Accounting
   FROM ApplicationState
   WHERE @ConversationGroupId = @ConversationGroupID;
END
```

With this information, you can now implement the LoadState method inside your managed stored procedure (see Listing 6-13).

Listing 6-13. *Implementation of the* LoadState *Method*

```
public override bool LoadState(
   SqlDataReader reader,
   SqlConnection connection,
   SqlTransaction transaction)
{
   if (reader.Read())
   {
      _conversationGroupId = new Guid(reader["ConversationGroupId"].ToString());
      _creditCardValidationStatus =
         bool.Parse(reader["CreditCardValidation"].ToString());
      _inventoryAdjustmentStatus =
         bool.Parse(reader["InventoryAdjustment"].ToString());
      _shippingStatus = bool.Parse(reader["Shipping"].ToString());
      _accountingStatus = bool.Parse(reader["Accounting"].ToString());

      return reader.NextResult();
   }
   else return false;
}
```

The most important aspect of the code in Listing 6-13 is that you must call the NextResult method on the supplied SqlDataReader. This is important because the SqlDataReader contains at least two result sets: the result set from your state table, and the result set with the received messages. Therefore, you must move inside the LoadState method to the last result set that contains the received messages. Otherwise, your managed stored procedure won't work.

As soon as your message is dispatched to the correct method for processing, the base class calls the virtual SaveState method that you can override in your implementation class. In this method, you can write the modified application state back to the state table. Listing 6-14 shows the implementation of the SaveState method.

Listing 6-14. *Implementation of the* SaveState *Method*

```
public override void SaveState(
   SqlConnection connection,
   SqlTransaction transaction)
{
   string sql = "UPDATE ApplicationState SET ";
   sql += "CreditCardValidation = @CreditCardValidationStatus, ";
   sql += "InventoryAdjustment = @InventoryAdjustmentStatus, ";
   sql += "Shipping = @ShippingStatus, ";
   sql += "Accounting = @AccountingStatus ";
   sql += "WHERE ConversationGroupId = @ConversationGroupId";
```

```
SqlCommand cmd = new SqlCommand(sql, connection);
cmd.Transaction = transaction;
cmd.Parameters.Add(new SqlParameter(
    "@CreditCardValidationStatus", SqlDbType.Bit);
cmd.Parameters.Add(new SqlParameter(
    "@InventoryAdjustmentStatus", SqlDbType.Bit);
cmd.Parameters.Add(new SqlParameter(
    "@ShippingStatus", SqlDbType.Bit);
cmd.Parameters.Add(new SqlParameter(
    "@AccountingStatus", SqlDbType.Bit);
cmd.Parameters.Add(new SqlParameter(
    "@ConversationGroupId", SqlDbType.UniqueIdentifier);

cmd.Parameters["@CreditCardValidationStatus"].Value =
    _creditCardValidationStatus;
cmd.Parameters["@InventoryAdjustmentStatus"].Value =
    _inventoryAdjustmentStatus;
cmd.Parameters["@ShippingStatus"].Value = _shippingStatus;
cmd.Parameters["@AccountingStatus"].Value = _accountingStatus;
cmd.Parameters["@ConversationGroupId"].Value = _conversationGroupId;

cmd.ExecuteNonQuery();
}
```

When you deploy this managed stored procedure into the database and use this managed stored procedure for the internal activation of the ProductOrderQueue, your sent messages get processed automatically, and the ApplicationState table reflects the state of your ongoing conversation groups (see Figure 6-10).

	ConversationGroupID	CreditCardValidation	InventoryAdjustment	Shipping	Accounting
1	F390C203-0EB3-DB11-864F-0014C2E615AA	1	0	0	0

Figure 6-10. *The stored application state in the* ApplicationState *table*

A Practical Example

Now that you know the basics about conversation groups and locking in Service Broker, let's combine all this knowledge into a complete Service Broker application. You'll enhance this sample in later chapters to refine and build a complete distributed message-based application.

Let's build a familiar application for order entry. The order-entry application will consist of several Service Broker services to fulfill an order. Figure 6-11 shows the relationship between these services.

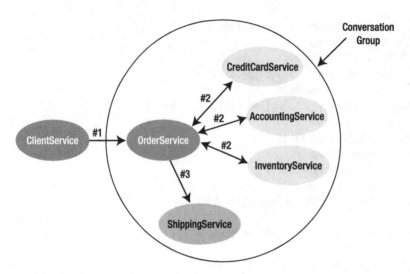

Figure 6-11. *The Service Broker services for the order-entry application*

As you can see in Figure 6-11, the ClientService starts a new conversation with OrderService. The OrderService starts three other conversations (on the same conversation group) with other services (which may be deployed to different machines) to process your order. The following three services are called concurrently:

- CreditCardService: This service creates a record of a credit card transaction showing that a credit card company, such as Visa, MasterCard, or American Express, drew money from your account.

- AccountingService: This service creates a record for the bookkeeping system, such as SAP.

- InventoryService: This service updates the available stocks for your ordered product.

When these three Service Broker services complete successfully, the OrderService starts a conversation with the ShippingService (which may be hosted by DHL or FedEx) that sends your ordered products directly to your specified delivery address. If the ShippingService returns successfully, the OrderService sends a response message back to the ClientService. The ClientService can then send an email to the customer and inform him that his order was processed successfully and will be delivered within the next few days. The exact period of time will be specified in the response message sent from the ShippingService back to the OrderService. When you implement this sample, all Service Broker services are hosted inside the same database. However, as you'll see in the next chapters, you can easily distribute these services to several individual databases to scale out this order-entry application.

The OrderService also holds some state so that the service can know when each of these three services (the CreditCardService, the AccountingService, and the InventoryService) have completed successfully. As soon as this happens, the OrderService calls the ShippingService. The OrderService stores this bit of state information in a state table. Let's start now with the Service Broker objects you need for this bigger sample. Table 6-3 shows all the message types, the contracts, the queues, and the services needed to run this sample on one dedicated database.

Table 6-3. *The Required Service Broker Objects*

Object Type	Used By	Object Name
Message type	ClientService, OrderService	OrderRequestMessage, OrderResponseMessage
Message type	OrderService, CreditCardService	CreditCardRequestMessage, CreditCardResponseMessage
Message type	OrderService, AccountingService	AccountingRequestMessage, AccountingResponseMessage
Message type	OrderService, InventoryService	InventoryRequestMessage, InventoryResponseMessage
Message type	OrderService, ShippingService	ShippingRequestMessage, ShippingResponseMessage
Contract	ClientService, OrderService	OrderContract
Contract	OrderService, CreditCardService	CreditCardContract
Contract	OrderService, AccountingService	AccountingContract
Contract	OrderService, InventoryService	InventoryContract
Contract	OrderService, ShippingService	ShippingContract
Queue	ClientService	ClientQueue
Queue	CreditCardService	CreditCardQueue
Queue	AccountingService	AccountingQueue
Queue	InventoryService	InventoryQueue
Queue	ShippingService	ShippingQueue

You can find further information about the exact definition of these objects in the T-SQL script OrderService.sql (in the folder OrderService) provided in this chapter's Source Code/Download area on the Apress website (http://www.apress.com). Before you develop the stored procedures for the service programs, Listing 6-15 shows the DDL you need to create the ApplicationState table used by the OrderService to track which service was already called successfully.

Listing 6-15. *The* ApplicationState *Table*

```
CREATE TABLE ApplicationState
(
   ConversationGroupID UNIQUEIDENTIFIER NOT NULL PRIMARY KEY,
   CreditCardStatus BIT NOT NULL,
   AccountingStatus BIT NOT NULL,
   InventoryStatus BIT NOT NULL,
   ShippingMessageSent BIT NOT NULL,
   ShippingStatus BIT NOT NULL
)
```

As you can see in Listing 6-15, each callable Service Broker service is reflected by one column of the BIT data type. Each column stores whether the service was called. Additionally, the ShippingMessageSent column stores the information that states whether the OrderService already sent the request message to the ShippingService. The sequence diagram in Figure 6-12 gives a good overview of which message types are exchanged between the individual Service Broker services involved in this sample.

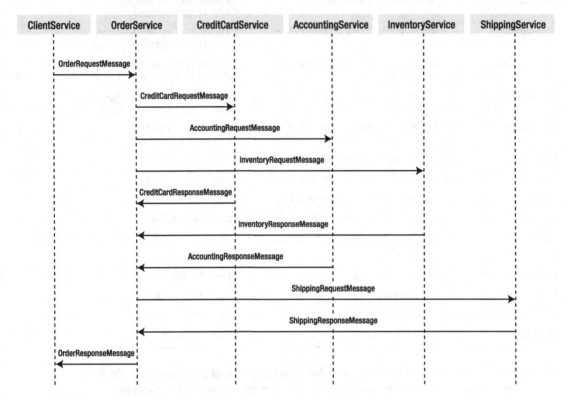

Figure 6-12. *The exchanged message types between the Service Broker services*

The OrderService

Listing 6-16 shows the code you need to write to send a message from the ClientService to the OrderService. Next, you'll look at what steps are executed while messages travel between the different services.

Listing 6-16. *Sending a New Message to the* OrderService

```
BEGIN TRANSACTION;
DECLARE @ch UNIQUEIDENTIFIER;
DECLARE @msg NVARCHAR(MAX);

BEGIN DIALOG CONVERSATION @ch
    FROM SERVICE [ClientService]
    TO SERVICE 'OrderService'
    ON CONTRACT [http://ssb.csharp.at/SSB_Book/c06/OrderContract]
    WITH ENCRYPTION = OFF;
```

```
SET @msg =
    '<OrderRequest>
        <Customer>
            <CustomerID>4242</CustomerID>
        </Customer>
        <Product>
            <ProductID>123</ProductID>
            <Quantity>5</Quantity>
            <Price>40.99</Price>
        </Product>
        <CreditCard>
            <Holder>Klaus Aschenbrenner</Holder>
            <Number>1234-1234-1234-1234</Number>
            <ValidThrough>2009-10</ValidThrough>
        </CreditCard>
        <Shipping>
            <Name>Klaus Aschenbrenner</Name>
            <Address>Wagramer Strasse 4/803</Address>
            <ZipCode>1220</ZipCode>
            <City>Vienna</City>
            <Country>Austria</Country>
        </Shipping>
    </OrderRequest>';

SEND ON CONVERSATION @ch MESSAGE TYPE
    [http://ssb.csharp.at/SSB_Book/c06/RequestMessage] (@msg);
COMMIT;
```

■**Note** Please note that this code won't work, because it's only a part of the whole solution. However, the code is useful to understand the message structure used for the request message sent to the OrderService.

As you can see in Listing 6-16, the request message sent to the OrderService contains all the information you need to process the order request submitted by a client application, such as a web application. When the sent message arrives at the OrderQueue, the internal activation mechanism of Service Broker starts the ProcessOrderRequestMessages stored procedure. This stored procedure also uses two loops to process the state information and the messages available on a given conversation group determined through a call to the GET CONVERSATION GROUP T-SQL statement. Listing 6-17 shows the relevant part of the outer loop of the ProcessOrderRequestMessages stored procedure that does the state processing for this sample.

Listing 6-17. *Outer Loop Implements the State-Processing Logic*

```
DECLARE @conversationGroup UNIQUEIDENTIFIER;
DECLARE @CreditCardStatus BIT;
DECLARE @AccountingStatus BIT;
DECLARE @InventoryStatus BIT;
DECLARE @ShippingMessageSent BIT;
DECLARE @ShippingStatus BIT;

WHILE (1 = 1)
BEGIN
   BEGIN TRANSACTION;

   -- Retrieve the next conversation group where messages are available
   -- for processing
   WAITFOR (
      GET CONVERSATION GROUP @conversationGroup FROM [OrderQueue]
   ), TIMEOUT 1000

   IF (@@ROWCOUNT = 0)
   BEGIN
      ROLLBACK TRANSACTION
      BREAK
   END

   -- Retrieve the application state for the current conversation group
   SELECT
      @CreditCardStatus = CreditCardStatus,
      @AccountingStatus = AccountingStatus,
      @InventoryStatus = InventoryStatus,
      @ShippingMessageSent = ShippingMessageSent,
      @ShippingStatus = ShippingStatus
   FROM ApplicationState
   WHERE ConversationGroupID = @conversationGroup;

   IF (@@ROWCOUNT = 0)
   BEGIN
      -- There is currently no application state available, so we insert the
      -- initial application state into the state table
      SET @CreditCardStatus = 0;
      SET @AccountingStatus = 0;
      SET @InventoryStatus = 0;
      SET @ShippingMessageSent = 0;
      SET @ShippingStatus = 0;
   END
```

```
-- Insert the new state record
INSERT INTO ApplicationState (ConversationGroupID, CreditCardStatus,
    AccountingStatus, InventoryStatus, ShippingMessageSent, ShippingStatus)
VALUES

(
    @conversationGroup,
    @CreditCardStatus,
    @AccountingStatus,
    @InventoryStatus,
    @ShippingMessageSent,
    @ShippingStatus
)
END

-- Here comes the message processing logic
-- ...

-- Update the application state
UPDATE ApplicationState SET
    CreditCardStatus = @CreditCardStatus,
    AccountingStatus = @AccountingStatus,
    InventoryStatus = @InventoryStatus,
    ShippingMessageSent = @ShippingMessageSent,
    ShippingStatus = @ShippingStatus
WHERE ConversationGroupID = @conversationGroup;

COMMIT TRANSACTION;
```

Let's have a more detailed look at the interesting parts of the ProcessOrderRequestMessages stored procedure. In the first step, you retrieve the stored state information from the ApplicationState table:

```
-- Retrieve the application state for the current conversation group
SELECT
    @CreditCardStatus = CreditCardStatus,
    @AccountingStatus = AccountingStatus,
    @InventoryStatus = InventoryStatus,
    @ShippingMessageSent = ShippingMessageSent,
    @ShippingStatus = ShippingStatus
FROM ApplicationState
WHERE ConversationGroupID = @conversationGroup;
```

If no state information is available (this is true for the first execution), the state variables will be initialized to their initial state:

```
IF (@@ROWCOUNT = 0)
BEGIN
    -- There is currently no application state available, so we insert the
    -- initial application state into the state table
    SET @CreditCardStatus = 0;
    SET @AccountingStatus = 0;
    SET @InventoryStatus = 0;
    SET @ShippingMessageSent = 0;
    SET @ShippingStatus = 0;
END
```

If no state information is available, the stored procedure will insert the new state information into the ApplicationState table:

```
-- Insert the new state record
INSERT INTO ApplicationState (ConversationGroupID, CreditCardStatus,
    AccountingStatus, InventoryStatus, ShippingMessageSent, ShippingStatus)
VALUES
(
    @conversationGroup,
    @CreditCardStatus,
    @AccountingStatus,
    @InventoryStatus,
    @ShippingMessageSent,
    @ShippingStatus
)
```

Now that you've retrieved the application state, let's take a look at the message-processing logic for the OrderQueue inside the ProcessOrderRequestMessages stored procedure. The first message type that the stored procedure must handle is [http://ssb.cshsarp.at/SSB_Book/c06/OrderRequestMessage]. This message type is sent from the ClientService to the OrderService when a new order is gathered through a client application. When this message type is received, the stored procedure must perform the following two actions:

- Retrieve the necessary information from the sent XML message.

- Begin a new conversation with the CreditCardService, AccountingService, and InventoryService on the same conversation group. These three services are all called concurrently.

Let's have a look at Listing 6-18, which shows how you implement the message-processing logic inside the ProcessOrderRequestMessages stored procedure.

Listing 6-18. *Inner Loop Handles the* OrderRequestMessage *Message Type*

```
IF (@messageTypeName = 'http://ssb.csharp.at/SSB_Book/c06/OrderRequestMessage')
BEGIN
  -- Variables for the conversation handles and the messages to be sent
  DECLARE @chCreditCardService UNIQUEIDENTIFIER;
  DECLARE @chAccountingService UNIQUEDIENTIFIER;
  DECLARE @chInventoryService UNIQUEIDENTIFIER;
  DECLARE @msgCreditCardService NVARCHAR(MAX);
  DECLARE @msgAccountingService NVARCHAR(MAX);
  DECLARE @msgInventoryService NVARCHAR(MAX);

  -- Variables needed to store the information extracted
  -- from the OrderRequestMessage
  DECLARE @creditCardHolder NVARCHAR(256);
  DECLARE @creditCardNumber NVARCHAR(256);
  DECLARE @validThrough NVARCHAR(10);
  DECLARE @quantity INT;
  DECLARE @price DECIMAL(18, 2);
  DECLARE @amount DECIMAL(18, 2);
  DECLARE @customerID NVARCHAR(256);
  DECLARE @productID INT;


  -- Extract the necessary information from the OrderRequestMessage
  SET @creditCardHolder =
    @messagebody.value('/OrderRequest[1]/CreditCard[1]/Holder[1]',
    'NVARCHAR(256)');
  SET @creditCardNumber =
    @messagebody.value('/OrderRequest[1]/CreditCard[1]/Number[]1]',
    'NVARCHAR(256)');
  SET @validThrough =
    @messagebody.value('/OrderRequest[1]/CreditCard[1]/ValidThrough[1]',
    'NVARCHAR(256)');
  SET @quantity =
    @messagebody.value('/OrderRequest[1]/Product[1]/Quantity[1]', 'INT');
  SET @price =
    @messagebody.value('/OrderRequest[1]/Product[1]/Price[1]', 'DECIMAL(18, 2)');
  SET @amount = @quantity * @price;
  SET @customerID =
    @messagebody.value('/OrderRequest[1]/Customer[1]/CustomerID[1]',
    'NVARCHAR(256)');
  SET @productID =
    @messagebody.value('/OrderRequest[1]/Product[1]/ProductID[1]', 'INT');
```

```
-- Begin a new conversation with the CreditCardService on the same
-- conversation group
BEGIN DIALOG CONVERSATION @chCreditCardService
   FROM SERVICE [OrderService]
   TO SERVICE 'CreditCardService'
   ON CONTRACT [http://ssb.csharp.at/SSB_Book/c06/CreditCardContract]
   WITH RELATED_CONVERSATION = @ch, ENCRYPTION = OFF;

-- Send a CreditCardRequestMessage to the CreditCardService
SET @msgCreditCardService =
   '<CreditCardRequest>
      <Holder>' + @creditCardHolder + '</Holder>
      <Number>' + @creditCardNumber + '</Number>
      <ValidThrough>' + @validThrough + '</ValidThrough>
      <Amount>' + CAST(@amount AS NVARCHAR(10)) + '</Amount>
   </CreditCardRequest>';

SEND ON CONVERSATION @chCreditCardService
   MESSAGE TYPE [http://ssb.csharp.at/SSB_Book/c06/CreditCardRequestMessage)
   (@msgCreditCardService);

-- Begin a new conversation with the AccountingService on the same
-- conversation group
BEGIN DIALOG CONVERSATION @chAccountingService
   FROM SERVICE [OrderService]
   TO SERVICE 'AccountingService'
   ON CONTRACT [http://ssb.csharp.at/SSB_Book/c06/AccountingContract]
   WITH RELATED_CONVERSATION = @ch, ENCRYPTION = OFF;


-- Send a message to the AccountingService
SET @msgAccountingService =
   '<AccountingRequest>
      <CustomerID>' + @customerID + '</CustomerID>
      <Amount>' + CAST(@amount AS NVARCHAR(10)) + '</Amount>
   <AccountingRequest>';

SEND ON CONVERSATION @chAccountingService
   MESSAGE TYPE [http://ssb.csharp.at/SSB_Book/c06/AccountingRequestMessage)
   (@msgAccountingService);

-- Begin a new conversation with the InventoryService on the same
-- conversation group
BEGIN DIALOG CONVERSATION @chInventoryService
   FROM SERVICE [OrderService]
   TO SERVICE 'InventoryService'
   ON CONTRACT [http://ssb.csharp.at/SSB_Book/c06/InventoryContract]
   WITH RELATED_CONVERSATION = @ch, ENCRYPTION = OFF;
```

```
-- Send a message to the InventoryService
SET @msgInventoryService =
    '<InventoryRequest>
        <ProductID> + CAST(@productID AS NVARCHAR(10)) + '</ProductID>
        <Quantity' + CAST(@quantity AS NVARCHAR(10)) + '</Quantity>
    </InventoryRequest>';

SEND ON CONVERSATION @chInventoryService
    MESSAGE TYPE [http://ssb.csharp.at/SSB_Book/c06/InventoryRequestMessage)
    (@msgInventoryService);
END
```

Let's have a more detailed look at the different parts of the message-processing logic for the OrderRequestMessage message type. In the first step, you declare some variables to store the conversation handles for the new started conversations and the messages that are sent over the new conversations:

```
-- Variables needed to store the information extracted
-- from the OrderRequestMessage
DECLARE @creditCardHolder NVARCHAR(256);
DECLARE @creditCardNumber NVARCHAR(256);
DECLARE @validThrough NVARCHAR(10);
DECLARE @quantity INT;
DECLARE @price DECIMAL(18, 2);
DECLARE @amount DECIMAL(18, 2);
DECLARE @customerID NVARCHAR(256);
DECLARE @productID INT;
```

XML DATA TYPE METHODS

The XML data type—first introduced with SQL Server 2005—offers several methods you can use to query and update the stored XML data directly inside the database. These methods are query(), value(), exist(), nodes(), and modify(). With the query() method, you can directly execute an XPath or XQuery statement that returns an XML fragment back to you.

When you want to get a scalar value out of the XML data, you can use the value() method on the XML data type. If you want to check if a specified node is available in the XML, you can use the exist() method. Finally, you can use the nodes() method to shred XML into multiple rows to propagate parts of the XML data into rowsets.

In the second step, you extract all required information from the received OrderRequestMessage. I use the value() XML data type method here to simplify this task to its minimum. This XML data type method returns the extracted value from the XML document as a scalar SQL Server data type, such as NVARCHAR, DECIMAL, or INT, as used in this example:

```
-- Extract the necessary information from the OrderRequestMessage
SET @creditCardHolder =
    @messagebody.value('/OrderRequest[1]/CreditCard[1]/Holder[1]',
    'NVARCHAR(256)');
SET @creditCardNumber =
    @messagebody.value('/OrderRequest[1]/CreditCard[1]/Number[]1]',
    'NVARCHAR(256)');
SET @validThrough =
    @messagebody.value('/OrderRequest[1]/CreditCard[1]/ValidThrough[1]',
    'NVARCHAR(256)');
SET @quantity =
    @messagebody.value('/OrderRequest[1]/Product[1]/Quantity[1]', 'INT');
SET @price =
    @messagebody.value('/OrderRequest[1]/Product[1]/Price[1]', 'DECIMAL(18, 2)');
SET @amount = @quantity * @price;
SET @customerID =
    @messagebody.value('/OrderRequest[1]/Customer[1]/CustomerID[1]',
    'NVARCHAR(256)');
SET @productID =
    @messagebody.value('/OrderRequest[1]/Product[1]/ProductID[1]', 'INT');
```

In the next step, you start three new conversations: one with the CreditCardService, one with the AccountingService, and one with the InventoryService. The associated conversation handles are stored in the variables declared in the first step. In the final step, you compose for each service the required request message (each message contains some information that was extracted from the OrderRequestMessage). The new message is sent over the opened conversation to the other Service Broker service that processes the message and sends a response message back to the OrderService:

```
-- Begin a new conversation with the CreditCardService on the same
-- conversation group
BEGIN DIALOG CONVERSATION @chCreditCardService
    FROM SERVICE [OrderService]
    TO SERVICE 'CreditCardService'
    ON CONTRACT [http://ssb.csharp.at/SSB_Book/c06/CreditCardContract]
    WITH RELATED_CONVERSATION = @ch, ENCRYPTION = OFF;


-- Send a CreditCardRequestMessage to the CreditCardService
SET @msgCreditCardService =
    '<CreditCardRequest>
        <Holder>' + @creditCardHolder + '</Holder>
        <Number>' + @creditCardNumber + '</Number>
        <ValidThrough>' + @validThrough + '</ValidThrough>
        <Amount>' + CAST(@amount AS NVARCHAR(10)) + '</Amount>
    </CreditCardRequest>';
```

```
SEND ON CONVERSATION @chCreditCardService
  MESSAGE TYPE [http://ssb.csharp.at/SSB_Book/c06/CreditCardRequestMessage)
  (@msgCreditCardService);

-- Begin a new conversation with the AccountingService on the same
-- conversation group
BEGIN DIALOG CONVERSATION @chAccountingService
  FROM SERVICE [OrderService]
  TO SERVICE 'AccountingService'
  ON CONTRACT [http://ssb.csharp.at/SSB_Book/c06/AccountingContract]
  WITH RELATED_CONVERSATION = @ch, ENCRYPTION = OFF;

-- Send a message to the AccountingService
SET @msgAccountingService =
  '<AccountingRequest>
    <CustomerID>' + @customerID + '</CustomerID>
    <Amount>' + CAST(@amount AS NVARCHAR(10)) + '</Amount>
  <AccountingRequest>';

SEND ON CONVERSATION @chAccountingService
  MESSAGE TYPE [http://ssb.csharp.at/SSB_Book/c06/AccountingRequestMessage)
  (@msgAccountingService);

-- Begin a new conversation with the InventoryService on the same
-- conversation group
BEGIN DIALOG CONVERSATION @chInventoryService
  FROM SERVICE [OrderService]
  TO SERVICE 'InventoryService'
  ON CONTRACT [http://ssb.csharp.at/SSB_Book/c06/InventoryContract]
  WITH RELATED_CONVERSATION = @ch, ENCRYPTION = OFF;

-- Send a message to the InventoryService
SET @msgInventoryService =
  '<InventoryRequest>
    <ProductID> + CAST(@productID AS NVARCHAR(10)) + '</ProductID>
    <Quantity' + CAST(@quantity AS NVARCHAR(10)) + '</Quantity>
  </InventoryRequest>';

SEND ON CONVERSATION @chInventoryService
  MESSAGE TYPE [http://ssb.csharp.at/SSB_Book/c06/InventoryRequestMessage)
  (@msgInventoryService);
```

After executing the message-processing logic, you write the modified state information back to the ApplicationState table with the UPDATE T-SQL statement:

```
-- Update the application state
UPDATE ApplicationState SET
    CreditCardStatus = @CreditCardStatus,
    AccountingStatus = @AccountingStatus,
    InventoryStatus = @InventoryStatus,
    ShippingMessageSent = @ShippingMessageSent,
    ShippingStatus = @ShippingStatus
WHERE ConversationGroupID = @conversationGroup;
```

Finally, you configure the ProcessOrderRequestMessages stored procedure for internal activation on the OrderQueue:

```
ALTER QUEUE OrderQueue
WITH ACTIVATION
(
    STATUS = ON,
    PROCEDURE_NAME = ProcessOrderRequestMessages,
    MAX_QUEUE_READERS = 1,
    EXECUTE AS SELF
)
GO
```

The OrderService retrieves OrderRequestMessages, processes them, and starts new conversations automatically. Now let's take a detailed look at how the credit card, accounting, and inventory services are implemented.

The CreditCardService

When CreditCardService starts a new conversation, the stored procedure receives messages and stores the messages in the CreditCardQueue on the target side. Listing 6-19 shows an example message.

Listing 6-19. *The* CreditCardRequestMessage *Message*

```
<CreditCardRequest>
    <Holder>Klaus Aschenbrenner</Holder>
    <Number>1234-1234-1234-1234</Number>
    <ValidThrough>2009-10</ValidThrough>
    <Amount>456.76</Amount>
</CreditCardRequest>
```

With this information, the CreditCardService can easily create a payment record that a credit card company can process. The generated payment record from this request message is finally stored in the CreditCardTransactions table. Listing 6-20 shows the definition of this table.

Listing 6-20. *The* CreditCardTransactions *Table*

```
CREATE TABLE CreditCardTransactions
(
    CreditCardTransactionID UNIQUEIDENTIFIER NOT NULL PRIMARY KEY,
    CreditCardHolder NVARCHAR(256) NOT NULL,
    CreditCardNumber NVARCHAR(50) NOT NULL,
    ValidThrough NVARCHAR(10) NOT NULL,
    Amount DECIMAL(18, 2) NOT NULL
)
```

Again, you use the XML data type methods to extract information from the XML message (as shown in Listing 6-19) and insert it into the CreditCardTransactions table. This task is done inside the ProcessCreditCardRequestMessages service program that processes received messages from CreditCardQueue. Listing 6-21 shows the implementation of this service program.

Listing 6-21. *Processing Messages from the* CreditCardQueue

```
CREATE PROCEDURE ProcessCreditCardRequestMessages
AS
    DECLARE @ch UNIQUEIDENTIFIER;
    DECLARE @messagetypename NVARCHAR(256);
    DECLARE @messagebody XML;
    DECLARE @responsemessage XML;

    WHILE (1=1)
    BEGIN
        BEGIN TRANSACTION

        WAITFOR (
            RECEIVE TOP(1)
                @ch = conversation_handle,
                @messagetypename = message_type_name,
                @messagebody = CAST(message_body AS XML)
            FROM CreditCardQueue
        ), TIMEOUT 1000

        IF (@@ROWCOUNT = 0)
        BEGIN
            ROLLBACK TRANSACTION
            BREAK
        END
```

```
IF (@messagetypename =
   'http://ssb.csharp.at/SSB_Book/c06/CreditCardRequestMessage')
BEGIN
   -- Create a new credit card transaction record
   INSERT INTO CreditCardTransactions (CreditCardTransactionID,
      CreditCardHolder, CreditCardNumber, ValidThrough, Amount)
   VALUES

   (
      NEWID(),
      @messagebody.value('/CreditCardRequest[1]/Holder[1]', 'NVARCHAR(256)'),
      @messagebody.value('/CreditCardRequest[1]/Number[1]', 'NVARCHAR(50)'),
      @messagebody.value('/CreditCardRequest[1]/ValidThrough[1]',
         'NVARCHAR(10)'),
      @messagebody.value('/CreditCardRequest[1]/Amount[1]', 'DECIMAL(18, 2)')
   )

   -- Create the response message for the OrderService
   SET @responsemessage = '<CreditCardResponse>1</CreditCardResponse>';

   -- Send the response message back to the OrderService
   SEND ON CONVERSATION @ch MESSAGE TYPE
      [http://ssb.csharp.at/SSB_Book/c06/CreditCardResponseMessage]
      (@responsemessage);

   -- End the conversation on the target's side
   END CONVERSATION @ch;
END

IF (@messagetypename =
   'http://schemas.microsoft.com/SQL/ServiceBroker/EndDialog')
BEGIN
   -- End the conversation
   END CONVERSATION @ch;
END

COMMIT TRANSACTION
END
GO
```

As you can see in Listing 6-21, this stored procedure handles the CreditCardRequestMessage and the EndDialog message sent by another Service Broker service. When the stored procedure receives a CreditCardRequestMessage, the required information is extracted from the XML message and a new record is created inside the CreditCardTransactions table that holds the values from the processed XML message:

```
-- Create a new credit card transaction record
INSERT INTO CreditCardTransactions (CreditCardTransactionID,
   CreditCardHolder, CreditCardNumber, ValidThrough, Amount)
VALUES
(
   NEWID(),
   @messagebody.value('/CreditCardRequest[1]/Holder[1]', 'NVARCHAR(256)'),
   @messagebody.value('/CreditCardRequest[1]/Number[1]', 'NVARCHAR(50)'),
   @messagebody.value('/CreditCardRequest[1]/ValidThrough[1]',
   'NVARCHAR(10)'),
   @messagebody.value('/CreditCardRequest[1]/Amount[1]', 'DECIMAL(18, 2)')
)
```

Here it depends on your business requirements how you implement the credit card payment of your customer. When everything goes fine, a response message is created that is finally sent through the SEND ON CONVERSATION T-SQL statement back to the initiator of the conversation—the OrderService:

```
-- Create the response message for the OrderService
SET @responsemessage = '<CreditCardResponse>1</CreditCardResponse>';

-- Send the response message back to the OrderService
SEND ON CONVERSATION @ch MESSAGE TYPE
   [http://ssb.csharp.at/SSB_Book/c06/CreditCardResponseMessage]
   (@responsemessage);

-- End the conversation on the target's side
END CONVERSATION @ch;
```

The AccountingService

The OrderService sends in parallel a message to the AccountingService that creates a booking record that a booking system such as SAP can use. Messages for the AccountingServices are described through the AccountingRequestMessage message type and are received on the target side on the AccountingQueue. Listing 6-22 shows the request message sent by the OrderService.

Listing 6-22. *The* AccountingRequestMessage *Message*

```
<AccountingRequest>
   <CustomerID>1223</CustomerID>
   <Amount>456.76</Amount>
</AccountingRequest>
```

The stored procedure can then transfer the extracted information from this message to a booking system. To simplify this sample, I stored the required information in a table stored in the same database as the AccountingService. Listing 6-23 shows the definition of the AccountingRecordings table that is used for this purpose.

Listing 6-23. *The* AccountingRecordings *Table*

```
CREATE TABLE AccountingRecordings
(
    AccountingRecordingsID UNIQUEIDENTIFIER NOT NULL PRIMARY KEY,
    CustomerID NVARCHAR(10) NOT NULL,
    Amount DECIMAL(18, 2) NOT NULL
)
```

As with the CreditCardService, the required information is extracted from the XML message and stored in this table. This task is handled by the ProcessAccountingRequestMessages stored procedure, which processes messages from the AccountingQueue. Listing 6-24 shows this stored procedure.

Listing 6-24. *The* ProcessAccountingRequestMessages *Stored Procedure*

```
CREATE PROCEDURE ProcessAccountingRequestMessages
AS
    DECLARE @ch UNIQUEIDENTIFIER;
    DECLARE @messagetypename NVARCHAR(256);
    DECLARE @messagebody XML;
    DECLARE @responsemessage XML;

    WHILE (1=1)
    BEGIN
        BEGIN TRANSACTION

        WAITFOR (
            RECEIVE TOP(1)
                @ch = conversation_handle,
                @messagetypename = message_type_name,
                @messagebody = CAST(message_body AS XML)
            FROM AccountingQueue
        ), TIMEOUT 1000

        IF (@@ROWCOUNT = 0)
        BEGIN
            ROLLBACK TRANSACTION
            BREAK
        END
```

```
    IF (@messagetypename =
        'http://ssb.csharp.at/SSB_Book/c06/AccountingRequestMessage')
    BEGIN
        -- Create a new booking record
        INSERT INTO AccountingRecordings
            (AccountingRecordingsID, CustomerID, Amount)
        VALUES
        (
            NEWID(),
            @messagebody.value('/AccountingRequest[1]/CustomerID[1]',
                'NVARCHAR(10)'),
            @messagebody.value('/AccountingRequest[1]/Amount[1]', 'DECIMAL(18, 2)')
        )

        -- Construct the response message
        SET @responsemessage = '<AccountingResponse>1</AccountingResponse>';

        -- Send the response message back to the OrderService
        SEND ON CONVERSATION @ch MESSAGE TYPE
            [http://ssb.csharp.at/SSB_Book/c06/AccountingResponseMessage]
            (@responsemessage);


        -- End the conversation on the target's side
        END CONVERSATION @ch;
    END

    IF (@messagetypename =
        'http://schemas.microsoft.com/SQL/ServiceBroker/EndDialog')
    BEGIN
        -- End the conversation
        END CONVERSATION @ch;
    END

    COMMIT TRANSACTION
END
GO
```

As you can see from Listing 6-24, the ProcessAccountingRequestMessages stored procedure handles the AccountingRequestMessage and the EndDialog message sent by another Service Broker service. When the stored procedure receives an AccountingRequestMessage, the information from the XML message is extracted and a new record in the AccountingRecordings table is created with the extracted values:

```
-- Create a new booking record
INSERT INTO AccountingRecordings
    (AccountingRecordingsID, CustomerID, Amount)
VALUES
(
    NEWID(),
    @messagebody.value('/AccountingRequest[1]/CustomerID[1]',
        'NVARCHAR(10)'),
    @messagebody.value('/AccountingRequest[1]/Amount[1]', 'DECIMAL(18, 2)')
)
```

It depends on your business requirements how you process an accounting message from your customer. Sometimes you must work with another back-end system, such as SAP, where you create a new booking record for the customer. When everything goes fine, a response message is created that is finally sent through the SEND ON CONVERSATION T-SQL statement back to the initiator of the conversation:

```
-- Construct the response message
SET @responsemessage = '<AccountingResponse>1</AccountingResponse>';

-- Send the response message back to the OrderService
SEND ON CONVERSATION @ch MESSAGE TYPE
    [http://ssb.csharp.at/SSB_Book/c06/AccountingResponseMessage]
    (@responsemessage);

-- End the conversation on the target's side
END CONVERSATION @ch;
```

The InventoryService

The third service that gets a request message when the OrderService processes an OrderRequestMessage from a client application is the InventoryService. Messages for the InventoryService are described through the InventoryRequestMessage message type and are received for processing on the InventoryQueue. The purpose of this service is for your inventory to get updated as soon as a customer orders a product through a client application, such as your company's website. Listing 6-25 shows the XML message that the InventoryService receives.

Listing 6-25. *The* InventoryRequestMessage *Message*

```
<InventoryRequest>
    <ProductID>123</ProductID>
    <Quantity>5</Quantity>
</InventoryRequest>
```

With this information, you can easily update the inventory so that it reflects the current available products in stock. To simplify this sample, I stored the whole inventory data in the Inventory table with some sample records (see Listing 6-26).

Listing 6-26. *The* Inventory *Table*

```
CREATE TABLE Inventory
(
   ProductID NVARCHAR(10) NOT NULL PRIMARY KEY,
   Quantity INT NOT NULL
)
GO

INSERT INTO Inventory (ProductID, Quantity) VALUES ('123', 50)
INSERT INTO Inventory (ProductID, Quantity) VALUES ('456', 80)
INSERT INTO Inventory (ProductID, Quantity) VALUES ('789', 563)
GO
```

The difference between the InventoryService and the OrderService is that the InventoryService checks in the first step to see if the quantity of the ordered product is available in the inventory. If it is, the ordered quantity is subtracted from the quantity available in the inventory. If the ordered quantity isn't available in the stock, a different response message is sent back to the OrderService. In this case, the OrderService must unroll all previous work done on this order request. This could involve the work done by the CreditCardService and AccountingService.

This concept is referred to as *compensation transactions*. In the "Compensation Logic with Service Broker" section later in this chapter, I'll show you how you can implement compensating transactions for this sample with the functionality provided by Service Broker. The update process of the inventory is handled by the ProcessInventoryRequestMessages stored procedure, which processes messages from the InventoryQueue. Listing 6-27 shows this stored procedure.

Listing 6-27. *The* ProcessInventoryRequestMessages *Stored Procedure*

```
CREATE PROCEDURE ProcessInventoryRequestMessages
AS
   DECLARE @ch UNIQUEIDENTIFIER;
   DECLARE @messagetypename NVARCHAR(256);
   DECLARE @messagebody XML;
   DECLARE @responsemessage XML;

   WHILE (1=1)
   BEGIN
      BEGIN TRANSACTION

      WAITFOR (
         RECEIVE TOP(1)
            @ch = conversation_handle,
            @messagetypename = message_type_name,
            @messagebody = CAST(message_body AS XML)
         FROM InventoryQueue
      ), TIMEOUT 1000
```

```sql
IF (@@ROWCOUNT = 0)
BEGIN
  ROLLBACK TRANSACTION
  BREAK
END

IF (@messagetypename =
    'http://ssb.csharp.at/SSB_Book/c06/InventoryRequestMessage')
BEGIN
  DECLARE @productID NVARCHAR(10);
  DECLARE @oldQuantity INT;
  DECLARE @newQuantity INT;
  DECLARE @quantity INT;

  -- Check if there is enough quantity of the specified product in stock
  SET @productID = @messagebody.value('/InventoryRequest[1]/ProductID[1]',
    'NVARCHAR(10)');
  SET @quantity = @messagebody.value('/InventoryRequest[1]/Quantity[1]',
    'INT');
  SELECT @oldQuantity = Quantity FROM Inventory
    WHERE ProductID = @productID;

  SET @newQuantity = @oldQuantity - @quantity;

  IF (@newQuantity <= 0)
  BEGIN
    -- There is not enough quantity of the specified product in stock
    SET @responsemessage = '<InventoryResponse>0</InventoryResponse>';

    -- Send the response message back to the OrderService
    SEND ON CONVERSATION @ch MESSAGE TYPE
      [http://ssb.csharp.at/SSB_Book/c06/InventoryResponseMessage]
      (@responsemessage);

    -- End the conversation on the target's side
    END CONVERSATION @ch;
  END
ELSE
BEGIN
  -- Update the inventory with the new quantity of the specified product
  UPDATE Inventory SET Quantity = @newQuantity WHERE ProductID = @productID;


  -- There is enough quantity of the specified product in stock
  SET @responsemessage = '<InventoryResponse>1</InventoryResponse>';
```

```
        -- Send the response message back to the OrderService
        SEND ON CONVERSATION @ch MESSAGE TYPE
            [http://ssb.csharp.at/SSB_Book/c06/InventoryResponseMessage]
            (@responsemessage);

        -- End the conversation on the target's side
        END CONVERSATION @ch;
    END
END

IF (@messagetypename =
    'http://schemas.microsoft.com/SQL/ServiceBroker/EndDialog')
    BEGIN
        -- End the conversation
        END CONVERSATION @ch;
    END

    COMMIT TRANSACTION
END
GO
```

Let's have a more detailed look at the tasks that this stored procedure executes. In the first step, you extract the ProductID and the Quantity from the received message:

```
-- Check if there is enough quantity of the specified product in stock
SET @productID = @messagebody.value('/InventoryRequest[1]/ProductID[1]',
    'NVARCHAR(10)');
SET @quantity = @messagebody.value('/InventoryRequest[1]/Quantity[1]', 'INT');
```

With the ProductID, you get the current available quantity of the product from the Inventory table. In the second step, you calculate the new quantity of the inventory and check if the quantity has fallen behind the available stock items:

```
SELECT @oldQuantity = Quantity FROM Inventory WHERE ProductID = @productID;
SET @newQuantity = @oldQuantity - @quantity;

IF (@newQuantity <= 0)
```

If it has, you send a response message with the value 0 back to the OrderService, which indicates that the order request can't be processed:

```
-- There is not enough quantity of the specified product in stock
SET @responsemessage = '<InventoryResponse>0</InventoryResponse>';

-- Send the response message back to the OrderService
SEND ON CONVERSATION @ch MESSAGE TYPE
    [http://ssb.csharp.at/SSB_Book/c06/InventoryResponseMessage]
    (@responsemessage);
```

```
-- End the conversation on the target's side
END CONVERSATION @ch;
```

If the ordered quantity is fine, the response message contains the value 1, indicating that everything is fine and that the order can be fulfilled:

```
-- Update the inventory with the new quantity of the specified product
UPDATE Inventory SET Quantity = @newQuantity WHERE ProductID = @productID;

-- There is enough quantity of the specified product in stock
SET @responsemessage = '<InventoryResponse>1</InventoryResponse>';

-- Send the response message back to the OrderService
SEND ON CONVERSATION @ch MESSAGE TYPE
    [http://ssb.csharp.at/SSB_Book/c06/InventoryResponseMessage]
    (@responsemessage);

-- End the conversation on the target's side
END CONVERSATION @ch;
```

With this return value, the OrderService must then decide if some compensation transaction must be executed on the services that already processed the order request. You'll find more about this in the "Compensation Logic with Service Broker" section.

Processing Response Messages

Now the OrderService must process and evaluate the response message that it gets back from the three called services. As soon as the response messages are processed, OrderService must also update the state information from the current conversation to indicate which conversation with the three services was already processed. Listing 6-28 shows how the response messages from these three services are processed inside the ProcessOrderRequestMessages stored procedure, which represents the service program for the OrderService.

Listing 6-28. *Processing the Response Messages*

```
IF (@messagetypename =
    'http://ssb.csharp.at/SSB_Book/c06/CreditCardResponseMessage')
BEGIN
    DECLARE @creditCardResult BIT;

    SET @creditCardResult = @messagebody.value('/CreditCardResponse[1]', 'BIT');

    -- Updating the state information, indicating that the CreditCardService
    -- was called
    SET @CreditCardStatus = 1;
END
```

```
IF (
  @messagetypename = 'http://ssb.csharp.at/SSB_Book/c06/AccountingResponseMessage'
BEGIN
  DECLARE @accountingResult BIT;

  SET @accountingResult = @messagebody.value('/AccountingResponse[1]', 'BIT');


  -- Updating the state information, indicating that the AccountingService
  -- was called
  SET @AccountingStatus = 1;
END

IF (
  @messagetypename = 'http://ssb.csharp.at/SSB_Book/c06/InventoryResponseMessage')
BEGIN
  DECLARE @inventoryResult BIT;

  SET @inventoryResult = @messagebody.value('/InventoryResponse[1]', 'BIT');

  -- Updating the state information, indicating that the InventoryService
  -- was called
  SET @InventoryStatus = 1;
END
```

As you can see in Listing 6-28, you can easily process the response messages from all three called services. Through the outer loop of this stored procedure, the changed state gets updated automatically, and the ApplicationState table reflects the changed state information. Finally, you need to implement a call to the ShippingService to ship the ordered products to the customer. You can implement this call only when you get a response from all three previously called services. You can do this check easily with the @CreditCardStatus, @AccountingStatus, and @InventoryStatus state variables.

The information for the request message sent to ShippingService must be extracted from the OrderRequestMessage sent by a client application. Listing 6-29 shows the content of this request message.

Listing 6-29. *The Request Message Sent by the Client Application*

```
<OrderRequest>
  <Customer>
    <CustomerID>4242</CustomerID>
  </Customer>
  <Product>
    <ProductID>123</ProductID>
    <Quantity>5</Quantity>
    <Price>40.99</Price>
  </Product>
```

```
<CreditCard>
    <Holder>Klaus Aschenbrenner</Holder>
    <Number>1234-1234-1234-1234</Number>
    <ValidThrough>2009-10</ValidThrough>
</CreditCard>
<Shipping>
    <Name>Klaus Aschenbrenner</Name>
    <Address>Wagramer Strasse 4/803</Address>
    <ZipCode>1220</ZipCode>
    <City>Vienna</City>
    <Country>Austria</Country>
</Shipping>
</OrderRequest>
```

MESSAGE RETENTION FOR COMPLEX MESSAGE PROCESSING

You can also use RETENTION as a staging area for complex message processing. Let's say that a service has to receive messages 1, 2, and 3, but it can only start processing when message 3 has arrived. One approach would be to have the sender send all the information from messages 1, 2, and 3 in one single complex message. However, often all three messages are simply not available at the same time.

Another approach would be to receive the messages and store them in a state table. When message 3 arrives, the service can select messages 1 and 2 from the state table. However, the simplest approach is to have RETENTION enabled. The target simply ignores messages 1 and 2, and when message 3 arrives, it looks up messages 1 and 2 in the queue, since they were retained.

You run into a big problem here, because the request message was processed and removed from OrderQueue when you sent out information to CreditCardService, AccountingService, and InventoryService. How can you access the shipping information stored in the <Shipping> node? There are two solutions. The first option is to store the request message in the state table when you receive it from the queue. However, this introduces some overhead in the message-processing logic and can degrade the performance of your messaging application.

The second option is to use the Service Broker RETENTION feature on OrderQueue. When a queue specifies message retention, Service Broker doesn't delete messages from the queue until the conversation ends. Furthermore, Service Broker also copies outgoing messages to the queue. This allows the service to maintain a precise record of the incoming and outgoing messages. Message retention allows you to maintain an exact record of a conversation for a queue while the conversation is active. For applications that require detailed auditing or that must perform compensating transactions when the conversation fails, it can be more efficient than copying each message to a state table while the conversation is in process.

Message retention increases the number of messages in the queue for active conversations and increases the amount of work that SQL Server performs when sending a message. Therefore, message retention reduces the performance. The exact performance impact depends on the communication pattern for the services that use that queue. In general, you should use message retention any time that message retention is required for an application to operate correctly. If the application doesn't require an exact record of all sent and received messages while the conversation is active, maintaining state in a state table may improve performance. Also, remember that when the conversation ends, the retained messages are removed from the queue, so if you're using retention for auditing purposes, you must be sure to copy the messages to another table before ending the conversation. To enable RETENTION on a queue, you must specify the RETENTION clause when you create or alter a queue (see Listing 6-30).

Listing 6-30. *Enabling* RETENTION *on a Queue*

```
CREATE QUEUE OrderQueue
   WITH STATUS = ON,
   RETENTION = ON
```

Listing 6-31 shows how you can send the final request message to the ShippingService that is part of the ProcessOrderRequestMessages stored procedure. This code assumes that the RETENTION support on the OrderQueue is activated.

Listing 6-31. *Sending the Final Message*

```
-- If we received all response messages from the other services we
-- can send the final message to the ShippingService
IF (@CreditCardStatus = 1 AND @AccountingStatus = 1 AND @InventoryStatus = 1
   AND @ShippingMessageSent = 0)
BEGIN
   DECLARE @chShippingService UNIQUEIDENTIFIER;
   DECLARE @msgShippingService NVARCHAR(MAX);

   -- Begin a new conversation with the ShippingService on the same
   -- conversation group
   BEGIN DIALOG CONVERSATION @chShippingService
      FROM SERVICE [OrderService]
      TO SERVICE 'ShippingService'
      ON CONTRACT [http://ssb.csharp.at/SSB_Book/c06/ShippingContract]
      WITH RELATED CONVERSATION = @ch, ENCRYPTION = OFF;

   -- Send the request message to the ShippingService
   DECLARE @msg XML;

   -- SELECT the original order request message -
   -- RETENTION makes it possible
   SELECT @msg = CAST(message_body AS XML) FROM OrderQueue
   WHERE
      conversation_group_id = @conversationGroup AND
      message_type_name = 'http://ssb.csharp.at/SSB_Book/c06/OrderRequestMessage';

   SET @msgShippingService =
      CAST(@msg.query('/OrderRequest[1]/Shipping[1]') AS NVARCHAR(MAX));
```

```
SEND ON CONVERSATION @chShippingService MESSAGE TYPE
    [http://ssb.csharp.at/SSB_Book/c06/ShippingRequestMessage]
    (@msgShippingService);

    SET @ShippingMessageSent = 1;
END
```

The ShippingService

The last service I want to describe is the ShippingService. The responsibility of this service is to ship the order from the customer directly to his supplied postal address. DHL or FedEx could host such a service. Messages for the ShippingService are described through the ShippingRequestMessage message type and are received for processing on the ShippingQueue. Listing 6-32 shows the XML message that the ShippingService receives from the OrderService.

Listing 6-32. *The* ShippingRequestMessage *Message*

```
<Shipping>
    <Name>Klaus Aschenbrenner</Name>
    <Address>Wagramer Strasse 4/803</Address>
    <ZipCode>1220</ZipCode>
    <City>Vienna</City>
    <Country>Austria</Country>
</Shipping>
```

With this information, you can easily ship the ordered products to the specified postal address. To simplify this sample, I've stored all the shipping information in the ShippingInformation table. Listing 6-33 shows the DDL script for this table.

Listing 6-33. *The* ShippingInformation *Table*

```
CREATE TABLE ShippingInformation
(
    ShippingID UNIQUEIDENTIFIER NOT NULL PRIMARY KEY,
    [Name] NVARCHAR(256) NOT NULL,
    Address NVARCHAR(256) NOT NULL,
    ZipCode NVARCHAR(10) NOT NULL,
    City NVARCHAR(256) NOT NULL,
    Country NVARCHAR(256) NOT NULL
)
```

The ProcessShippingRequestMessages stored procedure acts as the service program for the ShippingService. This stored procedure retrieves a new message from the ShippingQueue, extracts the required information from the XML message, inserts a new record into the ShippingInformation table, and sends a response message back to the OrderService. Listing 6-34 shows the implementation of this stored procedure.

Listing 6-34. *The* ProcessShippingRequestMessages *Stored Procedure*

```
CREATE PROCEDURE ProcessShippingRequestMessages
AS
BEGIN
   DECLARE @ch UNIQUEIDENTIFIER;
   DECLARE @messagetypename NVARCHAR(256);
   DECLARE @messagebody XML;
   DECLARE @responsemessage XML;

   WHILE (1=1)
   BEGIN
      BEGIN TRANSACTION


      WAITFOR (
         RECEIVE TOP(1)
            @ch = conversation_handle,
            @messagetypename = message_type_name,
            @messagebody = CAST(message_body AS XML)
         FROM ShippingQueue
      ), TIMEOUT 1000

      IF (@@ROWCOUNT = 0)
      BEGIN
         ROLLBACK TRANSACTION
         BREAK
      END

      IF (@messagetypename =
         'http://ssb.csharp.at/SSB_Book/c06/ShippingRequestMessage')
      BEGIN
         DECLARE @name NVARCHAR(256);
         DECLARE @address NVARCHAR(256);
         DECLARE @zipCode NVARCHAR(10);
         DECLARE @city NVARCHAR(256);
         DECLARE @country NVARCHAR(256);

         -- Extract the information from the ShippingRequestMessage
         SET @name = @messagebody.value('/Shipping[1]/Name[1]', 'NVARCHAR(256)');
         SET @address = @messagebody.value('/Shipping[1]/Address[1]',
            'NVARCHAR(256)');
         SET @zipCode = @messagebody.value('/Shipping[1]/ZipCode[1]',
            'NVARCHAR(10)');
         SET @city = @messagebody.value('/Shipping[1]/City[1]', 'NVARCHAR(256)');
         SET @country = @messagebody.value('/Shipping[1]/Country[1]',
            'NVARCHAR(256)');
```

```
        -- Insert the information into the shipping table
        INSERT INTO ShippingInformation
            (ShippingID, [Name], Address, ZipCode, City, Country)
        VALUES
        (
            NEWID(),
            @name,
            @address,
            @zipCode,
            @city,
            @country
        )

        -- Send the response message back to the OrderService
        SET @responsemessage = '<ShippingResponse>1</ShippingResponse>';
        SEND ON CONVERSATION @ch MESSAGE TYPE
            [http://ssb.csharp.at/SSB_Book/c06/ShippingResponseMessage]
            (@responsemessage);


        -- End the conversation on the target's side
        END CONVERSATION @ch;
    END

    IF (@messagetypename =
        'http://schemas.microsoft.com/SQL/ServiceBroker/EndDialog')
    BEGIN
        -- End the conversation
        END CONVERSATION @ch;
    END

    COMMIT TRANSACTION
    END
END
GO
```

The only thing left in this sample application is the logic that processes the sent
ShippingResponseMessage on the OrderQueue. If this message type arrives on that queue, you
only have to send a response message back to the ClientService to inform it about the outcome of the order request. Listing 6-35 shows the necessary code fragment from the
ProcessOrderRequestMessages stored procedure.

Listing 6-35. *Processing* ShippingResponseMessages

```
IF (@messageTypeName = 'http://ssb.csharp.at/SSB_Book/c06/ShippingResponseMessage')
BEGIN
    DECLARE @shippingResult BIT;
    DECLARE @orderResponseMessage NVARCHAR(MAX);
    DECLARE @chClientService UNIQUEIDENTIFIER;

    -- Create the response message for the ClientService
    SET @shippingResult = @messagebody.value('/ShippingResponse[1]', 'BIT');
    SET @orderResponseMessage = '<OrderResponse>' +
        CAST(@shippingResult AS CHAR(1)) + '</OrderResponse>';

    -- The order was shipped
    SET @ShippingStatus = 1;

    -- Get the conversation handle that is needed to send a response message
    -- back to the ClientService
    SELECT @chClientService = conversation_handle FROM sys.conversation_endpoints
    WHERE
        conversation_group_id = @conversationGroup AND
        far_service = 'ClientService';

    -- Send the response message back to the ClientService
    SEND ON CONVERSATION @chClientService MESSAGE TYPE
        [http://ssb.csharp.at/SSB_Book/c06/OrderResponseMessage]
        (@orderResponseMessage);

    -- End the conversation with the ClientService
    END CONVERSATION @chClientService;
END
```

The only difference in this code fragment is that you haven't stored the conversation handle back to the ClientService in a local variable. Therefore, you must retrieve the correct conversation handle from the sys.conversation_endpoints catalog view so that you can send a response message back to the ClientService. In this SELECT statement, you must restrict your returned result set by the conversation_group_id and far_service columns, so that you get back the correct conversation handle. For the ClientQueue, you can write a simple service program that prints the response message from the OrderService. In a real production application, you can send an email to the customer to inform her about the outcome of her order request. Listing 6-36 shows the simple ProcessOrderResponseMessages stored procedure.

Listing 6-36. *The* ProcessOrderResponseMessages *Stored Procedure*

```
CREATE PROCEDURE ProcessOrderResponseMessages
AS
BEGIN
    DECLARE @ch UNIQUEIDENTIFIER;
    DECLARE @messagetypename NVARCHAR(256);
    DECLARE @messagebody XML;
    DECLARE @responsemessage XML;

    WHILE (1 = 1)
    BEGIN
        BEGIN TRANSACTION;

        WAITFOR (
            RECEIVE TOP (1)
                @ch = conversation_handle,
                @messagetypename = message_type_name,
                @messagebody = CAST(message_body AS XML)
            FROM ClientQueue
        ), TIMEOUT 1000

        IF (@@ROWCOUNT = 0)
        BEGIN
            ROLLBACK TRANSACTION
            BREAK
        END

        IF (@messagetypename =
            'http://ssb.csharp.at/SSB_Book/c06/OrderResponseMessage')
        BEGIN
            -- Here you can send an email to the customer that his/her order
            -- was successfully processed
            PRINT 'Your order was successfully processed...';
        END

        IF (@messagetypename =
            'http://schemas.microsoft.com/SQL/ServiceBroker/EndDialog')
        BEGIN
            END CONVERSATION @ch;
        END


        COMMIT TRANSACTION;
    END
END
```

Now when you send an OrderRequestMessage to the OrderService, all the necessary steps are executed asynchronously in the background. After getting back the final response message from the OrderService, you can make a SELECT on all the tables. You'll get a result like the one shown in Figure 6-13.

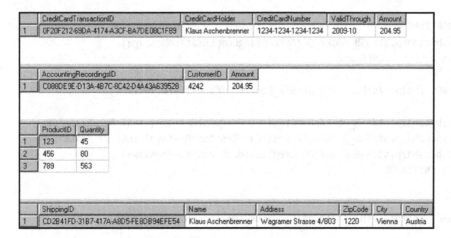

	CreditCardTransactionID	CreditCardHolder	CreditCardNumber	ValidThrough	Amount
1	0F20F212-69DA-4174-A3CF-BA7DE08C1F89	Klaus Aschenbrenner	1234-1234-1234-1234	2009-10	204.95

	AccountingRecordingsID	CustomerID	Amount
1	C088DE9E-D13A-4B7C-8C42-D4A43A639528	4242	204.95

	ProductID	Quantity
1	123	45
2	456	80
3	789	563

	ShippingID	Name	Address	ZipCode	City	Country
1	CD2B41FD-31B7-417A-A8D5-FE8DB94EFE54	Klaus Aschenbrenner	Wagramer Strasse 4/803	1220	Vienna	Austria

Figure 6-13. *The processed messages from the different Service Broker services*

Compensation Logic with Service Broker

As you've seen in the previous section, you can easily implement a Service Broker service that spans several dialogs. The conversation group concept also makes it easy to store application state between the individual dialogs that are spanned across the different Service Broker services. As you might expect, the sample application from the previous section has one drawback: what happens when the InventoryService can't process the order because too few items are in stock?

In this case, the response message contains a 0 (<InventoryResponse>0</InventoryResponse>), indicating that the request didn't process successfully. But what if the CreditCardService and the AccountingService already processed the request? In this case, your application will be in an invalid state, because the request would have been processed on some services and not on others. The solution to this problem is a concept referred to as *compensating transactions*.

With a compensation transaction, you can undo an action that already executed earlier. In this case, it means that a corresponding compensation transaction must undo the operations of the CreditCardService and the AccountingService. For this reason, you have to create two additional message types and the [http://ssb.csharp.at/SSB_Book/c06/CreditCardContract] and [http://ssb.csharp.at/SSB_Book/c06/AccountingContract] contracts. Take a look at Listing 6-37.

■**Note** Please make sure to create a new database for this sample.

Listing 6-37. *Defining the Message Types for the Compensation Transactions*

```
CREATE MESSAGE TYPE
   [http://ssb.csharp.at/SSB_Book/c06/CreditCardCompensationMessage]
   VALIDATION = WELL_FORMED_XML

CREATE MESSAGE TYPE
   [http://ssb.csharp.at/SSB_Book/c06/AccountingCompensationMessage]
   VALIDATION = WELL_FORMED_XML

CREATE CONTRACT [http://ssb.csharp.at/SSB_Book/c06/CreditCardContract]
(
   [http://ssb.csharp.at/SSB_Book/c06/CreditCardRequestMessage] SENT BY INITIATOR,
   [http://ssb.csharp.at/SSB_Book/c06/CreditCardResponseMessage] SENT BY TARGET,
   [http://ssb.csharp.at/SSB_Book/c06/CreditCardCompensationMessage]
      SENT BY INITIATOR
)

CREATE CONTRACT [http://ssb.csharp.at/SSB_Book/c06/AccountingContract]
(
   [http://ssb.csharp.at/SSB_Book/c06/AccountingRequestMessage] SENT BY INITIATOR,
   [http://ssb.csharp.at/SSB_Book/c06/AccountingResponseMessage] SENT BY TARGET,
   [http://ssb.csharp.at/SSB_Book/c06/AccountingCompensationMessage] SENT BY
      INITIATOR,
)
```

As you can see in Listing 6-37, the compensation messages are sent from the initiator of the conversation to the target—in this sample, from the OrderService to the CreditCardService and AccountingService. When the target side retrieves the compensation messages, the target service must undo the previous actions with the data contained in the compensation messages. Listing 6-38 shows both compensation messages that are sent from the OrderService to the corresponding target service.

Listing 6-38. *The Content of Both Compensation Messages*

```
<CreditCardCompensation>
    <Holder>Klaus Aschenbrenner</Holder>
    <Number>1234-1234-1234-1234</Number>
    <ValidThrough>2009-10</ValidThrough>
    <Amount>40.99</Amount>
</CreditCardCompensation>

<AccountingCompensation>
    <CustomerID>123</CustomerID>
    <Amount>40.99</Amount>
</AccountingCompensation>
```

Figure 6-14 shows a sequence diagram of the message exchange that occurs when a compensation transaction takes place.

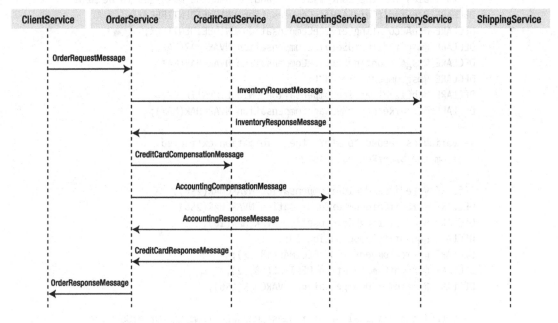

Figure 6-14. *Sequence diagram of the message exchange*

As you can see in Figure 6-14, the ShippingService isn't called when a compensation transaction takes place. This makes sense, because you don't want to ship the goods when you don't have them in stock. Now let's see how to implement the compensation logic in the ProcessOrderRequestMessage stored procedure that acts as the service program for the OrderQueue. The compensation transaction is initiated as soon as an InventoryResponseMessage is received from the InventoryService and when the response message contains a 0 in the message body. Listing 6-39 shows the T-SQL code that initiates both compensation transactions.

Listing 6-39. *Initiating the Compensation Transactions*

```
IF (@messageTypeName =
   'http://ssb.csharp.at/SSB_Book/c06/InventoryResponseMessage')
BEGIN
   DECLARE @inventoryResult BIT;
   SET @inventoryResult = @messageBody.Value('/InventoryResult[1]', 'BIT');

   -- Check if we must compensate any logic that has already taken place,
   -- because the order can not be fulfilled.
```

```sql
IF (@inventoryResult = 0)
BEGIN
    -- Variables for the conversation handles and the messages to be sent
    DECLARE @chCreditCardServiceCompensation UNIQUEIDENTIFER;
    DECLARE @chAccountingServiceCompensation UNIQUEIDENTIFER;
    DECLARE @msgCreditCardServiceCompensation NVARCHAR(MAX);
    DECLARE @msgAccountingServiceCompensation NVARCHAR(MAX);
    DECLARE @msgCompensation XML;
    DECLARE @chClientServiceCompensation UNIQUEIDENTIFIER;
    DECLARE @orderResponseMessageCompensation NVARCHAR(MAX);

    -- Variables needed to store the information extracted
    -- from the OrderRequestMessage

    DECLARE @creditCardHolderCompensation NVARCHAR(256);
    DECLARE @creditCardNumberCompensation NVARCHAR(256);
    DECLARE @validThroughCompensation NVARCHAR(10);
    DECLARE @quantityCompensation INT;
    DECLARE @priceCompensation DECIMAL(18, 2);
    DECLARE @amountCompensation DECIMAL(18, 2);
    DECLARE @customerIDCompensation NVARCHAR(256);

    -- SELECT the original order request message from the OrderQueue -
    -- RETENTION makes it possible
    SELECT @msgCompensation = CAST(message_body AS XML) FROM OrderQueue
    WHERE
        conversation_group_id = @conversationGroup AND
        message_type_name =
        'http://ssb.csharp.at/SSB_Book/c06/OrderRequestMessage'

    -- Extract the necessary information from the OrderRequestMessage
    SET @creditCardHolderCompensation =
        @msgCompensation.value('/OrderRequest[1]/CreditCard[1]/Holder[1]',
        'NVARCHAR(256)');
    SET @creditCardNumberCompensation =
        @msgCompensation.value('/OrderRequest[1]/CreditCard[1]/Number[1]',
        'NVARCHAR(256)');
    SET @validThroughCompensation =
        @msgCompensation.value('/OrderRequest[1]/CreditCard[1]/ValidThrough[1]',
        'NVARCHAR(10)');
    SET @quantityCompensation =
        @msgCompensation.value('/OrderRequest[1]/Product[1]/Quantity[1]',
        'INT');
    SET @priceCompensation =
        @msgCompensation.value('/OrderRequest[1]/Product[1]/Price[1]',
        'DECIMAL(18, 2)');
    SET @amountCompensation = @quantityCompensation * @priceCompensation;
```

```
SET @customerIDCompensation =
   @msgCompensation.value('/OrderRequest[1]/Customer[1]/CustomerID[1]',
   'NVARCHAR(256)');

-- Begin a new conversation with the CreditCardService on the same
-- conversation group to compensate the previous taken action
BEGIN DIALOG CONVERSATION @chCreditCardServiceCompensation
   FROM SERVICE [OrderService]
   TO SERVICE 'CreditCardService'
   ON CONTRACT [http://ssb.csharp.at/SSB_Book/c06/CreditCardContract]
   WITH RELATED_CONVERSATION = @ch, ENCRYPTION = OFF;

-- Send a CreditCardCompensationMessage to the CreditCardService
SET @msgCreditCardCompensation =
   '<CreditCardCompensation>
      <Holder>' + @creditCardHolderCompensation + '</Holder>
      <Number>' + @creditCardNumberCompensation + '</Number>
      <ValidThrough>' + @validThroughCompensation + '</ValidThrough>
      <Amount>' + CAST(@amountCompensation AS NVARCHAR(10)) + '</Amount>
   </CreditCardCompensation>';

SEND ON CONVERSATION @chCreditCardServiceCompensation MESSAGE TYPE
   [http://ssb.csharp.at/SSB_Book/c06/CreditCardCompensationMessage]
   (@msgCreditCardCompensation);

-- Begin a new conversation with the AccountingService on the same
-- conversation group to compensate the previous taken action
BEGIN DIALOG CONVERSATION @chAccountingServiceCompensation
   FROM SERVICE [OrderService]
   TO SERVICE 'AccountingService'
   ON CONTRACT [http://ssb.csharp.at/SSB_Book/c06/AccountingContract]
   WITH RELATED_CONVERSATION @ch, ENCRYPTION = OFF;

-- Send a AccountingCompensationMessage to the AccountingService
SET @msgAccountingMessage =
   '<AccountingCompensation
      <CustomerID>' + @customerIDCompensation + '</CustomerID>
      <Amount>' + CAST(@amountCompensation AS NVARCHAR(10)) + '</Amount>
   </AccountingCompensation>';

SEND ON CONVERSATION @chAccountingServiceCompensation MESSAGE TYPE
   [http://ssb.csharp.at/SSB_Book/c06/AccountingCompensationMessage]
   (@msgAccountingServiceCompensation);

-- End the conversation with the ClientService, because the order request
-- cannot be fulfilled. Get the conversation handle that is needed to
-- send a response message back to the ClientService.
```

```
        SELECT @chClientServiceCompensation = conversation_handle
        FROM sys.conversation_endpoints
        WHERE
            conversation_group_id = @conversationGroup AND
            far_service = 'ClientService';

        -- Send the response message back to the ClientService
        SET @orderResponseMessageCompensation = '<OrderResponse>0</OrderResponse>';
        SEND ON CONVERSATION @chClientServiceCompensation MESSAGE TYPE
            [http://ssb.csharp.at/SSB_Book/c06/OrderResponseMessage]
            (@orderResponseMessageCompensation);

        -- End the conversation with the ClientService
        END CONVERSATION @chClientServiceCompensation;
    END
END
```

In the first step of Listing 6-39, you extract the required information from the
OrderRequestMessage sent by the ClientService. This information is needed for the compensation messages sent to the CreditCardService and AccountingService. Therefore, you initiate a
new conversation with both services and send the corresponding messages as already described
in Listing 6-38. When both compensation transactions are started, you send a response message
back to the ClientService and immediately end the conversation with this service.

The only thing that is missing now is the processing of these compensation messages on
the CreditCardService and the AccountingService. For this simple application, I assume that
you can just delete the previously inserted record from the table, and that's all that the compensation transaction must do. In reality, however, it's always a little bit more complicated
when you execute compensation transactions, because normally there's more than one step in
a compensation transaction. Listing 6-40 shows the handling of the compensation message
for the CreditCardService inside the ProcessCreditCardMessages stored procedure that handles the incoming messages on the CreditCardQueue.

Listing 6-40. *Handling the Compensation Message for the* CreditCardService

```
IF (@messagetypename =
    'http://ssb.csharp.at/SSB_Book/c06/CreditCardCompensationMessage')
BEGIN
    -- Compensate the previous transaction through a DELETE
    DELETE FROM CreditCardTransactions
    WHERE
        CreditCardHolder = @messagebody.value('/CreditCardCompensation[1]/Holder[1]',
            'NVARCHAR(256)') AND
        CreditCardNumber = @messagebody.value('/CreditCardCompensation[1]/Number[1]',
            'NVARCHAR(50)') AND
        ValidThrough = @messagebody.value('/CreditCardCompensation[1]/Number[1]',
            'NVARCHAR(10)') AND
        Amount = @messagebody.value('/CreditCardCompensation[1]/Number[1]',
            'DECIMAL(18, 2)');
```

```
      -- The conversation on the target's side
      END CONVERSATION @ch;
END
```

As you can see in Listing 6-40, you just execute a `DELETE` on the `CreditCardTransactions` table and specify in the `WHERE` clause the column values that you inserted previously. Therefore, you can ensure that the correct record is deleted from the table `CreditCardTransactions`. Listing 6-41 shows the compensation transaction for the `AccountingService`.

Listing 6-41. *Handling the Compensation Message for the* `AccountingService`

```
IF (@messagetypename =
   'http://ssb.csharp.at/SSB_Book/c06/AccountingCompensationMessage')
BEGIN
   -- Compensate the previous transaction through a DELETE
   DELETE FROM AccountingRecordings
   WHERE
      CustomerID = @messagebody.value('/AccountingCompensation[1]/CustomerID[1]',
         'NVARCHAR(10)') AND
      Amount = @messagebody.value('/AccountingCompensation[1]/Amount[1]',
         'DECIMAL(18, 2)');

   -- End the conversation on the target's side
   END CONVERSATION @ch;
END
```

As soon as you implement the message-processing logic for the compensation messages, your sample application guarantees you data integrity when you send an `OrderRequestMessage` with more items specified than are available in stock, because both compensation transactions are executed automatically in the background when this event occurs. Figure 6-15 shows you the content of the application tables when a compensation transaction is executed. As you can see, the `CreditCardTransactions`, `AccountingRecords`, and `ShippingInformation` tables contain no records. Furthermore, the quantity of the specified product in the `Inventory` table is unchanged.

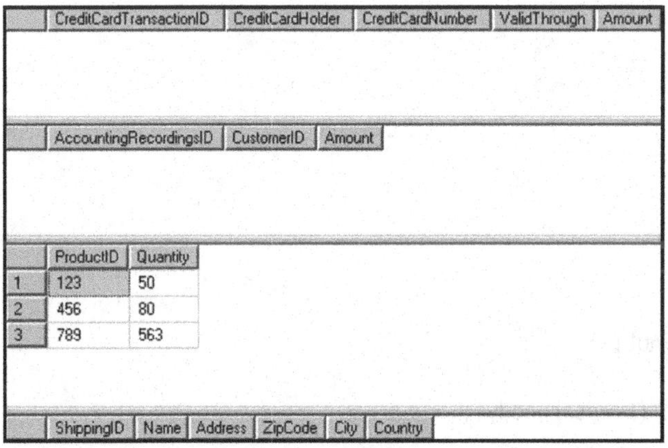

CreditCardTransactionID	CreditCardHolder	CreditCardNumber	ValidThrough	Amount

AccountingRecordingsID	CustomerID	Amount

	ProductID	Quantity
1	123	50
2	456	80
3	789	563

ShippingID	Name	Address	ZipCode	City	Country

Figure 6-15. *Data integrity due to compensation transactions*

Transaction Management

You can retrieve messages from a queue easily and process them accordingly. But in a production system where performance is crucial, you must carefully consider how to get the best possible performance and message throughput out of Service Broker. In this section, I'll talk about various transaction techniques and how they improve the overall performance of service programs.

Basic Receive Loop

One common practice in Service Broker programming is to implement a loop that runs as long as messages are available on a specified queue. Listing 6-42 shows a typical example of how to do this by creating a WHILE loop. The RECEIVE TOP (1) statement retrieves the next message from the queue and processes each message in an individual transaction.

Listing 6-42. *Basic Receive Loop for Message Processing*

```
CREATE PROCEDURE [BasicReceive]
AS
    DECLARE @ch UNIQUEIDENTIFIER
    DECLARE @messagetypename NVARCHAR(256)
    DECLARE @messagebody XML


    WHILE (1=1)
    BEGIN
        BEGIN TRANSACTION

        WAITFOR (
            RECEIVE TOP (1)
                @ch = conversation_handle,
                @messagetypename = message_type_name,
                @messagebody = CAST(message_body AS XML)
            FROM
                TargetQueue
        ), TIMEOUT 1000

        IF (@@ROWCOUNT = 0)
        BEGIN
            ROLLBACK TRANSACTION
            BREAK
        END

        IF (@messagetypename = 'DEFAULT')
        BEGIN
            SEND ON CONVERSATION @ch (@messagebody);
            END CONVERSATION @ch;
        END
```

```
    IF (@messagetypename =
        'http://schemas.microsoft.com/SQL/ServiceBroker/EndDialog')
    BEGIN
        -- End the conversation
        END CONVERSATION @ch;
    END

    COMMIT;
END
```

This stored procedure processes messages as long as they're available on the queue. When no messages are available, the loop exits, and the service program terminates. If you look at the ProcessedMessages table, you'll see that the stored procedure has processed the sent messages accordingly. Note that the RECEIVE T-SQL statement doesn't poll on the specified queue. It doesn't consume any processor cycles on the server. The only resource you're using is a thread that blocks until a result set is available on the queue.

Measuring Performance

Now the question is whether this is the fastest way to retrieve messages from a queue. First, you need a strategy for how you can measure the performance of the stored procedure from Listing 6-42. The simplest way is to preload the queue with a number of messages and then run the stored procedure. Next, you create a queue and load it with 100 conversations each with 100 messages (for a total of 10,000 messages).

Listing 6-43 shows the needed T-SQL batch.

Listing 6-43. *The* PreloadQueue *Stored Procedure for Preloading the Queue*

```
CREATE PROCEDURE PreloadQueue
    @ConversationCount INT,
    @MessagesPerConversation INT,
    @Payload VARBINARY(MAX)
AS
BEGIN
    DECLARE @batchCount INT
    DECLARE @ch UNIQUEIDENTIFIER

    SELECT @batchCount = 0;

    BEGIN TRANSACTION
    WHILE (@ConversationCount > 0)
    BEGIN
        BEGIN DIALOG CONVERSATION @ch
            FROM SERVICE [InitiatorService]
            TO SERVICE 'TargetService'
            WITH ENCRYPTION = OFF;

        DECLARE @messageCount INT;
        SELECT @messageCount = 0;
```

```
        WHILE (@messageCount < @messagesPerConversation)
        BEGIN
           SEND ON CONVERSATION @ch (@payload);

           SELECT @messageCount = @messageCount + 1, @batchCount = @batchCount + 1;

           IF (@batchCount >= 100)
           BEGIN
              COMMIT;
              SELECT @batchCount = 0;
              BEGIN TRANSACTION;
           END
        END

        SELECT @ConversationCount = @ConversationCount - 1
    END
    COMMIT;
END
```

After you create the stored procedure for the queue preload, you can measure the performance of the service program from Listing 6-43 with the T-SQL batch from Listing 6-44.

Listing 6-44. *Performance Measurement with a Basic Receive Loop*

```
DECLARE @payload VARBINARY(MAX);
SELECT @payload = CAST(N'<PerformanceMeasurements />' AS VARBINARY(MAX));
EXEC PreloadQueue 100, 100, @payload;
GO


DECLARE @messageCount FLOAT;
DECLARE @startTime DATETIME;
DECLARE @endTime DATETIME;

SELECT @messageCount = COUNT(*) FROM [TargetQueue];
SELECT @startTime = GETDATE();

EXEC BasicReceive;

SELECT @endTime = GETDATE();

SELECT
    @startTime AS [Start],
    @endTime AS [End],
    @messageCount AS [Count],
    DATEDIFF(second, @startTime, @endTime) AS [Duration],
    @messageCount / DATEDIFF(millisecond, @startTime, @endTime) * 1000 AS [Rate];
GO
```

First, you declare the variables you need to execute the PreloadQueue stored procedure from Listing 6-43. The stored procedure enqueues 100 conversations into the TargetQueue, where each conversation consists of 100 messages. All in all, you'll have 10,000 messages in the TargetQueue to process.

After the enqueuing process, you store the current time in the @startTime variable. Then you start the BasicReceive stored procedure, which processes the messages from the TargetQueue in a separate transaction. After this stored procedure executes successfully, the end time is stored in the @endTime variable. Finally, you calculate the processed message count (Count column), the duration (Duration column), and the message throughput per second (Rate column). When I ran this query on my notebook with 2 GB of RAM and a 2 GHz Intel Pentium processor, I got the values shown in Figure 6-16.

	Start	End	Count	Duration	Rate
1	2006-10-17 20:47:13.250	2006-10-17 20:47:36.873	10000	23	423.31625957753

Figure 6-16. *Measurements for a basic receive service program*

The basic stored procedure can process about 400 messages per second. This isn't a bad result, but let's see if we can beat it.

PERFORMANCE MEASUREMENTS

When you do some performance measurements with SQL Server 2008, you should fine-tune your system a bit so that you get the best possible performance out of it. For example, if you have two hard disks, it's always good to store the data files (*.mdf) and the log files (*.ldf) separately on each hard disk. You'll also get a performance benefit when you pre-grow your data files and log files under stress to an acceptable size to prevent dramatic alterations of the results due to file growth events.

Batched Commits

A drawback of the basic receive stored procedure from Listing 6-42 is that each message is processed in its own transaction. The first thing you can look at is changing the one-message-per-transaction processing into batching multiple messages into one transaction. This is the most simple and basic optimization any database application developer should think of first, as the commit rate is probably the first bottleneck any system will hit.

You can do a simple modification to the basic receive procedure from Listing 6-42: keep a counter of messages processed and commit only after 100 messages were processed. Everything else in the stored procedure stays the same. Listing 6-45 shows the modified stored procedure.

Listing 6-45. *Batched Commit in a Service Program*

```
CREATE PROCEDURE [BatchedReceive]
AS
BEGIN
   DECLARE @ch UNIQUEIDENTIFIER;
   DECLARE @messagetypename NVARCHAR(256);
   DECLARE @messagebody XML;
   DECLARE @batchCount INT;
   SELECT @batchCount = 0;

   BEGIN TRANSACTION
   WHILE (1=1)
   BEGIN
      BEGIN TRANSACTION

      WAITFOR (
         RECEIVE TOP (1)
            @ch = conversation_handle,
            @messagetypename = message_type_name,
            @messagebody = CAST(message_body AS XML)
         FROM
            TargetQueue
      ), TIMEOUT 1000

      IF (@@ROWCOUNT = 0)
      BEGIN
         ROLLBACK TRANSACTION
         BREAK
      END

      IF (@messagetypename = 'DEFAULT')
      BEGIN
         SEND ON CONVERSATION @ch (@messagebody);
         END CONVERSATION @ch;
      END


      IF (@messagetypename =
         'http://schemas.microsoft.com/SQL/ServiceBroker/EndDialog')
      BEGIN
         -- End the conversation
         END CONVERSATION @ch;
      END
```

```
        SELECT @batchCount = @batchCount + 1
        IF (@batchCount >= 100)
        BEGIN
            COMMIT;
            SELECT @batchCount = 0;
            BEGIN TRANSACTION;
        END
    END

    COMMIT;
END
```

Listing 6-46 shows the updated code to measure the performance with the stored procedure from Listing 6-45 again.

Listing 6-46. *Performance Measurement with a Batched Commit*

```
DECLARE @payload VARBINARY(MAX);
SELECT @payload = CAST(N'<PerformanceMeasurements />' AS VARBINARY(MAX));
EXEC PreloadQueue 100, 100, @payload;
GO

DECLARE @messageCount FLOAT;
DECLARE @startTime DATETIME;
DECLARE @endTime DATETIME;

SELECT @messageCount = COUNT(*) FROM [TargetQueue];
SELECT @startTime = GETDATE();

EXEC BatchedReceive;

SELECT @endTime = GETDATE();

SELECT
    @startTime AS [Start],
    @endTime AS [End],
    @messageCount AS [Count],
    DATEDIFF(second, @startTime, @endTime) AS [Duration],
    @messageCount / DATEDIFF(millisecond, @startTime, @endTime) * 1000 AS [Rate];
GO
```

The difference in this stored procedure is that you're not doing a COMMIT after each message. You defer the COMMIT after a batch of messages are processed, and then you do the COMMIT:

```
SELECT @batchCount = @batchCount + 1
IF (@batchCount >= 100)
BEGIN
    COMMIT;
    SELECT @batchCount = 0;
    BEGIN TRANSACTION;
END
```

The overall performance is much better than committing each message separately. When I executed this T-SQL batch, I got the results shown in Figure 6-17.

	Start	End	Count	Duration	Rate
1	2006-10-17 21:45:48.653	2006-10-17 21:46:09.420	10000	21	481,556390253299

Figure 6-17. *Measurements for a batched commit*

As you can see in Figure 6-17, the stored procedure now processes around 480 messages per second. This is about 20% faster than the single-message-per-transaction processing algorithm.

Cursor-Based Processing

You can take another approach that's completely different from the classic RECEIVE procedure. Instead of using the TOP (1) clause, you can use a cursor and process as many messages as the RECEIVE statement returns in one execution. Because you unfortunately can't declare T-SQL cursors on top of the RECEIVE result set, you need to use a trick: do a RECEIVE into a table variable and then iterate over the table variable using a cursor. The processing for each message will be identical to the previous two cases. Listing 6-47 shows the modified stored procedure.

Listing 6-47. *Cursor-Based Message Processing*

```
CREATE PROCEDURE CursorReceive
AS
BEGIN
    DECLARE @tableMessages TABLE
    (
        queuing_order BIGINT,
        conversation_handle UNIQUEIDENTIFIER,
        message_type_name SYSNAME,
        message_body VARBINARY(MAX)
    );

    DECLARE cursorMessages
        CURSOR FORWARD_ONLY READ_ONLY
        FOR SELECT
            queuing_order,
            conversation_handle,
            message_type_name,
            message_body
        FROM @tableMessages
        ORDER BY queuing_order;
```

```
DECLARE @ch UNIQUEIDENTIFIER;
DECLARE @messageTypeName SYSNAME;
DECLARE @payload VARBINARY(MAX);
DECLARE @order BIGINT;

WHILE (1 = 1)
BEGIN
  BEGIN TRANSACTION;

  WAITFOR (
    RECEIVE
      queuing_order,
      conversation_handle,
      message_type_name,
      message_body
    FROM [TargetQueue] INTO @tableMessages
  ), TIMEOUT 1000

  IF (@@ROWCOUNT = 0)
  BEGIN
    ROLLBACK;
    BREAK;
  END

  OPEN cursorMessages;

  WHILE (1 = 1)
  BEGIN
    FETCH NEXT FROM cursorMessages
    INTO @order, @ch, @messageTypeName, @payload;

    IF (@@FETCH_STATUS != 0)
    BREAK;

    IF (@messageTypeName = 'DEFAULT')
    BEGIN
      SEND ON CONVERSATION @ch (@payload);
    END

    IF (@messagetypename =
        'http://schemas.microsoft.com/SQL/ServiceBroker/EndDialog')
    BEGIN
      -- End the conversation
      END CONVERSATION @ch;
    END
  END
```

```
        CLOSE cursorMessages;
        DELETE FROM @tableMessages;
        COMMIT;
    END


    DEALLOCATE cursorMessages;
END
GO
```

The message processing changes in the CursorReceive stored procedure, making it dramatically different from Listing 6-46, which shows the stored procedure that does the batch commit. In the first step, you declare a table variable named @tableMessages that stores the received messages (with its columns) from the TargetQueue:

```
DECLARE @tableMessages TABLE
(
    queuing_order BIGINT,
    conversation_handle UNIQUEIDENTIFIER,
    message_type_name SYSNAME,
    message_body VARBINARY(MAX)
);
```

With the statement DECLARE cursorMessages CURSOR, you declare a cursor on top of this table variable so that you can iterate through it quickly:

```
DECLARE cursorMessages
    CURSOR FORWARD_ONLY READ_ONLY
    FOR SELECT
        queuing_order,
        conversation_handle,
        message_type_name,
        message_body
    FROM @tableMessages
    ORDER BY queuing_order;
```

When you execute the WAITFOR statement, you must fetch the messages from the TargetQueue directly into the declared table variable:

```
WAITFOR (
    RECEIVE (
        queuing_order,
        conversation_handle,
        message_type_name,
        message_body
    FROM [TargetQueue] INTO @tableMessages
), TIMEOUT 1000
```

Finally, you must open the cursor as soon as you've retrieved the messages from the TargetQueue and fetch the current row of the cursor into T-SQL variables for further processing:

```
OPEN cursorMessages;

WHILE (1 = 1)
BEGIN
   FETCH NEXT FROM cursorMessages;
      INTO @ch, @messageTypeName, @payload;

   IF (@@FETCH_STATUS != 0)
      BREAK;

   -- Process the message
END
```

Now when I did a performance measurement with this stored procedure, I got the results shown in Figure 6-18.

	Start	End	Count	Duration	Rate
1	2006-10-18 17:10:01.170	2006-10-18 17:10:13.077	10000	12	839.912649084495

Figure 6-18. *Measurements for cursor-based message processing*

Wow, great! The message throughput has increased to around 840 messages per second. This is about 75% faster than the approach with the batched commit. Do you think you can push the message throughput higher?

Set-Based Processing

The next approach is not a free one. Let's move away from processing message by message and see how you can do set-based processing. Note that not all messaging applications can do a set-based processing of incoming messages. Just assume that you get only a few messages per each conversation from different initiators.

Whenever one conversation side has to send long streams of messages without a response from the other side, you can usually apply this kind of processing. For example, with auditing, the front-end machines have to record user actions for auditing needs. Rather than connecting to a central database and inserting the audit record directly into the database, you can start a one-directional conversation on which you send the audit data as messages. The back-end processing of messages is straightforward: extract the audit data from the message payload and insert it into the audit tables. You can do this as a set-based operation, and you can insert the entire RECEIVE result set as a single set into the audit table.

Let's create a dummy audit backend: the messages consist of an XML payload containing the user name, the date, and some arbitrary audit payload. The back end has to store these records into a table, shredding the XML into relational columns first. As with any well-planned application that does this, it should also store the original XML received. Listing 6-48 shows the audit infrastructure consisting of the table and the message-processing stored procedure.

Listing 6-48. *Table and Stored Procedure for Set-Based Message Processing*

```
CREATE TABLE AuditingTrail
(
    Id INT NOT NULL IDENTITY(1, 1),
    Date DATETIME,
    Payload NVARCHAR(MAX),
    [User] NVARCHAR(256),
    OriginalXML XML
)
GO

CREATE PROCEDURE RowsetReceive
AS
BEGIN
    DECLARE @tableMessages TABLE

    (
        queuing_order BIGINT,
        conversation_handle UNIQUEIDENTIFIER,
        message_type_name SYSNAME,
        payload XML
    );

    WHILE (1 = 1)
    BEGIN
        BEGIN TRANSACTION;

        WAITFOR (
            RECEIVE
                queuing_order,
                conversation_handle,
                message_type_name,
                CAST(message_body AS XML) AS payload
            FROM [TargetQueue] INTO @tableMessages
        ), TIMEOUT 1000;

        IF (@@ROWCOUNT = 0)
        BEGIN
            COMMIT;
            BREAK;
        END
```

```
      ;WITH XMLNAMESPACES (DEFAULT 'http://ssb.csharp.at/SSB_Book/c06/Datagram')
      INSERT INTO AuditingTrail
      (
         Date,
         Payload,
         [User],
         OriginalXML
      )
      SELECT
         payload.value('(/Datagram/@date-time)[1]', 'DATETIME'),
         payload.value('(/Datagram/@payload)[1]', 'NVARCHAR(MAX)'),
         payload.value('(/Datagram/@user)[1]', 'NVARCHAR(256)'),
         payload
      FROM @tableMessages
      WHERE message_type_name = 'DEFAULT'
      ORDER BY queuing_order;

      COMMIT;

      DELETE FROM @tableMessages;
   END
END
GO
```

Take a detailed look at this stored procedure. You can see that the received messages are also stored in a table variable. The difference is that the content of the table variable now is directly shredded into the AuditingTrail table through the new methods of the XML data type:

```
;WITH XMLNAMESPACES (DEFAULT 'http://ssb.csharp.at/SSB_Book/c06/Datagram')
INSERT INTO AuditingTrail
(
   Date,
   Payload,
   [User],
   OriginalXML
)
SELECT
   payload.value('(/Datagram/@date-time)[1]', 'DATETIME'),
   payload.value('(/Datagram/@payload)[1]', 'NVARCHAR(MAX)'),
   payload.value('(/Datagram/@user)[1]', 'NVARCHAR(256)'),
   payload
FROM @tableMessages
WHERE message_type_name = 'DEFAULT'
ORDER BY queuing_order;
```

When you've created the AuditingTrail table and the RowsetReceive stored procedure, you can again do a performance measurement on top of this infrastructure. Listing 6-49 shows the code for this.

Listing 6-49. *Performance Measurement with Set-Based Message Processing*

```
DECLARE @xmlPayload XML;
DECLARE @payload VARBINARY(MAX);

;WITH XMLNAMESPACES (DEFAULT 'http://ssb.csharp.at/SSB_Book/c06/Datagram')
SELECT @xmlPayload = (SELECT
    GETDATE() AS [@date-time],
    SUSER_SNAME() AS [@user],
    'Some auditing data' AS [@payload]
FOR XML PATH('Datagram'), TYPE);

SELECT @payload = CAST(@xmlPayload AS VARBINARY(MAX));
EXEC PreloadQueue 100, 100, @payload;
GO

DECLARE @messageCount FLOAT;
DECLARE @startTime DATETIME;
DECLARE @endTime DATETIME;

SELECT @endTime = GETDATE();

SELECT
    @startTime AS [Start],
    @endTime AS [End],
    @messageCount AS [Count],
    DATEDIFF(second, @startTime, @endTime) AS [Duration],
    @messageCount / DATEDIFF(millsecond, @startTime, @endTime) * 1000 AS [Rate];
GO
```

As you can see in Listing 6-49, you use the FOR XML PATH clause to produce the required XML that the RowsetReceive stored procedure processes. Figure 6-19 shows the results of this processing technique.

	Start	End	Count	Duration	Rate
1	2006-10-18 21:40:55.263	2006-10-18 21:41:00.937	10000	5	1762,73576590869

Figure 6-19. *Measurements for set-based messaging processing*

Great, isn't it? You've now achieved a message throughput of about 1,750 messages per second. When you compare this with the previous results shown in Figure 6-17, this is a performance improvement of 100%. Now give me one last chance, and I'll try to overbid this result.

Binary Payload

You may like XML, but at the end of the day, XML is text. How much could you improve performance by moving to a binary payload for the audit records? Doing binary marshaling and unmarshaling in T-SQL code isn't for the faint of heart, but it's not only for the bravest. You need to create two stored functions: one that marshals the audit data into a binary BLOB and one that unmarshals the original data out of a BLOB. Listing 6-50 shows these two stored functions.

Listing 6-50. *Marshaling and Unmarshaling Binary Data*

```
CREATE FUNCTION BinaryMarshalPayload
(
   @DateTime DATETIME,
   @Payload VARBINARY(MAX),
   @User NVARCHAR(256)
)
RETURNS VARBINARY(MAX)
AS
BEGIN
   DECLARE @marshaledPayload VARBINARY(MAX);
   DECLARE @payloadLength BIGINT;
   DECLARE @userLength INT;

   SELECT @payloadLength = LEN(@Payload);
   SELECT @userLength = LEN(@User) * 2;

   SELECT @marshaledPayload =
      CAST(@DateTime AS VARBINARY(MAX)) +
      CAST(@payloadLength AS VARBINARY(MAX)) +
      @payload +
      CAST(@userLength AS VARBINARY(MAX)) +
      CAST(@User AS VARBINARY(MAX));

   RETURN @marshaledPayload;
END
GO



CREATE FUNCTION BinaryUnmarshalPayload
(
   @MessageBody VARBINARY(MAX)
)
RETURNS @UnmarshaledBody TABLE
(
   [DateTime] DATETIME,
   [Payload] VARBINARY(MAX),
   [User] NVARCHAR(256)
)
```

```
AS
BEGIN
    DECLARE @dateTime DATETIME;
    DECLARE @user NVARCHAR(256);
    DECLARE @userLength INT;
    DECLARE @payload VARBINARY(MAX);
    DECLARE @payloadLength BIGINT;

    SELECT @dateTime = CAST(SUBSTRING(@MessageBody, 1, 8) AS DATETIME);
    SELECT @payloadLength = CAST(SUBSTRING(@MessageBody, 9, 8) AS BIGINT);
    SELECT @payload = SUBSTRING(@MessageBody, 17, @payloadLength);
    SELECT @userLength = CAST(SUBSTRING(@MessageBody, @payloadLength + 17, 4)
        AS INT);
    SELECT @user = CAST(SUBSTRING(@MessageBody, @payloadLength + 21, @userLength)
        AS NVARCHAR(256));

    INSERT INTO @UnmarshaledBody
        VALUES (@datetime, @payload, @user);

    RETURN;
END
GO
```

The first stored function, `BinaryMarshalPayload`, makes one `VARBINARY(MAX)` from the given arguments and also stores the length of the payload and of the user inside the marshaled data. The second stored function, `BinaryUnmarshalPayload`, returns a table that includes the unmarshaled values from the given `VARBINARY(MAX)` parameter. With these two stored functions, you can now write a stored procedure that retrieves the marshaled messages from `TargetQueue` and processes them (see Listing 6-51).

Listing 6-51. *Processing Marshaled Messages*

```
CREATE TABLE PayloadData
(
    [Id] INT NOT NULL IDENTITY(1, 1),
    [DateTime] DATETIME,
    [Payload] NVARCHAR(MAX),
    [User] NVARCHAR(256)
)
GO
```

```
CREATE PROCEDURE RowsetBinaryDatagram
AS
BEGIN
   DECLARE @tableMessages TABLE
   (
      queuing_order BIGINT,
      conversation_handle UNIQUEIDENTIFIER,
      message_type_name SYSNAME,
      message_body VARBINARY(MAX)
   );

   WHILE (1 = 1)
   BEGIN
      BEGIN TRANSACTION;

      WAITFOR (
         RECEIVE
            queuing_order,
            conversation_handle,
            message_type_name,
            message_body
         FROM TargetQueue INTO @tableMessages
      ), TIMEOUT 1000;

      IF (@@ROWCOUNT = 0)
      BEGIN
         COMMIT;
         BREAK;
      END

      INSERT INTO PayloadData ([DateTime], [Payload], [User])
      SELECT [DateTime], [Payload], [User] FROM @tableMessages
         CROSS APPLY BinaryUnmarshalPayload(message_body)
      WHERE message_type_name = 'DEFAULT';

      COMMIT;

      DELETE FROM @tableMessages;
   END
END
GO
```

The stored procedure in Listing 6-51 uses the CROSS APPLY operator to unmarshal the binary message data and inserts the retrieved data in the PayloadData table. Figure 6-20 shows the result of the execution of this stored procedure.

	Start	End	Count	Duration	Rate
1	2006-10-18 21:35:45.263	2006-10-18 21:35:48.560	10000	3	3033.98058252427

Figure 6-20. *Measurements for processing a binary message payload*

You've now outperformed the last stored procedure by 70%! Think back to Listing 6-42, where you processed each message separately in a transaction and had a message throughput of 400 messages per second. Compared to this, the new result shows a performance benefit of 750%!

This means that you can theoretically process around 3,000 messages per second on a really low-end machine similar to my notebook. Now imagine that you do your message processing on an HP Superdome . . . The actual results you get in your application may differ from these results, because you must always include the message-processing logic itself, which could sometimes be the more time-consuming task. Figure 6-21 shows the results of these performance tests compared to each other.

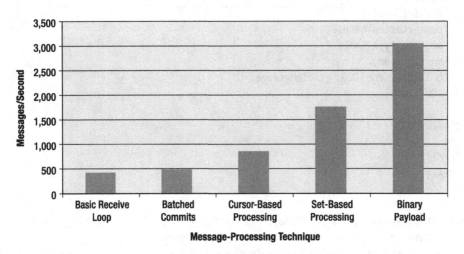

Figure 6-21. *Service Broker performance statistics*

Summary

This chapter featured two big logical sections. The first section covered Service Broker's locking support: conversation group locking. With this kind of lock, you can ensure that messages on the same conversation group are processed sequentially and in the correct message order.

The second section took a closer look at several message-processing technologies and their potential performance advantages. In the next chapter, you'll learn how to distribute Service Broker applications. Stay tuned.

CHAPTER 7

■ ■ ■

Distributed Service Broker Applications

One big advantage of Service Broker is that it easily lets you distribute Service Broker applications to different physical machines without any service implementation changes. In this chapter, I'll give you a general overview of distributed Service Broker applications and how they are created. This chapter will cover the following topics:

- *Communication*: Service Broker uses standard Transmission Control Protocol (TCP) connections for the communication between distributed Service Broker services. The communication protocol—the *adjacent broker protocol (ABP)*—is a proprietary protocol optimized for the efficient and reliable delivery of dialog messages.

- *Routing*: A Service Broker route maps a service name to a destination network address where the Service Broker service is deployed. Therefore, you can easily change the deployment topology of your Service Broker services.

- *Distributed applications*: You can easily distribute a Service Broker application. You simply have to deploy the Service Broker services on different machines and set up the security configuration and the routing information.

Communication

So far, each of the services has run in the same SQL Server instance. That's ideal during development, but in production, Service Broker services are typically spread across several SQL Server instances. For Service Broker applications, it doesn't matter whether a remote service is located on the same SQL Server instance, on an instance on the same computer, or on an instance on another computer connected through a local area network (LAN) or a wide area network (WAN).

Service Broker uses standard Transmission Control Protocol/Internet Protocol (TCP/IP) connections to send messages between SQL Server instances. Like many reliable messaging systems, the Service Broker communication protocol (the Adjacent Broker Protocol [ABP]) is a proprietary protocol optimized for the efficient, reliable delivery of dialog messages. The communication system architecture makes it easy to support other communication protocols, so it's likely that future releases of Service Broker will support web services protocols.

WCF CHANNEL FOR SERVICE BROKER

Even before SQL Server 2005 was finally released, Microsoft played around with and implemented a Windows Communication Foundation (WCF) channel for Service Broker. This channel was shown at Microsoft's Professional Developers Conference (PDC) 2005 in Los Angeles. Unfortunately, the WCF channel wasn't released with SQL Server 2005 and won't be part of a future SQL Server service pack or add-on.

The purpose of this demo was to prove that it is possible to write a WCF channel that directly supports Service Broker. Maybe a WCF channel will be available in the next version of SQL Server. Such a channel won't be a queued channel, such as the MSMQ channel available in WCF. It will be a reliable, full-duplex session channel, similar to a TCP channel, but with much stronger reliability and availability semantics.

In order for a remote system to open a TCP/IP connection to Service Broker, the Service Broker service must be listening on a TCP/IP port for incoming connections and requests. This port is configured through the creation of an endpoint object in SQL Server 2008. SQL Server 2008 uses endpoints to configure all incoming connection points, including T-SQL, Service Broker, database mirroring, and HTTP.

Service Broker Protocols

Multiple protocols are involved in a Service Broker conversation. At the high level, there is the dialog protocol (also called the *endpoint protocol*), which handles the exchange of messages between two dialog endpoints. This protocol manages message ordering, reliable delivery, dialog-level authentication, encryption, and dialog lifetime. Often hundreds of dialogs are opened between two Service Broker services (just remember the order service from the previous chapter), even though only a few of these are sending or receiving messages at any given moment.

The lower-level protocol is the ABP, which manages the TCP/IP connections between two Service Brokers. An ABP connection multiplexes messages from many dialogs over a single TCP/IP connection. As you'll see in Chapter 11, when we discuss forwarding services, a message between two dialog endpoints can traverse several adjacent broker connections as it is routed to its final destination, the target service.

One way to understand the difference between the two protocols is to think about the way the telephone network works. At the high level, you make a phone call from your phone to another phone. You and the other endpoint then carry on a conversation. At the low level, hundreds or even thousands of these conversations travel over a single wire or fiber. In the same way, many Service Broker conversations can be multiplexed over a single TCP/IP connection between two SQL Server instances.

Sending a Message

This section follows a message from a sending application to a receiving application on another SQL Server instance. The journey starts when the sending application issues a SEND command. As soon as the local SQL Server transaction commits, Service Broker tries to send the message asynchronously in the background to the specified destination. To handle this task, Service Broker uses a concept referred to as *routes*. A route specifies on which network address a Service Broker service is available.

Because of this abstraction, you always have to specify the TO SERVICE parameter in the BEGIN DIALOG T-SQL statement as a string literal. This string literal is used to find a route to the target service. A component referred to as a classifier does this lookup inside Service Broker. The logic of the classifier component uses the information in the sys.conversation_endpoints and the sys.routes catalog views to determine what to do with the message. If the destination for this message is a queue in the same SQL Server instance as the source, and if the queue is ready to receive messages, the message is inserted into the destination queue; otherwise, it is inserted into the sys.transmission_queue of the sending database. If the RETENTION option is set on the queue of the sending side, the message is also copied to the sending queue.

If the destination is a local queue, you're done with the send when the transaction commits. Otherwise, the message is committed into the sys.transmission_queue. A reference to the message is stored on an instance-wide list of messages to be sent. This global list ensures fairness in message dispatching across all the databases in the SQL Server instance. The message-sending order is independent of which transmission queue the messages come from.

Dialog messages routed to the same destination network address are assembled into transport messages to be sent over an adjacent broker connection to the remote Service Broker. For efficiency, Service Broker sends multiple dialog message fragments with each socket call when possible. This is referred to as *boxcaring*. Before each message is sent, it is signed to prevent alterations in the transmission and is optionally encrypted.

Service Broker also fragments large messages. This keeps a single large message from tying up all the available bandwidth for the amount of time it takes to transfer the contents to the network. Fragmentation allows messages from other dialogs to be interleaved with fragments of a large message. If an adjacent broker connection is open to the remote destination, the assembled boxcar is sent. If no connection is available, a connection is opened and authenticated. While the adjacent broker logic is waiting for the send to complete, another boxcar is assembled. This means an adjacent broker connection can effectively use all the bandwidth available. For this reason, only one connection is maintained between any two adjacent brokers.

Opening an adjacent broker connection can be relatively expensive, because several messages are exchanged to create and authenticate the connection. For this reason, adjacent broker connections are kept open for up to 90 seconds of idle time. As long as there is never a gap of more than 90 seconds between messages, the connection will stay open. When the message is received at the destination, Service Broker checks the signature and decrypts the message if necessary. The classifier component is called again to determine which queue the message should be inserted into. The sys.routes table in the msdb database is used for messages arriving from the network. If the message is bound for a queue in this instance, Service Broker inserts it into that queue. To maximize efficiency, several inserts are grouped into a single transaction if more messages are available.

Once the received message is successfully inserted into the queue, an acknowledgment message is sent back to the sender of the original message. The acknowledgment message can either be included in the header of another message that is returning on the same dialog, or it can be a separate message. An acknowledgment message can accept several different messages or message fragments with a single message. To maximize the possibility that the acknowledgment message will be returned as part of a normal dialog message and that it will acknowledge more than one message or fragment, the Service Broker receive logic waits for up to a second before acknowledging the current received message. This delay doesn't increase latency, because the message has already been successfully delivered to the target of the conversation. The delay just means the message will stay on the transmission queue at the sender's side a while longer than normal.

When the sender receives the acknowledgment message, the message status is marked as successfully sent, and the message is deleted from the sys.transmission_queue. If the adjacent broker logic has problems either sending the message or opening a connection to the remote Service Broker, the last_transmission_error column of the sys.transmission_queue will contain information about the error.

If an acknowledgment message for a message or fragment isn't received within the retry timeout, the message is sent again. The retry timeout starts at 4 seconds and doubles after each retry until it reaches a maximum of 64 seconds. After this maximum of 64 seconds, the message is resent again once every 64 seconds. This means that messages are not retried too often if the sends fail multiple times. It also means that when the destination server comes back online after a failure, it can take up to a minute for some of the messages to be resent. Messages that arrive at the destination in a bad state—that is, corrupted, incomplete, or with invalid signatures—are dropped by the destination and resent by the sender. You can use SQL Trace events available in the Broker events to find out why messages are dropped at the destination. Please refer to Chapter 12 for more information about this. If Service Broker drops a message, it won't return an error back to the original sender. Monitoring the dropped message trace is the only way to find out that messages are being dropped at the target of a conversation.

Routing

A Service Broker route maps a service name to a destination network address where messages to that service should be sent. As the previous section already mentioned, the classifier component of Service Broker uses this routing information to decide what to do with sent messages. All in all, four routes are involved in successfully delivering a message to its destination network address:

- A route from the local sys.routes table (ssb_db database, SQL Server A) to the destination network address

- A route from the remote msdb database to the correct database

- A route from the remote sys.routes table (ssb_db database, SQL Server B) back to the initiator's network address

- A route from the local msdb database to the correct database

Figure 7-1 illustrates this concept.

Let's have a look at each of these four routes. The first route (route #1 in Figure 7-1) is set up in the initiator's database and stores the network address of the remote Service Broker service. As soon as the SEND T-SQL command executes, the necessary route is picked up from the sys.routes table to determine where to send the message.

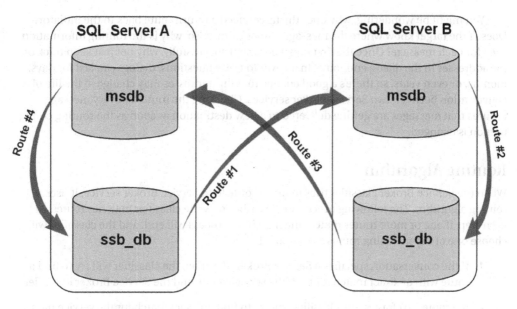

Figure 7-1. *The four routes involved in a distributed Service Broker scenario*

When the message arrives at the destination SQL Server instance, Service Broker uses a route from the sys.routes table in the msdb database to determine which database will receive the message. This is route #2 in Figure 7-1. This step is necessary because the same service may be defined in more than one database in the destination SQL Server instance. Once the message has been successfully committed in the proper queue in the destination database, an acknowledgment message is sent back to the sender, either as part of the header of another dialog message or as a separate message.

A route from the sys.routes table is used to determine where to send the acknowledgment message. This is route #3 in Figure 7-1. This is an important concept to understand. One of the most common configuration issues with distributed Service Broker scenarios is forgetting this return route back to the initiator of the conversation. If you forget the return route, messages will be delivered successfully to the destination queue, but they will never be acknowledged. Messages stay in the sys.transmission_queue on the sender's side and are resent periodically forever (or until someone adds the correct return route at the destination). If you notice successfully delivered messages still sitting in the sys.transmission_queue, or if you run SQL Profiler on the destination server and see a bunch of messages being dropped because of duplicates, check the route back to the sender's service in the destination database.

When the acknowledgment message arrives at the sender's SQL Server instance, Service Broker uses a route in the msdb database to route the message to the correct sending service queue in the sending database. This is route #4 in Figure 7-1.

These same four routes are used whether the message is sent from the initiator of the dialog to the target or from the target to the initiator. This explanation assumes that the sender and the receiver make a direct connection between Service Broker endpoints. In some cases, a message may be routed through multiple Service Broker instances to reach its destination. You can read more about forwarding in Chapter 11, where I talk about scale-out scenarios with Service Broker.

You might be wondering, why does the target need a return route back to the initiator? Doesn't the target know where the message comes from? Also, why is the routing information used for each message? Once the first message is sent successfully, why not just keep track of the addresses in the dialog endpoint? In answer to these questions, dialogs can last for days, months, or even years, so there's a good chance that the addresses may change in the life of a conversation between two Service Broker services. Checking the route for every message ensures that messages are getting delivered to a new destination as soon as the routing configuration is changed.

Routing Algorithm

When the Service Broker classifier tries to find a route for a Service Broker service, it uses a routing algorithm. The following procedure describes how the classifier matches routes. At each step, if one or more routes match, the matching process will end, and the classifier will choose one of the matching routes as described:

1. If the conversation specifies a Service Broker identifier, the classifier will try to find a route with an exact match for both the service name and the Service Broker identifier.

2. If a route isn't found, the classifier will try to find an exact match for the service name among the routes that don't specify a Service Broker identifier.

3. If the conversation doesn't specify a Service Broker identifier, the classifier will try to find an exact match for the service name among the routes that specify a Service Broker identifier. If the routing table contains routes that match the service name and have different Service Broker identifiers assigned, the classifier will randomly pick a route from among these routes. This is referred to as *load balancing*. Please refer to Chapter 11 for more information about this topic.

4. The classifier tries to find a route that doesn't specify either the service name or the Service Broker identifier.

5. If the conversation specifies a Service Broker identifier, and if the SQL Server instance contains one or more databases that contain Service Broker services with service names that match the name specified in the conversation, the message will be routed as through the routing table, which contains a route with the service name and the network address LOCAL.

6. If the classifier can't find a route, the conversation will be marked as DELAYED in sys.transmission_queue. When a conversation is marked as DELAYED, Service Broker performs the matching process again after a time-out period. Notice that failure to find a matching route is not considered an error.

Managing Routes

Service Broker routes are SQL Server metadata objects created with the DDL statement CREATE ROUTE. Listing 7-1 shows the syntax for this T-SQL statement.

Listing 7-1. *The* CREATE ROUTE *T-SQL Statement*

```
CREATE ROUTE route_name
[ AUTHORIZATION owner_name ]
WITH
   [ SERVICE_NAME = 'service_name' ]
   [ BROKER_INSTANCE = 'broker_instance_identifier' ]
   [ LIFETIME route_lifetime ]
   ADDRESS = 'next_hop_address'
   [ , MIRROR_ADDRESS = 'next_hop_mirror_address' ]
```

Table 7-1 describes the several parameters for this T-SQL statement.

Table 7-1. *Parameters for the* CREATE ROUTE *T-SQL Statement*

Parameter	Description
route_name	The name of the route to create in the current database and owned by the principal specified in the AUTHORIZATION clause. It must be a valid SYSNAME, and you cannot specify server, database, or schema names.
owner_name	The owner of the route. The default is the current user. It may be the name of any valid user or role if the current user is a member of the DB_OWNER fixed database role or a member of the SYSADMIN fixed server role. Otherwise, it must be the name of the current user, of a user that the current user has to impersonate permissions for, or of a role to which the current user belongs.
service_name	Sets the name of the remote Service Broker service that is addressed by this route. The comparison of the service_name is case-sensitive and doesn't use the current collation. If service_name isn't specified, the route matches any service name. It then has a lower priority in the matching process than a route that has a service_name specified.
broker_instance_identifier	Sets the Service Broker Globally Unique Identifier (GUID) of the database that hosts the target service specified in service_name. When broker_instance_identifier isn't specified, the created route matches any broker instance at the remote network address. A route without the broker_instance_identifier specified has a higher priority in the matching process than a route where the broker_instance_identifier is specified. For conversations where the broker_instance_identifier is specified, the route has a higher priority than a route that hasn't specified the broker_instance_identifier.
route_lifetime	Indicates the time (in seconds) of how long the route is stored in the routing table. After this time-out period, the route expires, and the classifier component doesn't consider this route when determining a route for a Service Broker service. If route_lifetime isn't specified, it is set to NULL and the route never expires.
next_hop_address	Specifies the network address used by this route. It must be a valid TCP address in the following format: TCP://{dns_name	netbios_name	ip_address}:port_number. Please make sure that the port number matches the port number of the Service Broker endpoint created at the specified network address.
next_hop_mirror_address	Specifies the network address for a mirrored database where one mirrored database is hosted at the specified network address. It must also be a valid TCP address with the format as described by the next_hop_address.

Listing 7-2 shows how you can set up a route with the CREATE ROUTE statement.

Listing 7-2. *Creating a Route*

```
CREATE ROUTE TargetServiceRoute
   WITH SERVICE_NAME = 'TargetService',
   ADDRESS = 'TCP://targetserver:4743'
```

The name of the route has no special meaning, because you only use the route name when you want to ALTER or DROP a route through the T-SQL commands ALTER ROUTE and DROP ROUTE. Listing 7-3 shows how you can alter and finally drop a route from a SQL Server database.

Listing 7-3. *Altering and Deleting a Route*

```
ALTER ROUTE TargetServiceRoute
   WITH SERVICE_NAME = 'TargetService',
   ADDRESS = 'TCP://new_targetserver:4743'
GO

DROP ROUTE TargetServiceRoute
GO
```

Distributed Applications

This section will show you how you can create a distributed application based on Service Broker. As I've already mentioned, it's normal that Service Broker applications in the first step are developed on a single SQL Server instance and then installed on several SQL Servers through the deployment process. Service Broker makes the physical distribution of your Service Broker services completely transparent from your service implementation code through the use of routes.

With routes, you can easily define where each Service Broker service is deployed and running. You don't have to make any changes to your service implementation, even when you want to scale out your Service Broker solution to thousands of concurrent users. This is an important point to understand in the Service Broker programming paradigm. For example, let's say you have to scale out an MSMQ messaging application that was developed on a single machine to support several thousand users. Here you have to change the whole implementation so that you can scale it out to handle the user load. With Service Broker, it's just a configuration issue—nothing more. Let's now take a look at the application as it was developed on a single SQL Server instance.

The Application

In this section, I want to show you how to deploy the different services of the Service Broker application you developed in Chapter 6 to several SQL Server instances and scale it out to any required size. I'll describe how to distribute CreditCardService and AccountingService to different SQL Server instances.

SECURITY IN SERVICE BROKER

When you distribute a Service Broker application to several SQL Server instances, you need to do a lot more than just setting up and configuring the necessary routes. After you configure the different routes success-fully, you also have to pay attention to security. Service Broker supports several kinds of security, and you must enable a minimum security set (the transport security) to allow distributed Service Broker applications to communicate with each other.

In this chapter, I'll show you only the basics of Service Broker security that you need to successfully set up and deploy the distributed Service Broker application. The next chapter gives more detailed information on the different kinds of security models that Service Broker supports.

Setting Up Routes

Let's begin in the first step with the setup of the necessary routes. Looking ahead to Figure 7-2, you can see that CreditCardService and AccountingService are running on different SQL Server machines. Therefore, you need routes to these services and from these services back to the OrderService. As you know, four routes are involved when setting up a route to another Service Broker service and back. To simplify this sample, you don't have to create routes from the msdb database to the correct application database, because the four Service Broker services are defined only once in each SQL Server instance (SQL Server B and SQL Server C).

Because of this simplification, you have to define the following four routes:

- A route from the local sys.routes table (named CreditCardServiceRoute) to the destination network address of SQL Server B

- A route from the local sys.routes table (named AccountingServiceRoute) to the destination network address of SQL Server C

- A route from the sys.routes table (named OrderServiceRoute) on SQL Server B back to the network address of SQL Server A

- A route from the sys.routes table (named OrderServiceRoute) on SQL Server C back to the network address of SQL Server A

MSDB ROUTES

You don't have to specify routes from the msdb database to the application database, because there is always a route named AutoCreatedLocal that is created as soon as SQL Server is installed. This route always routes your Service Broker messages to the correct service on that SQL Server instance as long as each Service Broker service is only deployed once in this SQL Server instance. Otherwise, Service Broker will randomly pick one of the available target services from this database. Refer to Chapter 11 for more informa-tion on this scale-out topic.

When you move your Service Broker application into production, it's always a good idea to delete the AutoCreatedLocal route and add a more specific route to the msdb database. Therefore, you can exactly ensure that messages are only traveling to the services you've explicitly defined through routes.

Figure 7-2 shows the direction of each route for the message flow.

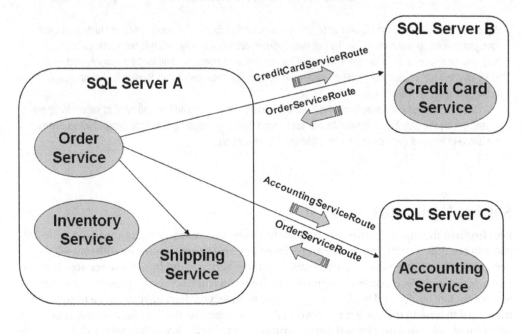

Figure 7-2. *The four necessary routes for the distributed application*

For this sample, you can assume that the various Service Broker services are deployed on the following computers:

- OrderService: NetBIOS name OrderServiceInstance

- CreditCardService: NetBIOS name CreditCardServiceInstance

- AccountingService: NetBIOS name AccountingServiceInstance

Listing 7-4 shows how you can assign a different NetBIOS name to your computer.

Listing 7-4. *Assigning Different NetBIOS Names to a Computer*

```
192.168.0.200      OrderServiceInstance
192.168.0.201      CreditCardServiceInstance
192.168.0.202      AccountingServiceInstance
```

DYNAMIC NETBIOS NAMES

It's very unlikely that your SQL Servers where you run this sample have the same NetBIOS names as used in the demo scripts for this distributed Service Broker sample. However, you can assign different NetBIOS names (aliases) to your computers so that you don't have to change the network addresses in the CREATE ROUTE T-SQL statement. In reality, my computers at home also have different NetBIOS names, so I've also assigned aliases to them to make the understanding of this sample a little bit clearer.

You can assign different NetBIOS names to a computer through a file called hosts. This file is located in the folder %systemroot%\system32\drivers\etc. In this file, you can assign different NetBIOS names to a computer. Refer to Listing 7-4 for a simple sample on this topic. When you're done with editing this file, just save it and ping the newly assigned NetBIOS name to verify your configured settings.

Before you create all the necessary routes between the several Service Broker services, you have to create on both new SQL Server instances the corresponding application databases that host the implementation of the CreditCardService and the AccountingService. Therefore, you have to deploy all needed tables and stored procedures for each Service Broker service. You also must deploy the message types and the contracts that are used between OrderService and CreditCardService/AccountingService into the application database. This is understandable, because the message types and the contracts form the communication protocol shared between OrderService and CreditCardService/AccountingService. Table 7-2 shows the SQL Server objects that you must deploy on the CreditCardServiceInstance machine where CreditCardService runs.

Table 7-2. *SQL Server Objects for the* CreditCardServiceInstance *Machine*

Object Type	Name
Message type	[http://ssb.csharp.at/SSB_Book/c07/CreditCardRequestMessage]
Message type	[http://ssb.csharp.at/SSB_Book/c07/CreditCardResponseMessage]
Contract	[http://ssb.csharp.at/SSB_Book/c07/CreditCardContract]
Queue	CreditCardQueue
Service	CreditCardService
Table	CreditCardTransactions
Stored procedure	ProcessCreditCardRequestMessages

Table 7-3 shows the SQL Server objects you have to create on the AccountingServiceInstance machine.

Table 7-3. *SQL Server Objects for the* AccountingServiceInstance *Machine*

Object Type	Name
Message type	[http://ssb.csharp.at/SSB_Book/c07/AccountingRequestMessage]
Message type	[http://ssb.csharp.at/SSB_Book/c07/AccountingResponseMessage]
Contract	[http://ssb.csharp.at/SSB_Book/c07/AccountingContract]
Queue	AccountingQueue
Service	AccountingService
Table	AccountingRecordings
Stored procedure	ProcessAccountingRequestMessages

Listing 7-5 shows the creation of the routes from OrderService to CreditCardService and AccountingService. You must run this T-SQL script on the SQL Server instance where OrderService is deployed (OrderServiceInstance).

Listing 7-5. *Setting Up the Routes from the* OrderService *to the Other Services*

```
CREATE ROUTE CreditCardServiceRoute
    WITH SERVICE_NAME = 'CreditCardService',
    ADDRESS = 'TCP://CreditCardServiceInstance:4741'
GO

CREATE ROUTE AccountingServiceRoute
    WITH SERVICE_NAME = 'AccountingService',
    ADDRESS = 'TCP://AccountingServiceInstance:4742'
GO
```

Listing 7-6 shows the creation of the returning route from the CreditCardService and the AccountingService back to the OrderService. You must create this route both on the CreditCardServiceInstance and AccountingServiceInstance.

Listing 7-6. *Setting Up the Route from the* CreditCardService *and from the* AccountingService *to the* OrderService

```
CREATE ROUTE OrderServiceRoute
    WITH SERVICE_NAME = 'OrderService',
    ADDRESS = 'TCP://OrderServiceInstance:4740'
GO
```

Establishing a Communication Channel

You've now created all the necessary routes between the Service Broker services that are deployed on different physical machines. However, if you try to send a message, it won't work. There are two important reasons why:

- You haven't yet configured the needed Service Broker endpoints.

- You haven't yet set up security between the different deployed Service Broker services.

In this section, I'll show you how you can create the Service Broker endpoints needed for the communication in this distributed Service Broker sample. As mentioned at the beginning of this chapter, Service Broker uses TCP/IP. A TCP/IP connection is able to multiplex several dialogs over a single connection. In Listings 7-5 and 7-6, you saw that each network address in the CREATE ROUTE statement also consists of a port number. This is the port number where the other Service Broker endpoint is listening for incoming TCP/IP connections from other Service Broker services. For the sample application, you need three different endpoints. You need to deploy each endpoint at each of the three SQL Server instances (OrderServiceInstance, CreditCardServiceInstance, and AccountingServiceInstance):

- OrderServiceEndpoint listening on port 4740

- CreditCardServiceEndpoint listening on port 4741

- AccountingServiceEndpoint listening on port 4742

SERVICE BROKER ENDPOINTS

Currently, SQL Server 2008 only supports one Service Broker endpoint per instance. If you host multiple Service Broker services on one SQL Server instance, they will all share the same endpoint with the same port number. In such a case, you should choose a more generic name for the endpoint that doesn't have a naming relationship with a Service Broker service, such as in this case.

SQL Server 2008 offers the T-SQL statement CREATE ENDPOINT for the creation of a new endpoint inside the current SQL Server instance. Listing 7-7 shows the syntax for this T-SQL statement. This listing only includes the relevant options for Service Broker, because endpoints are also used for web services support and for database mirroring.

Listing 7-7. *Syntax for the* CREATE ENDPOINT *T-SQL Statement*

```
CREATE ENDPOINT endPointName [ AUTHORIZATION login ]
STATE = { STARTED | STOPPED | DISABLED }
AS TCP
(
    LISTENER_PORT = listenerPort
)
FOR SERVICE_BROKER
(
    [ AUTHENTICATION = { WINDOWS [ { NTLM | KERBEROS | NEGOTIATE } ]
    | CERTIFICATE certificate_name
    | WINDOWS  [ { NTLM | KERBEROS | NEGOTIATE } ] CERTIFICATE certificate_name
    | CERTIFICATE certificate_name WINDOWS [ { NTLM | KERBEROS | NEGOTIATE } ] } ]
```

```
[ , ENCRYPTION = { DISABLED | SUPPORTED | REQUIRED }
[ ALGORITHM { RC4 | AES | AES RC4 | RC4 AES } ] ]
[ , MESSAGE_FORWARDING = { ENABLED | DISABLED } ]
[ , MESSAGE_FORWARDING_SIZE = forward_size ]
)
```

Table 7-4 describes the several parameters for the `CREATE ENDPOINT` T-SQL statement.

Table 7-4. *Parameters for the* `CREATE ENDPOINT` *T-SQL Statement*

Parameter	Description
endPointName	The name assigned to the endpoint and used during updating and deleting.
AUTHORIZATION login	Must be a valid SQL Server or Windows login that is assigned to the created endpoint. If the AUTHORIZATION clause isn't specified, the caller of the CREATE ENDPOINT statement becomes the owner of the created endpoint.
STATE	Specifies the state of the endpoint when it is created. When the state isn't specified, the endpoint's state is set to STOPPED, which means the endpoint isn't started and is therefore unavailable for other clients.
LISTENER_PORT	The endpoint uses the specified port listening for incoming TCP/IP Service Broker connections. If not specified, the default port number is 4022.
AUTHENTICATION	With this clause, you set the TCP/IP authentication requirements for the incoming Service Broker connection. The default authentication is WINDOWS. Service Broker supports the authentication methods NTLM or Kerberos, or both.
ENCRYPTION	Indicates whether or not encryption is used.
MESSAGE_FORWARDING	Indicates whether message forwarding is enabled on this endpoint. Please refer to Chapter 11 for more information about message forwarding.
MESSAGE_FORWARDING_SIZE	If message forwarding is enabled, MESSAGE_FORWARDING_SIZE specifies the amount of storage (in MB) that is allocated for the message forwarding endpoint in the RAM.

Listing 7-8 creates the various endpoints used for the communication between the different Service Broker services. You have to create each endpoint on the correct machine.

Listing 7-8. *Setting Up the Needed Endpoints for the Service Broker Communication*

```
-- Create this endpoint on the machine OrderServiceInstance
CREATE ENDPOINT OrderServiceEndpoint
STATE = STARTED
AS TCP
(
    LISTENER_PORT = 4740
)
```

```
FOR SERVICE_BROKER
(
   AUTHENTICATION = WINDOWS
)
GO

-- Create this endpoint on the machine CreditCardServiceInstance
CREATE ENDPOINT CreditCardServiceEndpoint
STATE = STARTED
AS TCP
(
   LISTENER_PORT = 4741
)
FOR SERVICE_BROKER

(
   AUTHENTICATION = WINDOWS
)
GO


-- Create this endpoint on the machine AccountingServiceInstance
CREATE ENDPOINT AccountingServiceEndpoint
STATE = STARTED
AS TCP
(
   LISTENER_PORT = 4742
)
FOR SERVICE_BROKER
(
   AUTHENTICATION = WINDOWS
)
GO
```

As you can see in Listing 7-8, each endpoint is created for the TCP protocol. This is a restriction of Service Broker, because Service Broker currently supports only TCP connections. The next version of Service Broker may offer more available protocols. After you set up the endpoints, you must also make sure that SQL Server allows incoming connections for the SQL Server instance.

When you create a new SQL Server instance, incoming connections from other machines are prohibited and must be enabled explicitly.

Setting Up Security

After configuring the endpoints, you must set up security between the distributed Service Broker services. By default, Service Broker doesn't allow two Service Broker services to communicate without configured security. This is a server-hardening feature provided by Service Broker, so you can ensure that only allowed services can talk to a deployed Service Broker service on your production machine. When talking about security in Service Broker, you must differentiate between two different security modes:

- Transport security

- Dialog security

Service Broker uses transport security to secure the TCP/IP connection between two Service Brokers that are connected through a network. Dialog security, on the other hand, secures each individual dialog between the Service Broker endpoints, regardless of how many networks the messages traverse as they travel between the conversation endpoints.

Transport security is easier to set up, while dialog security is significantly more efficient in complex networks where messages traverse multiple forwarding Service Brokers. In some cases where the highest level of security is required, using both may be appropriate. Because I want to make the distributed Service Broker application in this chapter as simple as possible, I will only demonstrate how to set up transport security. You'll learn more about dialog security in the next chapter.

Setting Up Windows-Based Transport Security

Transport security secures the TCP/IP connection between two SQL Server instances on different machines. Transport security covers the following two parts:

- Authentication

- Encryption

Authentication makes sure that each SQL Server instance knows the identity of the other SQL Server instance. Furthermore, both SQL Server instances must agree that they can talk with each other. Encryption defines whether the messages sent over the wire are encrypted. Authentication is always needed by a distributed Service Broker application where encryption is optional.

Service Broker offers two types of connection authentication: Windows and certificate-based authentication. Windows authentication uses the normal Windows authentication protocols such as NTLM or Kerberos to establish authentication between the two endpoints of the connection. Certificate-based authentication uses the Transport Layer Security (TLS) authentication protocol to authenticate the two endpoints. In general, you should use Windows authentication if both endpoints are in the same Windows domain, and you must use certificate-based authentication if the endpoints are in different Windows domains. Let's take a look at how to set up Windows authentication used by the transport security for your distributed Service Broker application.

In general, you can use Windows authentication only if a Windows domain is available and both SQL Server instances are registered in the same domain. It would even work if you have a trusted relationship between two Windows domains. When your SQL Server service account is LocalSystem or Network Service, then Windows authentication through Kerberos is the only option for you. You can use NTLM to authenticate these accounts. Kerberos authentication requires the registration of a Service Principal Name (SPN). You have to register this SPN using a tool such as setspn.exe, and the format of the SPN requested by Service Broker is MSSQLSvc/<MachineName>:<BrokerPort>.

If your network doesn't have Kerberos, you'll need to either run the SQL Server instance with a domain user account as the service account or use certificate-based authentication as already mentioned. For this sample, you can assume that Kerberos isn't available, so you must run both SQL Server instances with a domain user account that you can create inside the Computer Management Microsoft Management Console (MMC) snap-in. Table 7-5 shows the domain user accounts for each SQL Server machine.

Table 7-5. *The Domain User Accounts for the Various SQL Server Machines*

Machine	Domain User Account
OrderServiceInstance	OrderLogin
CreditCardServiceInstance	CreditCardLogin
AccountingServiceInstance	AccountingLogin

After you set up the domain user accounts, you have to use the Services MMC snap-in to configure SQL Server so that the new domain user account is used as the service account with which SQL Server is started. See Figure 7-3.

Figure 7-3. *Configuring the SQL Server service account*

After configuring the new SQL Server service accounts for each SQL Server machine, you now have to create SQL Server logins for the SQL Server that communicates with you. Note that this login represents the service account of the remote SQL Server machine, not the service account of the instance where you're creating the Service Broker endpoint. Figure 7-4 illustrates this.

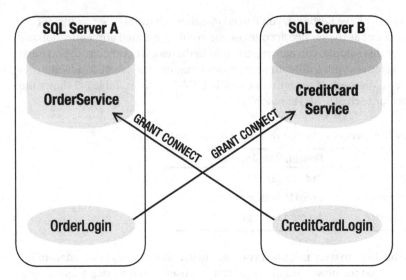

Figure 7-4. *Configuring Windows-based transport security*

Listing 7-9 shows how to add the necessary SQL Server logins to the master database.

■**Note** Please make sure to set up the necessary Service Broker services. Refer to the T-SQL scripts for this chapter in the Source Code/Download area of the Apress website (http://www.apress.com).

Listing 7-9. *Adding the Required SQL Server Logins*

```
-- Execute this T-SQL batch on machine OrderServiceInstance
USE master
GO

CREATE LOGIN [DOMAIN\CreditCardLogin] FROM WINDOWS
CREATE LOGIN [DOMAIN\AccountingLogin] FROM WINDOWS
GO

-- Execute this T-SQL batch on machine CreditCardServiceInstance
USE master
GO

CREATE LOGIN [DOMAIN\OrderLogin] FROM WINDOWS
GO
```

```
-- Execute this T-SQL batch on machine AccountingServiceInstance
USE master
GO

CREATE LOGIN [DOMAIN\OrderLogin] FROM WINDOWS
GO
```

You now must authorize the remote SQL Server machine to connect to the endpoint of
the local SQL Server machine by granting the login the CONNECT permission to the previously
created endpoint. Listing 7-10 shows this step.

Listing 7-10. *Granting the* CONNECT *Permission to the SQL Server Login*

```
-- Execute this T-SQL batch on machine OrderServiceInstance
USE master
GO

GRANT CONNECT ON ENDPOINT::OrderServiceEndpoint TO [DOMAIN\CreditCardLogin]
GRANT CONNECT ON ENDPOINT::OrderServiceEndpoint TO [DOMAIN\AccountingLogin]
GO

-- Execute this T-SQL batch on machine CreditCardServiceInstance
USE master
GO

GRANT CONNECT ON ENDPOINT::CreditCardServiceEndpoint TO [DOMAIN\OrderLogin]
GO

-- Granting the SEND permission
USE Chapter7_CreditCardService
GO

GRANT SEND ON SERVICE::[CreditCardService] TO PUBLIC
GO

-- Execute this T-SQL batch on machine AccountingServiceInstance
USE master
GO

GRANT CONNECT ON ENDPOINT::AccountingServiceEndpoint TO [DOMAIN\OrderLogin]
GO

-- Granting the SEND permission
USE Chapter7_AccountingService
GO

GRANT SEND ON SERVICE::[AccountingService] TO PUBLIC
GO
```

As you can see in Listing 7-10, you must also grant the SEND permission to the PUBLIC database role, so that the messages can be exchanged between the Service Broker services. This is only necessary for anonymous dialogs or dialogs without configured dialog security. You'll learn more about anonymous dialogs and dialog security in the next chapter.

You can now initiate a Service Broker conversation between your distributed deployed Service Broker services. Listing 7-11 shows the code to send a message.

Listing 7-11. *Starting a Conversation with Distributed Deployed Service Broker Services*

```
BEGIN TRANSACTION
    DECLARE @ch UNIQUEIDENTIFIER
    DECLARE @msg NVARCHAR(MAX);

    BEGIN DIALOG CONVERSATION @ch
        FROM SERVICE [ClientService]
        TO SERVICE 'OrderService'
        ON CONTRACT [http://ssb.csharp.at/SSB_Book/c07/OrderContract]
        WITH ENCRYPTION = OFF;

    SET @msg =
        '<OrderRequest>
            <Customer>
                <CustomerID>4242</CustomerID>
            </Customer>
            <Product>
                <ProductID>123</ProductID>
                <Quantity>5</Quantity>
                <Price>40.99</Price>
            </Product>
            <CreditCard>
                <Holder>Klaus Aschenbrenner</Holder>
                <Number>1234-1234-1234-1234</Number>
                <ValidThrough>2009-10</ValidThrough>
            </CreditCard>
            <Shipping>
                <Name>Klaus Aschenbrenner</Name>
                <Address>Wagramer Strasse 4/803</Address>
                <ZipCode>1220</ZipCode>
                <City>Vienna</City>
                <Country>Austria</Country>
            </Shipping>
        </OrderRequest>';

    SEND ON CONVERSATION @ch MESSAGE TYPE
        [http://ssb.csharp.at/SSB_Book/c07/OrderRequestMessage] (@msg);

COMMIT;
GO
```

The code in Listing 7-11 doesn't differ from the sending code you've used throughout this book. The only difference is in the configuration, because now Service Broker finds routing information when the classifier searches for the target network address of the requested Service Broker services. You don't have to change anything in your service implementation. Distributing Service Broker services to different machines is only a configuration issue. Easy, isn't it?

Setting Up Certificate-Based Transport Security

The other option that Service Broker provides for transport security is based on certificates. Windows-based transport security works well if both endpoints are in the same Windows domain. However, if they're in different domains, setup can be complex, and authentication can be very slow. It's rare that both Service Broker services are in the same domain when you communicate with your trading partners. In these cases, you should use certificate-based transport security. Before I go into the details of certificate-based transport security, I'll give you a short introduction to certificates, because this was a new feature first introduced with SQL Server 2005.

Certificates

One of the new features in SQL Server 2008 was the ability to create and store certificates inside a SQL Server database. Most modern distributed systems use certificates to establish user identity. If you've set up secure websites or web services, you're probably familiar with certificate authorities and trust chains.

For Service Broker, however, a certificate is a handy container for public-key/private-key pairs. I'll talk more about keys in the next section, but for now, it's sufficient to know that a certificate contains a key and that you can use the key to prove who you are to a remote user. For some scenarios, Service Broker uses certificates to authenticate the identity of the user who sent a message instead of using a password, as most other SQL Server features do. To see why this is, imagine sending a Service Broker message to a remote service that might be down, or perhaps to a batch service that only runs at night. This is no problem for Service Broker, because messages are persisted and reliably delivered.

The problem, though, is in how Service Broker can access the password for authenticating the other user who started the conversation. In fact, there is no way to access that password automatically in the background if no user is present. Therefore, you can only use certificates with Service Broker that are encrypted with the database master key. If you use certificates encrypted with a password, Service Broker doesn't allow you to use a certificate with a password when no database master key is present.

Public and Private Keys

Normally, you use the same key to lock and unlock things. Public and private keys (also called asymmetric keys) are different: there are two keys, and what you lock with one key can only be unlocked with the other key. If I encrypt something with my private key, you can decrypt it with my public key. If you encrypt something with my public key, only I can decrypt it, because I'm the only person who has my private key.

You can use this unique property of asymmetric keys to establish a secure communication channel. I can send my public key out to you and anyone else who wants to send me data securely. You can then encrypt the data with my public key and send it to me, secure in the knowledge that only I can decrypt it because only I have the corresponding private key. If you send me your public key, I can in turn send you data that only you can decrypt. As long as we are both careful to be sure that our private keys remain secret, we can reliably establish each other's identity through the exchange of public keys.

Service Broker just relies on the public key/private key aspect of certificates and not on building trust chains. In order to establish identity, each endpoint must have the opposite endpoint's public key. Whether that public key is obtained from a certificate authority or exchanged via email is a detail left up to the people deploying the system. You tell Service Broker which keys to use, and Service Broker uses them to securely establish identity.

Symmetric Keys

Using asymmetric keys to reliably establish identity and encrypt messages works conceptually, but in reality, it's not practical. The reason is that using asymmetric keys to encrypt and decrypt data is very slow. Sending a few megabytes of data using asymmetric keys can take hours. On the other hand, symmetric key encryption and decryption is very fast, but it's not so secure because you encrypt and decrypt data with the same key.

The disadvantage of symmetric keys is that both ends of the conversation must have the same key. Transferring a symmetric key between both endpoints is risky, because if it's intercepted, a hacker can decrypt all the information sent using the key. To get both the speed advantages of symmetric keys and the security advantages of asymmetric keys, Service Broker uses asymmetric keys to securely exchange a symmetric key, which can then be used to encrypt the messages exchanged between two endpoints. This concept is referred to as *hybrid encryption*.

Certificate-Based Transport Security

As you learned earlier, two systems can authenticate each other if each one has a certificate with its own private key and another certificate with the opposite endpoint's public key. Any data encrypted with the private key at one endpoint can only be decrypted with the corresponding public key at the opposite endpoint. Two endpoints can use this technique to securely establish each other's identity. One endpoint encrypts some data with its private key, and the opposite endpoint decrypts this data with the first endpoint's public key. If the data decrypts successfully, the decrypting endpoint knows that only the endpoint that owns the private key could have encrypted it.

When this exchange happens in both directions, both endpoints can be sure that they are talking to the opposite endpoint they expect. The advantage of this method is that authentication only requires the certificates. There is no need for the endpoints to contact a domain controller, as they need to do with Windows-based transport security. Each endpoint requires two certificates for this key exchange to succeed:

- The endpoint's own private key

- The corresponding public key of the opposite endpoint

This is a total of seven keys for the distributed Service Broker application. `OrderService` has its private key and the public keys of `CreditCardService` and `AccountingService`. `CreditCardService` and `AccountingService` have their own private keys and the public key of `OrderService`. Figure 7-5 shows these seven certificates and how they relate to each endpoint.

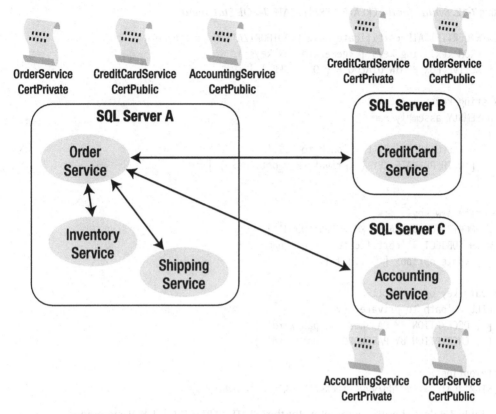

Figure 7-5. *Certificate-based transport security*

The private key certificate is associated with the endpoint, and the public key certificate is owned by a user that has the CONNECT permission on the endpoint. If you want to allow any Service Broker to connect to this SQL Server instance, you can grant the CONNECT permission to the PUBLIC database role. In this case, authentication between the two SQL Server instances will still be done, but if the authentication succeeds, the connection will be allowed unconditionally. This is useful when all the connecting machines are located in the same trusted network, and network security will prevent connections from untrusted machines.

Let's now look at how to set up certificate-based transport security with Service Broker. To simplify the example, you use certificates that are generated with SQL Server 2008. However, you can also use certificates obtained from a certificate authority or your organization. To create a certificate, SQL Server 2008 provides the CREATE CERTIFICATE T-SQL statement. Listing 7-12 shows the syntax for this statement.

Listing 7-12. *Syntax for the* CREATE CERTIFICATE *T-SQL Statement*

```
CREATE CERTIFICATE certificate_name [ AUTHORIZATION user_name ]
   { FROM <existing_keys | <generate_new_keys }
   [ ACTIVE FOR BEGIN DIALOG = { ON | OFF } ]

<existing_keys> ::=
   ASSEMBLY assembly_name
   | {
      [ EXECUTABLE ] FILE = 'path_to_file'
      [ WITH PRIVATE KEY ( <private_key_options> ) ]
   }

<generate_new_keys> ::=
   [ ENCRYPTION BY PASSWORD = 'password' ]
   WITH SUBJECT = 'certificate_subject_name'
   [ , <date_option> [ ,...n ] ]

<private_key_options> ::=
   FILE = 'path_to_private_key'
   [ , DECRYPTION BY PASSWORD = 'password' ]
   [ , ENCRYPTION BY PASSWORD = 'password' ]

<date_options> ::=
   START_DATE = 'mm/dd/yyy' | EXPIRY_DATE = 'mm/dd/yyyy'
```

Table 7-6 describes the parameters for the CREATE CERTIFICATE T-SQL statement.

Table 7-6. *Parameters for the* CREATE CERTIFICATE *T-SQL Statement*

Parameter	Description
certificate_name	Indicates the name under which the certificate is stored and referenced inside the database.
AUTHORIZATION user_name	Specifies the name of the user that owns this certificate.
[EXECUTABLE] FILE = 'path_to_file'	Specifies the complete path (including the file name) to a file that contains a Distinguished Encoding Rules (DER)-encoded certificate. path_to_file can be a local path, a Universal Naming Convention (UNC) file share, or a network location. The specified file is accessed under the security context of the SQL Server service account. Therefore, you must make sure that this account has the needed file system permissions to read the file.

Parameter	Description
WITH PRIVATE KEY	Specifies that the private key of the certificate is also imported in the database. You can only use this clause when the certificate is created from a file. If you want to load the private key of an assembly, use the ALTER CERTIFICATE T-SQL statement.
FILE = 'path_to_private_key'	Specifies the complete path (including the file name) to a private key file. path_to_private_key can be a local path, a UNC file share, or a network location. Service Broker accesses the specified file under the security context of the SQL Server service account. Therefore, you must make sure that this account has the needed file system permissions to read the file.
DECRYPTION BY PASSWORD = 'password'	Specifies the password that SQL Server uses to decrypt a private key loaded from a file. This clause is optional if the private key is protected by a null password. Be aware that saving a private key to a file without password protection is a dangerous risk. If the password is required and you don't supply one, the statement will fail.
ENCRYPTION BY PASSWORD = 'password'	Specifies the password used to encrypt the private key of the created certificate. If you omit this clause, the private key will be encrypted with the database master key of the current database. If you specify a password, the password must meet the configured password complexity policy.
SUBJECT = 'certificate_subject_name'	Specifies the subject of the certificate as defined in the X.509 standard. A specified subject can be up to 4,096 bytes long. If the subject is longer, SQL Server will truncate it.
START_DATE = 'mm/dd/yyyy'	Specifies the start date of the certificate when it will become valid. START_DATE must be set equal to the current date and can't be in the past.
EXPIRY_DATE = 'mm/dd/yyyy'	Specifies the expiration date of the certificate. If the clause is not specified, the EXPIRY_DATE is set to the date one year after START_DATE.
ACTIVE FOR BEGIN DIALOG	Makes the certificate available to the initiator of a Service Broker conversation. This clause is useful when you have to change a deployed certificate. Please refer to Chapter 8 for more information about this topic.

Listing 7-13 shows how to create the necessary certificates on each SQL Server machine. The code also exports the public key of each certificate in a file. The public key in the exported file can then be imported into other SQL Server machines to establish a trust relationship between the different deployed Service Broker services. As you can also see in Listing 7-13, each certificate must be created in the master database and associated with the Service Broker endpoint.

Listing 7-13. *Creating the Necessary Certificates to Establish a Trust Relationship Between the Service Broker Services*

```
-- Execute this T-SQL batch on OrderServiceInstance
USE master
GO

CREATE MASTER KEY ENCRYPTION BY PASSWORD = 'password1!'
GO

CREATE CERTIFICATE OrderServiceCertPrivate
   WITH SUBJECT = 'For Service Broker authentication',
   START_DATE = '01/01/2007'
GO

-- Create the Service Broker endpoint
CREATE ENDPOINT OrderServiceEndpoint
STATE = STARTED
AS TCP
(
   LISTENER_PORT = 4740
)
FOR SERVICE_BROKER
(
   AUTHENTICATION = CERTIFICATE OrderServiceCertPrivate
)
GO

BACKUP CERTIFICATE OrderServiceCertPrivate
   TO FILE = 'c:\OrderServiceCertPublic.cert'
GO

-- Execute this T-SQL batch on CreditCardServiceInstance
USE master
GO

CREATE MASTER KEY ENCRYPTION BY PASSWORD = 'password1!'
GO

CREATE CERTIFICATE CreditCardServiceCertPrivate
   WITH SUBJECT = 'For Service Broker authentication',
   START_DATE = '01/01/2007'
GO
```

```
-- Create the Service Broker endpoint
CREATE ENDPOINT CreditCardServiceEndpoint
STATE = STARTED
AS TCP
(
    LISTENER_PORT = 4741
)
FOR SERVICE_BROKER
(
    AUTHENTICATION = CERTIFICATE CreditCardServiceCertPrivate
)
GO


BACKUP CERTIFICATE CreditCardServiceCertPrivate
    TO FILE = 'c:\CreditCardServiceCertPublic.cert'
GO


-- Execute this T-SQL batch on AccountingServiceInstance
USE master
GO


CREATE MASTER KEY ENCRYPTION BY PASSWORD = 'password1!'
GO


CREATE CERTIFICATE AccountingServiceCertPrivate
    WITH SUBJECT = 'For Service Broker authentication',
    START_DATE = '01/01/2007'
GO


-- Create the Service Broker endpoint
CREATE ENDPOINT AccountingServiceEndpoint
STATE = STARTED
AS TCP
(
    LISTENER_PORT = 4742
)
FOR SERVICE_BROKER
(
    AUTHENTICATION = CERTIFICATE AccountingServiceCertPrivate
)
GO


BACKUP CERTIFICATE AccountingServiceCertPrivate
    TO FILE = 'c:\AccountingServiceCertPublic.cert'
GO
```

All three Service Broker endpoints now have private keys associated with them. Now you have to introduce the endpoints to each other by exchanging the public keys. Whether you exchange the public keys via File Transfer Protocol (FTP), over email, or on a floppy disk is up to you. Once you've exchanged the public keys, all you have to do is associate them with a SQL Server login that has a CONNECT permission for the endpoint. Listing 7-14 shows how you can import the public keys of the opposite endpoint into the master database.

Listing 7-14. *Importing the Public Keys*

```
-- Execute this T-SQL batch on OrderServiceInstance
USE master
GO

CREATE LOGIN CreditCardServiceLogin WITH PASSWORD = 'password1!'
GO

CREATE USER CreditCardServiceUser FOR LOGIN CreditCardServiceLogin
GO

CREATE CERTIFICATE CreditCardServiceCertPublic
    AUTHORIZATION CreditCardServiceUser
    FROM FILE = 'c:\CreditCardServiceCertPublic.cert'
GO


GRANT CONNECT ON ENDPOINT::OrderServiceEndpoint TO CreditCardServiceLogin
GO

CREATE LOGIN AccountingServiceLogin WITH PASSWORD = 'password1!'
GO

CREATE USER AccountingServiceUser FOR LOGIN AccountingServiceLogin
GO

CREATE CERTIFICATE AccountingServiceCertPublic
    AUTHORIZATION AccountingServiceUser
    FROM FILE = 'c:\AccountingServiceCertPublic.cert'
GO

GRANT CONNECT ON ENDPOINT::OrderServiceEndpoint TO AccountingServiceLogin
GO

-- Execute this T-SQL batch on CreditCardServiceInstance and
-- AccountingServiceInstance
USE master
GO
```

```
CREATE LOGIN OrderServiceLogin WITH PASSWORD = 'password1!'
GO

CREATE USER OrderServiceUser FOR LOGIN OrderServiceLogin
GO

CREATE CERTIFICATE OrderServiceCertPublic
    AUTHORIZATION OrderServiceUser
    FROM FILE = 'c:\OrderServiceCertPublic.cert'
GO

-- Execute this T-SQL batch on CreditCardServiceInstance
GRANT CONNECT ON ENDPOINT::CreditCardServiceEndpoint TO OrderServiceLogin
GO

-- Execute this T-SQL batch on AccountingServiceInstance
GRANT CONNECT ON ENDPOINT::AccountingServiceEndpoint TO OrderServiceLogin
GO
```

To revoke a remote Service Broker service's right to connect to your SQL Server instance, just drop the user or deny the login connection permission on the endpoint. By now, you've set up the whole certificate-based transport security. You're now able to send messages between the different deployed Service Broker services by executing the sending code from Listing 7-11. Again, you didn't have to change the message-sending code and the service implementation to reflect the different deployment and the different security model. You did everything just by configuring the Service Broker services.

Summary

In this chapter, I introduced distributed Service Broker applications. When you distribute Service Broker services to different SQL Server machines (maybe because of scale-out scenarios), you only have to configure the Service Broker applications. You don't have to change any service implementation or the message-sending code. Service Broker accomplishes this with routes. A route defines on which network address a Service Broker service is physically available.

It doesn't matter whether a Service Broker service is deployed locally or on a remote machine connected through a LAN or WAN. After setting up all necessary routes, you have to create endpoints on each SQL Server machine. An endpoint enables another SQL Server instance to communicate with you over a TCP/IP connection. The underlying communication protocol of Service Broker (the ABP) is also able to multiplex several different Service Broker conversations over a single TCP/IP connection.

After you set up your Service Broker endpoints, you have to configure transport security. Service Broker offers you two different modes: Windows-based and certificate-based transport security. Certificate-based transport security provides you more flexibility, because Windows-based transport security only works when both Service Broker endpoints are located in the same Windows domain, which is seldom the case when you communicate with your trading partners.

By now, you've seen everything about Service Broker that you need to implement asynchronous, reliable, distributed, and secure message-based applications with Service Broker. This chapter is also the end of the first part of this book, which was devoted to the general Service Broker programming model. In the second part of this book, which starts with the next chapter about advanced distributed Service Broker programming, I'll show you more complex Service Broker scenarios.

In the next part, I'll cover advanced security configurations, using Service Broker as the message bus for SODA architectures, using Service Broker in real-world scenarios, and scaling out Service Broker applications to any required size. Finally, I'll end with a chapter about the administration of Service Broker applications. Stay tuned.

PART 2

■ ■ ■

Advanced Service Broker Programming

CHAPTER 8

■■■

Advanced Distributed Service Broker Programming

The first part of this book covered the general aspects of Service Broker programming. By now, you can implement asynchronous, reliable, secure, and distributed Service Broker applications. The second part of this book will concentrate on advanced areas of Service Broker programming. In this chapter, I'll build on Chapter 7 and investigate advanced distributed Service Broker scenarios. I'll cover the following topics:

- *Transport security*: Service Broker offers you additional transport security features, such as the LOCAL route and the TRANSPORT route.

- *Dialog security*: Dialog security secures complete dialogs from the initiator of the dialog to the target of the dialog. The difference from transport security is that dialog security works between dialog endpoints instead of between transport endpoints.

- *Encryption*: Service Broker can also encrypt messages to prevent them from being monitored. If you use encryption, you have two different options: transport encryption and dialog encryption.

- *Transport protocol*: Service Broker uses a TCP-based transport protocol (Adjacent Broker Protocol, or ABP) to exchange Service Broker messages between two endpoints. I'll show you how you can trace the TCP communication between two Service Broker endpoints.

- *Replacing certificates*: By default, certificates expire and become unusable. Service Broker provides features you can use to replace certificates when they expire. You must distinguish between certificates used for transport security and certificates used for dialog security.

- *Service Listing Manager*: Service Listing Manager is a graphical tool for the setup and configuration of Service Broker security. I'll introduce this tool and show how you can use it to set up transport security and dialog security.

Let's start with more details about transport security.

Transport Security

In addition to the transport security features mentioned in Chapter 7, Service Broker offers two more: LOCAL routes and TRANSPORT routes. These routes are known as *wildcard routes*. With these kinds of routes, you're able to implement more complex distributed Service Broker applications. On the other hand, encryption makes it possible to encrypt messages that are transferred between two Service Broker endpoints. I'll give you more information in the "Encryption" section.

A Service Broker component called a *classifier* uses a combination of the service name and the broker identifier to select the route to use for a message. If the classifier can't find an exact match for the service name and the broker identifier specified in the BEGIN DIALOG command, it will look for a wildcard route. A route with no broker instance specified will match any broker instance, and a route with no service name specified will match any service name.

LOCAL Route

Two addresses have special meaning for Service Broker routes. When the route for a service name has an address of LOCAL, the classifier will look for the service name in the local instance to find which queue to put the message in. The first priority is the database where the route is located. If the classifier doesn't find the service there, it checks the services list, which contains all the services available in the local SQL Server instance. Listing 8-1 shows how you can create a route with the LOCAL address.

Listing 8-1. *Creating a* LOCAL *Route*

```
CREATE ROUTE InventoryRoute
    WITH SERVICE_NAME = 'InventoryService'
    ADDRESS = 'LOCAL'
GO
```

One possible unforeseen consequence of using a LOCAL route is that if the service name isn't found in the current database and is available in more than one other database in the current SQL Server instance, the classifier will see this as a load-balancing scenario and will randomly pick one of the services as the target of the dialog. This usually isn't what the application intends and can lead to strange behaviors. To avoid this, I recommend using a route with a BROKER_INSTANCE parameter to ensure that the dialog target is the database you intend. Because this is a common issue, Service Broker implicitly routes local dialogs that have a BROKER_INSTANCE parameter to the specified database even if there isn't a route specified for the target service.

If you look in the sys.routes catalog view of a newly created database, you'll find a route called AutoCreatedLocal. This route has no service name or broker identifier and an address of LOCAL. This route is the one you've used in all the examples so far that were deployed to only one SQL Server instance. Because it is a wildcard route, the classifier uses this route for any service name that doesn't have another route available. This is why you haven't had to create routes for any of the examples you deployed to one SQL Server instance. The AutoCreatedLocal route was sufficient, because they all sent messages to local services. While this route makes developing simple applications easy, I recommend dropping it when you deploy your distributed Service

Broker application into production. Without a wildcard route, you can be sure that messages only go where you intend them to go. Listing 8-2 shows the definition of the AutoCreatedLocal route that is always present in a newly created SQL Server database.

Listing 8-2. *Definition of the* AutoCreatedLocal *Route*

```
CREATE ROUTE AutoCreatedLocal
    WITH ADDRESS = 'LOCAL'
GO
```

TRANSPORT Route

The following question often arises: "If a Service Broker application has several hundred dialog initiators opening dialogs with the same target, does the target need to have routes back to all the initiators?" The short answer to this question is yes. Fortunately, Service Broker has a way to make a single route work for all the return messages. This shortcut is the TRANSPORT route. If the classifier finds a wildcard route with a TRANSPORT address after failing to find a more specific route, it will try to use the service name from the dialog as a return address to the initiator of the conversation.

This sounds a little bit curious, but just think of a Smart Client scenario where hundreds of different deployed Smart Client applications want to access a Service Broker service. You also have the requirement that deploying a new Smart Client application be as easy as possible. Therefore, you don't want to add a route for each new Smart Client application on the SQL Server, where the consumed Service Broker service is deployed back to the initiator of the conversation—the Smart Client application.

In this case, you can embed the address of the return route to the Smart Client application in the name of the Service Broker service. Therefore, you don't need to add routes on the SQL Server where the target service is located. Let's say you want to deploy the ClientService from Chapter 6 to a SQL Express Edition that is used by a Smart Client application. Figure 8-1 shows the final architecture after the distribution of this service to SQL Express Edition.

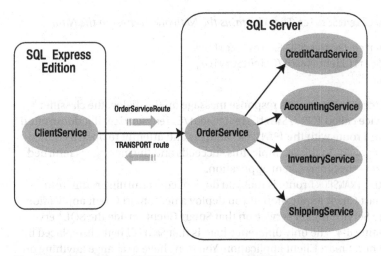

Figure 8-1. *Using the* TRANSPORT *route in a Smart Client scenario*

To configure this distributed scenario, follow these steps:

1. Create the endpoints on both SQL Server instances.

2. Configure the necessary routes between the ClientService and the OrderService.

3. Change the service name of the ClientService to include the network address in its name.

4. Set up transport security.

Because I've already talked about creating endpoints and setting up transport security in Chapter 7, I want to concentrate now on steps 2 and 3—configuring the Service Broker routes and changing the service name of ClientService. Listing 8-3 shows the code you need to set up the routes between ClientService and OrderService.

Listing 8-3. *Creating the Necessary Routes*

```
-- Execute this T-SQL batch on the SQL Express Edition
CREATE ROUTE OrderServiceRoute
    WITH SERVICE_NAME = 'OrderService',
    ADDRESS = 'TCP://OrderServiceInstance:4740'
GO

-- Execute this T-SQL batch on the OrderServiceInstance
CREATE ROUTE ClientServiceTransportRoute
    WITH ADDRESS = 'TRANSPORT'
GO
```

The returning route from OrderService uses the TRANSPORT address. This indicates to Service Broker that it needs to retrieve the complete returning route from the service name of the initiator service. Therefore, you have to change the name of the ClientService in the second step (see Listing 8-4).

Listing 8-4. *Creating a New* ClientService *That Contains the Network Address in the Name*

```
-- Execute this T-SQL batch on the SQL Express Edition
CREATE SERVICE [TCP://SmartClient1:4001/ClientService]
    ON QUEUE [ClientQueue]
```

When the OrderService needs to send a response message on the dialog, the classifier looks for a route for a service called TCP://SmartClient1:4001/ClientService. If it doesn't find one, it will find the wildcard route with the TRANSPORT address and attempt to open a connection to TCP://SmartClient1:4001. In this example, this succeeds and the message is returned successfully to the initiator—the Smart Client application.

The huge benefit of the TRANSPORT route is that you don't need a returning route from OrderService for each Smart Client application. If you deploy a new Smart Client application, you just have to create the Service Broker service on that Smart Client (inside the SQL Server Express Edition), as in Listing 8-4. The only difference here is that SmartClient1 is replaced by the NetBIOS name of the new Smart Client application. You don't have to change anything on the SQL Server instance where OrderService is deployed (when anonymous transport security is enabled). Easy, isn't it?

You can also use a TRANSPORT route in the TO SERVICE clause of the BEGIN DIALOG T-SQL statement. This allows ad hoc connections to services without creating the routing infrastructure normally required. The biggest disadvantage of using transport routes is that the address is embedded in the service name, so you can't move the service to another server without destroying all existing dialogs to the moved service. If you move the service, the service will be available on a different network address, and you must also reflect this change in the service name. So you have to change the service implementation.

Dialog Security

The default security model options that Service Broker provides for data sent between two connected Service Broker endpoints are adequate for most applications, but for certain applications, you may need to use dialog security in addition to transport security. This section explains what dialog security is and when you should consider using it in addition to transport security.

As the name implies, you use dialog security to secure complete dialogs, from the initiator of the dialog to the target of the dialog. The security features are similar to transport security: authentication, message integrity, and encryption. The difference is that dialog security works between dialog endpoints instead of between transport endpoints. This means that dialog messages that are routed through a complex network topology of different Service Broker forwarders to reach their final destination are encrypted at one of the dialog endpoints and decrypted at the other endpoint.

When you use dialog security, the messages going from the initiator to the target are encrypted at the initiator and decrypted at the target. If you use transport security instead, the messages will be decrypted and reencrypted at each forwarder, so the message will be encrypted and decrypted three times in route. The extra overhead can cause significant delays and increase processing loads.

Dialog security also provides authentication at the dialog level. This means that two services engaging in a dialog can reliably know that the service they are talking to is exactly who they think it is. Authentication is a harder problem in asynchronous dialogs than it is with normal connection-oriented network protocols. Dialogs are persistent and can last through multiple database server restarts, moving the database to a different server, failovers, and so on. Dialogs may last for years. Maintaining secure communication between dialog endpoints under these circumstances requires a different kind of security protocol.

Service Broker Security Protocol

Before getting into how to configure and manage dialog security, let's spend a little time understanding the basic security protocol used by Service Broker. Dialog authentication uses certificates to authenticate the endpoints with each other. The way this works is a little different from the certificate-based authentication approach used by the Service Broker transport security model. This difference occurs because dialog endpoints are authenticated with each other once, and this authentication lasts for the lifetime of the dialog. The asynchronous nature of dialogs also means that it's possible that the two services communicating over a dialog may never be running at the same time, so connection-oriented protocols won't work.

Dialog authentication requires a total of four certificates. Each SQL Server instance has its own private key certificate and a certificate with the public key of the opposite SQL Server instance. Because dialogs only exist between two endpoints, only these four certificates are required. The initiator of the dialog encrypts some data with both its own private key and the target endpoint's public key. This encrypted data is sent to the target in the header of the first dialog message. When this message arrives at the target endpoint, the public and private keys corresponding to the keys used to encrypt the data are used to decrypt it. If it is decrypted successfully, the two endpoints have reliably established each other's identity, because only the four keys at these two endpoints could have successfully encrypted and decrypted the data.

As mentioned in the previous chapter, asymmetric key encryption and decryption are expensive operations. If you used them every time a dialog was established, Service Broker throughput would degrade. To get around this problem, part of the data encrypted and decrypted during the authentication process is a symmetric key called the *key exchange key* (KEK). Once the KEK has been reliably transferred between the initiator and the target of the dialog, the two endpoints have a shared secret (the KEK) that only the two of them know. The shared KEK can be used to transfer more data between the two endpoints. Successfully transferring this data can now be used to establish the identities of the endpoints, because only the endpoints sharing this symmetric key can successfully encrypt and decrypt the data.

Using the KEK to establish authentication means that you only need to use the asymmetric key encryption and decryption when a new KEK must be exchanged. Because the KEK is cached in memory, the KEK must be reestablished whenever the database is restarted. The KEK also expires periodically, and a new KEK is created and exchanged. The KEK is transferred with the first message of every dialog so that it is always available when required.

The data transferred with the KEK is the session key for the dialog. The session key is the symmetric key used to encrypt and sign every message sent on the dialog. The initiator generates a session key, encrypts it with the KEK, and sends it to the target in the header of the first message. The target generates another session key and sends it back to the initiator in the header of the first message in that direction. I haven't discussed anonymous dialogs yet, but you should understand that an anonymous dialog uses the same session key in both directions.

To summarize, the dialog initiator generates a KEK if one isn't already available for the target and signs it with the initiator's private key. It then encrypts it with the target's public key. A session key is generated and encrypted with the KEK. The encrypted keys are copied into the header of the first message and cached locally. The KEK is stored in memory and never written to disk. The session key is encrypted with the database master key and stored in the conversation endpoint table. The KEK encrypted with the public key and private key is also cached in memory, so that Service Broker can use it in other messages without redoing the asymmetric encryption. The message is then hashed, signed, and encrypted with the session key and given to the transmission layer for transport to the target endpoint.

When the message arrives at the target endpoint, Service Broker checks its cache for the KEK used in the message. If it isn't already cached, the encrypted KEK from the message header is decrypted with the public key and the private key from the local certificates and is cached in memory. Service Broker decrypts the session key with the KEK, stores it in the conversation endpoint table, and uses it to decrypt and verify the sent message. When the first message is sent back to the initiator, a new session key for the return direction is generated, encrypted with the KEK, and used to sign and encrypt the return message.

The initiator includes the security header with the keys in every message it sends until it receives a message from the target. Once the first message is received from the target, the initiator can be sure that the target has the proper session key. The security header isn't then sent in subsequent messages. Messages include a timestamp and are valid for 30 seconds after they are sent. In reality, this time is 30 minutes and 30 seconds, because a 30-minute allowance for clock synchronization between the message sender and receiver is included in the time-out. KEKs are valid for six hours from the time they are generated. This time might be different from the time they are stored in memory.

Service Broker provides two types of dialog security: full dialog security and anonymous dialog security.

Full Dialog Security

Full dialog security helps to protect the initiating service from sending messages to an untrusted database and helps to protect the target service from receiving messages from an untrusted database. Service Broker encrypts messages transmitted over the network when the conversation uses full security.

Full security provides identification for both the initiating service and the target service. Full security requires that the initiating service trust the target service and also requires that the target service trust the initiating service. You can establish trust by exchanging certificates that contain public keys. For full dialog security, each side of the conversation contains a private key for a local user and a public key for a remote user. The database that hosts the initiating service contains a *remote service binding*.

The remote service binding specifies the local user who owns the certificate that corresponds to the private key in the remote database. Therefore, operations on behalf of the initiating service run as the designated user in the target database. The target database contains a user who owns a certificate that corresponds to a private key that is owned by the user who owns the initiating service. Therefore, operations on behalf of the target service run in the initiating database as the user who owns the initiating service.

Anonymous Dialog Security

Anonymous dialog security helps protect the initiating service against sending messages to an untrusted database. Service Broker encrypts messages transmitted over the network when the conversation uses anonymous security. Anonymous security identifies the target service to the initiating service, but doesn't identify the initiating service to the target service.

Because the target service can't verify the identity of the initiating service, operations on behalf of the initiating service run as members of the fixed [PUBLIC] database role in the target database. The target database receives no information about the user who initiated the conversation. The target database doesn't need to contain a certificate for the user who initiates the conversation. For dialogs that use anonymous security, both sides of the conversation use the session key generated by the initiating database. The target database doesn't return a session key to the initiating database.

Configuration

In the previous sections, you learned the theory about dialog security. In this section, I'll show you step by step how to configure full dialog security to secure the communication over a Service Broker conversation.

One important thing to know about dialog security is that you always need to set up transport security, because it establishes a secure communication channel between two Service Broker endpoints and allows two SQL Server instances to authenticate and authorize each other. Transport security also provides functionalities to protect and encrypt messages between two SQL Server instances.

In this example, let's use the OrderService sample application from Chapter 6 as a foundation and extend it to use dialog security for a secure exchange of dialog messages. You'll want to distribute CreditCardService and AccountingService to different SQL Server instances and set up dialog security between OrderService and the other two distributed Service Broker services. Figure 8-2 shows the architecture that you want to achieve with the distribution of the Service Broker services. As an additional exercise, you can distribute the other used Service Broker services (InventoryService and ShippingService) to different physical SQL Server machines and configure the needed security settings on your own.

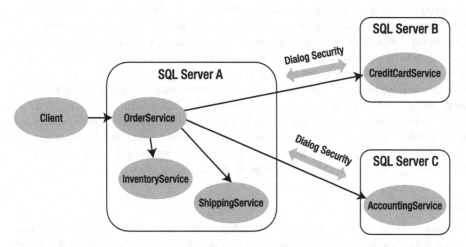

Figure 8-2. *Dialog security architecture*

When you set up transport security for this sample application, you'll use another option for certificate-based authentication. Service Broker allows you to grant the CONNECT permission of the endpoint to the [PUBLIC] database role. In this case, you don't need to deploy the certificate with the public key of the opposite endpoint to the local master database. This feature is needed to cover a scenario like an online shop.

Just imagine that an online shop offers a Service Broker service with which you can order products from the shop's website in a reliable manner. In this case, the Service Broker endpoint of the online shop must be able to authenticate millions of different users. The administrator of this Service Broker endpoint must deploy millions of certificates with the public key of each potential user and must configure the needed security settings (granting the CONNECT permission on that endpoint). Because of this, you can grant the CONNECT permission of the Service Broker endpoint to the [PUBLIC] database role. In this case, any incoming connection is authorized automatically, and you don't have to deploy the other endpoint's public key certificate.

Setting Up Anonymous Transport Security

If you set up anonymous transport security, you have to perform the following steps:

1. *Set up the certificate*: You have to create a certificate in the master database that holds the private key used for transport security.

2. *Set up the endpoint*: You have to create a Service Broker endpoint and authorize it on the previously created certificate.

3. *Grant permissions*: Finally, you grant the CONNECT permission on the created Service Broker endpoint to the [PUBLIC] database role.

Listing 8-5 shows the needed code for the initiator's endpoint, the OrderService.

Listing 8-5. *Setting Up Anonymous Transport Security on the Initiator's Side*

```
-- Execute this T-SQL batch on the OrderServiceInstance
USE master
GO

CREATE MASTER KEY ENCRYPTION BY PASSWORD = 'password1!'
GO

CREATE CERTIFICATE OrderServiceTransportCertPrivate
   WITH SUBJECT = 'For Service Broker authentication',
   START_DATE = '01/01/2008'
GO

-- Create the Service Broker endpoint
CREATE ENDPOINT OrderServiceEndpoint
STATE = STARTED
AS TCP
(
   LISTENER_PORT = 4740
)
FOR SERVICE_BROKER
(
   AUTHENTICATION = CERTIFICATE OrderServiceTransportCertPrivate
)
GO

-- Everyone (anonymous security) can now connect to this Service Broker endpoint!!!
GRANT CONNECT ON ENDPOINT::OrderServiceEndpoint TO [PUBLIC]
GO
```

Listing 8-6 shows the code needed on the SQL Server machine where the CreditCardService is hosted to set up anonymous transport security. The same code with the object names adjusted appropriately must be also executed on the SQL Server machine where AccountingService is deployed.

Listing 8-6. *Setting Up Anonymous Transport Security on the Target's Side*

```
-- Execute this T-SQL batch on the CreditCardInstance
USE master
GO

CREATE MASTER KEY ENCRYPTION BY PASSWORD = 'password1!'
GO

CREATE CERTIFICATE CreditCardServiceTransportCertPrivate
   WITH SUBJECT = 'For Service Broker authentication',
   START_DATE = '01/01/2008'
GO


-- Create the Service Broker endpoint
CREATE ENDPOINT CreditCardServiceEndpoint
STATE = STARTED
AS TCP
(
   LISTENER_PORT = 4741
)
FOR SERVICE_BROKER
(
   AUTHENTICATION = CERTIFICATE CreditCardServiceTransportCertPrivate
)
GO

-- Everyone (anonymous security) can now connect to this Service Broker endpoint!!!
GRANT CONNECT ON ENDPOINT::CreditCardServiceEndpoint TO [PUBLIC]
GO
```

As soon as you execute these T-SQL batches on each SQL Server machine, anonymous transport security is set up and ready to use. As you can see, you don't need to import the public key certificate from the opposite Service Broker endpoint when you use anonymous transport security. However, keep in mind that everyone is now able to connect to both Service Broker endpoints.

Setting Up Full Dialog Security

After you set up transport security, you can send messages between the Service Broker endpoints. The only disadvantage of transport security occurs when a message is forwarded through multiple Service Broker forwarders. In this case, Service Broker must encrypt and decrypt each sent message at each forwarder—and this stuff can hurt your overall Service Broker performance.

For this reason, Service Broker includes dialog security. With dialog security, you have the chance to encrypt the message once at the initiator and decrypt it finally only at the target of the conversation. When such a message passes a Service Broker forwarder, nothing happens (no decryption and encryption), because all necessary information (such as the final destination of the message) is stored in the header of the message, and the header isn't encrypted.

Let's look at how to set up dialog security for Service Broker conversations. Dialog security requires four certificates to secure a dialog: one public key and one private key for each direction. In this section, you'll learn how to create the certificates and the users required to make dialog security work. Figure 8-3 shows the SQL Server objects you must create for dialog security. The main difference from transport security is that the needed certificates are associated with database users instead of database logins.

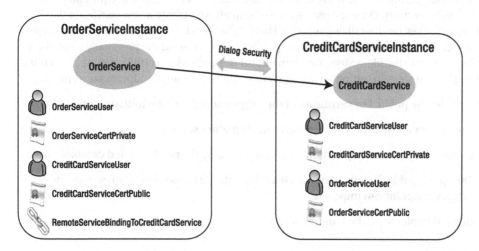

Figure 8-3. *Setting up dialog security*

Security configuration normally starts at the target endpoint. The target endpoint provides the service to one or more initiator endpoints. You set up the target once when the service is deployed, and you set up the initiator on any database that uses the service supplied by the target. Listing 8-7 shows the T-SQL code you need to create the database user who represents the CreditCardService.

Listing 8-7. *Dialog Security on the Target Service*

```
CREATE USER CreditCardServiceUser WITHOUT LOGIN
GO

-- Grant the CONTROL permission
GRANT CONTROL ON SERVICE::CreditCardService TO CreditCardServiceUser
GO

CREATE MASTER KEY ENCRYPTION BY PASSWORD = 'password1!'
GO
```

```
CREATE CERTIFICATE CreditCardServiceCertPrivate
   AUTHORIZATION CreditCardServiceUser
   WITH SUBJECT = 'Private certificate for CreditCardService',
   START_DATE = '01/01/2008'
GO

BACKUP CERTIFICATE CreditCardServiceCertPrivate
   TO FILE = 'c:\CreditCardServiceCertPublic.cert'
GO
```

The CREATE USER T-SQL statement creates a new database user who represents the user for the CreditCardService. You create the user with no login so that you can move the database between servers or duplicate it without moving the logins between servers. In the next step, you grant the CONTROL permission to this user on the CreditCardService. This is a requirement when you set up dialog security. Once the user setup is complete, you create a new certificate that stores the private key used for dialog security. This certificate is owned by the previously created database user. In the last step, you export the public key certificate of the previously created certificate and store it in the file system. You then import this public key certificate on the initiator's endpoint. The next steps in setting up dialog security on the initiator's endpoint are as follows:

1. Transfer the public key certificate of the target endpoint to the initiator's endpoint.

2. Create a database user who represents the initiator's service.

3. Create a new private key certificate that is owned by the newly created database user.

4. Dump the public key of the newly created certificate to the file system so that the target's endpoint can import it.

Listing 8-8 implements the required steps.

Listing 8-8. *Dialog Security on the Initiator Service*

```
CREATE USER OrderServiceUser WITHOUT LOGIN
GO

ALTER AUTHORIZATION ON SERVICE::OrderService TO OrderServiceUser
GO

CREATE MASTER KEY ENCRYPTION BY PASSWORD = 'password1!'
GO

CREATE CERTIFICATE OrderServiceCertPrivate
   AUTHORIZATION OrderServiceUser
   WITH SUBJECT = 'Private certificate for OrderService',
   START_DATE = '01/01/2008'
GO

BACKUP CERTIFICATE OrderServiceCertPrivate
   TO FILE = 'c:\OrderServiceCertPublic.cert'
GO
```

As you can see in Listing 8-8, you change the authorization of OrderService so that the newly created database user owns this Service Broker service. Now that you have established the identity of the initiator, you can import the target's public key certificate to authenticate the target. Listing 8-9 shows you how.

Listing 8-9. *Importing the Public Key Certificate of the Target*

```
CREATE USER CreditCardServiceUser WITHOUT LOGIN
GO

CREATE CERTIFICATE CreditCardServiceCertPublic
    AUTHORIZATION CreditCardServiceUser
    FROM FILE = 'c:\CreditCardServiceCertPublic.cert'
GO
```

The TargetService must also import the public key certificate of the initiator's service. You must also grant the SEND permission of the target service to the user who owns the public key certificate of the initiator service. Listing 8-10 shows the needed T-SQL code.

Listing 8-10. *Importing the Public Key Certificate of the Initiator*

```
CREATE USER OrderServiceUser WITHOUT LOGIN
GO

CREATE CERTIFICATE OrderServiceCertPublic
    AUTHORIZATION OrderServiceUser
    FROM FILE = 'c:\OrderServiceCertPublic.cert'
GO

GRANT SEND ON SERVICE::CreditCardService TO OrderServiceUser
GO
```

The only thing that is left now is to indicate which user the BEGIN DIALOG T-SQL statement will use to find the right certificate to authenticate with the target service. For this reason, Service Broker provides you with a *remote service binding*. A remote service binding establishes a relationship between a local database user, the certificate for the user, and the name of a remote Service Broker service. Service Broker determines the users for a conversation when a conversation begins, using the information in the database that hosts the initiating service. The remote service binding specifies the user for the target of the conversation. To create a new remote service binding, Service Broker provides the CREATE REMOTE SERVICE BINDING T-SQL statement. Listing 8-11 shows the syntax for this T-SQL statement.

Listing 8-11. *Syntax for the* CREATE REMOTE SERVICE BINDING *T-SQL Statement*

```
CREATE REMOTE SERVICE BINDING binding_name
    [ AUTHORIZATION owner_name ]
    TO SERVICE 'service_name'
    WITH USER = user_name [ , ANONYMOUS = { ON | OFF } ]
```

Table 8-1 describes the parameters for this T-SQL statement.

Table 8-1. *Parameters for the* CREATE REMOTE SERVICE BINDING *T-SQL Statement*

Parameter	Description
binding_name	Specifies the name of the remote service binding. The name must be a valid SYSNAME. Please note that you can't specify server, database, and schema.
owner_name	Sets the owner of the remote service binding.
service_name	Specifies the remote service to which you want to bind the user specified in the WITH USER clause.
user_name	Specifies the database principal who owns the certificate that is associated with the remote service specified with the TO SERVICE clause. Service Broker uses this certificate for encryption and authentication of the messages exchanged with the remote service.
ANONYMOUS	Specifies whether anonymous authentication is used when the communication with the remote service occurs. If you use anonymous authentication, operations in the remote database are executed as a member of the PUBLIC fixed database role. Otherwise, operations are executed as the specific user in that database. The default is OFF.

For dialog security to work, you must set up a remote service binding at the initiator's endpoint. Listing 8-12 shows the needed T-SQL code.

Listing 8-12. *Creating a Remote Service Binding*

```
CREATE REMOTE SERVICE BINDING RemoteServiceBindingToCreditCardService
    TO SERVICE 'CreditCardService'
    WITH USER = CreditCardServiceUser
GO
```

As you can see in Listing 8-12, the remote service binding associates the CreditCardServiceUser with the CreditCardService. Therefore, Service Broker now knows to use the CreditCardServiceCertPublic—the certificate that is associated with the CreditCardServiceUser—when sending new messages to CreditCardService. The remote service binding provides the necessary mapping information to the Service Broker infrastructure.

When you now send a new message from ClientService to OrderService, OrderService starts new conversations with CreditCardService, AccountingService, and InventoryService. The first two communication channels are secured by both transport security and dialog security. By using dialog security, you can also forward messages between OrderService, CreditCardService, and AccountingService through a Service Broker forwarder without performance losses, because messages are only encrypted at the initiator's endpoint and are decrypted at the final destination, the target endpoint. That's the power of dialog security.

Setting Up Anonymous Dialog Security

If the target service is going to supply services to a large number of dialog initiators, importing the certificates of the initiator services and provisioning users for all the initiators can be a significant administrative burden. There are other scenarios where the target service wants to

process requests from any initiator who makes the request without authenticating the initiator. Just think back to the scenario with the online shop. If you deploy these kinds of Service
Broker services to the general public, you can't authenticate each initiator to the target service.

To accommodate these scenarios, Service Broker includes the *anonymous dialog* feature.
In an anonymous dialog, the target service is authenticated to the initiator service, so that the
initiator service can be sure that the correct service processes its messages, but the initiator
service isn't authenticated with the target service.

To indicate to Service Broker that an anonymous dialog is used, you create the REMOTE
SERVICE BINDING on the initiator service with the ANONYMOUS option set to ON. The security
header in the first message from the initiator is sent with only the target's public key. The
owner of the initiator service doesn't need a private key certificate because it isn't used to
authenticate the connection. On the target side, you don't need to create a user to own the initiator's public key certificate. One implication of this is that there is no user to grant the SEND
permission for the target service, because the target has no way to know which user sent the
message. For this reason, you must grant the SEND permission to the database role PUBLIC for
the target service when anonymous dialogs are used.

Listing 8-13 shows how to set up anonymous dialog security on the target side.

Listing 8-13. *Anonymous Dialog Security on the Target Side*

```
USE Chapter8_CreditCardService
GO

CREATE USER CreditCardServiceUser WITHOUT LOGIN
GO

-- Grant the CONTROL permission to the previous created database user
GRANT CONTROL ON SERVICE::CreditCardService TO CreditCardServiceUser
GO

CREATE MASTER KEY ENCRYPTION BY PASSWORD = 'password1!'
GO

-- Create the certificate that represents the CreditCardService
CREATE CERTIFICATE CreditCardServiceCertPrivate
    AUTHORIZATION CreditCardServiceUser
    WITH SUBJECT = 'Private certificate for CreditCardService',
    START_DATE = '01/01/2008'
GO

-- Back up the public key of the certificate
BACKUP CERTIFICATE CreditCardServiceCertPrivate
    TO FILE = 'c:\CreditCardServiceCertPublic.cert'
GO

-- Grant the SEND permission to the database role [PUBLIC]
GRANT SEND ON SERVICE::CreditCardService TO [PUBLIC]
GO
```

As you can see in Listing 8-13, you create the private key certificate for CreditCardService and authorize the CreditCardServiceUser on that certificate. Finally, you dump the public key of the certificate to the file system so it can be imported from the initiator service. (And don't forget to grant the SEND permission to the PUBLIC database role.) Listing 8-14 shows how to set up anonymous dialog security on the initiator side.

Listing 8-14. *Anonymous Dialog Security on the Initiator Side*

```
USE Chapter8_OrderService
GO

-- Create the database master key
CREATE MASTER KEY ENCRYPTION BY PASSWORD = 'password1!'
GO

-- Create a database user that represents the CreditCardService
CREATE USER CreditCardServiceUser WITHOUT LOGIN
GO


-- Create the certificate that represents the CreditCardService
CREATE CERTIFICATE CreditCardServiceCertPublic
    AUTHORIZATION CreditCardServiceUser
    FROM FILE = 'c:\CreditCardServiceCertPublic.cert'
GO

-- Create the remote service binding, specifying that anonymous dialog
-- security is used
CREATE REMOTE SERVICE BINDING ServiceBindingToCreditCardService
    TO SERVICE 'CreditCardService'
    WITH USER = CreditCardServiceUser,
    ANONYMOUS = ON
GO
```

In the first step, you create a database master key in the application database. Then you create the database user who represents the target service, the CreditCardService. Next, you import the public key certificate of the target service and authorize the previously created user on this certificate. Finally, you create the REMOTE SERVICE BINDING and specify with the ANONYMOUS option that anonymous dialog security be used.

As soon as you set up the initiator side and the target side of the Service Broker conversation, you can send a new message. The message will arrive at the target, and the activated stored procedure will process it automatically. As you can see, it's an easy task to set up anonymous dialog security when you have a lot of initiator services and when you can't authorize each one separately to work together with the target service.

Encryption

Authentication is required for all transport connections. Along with authentication, all transport messages are checksummed and signed to ensure that the messages aren't altered during transport. Service Broker also encrypts messages to prevent them from being monitored, if desired. Message encryption is required by default. When you don't want to use encryption, you must indicate it separately. Encryption imposes some processor overhead, so if Service Broker traffic is being sent over a trusted LAN connection where tight security isn't required, you may want to turn off encryption to increase the efficiency of message transmission. Service Broker provides two different options for message encryption:

- *Transport encryption*: When you use transport encryption, Service Broker encrypts the whole message, including the header and payload. Transport encryption is configured through the Service Broker endpoint.

- *Dialog encryption*: When you use dialog encryption, the dialog encrypts the message payload. As such, only the target service can decrypt it. However, the message header is sent in clear text over the wire. Service Broker forwarders cannot decrypt the message payload, but they can see the unencrypted message header needed to correctly forward the message to the next hop on the route to the target service.

Message encryption gets more complex when you use transport and dialog encryption in combination. When you use both encryption options, Service Broker encrypts the message payload with dialog encryption and the message header with transport encryption. This is important, because often the message payload is the largest amount of the message (besides the message header), and if transport encryption would always encrypt everything (including the message header and message body), then the message payload would be encrypted twice (when you also use dialog encryption). This would be an unnecessary overhead, since encryption/decryption has a significant cost.

Transport Encryption

You can configure transport encryption through the Service Broker endpoint. When you create a new endpoint without specifying the encryption option, the Service Broker endpoint will be encrypted by default. Therefore, all the samples shown in this and in the previous chapter have used transport encryption by default. To turn off encryption, you can set the ENCRYPTION attribute of the endpoint to DISABLED with the CREATE ENDPOINT or ALTER ENDPOINT T-SQL statement. Listing 8-15 shows how to turn off encryption at OrderServiceEndpoint and CreditCardServiceEndpoint.

Listing 8-15. *Disabling Encryption for Service Broker Endpoints*

```
ALTER ENDPOINT OrderServiceEndpoint
STATE = STARTED
FOR SERVICE_BROKER
(
   AUTHENTICATION = CERTIFICATE OrderServiceTransportCertPrivate,
   ENCRYPTION = DISABLED
)
```

```
ALTER ENDPOINT CreditCardServiceEndpoint
STATE = STARTED
FOR SERVICE_BROKER
(
    AUTHENTICATION = CERTIFICATE CreditCardServiceTransportCertPrivate,
    ENCRYPTION = DISABLED
)
```

The ENCRYPTION attribute has three possible values:

- DISABLED: Specifies that data sent over a connection isn't encrypted.

- SUPPORTED: Indicates that the data is encrypted only if the opposite endpoint specifies either SUPPORTED or REQUIRED.

- REQUIRED: Specifies that connections to this endpoint must use encryption. Therefore, to connect to this endpoint, another endpoint must have ENCRYPTION set to either SUPPORTED or REQUIRED.

These three values let the administrator set up a complex network where some connections use encryption and others don't, even when these connections use the same endpoint. Table 8-2 shows the possible combinations of the ENCRYPTION attribute and whether or not data on the connection will be encrypted.

Table 8-2. *Setting Up Transport Security*

Endpoint A	Endpoint B	Encrypted?
Required	Required	Yes
Required	Supported	Yes
Required	Disabled	Error
Disabled	Disabled	No
Disabled	Supported	No
Supported	Supported	Yes

Dialog Encryption

Dialog encryption is specified when you begin a new conversation with the target service with the BEGIN DIALOG T-SQL statement. Here you use the ENCRYPTION = ON/OFF clause to specify whether dialog encryption should be used for the current conversation. When you use encryption, the whole message body is encrypted with the session key (refer back to the "Service Broker Security Protocol" section for more information).

This way, only the destination service can decrypt the message body. Because it has the corresponding private key for the remote service binding user's certificate, it can decrypt the KEK and then decrypt the session key. After the message is decrypted, the receiver can use the signature of the message to validate that the sender sent the message—the signature proves that the sender is in possession of the private key.

Even when you specify ENCRYPTION = OFF in the BEGIN DIALOG T-SQL statement, the conversation might end up encrypted. Why? Because the presence of a remote service binding overrides the ENCRYPTION = OFF option and enforces encryption on the conversation. Table 8-3 represents the interaction between the ENCRYPTION option of BEGIN DIALOG and the presence of a remote service binding (RSB).

Table 8-3. *Remote Service Binding and Encryption*

--	RSB Present	No RSB
ENCRYPTION = ON	Conversation is encrypted.	Conversation is delayed.
ENCRYPTION = OFF	Conversation is encrypted.	Conversation is clear text.
ENCRYPTION clause omitted	Conversation is encrypted.	Conversation is delayed.

In the case when the BEGIN DIALOG T-SQL statement has an ENCRYPTION = ON clause (or the ENCRYPTION clause is omitted) and there is no remote service binding present, the messages sent on this conversation will be delayed. They will remain in sys.transmission_queue with a transmission_status that indicates that a remote service binding is required.

At first glance, this seems wrong. Why is the ENCRYPTION = OFF option overridden by the presence of a remote service binding? The answer is that Service Broker has to consider the difference between encryption being required by the application (development time) or encryption being required by the environment (deployment time). The ENCRYPTION ON/OFF clause is hard-coded in the application that issues the BEGIN DIALOG T-SQL statement. You cannot change it by configuration. As such, this is the appropriate option to use if you determine at development time whether or not encryption is required.

On the other hand, a remote service binding is a configuration option. You create it when the application is deployed, and you can change it as conditions change in the environment in which the application is running. Even if the application doesn't require encryption, you can add it at deployment time by creating a remote service binding if you determine that it is needed. When you write an application, you have three different options to use ENCRYPTION in the BEGIN DIALOG T-SQL statement:

- *If there is no requirement for the conversations to be encrypted, you should explicitly use the* ENCRYPTION = OFF *clause*: This allows an administrator to configure your application by adding a remote service binding.

- *If the application requires secure conversations, you should use the* ENCRYPTION = ON *clause in the application code*: This forces the administrator to provide a remote service binding at deployment time.

- *If the* ENCRYPTION *clause is omitted, it is equivalent to specifying* ENCRYPTION = ON. ENCRYPTION = ON is the default value.

Recommendation

In general, the overhead of encrypting all the network traffic is high enough that you should look closely at whether or not to enable encryption on a connection. If your normal network security is adequate to protect Service Broker data or if the data isn't highly confidential, you probably shouldn't use encryption. Remember that authentication and signing of the data detects any data alterations on the network, so the only thing encryption adds is privacy.

Many companies use virtual private networks (VPNs) or other technologies to protect network data. If the data is already protected by one of these means, Service Broker encryption is probably redundant. Remember that Service Broker defaults to the most secure options. You must consciously decide that the default settings provide more security than required and configure a less secure connection.

Transport Protocol

When you disable the transport encryption between two different deployed Service Broker services, you're able to trace the TCP traffic between those two services. In this section, I'll show you how a simple message exchange between two Service Broker services occurs at the TCP protocol level. I won't investigate things such as message fragmentation, acknowledgment messages, and so on, because Microsoft doesn't document them officially.

Setting Up Tracing

To sniff the Service Broker network traffic, you need a tool that can display the traffic on the wire. I've chosen Microsoft Network Monitor 3.0. You can find more information about the Network Monitor at http://blogs.technet.com/netmon. Figure 8-4 shows this tool in action.

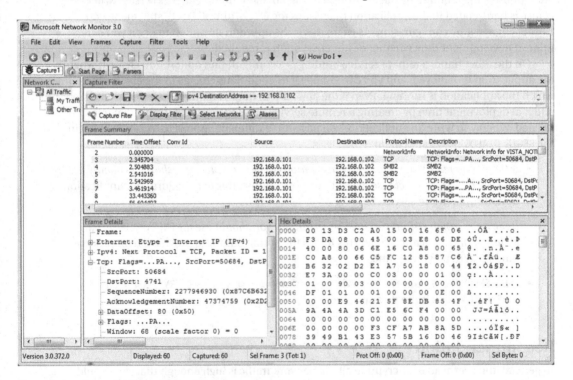

Figure 8-4. *Microsoft Network Monitor 3.0*

After you start a new capture with File ℅ New ℅ Capture, the first thing that you must do is add a filter. You can use the filter to specify which TCP packages should be traced. As you can see in Figure 8-4, I've chosen the following filter:

```
ipv4.DestinationAddress == 192.168.0.102
```

192.168.0.102 is the IP address where the CreditCardService is deployed in my network configuration. After you apply the filter, you can start the trace and send a request message from the ClientService to the OrderService. As soon as this message is sent, the ProcessOrderRequestMessages stored procedure starts automatically (because of internal activation) and sends a separate message to the CreditCardService and the AccountingService. If you've set up everything correctly, Microsoft Network Monitor should now show several TCP packages that are exchanged between your machine and the machine where the OrderService is deployed.

Inside Microsoft Network Monitor, you must search through the captured frames until you find the one where the message sent to the CreditCardService is contained. Figure 8-5 shows you the hexadecimal details of this frame.

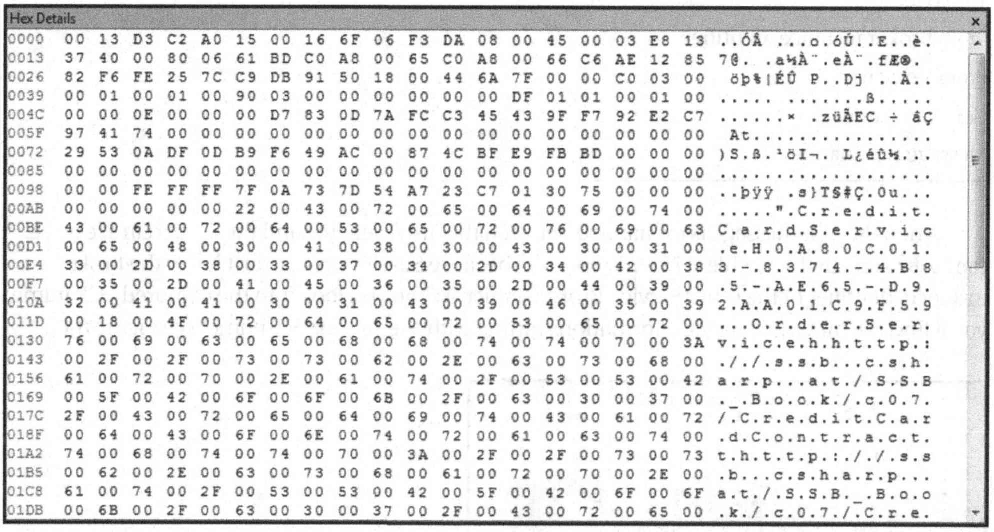

Figure 8-5. *The TCP frame with the captured Service Broker message*

The traced Service Broker message shown in Figure 8-5 contains the message header and the message body.

The Captured Service Broker Message

The message header contains all the information Service Broker needs to route the message from one Service Broker forwarder to the next until the message reaches its final destination. The current scenario is very simple, because the message is sent directly from the initiator to the target, and no Service Broker forwarders exist along the route. The message header of a Service Broker message contains the following information:

- *From service*: Contains the name of the initiator service—in this case, OrderService

- *To service*: Contains the name of the target service—in this case, CreditCardService

- *From broker instance identifier*: The Service Broker GUID of the sending database

- *To broker instance identifier*: The Service Broker GUID of the receiving database

- *Contract name*: The name of the used contract

- *Message type name*: The name of the used message type

Let's now take a look at where this information is located inside the captured TCP frame. Table 8-4 shows the message header format.

Table 8-4. *The Format of the Service Broker Message Header*

Service Broker Message Header
To broker instance identifier
To service
From broker instance identifier
From service
Contract name
Message type name

When the first message is exchanged between the OrderService and the CreditCardService, the To Broker Instance Identifier is omitted, because Service Broker can't know the broker instance identifier of the other Service Broker service. When you look into the captured TCP frame, you'll find the message header information starting with the To Service name (see Figure 8-6).

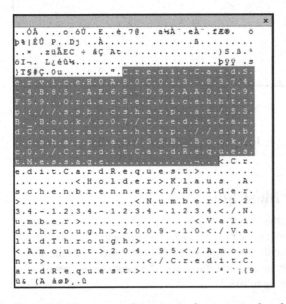

Figure 8-6. *The captured Service Broker message header*

As you can see in Figure 8-6, all information in the message header is transferred unencrypted across the wire. That's because transport encryption was disabled on the Service Broker endpoint. The message payload—the request message that is sent from OrderService to CreditCardService—follows the message header. Listing 8-16 shows the XML message. You can also find the message below the selected header in the captured TCP frame in Figure 8-6.

Listing 8-16. *The XML Message Sent to the* CreditCardService *Service*

```
<CreditCardRequest>
    <Holder>Klaus Aschenbrenner</Holder>
    <Number>1234-1234-1234-1234</Number>
    <ValidThrough>2009-10</ValidThrough>
    <Amount>204.95</Amount>
</CreditCardRequest>
```

Figure 8-7 shows the captured TCP frame that contains the response message sent back to the OrderService by the CreditCardService.

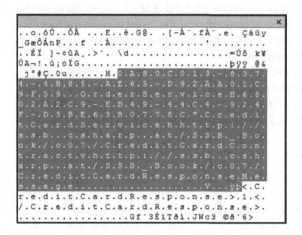

Figure 8-7. *The captured Service Broker response message*

As you can see in Figure 8-7, the message header (the selected part of the TCP frame) now contains the To Broker Instance Identifier (the first GUID in the selected part). This makes sense, because when Service Broker sends the response message, the To Broker Instance Identifier known from the first request message is sent to the CreditCardService (the From Broker Instance Identifier). You might be asking where this Broker Instance Identifier is stored inside SQL Server. Because a Service Broker service is always bound to a database, the sys.databases catalog view contains a column named service_broker_guid. This column stores the Broker Instance Identifier. When you capture the necessary TCP frames, you can compare the sent Broker Instance Identifier with the values in sys.databases, and you'll see that they're identical.

This section was a small excursion through the Service Broker transport protocol. The most important issue to remember here is that everyone is able to trace your Service Broker messages when you don't encrypt them! So make sure that you encrypt your messages when they contain sensitive data and are transferred across an unsecure connection.

Replaying Service Broker Messages

You might think that you can replay a Service Broker message with changed data when you capture one in the network (and also when the message is not signed). However, Service Broker provides a mechanism that prevents replaying captured messages.

Unlike initiator endpoints, target endpoints of a conversation are not deleted immediately. When you open a new conversation and close it, you can see on the target side in the sys.conversation_endpoints catalog view that the conversation is in the CLOSED state (state_desc column). But the conversation endpoint is deleted at least 30 minutes after receiving the first acknowledgment message for a message sent by the target. The threat Service Broker tries to mitigate is the possibility that an attacker will capture a message on the wire and replay it later, causing the opened dialog to perform the requested action again. Just imagine that you send a message to request the withdrawal of money from your account . . .

When the initiator sends such a message, the target accepts it, performs the action, and finally ends the dialog. Suppose that an attacker has intercepted this message and is capable of resending it again. If the target endpoint was deleted, there would be no evidence in the database that this dialog has already occurred once, so the target would be created again and the action would be performed again. The attacker might repeat this again and again while the message is valid. The messages have a timestamp on them, and the target accepts the messages with a timestamp tolerance of 30 minutes, so the attacker would be able to repeat the messages several times during those 30 minutes.

To prevent this, the target endpoint is not deleted for 30 minutes. If an attacker replays the message during those 30 minutes, the endpoint already exists (in the CLOSED state), so the message will be discarded. After 30 minutes, the target endpoint will be deleted, but by now the message will have become out of date and won't be accepted if replayed because the message timestamp has expired.

Replacing Certificates

By default, certificates expire and become unusable. In the previous examples, you created certificates without specifying an expiration date. In this case, the expiration date is set to one year after the specified start date. If you want to specify a longer or shorter expiration period, the CREATE CERTIFICATE T-SQL statement provides you with the EXPIRY_DATE option, where you can specify the needed expiration date of the certificate.

When a certificate is about to expire, you must replace it inside SQL Server 2008. How you do this depends on whether the certificate was used for transport security or for dialog security. Let's have a look at each of these two different options.

Transport Security

If you have to change the certificate in a Service Broker endpoint, all connections to the endpoint that don't have the new certificate will fail to deliver messages. However, an open dialog between two services won't fail, so when you replace the certificate, the open dialog will continue from where it left off. To avoid this, create a new certificate and send the public key certificate to all remote connections.

The remote Service Broker can associate this new certificate with the user who represents the SQL Server instance whose certificate will be changed. You can associate a user with multiple certificates by using the AUTHORIZATION clause in the CREATE CERTIFICATE T-SQL statement. Once all the remote endpoints have added the new certificate to their users, you can change the local endpoint (the side where the initiator's service lives) to point to the new certificate by using the ALTER ENDPOINT T-SQL statement. Once all the endpoints are using the new certificate, you can drop the old certificate from SQL Server 2008. This process can take a while, so don't wait until the certificate expires to change it.

Dialog Security

The certificates used for dialog security must also be replaced before they expire. This procedure also takes advantage of the fact that a single user can own multiple certificates. The message transmission logic chooses a private key certificate owned by the owner of the initiator's service. If this user owns more than one certificate, the certificate with the latest expiration date will be used. This can cause problems; when a new private key certificate is created for the user, the BEGIN DIALOG T-SQL statement will immediately start using it because it will have the latest expiration date.

These dialogs will fail until the public key for this certificate is exported and distributed to the target service. To get around this problem, the ACTIVE FOR BEGIN_DIALOG option on the CREATE CERTIFICATE T-SQL statement will allow you to create a certificate but prevent its use in the BEGIN DIALOG T-SQL statement until the target endpoint is ready. Listing 8-17 shows how you can use this option when you create a new certificate inside SQL Server 2008.

Listing 8-17. *The* ACTIVE FOR BEGIN_DIALOG *Option*

```
CREATE CERTIFICATE OrderServiceCertPrivate2
   WITH SUBJECT = 'A new private certificate for the OrderService',
   AUTHORIZATION OrderServiceUser
   ACTIVE FOR BEGIN_DIALOG = OFF
```

Back up the public key portion of this new certificate, and import it as a new certificate owned by the user who represents the initiator in the target database. When this is complete, the dialogs will be able to use the new certificate. Use the option from Listing 8-18 to switch the BEGIN DIALOG T-SQL statement to use the new certificate.

Listing 8-18. *Using the New Certificate*

```
ALTER CERTIFICATE OrderServiceCertPrivate2
   ACTIVE FOR BEGIN_DIALOG = ON
```

Now that both the initiator and the target are using the new certificate, you can drop the old certificate from both the initiator and the target database. This won't affect any existing dialogs, because they already exchanged a session key. They no longer need the certificates. You must also replace the certificate owned by the user who has the CONTROL permission of the target service, and you must distribute the corresponding public key to the initiators of the service. You should do this by first creating the private key certificate in the target database and then distributing the public key certificate to the initiators, where it will be owned by the user specified in the REMOTE SERVICE BINDING for the service.

Service Listing Manager

As you've seen, many steps are involved when you want to set up transport and dialog security. Unfortunately, SQL Server 2008 ships without some of the tools for easily setting up Service Broker security, creating routes between Service Broker services, and setting up the necessary permissions. That's bad, but the good thing is that the Service Broker development team provides a tool called *Service Listing Manager*, through http://www.codeplex.com/slm, for setting up and configuring Service Broker security. In this section, I'll introduce Service Listing Manager and show how you can use it to set up transport and dialog security in a few steps.

Service Listing Manager is a .NET Windows application that also uses some of the SQLCLR features of SQL Server 2008. Figure 8-8 shows the startup screen of Service Listing Manager.

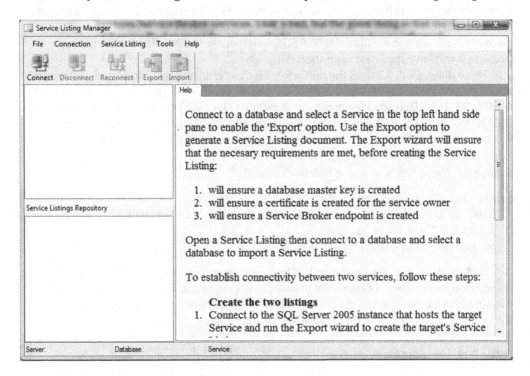

Figure 8-8. *Running Service Listing Manager*

Service Listing Manager is based on the Service Listing concept. A Service Listing is like an identity card for a service. It is an XML document that contains all the necessary information needed to establish a conversation with a Service Broker service. When two Service Broker services need to establish a connection between each other, they can exchange the Service Listing documents of the two services, and the tool will create the entire infrastructure needed to establish a connection between those two services. Optionally, the Service Listing Manager can also create the message types and the contracts supported by the target service in the initiator service database.

When you want to establish a connection between your service and another Service Broker service, you have to perform two steps:

1. *Export a Service Listing:* You have to export all the necessary security settings for your Service Broker services into a Service Listing document. The exported Service Listing document contains information such as the public key certificates used for transport and dialog security, the needed routes, and the used message types and contracts.

2. *Import a Service Listing:* When you want to establish a connection with another Service Broker service, you have to import the Service Listing document of this service. During the import, the tool creates all the necessary certificates, routes, logins, and users and sets up the required permissions.

When you set up a bidirectional connection between two Service Broker services (which is the standard case with Service Broker), you have to export your own Service Listing document, and you have to import the Service Listing document of the other Service Broker service and vice versa. Let's have a look at each of these two steps.

■**Note** In this section, I assume that you've set up an initiator service and a target service on different SQL Server machines, without any security settings (transport security and dialog security). You'll set up both transport security and dialog security with the Service Listing Manager.

Exporting a Service Listing

To export a Service Listing from an existing Service Broker service, you have to connect to your SQL Server instance and select the service from the correct database. Then use the Export button from the menu bar. In this case, Service Listing Manager starts the Export Service Listing Wizard, as shown in Figure 8-9.

The Export Service Listing Wizard ensures that the necessary requirements are met before creating the Service Listing:

- It ensures that the needed database master key is created in the application database and also inside the master database.

- It ensures that a certificate is created for the service owner.

- It ensures that a Service Broker endpoint is created.

If you haven't already created a database master key in your Service Broker database, the Export Service Listing Wizard will ask you to supply a password for the database master key that it creates automatically. Next, the wizard asks for a new certificate name if you haven't yet created a certificate for the exported Service Broker service.

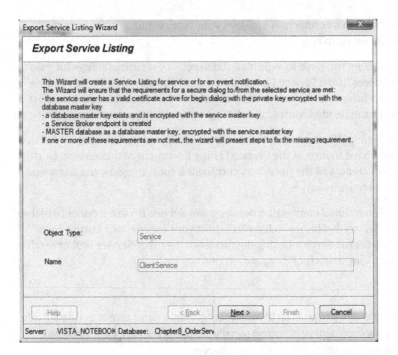

Figure 8-9. *Exporting a Service Listing*

The wizard then asks you to create a Service Broker endpoint for the SQL instance where the Service Broker service is deployed. Here you can supply an endpoint name and a TCP port number, and you can choose between Windows-based transport security and certificate-based transport security. If you choose certificate-based transport security, you have to supply the correct certificate used for transport security. In the final step, the Export Service Listing Wizard displays the Service Listing document that was created from the service definition and your inputs. You're also able to save the Service Listing document to the file system. The Service Listing document is an XML file that describes your exported Service Broker service. Listing 8-19 shows the most important information of the exported Service Listing document for OrderService.

Listing 8-19. *The* OrderService *Service Listing Document*

```
<definition author="vista_notebook\Klaus Aschenbrenner">
   <message
      name="http://ssb.csharp.at/SSB_Book/c08/OrderRequestMessage"
      validation="XML" />
   <message
      name="http://ssb.csharp.at/SSB_Book/c08/OrderResponseMessage"
      validation="XML" />
```

```
<contract name="http://ssb.csharp.at/SSB_Book/c08/OrderContract">
  <message
      name="http://ssb.csharp.at/SSB_Book/c08/OrderRequestMessage"
      sent-by="INITIATOR" />
  <message
      name="http://ssb.csharp.at/SSB_Book/c08/OrderResponseMessage"
      sent-by="TARGET" />
</contract>
<service
    name="OrderService"
    broker-instance="40E889B4-4802-41FE-8460-5E4B821D8BE9"
    public-access="No">
  <contract name="http://ssb.csharp.at/SSB_Book/c08/OrderContract" />
  <certificate
      issuer-name="Private certificate for OrderService"
      serial-number="...">
      <blob>...</blob>
  </certificate>
</service>
<endpoint
    machinename="VISTA_NOTEBOOK"
    tcp-port="4740"
    authentication="CERTIFICATE"
    encryption="RC4"
    public-access="No">
  <certificate
      issuer-name="For Service Broker authentication"
      serial-number="...">
      <blob>...</blob>
  </certificate>
</endpoint>
</definition>
```

As you can see in Listing 8-19, the Service Listing document contains the following XML nodes:

- <message>: Contains all the message types used by the exported Service Broker service.

- <contract>: Contains all the contracts used by the exported Service Broker service.

- <service>: Contains information about the exported Service Broker service. It also contains the <certificate> node. This node contains the public key certificate used by dialog security.

- <endpoint>: Contains information about the created Service Broker endpoint, such as the used TCP port, the authentication mode, and the used encryption algorithm. If you use certificate-based authentication, there is also a <certificate> node that contains the public key certificate of the certificate used for transport security.

■Note Please make sure to export the Service Listing document on both the initiator and the target side.

Importing a Service Listing

As soon as you export the Service Listing document, you can distribute it to the Service Broker service with which you want to establish a connection. You can exchange the Service Listing document in any way you want—whether by email or FTP, it doesn't matter.

When you get the Service Listing document from the other Service Broker service, you have to open it inside Service Listing Manager. Service Listing Manager shows you graphically the definition of the other Service Broker service (see Figure 8-10).

Services	
Service Name	**Broker Instance**
AccountingService	19D27851-4F27-
Certificate:Private certificate for AccountingService	4338-8EED-
SN:e7 c5 4f e1 50 9c 89 9c 48 3f 92 58 3b f4 96 b1	CF332806C343
Contracts	
http://ssb.csharp.at/SSB_Book/c08/AccountingContract	

Endpoint

Machine	WINDOWSVISTA
TCP port	4741
Authentication	CERTIFICATE

Certificate:For Service Broker authentication SN:34 ee cc e3 45 b8 2f 86 44 27 33 a4 0c e1 2d 4d

Service Interface

Contract	
http://ssb.csharp.at/SSB_Book/c08/AccountingContract	
Messages types	**Sent by**
http://ssb.csharp.at/SSB_Book/c08/AccountingRequestMessage	INITIATOR
http://ssb.csharp.at/SSB_Book/c08/AccountingResponseMessage	TARGET

Figure 8-10. *The Service Listing to import*

To start the import of the Service Listing document, click the Import button in the menu bar. This starts the Service Listing Import Wizard, which provides three different deployment options in the first step:

- *Initiator at Target*: The service in the Service Listing is an initiator service that needs to access a target service. This option deploys the proxy user and certificate, grants the SEND permission on a selected target service, and deploys the routing information.

- *Target at Initiator*: The service in the Service Listing is a target service that needs to be accessed by an initiator service. This option deploys the proxy user and certificate, the remote service binding, and the routing information.

- *Endpoint*: This additional option deploys the Service Broker endpoint proxy login and certificate, and it grants the CONNECT permission on the Service Broker endpoint. This option allows the SQL Server instance that hosts the service in the Service Listing to connect to the selected SQL Server instance. This option needs to be run only once per pair of SQL Server instances.

Initiator at Target

When you import a Service Listing document of an initiator service at a target service, you must configure the target service settings in the next step of the Service Listing Import Wizard (see Figure 8-11).

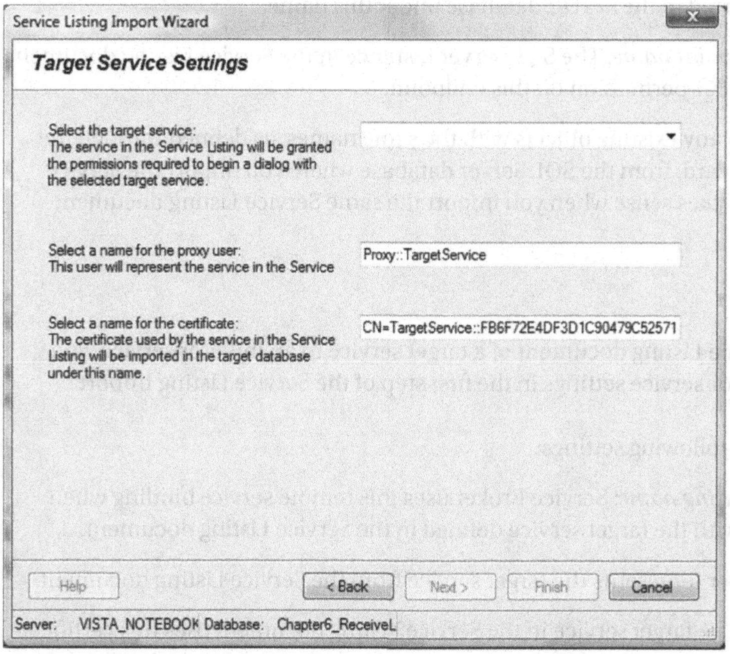

Figure 8-11. *Initiator at target*

You have to provide the following information:

- *Target service*: The service in the Service Listing document is granted the permissions required to begin a dialog with the provided target service.

- *Proxy user*: This database user represents the initiator service in the database of the target service.

- *Certificate name*: The public key certificate used by the service in the Service Listing document is imported in the target database under the specified name.

In the next step of the Service Listing Import Wizard, you have to provide the name of the route that points back to the initiator service. You configure Service Broker endpoint settings in the next step. You have to provide the following information:

- *Proxy login*: This login represents the SQL Server instance in the Service Listing document.

- *Login password*: The password for the login is used in the certificate-based transport authentication.

- *Certificate name*: The certificate used by the SQL Server instance in the Service Listing document is imported in the master database under this name.

- *Service Broker endpoint name*: The SQL Server instance in the Service Listing document is granted the CONNECT permission on this endpoint.

Finally, you can drop any existing objects with the same names, as defined through the Service Listing Import Wizard, from the SQL Server database where you import the Service Listing document. This makes sense when you import the same Service Listing document several times.

Target at Initiator

When you import a Service Listing document of a target service to an initiator service, you have to supply the initiator service settings in the first step of the Service Listing Import Wizard (see Figure 8-12).

You must supply the following settings:

- *Remote service binding name*: Service Broker uses this remote service binding when initiating dialogs with the target service defined in the Service Listing document.

- *Proxy user*: This user represents the target service from the Service Listing document.

- *Certificate name*: The target service in the Service Listing document uses this certificate.

- *Anonymous remote service binding*: This indicates whether you want to use an anonymous remote service binding.

- *Import service interface*: This indicates whether you want to import the service interface (such as message type contracts) of the target service.

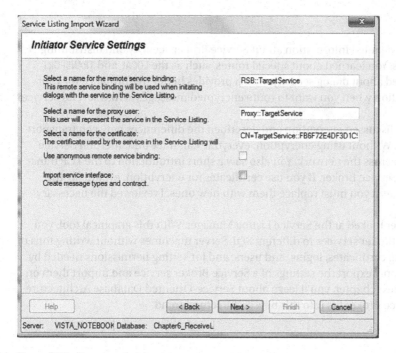

Figure 8-12. *Target at initiator*

In the next step of the wizard, you have to select a name for the route from the initiator service to the target service. Finally, you can configure the Service Broker endpoint settings. You have to provide the following information:

- *Authentication type*: You can choose between Windows-based and certificate-based authentication.

- *Proxy login*: This login represents the SQL Server instance in the Service Listing document.

- *Login password*: The password is used for login in certificate-based endpoint authentication.

- *Certificate name*: The certificate name used by the SQL Server instance in the Service Listing document is imported in the master database under this name.

- *Service Broker endpoint name*: The SQL Server instance in the Service Listing document is granted the CONNECT permission on this Service Broker endpoint.

Finally, you can also drop any existing objects with the same names, as defined through the Service Listing Import Wizard, from the SQL Server database from which you imported the Service Listing document. This makes sense when you import the same Service Listing document several times. After you import the opposite Service Listing document (on each side), the necessary Service Broker infrastructure between your two Service Broker services is set up, and you can exchange messages between these two Service Broker services. Easy, isn't it?

Summary

This chapter provided detailed information about Service Broker security and distributing Service Broker services. You learned about special routes, such as the LOCAL and TRANSPORT routes. You then learned about dialog security, which provides better performance for your Service Broker application when you want to route encrypted messages across several Service Broker forwarders.

This chapter also discussed encryption and described the differences between transport and dialog encryption. Without using encryption, everyone can trace and interpret Service Broker messages sent across the network. You also saw a short introduction to the TCP transport protocol used by Service Broker. If you use certificates for encryption, eventually the certificates will expire, and you must replace them with new ones. I reviewed the necessary steps for this.

Finally, this chapter looked at the Service Listing Manager. With this graphical tool, you can distribute Service Broker services to different SQL Server machines without writing tons of T-SQL code for creating certificates, logins, and users, and for setting permissions needed by Service Broker. You simply export the settings of a Service Broker service and import them on the other side. In the next chapter, you'll learn about Service-Oriented Database Architecture (SODA) and how Service Broker fits into this new architectural trend.

CHAPTER 9

■■■

Service-Oriented Database Architecture

In this chapter, you'll learn how to build Service-Oriented Database Architecture (SODA) database applications. This chapter will cover the following topics in detail:

- *Service-Oriented Database Architecture*: SODA is a new concept and builds on the foundation of SOA. With SODA, you can build, deploy, and run SOA applications directly inside a database, such as SQL Server 2008.

- *Data in SODA*: When you implement SODA applications, you deal with data outside and inside service boundaries.

- *SODA features in SQL Server 2008*: SQL Server provides you with several features to implement SODA. You'll get an introduction to them by using them in applications.

Service-Oriented Database Architecture

The dominant client/server and n-tier application architectures of the last decades raised serious scalability and availability issues. One of the major problems was that data tended to be stored in massive, centralized databases that all client components had direct access to. Virtually all communication with the database was in the form of SQL statements (or batches of them in stored procedures), producing a set of data for a specific task as a result.

Other problems arose when trying to incorporate legacy systems into newer applications. After decades of deploying a wide variety of systems using various proprietary technologies and platforms, the world was full of systems that did their job perfectly well but had no clear path to interact with other applications in an increasingly connected environment. Providing the agility needed by today's applications has been extremely difficult. Business-to-business (B2B) interactions complicate things even further, requiring standard, reliable ways of conducting business electronically. Clearly, systems that meet the needs of today's global business environments require an architecture that uses legacy systems efficiently and provides an agile commerce infrastructure.

SOA

In response to these problems, the past several years have seen the emergence of large-scale, loosely coupled, and distributed system architectures. SOA has emerged as the dominant, loosely coupled, service-centric architecture. Applications based on SOA are more resistant to failure, can be more easily scaled up by adding resources to meet changing demands, and support more flexible integration of legacy systems.

SOA service providers, consumers, and other components handle data as a natural feature of their roles in an SOA application. An SOA application typically still uses central databases to store and protect data, but is likely to use several large databases that hold classes of data—for example, separate databases for sales, manufacturing, and operations data and specialized subsets of each. Each service provider and consumer may have a localized need for cached data or its own specialized data store. Also, the messages that travel between the disparate parts of an application are themselves often data that is worth archiving. The "Data in SODA" section looks at the different kinds of data in SOA and SODA.

Figure 9-1 shows a few of the endpoints that might make up a loosely coupled application based on SOA. A *service consumer*, which could be a client application, a server application such as a web server, or any other kind of application, sends a message to a *service provider*. In complex systems, a message router might initially receive the message and apply some logic to route the request to the appropriate service provider. The service provider would then receive the message, perhaps unpack and reformat it, do whatever work is required for the message, and then send a response message back to the service consumer.

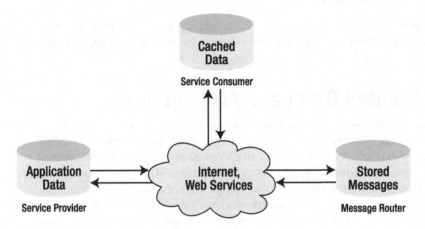

Figure 9-1. *An application based on SOA principles*

The important detail in Figure 9-1 is that each node in the transaction receives, stores, and transmits data in various forms. Sometimes the data is transient; at other times, each node might persist the data either to a cache or to its own local database. In light of these new ways of handling data within an application, the databases at the core of SOA applications face a different set of challenges than they did with monolithic, n-tier applications. Data integrity is just as important as ever, but now there are additional requirements:

- The database must operate in an environment where requests come from XML-based messages rather than dedicated connections from client applications.

- Repositories of cached data need to know when to refresh the data more dynamically than just doing a refresh on a set schedule.

- The database has to participate in dialogs that must occur in a set sequence.

- Complex logic must be hosted in or near the database.

XML makes a good message format for widely distributed systems. Almost any system can parse it easily, and it has a schema-modeling language to define the proper structure of the data. Systems exchanging messages can attach information to an XML message so that data accumulates in the message as it flows through the system. Systems can parse and process what they understand and ignore the rest. Simply put, XML is a highly adaptable format to support distributed systems.

Reasons for SODA Architectures

Microsoft recognized these architectural trends and built SQL Server 2008 to meet new challenges while continuing to support the many existing non-SOA applications. Many of the new features in SQL Server 2008 are part of an integrated architectural design that supports the use of the database as an SOA service provider. The SQL Server team at Microsoft calls this *Service-Oriented Database Architecture*, or SODA. There are a number of compelling reasons for implementing SOA features directly in the database engine, including the following:

- *Scaling up and down*: In even the largest enterprise SOA application, an individual service might be instantiated at almost any scale; a lightly used service might have less activity than a typical small departmental database. Integration with SQL Server means that a service program can take advantage of all the native support for scaling from embedded devices to the most substantial enterprise database server, without increasing administrative complexity. Service logic code can execute at any scale, and any implementation can scale out to a separate middle tier at deployment time. With SQL Server 2008, service logic can scale out to a separate middle tier at deployment time and can run either in the data tier or be deployed in the middle tier. If you design an application carefully, choosing how to scale can be a deployment decision rather than a design or development-time decision.

- *Scaling out*: You can scale out data-centric computing in a number of ways, generally either by scaling out the database or by distributing the processing based on SOA principles. Scaling out the database results in a database cluster that is relatively tightly coupled, while the service-oriented solution is more loosely coupled. Building support for SOA directly in the database reduces the component processes required for a true grid solution.

- *Messages are data*: Request and response messages are data that may have enough value to be archived in a database. Keeping messages available over time provides a history that allows you to audit and analyze business transactions. Because messages are stored in tables and have system catalog views available, you can easily use T-SQL to see the status of any part of the overall system.

These are enormous benefits to implementing SOA features in SQL Server so that it can act as a stand-alone service provider for an SOA application. But to do so, it must be able to act like a service provider, which demands a minimum set of capabilities.

Requirements for a SODA Service Provider

For SQL Server 2008 or any database engine to take on a role as a stand-alone SOA service program, it must implement several features beyond its native ability to handle data:

- *Endpoint support*: The SODA provider must provide support for communication to receive and transmit messages, typically as a TCP socket, HTTP GET or HTTP PUT, SOAP endpoint, or other type of endpoint.

- *Service request processing*: Most messages in SOA are formatted using XML, so the service provider must be able to process and possibly transform the enclosed data into other forms as needed by the components that make up the service. It must also be able to participate in complex dialogs and conversations as interdependent messages are received and sent to other components.

- *Service logic hosting*: The provider must be able to perform whatever complex logic is required to process the message and provide the necessary response, as well as possibly coordinate the input of several other services. This may require common application server tasks, such as pooling resources, activation, and scaling out logic processing.

The various new features of SQL Server 2008 provide support for these functions, besides plenty of other infrastructure to support data management. For example, a service provider must securely participate in an SOA system and be able to authenticate clients and in turn provide credentials to authenticate itself to others, provide durability, participate in conversations and transactions, and perform other application-level features. SQL Server 2008 built on the features of the SQL Server 2000 relational database engine as well as interim releases of new technologies since its original release, such as SQLXML 3.0, Notification Services, and other tools, to fully realize a SODA.

Data in SODA

When exploring the concepts behind SODA, it quickly becomes clear that each component in the overall system includes receiving, processing, and transmitting data among its primary functions. Even if a service provider's response to a message sent from a service consumer is to simply flip a bit to turn something on or off without interacting with a database, the service provider must process the data in the message in order to determine the work that is to be done. However, modern business applications deal extensively with data, so it's common for a SODA component to have access to either a local or centralized database, or frequently both. It's important to make a distinction between the data inside of services and the data outside of services. Let's have a more detailed look at data outside a service and data inside a service.

Outside Data

Data outside a service is sent between services as messages and must be defined in a way understandable to both the service consumer and the service provider. The need to interpret the data in at least two different services makes the existence and availability of a common schema imperative. The schema should also have certain characteristics. First, independent schema definition is important. This means the sender and the receiver of a message should be able to define message schemas without having to consult each other. Second, the message schema should be extensible. Extensibility allows the service provider to add information to the message beyond what is specified in the schema.

■**Note** The sender of the message may or may not be the definer of the message schema.

Sending Messages

Every message traveling through a network may be retransmitted in the event that the message is lost. Every message sent is guaranteed to be delivered zero or more times. Considerations are based on the following events:

- Networks losing messages
- Networks retrying messages
- Retries actually being delivered

It is important for retransmitted messages to remain unaltered no matter how many times they are sent. Therefore, all messages should be immutable.

IMMUTABLE DATA

Data exists in many forms. One type of data is immutable data. Essentially, immutable data is unchangeable once it is written. You can find immutable data almost anywhere in the real world: the first edition of a published book is unchangeable, the words spoken by the United States president on television are unchangeable, and the past stock prices of a company are unchangeable.

All immutable data has identifiers. An identifier ensures the same data is returned each time it is requested, no matter when it is requested or where it is requested. Therefore, if the same identifier is used, then the same data is returned.

Reference Data

Reference data is information published across service boundaries. For each collection of reference data, one service creates it, publishes it, and periodically sends it to other services. There are three broad uses for reference data:

- *Operands*: Operands add crucial information, such as parameters or options, to the operator requests sent out for processing. Examples of operands are the customer ID for the customer placing the order, the part numbers for the parts being ordered, or the expected shipment date and the price agreed to for the order.

- *Historical artifacts*: Historical artifacts are another type of reference data. Their purpose is documenting past information within a transmitting service. Related services receive and use historical artifacts to perform other business operations. Examples of historical data include quarterly sales results, monthly banking statements, and monthly bills.

- *Shared collections of data*: Reference data sometimes shares the same collection of data across an enterprise or different enterprises. Even after this collection of data is accessed across an enterprise, it continues to evolve and change. Typically, one special service owns this information and is responsible for updating and distributing new versions of the data across systems. Examples of shared collections of data include customer databases (which contain all the relevant information about the customers of the enterprise), employee databases (which contain information about every employee in the enterprise), parts databases, and price lists.

Inside Data

Unlike data outside services, data on the inside is private to the service. In fact, it is only loosely correlated to the data on the outside. Data on the inside is always encapsulated by service code, so the only way of accessing it is through the business logic of the service. Data on the inside comprises the tables where you store your transactional data. Just think back to the CreditCardTransaction table from Chapter 6, where you implemented the CreditCardService.

Messages

All services receive messages. These messages contain operations asking the service to perform a function. The function may be a business instruction or perhaps a product order. The function may also be to accept some incoming reference data.

Once a service receives messages, it records and commits them as data in a database table. This ensures that the data is stored and retrievable. In the next step, a transaction takes place that marks the incoming messages as consumed. As a part of the transaction, outgoing messages are queued in the local database for later transmission. Finally, the whole transaction is committed. If the transaction terminates before the entire operation is committed, the incoming message will reappear in the queue, and the transaction will be retried. With the possibility that a transaction may abort, outgoing messages are never sent until the transaction is processed to ensure message transmission is atomic with the rest of the transaction. If, for instance, a message is sent and then the transaction is aborted, the message may still be processed even when the transaction fails. The atomicity of the transaction is violated in this situation, because the transaction has not been completely undone.

In addition to the transactional support achieved by storing incoming messages in the database, there are also business benefits. The contents of the messages can be easily retrieved for different purposes, such as audits and business intelligence analysis. As an added benefit, data in a database allows for management and monitoring of the ongoing work to be based on SQL queries.

Reference Data

You use reference data to create service requests, such as a product catalog. Reference data must be in a format that is usable by both the service provider and the service consumer and is identified in a way that doesn't change over time, such as a catalog date. Reference data may also be imported into a service. As it is read into a service, it may be processed, reformatted, and indexed. Reference data stored in the service remains immutable. While the syntax and the internal representation of the reference data may be changed to suit the needs of the service, the semantics remain intact and are considered a representation of the same immutable data.

Activity Data

Activity data is data used to perform a specific activity, such as a pick list that is used to retrieve purchased items from an inventory. Since it is private to the service, other services don't need to understand the format. The lifetime of activity data is generally bound to the executed business transaction.

Resource Data

Resource data is long-lived data that is used internally by a service, such as a stock-keeping unit (SKU), customer data, or accounting data. The format and the update period of resource data is an internal detail left up to the service.

Service Interaction Data

Service interaction data is used to communicate between services. It must be in a format that all incorporated services understand, and it must remain constant over time. For example, an order form is communicated between services. If the order is lost, it must be able to be regenerated in the same form as the original and transmitted again.

SODA Features in SQL Server 2008

Now that you've had a short tour of the different types of data encountered in SODA architectures, let's concentrate on the SQL Server 2008 features that make it possible to create a SODA architecture:

- *XML support*: With the 2005 version, SQL Server began providing the new XML data type. This data type makes it possible to store XML data directly in the database and execute queries against the stored XML data. SQL Server 2005 also made it possible to modify XML data directly inside the database, without leaving the database.

- *Native web services*: Native web service support allows message-based communication based on SOAP and other protocols that take advantage of the Windows Server 2003 HTTP kernel-mode driver, http.sys. With this support, you're now able to publish stored procedures that implement Service Broker message-sending logic directly as a web service that can be used by other client applications that have no direct access to the SQL Server where your Service Broker application is deployed.

- *SQLCLR*: SQL Server provides support for integrating the .NET runtime into the database. You can use the SQLCLR feature of SQL Server to write .NET code that runs within a SQL Server process. With .NET code executed in the database, you can increase the performance, the functionality, and the maintainability of your Service Broker applications compared to those implemented completely in T-SQL.

- *Query notifications*: One of the most useful ways to improve the performance of a widely distributed, loosely coupled application is to cache data. Such a system needs a way to refresh data when the data has changed at the source. Query notifications provide you a way to become informed automatically when your cached data has changed.

- *Service Broker*: Service Broker acts as an asynchronous, reliable, and secure message bus in SODA architectures. As you've already seen from the previous chapters, you can easily build powerful, distributed solutions based on Service Broker. In SODA-based architectures, Service Broker acts as a reliable messaging bus.

As you can see, SQL Server 2008 provides a lot of new technologies and functionalities. But you can only take best advantage of them by using the technologies in conjunction to implement SODA applications. In the next sections, I'll show you how you can incorporate these features into the OrderService from the previous chapters to make it a more SODA-based one.

XML Support

SQL Server 2005 was the first version of SQL Server that supports storing native XML data directly in the database. In the previous versions of SQL Server, you had to store XML data in data types such as NVARCHAR. The XML data type lets you store XML documents and fragments in a column. An XML fragment is an XML instance that is missing a single top-level element. You can create columns, parameters, and variables of the XML data type and store XML instances in them. Note that the stored representation of the XML data type cannot exceed 2GB per instance.

You can also optionally associate an XML schema collection with a column, a parameter, or a variable of the XML data type. The schemas in the collection are used to validate and type the XML instance stored in the XML data type. In this case, the XML is said to be *typed*; otherwise, it's *untyped*.

The XML data type provides methods to query and transform the XML data directly inside SQL Server 2008. These methods are convenient, considering that Service Broker sends messages as XML data. In this case, you can process and create messages for other Service Broker services directly inside SQL Server 2008 without leaving SQL Server 2008 for further message processing.

XML Data Type Methods

The XML data type also offers so-called data type methods. With these data type methods, you're able to query and modify the XML data type instance directly inside SQL Server 2008. The XML data type offers you the following five data type methods:

- query(): Use this method to execute an XQuery-based query over an XML instance. The result of the query is also XML data.

- value(): Use this method to retrieve a scalar SQL Server value from an XML instance.

- exist(): Use this method to determine whether a query returns a non-empty result.

- modify(): Use this method to specify XML Data Modification Language (DML) statements to perform updates in the XML instance.

- nodes(): Use this method to shred XML into multiple rows to propagate parts of XML documents into row sets.

Let's take a more detailed look at each of these methods.

query()

With the query() method, you can execute an XQuery statement over an XML instance. Listing 9-1 shows a simple example of this method.

Listing 9-1. *Using the* query() XML *Data Type Method*

```
DECLARE @myDoc XML
SET @myDoc =
'<OrderRequest>
   <Customer>
      <CustomerID>4242</CustomerID>
   </Customer>
   <Product>
      <ProductID>123</ProductID>
      <Quantity>5</Quantity>
      <Price>40.99</Price>
   </Product>
   <CreditCard>
      <Holder>Klaus Aschenbrenner</Holder>
      <Number>1234-1234-1234-1234</Number>
      <ValidThrough>2009-10</ValidThrough>
   </CreditCard>
   <Shipping>
      <Name>Klaus Aschenbrenner</Name>
      <Address>Wagramer Strasse 4/803</Address>
      <ZipCode>1220</ZipCode>
      <City>Vienna</City>
      <Country>Austria</Country>
   </Shipping>
</OrderRequest>'


-- Extracting some information from the XML data
SELECT
   @myDoc.query('/OrderRequest/Customer') AS 'Customer',
   @myDoc.query('/OrderRequest/Product') AS 'Product',
   @myDoc.query('/OrderRequest/CreditCard') AS 'CreditCard',
   @myDoc.query('/OrderRequest/Shipping') AS 'Shipping'
GO
```

Figure 9-2 shows the result of the T-SQL batch from Listing 9-1.

	Customer	Product	CreditCard	Shipping
1	<Customer><CustomerID>4242</C...	<Product><ProductID>123</...	<CreditCard><Holder>Klaus Asch...	<Shipping><Name>Klaus Aschenbre...

Figure 9-2. *Using the* query() XML *data type method*

value()

With the value() method, you can perform an XQuery statement against an XML instance. value() returns a scalar SQL Server value as a result. You typically use this method to extract a value from an instance stored in an XML column, parameter, or variable. In this way, you can specify SELECT queries that combine or compare XML data with data in non-XML columns. Listing 9-2 shows how you can use this method to work with XML data.

Listing 9-2. *Using the* value() XML *Data Type Method*

```
DECLARE @myDoc XML
-- @myDoc is initialized as in Listing 9-1
SELECT
   @myDoc.value('/OrderRequest[1]/CreditCard[1]/Holder[1]',
      'NVARCHAR(256)') AS 'CreditCardHolder',
   @myDoc.value('/OrderRequest[1]/CreditCard[1]/Number[1]',
      'NVARCHAR(256)') AS 'CreditCardNumber',
   @myDoc.value('/OrderRequest[1]/CreditCard[1]/ValidThrough[1]',
      'NVARCHAR(256)') AS 'ValidThrough',
   @myDoc.value('/OrderRequest[1]/Product[1]/Quantity[1]',
      'INT') AS 'Quantity',
   @myDoc.value('/OrderRequest[1]/Product[1]/Price[1]',
      'DECIMAL(18, 2)') AS 'Price',
   @myDoc.value('/OrderRequest[1]/Customer[1]/CustomerID[1]',
      'NVARCHAR(256)') AS 'CustomerID',
   @myDoc.value('/OrderRequest[1]/Product[1]/ProductID[1]',
      'INT') AS 'ProductID'
```

Figure 9-3 shows the result of the T-SQL batch from Listing 9-2.

	CreditCardHolder	CreditCardNumber	ValidThrough	Quantity	Price	CustomerID	ProductID
1	Klaus Aschenbrenner	1234-1234-1234-1234	2009-10	5	40.99	4242	123

Figure 9-3. *Using the* value() XML *data type method*

exist()

With the exist() method, you can check whether a specific element or value is stored inside an XML instance. This method is easy to use, as you can see in Listing 9-3.

Listing 9-3. *Using the* exist() XML *Data Type Method*

```
DECLARE @myDoc XML
-- @myDoc is initialized as in Listing 9-1
SELECT
    @myDoc.exist('/OrderRequest[1]/CreditCard') AS 'CreditCardAvailable',
    @myDoc.exist('/OrderRequest[1]/Inventory') AS 'InventoryDataAvailable'
```

Figure 9-4 shows the result of the T-SQL batch from Listing 9-3.

	CreditCardAvailable	InventoryDataAvailable
1	1	0

Figure 9-4. *Using the* exist() XML *data type method*

modify()

With the modify() method, you can modify an XML instance directly inside SQL Server 2008. This method takes an XML DML statement to insert, update, or delete nodes from XML data. You can only use the modify() method with the SET clause in the UPDATE T-SQL statement. See Listing 9-4.

Listing 9-4. *Using the* modify() XML *Data Type Method*

```
DECLARE @myDoc XML
-- @myDoc is initialized as in Listing 9-1
SET @myDoc.modify('insert <MyNewNode></MyNewNode> as first into (/OrderRequest)[1]')
SELECT @myDoc
```

nodes()

The nodes() method is useful when you want to shred an XML instance into relational data. It allows you to identify nodes that will be mapped into a new row. The result of the nodes() method is a result set that contains logical copies of the original XML instance. See Listing 9-5.

Listing 9-5. *Using the* nodes() XML *Data Type Method*

```
SELECT T.c.query('.') AS result FROM @myDoc.nodes('/OrderRequest') T(c)
```

Native Web Services

For years, the only real way to communicate from a client to a server running SQL Server was by using the proprietary Tabulator Data Stream (TDS) protocol of SQL Server. TDS is still the fastest and most efficient data access method, but to communicate with the server, the client must have the proper libraries installed. Sometimes, SQL Server clients must use Microsoft Data Access Components (MDAC). The MDAC stack is installed on the client computer that connects to SQL Server. For SQL Server 2008 to be a full SODA service provider, it must support standards-based protocols to provide endpoints for accepting and processing service requests for any kind of service consumer.

The SQLXML extensions to SQL Server 2000 laid the foundation for this feature by including an Internet Server API (ISAPI) filter to use with Internet Information Services (IIS) to allow HTTP web service–based communication with SQL Server. SQL Server 2008 includes a formal endpoint abstraction that you can use to support a variety of endpoint types, including TDS, database mirroring, web services, and Service Broker. The HTTP endpoint allows the SQL Server instance to serve as a service provider for any kind of application on any kind of device that has support for web services over HTTP.

http.sys

Full native web service access requires that SQL Server 2008 be installed on Windows Server 2003 to take advantage of the Windows Server kernel-mode driver, http.sys. SQL Server can register in this kernel-mode driver to reserve portions of the URL namespace. Figure 9-5 shows the tight integration and direct connection between the kernel-mode driver and the SQL Server database. When the HTTP listener detects an HTTP request over a configured port, it routes the request directly to the endpoint that you define within SQL Server. SQL Server then does whatever processing is required and returns a response back to the caller.

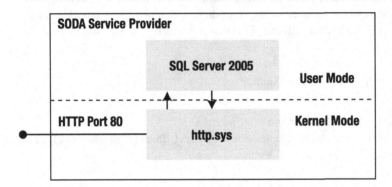

Figure 9-5. *Integration of the kernel-mode driver http.sys in SQL Server 2008*

Because the installation doesn't require IIS and because requests are sent directly from the kernel-mode driver http.sys to SQL Server, such requests are efficient and simple to administer. http.sys provides kernel-based process isolation between the various applications that might own different portions of the URL namespace. Therefore, different endpoints in the same and other instances of SQL Server cannot interfere with each other.

HTTP Endpoints

To use native web services in SQL Server 2008, an HTTP endpoint must be established at the server. This endpoint is essentially the gateway through which HTTP-based clients can query the server. After you establish an HTTP endpoint, you can add stored procedures and user-defined functions to make them available to endpoint users. This can occur when the endpoint is either created or updated. When procedures and functions are enabled, they are specified as *web methods*. A collection of web methods that are designed to be used together can be called a *web service*.

You can describe these web services by using the Web Services Description Language (WSDL) format. The WSDL format is generated by an instance of SQL Server and returned to SOAP clients for any HTTP endpoint on which WSDL generation is enabled, as shown in Figure 9-6. If required, the WSDL format can be a custom solution instead of one generated by SQL Server. The endpoint can optionally be configured to not answer WSDL requests.

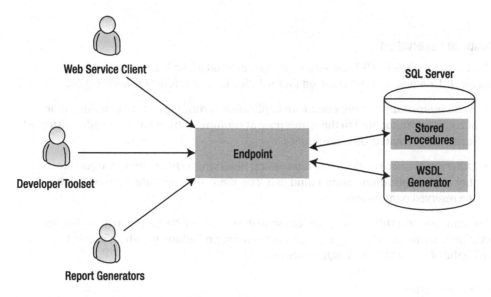

Figure 9-6. *HTTP endpoints in SQL Server 2008*

A web method that is bound to an HTTP endpoint can be a stored procedure or a scalar-valued user-defined function. The name of the method within SQL Server doesn't have to be the same as the publicly defined web method name. The implementation of the web method doesn't have any code to parse the request or to format the result for return to the service consumer, because SQL Server 2008 manages that functionality for you.

Endpoints support *basic authentication, digest authentication, Windows integrated authentication* (NTLM or Kerberos), and SQL Server authentication, but they don't support anonymous requests. This selection of authentication methods supports almost any client in a mixed-platform SODA application. You can use Windows integrated authentication with Windows consumers, and you can use SQL Server authentication for all other consumers. SQL Server 2008 also supports the Web Services Security (WS-Security) specification, so you can pass credentials by using the username token headers for SQL Server authentication. You can further restrict or allow requests based on the consumer's IP address.

HTTP endpoints are off by default, so a newly installed SQL Server instance is secure by default. This means that attacks aren't possible unless an administrator explicitly enables HTTP endpoints. Only members of the SYSADMIN fixed server role or the endpoint creator can initially connect to the endpoint. Other users can connect to the endpoint when you explicitly grant permissions, by using the GRANT CONNECT T-SQL statement. As with any HTTP connection, you can secure the channel by using Secure Sockets Layer (SSL) to protect any clear-text credentials that some of the authentication methods transmit. As soon as you enable an HTTP endpoint (through the ALTER ENDPOINT T-SQL statement), the endpoint is accessible from a client application.

■**Caution** HTTP endpoints are marked as deprecated in SQL Server 2008, because they are removed in a future version of SQL Server. Microsoft refers to the ADO.NET Data Services (formerly known as Project Astoria) as a replacement for HTTP endpoints.

Namespace Reservation

An HTTP endpoint uses a URL namespace that is reserved in the kernel-mode driver http.sys. URL namespaces are reserved for the following reasons in SQL Server 2008:

- *Nonadministrative permissions*: If an application is running as a nonadministrator account, it cannot bind to the namespace at runtime without having an administrator reserve the required URL namespace.

- *Other applications can't use the namespace*: Reserving a URL namespace guarantees that other applications cannot bind to it. Therefore, the application has ownership of the reserved namespace.

You can reserve a URL namespace for use with SQL Server 2008 either with an explicit reservation with the sp_reserve_http_namespace stored procedure or with an implicit reservation with the CREATE ENDPOINT T-SQL statement.

Explicit Reservation

To create an explicit reservation, an administrator who wants to expose an HTTP endpoint has to reserve a URL namespace by using the sp_reserve_http_namespace stored procedure. For example, you can connect to an instance of SQL Server 2008 and execute the T-SQL code, as shown in Listing 9-6, to make a URL namespace reservation.

Listing 9-6. *Explicit URL Namespace Reservation*

```
USE master
GO

sp_reserve_http_namespace N'http://csharp.at:80/sql'
GO
```

Implicit Reservation

SQL Server 2008 creates an implicit namespace reservation when you use the CREATE ENDPOINT T-SQL statement. When an implicit reservation is made, other applications can take the namespace if the SQL Server instance isn't running. In the "Exposing Web Services" section, you'll see how to use the CREATE ENDPOINT T-SQL statement.

Verifying HTTP Namespace Reservations

To determine what namespaces are reserved in http.sys, you can run the HTTP configuration utility httpcfg.exe. Listing 9-7 shows an example of using httpcfg.exe to return the list of reserved HTTP namespaces.

Listing 9-7. *Verifying HTTP Namespace Reservations*

```
-- Execute from the command line
httpcfg.exe query urlacl

-- Here is a typical output for this command
URL: http://csharp.at:80/sql
ACL: D:(A;;GA;;;S-1-5-21-123456789-1234567890-1262470759-1010)
------------------------------------------------------------------

URL : https://csharp.at:443/sql/
ACL : D:(A;;GA;;;NS)
------------------------------------------------------------------
```

Note httpcfg.exe is a tool available in the Windows Support Tools of Windows Server 2003. This tool is not installed by default and must be installed additionally on a Windows Server 2003 installation. Refer to the Books Online topic "Configuring the HTTP Kernel-Mode Driver (Http.sys)" for more information.

Exposing Web Services

You use the CREATE ENDPOINT T-SQL statement to create an HTTP endpoint and expose a stored procedure as a web method. Listing 9-8 shows the syntax for the CREATE ENDPOINT T-SQL statement for creating an HTTP endpoint. You've already seen the CREATE ENDPOINT T-SQL statement in Chapter 7, where you created a Service Broker endpoint with it. Now you create an HTTP endpoint.

Listing 9-8. *Syntax for the* CREATE ENDPOINT *T-SQL Statement*

```
CREATE ENDPOINT endPointName [ AUTHORIZATION login ]
[ STATE = { STARTED | STOPPED | DISABLED } ]
AS HTTP
(
   PATH = 'url',
   AUTHENTICATION = ( { BASIC | DIGEST | INTEGRATED | NTLM | KERBEROS } [ ,...n ] ),
   PORTS  = ( { CLEAR | SSL } [ ,... n ] )
   [ SITE = { '*' | '+' | 'website' } , ]
   [ [ , ] CLEAR_PORT = clearPort ]
   [ [ , ] SSL_PORT = sslPort ]
   [ [ , ] AUTH_REALM = { 'realm' | NONE } ]
   [ [ , ] DEFAULT_LOGON_DOMAIN = { 'domain' | NONE } ]
   [ [ , ] COMPRESSION = { ENABLED | DISABLED } ]
)
```

```
FOR SOAP
(
   [ { WEBMETHOD [ 'namespace' .] 'method_alias'
     (
         NAME = 'database.schema.name'
         [ [ , ] SCHEMA = { NONE | STANDARD | DEFAULT } ]
         [ [ , ] FORMAT = { ALL_RESULTS | ROWSETS_ONLY | NONE } ]
     )
   } [ ,...n ] ]
   [ [ , ] BATCHES = { ENABLED | DISABLED } ]
   [ [ , ] WSDL = { NONE | DEFAULT | 'sp_name' } ]
   [ [ , ] SESSIONS = { ENABLED | DISABLED } ]
   [ [ , ] LOGIN_TYPE = { MIXED | WINDOWS } ]
   [ [ , ] SESSION_TIMEOUT = { timeoutInterval | NEVER } ]
   [ [ , ] DATABASE = { 'database_name' | DEFAULT } ]
   [ [ , ] NAMESPACE = { 'namespace' | DEFAULT } ]
   [ [ , ] SCHEMA = { NONE | STANDARD } ]
   [ [ , ] CHARACTER_SET = { SQL | XML } ]
   [ [ , ] HEADER_LIMIT = int ]
)
```

Table 9-1 describes the arguments for the CREATE ENDPOINT T-SQL statement.

Table 9-1. *Arguments for the* CREATE ENDPOINT *T-SQL Statement*

Argument	Description
endpointName	Specifies the name for the endpoint.
AUTHORIZATION login	A valid SQL Server or Windows login to be assigned to the newly created endpoint object.
STATE = { STARTED	STOPPED	DISABLED }	Specifies the state of the endpoint when it is created.
PATH = 'url'	Specifies the location of the endpoint on the host computer as a URL (as specified in the SITE argument). It is a logical partitioning of the URL namespace that is used by http.sys to route requests.
AUTHENTICATION = { BASIC	DIGEST	INTEGRATED	NTLM	KERBEROS }	The authentication type used to authenticate users that access the endpoint.
PORTS = ({ CLEAR | SSL } [,...n])	Associates one or more listening port types with this endpoint.
SITE = { '*'	'+'	'website' }	The name of the host computer. If you don't specify this parameter, the asterisk ('*') is the default. If you use the sp_reserve_http_namespace stored procedure, pass the host part to this argument. '+' implies that a listening operation applies to all possible host names for the computer; website is the specific host name for the computer.
CLEARPORT = clearPort	The clear port number of the endpoint. If PORTS = (CLEAR), clearPort specifies the clear port number.

Argument	Description
SSL_PORT = sslPort	Specifies the SSL port number.
AUTH_REALM = { 'realm'	NONE }	If you use AUTHENTICATION = DIGEST, AUTH_REALM specifies the hint that returns to the client, which sent the SOAP request to the endpoint, as part of HTTP authentication challenge.
DEFAULT_LOGON_DOMAIN = { 'domain'	NONE }	If you use AUTHENTICATION = BASIC, DEFAULT_LOGON_DOMAIN specifies the default login domain.
COMPRESSION = { ENABLED	DISABLED }	If you set this parameter to ENABLED, SQL Server will honor requests where gzip encoding is requested, and will return compressed responses.
WEBMETHOD ['namespace'.] 'method_alias'	Specifies a method for which you can send HTTP SOAP requests to an endpoint. Each WEBMETHOD clause describes one method. You can expose multiple methods through the endpoint.
NAME = 'database.schema.name'	Specifies the stored procedure name or user-defined function name that is exposed as a web method. You must supply the three-part name of the stored procedure or user-defined function you want to expose.
SCHEMA = { NONE	STANDARD	DEFAULT }	Specifies if inline XSD schemas are returned for the web method in a SOAP response.
FORMAT = { ALL_RESULTS	ROWSETS_ONLY	NONE }	Specifies if a row count, error messages, and warnings are returned with the result set.
BATCHES = { ENABLED	DISABLED }	Specifies if ad hoc SQL requests are supported on the endpoint.
WSDL = { NONE	DEFAULT	'sp_name' }	Specifies if WSDL document generation is supported for this endpoint.
SESSIONS = { ENABLED	DISABLED }	Specifies if the SQL Server instance allows session support. If allowed, multiple SOAP request/response message pairs can be identified as part of a single SOAP session.
LOGIN_TYPE = { MIXED	WINDOWS }	Specifies the SQL Server authentication mode for this endpoint.
SESSION_TIMEOUT = { timeoutInterval	NEVER }	Specifies the time in seconds (as an integer) that is available before a SOAP session expires at the server when no further requests are received.
DATABASE = { 'database_name'	DEFAULT }	Specifies the database in the context of which the requested operation is executed.
NAMESPACE = { 'namespace'	DEFAULT }	Specifies the namespace for the endpoint.
SCHEMA = { NONE	STANDARD }	Specifies whether an XSD schema is returned by the endpoint when SOAP results are sent.
CHARACTER_SET = { SQL	XML }	Defines the behavior when the result of an operation includes characters that are not valid in XML.
HEADER_LIMIT	Specifies the maximum size, in bytes, of the header section in the SOAP envelope.

Let's see how you can use this T-SQL statement to expose a stored procedure as a web service. In SODA architectures, stored procedures are often used to expose the Service Broker message-sending logic (from the initiating service to the target service) to clients that have no direct access to the SQL Server hosting the initiating service.

Let's take the OrderService application from previous chapters and wrap the message-sending logic from the ClientService into a stored procedure that is then exposed as a web service to other clients. You can then call the message-sending logic from other applications through the web service—it doesn't matter if the client is written in C#, PHP, Java, or even Perl.

Listing 9-9 shows the T-SQL statement needed to create the stored procedure that sends a message of the message type OrderRequestMessage from the ClientService to the OrderService.

■**Note** Please make sure that you create a new database for the following samples and that you deploy all the necessary Service Broker objects.

Listing 9-9. *Stored Procedure with the Message-Sending Logic*

```
CREATE PROCEDURE SendOrderRequestMessage
@RequestMessage XML
AS
    BEGIN TRY
        BEGIN TRANSACTION;
            DECLARE @ch UNIQUEIDENTIFIER
            DECLARE @msg NVARCHAR(MAX);

            BEGIN DIALOG CONVERSATION @ch
                FROM SERVICE [ClientService]
                TO SERVICE 'OrderService'
                ON CONTRACT [http://ssb.csharp.at/SSB_Book/c09/OrderContract]
                WITH ENCRYPTION = OFF;

            SET @msg = CAST(@RequestMessage AS NVARCHAR(MAX));

            SEND ON CONVERSATION @ch
                MESSAGE TYPE [http://ssb.csharp.at/SSB_Book/c09/OrderRequestMessage]
                (@msg);
        COMMIT;
    END TRY
    BEGIN CATCH
        ROLLBACK TRANSACTION;
    END CATCH
```

After you create the SendOrderRequestMessage stored procedure, you can easily send a new Service Broker message to the OrderService. Refer to Listing 9-10.

Listing 9-10. *Sending a New Service Broker Message with the Created Stored Procedure*

```
EXEC SendOrderRequestMessage
'<OrderRequest>
   <Customer>
      <CustomerID>4242</CustomerID>
   </Customer>
   <Product>
      <ProductID>123</ProductID>
      <Quantity>5</Quantity>
      <Price>40.99</Price>
   </Product>
   <CreditCard>
      <Holder>Klaus Aschenbrenner</Holder>
      <Number>1234-1234-1234-1234</Number>
      <ValidThrough>2009-10</ValidThrough>
   </CreditCard>
   <Shipping>
      <Name>Klaus Aschenbrenner</Name>
      <Address>Wagramer Strasse 4/803</Address>
      <ZipCode>1220</ZipCode>
      <City>Vienna</City>
      <Country>Austria</Country>
   </Shipping>
</OrderRequest>'
```

The only thing left to do is to create the HTTP endpoint that exposes this stored procedure as a web service to other clients. Listing 9-11 shows the CREATE ENDPOINT T-SQL command that creates the necessary HTTP endpoint.

Listing 9-11. *Creating the HTTP Endpoint*

```
CREATE ENDPOINT WebServiceEndpoint
STATE = STARTED
AS HTTP
(
   PATH = '/SendOrderRequestMessage',
   AUTHENTICATION = (INTEGRATED),
   PORTS = (CLEAR),
   SITE = '*'
)
```

```
FOR SOAP
(
    WEBMETHOD 'SendOrderRequestMessage'
    (
        NAME = 'Chapter9_SODA_Services.dbo.SendOrderRequestMessage'
    ),
    WSDL = DEFAULT,
    SCHEMA = STANDARD,
    DATABASE = ' Chapter9_SODA_Services',
    NAMESPACE = 'http://www.csharp.at'
)
GO
```

As soon as you create the HTTP endpoint, the endpoint becomes browsable through your web browser. Just navigate to the URL `http://your-computer-name/SendOrderRequestMessage?wsdl` to view the WSDL document for the exposed web service. Make sure to replace `http://your-computer-name` with the value you've specified in the SITE argument of the CREATE ENDPOINT T-SQL statement. Figure 9-7 shows the generated WSDL document for the web service.

Caution Don't use `http://localhost` when you want to connect to the SQL Server web service! You must always use the NetBIOS name of the computer you've specified in the SITE argument in the CREATE ENDPOINT T-SQL statement.

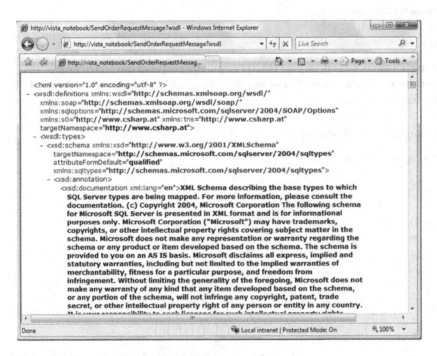

Figure 9-7. *Browsing the deployed SQL Server web service*

Using Web Services

After you deploy the stored procedure SendOrderRequestMessages as a web service, you can easily call the stored procedure from a client application, thereby sending a Service Broker message in the background when the stored procedure executes. Listing 9-12 shows a simplified console application that calls the web service for sending a Service Broker message.

Listing 9-12. *Using the Web Service*

```
public static void Main(string [] args)
{
    string message =
    "<OrderRequest>" +
        "<Customer>" +
            "<CustomerID>4242</CustomerID>" +
        "</Customer>" +
        "<Product>" +
            "<ProductID>123</ProductID>" +
            "<Quantity>5</Quantity>" +
            "<Price>40.99</Price>" +
        "</Product>" +
        "<CreditCard>" +
            "<Holder>Klaus Aschenbrenner</Holder>" +
            "<Number>1234-1234-1234-1234</Number>" +
            "<ValidThrough>2009-10</ValidThrough>" +
        "</CreditCard>" +
        "<Shipping>" +
            "<Name>Klaus Aschenbrenner</Name>" +
            "<Address>Wagramer Strasse 4/803</Address>" +
            "<ZipCode>1220</ZipCode>" +
            "<City>Vienna</City>" +
            "<Country>Austria</Country>" +
        "</Shipping>" +
    "</OrderRequest>";

    ClientApplication.vista_notebook.WebServiceEndpoint svc =
        new WebServiceEndpoint();
    XmlDocument doc = new XmlDocument();
    doc.LoadXml(message);

    xml requestMessage = new xml();
    requestMessage.Any = new XmlNode[1] { doc.DocumentElement.ParentNode };

    svc.UseDefaultCredentials = true;
    svc.SendOrderRequestMessage(requestMessage);

    Console.WriteLine("Done");
    Console.ReadLine();
}
```

When you execute this simple C# program and then look into the various queues of the different Service Broker services, you'll see that your sent message gets processed automatically. As you can see, you can easily provide Service Broker functionality to other clients that have no direct access to your SQL Service where your initiating service is hosted.

Web services for exposing SQL Server functionality are one pillar of SODA in SQL Server 2008. Let's now look at another interesting SODA feature, the SQLCLR.

SQLCLR

One critical ingredient in SODA is the logic itself—that is, the ability to run high-level code to control all aspects of the system, process input, and respond to changing conditions in the environment. SQL Server has long included T-SQL and the ability to invoke external applications, such as COM components, using the sp_OA system stored procedure.

However, a viable SODA service provider must be able to run integrated, high-level, efficient code capable of implementing highly complex business logic functionality. T-SQL is great for manipulating set-based, relational data, but it's not a programming language for coding complex, high-performance, business-logic code. The .NET Base Class Library (BCL) provides exactly the programming infrastructure needed to write this kind of code.

.NET 2.0 has a CLR hosting API that lets you execute CLR applications within a host process such as SQL Server 2008. You can use the SQLCLR feature of SQL Server 2008 to write .NET code that runs within the SQL Server process. The SQLCLR is close to the data and to the other SODA features, and it's integrated with database security. .NET assemblies are stored and loaded directly from the database instead of the file system. This improves efficiency and reduces administrative complexity when you back up and restore databases with .NET code inside.

You can use SQLCLR to write functions as replacements for extended stored procedures and to create user-defined functions and data types. It has a variety of other uses within the database for more traditional applications (although it doesn't replace all T-SQL applications). In an application that is based on SODA, hosting the CLR provides a code execution environment that supports multiple programming languages, garbage collection, memory management, resource pooling, system resource management, and code-access security. The primary SQL Server process works with the CLR to control global process resources such as memory, concurrency primitives, and threads.

SQLCLR radically changes and expands the programming paradigm supported by SQL Server 2008. It allows you to develop the following database objects in a .NET language of your choice:

- *Managed stored procedures*: Managed stored procedures provide you with the ability to implement a stored procedure in a .NET language such as C# or VB. Managed stored procedures also improve the performance of your business logic compared to when it is written in T-SQL, because T-SQL is a more data-centric programming language.

- *User-defined functions*: With user-defined functions, you can write scalar- and table-valued functions directly in .NET code.

- *User-defined data types*: With a custom data type, you're able to extend the type system of SQL Server 2008. You can use a custom data type everywhere you can use a built-in data type. Custom data types contain both logic and data.

- *User-defined aggregates*: You can also develop a set of custom aggregate functions on top of your custom data type.

- *Triggers*: With SQLCLR, you can write triggers in a .NET language.

These sophisticated features are required by a service program within SODA architectures. You can place any or all of the logic within the database rather than develop and deploy a separate application external to the database for business-logic processing. For more traditional three- or n-tier applications, the line between hosting data-processing code in the database and business logic in a middle tier is blurred. However, it is now relatively easy to develop one code base that you can deploy either to the database or to a middle-tier application server as demands placed on the system change.

You can use SQLCLR to extend the built-in T-SQL functions. Once deployed to the database, each managed code object is available for use within any query. Since the CLR functions are compiled into intermediate language (IL) and ultimately into native machine instructions, the functions can run much faster than equivalent functions written in T-SQL, which are interpreted at runtime rather than compiled.

SQLCLR also provides a data access library, which can run inside the relational data engine. When the SQLCLR data access code is executed within a SQL Server process, latencies and the transaction costs of connecting to a remote database and acquiring data are significantly reduced. Data that is required to process a service request from an external server doesn't have to travel across a portion of the network or even from an adjacent machine on the server rack.

Writing .NET Service Logic

As you saw in Chapter 5, the ServiceBrokerInterface managed assembly enables you to write Service Broker service programs and also client applications for Service Broker in a .NET language. With this managed assembly, you can easily implement Service Broker message-processing logic in C# or VB. In Chapter 5, you also saw the CREATE ASSEMBLY T-SQL statement with which you can register a managed assembly in SQL Server 2008.

To give you a practical example of how to use SQLCLR in SODA, let's transform all the T-SQL service programs from the OrderService application into managed stored procedures that leverage the .NET support in SQL Server 2008. This approach has different advantages:

- *Performance*: If you have complex business logic in your service program (which isn't the case in this example), then SQLCLR will boost the performance of your service program, since SQLCLR handles the execution of complex business logic more efficiently than T-SQL.

- *Extensibility*: As you saw in Chapter 6, the ProcessOrderRequestMessages stored procedure was complex and long, because all the different message types were processed in one stored procedure. When you implement the message-processing logic with the ServiceBrokerInterface managed assembly, you can assign each message type a separate method that does its message processing.

Implementing State Handling

Before you implement the whole message-processing logic of the different Service Broker services, let's write the code that does the state handling inside OrderService. As you learned in Chapter 6, you need a state table that stores the state of the ongoing conversations between the different services. Figure 9-8 shows the structure of the ApplicationState table.

Column Name	Data Type	Allow Nulls
ConversationGroupID	uniqueidentifier	☐
CreditCardStatus	bit	☐
AccountingStatus	bit	☐
InventoryStatus	bit	☐
ShippingMessageSent	bit	☐
ShippingStatus	bit	☐

Figure 9-8. *The* ApplicationState *table*

After creating the state table, you have to override the LoadState and SaveState methods in the OrderService that represent your Service Broker service. Listing 9-13 shows the LoadState method.

Listing 9-13. *Implementation of the* LoadState *Method*

```
public override bool LoadState(SqlDataReader reader, SqlConnection connection,
    SqlTransaction transaction)
{
    if (reader.Read())
    {
        _conversationGroupId = new Guid(reader["ConversationGroupID"].ToString());
        _creditCardStatus = bool.Parse(reader["CreditCardStatus"].ToString());
        _accountingStatus = bool.Parse(reader["AccountingStatus"].ToString());
        _inventoryStatus = bool.Parse(reader["InventoryStatus"].ToString());
        _shippingMessageSent =
          bool.Parse(reader["ShippingMessageSent"].ToString());
        _shippingStatus = bool.Parse(reader["ShippingStatus"].ToString());

        // Advances the cursor to the next result set that contains
        // the received message(s)
        return reader.NextResult();
    }
    else
        // Something went wrong...
        return false;
}
```

The most important part of Listing 9-13 is the line where the database cursor is moved to the next result set inside the SqlDataReader instance:

```
return reader.NextResult();
```

This is necessary, because the SqlDataReader contains two result sets, and you must move the cursor to the result set that contains the retrieved message:

- The first result set contains the state data from the state table.

- The second result set contains the message retrieved from the queue.

Listing 9-14 shows the implementation of the SaveState method.

Listing 9-14. *Implementation of the* SaveState *Method*

```
public override void SaveState(SqlConnection connection, SqlTransaction transaction)
{
    // Create the T-SQL command for updating the application state
    string sql = "UPDATE ApplicationState SET ";
    sql += "CreditCardStatus = @CreditCardStatus, ";
    sql += "AccountingStatus = @AccountingStatus, ";
    sql += "InventoryStatus = @InventoryStatus, ";
    sql += "ShippingMessageSent = @ShippingMessageSent, ";
    sql += "ShippingStatus = @ShippingStatus ";
    sql += "WHERE ConversationGroupID = @ConversationGroupID";

    // Create the necessary T-SQL parameters
    SqlCommand cmd = new SqlCommand(sql, connection);
    cmd.Transaction = transaction;
    cmd.Parameters.Add("@CreditCardStatus", SqlDbType.Bit);
    cmd.Parameters.Add("@AccountingStatus", SqlDbType.Bit);
    cmd.Parameters.Add("@InventoryStatus", SqlDbType.Bit);
    cmd.Parameters.Add("@ShippingMessageSent", SqlDbType.Bit);
    cmd.Parameters.Add("@ShippingStatus", SqlDbType.Bit);
    cmd.Parameters.Add("@ConversationGroupID", SqlDbType.UniqueIdentifier);

    // Set the T-SQL parameters
    cmd.Parameters["@CreditCardStatus"].Value = _creditCardStatus;
    cmd.Parameters["@AccountingStatus"].Value = _accountingStatus;
    cmd.Parameters["@InventoryStatus"].Value = _inventoryStatus;
    cmd.Parameters["@ShippingMessageSent"].Value = _shippingMessageSent;
    cmd.Parameters["@ShippingStatus"].Value = _shippingStatus;
    cmd.Parameters["@ConversationGroupID"].Value = _conversationGroupId;

    // Execute the query
    cmd.ExecuteNonQuery();
}
```

As you can see in Listing 9-14, SaveState is straightforward, because it just executes a simple UPDATE T-SQL statement that updates the ApplicationState table.

Implementing the OrderService

Once you implement state handling, you're ready to write the message-processing logic. The main logic of OrderService is executed when an OrderRequestMessage is received from ClientService. You implement the message-processing logic for the OrderRequestMessage message type in ProcessOrderRequestMessage. Listing 9-15 shows the concrete implementation.

Listing 9-15. *Implementation of the* ProcessOrderRequestMessage *Method*

```
[BrokerMethod("http://ssb.csharp.at/SSB_Book/c09/OrderRequestMessage")]
public void ProcessOrderRequestMessage(Message ReceivedMessage,
    SqlConnection Connection, SqlTransaction Transaction)
{
    BeginConversationWithCreditCardService(ReceivedMessage, Connection, Transaction);
    BeginConversationWithAccountingService(ReceivedMessage, Connection, Transaction);
    BeginConversationWithInventoryService(ReceivedMessage, Connection, Transaction);
}
```

You simply call three methods: BeginConversationWithCreditCardService, BeginConversationWithAccountingService, and BeginConversationWithInventoryService. In each method, you send the required request message to each Service Broker service (CreditCardService, AccountingService, InventoryService) for further processing. The main difference between these three methods is the creation of the message structure, because the XML message is different for each service. Listing 9-16 shows the implementation of the BeginConversationWithAccountingService method.

Listing 9-16. *Implementation of the* BeginConversationWithAccountingService *Method*

```
private void BeginConversationWithAccountingService(Message ReceivedMessage,
    SqlConnection Connection, SqlTransaction Transaction)
{
    XmlDocument doc = new XmlDocument();
    doc.LoadXml(ReceivedMessage.BodyAsString);

    int quantity = int.Parse(doc.GetElementsByTagName("Quantity").Item(0).InnerText);
    double price = double.Parse(doc.GetElementsByTagName("Price").Item(0).InnerText);

    XmlDocument accountingDoc = new XmlDocument();
    XmlElement root = accountingDoc.CreateElement("AccountingRequest");
    XmlElement accountingCustomerID = accountingDoc.CreateElement("CustomerID");
    XmlElement accountingAmount = accountingDoc.CreateElement("Amount");

    accountingCustomerID.InnerText =
        doc.GetElementsByTagName("CustomerID").Item(0).InnerText;
    accountingAmount.InnerText = (price * quantity).ToString();
```

```
root.AppendChild(accountingCustomerID);
root.AppendChild(accountingAmount);
accountingDoc.AppendChild(root);

Conversation conv = this.BeginDialog("AccountingService", null,
    "http://ssb.csharp.at/SSB_Book/c09/AccountingContract",
    TimeSpan.FromMinutes(99999), false, ReceivedMessage.Conversation, Connection,
    Transaction);
conv.Send(new Message(
    "http://ssb.csharp.at/SSB_Book/c09/AccountingRequestMessage",
    new MemoryStream(Encoding.Unicode.GetBytes(accountingDoc.InnerXml))),
    Connection, Transaction);
}
```

The last lines where you begin a new dialog with the AccountingService and send a request message to this service are the most important part:

```
Conversation conv = this.BeginDialog("AccountingService", null,
    "http://ssb.csharp.at/SSB_Book/c09/AccountingContract",
    TimeSpan.FromMinutes(99999), false, ReceivedMessage.Conversation, Connection,
    Transaction);
conv.Send(new Message(
    "http://ssb.csharp.at/SSB_Book/c09/AccountingRequestMessage",
    new MemoryStream(Encoding.Unicode.GetBytes(accountingDoc.InnerXml))),
    Connection, Transaction);
```

When you begin the dialog, you must ensure that you also specify the existing conversation (ReceivedMessage.Conversation). If you forget this, the newly created dialog will belong to a new conversation group, and the previously implemented state-handling logic won't work. For the implementation of all the other mentioned methods, refer to the source code provided in this chapter's Source Code/Download area on the Apress website (http://www.apress.com).

Implementing the Other Services

By now, you've seen how OrderService handles the OrderRequestMessage message type. In this section, I want to show how the other Service Broker services (AccountingService, CreditCardService, and InventoryService) are implemented with SQLCLR. Because they just differ in the INSERT T-SQL statement that inserts the data of a newly received message into a table, I'll present only the implementation of the AccountingService. For the implementation of the other two services, refer to this chapter's enclosed source code. The AccountingService service has to handle the following two message types:

- http://ssb.csharp.at/SSB_Book/c09/AccountingRequestMessage

- http://schemas.microsoft.com/SQL/ServiceBroker/EndDialog

Listing 9-17 shows how AccountingService handles the AccountingRequestMessage message type.

Listing 9-17. *Processing the* AccountingRequestMessage *Message Type*

```
[BrokerMethod("http://ssb.csharp.at/SSB_Book/c09/AccountingRequestMessage")]
public void ProcessAccountingRequestMessage(Message ReceivedMessage,
    SqlConnection Connection, SqlTransaction Transaction)
{
    XmlDocument doc = new XmlDocument();
    doc.LoadXml(ReceivedMessage.BodyAsString);

    // Create the T-SQL command for updating the application state
    string sql = "INSERT INTO AccountingRecordings (AccountingRecordingsID, " +
        "CustomerID, Amount) VALUES ";
    sql += "(NEWID(), @CustomerID, @Amount)";

    // Create the necessary T-SQL parameters
    SqlCommand cmd = new SqlCommand(sql, Connection);
    cmd.Transaction = Transaction;
    cmd.Parameters.Add("@CustomerID", SqlDbType.NVarChar);
    cmd.Parameters.Add("@Amount", SqlDbType.Decimal);

    // Set the T-SQL parameters
    cmd.Parameters["@CustomerID"].Value =
        doc.GetElementsByTagName("CustomerID").Item(0).InnerText;
    cmd.Parameters["@Amount"].Value =
        decimal.Parse(doc.GetElementsByTagName("Amount").Item(0).InnerText);

    // Execute the query
    cmd.ExecuteNonQuery();

    // Construct the response message
    XmlDocument responseDoc = new XmlDocument();
    XmlElement root = responseDoc.CreateElement("AccountingResponse");
    root.InnerText = "1";
    responseDoc.AppendChild(root);


    // Send the response message back to the OrderService
    ReceivedMessage.Conversation.Send(
        new Message("http://ssb.csharp.at/SSB_Book/c09/AccountingResponseMessage",
        new MemoryStream(Encoding.Unicode.GetBytes(responseDoc.InnerXml))),
        Connection, Transaction);

    // End the conversation with the OrderService
    ReceivedMessage.Conversation.End(Connection, Transaction);
}
```

The ProcessAccountingRequestMessage method first constructs a new XML structure that represents the message sent back to OrderService. You use classes in the System.Xml namespace—in particular, XmlDocument and XmlElement. After constructing the message, you send it back to OrderService with the Send method of the Conversation class available in the ServiceBrokerInterface managed assembly. Finally, you end the conversation with OrderService by calling ReceivedMessage.Conversation.End.

Processing Response Messages

Processing the response messages from the three other services (AccountingService, CreditCardService, and InventoryService) is easy, because you just have to update the corresponding status variable in the OrderService instance. Because of the state-handling logic you already implemented (see Listings 9-13 and 9-14), the updated application status is reflected automatically in the ApplicationState table by the SaveState method in the ServiceBrokerInterface managed assembly described in Listing 9-14.

Listing 9-18 shows how easy it is to update the application state when a response message arrives from the three other services.

Listing 9-18. *Updating the Application State*

```
[BrokerMethod("http://ssb.csharp.at/SSB_Book/c09/AccountingResponseMessage")]
public void ProcessAccountingResponseMessage(Message ReceivedMessage,
    SqlConnection Connection, SqlTransaction Transaction)
{
    // The AccountingResponseMessage was successfully received
    _accountingStatus = true;
}
```

Interaction with the ShippingService

More interesting is the interaction with the ShippingService. I've written the SendShippingRequestMessage method to send the ShippingRequestMessage as soon as all the other three services have successfully returned their response messages. This method checks first for the response messages from the three other services. If this is the case, it retrieves the original OrderRequestMessage from OrderQueue (the retention support of the queue makes this possible). Finally, you send the <Shipping> node of this message to ShippingService. Listing 9-19 shows the implementation of the SendShippingRequestMessage method.

Listing 9-19. *The* SendShippingRequestMessage *Method*

```
private void SendShippingRequestMessage(Message ReceivedMessage,
    SqlConnection Connection, SqlTransaction Transaction)
{
    // If we received all response messages from all the other services,
    // we can send the final message to the shipping service
    if (_accountingStatus && _creditCardStatus && _inventoryStatus)
```

```
{
    // SELECT the original order request message from the OrderQueue -
    // RETENTION makes it possible
    string sql = "SELECT CAST(message_body AS XML) FROM OrderQueue " +
        "WHERE conversation_group_id = @ConversationGroupID AND " +
        "message_type_name = " +
        "'http://ssb.csharp.at/SSB_Book/c09/OrderRequestMessage'";

    SqlCommand cmd = new SqlCommand(sql, Connection);
    cmd.Transaction = Transaction;

    // Create and set the parameters for the T-SQL command
    cmd.Parameters.Add("@ConversationGroupID", SqlDbType.UniqueIdentifier);
    cmd.Parameters["@ConversationGroupID"].Value = _conversationGroupId;

    // Execute the T-SQL command
    SqlDataReader reader = cmd.ExecuteReader();

    if (reader.Read())
    {
        // Get the <ShippingNode> from the original order request message
        SqlXml xml = reader.GetSqlXml(0);
        XmlDocument requestDoc = new XmlDocument();
        requestDoc.LoadXml(reader.GetSqlXml(0).Value);
        reader.Close();
        string shippingNode =
            requestDoc.SelectSingleNode("OrderRequest/Shipping").OuterXml;

        // Send the request message to the shipping service
        Conversation conv = this.BeginDialog("ShippingService", null,
            "http://ssb.csharp.at/SSB_Book/c09/ShippingContract",
            TimeSpan.FromSeconds(999999), false, ReceivedMessage.Conversation,
            Connection, Transaction);
        conv.Send(new Message(
            "http://ssb.csharp.at/SSB_Book/c09/ShippingRequestMessage",
            new MemoryStream(Encoding.Unicode.GetBytes(shippingNode))),
            Connection, Transaction);

        // The shipping request message was successfully sent
        _shippingMessageSent = true;
    }
}
}
```

You retrieve the original request message easily from OrderQueue with this code:

```
// SELECT the original order request message from the OrderQueue -
// RETENTION makes it possible
string sql = "SELECT CAST(message_body AS XML) FROM OrderQueue " +
   "WHERE conversation_group_id = @ConversationGroupID AND " +
   "message_type_name = " +
   "'http://ssb.csharp.at/SSB_Book/c09/OrderRequestMessage'";

SqlCommand cmd = new SqlCommand(sql, Connection);
cmd.Transaction = Transaction;

// Create and set the parameters for the T-SQL command
cmd.Parameters.Add("@ConversationGroupID", SqlDbType.UniqueIdentifier);
cmd.Parameters["@ConversationGroupID"].Value = _conversationGroupId;

// Execute the T-SQL command
SqlDataReader reader = cmd.ExecuteReader();
```

More interesting is how OrderService processes the ShippingResponseMessage. This functionality is implemented in the ProcessShippingResponseMessage method of the OrderService class. You must determine the correct conversation handle that leads you back to the ClientService. You obtain the conversation handle from the sys.conversation_endpoints catalog view and create a new Conversation object that represents the ongoing conversation with ClientService. Finally, you send an OrderResponseMessage over this conversation back to ClientService. See Listing 9-20 for the detailed implementation.

Listing 9-20. *The* ProcessShippingResponseMessage *Method*

```
[BrokerMethod("http://ssb.csharp.at/SSB_Book/c09/ShippingResponseMessage")]
public void ProcessShippingResponseMessage(Message ReceivedMessage,
   SqlConnection Connection, SqlTransaction Transaction)
{
   XmlDocument doc = new XmlDocument();
   doc.LoadXml(ReceivedMessage.BodyAsString);

   // Create the order response message
   XmlDocument responseDoc = new XmlDocument();
   XmlElement root = responseDoc.CreateElement("OrderResponse");
   root.InnerText = doc.GetElementsByTagName("ShippingResponse").Item(0).InnerText;
   responseDoc.AppendChild(root);

   // Create the T-SQL command to retrieve the conversation handle
   // back to the client service
   string sql = "SELECT conversation_handle FROM sys.conversation_endpoints " +
      "WHERE conversation_group_id = @ConversationGroupID " +
      "AND far_service = 'ClientService'";
   SqlCommand cmd = new SqlCommand(sql, Connection);
   cmd.Transaction = Transaction;
```

```
    cmd.Parameters.Add("@ConversationGroupID", SqlDbType.UniqueIdentifier);
    cmd.Parameters["@ConversationGroupID"].Value = _conversationGroupId;


    // Execute the T-SQL command
    SqlDataReader reader = cmd.ExecuteReader();

    if (reader.Read())
    {
        // Re-create the conversation object that represents the conversation
        // back to the client service
        Conversation conv = new Conversation(reader.GetGuid(0));
        reader.Close();

        // Send the response message back to the OrderService
        conv.Send(new Message(
            "http://ssb.csharp.at/SSB_Book/c09/OrderResponseMessage",
            new MemoryStream(Encoding.Unicode.GetBytes(responseDoc.InnerXml))),
            Connection, Transaction);

        // End the conversation with the OrderService
        conv.End(Connection, Transaction);
    }

    // The shipment was successfully completed
    _shippingStatus = true;
}
```

The most interesting part of Listing 9-20 is retrieving the conversation handle back to ClientService and creating the Conversation object with it:

```
string sql = "SELECT conversation_handle FROM sys.conversation_endpoints " +
    "WHERE conversation_group_id = @ConversationGroupID " +
    "AND far_service = 'ClientService'";

// ...

Conversation conv = new Conversation(reader.GetGuid(0));
reader.Close();

// Send the response message back to the OrderService
conv.Send(new Message(
    "http://ssb.csharp.at/SSB_Book/c09/OrderResponseMessage",
    new MemoryStream(Encoding.Unicode.GetBytes(responseDoc.InnerXml))),
    Connection, Transaction);
```

As you can see, you can write all your Service Broker service programs completely with SQLCLR instead of T-SQL. But be careful in choosing between .NET code and T-SQL. In these simple examples, it might be better in some circumstances to use T-SQL, because there isn't a lot of business logic—only message retrieval and data logic. But as your service programs get bigger and more complex and need to support additional message types, it's easier to use SQLCLR with the ServiceBrokerInterface methods. You can easily access the complete .NET BCL, and you have a powerful programming language and environment for coding business logic.

Query Notifications

One of the classic problems when writing distributed database applications is refreshing data. Imagine a website or smart client application where you display products and price lists. The same data is retrieved from the database over and over again. This is inefficient if the data rarely changes, and it wastes resources and execution time on the database server.

Caching is one technique for minimizing demands on the database server. The data is queried once and stored in a cache on the client side, and the application then repeatedly accesses the cache. Occasionally, the cache is updated to refresh the data. The issue is deciding when to update the cache. If you don't do it often enough, users see old data; if you update the cache too often, then you don't optimally reduce your demand on the server side.

Query notifications help you to solve this tricky problem. Query notifications allow you to cache data and be notified by SQL Server when data has been changed. You can then refresh your cache or take whatever other action you need. Why mention query notifications in a chapter about SODA? There are two main reasons:

- *Query notifications are needed for SODA*: Query notifications are the fourth technology offered by SQL Server 2008 to support SODA. Query notifications are mainly used on the middle tier to update caches when they have changed on the database server.

- *Query notifications are based on Service Broker*: Query notifications are internally implemented with Service Broker. As soon as a data change is detected on the database server, query notifications generate a new Service Broker message that gets sent to the subscriber that's caching the data. It doesn't matter if the subscriber is implemented in the middle tier, as a web service, or as a Smart Client—the reliability and routing features of Service Broker ensure that the message is sent successfully to the subscriber.

Query Notifications Implementation

Clients can submit a query that requests to be notified when data is modified in a manner that would change the query result, and the database server sends a notification when such changes occur. This notification is sent through a Service Broker message to the subscriber. These requests are called *query notification subscriptions*. You can find the list of notification subscriptions in the sys.dm_qn_subscriptions server-level view. Table 9-2 describes the available columns of this catalog view.

Although you must take a number of actions to allow SQL Server to provide this service to .NET clients, the key is that queries sent to SQL Server have a flag attached to them telling SQL Server that in addition to returning the result set, SQL Server should register the query (and its subscriber) into query notifications. It does this by using a queue that is aware of the query and a Service Broker service that is attached to the queue and knows how to get back to the client (through the routing configuration). If any of the rows in that result set get updated in the database, the item in the related queue is triggered and in turn, sends a Service Broker message to its service and then sends a notice back to the application that initiated the request.

Table 9-2. *Columns of the* sys.dm_qn_subscriptions *Catalog View*

Column	Data Type	Description
id	INT	Stores the query notification subscription ID.
database_id	INT	The ID of the database in which the query notification was executed. In this database, you'll find related information about the query notification subscription.
sid	VARBINARY(85)	The security ID of the server principal that created and owns the query notification subscription.
object_id	INT	The ID of the internal table that stores information about the query notification subscription parameters.
created	DATETIME	The date and time when the query notification subscription was created.
timeout	INT	The time-out value of the query notification subscription. The query notification will be flagged to fire after this time has elapsed.
status	INT	The status of the query notification subscription.

You've seen that the notification is not delivered back to the subscriber, but a Service Broker message is instead sent to the service that the subscriber provided in the subscription request. All normal rules for delivery, routing, and dialog security apply to the dialog used to send this message. This means that the notification message can be sent to a service hosted in the same database, in a different database, or even on a remote machine (such as a SQL Express Edition running on a Smart Client). Also, there is no need for the subscriber to be connected to receive the notification. It is perfectly acceptable for a subscriber to submit a query for a query notification subscription and then disconnect and shut down.

The subscriber consumes the notification message just like any other Service Broker message: by receiving it from the service queue. The notification message will be of the message type [http:// schemas.microsoft.com/SQL/Notifications/QueryNotification], an XML message type. This message type is part of the [http://schemas.microsoft.com/SQL/Notifications/PostQueryNotification] contract, which means that the service that receives the notification message must be bound to this contract. After the subscriber receives the message, the subscriber is supposed to end the conversation on which the message was received, using the END CONVERSATION T-SQL statement.

Clients can submit query notification subscription requests by programming directly against the SQL Native Client, using native web services support to access SQL Server, or, most commonly, using the ADO.NET client components. You must understand several important things when you want to use query notifications successfully:

- *There are rules about what types of queries are acceptable to SQL Server*: Therefore, subscribers can't subscribe to all types of queries.

- *The information returned to the subscriber isn't much more than something has changed*: The subscriber doesn't get notified about what was changed.

- *Although the dependency is tied to the rows that are returned from the query, it isn't filtered by the individual columns of the query*: If you have a query that returns the first and the last names of a customer, and the addresses of those customers change (but their first or last name doesn't change), this also triggers a query notification.

- *Notifications are returned through a single* System.Data.SqlClient.SqlConnection *that is established solely for this purpose*: This connection isn't engaged in connection pooling.

When you want to use query notifications in the middle tier or on a Smart Client, the .NET Framework provides classes with which you can directly interact with the query notifications implementation on the database server. .NET offers two possibilities:

- SqlDependency: The .NET class System.Data.SqlDependency is a high-level implementation to access the query notifications feature on SQL Server 2008. This class allows you to use a dependency to detect changes on the database server. In most cases, this is the simplest and most effective way to leverage the SQL Server 2008 notifications capability by managed client applications using the .NET Framework data provider for SQL Server.

- SqlNotificationRequest: The low-level implementation is provided by the System.Data.SqlNotificationRequest class that exposes server-side functionality, enabling you to execute a command with a notification request.

■**Note** When you use query notifications, you must be sure to enable Service Broker for the database. You can use the ALTER DATABASE MyDatabase SET ENABLE_BROKER T-SQL statement.

SqlDependency

If you want to use query notifications without paying attention to the underlying Service Broker infrastructure, the SqlDependency .NET class from the namespace System.Data is your choice. The SqlDependency class represents a query notification dependency between an application and an instance of SQL Server 2008. When you use query notifications, SQL Server 2008 provides the queue and the service object, because they are created automatically when you create a new database:

- [QueryNotificationErrorsQueue]

- [http://schemas.microsoft.com/SQL/Notifications/QueryNotificationService]

■**Note** As you'll see in the upcoming "SqlNotificationRequest" section, it's also possible for you to use your own created queue and service objects with query notifications.

Figure 9-9 shows both Service Broker objects within SQL Server Management Studio.

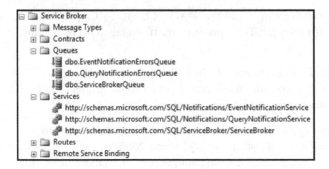

Figure 9-9. *The query notifications objects of a new database*

An application can create a SqlDependency object and register to receive notifications via an event handler. Table 9-3 shows the most important members of the SqlDependency class.

Table 9-3. *Members of the* SqlDependency *Class*

Member	Description
Start	This static method starts the listener for receiving dependency change notifications.
Stop	This static method stops the listener specified in the previous call to the Start method.
AddCommandDependency	This method associates a SqlCommand object with the SqlDependency object.
OnChange	This event occurs when a notification is received for any of the commands associated with the SqlDependency object.

To set up a dependency, you have to do the following:

1. Call SqlDependency.Start to start the listener for receiving dependency change notifications.

2. Associate a SqlDependency object with one or more SqlCommand objects.

3. Subscribe to the OnChange event of the SqlDependency object.

4. Implement the event handler of the OnChange event accordingly.

Let's take a detailed look at each of these steps. I've written a simple Windows Forms application called SimpleQueryNotification, which demonstrates how to use query notifications in a Smart Client application. This sample application shows the rows from the Products table in a DataGridView. Listing 9-21 shows the CREATE TABLE T-SQL statement needed to create this table.

Listing 9-21. *Creating the* Products *Table*

```
CREATE TABLE Products
(
   ID INT PRIMARY KEY IDENTITY(1, 1) NOT NULL,
   ProductName NVARCHAR(256) NOT NULL,
   ProductDescription NVARCHAR(256) NOT NULL
)
```

Inside the MainForm class of the sample application, you define various member variables used for the data retrieval, as shown in Listing 9-22.

Listing 9-22. *The Member Variables*

```
public partial class MainForm : Form
{
   private string _connectionString =
      "Data Source=localhost;Initial Catalog=Chapter9_QueryNotifications;" +
      "Integrated Security=SSPI;";
   private SqlConnection _cnn;
   private SqlCommand _cmd;
   private DataSet _dataToWatch;
}
```

The user interface (UI) of the MainForm class is simple: it's a DataGridView control that shows the records from the Products table and a button for retrieving the records. Figure 9-10 shows the UI.

Figure 9-10. *The UI of the sample application*

When you click the Get Data button, the cmdGetData_Click method is called, which then calls the GetData method. Listing 9-23 shows the implementation of both methods.

Listing 9-23. *Implementation of the* cmdGetData_Click *and* GetData *Methods*

```
private void cmdGetData_Click(object sender, EventArgs e)
{
    SqlDependency.Stop(_connectionString);
    SqlDependency.Start(_connectionString);

    if (_cnn == null)
        _cnn = new SqlConnection(_connectionString);

    if (_cmd == null)
        _cmd = new SqlCommand(
            "SELECT ProductName, ProductDescription FROM Products", _cnn);

    if (_dataToWatch == null)
        _dataToWatch = new DataSet();

    GetData();
}

private void GetData()
{
    _dataToWatch.Clear();
    _cmd.Notification = null;


    SqlDependency dependency = new SqlDependency(_cmd);
    dependency.OnChange += new OnChangeEventHandler(dependency_OnChange);

    using (SqlDataAdapter adapter = new SqlDataAdapter(_cmd))
    {
        adapter.Fill(_dataToWatch, "Products");
        dataGridView1.DataSource = _dataToWatch;
        dataGridView1.DataMember = "Products";
        lblCount.Text = _dataToWatch.Tables["Products"].Rows.Count.ToString();
    }
}
```

As you can see in Listing 9-23, cmdGetData_Click stops and starts the query notifications for the current database connection. On first execution, the SqlConnection and SqlCommand objects are created and used inside GetData. GetData creates a new SqlDependency object and registers an event handler for the OnChange event of the SqlDependency object. In the last step, you retrieve the available data from the Products table through the SqlDataAdapter class. Listing 9-24 is the event handler for the OnChange event of the SqlDependency class.

Listing 9-24. *The* OnChange *Event Handler for the* SqlNotification *Class*

```
private void dependency_OnChange(object sender, SqlNotificationEventArgs e)
{
    ISynchronizeInvoke i = (ISynchronizeInvoke)this;

    if (i.InvokeRequired)
    {
        OnChangeEventHandler tempDelegate =
            new OnChangeEventHandler(dependency_OnChange);
        object[] args = { sender, e };

        i.BeginInvoke(tempDelegate, args);
        return;
    }

    SqlDependency dependency = (SqlDependency)sender;
    dependency.OnChange -= dependency_OnChange;

    GetData();
}
```

You retrieve the changed data from the database with GetData, as shown in Listing 9-23. Prior to calling GetData, you check if the dependency_OnChange method is executing on a background thread. If this is the case, you transition to the UI thread with BeginInvoke of the ISynchronizeInvoke interface. This is necessary because you can only update UI controls from the UI thread. As you can see in GetData, you're changing the content of the DataGridView control.

Take a careful look at Listing 9-24. You'll see that the OnChange event handler of the SqlNotification class has a second parameter that specifies an instance of the SqlNotificationEventArgs class. Table 9-4 describes the properties of the SqlNotificationEventArgs class.

Table 9-4. *Properties of the* SqlNotificationEventArgs *Class*

Property	Description
Info	Gets a value of the SqlNotificationInfo enum that indicates the reason for the notification event
Source	Gets a value of the SqlNotificationSource enum that indicates the source that generated the notification
Type	Gets a value of the SqlNotificationType enum that indicates whether the notification is generated because of an actual change or by the subscription

The properties of the SqlNotificationEventArgs class provide further information about the raised query notification. However, keep in mind that the properties don't tell you what data was changed on the database server. The properties give you most details you're going to see in a notification and can be useful for troubleshooting. You can find detailed information about the provided enumerations at http://msdn2.microsoft.com/en-us/library/system. data.sqlclient.sqlnotificationeventargs.aspx.

SqlNotificationRequest

The `SqlDependency` class is a high-level implementation of the `SqlNotificationRequest` class. With the `SqlNotificationRequest` class, you're required to create your own Service Broker services and queues in SQL Server as well as your own listener to process the sent notification accordingly. You may choose to use this lower-level class for more granular control over the notification architecture. Another benefit is that you can create your own messages that are returned along with the notification, similar to the `SqlNotificationInfo` enumeration. Let's have a look at how the `SqlNotificationRequest` class is used. Three steps are involved:

1. Set up the Service Broker service and queue.

2. Create an instance of the `SqlNotificationRequest` class and attach it to the `SqlCommand.Notification` property.

3. Write a listener that retrieves and reacts to the received query notifications message.

Let's have a look at each of these steps.

Setting Up the Service Broker Service and Queue

The first step is to set up the required Service Broker objects: a service with an associated queue. The queue used for query notifications must support the contract [http://schemas.microsoft.com/SQL/ Notifications/PostQueryNotification]. Listing 9-25 shows the required T-SQL code.

Listing 9-25. *Setting Up the Required Service Broker Objects Needed for Query Notifications*

```
CREATE QUEUE QueryNotificationQueue
GO

CREATE SERVICE QueryNotificationService
ON QUEUE QueryNotificationQueue
(
    [http://schemas.microsoft.com/SQL/Notifications/PostQueryNotification]
)
GO
```

■**Note** Make sure that you enable Service Broker in the database and that you create the `Products` table from Listing 9-21.

Creating the SqlNotificationRequest Object

Next, create a `SqlNotificationRequest` object and associate a `SqlCommand` object with it. Listing 9-26 shows the `cmdGetData_Click` and `GetData` methods where `cmdGetData_Click` is called when the user clicks the Get Data button.

Listing 9-26. *Creating a* SqlNotificationRequest *Object*

```
private void cmdGetData_Click(object sender, EventArgs e)
{
   if (_cnn == null)
     _cnn = new SqlConnection(_connectionString);

   if (_cmd == null)
     _cmd = new SqlCommand(
        "SELECT ProductName, ProductDescription FROM Products", _cnn);

   if (_dataToWatch == null)
     _dataToWatch = new DataSet();

   GetData();
}

private void GetData()
{
   _dataToWatch.Clear();
   _cmd.Notification = null;

   SqlNotificationRequest request = new SqlNotificationRequest();
   request.UserData = Guid.NewGuid().ToString();
   request.Options = "service=" + _serviceName + ";";
   request.Timeout = _notificationTimeout;
   _cmd.Notification = request;

   using (SqlDataAdapter adapter = new SqlDataAdapter(_cmd))
   {
      adapter.Fill(_dataToWatch, "Products");
      dataGridView1.DataSource = _dataToWatch;
      dataGridView1.DataMember = "Products";

      StartListener();
   }
}
```

Note that you must set the UserData and Options properties of the SqlNotificationRequest object. With UserData, you can assign an application-specific identifier for this notification. This value is not used by the notification infrastructure. Instead, it is a mechanism that allows an application to associate notifications with application state.

The Options property is used to set the Service Broker service name, the database, or the Service Broker instance GUID where the notification messages are sent. The value of the Options property has the following format:

```
service=<service-name>
   {;(local database=<database>|broker instance=<broker instance>)}
```

Finally, you fill the DataGridView control with the data retrieved by the SqlDataAdapter and call StartListener to retrieve and react on the sent query notification.

Writing a Listener

The last step to set up query notifications with SqlNotificationRequest is to write a listener method that processes the incoming query notifications. You called the listener, StartListener, in Listing 9-26. Listing 9-27 is the implementation of this method.

Listing 9-27. *Starting Up the Listener*

```
private void StartListener()
{
   Thread listener = new Thread(Listen);
   listener.Name = "Query Notification Watcher";
   listener.Start();
}
```

You just start a new thread and pass the Listen method as a parameter. This means that the query notifications are retrieved by Listen. Refer to Listing 9-28.

Listing 9-28. *Implementation of the Listener*

```
private void Listen()
{
   using (SqlConnection cnn = new SqlConnection(_connectionString))
   {
      using (SqlCommand cmd = new SqlCommand(
         "WAITFOR ( RECEIVE * FROM QueryNotificationQueue);", cnn))
      {
         // cmd.CommandTimeout = _notificationTimeout + 100;
         cnn.Open();
         SqlDataReader reader = cmd.ExecuteReader();

         while (reader.Read())
         {
         }

         object[] args = { this, EventArgs.Empty };
         EventHandler notify = new EventHandler(OnNotificationComplete);

         // Switch back to the UI-Thread
         this.BeginInvoke(notify, args);
      }
   }
}
```

As soon as the query notifications are received from the queue through the RECEIVE T-SQL statement, the method OnNotificationComplete is called, and it calls GetData from Listing 9-26. Also make sure that you switch back from the background thread to the UI thread so that the runtime can update the DataGridView control.

When you click Get Data the first time, the query notifications are set up. You can now change the data in the Products table through an INSERT, DELETE, or UPDATE T-SQL statement, and your changes will be reflected in the application. See Figure 9-11.

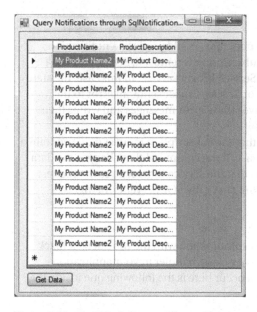

Figure 9-11. *The UI of the sample application*

Troubleshooting Query Notifications

While the SqlDependency class provides access to query notifications without knowing anything about the underlying Service Broker infrastructure, it's hard to troubleshoot query notifications without this essential knowledge. The profiler can show the query notification events that are reported when a new subscription is registered. Once a query notification subscription is notified, the notification message is delivered using Service Broker. If the notification message isn't delivered, the first place to look is the transmission_status column in the sys.tranmission_queue in the sender's database. Let's have a look at some helpful information for diagnosing common query notifications problems.

Checking a Subscription

Subscriptions for notifications are stored in the database where the query is executed. If your application isn't receiving notifications, request a notification and then immediately check to see if the subscription appears in the sys.dm_qn_subscriptions server-level view. If SQL Server doesn't produce a notification event and no notification subscription appears, the parameter for the request is invalid. In this case, SQL Server refuses the notification request. SQL Server reports information on refused requests in two places:

- The event log

- The SQL Profiler

Notice that notification subscriptions are tracked using the query and the notification message. When you submit a subscription with the same message, the same query, and the same delivery service as an existing subscription, SQL Server updates the time-out for the existing subscription rather than creating a new subscription.

Notification Message Not Produced

If a subscription is registered successfully but a query that should produce a notification doesn't produce a notification even though the subscription is removed, SQL Server can't deliver the notification message to the specified Service Broker service. In this case, the statement that updated the data may return an error, or Service Broker sends an error to the QueryNotificationErrorsQueue. SQL Server receives these error messages and writes them to the SQL Server error log.

The most common cause of this problem is that the subscription request didn't contain a service name that matched a service in the database. If the command that changes the data doesn't report an error, the most likely problem is that the service that receives the request isn't configured correctly. To diagnose this problem, check the SQL Server error log.

Callback Problems

A common problem with query notifications is in combination with the provided callback (the OnChange event handler inside the SqlDependency class) handler in your application. One of the most common error messages that can occur here is the following one inside the event log:

```
The query notification dialog on conversation handle
'{5925E62A-A3BA-DC11-9E8E-000C293EC5A4}.'closed due to the following error:
'<?xml version="1.0"?>
<Error xmlns="http://schemas.microsoft.com/SQL/ServiceBroker/Error">
    <Code>-8470</Code>
    <Description>Remote service has been dropped.</Description>
</Error>'
```

As you can see from the error description, the remote service has been dropped. But what happened here? The immediate cause of the error message is clear, because the target service of the query notification was dropped. But the real question is why this happens. Is it a programming error or a configuration error? As you'll see in a moment, it's neither of these errors.

The first solution to this problem is that the SqlDependency.Stop method is called too often in the application code. The general recommendation here is to call SqlDependency. Start when the application starts up and SqlDependency.Stop when the application shuts down.

However, sometimes it turns out that this approach doesn't solve the problem itself. Let's look how SqlDependency waits for notification messages. When you look at SQL Profiler when you call SqlDependency.Start, you'll see the T-SQL query submitted by the SqlDependency background thread that waits for incoming notifications. See Listing 9-29.

Listing 9-29. *T-SQL Code Produced by* SqlDependency.Start

```
exec sp_executesql
  N'BEGIN CONVERSATION TIMER (''9c0b82d5-a3ba-dc11-9e8e-000c293ec5a4'')
  TIMEOUT = 120; WAITFOR(RECEIVE TOP (1) message_type_name, conversation_handle,
  cast(message_body AS XML) as message_body from
  [SqlQueryNotificationService-6f91483f-089c-425e-afa6-0c1553ad1b52]),
  TIMEOUT @p2;',N'@p2 int',@p2=60000
```

This query will start a new conversation timer with a time-out of two minutes (120 seconds) and then posts a WAITFOR T-SQL statement with a time-out of one minute (60,000 milliseconds). The idea here is that if the application exits abruptly the conversation timer will fire and this will cause the activated procedure attached to the queue to run; this in turn will clean up the SqlDependency infrastructure (the activated procedure itself, the Service Broker service, and the queue). Normally the application will not disconnect abruptly, so the WAITFOR T-SQL statement will time out after one minute, causing the SqlDependency to post back the same query, which will reset the conversation timer again to two minutes. This means the timer is actually never firing because it is continuously moved back two minutes. If a notification is received, then the WAITFOR T-SQL statement will dequeue the notification before the one-minute time-out occurs, and after the application callback is notified, the SqlDependendy will again post the same query, resetting the timer again.

The problem here is that the same query is only posted again after the application callback is notified. This means when the callback function is lasting longer than two minutes (or more precisely, the time left from the original two minutes when the query was first launched), then the conversation will fire and the SqlDependency infrastructure will be removed!

The application callback (the SqlDependency.OnChange event handler) is called synchro-nously in the context of processing the WAITFOR T-SQL statement query result. If this callback exceeds what's left from the original timer of two minutes, then the conversation timer will fire and the SqlDependency infrastructure will be removed. You can easily verify this behavior by simply waiting in the debugger on a breakpoint set inside this callback. Shortly the SQL Profiler will show that the activated stored procedure was launched and the procedure itself, the Service Broker service, and the queue were dropped. Interestingly enough, after the appli-cation is resumed, the SqlDependency class creates a new infrastructure by deploying a new stored procedure, a new Service Broker service, and a new queue.

Of course, a two-minute time frame to process a callback seems long enough. But there is one very common scenario that results in much more time: debugging. When you develop applications, you often spend several minutes inside the debugger before you move on. So please be careful when you debug an application that uses the SqlDependency class.

When to Use Query Notifications

Query notifications are designed for data that doesn't change frequently. They are also best used in server-side applications rather than client-side applications. Remember that each request for a notification is registered in SQL Server. If thousands of client applications each request a notification, this can create a scalability problem on your database server. Microsoft's recommendation is that for client-side applications, you should limit the use of query notifications to no more than ten concurrent users.

For large-scale applications, query notifications can be a powerful addition to meet high load demands. Imagine a large-scale website that provides online information to thousands or even millions of users. Rather than having each user's update trigger yet another query on the server to see which information is available, the query can be cached, and matching queries can be served directly from the cache.

On a smaller scale, drop-down lists are another typical set of data that is requested frequently but not updated often. Product lists, state lists, country lists, vendors, salespeople, and other information that changes at a much lower frequency than it is requested are great candidates for notifications.

■**Note** If your query notifications stop working after five minutes, have a look at this Microsoft Knowledge Base article: http://support.microsoft.com/Default.aspx?kbid=913364.

Summary

In this chapter, I've shown how SQL Server 2008 enables a SODA architecture. I first introduced the various data types that are used inside and outside a service boundary. These are important concepts to understand. Next, I introduced the SODA features of SQL Server 2008. The XML support of SQL Server 2008 makes it possible to store XML data inside SQL Server. Combined with the native web service support in SQL Server 2008, XML and web services provide all the features needed to connect your Service Broker application to other clients—even those written on different platforms.

The integration of the .NET runtime into SQL Server 2008 makes it possible to write service logic for Service Broker applications directly with managed programming languages such as C# or VB. Therefore, you can move your externally implemented business logic directly inside SQL Server 2008 without learning new things. The last SODA feature I covered was query notifications. Query notifications provide notification from the database server as soon as cached data has changed. The use of query notifications makes it possible to write fast data-driven applications. In the next chapter, I'll show you several real-world application scenarios with Service Broker.

■ ■ ■

## CHAPTER 10

Real-World Application Scenarios

In this chapter, I'll show you several real-world application scenarios where you can use Service Broker to implement scalable and reliable database solutions based on SQL Server 2008. This chapter will cover the following topics:

- *Reliable web service requests*: Calls to ASP.NET 2.0 web services aren't very reliable because of the underlying unreliable HTTP protocol. I'll provide you with a complete solution for using Service Broker to call ASP.NET 2.0 web services in a reliable way.

- *Asynchronous triggers*: Under normal conditions, a database trigger is executed synchronously. But what if the trigger has to do a lot of time-consuming work? In this case, it would be great if the functionality of the trigger could be executed in an asynchronous fashion. With the use of Service Broker, this is possible. I'll show you a complete sample that implements an asynchronous trigger with the use of Service Broker.

- *Workflow-driven Service Broker solutions*: When you implement Service Broker solutions, you are always modeling a message exchange workflow between several Service Broker services. Think back to Chapter 6, where the OrderService initiated additional conversations with several other Service Broker services. The .NET Framework 3.0 consists of the Windows Workflow Foundation (WF), a technology for implementing workflow-driven applications. I'll show you how you can combine Service Broker and WF to build Service Broker applications directly with WF.

- *Batch frameworks*: Many people around the world have implemented various batch job systems with SQL Server. But what would you say if you could use the features provided by Service Broker to implement an asynchronous, reliable, secure, and distributed batch framework based on the SQLCLR? I'll show you how to make this possible.

- *Publish-subscribe frameworks*: Service Broker doesn't provide out-of-the-box functionalities for publish-subscribe scenarios. However, this doesn't mean that you can't achieve such scenarios with Service Broker. I'll show you how to implement a complete publish-subscribe framework with Service Broker.

- *Workload throttling through Service Broker*: Sometimes you may have the requirement to call some functionality in a synchronous way. Consider a resource (like a mainframe application) where you just have one dedicated connection available that you have to share between your different connected clients. With Service Broker and its activation mechanism, you're able to implement the needed workload throttling mechanism out of the box.

- *Priority-based message processing*: Priority-based messaging for conversations in Service Broker can get a bit tricky because of the complexity involved in those scenarios. I'll provide you with a complete sample that implements priority-based message processing for conversation groups in Service Broker.

Reliable Web Service Requests

Service Broker provides reliability features out of the box through its adjacent message-sending protocol. Web services are a messaging technology that you can also use for communication between distributed application components. However, one big drawback of using web services is that they're based on HTTP, and HTTP isn't a very reliable or secure protocol.

Fortunately, you can use Service Broker to add reliability to web service calls. The application that calls the web service can simply begin a Service Broker conversation and send a web service request over to a proxy Service Broker service that handles the task of performing the web service request and sending the response back over the conversation in a reliable manner. The proxy Service Broker service can perform all the magic of determining transient errors and retrying the web service requests. This section shows you how to implement this proxy Service Broker service and how to use it in your own Smart Client applications to add reliability to your web service requests.

Service Broker Infrastructure

Figure 10-1 shows the basic architecture for the next example.

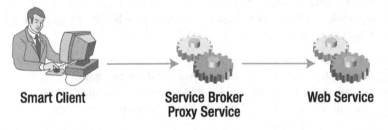

    Smart Client   Service Broker   Web Service
                     Proxy Service

Figure 10-1. *Architecture for doing reliable web service calls*

The Smart Client application doesn't communicate directly with the web service. Instead, the client opens a new Service Broker conversation with a Service Broker service deployed in a SQL Server 2008 Edition of your choice (it would also work with a SQL Server Express Edition) on the computer where the Smart Client is running. When the conversation is established, the client sends a Service Broker message to the Service Broker service. This sent message contains the complete HTTP request needed to call the real web service.

As soon as the message from the client application is put into the service queue, a stored procedure, written in managed code, is activated by Service Broker. Inside the managed stored procedure, the HTTP request is forwarded to the real web service. If an error occurs (such as network unavailability, an HTTP error, or a broken connection), the message containing the HTTP request will be put in a table that stores all the pending (in other words, incomplete) web service requests. After a configured retry period, the pending HTTP request is taken from this table, and the stored procedure tries again to forward the HTTP request to the web service. This continues until the web service request completes successfully or until a configured maximum retry count is reached.

Configuration Information

As you will see soon, the Service Broker service uses different configuration information, such as a retry count and a retry period to configure the behavior of the proxy Service Broker service. All of this information is stored primarily in the two following tables:

- RequestFilter: This table maps an incoming request from a client application to the action to be taken (such as deny or accept the web service call). If the request is to be accepted, additional columns will indicate how the service is to behave in case of failures.

- ResponseFilter: This table maps HTTP responses to the action to be taken (such as respond, retry, or error).

Let's have a detailed look at each of these two tables. Listing 10-1 shows the structure of the RequestFilter table.

Listing 10-1. *The Structure of the* RequestFilter *Table*

```
CREATE TABLE RequestFilter
(
    RequestFilterID INT IDENTITY(1, 1) NOT NULL
        CONSTRAINT PkRequestFilter PRIMARY KEY,
    Method NCHAR(10),
    UrlPattern NVARCHAR(256),
    Timeout INT NOT NULL,
    NumberOfRetries TINYINT NOT NULL,
    RetryDelay INT NOT NULL,
    BackoffFactor REAL NOT NULL,
    [Action] TINYINT NOT NULL
        CONSTRAINT CkRequestAction CHECK (Action >= 0 AND Action <= 1)
)
GO
```

Table 10-1 describes the columns of the RequestFilter table.

Table 10-1. *Columns of the* RequestFilter *Table*

Column	Data Type	Description
RequestFilterID	INT	Identifier for the rule.
Method	NCHAR(10)	HTTP method used in the request—such as GET or POST.
UrlPattern	NVARCHAR(256)	Regular expression to match the URL.
Timeout	INT	Amount of time (in milliseconds) to wait for the HTTP response from the target server before failing and retrying the HTTP request.
NumberOfRetries	TINYINT	Number of times to try before giving up and failing the HTTP request.
RetryDelay	INT	Number of seconds to wait before the next retry occurs.
BackoffFactor	REAL	Factor to multiply the time-out with each retry.
Action	TINYINT	0 indicates DENY; 1 indicates ACCEPT.

Listing 10-2 shows the definition of the ResponseFilter table.

Listing 10-2. *The Structure of the* ResponseFilter *Table*

```
CREATE TABLE ResponseFilter
(
    ResponsePolicyID INT IDENTITY(1, 1) NOT NULL
        CONSTRAINT PkResponsePolicy PRIMARY KEY,
    StatusCodeLower SMALLINT NOT NULL,
    StatusCodeUpper SMALLINT,
    [Action] TINYINT NOT NULL
        CONSTRAINT CkResponseAction CHECK (Action >= 0 AND Action <= 2)
)
GO
```

Table 10-2 describes the columns of the ResponseFilter table.

Table 10-2. *Columns of the* ResponseFilter *Table*

Column	Data Type	Description
ResponseFilterID	INT	Identifier for the rule.
StatusCodeLower	SMALLINT	Lower bound of the HTTP status code interval.
StatusCodeUpper	SMALLINT	Upper bound of the HTTP status code interval.
Action	TINYINT	0 indicates RESPOND; 1 indicates RETRY; and 2 indicates ERROR.

Finally, you use the sp_MatchRequestFilter and sp_MatchResponseFilter stored procedures to return the correct request and response filters used by the managed stored procedure to process an HTTP request or an HTTP response. The "Implementation of the Web Proxy" section looks at the usage of these stored procedures. Listing 10-3 shows the implementation of both stored procedures to give you an understanding about both of them.

Listing 10-3. *The* sp_MatchRequestFilter *and* sp_MatchResponseFilter *Stored Procedures*

```
CREATE PROCEDURE sp_MatchRequestFilter
@Method NCHAR(10),
@Url NVARCHAR(256)
AS
BEGIN
   SELECT TOP (1) [Action], Timeout, NumberOfRetries, RetryDelay, BackoffFactor
   FROM RequestFilter
   WHERE
      (Method IS NULL OR Method = @Method)
      AND (UrlPattern IS NULL OR dbo.RegEx(UrlPattern, @Url) = 1)
   ORDER BY
      CASE
         WHEN [Action] = 0 THEN 0
         WHEN Method IS NOT NULL AND UrlPattern IS NOT NULL THEN 1
         WHEN Method IS NULL AND UrlPattern IS NOT NULL THEN 2
         WHEN Method IS NULL AND UrlPattern IS NULL THEN 3
         ELSE 4
      END;
END
GO


CREATE PROCEDURE sp_MatchResponseFilter
@StatusCode SMALLINT
AS
BEGIN
   SELECT TOP(1) [Action]
   FROM ResponseFilter
   WHERE
      (StatusCodeLower = @StatusCode AND StatusCodeUpper IS NULL)
      OR (StatusCodeLower <= @StatusCode AND StatusCodeUpper >= @StatusCode)

   ORDER BY
      CASE
         WHEN StatusCodeLower = @StatusCode AND StatusCodeUpper IS NULL THEN 0
         ELSE 1
      END
END
GO
```

Service Broker Objects

Now that you know the details about the configuration information in this sample, let's concentrate on the necessary Service Broker objects. First, you need two message types. The first message type, [http://ssb.csharp.at/SSB_Book/c10/HttpRequestMessageType], represents the HTTP request message sent by the client application to the proxy Service Broker service. The second message type, [http://ssb.csharp.at/SSB_Book/c10/HttpResponseMessageType], represents the HTTP response message returned by the web service.

Each message type is also associated with an XML schema collection to use typed XML data in the messages. Listing 10-4 shows the HttpRequestSchema XML schema collection used by the request message. You can find the HttpResponseSchema collection in this chapter's source code.

Listing 10-4. *The* HttpRequestSchema *XML Schema Collection*

```
CREATE XML SCHEMA COLLECTION HttpRequestSchema AS
N'<xsd:schema xmlns:xsd="http://www.w3.org/2001/XMLSchema"
    targetNamespace="http://ssb.csharp.at/SSB_Book/c10/ReliableWebRequestsSchema"
    xmlns:tns="http://ssb.csharp.at/SSB_Book/c10/ReliableWebRequestsSchema">
    <xsd:complexType name="headerType">
        <xsd:attribute name="name" type="xsd:string" use="required" />
        <xsd:attribute name="value" type="xsd:string" use="required" />
    </xsd:complexType>
    <xsd:complexType name="headersType">
        <xsd:sequence>
            <xsd:element name="header" type="tns:headerType" minOccurs="1"
                maxOccurs="unbounded" />
        </xsd:sequence>
    </xsd:complexType>
    <xsd:complexType name="httpRequestType">
        <xsd:sequence>
        <xsd:element name="headers" type="tns:headersType" minOccurs="0"
            maxOccurs="1" />
        <xsd:element name="body" type="xsd:base64Binary" minOccurs="0"
            maxOccurs="1" />
        </xsd:sequence>
        <xsd:attribute name="method" type="xsd:string" use="optional" default="GET" />
        <xsd:attribute name="url" type="xsd:anyURI" use="required" />
        <xsd:attribute name="protocolVersion" type="xsd:string" use="optional"
            default="HTTP/1.1"/>
    </xsd:complexType>
    <xsd:element name="httpRequest" type="tns:httpRequestType" />
</xsd:schema>'
GO
```

In Listing 10-4, the HTTP request message contains the root element <httpRequest>, which includes several attributes (method, url, protocolVersion) and the child elements <headers> and <body>. In the <headers> element, you can define the needed header information (each header entry is represented by a <header> element). Finally, the <body> element contains the actual body sent to the web service. Note that you must supply the body as a Base64-encoded string. You'll see how this is achieved in the "Using the Web Proxy in a Smart Client" section.

After you define both XML schema collections, you can define the mentioned message types and group them together in the [http://ssb.csharp.at/SSB_Book/c10/ ReliableWebRequestContract] contract (see Listing 10-5).

Listing 10-5. *Creation of the Message Types and the Contract*

```
CREATE MESSAGE TYPE [http://ssb.csharp.at/SSB_Book/c10/HttpRequestMessageType]
VALIDATION = VALID_XML WITH SCHEMA COLLECTION HttpRequestSchema;

CREATE MESSAGE TYPE [http://ssb.csharp.at/SSB_Book/c10/HttpResponseMessageType]
VALIDATION = VALID_XML WITH SCHEMA COLLECTION HttpResponseSchema;
GO

CREATE CONTRACT [http://ssb.csharp.at/SSB_Book/c10/ReliableWebRequestContract]
(
    [http://ssb.csharp.at/SSB_Book/c10/HttpRequestMessageType]  SENT BY INITIATOR,
    [http://ssb.csharp.at/SSB_Book/c10/HttpResponseMessageType] SENT BY TARGET
)
GO
```

Finally, you have to create the initiator WebClientService used by the client application to communicate with the target service, the WebProxyService. Refer to Listing 10-6 for more information.

Listing 10-6. *Creation of the Service Broker Services*

```
CREATE QUEUE [WebClientQueue];
CREATE SERVICE [WebClientService] ON QUEUE [WebClientQueue];
GO

CREATE QUEUE [WebProxyQueue];
CREATE SERVICE [WebProxyService] ON QUEUE [WebProxyQueue]
(
    [http://ssb.csharp.at/SSB_Book/c10/ReliableWebRequestContract]
);
GO
```

Implementation of the Web Proxy

By now, you've implemented the whole infrastructure used by Service Broker. The only thing left is the stored procedure that acts as a service program for the WebProxyService. As I've already mentioned, this stored procedure is an internal activated stored procedure that uses the features of the SQLCLR and of the ServiceBrokerInterface managed assembly I introduced you to in Chapter 5. You implement this stored procedure in the Run method of the WebProxyService class. Listing 10-7 shows the implementation of this method.

Listing 10-7. *The* Run *Method of the Managed Stored Procedure*

```
public static void Run()
{
    using (SqlConnection conn = new SqlConnection("context connection=true"))
    {
        conn.Open();

        // Create a new WebProxyService on this in-proc connection.
        Service service = new WebProxyService(conn);

        bool success = false;

        // Loop until you can exit successfully
        while (!success)
        {
            try
            {
                service.Run(true, conn, null);
                success = true;
            }
            catch (ServiceException svcex)
            {
                // Let us end the current dialog with the exception
                // wrapped up in the error message.
                if (svcex.CurrentConversation != null)
                {
                    svcex.CurrentConversation.EndWithError(2, svcex.Message,
                        svcex.Connection, svcex.Transaction);
                }

                success = false;
            }
        }
    }
}
```

In Listing 10-7, the Service Broker service program starts and waits to receive new messages from other Service Broker clients. As soon as a client sends the [http://ssb.csharp. at/SSB_Book/ c10/HttpRequestMessageType] message type, the OnHttpRequest method gets called. Listing 10-8 shows the implementation of this method.

Listing 10-8. *Implementation of the* OnHttpRequest *Method*

```
[BrokerMethod(WebProxyService.x_httpRequestMessageType)]
public void OnHttpRequest(
   Message msgReceived,
   SqlConnection connection,
   SqlTransaction transaction)

{

   s_connection = connection;
   s_transaction = transaction;
   s_currentConversation = msgReceived.Conversation;
   s_msgReceived = msgReceived;

   try
   {
      XmlSerializer xs = new XmlSerializer(typeof(httpRequestType));
      httpRequestType request = (httpRequestType)xs.Deserialize(msgReceived.Body);
      ServiceRequest(request);
   }
   catch (Exception e)
   {
      SqlContext.Pipe.Send(e.StackTrace);

      if (connection.State == ConnectionState.Open)
      {
         msgReceived.Conversation.EndWithError(1, e.Message + "\n" + e.StackTrace,
            connection, transaction);
      }
   }
}
```

The important part of Listing 10-8 is how the XmlSerializer class is used. As you can see, you use the XmlSerializer class to deserialize the message body of the received message to an instance of the httpRequestType class. The definition of this class is generated automatically from Visual Studio 2008 from the XML schema definition, as shown in Listing 10-4. Figure 10-2 shows a class diagram of the generated classes.

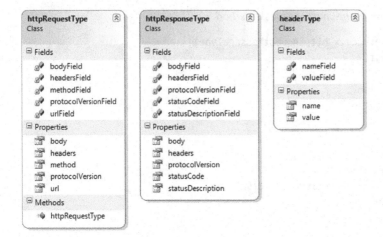

Figure 10-2. *The generated classes*

As soon as the message body is deserialized, the instance of the httpRequestType class is passed as a parameter to the ServiceRequest method call. The main responsibility of this method is to execute the requested web service request. Listing 10-9 shows the part of the method responsible for executing the request.

Listing 10-9. *Web Service Request Execution*

```
RequestFilterAction reqAction = MatchRequestFilter(incomingRequest);

switch (reqAction)
{
   case RequestFilterAction.Deny:
      ErrorConversation(2,
         "Proxy does not accept this type of request to given URL.");
   return;
}

HttpWebRequest outgoingRequest = CreateWebRequest(incomingRequest);

if (outgoingRequest == null)
{
   ErrorConversation(3, m_lastError);
   return;
}

HttpWebResponse incomingResponse = null;
ResponseFilterAction respAction = TryWebRequest(outgoingRequest,
   out incomingResponse);
SqlContext.Pipe.Send(respAction.ToString());
```

In the first step, the ServiceRequest method retrieves the matching request filter from the RequestFilter table. This is done through the MatchRequestFilter method call. Internally, this method uses the sp_MatchRequestFilter stored procedure you've seen in Listing 10-3. Listing 10-10 shows the implementation of the MatchRequestFilter method.

Listing 10-10. *Implementation of the* MatchRequestFilter *Method*

```
private RequestFilterAction MatchRequestFilter(httpRequestType incomingRequest)
{
    SqlCommand cmd = s_connection.CreateCommand();
    cmd.CommandText = "sp_MatchRequestFilter";
    cmd.CommandType = CommandType.StoredProcedure;
    cmd.Transaction = s_transaction;

    SqlParameter prmMethod = cmd.Parameters.AddWithValue(
        "@Method", incomingRequest.method);
    SqlParameter prmUrl = cmd.Parameters.AddWithValue("@Url", incomingRequest.url);
    SqlDataReader reader = cmd.ExecuteReader();

    if (!reader.Read())
    {
        reader.Close();
        return RequestFilterAction.Deny;
    }


    RequestFilterAction action = (RequestFilterAction)reader.GetByte(0);

    if (!reader.IsDBNull(1))
        m_timeout = TimeSpan.FromSeconds(reader.GetInt32(1));

    if (!reader.IsDBNull(2))
        m_numRetries = (int) reader.GetByte(2);

    if (!reader.IsDBNull(3))
        m_retryDelay = reader.GetInt32(3);

    if (!reader.IsDBNull(4))
        m_backoffFactor = reader.GetFloat(4);

    reader.Close();

    return action;
}
```

In Listing 10-10, various columns from the RequestFilter records are stored in the m_timeout, m_retryDelay, and m_backoffFactor member variables of the WebProxyService class. When the request filter is retrieved from the database, the ServiceRequest method calls the CreateWebRequest method. The responsibility of this method is to create an instance of the HttpWebRequest class that encapsulates all the necessary things to make a web request. Listing 10-11 shows the implementation of the CreateWebRequest method.

Listing 10-11. *Implementation of the* CreateWebRequest *Method*

```
private HttpWebRequest CreateWebRequest(httpRequestType incomingRequest)
{
    HttpWebRequest outgoingRequest;

    try
    {
        outgoingRequest = (HttpWebRequest)HttpWebRequest.Create(incomingRequest.url);
    }
    catch (NotSupportedException nse)
    {
        m_lastError = nse.Message;
        return null;
    }
    catch (UriFormatException ufe)
    {
        m_lastError = ufe.Message;
        return null;
    }


    outgoingRequest.Method = incomingRequest.method;
    outgoingRequest.Timeout = (int) m_timeout.TotalMilliseconds;

    if (incomingRequest.protocolVersion != null)
    {
        try
        {
            string[] s = incomingRequest.protocolVersion.Split(new char[] { '/' });

            if (s.Length > 1)
            {
                outgoingRequest.ProtocolVersion = new Version(s[1]);
            }
        }
        catch
        { }
    }
```

```
    if (incomingRequest.headers != null)
    {
        foreach (headerType h in incomingRequest.headers)
        {
            // Assigning the HTTP header values
            // See enclosed source code...
            // ...
            SqlContext.Pipe.Send(h.name + ": " + h.value);
        }
    }

    byte[] buffer = incomingRequest.body;

    if (buffer != null && buffer.Length > 0)
    {
        Stream body = outgoingRequest.GetRequestStream();
        body.Write(buffer, 0, buffer.Length);
        body.Close();
    }

    return outgoingRequest;
}
```

In Listing 10-11, the CreateWebRequest method initializes the HttpWebRequest object with the information contained in the sent request message. To simplify this example, I omitted the creation of the HTTP header because it uses a lot of code. Refer to the enclosed source code for more information about this. As soon as you construct the HttpRequestObject, the ServiceRequest method calls the TryWebRequest method, which actually performs the web service request over the network. Listing 10-12 shows the implementation of this method.

Listing 10-12. *Implementation of the* TryWebRequest *Method*

```
private ResponseFilterAction TryWebRequest(HttpWebRequest outgoingRequest,
    out HttpWebResponse incomingResponse)
{
    try
    {
        incomingResponse = (HttpWebResponse)outgoingRequest.GetResponse();
        return MatchResponseFilter(incomingResponse);
    }
    catch (ProtocolViolationException pve)
    {
        incomingResponse = null;
        m_lastError = pve.Message;
        return ResponseFilterAction.Error;
    }
```

```
    catch (WebException we)
    {
        incomingResponse = we.Response as HttpWebResponse;
        m_lastError = we.Message;

        if (incomingResponse != null)
            return MatchResponseFilter(incomingResponse);

        return ResponseFilterAction.Retry;
    }
    catch (InvalidOperationException ioe)
    {
        incomingResponse = null;
        m_lastError = ioe.Message;
        return ResponseFilterAction.Error;
    }
}
```

In Listing 10-12, the `MatchResponseFilter` method is called when the `GetResponse` method of the `HttpWebRequest` class is called. Internally, the `MatchResponseFilter` method calls the `sp_MatchResponseFilter` stored procedure to retrieve the response filter from the `ResponseFilter` table. Refer to Listing 10-3 for the implementation details of this stored procedure. In the error case, the `TryWebRequest` method returns the `ResponseFilterAction.Error` enumeration value. This indicates to the caller that the web service request wasn't completed successfully. In this case, the web service request is queued for a retry. You implement the queuing mechanism for a retry in the `SavePendingRequest` method. You'll learn about the retry mechanism later in this section.

When the web service request completes successfully, a response message with the web service result is sent to the initiator of the conversation. Finally, the conversation is ended. You use the `SendResponse` method to send the result, and you use the `EndConversation` method to end the conversation. Listing 10-13 shows the `SendResponse` method.

Listing 10-13. *Implementation of the* `SendResponse` *Method*

```
private void SendResponse(httpResponseType outgoingResponse)
{
    MemoryStream msgBody = new MemoryStream();
    XmlSerializer xs = new XmlSerializer(typeof(httpResponseType));
    xs.Serialize(msgBody, outgoingResponse);

    Message msgResponse = new Message(x_httpResponseMessageType, msgBody);
    s_currentConversation.Send(msgResponse, s_connection, s_transaction);
}
```

After sending the response message and ending the conversation, the whole process of executing the web service request is complete. Let's concentrate now on the implementation details of the retry mechanism. As soon as an error is returned from the `TryWebRequest` method, the retry mechanism does the following two things:

- *Saves the request*: The retry mechanism stores the failed web request in the PendingRequest table. Then it retries the pending web request until the configured maximum value is reached (which is stored in the NumberOfRetries column in the RequestFilter table).

- *Starts a dialog timer*: Finally, a Service Broker dialog timer is started. A dialog timer sends a message after a configured period of time. When the service program receives this dialog timer message, the execution of the pending web request is tried again.

Let's have a look at each of these two points. The PendingRequest table stores all the web requests that weren't executed successfully. These web requests are retried again as soon as the service program receives the associated dialog timer message. Listing 10-14 shows the CREATE TABLE T-SQL statement for this table.

Listing 10-14. *The* CREATE TABLE *T-SQL Script for the* PendingRequest *Table*

```
CREATE TABLE PendingRequest
(
    ConversationHandle UNIQUEIDENTIFIER NOT NULL
        CONSTRAINT PkPendingRequest PRIMARY KEY,
    RequestBody VARBINARY(MAX) NOT NULL,
    RetriesUsed TINYINT NOT NULL,
    Status NVARCHAR(MAX)
)
GO
```

PendingRequest stores the conversation handle that is associated with the failed web service request. The table also stores the number of retries already executed. Therefore, you can easily determine how many retries are still left. You use the sp_AddOrUpdatePendingRequest stored procedure to insert the pending web service request. Listing 10-15 shows the implementation of this stored procedure.

Listing 10-15. *Implementation of the* sp_AddOrUpdatePendingRequest *Stored Procedure*

```
CREATE PROCEDURE sp_AddOrUpdatePendingRequest
    @ConversationHandle UNIQUEIDENTIFIER,
    @RequestBody VARBINARY(MAX),
    @RetriesUsed TINYINT,
    @Status NVARCHAR(256)
AS
BEGIN
    BEGIN TRANSACTION;

    IF (EXISTS
    (
        SELECT * FROM PendingRequest WHERE ConversationHandle = @ConversationHandle
    ))
```

```
BEGIN
    UPDATE PendingRequest SET
        RetriesUsed = @RetriesUsed,
        Status = @Status
    WHERE ConversationHandle = @ConversationHandle
END
ELSE
BEGIN
    INSERT INTO PendingRequest
        (ConversationHandle, RequestBody, RetriesUsed, Status)
    VALUES
    (
        @ConversationHandle,
        @RequestBody,
        @RetriesUsed,
        @Status
    );
END

    COMMIT;
END
GO
```

You can use the sp_AddOrUpdatePendingRequest stored procedure to insert a new failed web request into the PendingRequest table. This is done when the web request fails for the first time. On the other hand, you can use the sp_AddOrUpdatePendingRequest stored procedure to update the RetriesUsed and the Status column of the PendingRequest table. This is done when the execution of a pending web request fails again (until the configured maximum limit is reached).

Inside the managed service program, the SavePendingRequest method uses the sp_AddOrUpdatePendingRequest stored procedure to put the failed web request into the PendingRequest table. Listing 10-16 shows the implementation of the SavePendingRequest method.

Listing 10-16. *Implementation of the* SavePendingRequest *Method*

```
private void SavePendingRequest(httpRequestType incomingRequest)
{
    SqlCommand cmd = s_connection.CreateCommand();
    cmd.CommandText = "sp_AddOrUpdatePendingRequest";
    cmd.CommandType = CommandType.StoredProcedure;
    cmd.Transaction = s_transaction;
    cmd.Parameters.AddWithValue("@ConversationHandle", s_currentConversation.Handle);
    cmd.Parameters.AddWithValue("@RetriesUsed", ++m_numRetriesUsed);
```

```
if (s_msgReceived.Type == x_httpRequestMessageType)
{
   MemoryStream stream = new MemoryStream();
   XmlSerializer xs = new XmlSerializer(typeof(httpRequestType));
   xs.Serialize(stream, incomingRequest);
   cmd.Parameters.AddWithValue("@RequestBody", stream.ToArray());
}
else
   {
      cmd.Parameters.Add("@RequestBody", SqlDbType.VarBinary).Value =
         DBNull.Value;
   }

if (m_lastError == null)
   cmd.Parameters.AddWithValue("@Status", DBNull.Value);
else
   cmd.Parameters.AddWithValue("@Status", m_lastError);

try
{
   cmd.ExecuteNonQuery();
}
catch (SqlException e)
{
   SqlContext.Pipe.Send(e.Message);
}
}
```

The SavePendingRequest method calls the sp_AddOrUpdatePendingRequest stored procedure to update the PendingRequest table. The method also increments the m_numRetriesUsed
member variable to reflect the retry count of the current failed web request. After the retry
mechanism stores the pending web request in the PendingRequest table, the BeginTimer
method is called from the ServiceRequest method.

The main purpose of this method is to start a Service Broker conversation timer. You use
the BEGIN CONVERSATION TIMER T-SQL statement to do this. Listing 10-17 shows the syntax of
this T-SQL statement.

Listing 10-17. *Syntax of the* BEGIN CONVERSATION TIMER *T-SQL Statement*

```
BEGIN CONVERSATION TIMER (conversation_handle)
TIMEOUT = timeout
```

Table 10-3 describes the arguments of the BEGIN CONVERSATION TIMER T-SQL statement.

Table 10-3. *Arguments of the* BEGIN CONVERSATION TIMER *T-SQL Statement*

Argument	Description
conversation_handle	Specifies the conversation for which the dialog timer is set up. The conversation_handle must be a UNIQUEIDENTIFIER data type.
timeout	Specifies the amount of time (in seconds) to wait before putting the message on the queue.

A conversation timer provides a way for an application to receive a message on a conversation after a specific amount of time. Calling BEGIN CONVERSATION TIMER on a conversation before the timer has expired sets the time-out to the new value. Unlike the conversation lifetime, each side of the conversation has an independent conversation timer. The sent conversation timer message arrives on the local queue without affecting the remote side of the conversation. Therefore, an application can use a timer message for any purpose.

For example, you can use the conversation timer to keep an application from waiting too long for an overdue response. If you expect the application to complete a dialog in 30 seconds, you might set the conversation timer for that dialog to 60 seconds (30 seconds plus a 30-second grace period). If the dialog is still open after 60 seconds, the application will receive a time-out message on the queue for that dialog.

Alternatively, an application can use a conversation timer to request activation at a particular time. For example, you might create a service that reports the number of active connections every few minutes, or a service that reports the number of open purchase orders every evening. The service sets a conversation timer to expire at the desired time. When the timer expires, Service Broker sends a DialogTimer message. The DialogTimer message causes Service Broker to start the configured stored procedure for the queue. The stored procedure sends a message to the remote service and restarts the conversation timer. Listing 10-18 shows the implementation of the BeginTimer method that starts the conversation timer when the execution of a web service request fails.

Listing 10-18. *Implementation of the* BeginTimer *Method*

```
private void BeginTimer()
{
    int timeout = (int)
        (m_retryDelay * Math.Pow(m_backoffFactor, m_numRetriesUsed));
    SqlCommand cmd = s_connection.CreateCommand();
    cmd.CommandText = @"BEGIN CONVERSATION TIMER (@dh) TIMEOUT = @to";
    cmd.Transaction = s_transaction;
    cmd.Parameters.AddWithValue("@dh", s_currentConversation.Handle);
    cmd.Parameters.AddWithValue("@to", timeout);
    cmd.ExecuteNonQuery();
    SqlContext.Pipe.Send("set timer");
}
```

The conversation timer message is delivered to the local queue as soon as the specified time-out is over. This message follows the [http://schemas.microsoft.com/SQL/ServiceBroker/DialogTimer] Service Broker message type. As soon as this message type is received on the local queue, the OnTimer method gets called automatically through the functionality of the ServiceBrokerInterface managed assembly. Listing 10-19 shows the implementation of the OnTimer method.

Listing 10-19. *Implementation of the* OnTimer *Method*

```
[BrokerMethod(Message.DialogTimerType)]
public void OnTimer(
    Message msgReceived,
    SqlConnection connection,
    SqlTransaction transaction)
{
    s_connection = connection;
    s_transaction = transaction;
    s_currentConversation = msgReceived.Conversation;
    s_msgReceived = msgReceived;

    httpRequestType pendingRequest = GetPendingRequest();

    if (pendingRequest == null)
    {
        ErrorConversation(6, "Your pending request was mysteriously lost.");
        return;
    }

    SqlContext.Pipe.Send("retrieved: " + pendingRequest.url);
    SqlContext.Pipe.Send("num used: " + m_numRetriesUsed);
    ServiceRequest(pendingRequest);
}
```

As you can see, the OnTimer method uses the GetPendingRequest method to retrieve the pending web service request from the PendingRequest table. When the web service request is retrieved, it is handed over to the ServiceRequest method (see Listing 10-9 for reference), which tries to execute the web service request. Listing 10-20 shows the implementation of the GetPendingRequest method.

Listing 10-20. *Implementation of the* GetPendingRequest *Method*

```
private httpRequestType GetPendingRequest()
{
    SqlCommand cmd = s_connection.CreateCommand();
    cmd.CommandText =
        @"SELECT RequestBody, RetriesUsed FROM PendingRequest WHERE " +
        "ConversationHandle = @ConversationHandle";
    cmd.Transaction = s_transaction;
    cmd.Parameters.AddWithValue("@ConversationHandle", s_currentConversation.Handle);
    SqlDataReader reader = cmd.ExecuteReader();
```

```
    if (!reader.Read())
    {
        reader.Close();
        return null;
    }

    SqlBytes requestBytes = reader.GetSqlBytes(0);
    XmlSerializer xs = new XmlSerializer(typeof(httpRequestType));
    httpRequestType pendingRequest =
        xs.Deserialize(requestBytes.Stream) as httpRequestType;

    m_numRetriesUsed = (int) reader.GetByte(1);
    reader.Close();

    return pendingRequest;
}
```

In Listing 10-20, the retry mechanism retrieves the pending web service from the PendingRequest table. As soon as the web service request is retrieved, the request is deserialized to an object of the httpRequestType type. The newly created object instance is finally returned to the caller that hands the pending request over to the ServiceRequest method for further execution. Listing 10-21 shows how to register the managed service program inside the database. Be sure to load the ServiceBrokerInterface.dll assembly from the correct path in your file system.

Listing 10-21. *Registration of the Managed Service Program*

```
CREATE ASSEMBLY [ServiceBrokerInterface]
FROM 'c:\ServiceBrokerInterface.dll'
WITH PERMISSION_SET = EXTERNAL_ACCESS
GO

CREATE ASSEMBLY [WebProxy]
FROM 'c:\WebProxy.dll'
WITH PERMISSION_SET = EXTERNAL_ACCESS;
GO

CREATE ASSEMBLY [WebProxy.XmlSerializers]
FROM 'c:\WebProxy.XmlSerializers.dll'
WITH PERMISSION_SET = EXTERNAL_ACCESS;
GO

CREATE PROCEDURE sp_WebProxyService
AS EXTERNAL NAME [WebProxy].[Microsoft.Samples.SqlServer.WebProxyService].Run
GO
```

```
ALTER QUEUE WebProxyQueue
WITH ACTIVATION
(
    STATUS = ON,
    PROCEDURE_NAME = sp_WebProxyService,
    MAX_QUEUE_READERS = 1,
    EXECUTE AS SELF
)
GO
```

Using the Web Proxy in a Smart Client

Now let's have a look at how you can use the reliable web service proxy. First, you need to take a more detailed look at the request message sent by a client service. The sent request message follows the [http://ssb.csharp.at/SSB_Book/c10/HttpRequestMessageType] message type, which is associated with the HttpRequestSchema XML schema collection. Listing 10-22 shows the basic structure of the request message.

Listing 10-22. *The Sent Request Message*

```
<tns:httpRequest
    url="http://localhost:8080/WebService/Service.asmx"
    method="POST"
    xsi:schemaLocation=
       "http://ssb.csharp.at/SSB_Book/c10/ReliableWebRequestsSchema/MessageTypes.xsd"
    xmlns:tns="http://ssb.csharp.at/SSB_Book/c10/ReliableWebRequestsSchema"
    xmlns:xsi="http://www.w3.org/2001/XMLSchema-instance">
    <headers>
       <header name="SOAPAction" value="http://tempuri.org/HelloWorld" />
       <header name="Content-Type" value="text/xml; charset=utf-8" />
    </headers>
    <body>
    -- Here comes the SOAP body for the Web service request...
    </body>
</tns:httpRequest>
```

In Listing 10-22, the <httpRequest> XML element contains some attributes, the most important of which are url and method. With the url attribute, you specify to which network address the web service request is forwarded. In this case, the request is forwarded to http://localhost:8080/ WebService/Service.asmx, where an ASP.NET 2.0 web service is deployed. With the method attribute, you specify the HTTP action GET or POST. Finally, you can specify in the <body> XML element the SOAP message you want to send to the web service specified in the url attribute. Before concentrating on the SOAP message, take a look at Listing 10-23, which shows the implementation of the ASP.NET web service.

Listing 10-23. *Registration of the Managed Service Program*

```
using System;
using System.Web;
using System.Web.Services;
using System.Web.Services.Protocols;

[WebService(Namespace = "http://www.csharp.at")]
[WebServiceBinding(ConformsTo = WsiProfiles.BasicProfile1_1)]
public class Service : System.Web.Services.WebService
{
    public Service ()
    {
    }

    [WebMethod]
    public string HelloWorld()
    {
        return "Hello World from our reliable web service.";
    }
}
```

In Listing 10-23, this web service implementation returns the famous *Hello World* phrase as a result back to the client. When you navigate to this web service in your web browser, the web service helper page displays, as shown in Figure 10-3.

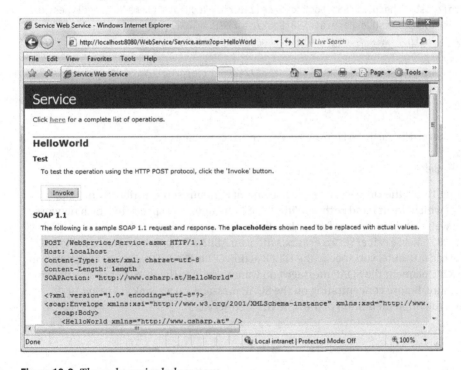

Figure 10-3. *The web service helper page*

The web service helper page also shows you the SOAP request that you must send to the web service to invoke the HelloWorld method. Listing 10-24 shows the SOAP request in detail.

Listing 10-24. *The SOAP Request Sent to the Web Service*

```
POST /WebService/Service.asmx HTTP/1.1
Host: localhost
Content-Type: text/xml; charset=utf-8
Content-Length: length
SOAPAction: "http://www.csharp.at/HelloWorld"

<?xml version="1.0" encoding="utf-8"?>
<soap:Envelope
    xmlns:xsi="http://www.w3.org/2001/XMLSchema-instance"
    xmlns:xsd="http://www.w3.org/2001/XMLSchema"
    xmlns:soap="http://schemas.xmlsoap.org/soap/envelope/">
    <soap:Body>
        <HelloWorld xmlns="http://www.csharp.at" />
    </soap:Body>
</soap:Envelope>
```

Now the question is how to embed this SOAP request into the <body> XML element of the Service Broker request message. The problem is that you can't just add the SOAP request directly into the <body> XML element, because you can't put an XML fragment into the <body> XML element (according to the defined XML schema collection). When you look at the HttpRequestSchema XML schema collection, you can see that the <body> XML element has the data type xsd:base64binary.

Because of this, you must convert the SOAP request shown in Listing 10-24 to the binary Base64 format. The same applies to the response message sent back from the called web service: here you must also convert the response message to the binary Base64 format and place it inside the <body> XML element of the Service Broker response message. Because of these requirements, you'll write two managed stored functions that do the conversion from and to the binary Base64 format. Listing 10-25 shows the implementation of these two methods.

Listing 10-25. *Managed Stored Functions for Manipulating Base64 Formats*

```
public static string EncodeToBase64(string Content)
{
    return System.Convert.ToBase64String(new ASCIIEncoding().GetBytes(Content));
}

public static string EncodeFromBase64(string Content)
{
    return new ASCIIEncoding().GetString(System.Convert.FromBase64String(Content));
}
```

After you implement these two functions, you must register them inside the SQL Server 2008 database. You can use the CREATE FUNCTION T-SQL statement, as shown in Listing 10-26.

Listing 10-26. *Creation of the Managed Stored Functions in the SQL Server 2008 Database*

```
CREATE FUNCTION EncodeToBase64
(
@Content NVARCHAR(MAX)
)
RETURNS NVARCHAR(MAX)
AS EXTERNAL NAME
    [WebProxy].[Microsoft.Samples.SqlServer.WebProxyService].
    EncodeToBase64
GO

CREATE FUNCTION EncodeFromBase64
(
@Content NVARCHAR(MAX)
)
RETURNS NVARCHAR(MAX)
AS EXTERNAL NAME
    [WebProxy].[Microsoft.Samples.SqlServer.WebProxyService].
    EncodeFromBase64
GO
```

With these managed stored functions, you can easily create a Service Broker request message that contains the <body> XML element of the SOAP request message. Listing 10-27 shows the necessary T-SQL code that constructs the request message and sends the message to the WebProxyService that processes it.

Listing 10-27. *Sending the Service Broker Request Message*

```
BEGIN TRANSACTION
DECLARE @conversationHandle UNIQUEIDENTIFIER
DECLARE @messageBody NVARCHAR(MAX)

SET @messageBody =
'
<soap:Envelope
    xmlns:xsi="http://www.w3.org/2001/XMLSchema-instance"
    xmlns:xsd="http://www.w3.org/2001/XMLSchema"
    xmlns:soap="http://schemas.xmlsoap.org/soap/envelope/">
    <soap:Body>
        <HelloWorld xmlns="http://tempuri.org/" />
    </soap:Body>
</soap:Envelope>
'
```

```
BEGIN DIALOG @conversationHandle
    FROM SERVICE [WebClientService]
    TO SERVICE 'WebProxyService'
    ON CONTRACT [http://ssb.csharp.at/SSB_Book/c10/ReliableWebRequestContract]
    WITH ENCRYPTION = OFF;

SEND ON CONVERSATION @conversationHandle
MESSAGE TYPE [http://ssb.csharp.at/SSB_Book/c10/HttpRequestMessageType]
(
    CAST(N'
        <tns:httpRequest
            url="http://localhost:8080/WebService/Service.asmx"
            method="POST"
            xsi:schemaLocation="http://ssb.csharp.at/SSB_Book/c10/
                ReliableWebRequestsSchema/MessageTypes.xsd"
            xmlns:tns="http://ssb.csharp.at/SSB_Book/c10/ReliableWebRequestsSchema"
            xmlns:xsi="http://www.w3.org/2001/XMLSchema-instance">
            <headers>
                <header name="SOAPAction" value="http://tempuri.org/HelloWorld" />
                <header name="Content-Type" value="text/xml; charset=utf-8" />
            </headers>
            <body>' + dbo.EncodeToBase64(@messageBody) +
            '</body>
        </tns:httpRequest>
        '
    AS XML)
)
COMMIT
GO
```

As soon as you execute the T-SQL batch in Listing 10-27, the request message is sent to the WebProxyService, where it is executed automatically by the sp_WebProxyService stored procedure that you configured for internal Service Broker activation. As soon as the stored procedure executes the web request (this could take a few seconds because of the web service call), you can query the WebClientQueue for the received web service response message. Listing 10-28 shows how you extract the SOAP response from the Service Broker response message and convert it from the binary Base64 format to plain text.

Listing 10-28. *Retrieving the SOAP Response from the Web Service Call*

```
DECLARE @response XML

SELECT
    TOP (1) @response = message_body
FROM WebClientQueue
WHERE
    message_type_name = 'http://ssb.csharp.at/SSB_Book/c10/HttpResponseMessageType'
```

```
SELECT
    dbo.EncodeFromBase64(@response.value('
    declare namespace
    WS="http://ssb.csharp.at/SSB_Book/c10/ReliableWebRequestsSchema";
    /WS:httpResponse[1]/body[1]', 'NVARCHAR(MAX)'))
GO
```

As you can see, you simply call the EncodeFromBase64 managed stored function to convert the binary Base64 string to plain text. If an error occurs during the web service request, then the request will move to the PendingRequest table. Don't worry if you get no response message—just look into the PendingRequest table to see if the web service request has failed. If this is the case, the managed service program will try it again until it reaches the configured maximum retry count (configured through the NumberOfRetries column in the RequestFilter table).

Asynchronous Triggers

When you combine database triggers with Service Broker functionality, you can achieve great results. Let's assume you have a table in your database with some data. Each time you insert or update a new record in the table, you must execute a business functionality that takes some amount of time. Just imagine when you have to call a web service to validate a credit card number, or when you have to communicate with other systems. Or think about when you must start a workflow, such as in BizTalk Server or Windows Workflow Foundation. It would be tedious if you did this directly in the trigger. The only solution here is to use an asynchronous approach, such as the one that Service Broker provides you.

Defining the Problem

A quick and dirty solution would be to write a trigger that calls the desired business functionality directly. But what if your database is part of a high-performance, mission-critical, enterprise application? In that case, you must always make an expensive (in terms of time) synchronous call to your business functionality. As soon as you insert or update more records simultaneously in the table, the performance of your solution will get slower and slower. In addition, you'll probably have locks on the inserted or updated records, so other writers and readers will have to wait until the trigger finishes and releases the locks. You can see that this simple and quick approach is not suitable for scalable, mission-critical, enterprise applications.

Instead, I suggest that you use a trigger that fires when you insert a record in a specified table. You use this trigger to send a Service Broker message to a Service Broker service that contains all the needed information for further processing. As soon as the message arrives on the other Service Broker endpoint, the activation feature starts a managed stored procedure (written with the managed assembly ServiceBrokerInterface I introduced in Chapter 5) that handles this message. Within the managed stored procedure, you can then execute whatever business functionality you need—it doesn't matter how long the execution takes. Therefore, all the other stuff (sending the message, retrieving the message, processing the message, and executing the business functionality) is done in an asynchronous way. Because of this approach, the trigger finishes in a short time, and the acquired locks on the data are held as little as possible. The result is an asynchronous solution that is suitable for high-performance, scalable, enterprise applications. Figure 10-4 shows the architecture of this application.

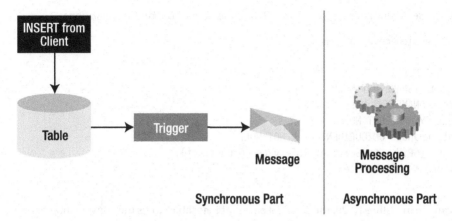

Figure 10-4. *An asynchronous trigger with Service Broker*

Implementing the Trigger

As you have seen in Figure 10-4, it is just a one-way message sending process between the database trigger and the message processing logic. This is one of the most common deployed patterns when Service Broker conversations are used to send data one way only (from the initiator to the target). In this pattern, the target never sends any message back to the initiator.

But one question arises with this pattern: what if you want to start a new conversation for each sent message, or if you want to try to reuse conversations because of performance reasons? My recommendation is to reuse conversations whenever possible. Here are some arguments for reusing conversations:

- Conversations are the only elements that are guaranteed to preserve order in transmission. When the order of the sent messages is important, the messages have to be sent on the same conversation.

- Reusing conversations has a significant performance impact. The cost of setting up and tearing down a conversation for each message can influence the performance by a factor of about 4.

- The advantage of having multiple messages on the same conversation can speed up processing on the receiver's side by a factor of about 10.

- Conversations are the unit of work for the Service Broker background, and as such, resources are allocated in the system according to the number of active conversations. The number of pending messages has less influence on resource allocation—two dialogs with 500 messages each will allocate far fewer resources than 1,000 dialogs with one message each.

The asynchronous trigger in this example uses the SessionConversations table to store opened Service Broker conversations so that they can be reused at a later time. Listing 10-29 shows the definition of this table.

Listing 10-29. *The* SessionConversations *Table That Stores Service Broker Conversations*

```
CREATE TABLE SessionConversations
(
    SPID INT NOT NULL,
    FromService SYSNAME NOT NULL,
    ToService SYSNAME NOT NULL,
    OnContract SYSNAME NOT NULL,
    ConversationHandle UNIQUEIDENTIFIER NOT NULL,
    PRIMARY KEY (SPID, FromService, ToService, OnContract),
    UNIQUE (ConversationHandle)
)
```

As you can see in Listing 10-29, the SessionConversations table stores the conversation handle tied to the combination of a SPID, the initiator service, the target service, and the contract. As soon as the OnCustomerInserted database trigger starts a new Service Broker conversation with the target service, it also inserts the current conversation handle into this table for further use. Listing 10-30 shows the T-SQL code of the OnCustomerInserted database trigger.

Listing 10-30. *The* OnCustomerInserted *Database Trigger*

```
CREATE TRIGGER OnCustomerInserted ON Customers FOR INSERT
AS
    DECLARE @conversationHandle UNIQUEIDENTIFIER
    DECLARE @fromService SYSNAME
    DECLARE @toService SYSNAME
    DECLARE @onContract SYSNAME
    DECLARE @messageBody XML

    SET @fromService = 'CustomerInsertedClient'
    SET @toService = 'CustomerInsertedService'
    SET @onContract = 'http://ssb.csharp.at/SSB_Book/c10/CustomerInsertContract'

    -- Check if there is already an ongoing conversation with the TargetService
    SELECT @conversationHandle = ConversationHandle FROM SessionConversations
        WHERE SPID = @@SPID
        AND FromService = @fromService
        AND ToService = @toService
        AND OnContract = @onContract

    IF @conversationHandle IS NULL
    BEGIN
        -- We have to begin a new Service Broker conversation with the TargetService
        BEGIN DIALOG CONVERSATION @conversationHandle
            FROM SERVICE @fromService
            TO SERVICE @toService
            ON CONTRACT @onContract
            WITH ENCRYPTION = OFF;
```

```
-- Create the dialog timer for ending the ongoing conversation
BEGIN CONVERSATION TIMER (@conversationHandle) TIMEOUT = 5;

-- Store the ongoing conversation for further use
INSERT INTO SessionConversations (SPID, FromService, ToService, OnContract,
    ConversationHandle)
VALUES
(
    @@SPID,
    @fromService,
    @toService,
    @onContract,
    @conversationHandle
)
END

-- Construct the request message
SET @messageBody = (SELECT * FROM INSERTED FOR XML AUTO, ELEMENTS);

-- Send the message to the TargetService
;SEND ON CONVERSATION @conversationHandle
MESSAGE TYPE [http://ssb.csharp.at/SSB_Book/c10/CustomerInsertedRequestMessage]
    (@messageBody);
GO
```

Let's have a more detailed look at the T-SQL code of the OnCustomerInserted database trigger. In the first step, the trigger checks if there is already an opened Service Broker conversation between the initiator service and the target service based on the current contract:

```
SET @fromService = 'CustomerInsertedClient'
SET @toService = 'CustomerInsertedService'
SET @onContract = 'http://ssb.csharp.at/SSB_Book/c10/CustomerInsertContract'

-- Check if there is already an ongoing conversation with the TargetService
SELECT @conversationHandle = ConversationHandle FROM SessionConversations
    WHERE SPID = @@SPID
    AND FromService = @fromService
    AND ToService = @toService
    AND OnContract = @onContract
```

If there is no opened conversation available, a new Service Broker conversation is started with the BEGIN DIALOG CONVERSATION T-SQL statement. Before the conversation handle of the created conversation is inserted into the SessionConversations table, a dialog timer is instantiated on the current conversation. As you already have learned in the previous section about making reliable web requests with Service Broker, a dialog timer sends you a timer message in the specified amount of time—in this case, after 5 seconds.

The received dialog timer message is then used to indicate to the target service that the current conversation should be closed—in other words, the message deletes the corresponding conversation record from the SessionConversations table. If this is the case the next time, the database trigger creates a new conversation between the initiator service and the target service, and a new conversation is re-created at the initiator service.

```
-- We have to begin a new Service Broker conversation with the TargetService
BEGIN DIALOG CONVERSATION @conversationHandle
    FROM SERVICE @fromService
    TO SERVICE @toService
    ON CONTRACT @onContract
    WITH ENCRYPTION = OFF;

-- Create the dialog timer for ending the ongoing conversation
BEGIN CONVERSATION TIMER (@conversationHandle) TIMEOUT = 5;

-- Store the ongoing conversation for further use
INSERT INTO SessionConversations (SPID, FromService, ToService, OnContract,
    ConversationHandle)
VALUES
(
    @@SPID,
    @fromService,
    @toService,
    @onContract,
    @conversationHandle
)
```

Creating the Service Broker Infrastructure

In Listing 10-30, a message is sent from the CustomerInsertedClient to the CustomerInsertedService based on the [http://ssb.csharp.at/SSB_Book/c10/CustomerInsertContract] contract. Figure 10-5 shows the Service Broker objects needed for this solution.

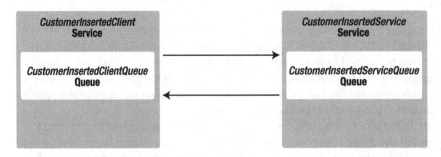

Figure 10-5. *The needed Service Broker objects*

Listing 10-31 shows the T-SQL code needed to create the various Service Broker objects used by this sample.

Listing 10-31. *Creation of the Needed Service Broker Objects*

```
CREATE MESSAGE TYPE
    [http://ssb.csharp.at/SSB_Book/c10/CustomerInsertedRequestMessage]
    VALIDATION = WELL_FORMED_XML
GO

CREATE MESSAGE TYPE
    [http://ssb.csharp.at/SSB_Book/c10/EndOfMessageStream]
    VALIDATION = WELL_FORMED_XML
GO

CREATE CONTRACT [http://ssb.csharp.at/SSB_Book/c10/CustomerInsertContract]
(
    [http://ssb.csharp.at/SSB_Book/c10/CustomerInsertedRequestMessage]
        SENT BY INITIATOR,
    [http://ssb.csharp.at/SSB_Book/c10/EndOfMessageStream]
        SENT BY INITIATOR
)
GO

CREATE QUEUE [CustomerInsertedServiceQueue]
GO

CREATE QUEUE [CustomerInsertedClientQueue]
GO

CREATE SERVICE [CustomerInsertedService]
    ON QUEUE [CustomerInsertedServiceQueue]
(
    [http://ssb.csharp.at/SSB_Book/c10/CustomerInsertContract]
)
GO

CREATE SERVICE [CustomerInsertedClient]
    ON QUEUE [CustomerInsertedClientQueue]
(
    [http://ssb.csharp.at/SSB_Book/c10/CustomerInsertContract]
)
GO
```

As you can see in Listing 10-31, you have to create two different message types that are sent from the initiator service to the target service:

- [http://ssb.csharp.at/SSB_Book/c10/CustomerInsertedRequestMessage]

- [http://ssb.csharp.at/SSB_Book/c10/EndOfMessageStream]

The [http://ssb.csharp.at/SSB_Book/c10/CustomerInsertedRequestMessage] message type is sent to the target service as soon as the trigger gets fired and the initiator service pushes the inserted data asynchronously to the target service. The [http://ssb.csharp.at/SSB_Book/c10/EndOfMessageStream] message type is also sent from the initiator service to the target service as soon as the setup dialog timer message arrives after the configured expire timeout (5 seconds), indicating that the current conversation between the initiator service and the target service should be closed.

Let's now have a more detailed look at the ProcessCustomerInsertedClientQueue stored procedure that is automatically activated at the initiator's queue CustomerInsertedClientQueue as soon as a dialog timer message or EndDialog message arrives. Listing 10-32 shows the implementation of this stored procedure.

Listing 10-32. *Implementation of the* ProcessCustomerInsertedClientQueue *Stored Procedure*

```
CREATE PROCEDURE ProcessCustomerInsertedClientQueue
AS
    DECLARE @conversationHandle UNIQUEIDENTIFIER;
    DECLARE @messageTypeName SYSNAME;

    BEGIN TRANSACTION;

    RECEIVE TOP(1)
        @conversationHandle = conversation_handle,
        @messageTypeName = message_type_name
    FROM CustomerInsertedClientQueue;

    IF @conversationHandle IS NOT NULL
    BEGIN
        DELETE FROM SessionConversations
        WHERE ConversationHandle = @conversationHandle;

        IF @messageTypeName =
            'http://schemas.microsoft.com/SQL/ServiceBroker/DialogTimer'
        BEGIN
            SEND ON CONVERSATION @conversationHandle MESSAGE TYPE
                [http://ssb.csharp.at/SSB_Book/c10/EndOfMessageStream];
        END

        ELSE IF @messageTypeName =
            'http://schemas.microsoft.com/SQL/ServiceBroker/EndDialog'
        BEGIN
            END CONVERSATION @conversationHandle;
        END
    END

    COMMIT TRANSACTION;
GO
```

As you can see in Listing 10-32, the ProcessCustomerInsertedClientQueue stored procedure handles the [http://schemas.microsoft.com/SQL/ServiceBroker/DialogTimer] and the
[http://schemas.microsoft.com/SQL/ServiceBroker/EndDialog] message types. The more
interesting message type is [http://schemas.microsoft.com/SQL/ServiceBroker/
DialogTimer], because this message type arrives at the CustomerInsertedClientQueue queue
as soon as the setup dialog timer gets fired on the current conversation by Service Broker.
In this case, the stored procedure just sends the [http://ssb.csharp.at/SSB_Book/c10/
EndOfMessageStream] message type to the target service, indicating that the current conversation between the initiator service and the target service can be closed.

Let's now have a look at the service program hosted at the target service that processes
the incoming [http://ssb.csharp.at/SSB_Book/c10/CustomerInsertedRequestMessage] and
the [http://ssb.csharp.at/SSB_Book/c10/EndOfMessageStream] message types.

Writing the Service Program

After you set up the whole Service Broker infrastructure, you need to write a service program
that processes the incoming message from the CustomerInsertedClient and executes the
required business functionality. For this sample, you'll create the managed stored procedure,
ProcessInsertedCustomer, which is activated automatically as soon as a new message arrives
on the CustomerInsertedServiceQueue.

The stored procedure is implemented in conjunction with the ServiceBrokerInterface
managed assembly that I introduced in Chapter 5. The stored procedure is able to consume
and process the incoming [http://ssb.csharp.at/SSB_Book/c10/
CustomerInsertedRequestMessage] and [http://ssb.csharp.at/SSB_Book/c10/
EndOfMessageStream] message types. Listing 10-33 shows how the [http://ssb.csharp.at/
SSB_Book/c10/CustomerInsertedRequestMessage] message type is processed within the
managed stored procedure.

Listing 10-33. *Processing the* [http://ssb.csharp.at/SSB_Book/c10/
CustomerInsertedRequestMessage] *Message Type*

```
[BrokerMethod("http://ssb.csharp.at/SSB_Book/c10/CustomerInsertedRequestMessage")]
public void OnCustomerInsertedRequestMessage(
    Message ReceivedMessage,
    SqlConnection Connection,
    SqlTransaction Transaction)
{
    WriteCustomerDetails(ReceivedMessage.BodyAsString);
}

private static void WriteCustomerDetails(string xmlMessage)
{
    // Loading the message into a XmlDocument
    XmlDocument xmlDoc = new XmlDocument();
    xmlDoc.LoadXml(xmlMessage);
```

```
// Appending data to the text file
using (StreamWriter writer = new StreamWriter(@"c:\InsertedCustomers.txt", true))
{
    // Writing the message to the file system
    writer.WriteLine("New Customer arrived:");
    writer.WriteLine("=====================");
    writer.WriteLine("CustomerNumber: " +
        xmlDoc.SelectSingleNode("//CustomerNumber").InnerText);
    writer.WriteLine("CustomerName: " +
        xmlDoc.SelectSingleNode("//CustomerName").InnerText);
    writer.WriteLine("CustomerAddress: " +
        xmlDoc.SelectSingleNode("//CustomerAddress").InnerText);
    writer.WriteLine("EmailAddress: " +
        xmlDoc.SelectSingleNode("//EmailAddress").InnerText);

    writer.Close();
}
}
```

As you can see in Listing 10-33, the OnCustomerInsertedRequestMessage method uses the WriteCustomerDetails method to write the details about the inserted record (retrieved through the incoming XML message) to the file system. Finally, Listing 10-34 shows how the [http://ssb.csharp.at/SSB_Book/c10/EndOfMessageStream] message type is processed inside the managed stored procedure.

Listing 10-34. *Processing the* [http://ssb.csharp.at/SSB_Book/c10/EndOfMessageStream] *Message Type*

```
[BrokerMethod("http://ssb.csharp.at/SSB_Book/c10/EndOfMessageStream")]
public void EndConversation(
    Message ReceivedMessage,
    SqlConnection Connection,
    SqlTransaction Transaction)
{
    // Ends the current Service Broker conversation
    ReceivedMessage.Conversation.End(Connection, Transaction);
}
```

As you can see in Listing 10-34, as soon as the [http://ssb.csharp.at/SSB_Book/c10/EndOfMessageStream] message type arrives at the target service, the current conversation is ended. In this case, Service Broker sends an EndDialog message back to the initiator service, which also ends the conversation on its side (refer back to Listing 10-32 for more details on this). After you deploy all needed objects (such as the Service Broker objects and the managed assembly) to the database, you can try to insert a new record into the Customers table. See Listing 10-35.

Listing 10-35. *Inserting a New Record into the* Customers *Table*

```
INSERT INTO Customers
(
    ID,
    CustomerNumber,
    CustomerName,
    CustomerAddress,
    EmailAddress
)
VALUES
(
    NEWID(),
    'AKS',
    'Aschenbrenner Klaus',
    'A-1220 Vienna',
    'Klaus.Aschenbrenner@csharp.at'
)
```

■**Note** Please make sure that the .NET Framework execution support is enabled in the target database. You can activate it with sp_configure 'clr enabled', 1 and then run the RECONFIGURE T-SQL statement.

As soon as you execute the T-SQL batch in Listing 10-35, the trigger fires and executes the managed stored procedure. This stored procedure retrieves the inserted record and creates a new XML message out of this data. This message is then sent to the CustomerInsertedService, where the ProcessInsertedCustomer stored procedure is activated automatically through Service Broker. Inside this stored procedure, you write the content of the retrieved message to the file system. Figure 10-6 shows the content of the created file.

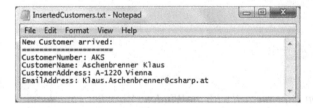

Figure 10-6. *The content of the created file*

Workflow-Driven Service Broker Solutions

When you start to implement Service Broker applications, you are always modeling a message exchange between several Service Broker services. Let's just think back to Chapter 6, where the OrderService initiated additional conversations with other Service Broker services, like the AccountingService, the InventoryService, the CreditCardService, and the ShippingService.

In this example, you modeled directly inside the T-SQL code the message exchange between those Service Broker services. If you have a more detailed look at the written T-SQL code, the code appears to be a workflow that does the message exchange rather than the T-SQL code you know from other scenarios. As you have seen, the ProcessOrderRequestMessages stored procedure is about 300 lines of T-SQL code, which just coordinates the Service Broker services with one another. In other words, the stored procedure implements a workflow that coordinates your Service Broker services.

Wouldn't it be nicer to model such an interaction between Service Broker services with a workflow technology instead of using pure T-SQL code, which isn't the best language in this case? In this section, I'll show you how you can use the programming model of WF to build more advanced workflow-driven Service Broker solutions with much less code than you would need with a pure T-SQL solution. Figure 10-7 shows the OrderService from Chapter 6 implemented with a WF workflow, designed graphically inside Visual Studio 2008.

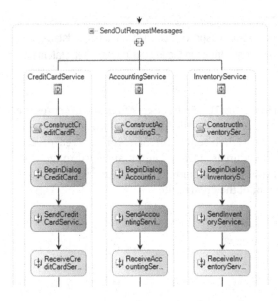

Figure 10-7. *A Service Broker application implemented with the Windows Workflow Foundation*

As you can see in Figure 10-7, it is more natural to implement Service Broker applications directly with the WF instead of using traditional T-SQL code. One further advantage of this approach is that your Service Broker applications are self-documented, because a picture says more than a thousand words—or a thousand lines of T-SQL code.

The workflow in Figure 10-7 tells you at one glance that your Service Broker application creates new conversations with the CreditCardService, the AccountingService, and the InventoryService—in parallel, because the ParallelActivity of WF was used here.

Furthermore, a request message is sent out to each service, and each branch waits until a response message from each service is sent back to the OrderService. So this workflow accomplishes the same as the T-SQL code presented in Chapter 6.

Combining Service Broker and WF

When I combined the programming model of Service Broker with the WF technology offered by.NET Framework 3.0, my first step was the implementation of a simple framework on top of WF that incorporates all the necessary Service Broker functionality. In this section I'll explore the architecture and the implementation of this framework, before you start to implement a concrete Service Broker application on top of it.

The WF provides you with several extensibility mechanisms that you can use to incorporate the functionality of Service Broker into workflow-driven applications. One of these extensibility mechanisms is referred to as *Local Services*. A Local Service offers a workflow the possibility to communicate with the host process that hosts and executes the workflow runtime with your workflows. The communication with the host process can be accomplished in two different directions:

- Host ➤ Workflow

- Workflow ➤ Host

Figure 10-8 illustrates both communication possibilities.

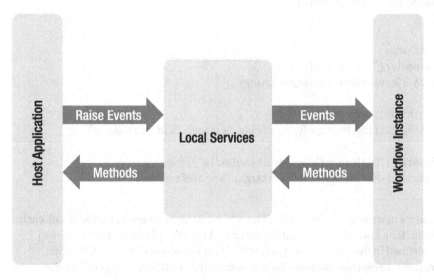

Figure 10-8. *Interaction between Local Services and the WF host process*

As you can see in Figure 10-8, the host process can raise events on the Local Service that are forwarded by the Local Service to the workflow instance itself. In such a case, a workflow is automatically idled by the workflow runtime until a configured event is raised by the host process on a configured Local Service. On the other hand, a workflow can call a method on the host process through a configured Local Service. This is the second option shown in Figure 10-8.

Before you can develop a Local Service for the WF, you have to define in the first step the interface that describes the capabilities of the Local Service. This interface defines the events that can be raised by the host process and the methods that can be called by a workflow instance on the hosting process. Once you've defined the interface, you can implement it on a .NET class, which is then registered inside the workflow runtime so that it can act as a Local Service. If you want to use the Local Service inside a workflow, you have to use the HandleExternalEventActivity and CallExternalMethodActivity activities offered by the WF that work in conjunction with the Local Service.

The definition of the interface for the Local Service is split into the following two interfaces:

- IServiceBrokerMethods

- IServiceBrokerMessageExchange

Listing 10-36 shows the definition of both interfaces.

Listing 10-36. *Interface Definition for the Local Service*

```
[ExternalDataExchange]
public interface IServiceBrokerMethods
{
    void BeginDialog(string ToService, string Contract, out Guid DialogHandle);
    void EndDialog(Guid DialogHandle);
}


[ExternalDataExchange]
[CorrelationParameter("DialogHandle")]
public interface IServiceBrokerMessageExchange
{
    [CorrelationInitializer]
    void SendMessage(string MessageType, string Message, Guid DialogHandle);

    [CorrelationAlias("DialogHandle", "e.DialogHandle")]
    event EventHandler<MessageReceivedEventArgs> MessageReceived;
}
```

Let's now have a more detailed look at both interfaces. As you can see in Listing 10-36, each interface definition for a Local Service has to be decorated with the [ExternalDataExchange] attribute that is defined in the System.Workflow.Activities namespace of the WF. The first interface, IserviceBrokerMethods, defines the methods that a Local Service can call on the host process.

The interface defines the BeginDialog method for beginning a new Service Broker dialog and the EndDialog method for ending a dialog between two Service Broker services. The BeginDialog method returns the conversation handle as an output parameter. The returned conversation handle is used later for sending messages over this opened conversation. The EndDialog method accepts the conversation handle as an input parameter indicating that the conversation should end.

The ISserviceBrokerMessageExchange interface defines the SendMessage method and the MessageReceived event. As you can see, both interface members are correlated to each other with the [CorrelationParameter], [CorrelationInitializer], and [CorrelationAlias] attributes. This means that when you are sending out several messages through the SendMessage method, you can ensure that you get back the correct response message through the MessageReceived event that is raised by the host process as soon as a new Service Broker message is available on the queue.

As you can see in the MessageReceived event, it accepts a MessageReceivedEventArgs class instance as an input parameter. This class wraps an incoming Service Broker message with additional information and is then available through the MessageReceived event in the Local Service. Listing 10-37 shows the definition of the MessageReceivedEventArgs class.

Listing 10-37. *The* MessageReceivedEventArgs *Class*

```
[Serializable]
public class MessageReceivedEventArgs : ExternalDataEventArgs
{
    private Guid _dialogHandle;
    private string _messageType;
    private string _message;

    public Guid DialogHandle
    {
        get { return _dialogHandle; }
    }

    public string MessageType
    {
        get { return _messageType; }
    }

    public string Message
    {
        get { return _message; }
    }

    public MessageReceivedEventArgs(
        Guid WorkflowInstanceID,
        Guid DialogHandle,
        string MessageType,
        string Message)
        : base(WorkflowInstanceID)
    {
        this._dialogHandle = DialogHandle;
        this._messageType = MessageType;
        this._message = Message;
    }
}
```

The most important thing to remember from Listing 10-37 is that you have to mark the MessageReceivedEventArgs class serializable through the [Serializable] attribute.

Implementing the Local Service

After you've defined the functionality of the Local Service through an interface, it's now time to implement the interface on a concrete class that then can act as a Local Service. In our case I've implemented both the IServiceBrokerMethods and the IServiceBrokerMessageExchange interface on the class ServiceBrokerLocalService. Listing 10-38 shows the definition of this class.

Listing 10-38. *The Implementation of the* ServiceBrokerLocalService *Class*

```
public class ServiceBrokerLocalService :
    IServiceBrokerMethods,
    IServiceBrokerMessageExchange
{
    private ServiceBrokerImpl _broker;

    public ServiceBrokerImpl Broker
    {
        get { return _broker; }
        set { _broker = value; }
    }

    public event EventHandler<MessageReceivedEventArgs> MessageReceived;

    public void BeginDialog(string ToService, string Contract, out Guid DialogHandle)
    {
        _broker.BeginDialog(
            ToService,
            Contract,
            WorkflowEnvironment.WorkflowInstanceId,
            out DialogHandle);
    }

    public void EndDialog(Guid DialogHandle)
    {
        _broker.EndDialog(DialogHandle);
    }

    public void SendMessage(string MessageType, string Message, Guid DialogHandle)
    {
        _broker.SendMessage(MessageType, Message, DialogHandle);
    }
```

```
    public void OnMessageReceived(MessageReceivedEventArgs e)
    {
        if (this.MessageReceived != null)
            this.MessageReceived(null, e);
    }
}
```

As you can see in Listing 10-38, the ServiceBrokerLocalService class forwards all method calls defined in the interface to the local variable _broker, which is an instance of the type ServiceBrokerImpl. Furthermore, the ServiceBrokerLocalService class also provides the additional method OnMessageReceived, which wraps the logic for raising the MessageReceived event.

The ServiceBrokerImpl class implements all functionality to interact with Service Broker. That means that this class implements through ADO.NET the following methods:

- BeginDialog: Begins a new dialog between two Service Broker services through the BEGIN DIALOG CONVERSATION T-SQL statement

- SendMessage: Sends a message over an existing conversation to a remote Service Broker service through the SEND ON CONVERSATION T-SQL statement

- ReceiveMessage: Receives a message from the queue through the RECEIVE T-SQL statement

- EndDialog: Ends the dialog between two Service Broker services through the END DIALOG T-SQL statement

Listing 10-39 shows the implementation of the class constructor of the ServiceBrokerImpl class.

Listing 10-39. *Default Constructor of the* ServiceBrokerImpl *Class*

```
public ServiceBrokerImpl()
{
    _cnn = new SqlConnection(
        ConfigurationManager.ConnectionStrings["Database"].ConnectionString);
    _cnn.Open();

    _queueName = ConfigurationManager.AppSettings["QueueName"];
    _serviceName = ConfigurationManager.AppSettings["ServiceName"];
}
```

As you can see in Listing 10-39, the constructor initializes the private member variables _cnn (which represents the current SQL connection), _queueName (which represents the queue of the initiator service), and _serviceName (which specifies the name of the initiator service). All this information is read from the app.config file of the hosting application. Therefore, you have to supply the app.config configuration file for the application that hosts the workflow runtime for you. Listing 10-40 shows a typical app.config configuration file.

Listing 10-40. *An* app.config *file for the* ServiceBrokerImpl *Class*

```xml
<?xml version="1.0" encoding="utf-8" ?>
<configuration>
    <connectionStrings>
        <add
            name="Database"
            connectionString="Data Source=localhost;
            Initial Catalog=Chapter10_Workflows;Integrated Security=SSPI;" />
    </connectionStrings>
    <appSettings>
        <add key="QueueName" value="InitiatorQueue" />
        <add key="ServiceName" value="InitiatorService" />
    </appSettings>
</configuration>
```

Finally, Listing 10-41 shows the implementation of the BeginDialog method inside the ServiceBrokerImpl class. For the implementation of all the other methods, please refer to the source code for this book.

Listing 10-41. *Implemention of the* BeginDialog *Method*

```csharp
public void BeginDialog(
    string ToService,
    string Contract,
    Guid ConversationGroupID,
    out Guid DialogHandle)
{
    DialogHandle = Guid.Empty;

    SqlCommand cmd = _cnn.CreateCommand();
    cmd.Transaction = _trans;

    SqlParameter paramDialogHandle = new SqlParameter("@dh",
        SqlDbType.UniqueIdentifier);
    paramDialogHandle.Direction = ParameterDirection.Output;
    cmd.Parameters.Add(paramDialogHandle);

    // Build the BEGIN DIALOG T-SQL statement
    cmd.CommandText = "BEGIN DIALOG CONVERSATION @dh " +
        "   FROM SERVICE [" + _serviceName +
        "]  TO SERVICE     '" + ToService + "'" +
        "   ON CONTRACT     [" + Contract +
        "]  WITH RELATED_CONVERSATION_GROUP = '" + ConversationGroupID.ToString() +
        "', ENCRYPTION = OFF";
```

```
try
{
    cmd.ExecuteNonQuery();
    DialogHandle = (System.Guid)paramDialogHandle.Value;
}
catch (SqlException ex)
{
    Console.WriteLine("BEGIN DIALOG failed " + ex.Message);
}
}
```

As you can see in Listing 10-41, the implementation uses an instance of the `SqlCommand` class to send the `BEGIN DIALOG CONVERSATION` T-SQL statement to the database. The output parameter `DialogHandle` finally stores the conversation handle of the previously created conversation between the initiator service and the target service.

Implementing the TargetService

By now you've seen how you can communicate with Local Services between a running workflow instance and Service Broker. Next, I'll show you how to use the implemented Local Service in a workflow-driven Service Broker solution. In the first step, I want to develop a workflow that implements a target service in a traditional Service Broker application. Listing 10-42 shows the T-SQL script for the creation of the Service Broker objects you need for this sample.

Listing 10-42. *Creating the Necessary Service Broker Objects*

```
CREATE MESSAGE TYPE
[http://ssb.csharp.at/SSB_Book/c10/ResponseMessage]
VALIDATION = WELL_FORMED_XML
GO

CREATE CONTRACT [http://ssb.csharp.at/SSB_Book/c10/HelloWorldContract]
(
    [http://ssb.csharp.at/SSB_Book/c10/RequestMessage] SENT BY INITIATOR,
    [http://ssb.csharp.at/SSB_Book/c10/ResponseMessage] SENT BY TARGET
)
GO

CREATE QUEUE InitiatorQueue
WITH STATUS = ON
GO

CREATE QUEUE TargetQueue
WITH STATUS = ON
GO
```

```
CREATE SERVICE InitiatorService
ON QUEUE InitiatorQueue
(
    [http://ssb.csharp.at/SSB_Book/c10/HelloWorldContract]
)
GO

CREATE SERVICE TargetService
ON QUEUE TargetQueue
(
    [http://ssb.csharp.at/SSB_Book/c10/HelloWorldContract]
)
GO
```

As you can see, you're sending a RequestMessage from the InitiatorService to the TargetService, and the TargetService sends a ResponseMessage back to the InitiatorService. As soon as you've created the necessary Service Broker objects, you're now able to create the workflow that acts as the TargetService. Figure 10-9 shows the completed workflow.

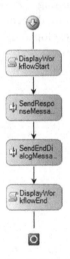

Figure 10-9. *The* TargetService, *implemented as a workflow*

As you can see in Figure 10-9, the workflow consists of the following activities:

- DisplayWorkflowStart: This is a CodeActivity that writes a message to the console when the workflow starts.

- SendResponseMessage: This is a CallExternalMethodActivity that calls the SendMessage method on the IServiceBrokerMessageExchange interface. This activity sends a ResponseMessage back to the InitiatorService.

- SendEndDialogMessage: This is also a CallExternalMethodActivity that calls the SendMessage method on the IServiceBrokerMessageExchange interface. This activity sends an EndDialog message back to the InitiatorService.

- DisplayWorkflowEnd: This is a CodeActivity that writes a message to the console when the workflow ends.

You can refer to the book's source code for detailed information about the configuration of each activity. As soon as you've implemented the workflow, you need an application that acts as a hosting process for the workflow. In this example, I've used a simple console application as a hosting process. In a production environment, a Windows service will provide you more benefits and better flexibility, because a Windows service can be started automatically when the operating system is started. Listing 10-43 shows the WF hosting code inside the console application TargetService.

Listing 10-43. *The WF Hosting Code for the* TargetService

```
using (WorkflowRuntime runtime = new WorkflowRuntime())
{
    ServiceBrokerImpl _broker = new ServiceBrokerImpl();
    AutoResetEvent waitHandle = new AutoResetEvent(false);

    // Handle the various WF Runtime Events
    runtime.WorkflowCompleted
        += delegate(object sender, WorkflowCompletedEventArgs e)
    {
        // ssbPresistence.wfStateCleanup(e.WorkflowInstance.InstanceId);
        waitHandle.Set();
    };

    runtime.WorkflowTerminated
        += delegate(object sender, WorkflowTerminatedEventArgs e)
    {
        Console.WriteLine(e.Exception.Message);
        // ssbPresistence.wfStateCleanup(e.WorkflowInstance.InstanceId);
        waitHandle.Set();
    };

    runtime.WorkflowSuspended
        += delegate(object sender, WorkflowSuspendedEventArgs e)
    {
        waitHandle.Set();
    };

    runtime.WorkflowIdled
        += delegate(object sender, WorkflowEventArgs e)
    {
        waitHandle.Set();
    };
```

```
// Setup local Event handlers
ExternalDataExchangeService exchangeService = new ExternalDataExchangeService();
runtime.AddService(exchangeService);

ServiceBrokerLocalService localSvc = new ServiceBrokerLocalService();
localSvc.Broker = _broker;
exchangeService.AddService(localSvc);

// Here comes the message loop for processing Service Broker messages
...
}
```

As you can see in Listing 10-43, the first step is to create a new instance of the WorkflowRuntime class. After you've created an instance of that class, the code in Listing 10-43 registers event handlers for several events that are raised internally by the WorkflowRuntime class. The most important code in Listing 10-43 is at the end, where you register the Local Service you developed in the last step. You have to register your Local Service inside an instance of the ExternalDataExchangeService class. This class is needed to manage your registered Local Services between an actual workflow instance and the host process itself.

As soon as your Local Service is registered inside the workflow runtime, you have to create a simple message loop that processes the received Service Broker messages. Listing 10-44 shows the implementation of the message loop used by the TargetService.

Listing 10-44. *The Message Loop of the* TargetService

```
while (true)
{
    string messageType;
    string message;
    Guid dialogHandle;
    Guid conversationGroupID;

    // Begin a new local SQL Server transaction
    _broker.Transaction = _broker.Connection.BeginTransaction();

    // Receive a new Service Broker message from the local queue
    _broker.ReceiveMessage(
        out messageType,
        out message,
        out conversationGroupID,
        out dialogHandle);

    if (dialogHandle == Guid.Empty)
    {
        _broker.Transaction.Rollback();
        continue;
    }
```

```csharp
else
{
    switch (messageType)
    {
        case "http://ssb.csharp.at/SSB_Book/c10/RequestMessage":
            // Create dictionary for parameters
            Dictionary<String, Object> wfMessage = new Dictionary<string, object>();
            wfMessage.Add("MessageType", messageType);
            wfMessage.Add("Message", message);
            wfMessage.Add("DialogHandle", dialogHandle);

            try
            {
                WorkflowInstance instance =
                    runtime.CreateWorkflow(
                        typeof(SimpleWorkflowTargetService),
                        wfMessage,
                        conversationGroupID);
                instance.Start();
            }
            catch (Exception exception)
            {
                Console.WriteLine(
                    "Failed to create workflow instance " + exception.Message);
            }

            waitHandle.WaitOne();
            break;
        case "http://schemas.microsoft.com/SQL/ServiceBroker/EndDialog":
            _broker.EndDialog(dialogHandle);
            break;

        case "http://schemas.microsoft.com/SQL/ServiceBroker/Error":
            _broker.EndDialog(dialogHandle);
            break;
        default:
            try
            {
                // Construct the events args for the MessageReceived event
                MessageReceivedEventArgs msgReceivedArgs =
                    new MessageReceivedEventArgs(
                        conversationGroupID,
                        dialogHandle,
                        messageType,
                        message);
```

```
            // Load the correct workflow to handle the received
            // Service Broker message
            runtime.GetWorkflow(conversationGroupID).Resume();

            // Call the MessageReceived event inside the
            // current workflow instance
            localSvc.OnMessageReceived(msgReceivedArgs);
            waitHandle.WaitOne();
          }
          catch (Exception exception)
          {
            Console.WriteLine(
                "Failure calling received message event " + exception.Message);
          }

          break;
        }
      }

      // Commit the whole SQL Server transaction
      _broker.Transaction.Commit();
    }
  }
}
```

Let's go step by step through the code of Listing 10-44. In the first step, a new SQL Server transaction is started. In the next step, you have to call the ReceiveMessage method of the ServiceBrokerImpl class to retrieve a new message from the TargetQueue. Then, you can check whether you got a new message; otherwise you have to roll back the current transaction:

```
string messageType;
string message;
Guid dialogHandle;
Guid conversationGroupID;

// Begin a new local SQL Server transaction
_broker.Transaction = _broker.Connection.BeginTransaction();

// Receive a new Service Broker message from the local queue
_broker.ReceiveMessage(
    out messageType,
    out message,
    out conversationGroupID,
    out dialogHandle);

if (dialogHandle == Guid.Empty)
{
    _broker.Transaction.Rollback();
    continue;
}
```

When you have retrieved a new message from the TargetQueue, you have to check which message type the received message has. If you got a RequestMessage, you add the message type, the current conversation handle, and the message itself to the dictionary wfMessage. Then you have to create a new instance of the SimpleWorkflowTargetService workflow class, pass in the dictionary as input parameters, and start the created workflow instance:

```
case "http://ssb.csharp.at/SSB_Book/c10/RequestMessage":
   // Create dictionary for parameters
   Dictionary<String, Object> wfMessage = new Dictionary<string, object>();
   wfMessage.Add("MessageType", messageType);
   wfMessage.Add("Message", message);
   wfMessage.Add("DialogHandle", dialogHandle);

   try
   {
      WorkflowInstance instance = runtime.CreateWorkflow(
         typeof(SimpleWorkflowTargetService),
         wfMessage,
         conversationGroupID);
      instance.Start();
   }
   catch (Exception exception)
   {
      ConsoOle.WriteLine(
         "Failed to create workflow instance " + exception.Message);
   }

   waitHandle.WaitOne();
   break;
```

After you have started the workflow, the workflow schedules the activities for execution as shown in Figure 10-9. Therefore, the workflow automatically sends a ResponseMessage and an EndDialog message back to the InitiatorService. When you have a more detailed look at Listing 10-44, you'll see that the message loop is also able to process the message types EndDialog, Error, and any other message type received on the TargetQueue (indicated by the default branch of the switch statement):

```
case "http://schemas.microsoft.com/SQL/ServiceBroker/EndDialog":
   _broker.EndDialog(dialogHandle);
   break;

case "http://schemas.microsoft.com/SQL/ServiceBroker/Error":
   _broker.EndDialog(dialogHandle);
   break;
default:
```

```
    try
    {
        // Construct the events args for the MessageReceived event
        MessageReceivedEventArgs msgReceivedArgs =new MessageReceivedEventArgs(
            conversationGroupID,
            dialogHandle,
            messageType,
            message);

        // Load the correct workflow to handle the received Service Broker message
        runtime.GetWorkflow(conversationGroupID).Resume();

        // Call the MessageReceived event inside the current workflow instance
        localSvc.OnMessageReceived(msgReceivedArgs);
        waitHandle.WaitOne();
    }
    catch (Exception exception)
    {
        Console.WriteLine(
        "Failure calling received message event " + exception.Message);
    }

    break;
```

Any other message type refers to the message types sent from the InitiatorService to the TargetService. As you can see in Listing 10-44, the code constructs an instance of the MessageReceivedEventArgs class and wraps the received Service Broker message within it. Then you have to load the correct workflow instance from the workflow runtime. This is done by calling the GetWorkflow method on the workflow runtime class.

You pass in as a parameter the current conversation group ID, because this ID is always the same ID as the workflow instance ID. It's just a one-to-one mapping between workflow instance ID and conversation group ID. You have to load the correct workflow, because when you use a persistence service inside your workflow runtime, it could be the case that the original workflow where you just received a new incoming message was already persisted to disk.

After you have loaded the correct workflow, you just have to call the OnMessageReceived method of the Local Service that internally raises the MessageReceived event. When you have a HandleExternalMethodActivity inside your workflow that waits for the MessageReceived event, your workflow is then scheduled for further execution and also gets the received Service Broker message as an event parameter for further processing. In the next section, you'll see how this is accomplished.

You might be asking why you need a dedicated case branch for the RequestMessage sent by the InitiatorService to the TargetService. The dedicated case branch is needed because the RequestMessage is the first message sent from the InitiatorService to the TargetService, which means that you have to create a new instance of the workflow as soon as the RequestMessage is received at the TargetService. Therefore, you have to handle this message type explicitly, instead of handling it in the default branch of the switch statement. Listing 10-45 shows the needed T-SQL code for sending a new RequestMessage to the TargetService, where it is automatically processed by the implemented workflow.

Listing 10-45. *Sending a Request Message to the* TargetService

```
BEGIN TRY
   BEGIN TRANSACTION;
      DECLARE @ch UNIQUEIDENTIFIER
      DECLARE @msg NVARCHAR(MAX);

      BEGIN DIALOG CONVERSATION @ch
         FROM SERVICE [InitiatorService]
         TO SERVICE 'TargetService'
         ON CONTRACT [http://ssb.csharp.at/SSB_Book/c10/HelloWorldContract]
         WITH ENCRYPTION = OFF;

      SET @msg =
         '<HelloWorldRequest>
            Klaus Aschenbrenner
         </HelloWorldRequest>';

      SEND ON CONVERSATION @ch MESSAGE TYPE
         [http://ssb.csharp.at/SSB_Book/c10/RequestMessage] (@msg);
   COMMIT
END TRY
BEGIN CATCH
   ROLLBACK TRANSACTION
END CATCH
```

As soon as the request message is received at the TargetService, you just have to start the TargetService console application that itself starts the workflow that processes the received request message from the InitiatorService. Figure 10-10 shows the output from the console application.

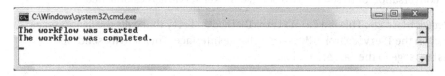

Figure 10-10. *The output of the console application that hosts the workflow for the* TargetService

Implementing the InitiatorService

Now that you've seen how to implement a workflow for a TargetService, I'll show in this section how you can implement a workflow for an InitiatorService. Before I go into the details, Figure 10-11 shows you the final workflow you will implement in this section for the InitiatorService that is part of this sample.

Figure 10-11. *The* InitiatorService, *implemented as a workflow*

As you can see in Figure 10-11, the workflow consists of the following activities:

- BeginDialog: This is a CallExternalMethodActivity that calls the BeginDialog method on the IServiceBrokerMessageExchange interface. This activity begins a new dialog between the InitiatorService and the TargetService.

- DisplayBeginDialog: This is a CodeActivity that writes a message to the console as soon as the conversation between the two Service Broker services is established.

- SendRequestMessage: This is a CallExternalMethodActivity that calls the SendMessage method on the IServiceBrokerMessageExchange interface. This activity sends a RequestMessage to the TargetService.

- DisplayRequestMessageSent: This is a CodeActivity that writes a message to the console as soon as the request message is sent to the TargetService.

- WaitForResponseMessage: This is a HandleExternalEventActivity that stops the workflow execution until a response message is received from the TargetService.

- DisplayResponseMessageReceived: This is a CodeActivity that writes a message to the console as soon as the response message is received from the TargetService.

You can refer to the book's source code for detailed information about the configuration of each activity. As soon as you've implemented the workflow, you also need an application that acts as a hosting process for the workflow. As in the previous example, I used here a simple console application as a hosting process. Listing 10-46 shows the WF hosting code inside the console application InitiatorService.

Listing 10-46. *The WF Hosting Code for the* InitiatorService

```
using (WorkflowRuntime runtime = new WorkflowRuntime())
{
    ServiceBrokerImpl _broker = new ServiceBrokerImpl();
    AutoResetEvent waitHandle = new AutoResetEvent(false);

    // Handle the various WF Runtime Events
    runtime.WorkflowCompleted +=
        delegate(object sender, WorkflowCompletedEventArgs e)
    {
        waitHandle.Set();
    };

    runtime.WorkflowTerminated +=
        delegate(object sender, WorkflowTerminatedEventArgs e)
    {
        Console.WriteLine(e.Exception.Message);
        waitHandle.Set();
    };

    runtime.WorkflowSuspended +=
        delegate(object sender, WorkflowSuspendedEventArgs e)
    {
        waitHandle.Set();
    };

    runtime.WorkflowIdled += delegate(object sender, WorkflowEventArgs e)
    {
        waitHandle.Set();
    };

    // Setup local Event handlers
    ExternalDataExchangeService exchangeService = new ExternalDataExchangeService();
    runtime.AddService(exchangeService);

    ServiceBrokerLocalService localSvc = new ServiceBrokerLocalService();
    localSvc.Broker = _broker;
    exchangeService.AddService(localSvc);

    try
    {
        // Begin a new local SQL Server transaction
        _broker.Transaction = _broker.Connection.BeginTransaction();
```

```
        // Start the workflow and wait until the workflow is idle...
        WorkflowInstance instance =
            runtime.CreateWorkflow(typeof(SimpleWorkflowInitiatorService));
        instance.Start();
        waitHandle.WaitOne();

        // Commit the whole SQL Server transaction
        _broker.Transaction.Commit();
    }
    catch (Exception exception)
    {
        Console.WriteLine("Failed to create workflow instance " + exception.Message);
    }

    // Here comes the message loop for processing Service Broker messages
    ...
}
```

When you look at Listing 10-46, you'll see that it only differs in a few lines from the hosting code you used at the TargetService (presented in Listing 10-43). The only difference here is that the workflow gets started immediately instead of waiting for a specified message arriving from the other Service Broker service:

```
try
{
    // Begin a new local SQL Server transaction
    _broker.Transaction = _broker.Connection.BeginTransaction();

    // Start the workflow and wait until the workflow is idle...
    WorkflowInstance instance =
        runtime.CreateWorkflow(typeof(SimpleWorkflowInitiatorService));
    instance.Start();
    waitHandle.WaitOne();

    // Commit the whole SQL Server transaction
    _broker.Transaction.Commit();
}
catch (Exception exception)
{
    Console.WriteLine("Failed to create workflow instance " + exception.Message);
}
```

As soon as your Local Service is registered inside the workflow runtime and your workflow instance is started, you have to create a simple message loop that processes the received Service Broker messages from the InitiatorService. Listing 10-47 shows the implementation of the message loop used by the InitiatorService.

Listing 10-47. *The Message Loop of the* InitiatorService

```
while (true)
{
    string messageType;
    string message;
    Guid dialogHandle;
    Guid conversationGroupID;

    // Begin a new local SQL Server transaction
    _broker.Transaction = _broker.Connection.BeginTransaction();

    // Receive a new Service Broker message from the local queue
    _broker.ReceiveMessage(
        out messageType,
        out message,
        out conversationGroupID,
        out dialogHandle);

    if (dialogHandle == Guid.Empty)
    {
        _broker.Transaction.Rollback();
        continue;
    }
    else
    {
        switch (messageType)
        {
            case "http://schemas.microsoft.com/SQL/ServiceBroker/EndDialog":
                _broker.EndDialog(dialogHandle);
                _broker.Transaction.Commit();

                // Press any key to exit the host process at the Initiator's side
                Console.WriteLine("Press ENTER to exit");
                Console.ReadLine();
                return;

            case "http://schemas.microsoft.com/SQL/ServiceBroker/Error":
                _broker.EndDialog(dialogHandle);
                _broker.Transaction.Commit();

                // Press any key to exit the host process at the Initiator's side
                Console.WriteLine("Press ENTER to exit");
                Console.ReadLine();
                return;
```

```
        default:
          try
          {
            // Construct the events args for the MessageReceived event
            MessageReceivedEventArgs msgReceivedArgs =
              new MessageReceivedEventArgs(
                conversationGroupID,
                dialogHandle,
                messageType,
                message);

            // Load the correct workflow to handle the received
            // Service Broker message
            runtime.GetWorkflow(conversationGroupID).Resume();

            // Call the MessageReceived event inside the current
            // workflow instance
            localSvc.OnMessageReceived(msgReceivedArgs);
            waitHandle.WaitOne();
          }
          catch (Exception exception)
          {
            Console.WriteLine("Failure calling received message event " +
              exception.Message);
          }

          break;
      }
    }

    // Commit the whole SQL Server transaction
    _broker.Transaction.Commit();
  }
}
```

As you can see in Listing 10-47, the message loop of the InitiatorService is also able to process the Error and the EndDialog messages sent internally by Service Broker. All other received messages are processed inside the default branch of the switch statement. Here you can see that each received message is packaged into an instance of the MessageReceivedEventArgs class. In the same manner as at the TargetService, the correct workflow instance is loaded into memory with the Resume method. Finally, the OnMessageReceived method is called on the Local Service that internally raises the MessageReceived event.

In this example, the message loop goes into the default branch of the switch statement as soon as the ResponseMessage from the TargetService is received. This means that in the meantime the whole workflow instance is idled and perhaps unloaded from memory if you're using a WF persistence service. As soon as the ResponseMessage arrives, the host reloads the workflow instance (inside the default branch) and handles the received ResponseMessage over to the workflow instance through the OnMessageReceived method call on the Local Service. If this is done, the WaitForResponseMessage activity in the workflow is reactivated and the next activity (DisplayResponseMessageReceived) is scheduled for execution.

You can now start a new instance of the InitiatorService console application. The console application executes until the RequestMessage is sent to the TargetService. After that activity, the workflow is idled and unloaded from memory if you're using a WF persistence service.

As soon as the RequestMessage is delivered to the TargetQueue, you can start another instance of the TargetService console application. This console application will now receive the sent message from the TargetQueue, process it, and return a ResponseMessage back to the InitiatorService. As soon as this message is delivered to the InitiatorQueue, the workflow of the InitiatorService console application will continue its execution until the workflow is completed. Figure 10-12 shows the output of the InitiatorService console application.

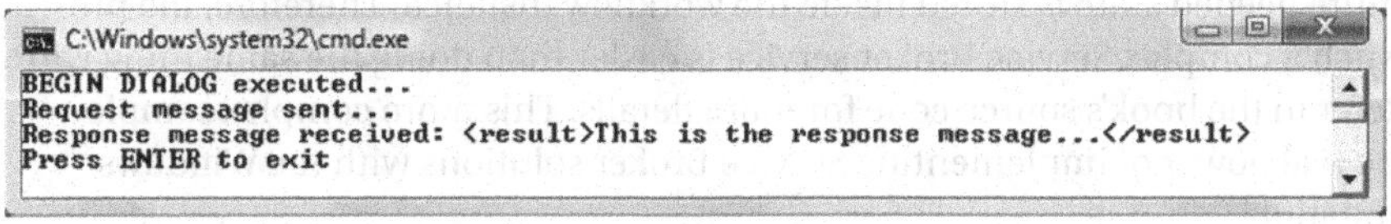

Figure 10-12. *The output of the console application that hosts the workflow for the* TargetService

Implementing a More Complex TargetService

Do you remember the OrderService from Chapter 6? At the beginning of this section, I'd shown in Figure 10-7 how this complex Service Broker service can be implemented with a simple workflow and the Local Service I've developed so far. When you're investigating this example using the source code, you'll see that the most complex work was to arrange the different activities on the designer surface.

The C# code that does the real work is very simplified compared with the needed T-SQL code from the OrderService of Chapter 6. Listing 10-48 shows a simple method that constructs the ShippingRequestMessage sent to the ShippingService as soon as the OrderService has received response messages from the CreditCardService, the AccountingService, and the InventoryService.

Listing 10-48. *Construction of the* ShippingRequestMessage

```
private void ConstructShippingServiceRequestMessage_ExecuteCode(
   object sender, EventArgs e)
{
   string name =
      OrderRequestMessage.GetElementsByTagName("Name")[0].InnerText;
   string address =
      OrderRequestMessage.GetElementsByTagName("Address")[0].InnerText;
   string zipCode =
      OrderRequestMessage.GetElementsByTagName("ZipCode")[0].InnerText;
   string city =
      OrderRequestMessage.GetElementsByTagName("City")[0].InnerText;
   string country =
      OrderRequestMessage.GetElementsByTagName("Country")[0].InnerText;
```

```
ShippingServiceRequestMessage = string.Format(
    "<Shipping>" +
        "<Name>{0}</Name>" +
        "<Address>{1}</Address>" +
        "<ZipCode>{2}</ZipCode>" +
        "<City>{3}</City>" +
        "<Country>{4}</Country>" +
    "</Shipping>", name, address, zipCode, city, country);

Console.WriteLine("Starting dialog with the ShippingService...");
}
```

As you'll also see in this sample, the ApplicationState table is now also obsolete, because the entire needed state is stored inside the workflow instance. Therefore, the programming of such a complex Service Broker service is easier than doing the same thing with T-SQL code. Refer to the book's source code for more details. This more complex sample showed you the real power of implementing Service Broker solutions with the Windows Workflow Foundation!

Batch Frameworks

Another useful example of when you can use Service Broker to realize a scalable solution is when processing batch jobs in an asynchronous way. In this section, you'll write a simple batch framework that processes batch jobs submitted from client applications. The batch framework itself is completely extensible through new types of batch jobs, so it's completely up to you which types of batch jobs you want to support. Figure 10-13 shows the overall architecture of the batch framework.

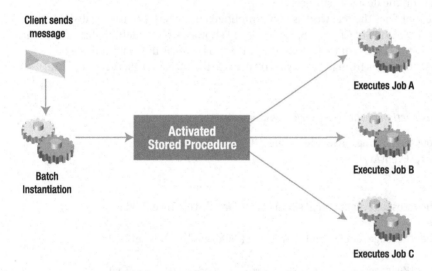

Figure 10-13. *The architecture of the batch job framework*

First, the client sends a Service Broker message to a Service Broker service that acts as the batch job processor. The request message sent by the client contains the following important information:

- *General information about the batch job*: The request message contains general information about the submitted batch job, such as the submission time, the sender (the client), the owner of the job, and so on.

- *Batch job type*: The request message contains an identifier that describes which batch job must be instantiated to process this batch job request successfully.

- *Payload for the batch job*: The request message contains the payload that the concrete batch job needs to process the batch job request.

As you can see, each submitted batch job request contains a *batch job type*. The client can use this batch job type to control which concrete batch job is executed. Because of this, you have the possibility to extend the batch job framework with additional batch job types.

Creating the Service Broker Infrastructure

Let's have a look at which Service Broker objects you need for the batch job framework. As with every Service Broker solution, you must define in the first step the needed message types and contracts that are used between the initiator service (the BatchJobSubmissionService) and the target service (the BatchJobProcessingService). These are the [http://ssb.csharp.at/ SSB_Book/c10/ BatchJobRequestMessage] and the [http://ssb.csharp.at/SSB_Book/c10/ BatchJobResponseMessage] message types. Both message types are used in the [http://ssb. csharp.at/SSB_Book/c10/ SubmitBatchJobContract] contract. Figure 10-14 shows these Service Broker objects in more detail.

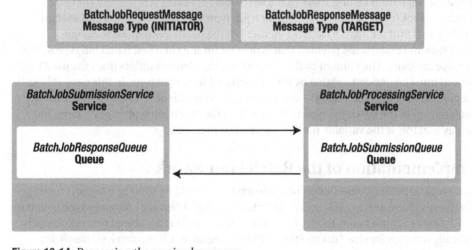

Figure 10-14. *Processing the received message*

Let's take a more detailed look at the request message that the client sends. As you already know, this request message contains a lot of information needed by the BatchJobProcessingService to process the batch job request message correctly. Listing 10-49 shows a typical request message sent from the initiator service to the target service.

Listing 10-49. *The Batch Job Request Message*

```
<BatchJobRequest
    Submittor="vista_notebook\Klaus Aschenbrenner"
    SubmittedTime="06.01.2007 14:23:45"
    ID="D8E97781-0151-4DBF-B983-F1B4AE6F2445"
    MachineName="win2003dev"
    BatchJobType="http://ssb.csharp.at/SSB_Book/c10/BatchJobTypeA">
    <BatchJobData>
        <ContentOfTheCustomBatchJob>
            <FirstElement>This is my first information for the batch job</FirstElement>
            <SecondElement>
                This is my second information for the batch job
            </SecondElement>
            <ThirdElement>This is my third information for the batch job</ThirdElement>
        </ContentOfTheCustomBatchJob>
    </BatchJobData>
</BatchJobRequest>
```

In Listing 10-49, the <BatchJobRequest> element includes several attributes that contain additional information about the submitted batch job request. The most important attribute here is the BatchJobType attribute. With this attribute, you can control which concrete batch job is instantiated and executed on the database server. In the next section, "The Implementation of the Batch Framework," you'll see how this instantiation works in detail. When you send the request message from Listing 10-49 to the BatchJobProcessingService, the [http://ssb. csharp.at/SSB_Book/c10/ BatchJobTypeA] batch job type will be instantiated and executed.

Finally, you'll find the <BatchJobData> element in the batch job request message. This XML element contains the payload that is needed for the specified batch job type in the BatchJobType attribute. The content of the <BatchJobData> element differs from the used batch job type and must be understandable by the instantiated batch job type. In this case, this XML element contains the child elements <FirstElement>, <SecondElement>, and <ThirdElement>. It's completely up to the batch job type which payload the batch job type expects here. You can also say that this is the variable part of the request message.

The Implementation of the Batch Framework

Let's take a look at the implementation of the batch framework. As soon as a request message of the [http://ssb.csharp.at/SSB_Book/c10/BatchJobRequestMessage] message type is sent to the BatchJobProcessingService, the sp_ProcessBatchJobSubmissions stored procedure starts automatically through Service Broker. This stored procedure reads the received batch job request message from the BatchJobSubmissionQueue and finally calls the ProcessBatchJobs stored procedure that you write in C# with the features provided by the SQLCLR. Listing 10-50 shows the implementation of the sp_ProcessBatchJobSubmissions stored procedure.

Listing 10-50. *The Implementation of the* sp_ProcessBatchJobSubmissions *Stored Procedure*

```
CREATE PROCEDURE sp_ProcessBatchJobSubmissions
AS
    DECLARE @conversationHandle AS UNIQUEIDENTIFIER;
    DECLARE @messageBody AS XML;

    BEGIN TRY
        BEGIN TRANSACTION;

        RECEIVE TOP (1)
            @conversationHandle = conversation_handle,
            @messageBody = CAST(message_body AS XML)
        FROM [BatchJobSubmissionQueue]

        IF @conversationHandle IS NOT NULL
        BEGIN
            EXECUTE dbo.ProcessBatchJob @messageBody, @conversationHandle;

            DECLARE @data NVARCHAR(MAX)
            SET @data = CAST(@messageBody as NVARCHAR(MAX))
            INSERT INTO MessageLog VALUES (GETDATE(), @data);
        END

        COMMIT TRANSACTION
    END TRY
    BEGIN CATCH
        -- Log error (eg. in an error table)
        PRINT ERROR_MESSAGE()
        ROLLBACK TRANSACTION
    END CATCH
GO
```

In Listing 10-50, the ProcessBatchJob managed stored procedure accepts two parameters: the message body of the received message, and the conversation handle of the ongoing conversation with the submitter of the batch job. The received message is also inserted in the MessageLog table for auditing purposes. You can easily check whether the batch framework successfully processed a sent message. Listing 10-51 shows the definition of the MessageLog table.

Listing 10-51. *Definition of the* MessageLog *Table*

```
CREATE TABLE MessageLog
(
    Date DATETIME,
    LogData NVARCHAR(MAX)
)
GO
```

After you call the ProcessBatchJobs managed stored procedure, this stored procedure performs the following steps:

1. *Instantiate the batch job*: With the information in the BatchJobType attribute of the request message, the stored procedure is able to instantiate the concrete batch job.

2. *Execute the batch job*: After the instantiation of the batch job, the received message is handed over to the batch job, and the batch job itself is executed.

Let's have a more detailed look at each of these two steps.

Batch Job Instantiation

Each supported batch job in the batch framework is implemented as a .NET class and must implement the IBatchJob interface. Listing 10-52 shows the definition of this interface.

Listing 10-52. *Definition of the* IBatchJob *Interface*

```
public interface IBatchJob
{
    // This method is called, when the batch job gets executed
    // through the batch framework.
    void Execute(SqlXml Message, Guid ConversationHandle, SqlConnection Connection);
}
```

In Listing 10-52, the IBatchJob interface defines only one method—the Execute method. The batch framework calls this method as soon as a batch job gets instantiated and executed. Let's have a look at how the batch framework does this.

Each batch job that the BatchJobType attribute requests must be mapped to a concrete CLR class that implements the IBatchJob interface. For this reason, the batch job framework comes with a lookup table that achieves this mapping—the BatchJobs table. Listing 10-53 shows the definition of this table.

Listing 10-53. *Definition of the* BatchJobs *Table*

```
CREATE TABLE BatchJobs
(
    ID UNIQUEIDENTIFIER NOT NULL PRIMARY KEY,
    BatchJobType NVARCHAR(255) NOT NULL,
    CLRTypeName NVARCHAR(255) NOT NULL
)
GO
```

To support the [http://ssb.csharp.at/SSB_Book/c10/BatchJobTypeA] batch job type (as defined in the batch job request message in Listing 10-49), you must map this batch job type to a concrete CLR class, such as the BatchJobTypeA class. Listing 10-54 shows the mapping information needed in the BatchJobs table.

Listing 10-54. *The Needed Mapping Information for* BatchJobTypeA

```
INSERT INTO BatchJobs
(
    ID,
    BatchJobType,
    CLRTypeName
)
VALUES
(
    NEWID(),
    'http://ssb.csharp.at/SSB_Book/c10/BatchJobTypeA',
    'BatchFramework.Implementation.BatchJobTypeA,BatchFramework.Implementation,
    Version=1.0.0.0,Culture=neutral, PublicKeyToken=neutral'
)
```

After you know the required mapping information is stored in the database, you can have a look at the code that instantiates a specified batch job. This code is encapsulated inside the BatchJobFactory class. This class contains only one method, the GetBatchJob method. Listing 10-55 shows the implementation of this method.

Listing 10-55. *Implementation of the* GetBatchJob *Method*

```
public static IBatchJob GetBatchJob(string BatchJobType)
{
    SqlConnection cnn = new SqlConnection("context connection=true");

    try
    {
        SqlCommand cmd = new SqlCommand(
            "SELECT CLRTypeName FROM BatchJobs WHERE BatchJobType = @BatchJobType",
            cnn);
        cmd.Parameters.Add("@BatchJobType", SqlDbType.NVarChar, 255);
        cmd.Parameters["@BatchJobType"].Value = MessageType;

        cnn.Open();
        SqlDataReader reader = cmd.ExecuteReader();

        if (reader.Read())
        {
            string typeName = (string)reader["CLRTypeName"];
            reader.Close();

            return InstantiateBatchJob(typeName);
        }
        else
            throw new ArgumentException(
                "The given BatchJobType was not found.", BatchJobType);
    }
```

```
    finally
    {
        cnn.Close();
    }
}
```

In Listing 10-55, you retrieve the CLR type name from the BatchJobs table. After the retrieval, the InstantiateBatchJob method instantiates the specified CLR type name and returns it as a type of IBatchJob back to the caller of the method. Listing 10-56 shows the implementation of the InstantiateBatchJob method.

Listing 10-56. *Implementation of the* InstantiateBatchJob *Method*

```
private static IBatchJob InstantiateBatchJob(string fqAssemblyName)
{
    if (null == fqAssemblyName || fqAssemblyName.Length == 0)
        throw new ArgumentException("AssemblyName parameter cannot be null or empty",
            fqAssemblyName);

    Type type = Type.GetType(fqAssemblyName);

    if (null == type)
    {
        throw new ArgumentException(string.Format(CultureInfo.InvariantCulture,
            "Requested type {0} not found, unable to load", fqAssemblyName),
            "fqAssemblyName");
    }

    ConstructorInfo ctor = type.GetConstructor(new Type[] { });
    IBatchJob job = (IBatchJob)ctor.Invoke(new object[] { });

    return job;
}
```

Batch Job Execution

As soon as the BatchJobFactory.InstantiateBatchJob method returns, the Execute method is called through the IBatchJob interface. It's now up to you how you implement the Execute method in your batch job. Listing 10-57 shows a simple implementation of this method that only ends the Service Broker conversation with the initiator service. In the next section, "Extending the Batch Framework," you'll find a more complex implementation of this interface.

Listing 10-57. *Implementation of the* Execute *Method of a Batch Job*

```
public class BatchJobTypeA : IBatchJob
{
   public void Execute(System.Data.SqlTypes.SqlXml Message, Guid ConversationHandle)
   {
      new ServiceBroker("context connection=true;").EndDialog(ConversationHandle);
   }
}
```

Listing 10-58 shows the implementation of the ProcessBatchJobTasks method that receives the sent message as a parameter, instantiates the concrete batch job, and executes it.

Listing 10-58. *Implementation of the* ProcessBatchJobTasks *Method*

```
public static void ProcessBatchJobTasks(SqlXml Message, Guid ConversationHandle)
{
   if (Message.IsNull)
   {
      SqlContext.Pipe.Send("No message was supplied for processing.");
      new ServiceBroker("context connection=true;").EndDialog(ConversationHandle);
      return;
   }

   XmlDocument doc = new System.Xml.XmlDocument();
   doc.LoadXml(Message.Value);

   // Execute the requested batch job
   IBatchJob task = BatchJobFactory.GetBatchJob(
      doc.DocumentElement.Attributes["BatchJobType"].Value);
   task.Execute(Message, ConversationHandle);
}
```

Finally, you must deploy to the database the managed assembly that contains the implementation of the batch framework. As you already know, you can do this through the CREATE ASSEMBLY T-SQL statement. Listing 10-59 shows the needed T-SQL code.

Listing 10-59. *Deployment of the Managed Assembly*

```
-- Register the managed assembly
CREATE ASSEMBLY [BatchFramework.Implementation]
FROM 'c:\BatchFramework.Implementation.dll'
GO

-- Add the debug information to the registered assembly
ALTER ASSEMBLY [BatchFramework.Implementation]
ADD FILE FROM 'c:\BatchFramework.Implementation.pdb'
GO
```

```
-- Register the managed stored procedure "ProcessBatchJobs"
CREATE PROCEDURE ProcessBatchJobs
(
    @Message XML,
    @ConversationHandle UNIQUEIDENTIFIER
)
AS
EXTERNAL NAME
    [BatchFramework.Implementation].
    [BatchFramework.Implementation.BatchFramework].ProcessBatchJobs
GO
```

After you deploy the managed assembly and you set up the required mapping information, you're able to submit a new batch job to the BatchJobProcessingService. Listing 10-60 shows the required code.

Listing 10-60. *Submitting a New Batch Job to the* BatchJobProcessingService

```
BEGIN TRANSACTION
DECLARE @conversationHandle UNIQUEIDENTIFIER

BEGIN DIALOG @conversationHandle
    FROM SERVICE [BatchJobSubmissionService]
    TO SERVICE 'BatchJobProcessingService'
    ON CONTRACT [http://ssb.csharp.at/SSB_Book/c10/SubmitBatchJobContract]
    WITH ENCRYPTION = OFF;

SEND ON CONVERSATION @conversationHandle
    MESSAGE TYPE [http://ssb.csharp.at/SSB_Book/c10/BatchJobRequestMessage]
    (
    -- Please use here the message as shown in Listing 10-49...
    )
COMMIT
GO
```

When the message is processed successfully, you should see one record in the MessageLog table, as shown in Figure 10-15.

	Date	LogData
1	2007-01-18 22:27:50.083	<BatchJobRequest xmlns="http://ssb.csharp.at/JobServer/TaskRequest" Submittor="win2003dev\Klaus ...

Figure 10-15. *The processed message in the* MessageLog *table*

Extending the Batch Framework

By now, you've seen the complete implementation of the batch framework. The great thing about this framework is that you can extend it easily by just adding a new batch job type. In this section, you'll implement a batch job with which you can order flight tickets from a website. You'll discover the necessary steps to implement and use the new batch job.

Implementing the New Batch Job Type

First, you must implement the new batch job type. But you must first create a table that stores the entered flight ticket information from the website. Let's call this table FlightTickets. Listing 10-61 shows the definition of this table.

Listing 10-61. *Definition of the* FlightTickets *Table*

```
CREATE TABLE FlightTickets
(
    ID UNIQUEIDENTIFIER NOT NULL PRIMARY KEY,
    [From] NVARCHAR(255) NOT NULL,
    [To] NVARCHAR(255) NOT NULL,
    FlightNumber NVARCHAR(255) NOT NULL,
    Airline NVARCHAR(255) NOT NULL,
    Departure NVARCHAR(255) NOT NULL,
    Arrival NVARCHAR(255) NOT NULL
)
```

After you define the data storage for the new batch job, you create the batch job itself. Before learning how to implement the batch job, take a look at the request message that is sent for this new batch job request. Listing 10-62 shows the request message with the payload that is expected by the new batch job.

Listing 10-62. *The Request Message for the New Batch Job Type*

```
<BatchJobRequest
    Submittor="vista_notebook\Klaus Aschenbrenner"
    SubmittedTime="06.01.2007 14:23:45"
    ID="D8E97781-0151-4DBF-B983-F1B4AE6F2445"
    MachineName="vista_notebook"
    BatchJobType="http://ssb.csharp.at/SSB_Book/c10/TicketReservationTask">
    <BatchJobData>
        <FlightTicketReservation>
            <From>IAD</From>
            <To>SEA</To>
            <FlightNumber>UA 119</FlightNumber>
            <Airline>United Airlines</Airline>
            <Departure>2008-11-10 08:00</Departure>
            <Arrival>2008-11-10 09:10</Arrival>
        </FlightTicketReservation>
    </BatchJobData>
</BatchJobRequest>
```

In Listing 10-62, you can easily map each XML element in the `<FlightTicketReservation>` element to the `FlightTickets` table shown in Listing 10-61. Because you can implement a new batch job independent of the batch framework, let's add a new class library called `BatchFramework`. `FlightTicketJob` to the Visual Studio 2008 solution. In this library, you can add the `FlightTicketJob` class that implements the new batch job. See Listing 10-63 for further details.

Listing 10-63. *Implementation of the* `FlightTicketJob` *Class*

```
public class TicketReservationTask : IBatchJob
{
    public void Execute(
        System.Data.SqlTypes.SqlXml Message,
        Guid ConversationHandle,
        SqlConnection Connection)
    {
        XmlDocument doc = new XmlDocument();
        doc.LoadXml(Message.Value);

        try
        {
            // Construct the SqlCommand
            SqlCommand cmd = new SqlCommand(
                "INSERT INTO FlightTickets (ID, [From], [To], FlightNumber, Airline,
                Departure, Arrival) VALUES ("
                + "@ID, @From, @To, @FlightNumber, @Airline, @Departure, @Arrival)",
                Connection);

            cmd.Parameters.Add(new SqlParameter("@ID", SqlDbType.UniqueIdentifier));
            cmd.Parameters.Add(new SqlParameter("@From", SqlDbType.NVarChar));
            cmd.Parameters.Add(new SqlParameter("@To", SqlDbType.NVarChar));
            cmd.Parameters.Add(new SqlParameter("@FlightNumber", SqlDbType.NVarChar));
            cmd.Parameters.Add(new SqlParameter("@Airline", SqlDbType.NVarChar));
            cmd.Parameters.Add(new SqlParameter("@Departure", SqlDbType.NVarChar));
            cmd.Parameters.Add(new SqlParameter("@Arrival", SqlDbType.NVarChar));
            cmd.Parameters["@ID"].Value = Guid.NewGuid();
            cmd.Parameters["@From"].Value =
                doc.GetElementsByTagName("From").Item(0).InnerText;
            cmd.Parameters["@To"].Value =
                doc.GetElementsByTagName("To").Item(0).InnerText;
            cmd.Parameters["@FlightNumber"].Value =
                doc.GetElementsByTagName("FlightNumber").Item(0).InnerText;
            cmd.Parameters["@Airline"].Value =
                doc.GetElementsByTagName("Airline").Item(0).InnerText;
            cmd.Parameters["@Departure"].Value =
                doc.GetElementsByTagName("Departure").Item(0).InnerText;
            cmd.Parameters["@Arrival"].Value =
                doc.GetElementsByTagName("Arrival").Item(0).InnerText;
```

```
        // Execute the query
        cmd.ExecuteNonQuery();
    }
    finally
    {
        // End the ongoing conversation between the two services
        new ServiceBroker(Connection).EndDialog(ConversationHandle);
    }
  }
}
```

In Listing 10-63, the needed information from the flight ticket reservation is extracted from the received message and is finally inserted in the FlightTickets table through a SqlCommand.

Registering the New Batch Job Type

After you implement the new batch job, it's time to register it within the batch framework. First, you must register the newly created managed assembly inside the database. Listing 10-64 shows the necessary T-SQL code.

Listing 10-64. *Registration of the New Managed Assembly*

```
-- Register the new managed assembly
CREATE ASSEMBLY [BatchFramework.TicketReservationTask]
FROM 'c:\BatchFramework.TicketReservationTask.dll'
GO


-- Add the debug information about the assembly
ALTER ASSEMBLY [BatchFramework.TicketReservationTask]
ADD FILE FROM 'c:\BatchFramework.TicketReservationTask.pdb'
GO
```

Finally, add the required mapping information to the BatchJobs table (see Listing 10-65).

Listing 10-65. *Registration of the New Batch Job Inside the Batch Framework*

```
INSERT INTO BatchJobs
(
   ID,
   BatchJobType,
   CLRTypeName
)
VALUES
(
   NEWID(),
   'http://ssb.csharp.at/SSB_Book/c10/TicketReservationTask',
   ,BatchFramework.TicketReservationTask.TicketReservationTask,
   BatchFramework.TicketReservationTask, Version=1.0.0.0,Culture=neutral,
   PublicKeyToken=neutral'
)
GO
```

Your new batch job is now ready to use. Try to send the request message from Listing 10-62 to the `BatchJobProcessingService`. If everything goes fine, you should see a new record in the `MessageLog` and in the `FlightTickets` table. See Figure 10-16.

	Date	LogData
1	2007-01-18 22:29:40.540	<BatchJobRequest xmlns="http://ssb.csharp.at/JobServer/TaskRequest" Submittor="win2003dev\Klaus ...
2	2007-01-18 22:29:40.727	<BatchJobRequest xmlns="http://ssb.csharp.at/JobServer/TaskRequest" Submittor="win2003dev\Klaus ...

	ID	From	To	FlightNumber	Airline	Departure	Arrival
1	7BEA7084-10FE-4875-B6E2-3A719E1E549E	IAD	SEA	UA 119	United Airlines	2006-11-10 08:00	2006-11-10 09:10

Figure 10-16. *The processed flight ticket reservation*

As you've seen from this sample, you can easily extend this batch framework with additional custom batch jobs. In this case, you don't have to worry about defining message types, contracts, queues, and services for your additional business functionality. Simply implement the `IBatchJob` interface and add the necessary mapping information into the `BatchJobs` table, and the plumbing (like security) is done for you by the batch framework.

Publish-Subscribe Frameworks

Service Broker can also realize a publish-subscribe scenario in which a sent Service Broker message (referred as an *article*) from an *author* is sent to a *publisher*. The publisher itself distributes the message to different *subscribers*. Each subscriber has subscribed to the received messages through a *subscription*. Figure 10-17 illustrates this concept.

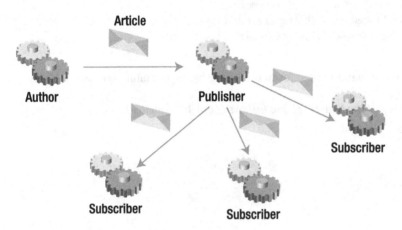

Figure 10-17. *A publish-subscribe scenario*

Let's have a look at how to implement this scenario with the functionality of Service Broker.

Defining the Infrastructure

You implement the author, publisher, and different subscribers as Service Broker services. Articles are published by the AuthorService, which begins a new conversation with the PublisherService. Before the AuthorService sends the actual articles, it notifies the PublisherService about the *subject* of the articles that are sent along with this conversation.

Subscribers are also Service Broker services that begin conversations with the PublisherService. They request a subject of interest and then receive all published articles on that subject as they are published. Because of these requirements, the interface for the PublisherService needs to support the following two contracts:

- A contract on which author services publish articles

- A contract on which the subscribers subscribe to a subject and receive published articles

Listing 10-66 shows the definition of all Service Broker objects needed for this sample.

Listing 10-66. *Defining the Service Broker Infrastructure*

```
CREATE MESSAGE TYPE [http://ssb.csharp.at/SSB_Book/c10/PublishMessage]
VALIDATION = WELL_FORMED_XML;
GO


CREATE MESSAGE TYPE [http://ssb.csharp.at/SSB_Book/c10/ArticleMessage]
VALIDATION = NONE;
GO


CREATE MESSAGE TYPE [http://ssb.csharp.at/SSB_Book/c10/SubscribeMessage]
VALIDATION = WELL_FORMED_XML;
GO



CREATE CONTRACT [http://ssb.csharp.at/SSB_Book/c10/PublishContract]
(
   [http://ssb.csharp.at/SSB_Book/c10/PublishMessage] SENT BY INITIATOR,
   [http://ssb.csharp.at/SSB_Book/c10/ArticleMessage] SENT BY INITIATOR
)
GO


CREATE CONTRACT [http://ssb.csharp.at/SSB_Book/c10/SubscribeContract]
(
   [http://ssb.csharp.at/SSB_Book/c10/SubscribeMessage] SENT BY INITIATOR,
   [http://ssb.csharp.at/SSB_Book/c10/ArticleMessage] SENT BY TARGET
)
GO


CREATE QUEUE [PublisherQueue]
GO
```

```
CREATE SERVICE [PublisherService] ON QUEUE [PublisherQueue]
(
    [http://ssb.csharp.at/SSB_Book/c10/PublishContract],
    [http://ssb.csharp.at/SSB_Book/c10/SubscribeContract]
)
GO

CREATE QUEUE SubscriberQueue1;
GO

CREATE SERVICE SubscriberService1 ON QUEUE SubscriberQueue1;
GO

CREATE QUEUE SubscriberQueue2;
GO

CREATE SERVICE SubscriberService2 ON QUEUE SubscriberQueue2;
GO

CREATE QUEUE AuthorQueue;
GO

CREATE SERVICE AuthorService ON QUEUE AuthorQueue;
GO
```

After you create the Service Broker infrastructure, you need two tables to store the various publications and subscriptions. For this sample, you'll create the Publications and the Subscriptions tables. Listing 10-67 shows the T-SQL code needed to create these two tables.

Listing 10-67. *Creation of the* Publications *and* Subscriptions *Tables*

```
CREATE TABLE Publications
(
    Publication UNIQUEIDENTIFIER NOT NULL PRIMARY KEY,
    Subject NVARCHAR(MAX) NOT NULL,
    OriginalXml XML NOT NULL
)
GO

CREATE TABLE Subscriptions
(
    Subscriber UNIQUEIDENTIFIER NOT NULL PRIMARY KEY,
    Subject NVARCHAR(MAX) NOT NULL,
    OriginalXml XML NOT NULL
)
GO
```

With these two tables, you're able to match an incoming publication from the AuthorService to the subscribers. You simply join both tables through the Subject column, as you'll see in the next section, "Applying Publisher Logic." Let's have a look at the service program that runs on the PublisherService.

Applying Publisher Logic

You implement the entry point of the service program for the PublisherService in the sp_PublisherService stored procedure. This stored procedure activates automatically as soon as a new message arrives at the PublisherQueue and starts to process the message. This stored procedure is able to process the following message types:

- [http://ssb.csharp.at/SSB_Book/c10/PublishMessage]: The stored procedure receives this message type from the AuthorService when the stored procedure wants to start publishing several articles. This message contains the subject to which the following articles belongs.

- [http://ssb.csharp.at/SSB_Book/c10/SubscribeMessage]: The stored procedure receives this message type from the subscriber service when it wants to subscribe to a subject. This message contains the requested subject to subscribe.

- [http://ssb.csharp.at/SSB_Book/c10/ArticleMessage]: The stored procedure receives this message type from the AuthorService when it publishes an article.

- [http://schemas.microsoft.com/SQL/ServiceBroker/EndDialog]: The stored procedure receives this message type from the AuthorService or a subscriber service when it wants to close the opened conversation with the PublisherService.

- [http://schemas.microsoft.com/SQL/ServiceBroker/Error]: The stored procedure receives this message type from the PublisherService when a requested subject isn't available.

Listing 10-68 shows the sp_PublisherService stored procedure that processes these message types.

Listing 10-68. *The* sp_PublisherService *Service Program*

```
CREATE PROCEDURE sp_PublisherService
AS
BEGIN
    DECLARE @Conversation UNIQUEIDENTIFIER;
    DECLARE @Message VARBINARY(MAX);
    DECLARE @MessageTypeName SYSNAME;

    BEGIN TRANSACTION;
```

```
WAITFOR
(
   RECEIVE TOP(1)
      @Conversation = conversation_handle,
      @Message = message_body,
      @MessageTypeName = message_type_name
   FROM PublisherQueue
), TIMEOUT 1000;

WHILE (@Conversation IS NOT NULL)
BEGIN
   IF (@MessageTypeName = 'http://ssb.csharp.at/SSB_Book/c10/PublishMessage')
   BEGIN
      EXEC sp_ProcessPublicationRequest @Conversation, @Message;
   END
   ELSE IF (@MessageTypeName =
      'http://ssb.csharp.at/SSB_Book/c10/SubscribeMessage')
   BEGIN
      EXEC sp_ProcessSubscriptionRequest @Conversation, @Message;
   END
   ELSE IF (@MessageTypeName =
      'http://ssb.csharp.at/SSB_Book/c10/ArticleMessage')
   BEGIN
      EXEC sp_SendOnPublication @Conversation, @Message;
   END
   ELSE IF (@MessageTypeName IN (
      N'http://schemas.microsoft.com/SQL/ServiceBroker/Error',
      N'http://schemas.microsoft.com/SQL/ServiceBroker/EndDialog'))
   BEGIN
      END CONVERSATION @Conversation;

      IF (EXISTS (SELECT * FROM Publications
      WHERE Publication = @Conversation))
      BEGIN
         EXEC sp_RemovePublication @Conversation;
      END


      IF (EXISTS (SELECT * FROM Subscribers))
      BEGIN
         EXEC sp_RemoveSubscriber @Conversation;
      END
   END
```

```
    ELSE
    BEGIN
        -- Unexpected message
        RAISERROR (N'Received unexpected message type: %s', 16, 1,
            @MessageTypeName);
        ROLLBACK;
        RETURN;
    END
    COMMIT;

    SELECT @Conversation = NULL;
    BEGIN TRANSACTION;

    WAITFOR
    (
        RECEIVE TOP(1)
            @Conversation = conversation_handle,
            @Message = message_body,
            @MessageTypeName = message_type_name
        FROM PublisherQueue
    ), TIMEOUT 1000;
    END
    COMMIT;
END
GO
```

In Listing 10-68, you retrieve a new message from the PublisherQueue. If it is the
[http://ssb.csharp.at/SSB_Book/c10/PublishMessage] message type, you call the
sp_ProcessPublicationRequest stored procedure to store the received publication in the
Publications table. If the [http://ssb.csharp.at/SSB_Book/c10/SubscribeMessage] message
type is received, the sp_ProcessSubscriptionRequest stored procedure is called. Within this
stored procedure, the received subscription is stored in the Subscriptions table. Finally, if
the [http://ssb.csharp.at/SSB_Book/c10/ArticleMessage] message type is received, the
sp_PublisherService stored procedure calls the sp_SendOnPublication stored procedure,
which sends all publications to the matching subscribers.

You do the publication and subscription management through the
sp_ProcessPublicationRequest and sp_ProcessSubscriptionRequest stored procedures.
These stored procedures call other stored procedures that do an insert into the
Publications or Subscriptions table with the data from the received message.
Listing 10-69 shows the sp_ProcessPublicationRequest stored procedure. I've omitted
the sp_ProcessSubscription-Request stored procedure, because it's similar to the
sp_ProcessPublicationRequest stored procedure.

Listing 10-69. *The* sp_ProcessPublicationRequest *Stored Procedure*

```
CREATE PROCEDURE sp_ProcessPublicationRequest
   @Conversation UNIQUEIDENTIFIER,
   @Message VARBINARY(MAX)
AS
BEGIN
   DECLARE @Request XML;
   DECLARE @Subject NVARCHAR(MAX);

   SELECT @Request = CAST(@Message AS XML);

   WITH XMLNAMESPACES (DEFAULT 'http://ssb.csharp.at/SSB_Book/c10/PublishSubscribe')
   SELECT @Subject = @Request.value(N'(//Publish/Subject)[1]', N'NVARCHAR(MAX)');

   IF (@Subject IS NOT NULL)
   BEGIN
      EXEC sp_PublishPublication @Conversation, @Subject, @Message;
   END
   ELSE
   BEGIN
      END CONVERSATION @Conversation
         WITH ERROR = 1
         DESCRIPTION = N'The publication is missing a subject';
      EXEC sp_RemovePublication @Conversation;
   END
END
GO
```

In Listing 10-69, the sp_ProcessPublicationRequest stored procedure calls the sp_PublishPublication stored procedure with the conversation handle, the subject, and the message as parameters. Listing 10-70 shows the sp_PublishPublication stored procedure.

Listing 10-70. *The* sp_PublishPublication *Stored Procedure*

```
CREATE PROCEDURE sp_PublishPublication
   @Publication UNIQUEIDENTIFIER,
   @Subject NVARCHAR(MAX),
   @OriginalXml XML
AS
BEGIN
   INSERT INTO Publications (Publication, Subject, OriginalXml)
   VALUES
   (
      @Publication,
      @Subject,
      @OriginalXml
   )
END
GO
```

In Listing 10-70, the Publication column in the Publications table and the Subscription column in the Subscriptions table are just storing the conversation handles. You need these conversation handles to send a published article to the subscribers. The only stored procedure that's left is the sp_SendOnPublication stored procedure, which is called from the service program as soon as the message type [http://ssb.csharp.at/SSB_Book/c10/ArticleMessage] is received from the AuthorService. Listing 10-71 shows the definition of the sp_SendOnPublication stored procedure.

Listing 10-71. *The* sp_SendOnPublication *Stored Procedure*

```
CREATE PROCEDURE sp_SendOnPublication
    @Publication UNIQUEIDENTIFIER,
    @Article VARBINARY(MAX)
AS
BEGIN
    DECLARE @Subscription UNIQUEIDENTIFIER;
    DECLARE @cursorSubscriptions CURSOR;

    SET @cursorSubscriptions = CURSOR LOCAL SCROLL FOR
        SELECT Subscriber
        FROM Subscriptions s
        JOIN Publications p ON s.Subject = p.Subject
        WHERE p.Publication = @Publication;

    BEGIN TRANSACTION;
    OPEN @cursorSubscriptions;

    FETCH NEXT FROM @cursorSubscriptions
    INTO @Subscription;

    WHILE (@@fetch_status = 0)
    BEGIN
        IF (@Article IS NOT NULL)
        BEGIN
            SEND ON CONVERSATION @Subscription
            MESSAGE TYPE [http://ssb.csharp.at/SSB_Book/c10/ArticleMessage] (@Article);
        END
        ELSE
        BEGIN
            SEND ON CONVERSATION @Subscription
            MESSAGE TYPE [http://ssb.csharp.at/SSB_Book/c10/ArticleMessage];
        END
        FETCH NEXT FROM @cursorSubscriptions
        INTO @Subscription;
    END
```

```
    CLOSE @cursorSubscriptions;
    DEALLOCATE @cursorSubscriptions;
    COMMIT;
END
GO
```

In Listing 10-71, the sp_SendOnPublication stored procedure uses a cursor to send the received article from the AuthorService to the matched subscribers:

```
SEND ON CONVERSATION @Subscription
MESSAGE TYPE [http://ssb.csharp.at/SSB_Book/c10/ArticleMessage] (@Article);
```

The matching is done through a join between the Publications and the Subscriptions tables— through the Subject column:

```
SELECT Subscriber
FROM Subscriptions s
JOIN Publications p ON s.Subject = p.Subject
WHERE p.Publication = @Publication;
```

When the [http://schemas.microsoft.com/SQL/ServiceBroker/EndDialog] message type is received—either from the AuthorService or a subscriber service—the corresponding publication or subscription is removed from the Publications or Subscriptions table. This is done through the sp_RemovePublication or sp_RemoveSubscriptions stored procedure. Listing 10-72 shows the sp_RemovePublication stored procedure.

Listing 10-72. *The* sp_RemovePublication *Stored Procedure*

```
CREATE PROCEDURE sp_RemovePublication
    @Publication UNIQUEIDENTIFIER
AS
BEGIN
    DELETE FROM Publications
    WHERE Publication = @Publication
END
GO
```

Publishing Information

This section takes a look at how a subscriber can request information from the PublisherService through a subscription and how the AuthorService can send new articles to the PublisherService for distribution. Before a subscriber service receives new articles from the PublisherService, it must request a subscription. It does this through the [http://ssb.csharp.at/SSB_Book/c10/SubscribeMessage] message type, as shown in Listing 10-73.

Listing 10-73. *Requesting a Subscription*

```
DECLARE @ch UNIQUEIDENTIFIER;

BEGIN DIALOG CONVERSATION @ch
    FROM SERVICE [SubscriberService1]
    TO SERVICE 'PublisherService'
    ON CONTRACT [http://ssb.csharp.at/SSB_Book/c10/SubscribeContract]
    WITH ENCRYPTION = OFF;

SEND ON CONVERSATION @ch
MESSAGE TYPE [http://ssb.csharp.at/SSB_Book/c10/SubscribeMessage]
(
    N'<?xml version="1.0"?>
    <Request xmlns="http://ssb.csharp.at/SSB_Book/c10/PublishSubscribe">
        <Subject>Subject1</Subject>
    </Request>'
);
GO
```

In Listing 10-73, you must specify in the sent message the subject for which you want to get publications from the PublisherService. As soon as the subscribers set up subscriptions, the AuthorService can begin to send articles to the PublisherService. Listing 10-74 shows the code needed to start sending articles.

Listing 10-74. *Sending Articles*

```
DECLARE @ch UNIQUEIDENTIFIER;

BEGIN DIALOG CONVERSATION @ch
    FROM SERVICE [AuthorService]
    TO SERVICE 'PublisherService'
    ON CONTRACT [http://ssb.csharp.at/SSB_Book/c10/PublishContract]
    WITH ENCRYPTION = OFF;

SEND ON CONVERSATION @ch
MESSAGE TYPE [http://ssb.csharp.at/SSB_Book/c10/PublishMessage]
(
    N'<?xml version="1.0"?>
    <Publish xmlns="http://ssb.csharp.at/SSB_Book/c10/PublishSubscribe">
        <Subject>Subject1</Subject>
    </Publish>'
);
```

In Listing 10-74, the AuthorService must first specify to which subject the following sent articles belong. It does this by sending the [http://ssb.csharp.at/SSB_Book/c10/PublishMessage] message type. Finally, the AuthorService sends the various articles that belong to the previously specified subject (see Listing 10-75).

Listing 10-75. *Sending Articles for the Specified Subject*

```
SEND ON CONVERSATION @ch
MESSAGE TYPE [http://ssb.csharp.at/SSB_Book/c10/ArticleMessage]
(
   N'This is an article on Subject1'
);

SEND ON CONVERSATION @ch
MESSAGE TYPE [http://ssb.csharp.at/SSB_Book/c10/ArticleMessage]
(
   N'And this is another article on Subject1'
);
GO
```

As soon as the articles are sent from the AuthorService to the PublisherService, they are forwarded automatically to the subscribed subscriber services through the sp_PublisherService service program. Now, when you take a look at the associated queues of the subscriber services, you'll see that the sent articles were forwarded successfully, as shown in Figure 10-18.

■**Note** Because of the asynchronous processing nature of Service Broker, you have to wait a few seconds (until the sent messages are processed) before you can look into the SubscriberQueue1 and SubscriberQueue2.

	(No column name)	status	priority	queuing_order	conversation_group_id	conversation_handle
1	This is an article on Subject 1	1	0	0	632551FE-6E9E-DB11-8D23-0014C2E615AA	622551FE-6E9E-DB11-8D23-0014C2E615AA
2	And this is another article on Subject1	1	0	1	632551FE-6E9E-DB11-8D23-0014C2E615AA	622551FE-6E9E-DB11-8D23-0014C2E615AA

Figure 10-18. *The articles forwarded to the subscriber services*

Workload Throttling Through Service Broker

Now that you've seen how you can use Service Broker to implement scalable, distributed, and multithreaded database applications, what about the opposite? Suppose you have the requirement to call some application functionality in a synchronous way. The requirements dictate that you call some functionality inside a mainframe application or inside another resource where you have just one dedicated connection available that you have to share among your various connected clients.

Or consider a scenario where you have to call a legacy COM component that is not thread-safe by its design. I had this requirement in 2002 in a customer project where I had no SQL Server 2008 available and therefore no Service Broker functionality. I wrote a component that accepted calls from clients, queued them up in a table, and finally forwarded the queued calls one by one to the legacy COM component.

The same functionality can be also implemented with Service Broker and the activation feature. Follow these steps:

- Write a stored procedure that calls your resource (like a mainframe application or a legacy COM component), where you have only one dedicated connection available or where your resource must be accessed in a synchronous way.

- Use the stored procedure for internal activation on your target queue of your target service.

- Configure internal activation so that only one parallel queue reader is executed at a time. Because of this, you're gaining synchronous access to your resource or to your dedicated connection.

- Clients that are requesting access to your resource are just sending Service Broker messages to your target service, which does the real synchronous processing through the internal activation mechanism of Service Broker in the background.

- For urgent calls to your synchronous accessible resource, you can use the conversation priority feature of Service Broker to handle some conversations with a higher priority than others.

Let's now have a look at how you can implement such a system. In this example, I want to show how you can access a Simple Mail Transfer Protocol (SMTP) server in a synchronous way. Imagine that you've implemented a large customer relationship management (CRM) application that must send out newsletters to several thousand customers at the beginning of each month.

In this case, it is unusual to send all several thousand emails in one big chunk out to your customers, because this would impact the scalability as well as the overall availability of your SMTP server. Maybe your SMTP server would also go down, because of this critical workload. In this case you can use the approach I've described so far to access your SMTP server in a synchronous way to achieve a better availability of your SMTP server. Let's have a look at the first step: creating the Service Broker objects you need for this example.

Implementing the Service Broker Infrastructure

Before you implement your service program with a stored procedure, you have to create all the Service Broker objects needed for this example. This example uses the [http://ssb.csharp.at/SSB_Book/c10/EmailContract] contract that references the [http://ssb.csharp.at/SSB_Book/c10/EmailRequestMessageType] and the [http://ssb.csharp.at/SSB_Book/c10/EmailResponseMessageType] message types. Listing 10-76 shows the definition of these three objects.

Listing 10-76. *Creating All Necessary Service Broker Objects*

```
CREATE MESSAGE TYPE [http://ssb.csharp.at/SSB_Book/c10/EmailRequestMessageType]
   VALIDATION = WELL_FORMED_XML
GO

CREATE MESSAGE TYPE [http://ssb.csharp.at/SSB_Book/c10/EmailResponseMessageType]
   VALIDATION = WELL_FORMED_XML
GO

CREATE CONTRACT [http://ssb.csharp.at/SSB_Book/c10/EmailContract]
(
   [http://ssb.csharp.at/SSB_Book/c10/EmailRequestMessageType] SENT BY INITIATOR,
   [http://ssb.csharp.at/SSB_Book/c10/EmailResponseMessageType] SENT BY TARGET
)
GO
```

Once you've defined your message types and the needed contract, you have to create the target service that does the real communication with your synchronous accessible resource. Listing 10-77 shows the definition of our target service.

Listing 10-77. *The Target Service*

```
CREATE QUEUE TargetQueue
GO

CREATE SERVICE TargetService
ON QUEUE TargetQueue
(
   [http://ssb.csharp.at/SSB_Book/c10/EmailContract]
)
GO
```

As you can see in Listing, 10-77 the target service supports the one and only [http://ssb.csharp.at/SSB_Book/c10/EmailContract] contract.

Writing the Stored Procedure

Now that you've implemented the Service Broker infrastructure, you can write the stored procedure that acts as your service program and implements the synchronous access to your SMTP server. In this case, the stored procedure is called ProcessRequestMessages and processes all received messages from the TargetQueue. Listing 10-78 shows the definition of the ProcessRequestMessages stored procedure.

Listing 10-78. *Implementation of the* ProcessRequestMessages *Stored Procedure*

```sql
CREATE PROCEDURE ProcessRequestMessages
AS
   DECLARE @ch UNIQUEIDENTIFIER;
   DECLARE @messagetypename NVARCHAR(256);
   DECLARE @messagebody XML;
   DECLARE @responsemessage XML;
   DECLARE @priority INT;

   WHILE (1=1)
   BEGIN
      BEGIN TRY
         BEGIN TRANSACTION;

         RECEIVE TOP(1)
            @ch = conversation_handle,
            @messagetypename = message_type_name,
            @messagebody = CAST(message_body AS XML),
            @priority = priority
         FROM TargetQueue;

         IF (@@ROWCOUNT = 0)
         BEGIN
            ROLLBACK TRANSACTION
            BREAK
         END

         IF (@messagetypename =
            'http://ssb.csharp.at/SSB_Book/c10/EmailRequestMessageType')
         BEGIN
            DECLARE @recipients VARCHAR(MAX);
            DECLARE @subject NVARCHAR(256);
            DECLARE @body NVARCHAR(MAX);
            DECLARE @profileName SYSNAME = 'KlausProfile';

            -- Get the needed information from the received message
            SELECT @recipients = @messagebody.value(
               '/Email[1]/Recipients[1]', 'NVARCHAR(MAX)')
            SELECT @subject = @messagebody.value(
               '/Email[1]/Subject[1]', 'NVARCHAR(MAX)')
            SELECT @body = @messagebody.value('/Email[1]/Body[1]', 'NVARCHAR(MAX)')

            -- Store the received request message in a table
            INSERT INTO ProcessedEmailMessages
               (ID, Recipients, Subject, Body, Priority)
            VALUES (NEWID(), @recipients, @subject, @body, @priority)
```

```
                -- Send the email
                EXEC msdb.dbo.sp_send_dbmail
                    'KlausProfile', @recipients, NULL, NULL, @subject, @body;

                -- Construct the response message
                SET @responsemessage =
                    '<EmailResponse>Your email message was queued for further
                    processing.</EmailResponse>';

                -- Send the response message back to the initiating service
                SEND ON CONVERSATION @ch MESSAGE TYPE
                    [http://ssb.csharp.at/SSB_Book/c10/EmailResponseMessageType]
                    (@responsemessage);

                -- End the conversation on the target's side
                END CONVERSATION @ch;
            END

            IF (@messagetypename =
                'http://schemas.microsoft.com/SQL/ServiceBroker/EndDialog')
            BEGIN
                -- End the conversation
                END CONVERSATION @ch;
            END

            COMMIT TRANSACTION
        END TRY
        BEGIN CATCH
            ROLLBACK TRANSACTION
        END CATCH
    END
GO
```

As you can see in Listing 10-78, the implementation of the ProcessRequestMessages stored procedure is straightforward. As soon as the stored procedure receives the [http://ssb. csharp.at/SSB_Book/c10/EmailRequestMessageType] message type, the recipients, the subject, and the body are extracted through the XML data type method value() from the received request message:

```
-- Get the needed information from the received message
SELECT @recipients = @messagebody.value('/Email[1]/Recipients[1]', 'NVARCHAR(MAX)')
SELECT @subject = @messagebody.value('/Email[1]/Subject[1]', 'NVARCHAR(MAX)')
SELECT @body = @messagebody.value('/Email[1]/Body[1]', 'NVARCHAR(MAX)')
```

After the information is extracted from the request message, a new record is inserted into the ProcessedEmailMessages table for logging purposes. Listing 10-79 shows the definition of this table.

Listing 10-79. *Definition of the* ProcessedEmailMessages *Table*

```
CREATE TABLE ProcessedEmailMessages
(
    ID UNIQUEIDENTIFIER NOT NULL PRIMARY KEY,
    Recipients NVARCHAR(MAX) NOT NULL,
    Subject NVARCHAR(256) NOT NULL,
    Body NVARCHAR(MAX) NOT NULL,
    Priority INT NOT NULL
)
GO
```

After the logging record is inserted into the ProcessedEmailMessages table, the actual email is sent out through a call to the sp_send_dbmail stored procedure that is located inside the msdb database:

```
-- Send the email
EXEC msdb.dbo.sp_send_dbmail
    'KlausProfile', @recipients, NULL, NULL, @subject, @body;
```

■**Note** Please make sure that you have configured a Database Mail profile named KlausProfile as used in this example.

Once the email has been sent out to the actual recipient, the response message is constructed, sent back to the initiator, and the Service Broker conversation is ended:

```
-- Construct the response message
SET @responsemessage =
    '<EmailResponse>Your email message was queued for further
    processing.</EmailResponse>';

-- Send the response message back to the initiating service
SEND ON CONVERSATION @ch MESSAGE TYPE
    [http://ssb.csharp.at/SSB_Book/c10/EmailResponseMessageType] (@responsemessage);

-- End the conversation on the target's side
END CONVERSATION @ch;
```

As soon as the current conversation is ended, Service Broker starts a new conversation when a new request message is available in the TargetQueue.

■**Note** Be sure to sign the ProcessRequestMessages stored procedure (as described in Chapter 4), because you're creating stored procedure calls between databases. The shorthand available to you is to quickly enable the TRUSTWORTHY property on your database.

Configuring Internal Activation

After you've implemented the ProcessRequestMessages stored procedure, you have to configure internal activation for the TargetQueue that receives request messages from an initiator service. Listing 10-80 shows the T-SQL code needed to enable internal activation for the TargetQueue.

Listing 10-80. *Enabling Internal Activation for the* TargetQueue

```
ALTER QUEUE [TargetQueue]
WITH ACTIVATION
(
    STATUS = ON,
    PROCEDURE_NAME = [ProcessRequestMessages],
    MAX_QUEUE_READERS = 1,
    EXECUTE AS SELF
)
GO
```

The important point here is that you configure the property MAX_QUEUE_READERS with a value of 1. This means that Service Broker activates at least one instance of the stored procedure at a time. Therefore, all your received messages in the TargetQueue are being processed synchronously, one by one. This also means that the email sending process is done synchronously, one email after another, instead of a big chunk that blocks your SMTP server for a huge amount of time. This means you can ensure a better availability of your SMTP server for other applications that are sending out emails through this SMTP server.

Queuing Up Some Synchronous Work

The only thing left to do is set up an initiator service that sends out several [http://ssb. csharp.at/SSB_Book/c10/EmailRequestMessageType] messages to queue up emails that must be sent out to their recipients. Listing 10-81 shows the definition of the InitiatorService1.

Listing 10-81. *Definition of the* InitiatorService1

```
CREATE QUEUE InitiatorQueue1
GO

CREATE SERVICE InitiatorService1
ON QUEUE InitiatorQueue1
(
    [http://ssb.csharp.at/SSB_Book/c10/EmailContract]
)
GO
```

After you've created the InitiatorService1, you're now able to send some email sending requests to the TargetService. Listing 10-82 shows the necessary T-SQL sending code.

Listing 10-82. *Sending Some Email Sending Requests*

```
DECLARE @dh UNIQUEIDENTIFIER;
DECLARE @i INT = 0;
DECLARE @message XML;

SET @message =
'
<Email>
    <Recipients>Klaus.Aschenbrenner@csharp.at</Recipients>
    <Subject>SQL Service Broker email</Subject>
    <Body>This is a test email from SQL Server 2008 using Conversation
        Priorities</Body>
</Email>
'

WHILE @i < 10
BEGIN
    BEGIN TRANSACTION;

    -- Begin a high priority conversation
    BEGIN DIALOG CONVERSATION @dh
        FROM SERVICE [InitiatorService1]
        TO SERVICE N'TargetService'
        ON CONTRACT [http://ssb.csharp.at/SSB_Book/c10/EmailContract]
        WITH ENCRYPTION = OFF;

    SEND ON CONVERSATION @dh
        MESSAGE TYPE [http://ssb.csharp.at/SSB_Book/c10/EmailRequestMessageType]
        (@message);

    COMMIT;
END
GO
```

As you can see in Listing 10-82, the T-SQL code just sent out ten [http://ssb.csharp.at/SSB_Book/c10/EmailRequestMessageType] messages on ten different conversations. These messages are put into the TargetQueue and are automatically processed by the ProcessRequestMessages stored procedure in the background through the configured internal activation. The big difference in this example is that the received message from each conversation is processed synchronously—one by one—configured with the internal activation. So you can ensure that you can access some of your application resources (such as an SMTP server, a legacy COM component, or a mainframe application) synchronously.

Enabling Conversation Priorities

Processing all conversations synchronously one by one sounds good for some scenarios. But what happens when you have some customers with initiator services, where those conversations should be processed faster than other conversations because they paid a higher royalty fee? In this case, you need a functionality to prioritize these conversations with a higher priority than conversations from normal paid customers.

To achieve this prioritization, you can use the *Conversation Priority* feature of Service Broker, first introduced with SQL Server 2008. The Conversation Priority feature allows you to give a conversation a priority from 1 to 10, where 1 is the lowest priority and 10 is the highest priority. Conversation priorities can be seen as a set of user-defined rules, where each rule specifies the priority level and the criteria for determining which Service Broker conversation to assign to this conversation priority. Messages from conversations with a higher priority level are sent and received faster than messages from conversations with a lower priority level.

You create conversation priority objects through the CREATE BROKER PRIORITY T-SQL statement inside your application database. Listing 10-83 shows the syntax of the CREATE BROKER PRIORITY T-SQL statement.

Listing 10-83. *Syntax of the* CREATE BROKER PRIORITY *T-SQL Statement*

```
CREATE BROKER PRIORITY ConversationPriorityName
FOR CONVERSATION
[
   SET (
      [ CONTRACT_NAME = { ContractName | ANY } ]
      [ [ , ] LOCAL_SERVICE_NAME = { LocalServiceName | ANY } ]
      [ [ , ] REMOTE_SERVICE_NAME = { 'RemoteServiceName' | ANY } ]
      [ [ , ] PRIORITY_LEVEL = { PriorityValue | DEFAULT } ]
   )
]
```

Table 10-4 describes the several arguments for the CREATE BROKER PRIORITY T-SQL statement.

Table 10-4. *Arguments for* CREATE BROKER PRIORITY

Argument	Description
ConversationPriorityName	The name of the conversation priority object. The name must be unique inside the current database.
ContractName	Specifies the name of the Service Broker contract to be used as a criterion for determining whether the conversation priority applies to a conversation.
LocalServiceName	Specifies the name of a Service Broker service to be used as a criterion to determine whether the conversation priority applies to a conversation.
RemoteServiceName	Specifies the name of a Service Broker service to be used as a criterion to determine whether the conversation priority applies to a conversation. This argument must be specified as a string literal.
PriorityValue	Specifies the priority to assign to any conversations that use the contracts and services specified previously. This value must be an integer between 1 (lowest priority) and 10 (highest priority). The default value is 5.

Before you can create conversation priority objects in a database, you have to set the `HONOR_BROKER_PRIORITY` database option to `ON`:

```
ALTER DATABASE Chapter10_ConversationPriority SET HONOR_BROKER_PRIORITY ON
```

After you've created a conversation priority object, Service Broker is able to assign a priority to a Service Broker conversation. Service Broker assigns conversation priority levels when conversation endpoints are created. The conversation endpoint retains the priority level until the conversation ends. Service Broker assigns the conversation endpoint the priority level from the conversation priority whose contract and services criteria best match the endpoint properties. Table 10-5 shows the match precedence.

Table 10-5. *Conversation Priority Match Precedence*

Endpoint Contract	Endpoint Local Service	Endpoint Remote Service
Priority Contract	Priority Local Service	Priority Remote Service
Priority Contract	Priority Local Service	ANY
Priority Contract	ANY	Priority Remote Service
Priority Contract	ANY	ANY
ANY	Priority Local Service	Priority Remote Service
ANY	Priority Local Service	ANY
ANY	ANY	Priority Remote Service
ANY	ANY	ANY

Service Broker first looks for a priority whose specified contract, local service, and remote service match those used by the conversation endpoint. If one is not found, Service Broker then looks for a priority with a contract and local service that match those used by the endpoint, and where the remote service was specified as ANY. This continues for all variations listed in Table 10-5. If no match is found, the endpoint gets the default priority of 5.

The Service Broker communication protocol doesn't transmit priority levels between conversation endpoints. Service Broker independently assigns a priority level to each endpoint. To have Service Broker assign priority levels to both the initiator and the target conversation endpoints, you must ensure that both endpoints are covered by conversation priorities. If the initiator and target conversation endpoints are in separate databases, you must create conversation priorities in each database.

The same priority level is usually specified for both conversation endpoints for a given conversation. While you can specify different priority levels for each endpoint, doing this doesn't mean that messages are sent faster in one direction than the other. All conversation endpoints in a database are assigned with a default priority of 5 if no conversation priorities have been created for the database. Conversation priorities don't affect message forwarding (refer to Chapter 11 for more information about message forwarding), which always operates at the default priority level of 5.

In this example, I created a new initiator service called `InitiatorService2` that gets a higher conversation priority than the original initiator service named `InitiatorService1`. Listing 10-84 shows the definition of the `InitiatorService2` and the needed conversation priorities.

Listing 10-84. *Creating Conversation Priorities*

```
CREATE QUEUE InitiatorQueue2
GO

CREATE SERVICE InitiatorService2
ON QUEUE InitiatorQueue2
(
    [http://ssb.csharp.at/SSB_Book/c10/EmailContract]
)
GO

CREATE BROKER PRIORITY LowPriorityInitiatorToTarget FOR CONVERSATION SET
(
    CONTRACT_NAME = [http://ssb.csharp.at/SSB_Book/c10/EmailContract],
    LOCAL_SERVICE_NAME = InitiatorService1,
    REMOTE_SERVICE_NAME = 'TargetService',
    PRIORITY_LEVEL = 1
)
GO

CREATE BROKER PRIORITY LowPriorityTargetToInitiator FOR CONVERSATION SET
(
    CONTRACT_NAME = [http://ssb.csharp.at/SSB_Book/c10/EmailContract],
    LOCAL_SERVICE_NAME = TargetService,
    REMOTE_SERVICE_NAME = 'InitiatorService1',
    PRIORITY_LEVEL = 1
)
GO

CREATE BROKER PRIORITY HighPriorityInitiatorToTarget FOR CONVERSATION SET
(
    CONTRACT_NAME = [http://ssb.csharp.at/SSB_Book/c10/EmailContract],
    LOCAL_SERVICE_NAME = InitiatorService2,
    REMOTE_SERVICE_NAME = 'TargetService',
    PRIORITY_LEVEL = 10
)
GO

CREATE BROKER PRIORITY HighPriorityTargetToInitiator FOR CONVERSATION SET
(
    CONTRACT_NAME = [http://ssb.csharp.at/SSB_Book/c10/EmailContract],
    LOCAL_SERVICE_NAME = TargetService,
    REMOTE_SERVICE_NAME = 'InitiatorService2',
    PRIORITY_LEVEL = 10
)
GO
```

As you can see from Listing 10-84, we have created four conversation priority objects that describe the conversation priority between the InitiatorService1 and the TargetService, and the InitiatorService2 and the TargetService, in both directions. As soon as you have created the required conversation priorities, you can query the sys.conversation_priorities catalog view for more information about the created conversation priorities objects. Table 10-6 shows the columns returned by the sys.conversation_priorities catalog view.

Table 10-6. *The* sys.conversation_priorities *Catalog View*

Column	Data Type	Description
name	SYSNAME	Name of the conversation priority
service_contract_id	INT	The identifier of the contract that is specified for the conversation priority
local_service_id	INT	The identifier of the service that is specified as the local service for the conversation priority
remote_service_name	NVARCHAR(256)	The name of the service that is specified as the remote service for the conversation priority
priority	TINYINT	The priority level that is specified for this conversation priority

Figure 10-19 shows the output of the sys.conversations_priorities catalog view after creating the four conversation priority objects from Listing 10-84.

	priority_id	name	service_contract_id	local_service_id	remote_service_name	priority
1	65536	LowPriorityInitiatorToTarget	65536	65536	TargetService	1
2	65537	LowPriorityTargetToInitiator	65536	65537	InitiatorService1	1
3	65538	HighPriorityInitiatorToTarget	65536	65538	TargetService	10
4	65539	HighPriorityTargetToInitiator	65536	65537	InitiatorService2	10

Figure 10-19. *Querying the* sys.conversation_priorities *catalog view*

After you've created the needed conversation priority objects, you can start several conversations from the InitiatorService1 and InitiatorService2 to the TargetService. All conversations from the InitiatorService1 will be assigned the conversation priority 1, and all conversations from the InitiatorService2 will be assigned the conversation priority 10. Listing 10-85 shows the modified message sending code.

Listing 10-85. *Creating Conversations with Different Assigned Conversation Priorities*

```
DECLARE @dh UNIQUEIDENTIFIER;
DECLARE @i INT = 0;
DECLARE @message XML;

SET @message =
'
```

```
<Email>
    <Recipients>Klaus.Aschenbrenner@csharp.at</Recipients>
    <Subject>SQL Service Broker email</Subject>
    <Body>This is a test email from SQL Server 2008 using Conversation
Priorities</Body>
</Email>
'


WHILE @i < 10
BEGIN
    BEGIN TRANSACTION;

    -- Every 10 requests we're sending the message from a different
    -- initiator service to get a different priority
    IF (@i % 10) = 0
    BEGIN
        -- Begin a high priority conversation
        BEGIN DIALOG CONVERSATION @dh
            FROM SERVICE [InitiatorService1]
            TO SERVICE N'TargetService'
            ON CONTRACT [http://ssb.csharp.at/SSB_Book/c10/EmailContract]
            WITH ENCRYPTION = OFF;

        SEND ON CONVERSATION @dh
            MESSAGE TYPE [http://ssb.csharp.at/SSB_Book/c10/EmailRequestMessageType]
            (@message);
    END
    ELSE
    BEGIN
        -- Begin a low priority conversation
        BEGIN DIALOG CONVERSATION @dh
            FROM SERVICE [InitiatorService2]
            TO SERVICE N'TargetService'
            ON CONTRACT [http://ssb.csharp.at/SSB_Book/c10/EmailContract]
            WITH ENCRYPTION = OFF;

        SEND ON CONVERSATION @dh
            MESSAGE TYPE [http://ssb.csharp.at/SSB_Book/c10/EmailRequestMessageType]
            (@message);
    END

    COMMIT;

    SELECT @i += 1;
END
GO
```

As you can see in Listing 10-85, every tenth conversation is created through the InitiatorService2. This means that every tenth conversation is assigned the conversation priority 10, and all other conversations (that are started from the InitiatorService1) are assigned the conversation priority 1.

When you now have a look at the sys.conversation_endpoints catalog view, you can see the conversation priority assignment in the priority column. See Figure 10-20 for more information.

	priority	conversation_handle	conversation_id	is_initiator	service_contract_id	conversation_group_id
1	10	A3C597D9-7FBB-DC11-8BC7-0003FFC30DDD	C91C09F6-6E1F-4BC9-968B-02EF374EF078	0	0	00000000-0000-0000-0000-000000000000
2	10	A0C597D9-7FBB-DC11-8BC7-0003FFC30DDD	C91C09F6-6E1F-4BC9-968B-02EF374EF078	1	65536	A1C597D9-7FBB-DC11-8BC7-0003FFC30DDD
3	5	8789FE80-7FBB-DC11-8BC7-0003FFC30DDD	8FC4DF68-FCD4-4C10-A6B6-04CEAEA19488	0	0	00000000-0000-0000-0000-000000000000
4	5	8489FE80-7FBB-DC11-8BC7-0003FFC30DDD	8FC4DF68-FCD4-4C10-A6B6-04CEAEA19488	1	65536	8589FE80-7FBB-DC11-8BC7-0003FFC30DDD
5	10	97C597D9-7FBB-DC11-8BC7-0003FFC30DDD	02EE0834-A274-45B9-B0E1-08C51375C576	0	0	00000000-0000-0000-0000-000000000000
6	10	94C597D9-7FBB-DC11-8BC7-0003FFC30DDD	02EE0834-A274-45B9-B0E1-08C51375C576	1	65536	95C597D9-7FBB-DC11-8BC7-0003FFC30DDD
7	5	8F89FE80-7FBB-DC11-8BC7-0003FFC30DDD	C7F4133C-213A-4958-B4F3-178E5325D5F6	0	0	00000000-0000-0000-0000-000000000000
8	5	8C89FE80-7FBB-DC11-8BC7-0003FFC30DDD	C7F4133C-213A-4958-B4F3-178E5325D5F6	1	65536	8D89FE80-7FBB-DC11-8BC7-0003FFC30DDD
9	10	AFC597D9-7FBB-DC11-8BC7-0003FFC30DDD	CBB8D2D4-2028-4E65-8606-1819FE172E8A	0	0	00000000-0000-0000-0000-000000000000
10	10	ACC597D9-7FBB-DC11-8BC7-0003FFC30DDD	CBB8D2D4-2028-4E65-8606-1819FE172E8A	1	65536	ADC597D9-7FBB-DC11-8BC7-0003FFC30DDD
11	10	B7C597D9-7FBB-DC11-8BC7-0003FFC30DDD	DB2D12EB-9864-4061-AE74-2943C711D751	0	0	00000000-0000-0000-0000-000000000000
12	10	B4C597D9-7FBB-DC11-8BC7-0003FFC30DDD	DB2D12EB-9864-4061-AE74-2943C711D751	1	65536	B5C597D9-7FBB-DC11-8BC7-0003FFC30DDD
13	10	B3C597D9-7FBB-DC11-8BC7-0003FFC30DDD	6949773F-9F17-449E-9A7B-429C973CDA27	0	0	00000000-0000-0000-0000-000000000000

Figure 10-20. *Conversation priorities at the conversation endpoints*

When you have a look at the TargetQueue for the received messages (with disabled internal activation, of course), you can also see the given priority of a received message in the priority column. See Figure 10-21.

	status	priority	queuing_order	conversation_group_id	conversation_handle	message_sequence_number	service_name	service_id
1	1	1	20	C2338C1C-80BB-DC11-8BC7-0003FFC30DDD	C3338C1C-80BB-DC11-8BC7-0003FFC30DDD	0	TargetService	65537
2	1	10	21	C6338C1C-80BB-DC11-8BC7-0003FFC30DDD	C7338C1C-80BB-DC11-8BC7-0003FFC30DDD	0	TargetService	65537
3	1	10	22	CA338C1C-80BB-DC11-8BC7-0003FFC30DDD	CB338C1C-80BB-DC11-8BC7-0003FFC30DDD	0	TargetService	65537
4	1	10	23	CE338C1C-80BB-DC11-8BC7-0003FFC30DDD	CF338C1C-80BB-DC11-8BC7-0003FFC30DDD	0	TargetService	65537
5	1	10	24	D2338C1C-80BB-DC11-8BC7-0003FFC30DDD	D3338C1C-80BB-DC11-8BC7-0003FFC30DDD	0	TargetService	65537
6	1	10	25	D6338C1C-80BB-DC11-8BC7-0003FFC30DDD	D7338C1C-80BB-DC11-8BC7-0003FFC30DDD	0	TargetService	65537
7	1	10	26	DA338C1C-80BB-DC11-8BC7-0003FFC30DDD	DB338C1C-80BB-DC11-8BC7-0003FFC30DDD	0	TargetService	65537
8	1	10	27	DE338C1C-80BB-DC11-8BC7-0003FFC30DDD	DF338C1C-80BB-DC11-8BC7-0003FFC30DDD	0	TargetService	65537
9	1	10	28	E2338C1C-80BB-DC11-8BC7-0003FFC30DDD	E3338C1C-80BB-DC11-8BC7-0003FFC30DDD	0	TargetService	65537
10	1	10	29	E6338C1C-80BB-DC11-8BC7-0003FFC30DDD	E7338C1C-80BB-DC11-8BC7-0003FFC30DDD	0	TargetService	65537

Figure 10-21. *Conversation priorities at the TargetQueue*

Finally the sys.transmission_queue catalog view is also enhanced with the priority column, if you're sending messages between SQL Server instances. Service Broker sends and receives messages for higher-priority conversations before sending and receiving messages for low-priority conversations. Messages from high-priority conversations spend less time in queues than messages from low-priority conversations.

Priority levels are always applied to operations that receive messages or conversation group identifiers from a queue. Priority level is one of the factors determining the set of messages retrieved by a RECEIVE T-SQL statement and the sequence in which the messages are retrieved:

- Each RECEIVE T-SQL statement always retrieves messages from one conversation group. A RECEIVE T-SQL statement that has no WHERE clause retrieves messages that belong to the highest priority unlocked conversation group that has messages in the queue. A RECEIVE T-SQL statement that has a WHERE clause retrieves the messages for the conversation group specified in the WHERE clause.

- Within a conversation group, the RECEIVE T-SQL statement retrieves messages depending on the priority level of the conversations in the conversation group. All of the messages from the conversation with the highest priority level are retrieved first, then the messages for the conversation with the next highest priority level, and so on.

- Within a conversation, the messages are retrieved in the same sequence as they were sent (exactly once in order delivery).

The GET CONVERSATION GROUP T-SQL statement returns the group with the highest priority level from the set of unlocked conversation groups that have messages in the queue. Messages in the transmission queues for an instance are transmitted in sequence based on

- The priority level of their associated conversation endpoint

- Within priority level, their send sequence in the conversation

Service Broker coordinates priority levels across all of the transmission queues in an instance of the database engine. Service Broker first transmits messages from the priority 10 conversations in all of the transmission queues, then messages from priority 9 conversations, and so on.

The relative difference in message performance increases with the difference in priority levels. In a system using two different priority levels, such as 5 and 6, the messages with the higher priority level will have a small performance advantage. In a system using two widely separated priority levels, such as 1 and 10, the messages with the higher priority level have a larger performance advantage. In systems using multiple priority levels, most of the processing is allocated to the top two or three priority levels.

Priority levels specified in conversation priorities are only applied to messages in the transmission queue if the HONOR_BROKER_PRIORITY database option is set to ON. If HONOR_BROKER_PRIORITY is set to OFF, all messages placed in the transmission queue for that database are sent using the default priority level of 5.

Keep in mind that messages and message fragments may be sent out of priority order for the following reasons:

- Service Broker sends messages between instances of the Database Engine using blocks of message fragments. If there are several message fragments with different priorities ready to send to one instance, Service Broker may send all of the fragments in one block. Some of the fragments at the end of the block may have a lower priority level than message fragments waiting for transmission to another instance.

- Service Broker includes a starvation prevention mechanism to help keep large numbers of high-priority messages from blocking low-priority messages. A low-priority message that has been waiting for a long time can be sent even if there are higher-priority messages in the queue.

In the next section, I'll show how you can implement priority-based message processing for Service Broker applications on your own without using the underlying infrastructure provided by Service Broker in SQL Server 2008.

Priority-Based Message Processing

One of the most frequent questions about Service Broker is whether it supports any sort of priority messages. Service Broker does offer message priority, because every message has a priority column, and messages are received in priority order within a dialog or conversation group. However, Service Broker doesn't have a way to set message priority within a conversation, because having priority within a conversation would conflict directly with the exactly-once-in-order delivery of a Service Broker conversation. In a good SOA design, the two Service Broker services involved in a conversation are independent. If one service could set the priority of an individual message without the consent of the others, this action would disturb how the messages are processed, since the other services may expect the messages in order. Two priority-based messaging options are possible with Service Broker:

- *Message priority within a conversation*: You must realize that with Service Broker priority, messages can't have priority—only dialogs can have priority. Because dialogs guarantee message ordering, it makes no sense to prioritize messages within a dialog. Message 10 can't be processed until messages 1–9 have been processed, no matter what their priority.

- *Message priority for individual conversations*: However, you can have assigned priorities for individual conversations. Conversations are independent and atomic; the processing order shouldn't matter, so having the ability to set a priority for a conversation makes sense.

Once you set priorities, you need to consider what to do with the priority. Normally, you should receive messages in priority order. Does that mean that as long as first-priority messages exist in the queue, you can never receive second-priority messages? That's the normal interpretation, but it means that low-priority messages will never be processed if enough high-priority messages are available.

Let's say you want to ensure that high-priority messages always have priority. What happens if all the queue readers are processing low-priority messages when a high-priority message arrives? If another reader is started, will it have enough resources to process the message while all the low-priority messages are being processed? Should a low-priority message be rolled back to make room for the high-priority message, or should the high-priority message wait for one of the low-priority messages to finish?

Another possibility is that both high- and low-priority messages are being processed, but more resources are being dedicated to the high-priority messages. For example, you might have ten queue readers for high-priority messages and one queue reader for low-priority messages. This ensures that low-priority messages are processed but at a lower rate than high-priority messages.

Implementing Priority-Based Messaging

Given all this, let's look at a way to implement priorities in Service Broker. The solution presented here applies to a case when messages are taking a long time to be processed. The service queue will accumulate a long list of pending messages during peak hours and will slowly progress through the queue.

In principle, you can easily achieve priority-based messaging with Service Broker by using the RECEIVE T-SQL statement, which has the WHERE clause that you can use to specify the desired conversation to process. However, you need a way to pass the conversation IDs and the desired priority to the processing service.

CONVERSATIONS VS. CONVERSATION GROUPS

In practice, you'll quickly notice that you want to control the priority of conversation groups instead of individual conversations. This is because the RECEIVE T-SQL statement locks an entire conversation group and naturally returns all messages for an entire conversation group in one result set. When you don't use related conversations, then conversation groups map one-to-one to individual conversations, and it makes no difference for you.

You can't just insert a message that sets the priority of a conversation group into the service queue, simply because the message will be at the bottom of the service queue. A solution to this problem is to split the service into two services: a front-end service, to which the clients are opening conversations, and a back-end service, which does the real, long-timed processing. Figure 10-22 shows the architecture of this solution.

Client   **Frontend Service**   **Backend Service**

Figure 10-22. *Priority-based message processing*

Service Broker Infrastructure

Let's have a look at how to implement this solution. First, you must define the used message types and contracts. In this sample, you define the following three message types:

- [http://ssb.csharp.at/SSB_Book/c10/LongWorkloadRequestMessageType]: This message type is sent when the client wants to enqueue a long work request at the target service.

- [http://ssb.csharp.at/SSB_Book/c10/SetPriorityRequestMessageType]: This message type is sent when the client wants to promote the priority of a conversation group to a higher level.

- [http://ssb.csharp.at/SSB_Book/c10/LongWorkloadResponseMessageType]: This message type is sent from the target service as an answer back to the client.

Because you have the front-end and the back-end Service Broker service in this solution, you also need to separate contracts. The first contract—the [http://ssb.csharp.at/SSB_Book/ c10/RequestWithPriorityContract] contract—defines the communication between the clients and the frontend service. The second contract—the [http://ssb.csharp.at/SSB_Book/ c10/ RequestInternalContract] contract—defines the communication between the front-end service and the back-end service. Finally, you have to define the two Service Broker services with their corresponding service queues. Listing 10-86 shows the necessary T-SQL code.

Listing 10-86. *Creating the Service Broker Infrastructure*

```
CREATE MESSAGE TYPE
    [http://ssb.csharp.at/SSB_Book/c10/LongWorkloadRequestMessageType]
    VALIDATION = WELL_FORMED_XML
GO

CREATE MESSAGE TYPE
    [http://ssb.csharp.at/SSB_Book/c10/SetPriorityMessageType]
    VALIDATION = WELL_FORMED_XML
GO

CREATE MESSAGE TYPE
    [http://ssb.csharp.at/SSB_Book/c10/LongWorkflowResponseMessageType]
    VALIDATION = WELL_FORMED_XML;
GO

CREATE CONTRACT [http://ssb.csharp.at/SSB_Book/c10/RequestWithPriorityContract]
(
    [http://ssb.csharp.at/SSB_Book/c10/LongWorkloadRequestMessageType]
        SENT BY INITIATOR,
    [http://ssb.csharp.at/SSB_Book/c10/SetPriorityMessageType]
        SENT BY INITIATOR,
    [http://ssb.csharp.at/SSB_Book/c10/LongWorkflowResponseMessageType]
        SENT BY TARGET
)
GO

CREATE CONTRACT [http://ssb.csharp.at/SSB_Book/c10/RequestInternalContract]
(
    [http://ssb.csharp.at/SSB_Book/c10/LongWorkloadRequestMessageType]
        SENT BY INITIATOR,
    [http://ssb.csharp.at/SSB_Book/c10/LongWorkflowResponseMessageType]
        SENT BY TARGET
)
GO

CREATE QUEUE FrontEndQueue
GO
```

```
CREATE QUEUE BackEndQueue
GO

CREATE SERVICE [FrontEndService]
ON QUEUE [FrontEndQueue]
(
    [http://ssb.csharp.at/SSB_Book/c10/RequestWithPriorityContract]
)
GO


CREATE SERVICE [BackEndService]
ON QUEUE [BackEndQueue]
(
    [http://ssb.csharp.at/SSB_Book/c10/RequestInternalContract]
)
GO
```

In Listing 10-86, the only difference between the two created contracts is that the
[http://ssb.csharp.at/SSB_Book/c10/RequestWithPriorityContract] contract also supports
setting the priority of a conversation group through the [http://ssb.csharp.at/SSB_Book/
c10/ SetPriorityRequestMessageType] message type.

Request Bindings

After you define the Service Broker infrastructure, you're ready to implement the priority-
based messaging. Because the front-end service only forwards incoming requests from clients
directly to the back-end service, you need a table that stores the established link between an
incoming conversation from a client and the corresponding conversation with the backend
service. I've called this table RequestsBindings, as shown in Listing 10-87.

Listing 10-87. *Creation of the* RequestsBindings *Table*

```
CREATE TABLE RequestsBindings
(
    FrontendConversation UNIQUEIDENTIFIER PRIMARY KEY,
    BackendConversation UNIQUEIDENTIFIER UNIQUE
)
GO
```

After you create the RequestsBindings table, you need some logic to manipulate the
records inside the table. You implement this logic in the following two stored procedures:

- sp_BindingGetPeer: This stored procedure retrieves the opposite side's conversation
  from the bindings table. It retrieves the front-end conversation from the back-end
  conversation, and vice versa.

- sp_BindingGetBackend: This stored procedure retrieves a back-end conversation for a
  front-end conversation. It will initiate a new conversation with the BackEndService if
  one doesn't already exist.

Listing 10-88 shows the implementation of the sp_BindingGetPeer stored procedure.

Listing 10-88. *The* sp_BindingGetPeer *Stored Procedure*

```
CREATE PROCEDURE sp_BindingGetPeer (
   @Conversation UNIQUEIDENTIFIER,
   @Peer UNIQUEIDENTIFIER OUTPUT)
AS
SET NOCOUNT ON;
SELECT @Peer =

(
   SELECT
      BackendConversation
      FROM RequestsBindings
   WHERE FrontendConversation = @Conversation

   UNION ALL

   SELECT FrontendConversation
      FROM RequestsBindings
      WHERE BackendConversation = @Conversation
)

IF (@@ROWCOUNT = 0)
BEGIN
   SELECT @Peer = NULL;
END
GO
```

In Listing 10-88, the sp_BindingGetPeer stored procedure does two lookups in the RequestsBindings table and joins both result sets through the UNION ALL T-SQL operator. Therefore, it's possible to retrieve the front-end conversation from the back-end conversation, and vice versa.

More interesting is the sp_BindingGetBackend stored procedure, which retrieves the back-end conversation for the specified front-end conversation supplied as a parameter. If the back-end conversation isn't already initiated, the stored procedure will start a new conversation with the BackEndService and store the link between the front-end and back-end conversation in the RequestsBindings table. Listing 10-89 shows the implementation of the sp_BindingGetBackend stored procedure.

Listing 10-89. *The* sp_BindingGetBackend *Stored Procedure*

```
CREATE PROCEDURE sp_BindingGetBackend (
   @FrontendConversation UNIQUEIDENTIFIER,
   @BackendConversation UNIQUEIDENTIFIER OUTPUT)
AS
SET NOCOUNT ON;
BEGIN TRANSACTION;
```

```
SELECT @BackendConversation = BackendConversation
    FROM RequestsBindings
    WHERE FrontendConversation = @FrontendConversation;

IF (@@ROWCOUNT = 0)
BEGIN
    BEGIN DIALOG CONVERSATION @BackendConversation
        FROM SERVICE [FrontEndService]
        TO SERVICE N'BackEndService', N'current database'
        ON CONTRACT [http://ssb.csharp.at/SSB_Book/c10/RequestInternalContract]
        WITH
            RELATED_CONVERSATION = @FrontendConversation,
            ENCRYPTION = OFF;


    INSERT INTO RequestsBindings (FrontendConversation, BackendConversation)
    VALUES
    (
        @FrontendConversation,
        @BackendConversation
    );
END
COMMIT;
GO
```

Priority Table

After you implement the request binding between the front-end and the back-end service, it's time to create the priority table and implement the logic on top of this table. I've simply called this the Priority table. This table stores the current priority for a conversation group. Listing 10-90 shows the table definition.

Listing 10-90. *Creating the* Priority *Table*

```
CREATE TABLE Priority
(
    ConversationGroup UNIQUEIDENTIFIER UNIQUE,
    Priority TINYINT,
    EnqueueTime TIMESTAMP,
    PRIMARY KEY CLUSTERED
    (
        Priority DESC,
        EnqueueTime ASC,
        ConversationGroup
    )
)
GO
```

In Listing 10-90, the primary key of the table is defined on the columns Priority, EnqueueTime, and ConversationGroup. To manipulate the content of the Priority table, you can write the following two stored procedures:

- sp_DequeuePriority: This stored procedure dequeues the next conversation from the Priority table.

- sp_EnqueuePriority: This stored procedure enqueues a new conversation group into the Priority table.

Listing 10-91 shows the implementation of the sp_DequeuePriority stored procedure.

Listing 10-91. *Implementation of the* sp_DequeuePriority *Stored Procedure*

```
CREATE PROCEDURE sp_DequeuePriority
@ConversationGroup UNIQUEIDENTIFIER OUTPUT
AS
SET NOCOUNT ON;
BEGIN TRANSACTION;


SELECT @ConversationGroup = NULL;
DECLARE @cgt TABLE (ConversationGroup UNIQUEIDENTIFIER);

DELETE FROM Priority WITH (READPAST)
OUTPUT DELETED.ConversationGroup INTO @cgt
WHERE ConversationGroup =
(
    SELECT TOP (1) ConversationGroup
    FROM Priority WITH (READPAST)
    ORDER BY Priority DESC, EnqueueTime ASC
)

SELECT @ConversationGroup = ConversationGroup
FROM @cgt;

COMMIT;
GO
```

Listing 10-92 shows the implementation of the sp_EnqueuePriority stored procedure.

Listing 10-92. *Implementation of the* sp_EnqueuePriority *Stored Procedure*

```
CREATE PROCEDURE sp_EnqueuePriority
@ConversationGroup UNIQUEIDENTIFIER,
@Priority TINYINT
AS
SET NOCOUNT ON;
BEGIN TRANSACTION;
```

```
DELETE FROM Priority
WHERE ConversationGroup = @ConversationGroup;

INSERT INTO Priority (ConversationGroup, Priority)
VALUES (@ConversationGroup, @Priority);

COMMIT;
```

In Listing 10-92, the stored procedure deletes a priority for the given conversation group in the first step. This is necessary when a priority is assigned twice to a conversation group.

Front-end Service Program

After you implement the complete infrastructure and logic for the priority-based messaging, it's time to implement the service program for the FrontEndService. This service program is implemented in the sp_FrontendService stored procedure and is the more interesting part in this sample. The main functionality of the stored procedure is to accept incoming requests from a client and forward them to the BackEndService. It also sets the priority of a conversation group when the [http://ssb.csharp.at/SSB_Book/c10/SetPriorityMessageType] message type is processed from the FrontEndQueue. Because the sp_FrontendService stored procedure is quite complex, I've split the description into several steps. The first step begins with the message retrieval from the FrontEndQueue (see Listing 10-93).

Listing 10-93. *Message Retrieval in the* FrontEndService

```
CREATE PROCEDURE sp_FrontendService
AS
SET NOCOUNT ON
DECLARE @dh UNIQUEIDENTIFIER;
DECLARE @bind_dh UNIQUEIDENTIFIER;
DECLARE @message_type_name SYSNAME;
DECLARE @message_body VARBINARY(MAX);

BEGIN TRANSACTION;

WAITFOR
(
    RECEIVE TOP (1)
        @dh = conversation_handle,
        @message_type_name = message_type_name,
        @message_body = message_body
    FROM [FrontEndQueue]
), TIMEOUT 1000;
```

As soon as a new message is received from the FrontEndQueue, the actual message processing starts. Listing 10-94 shows how the [http://ssb.csharp.at/SSB_Book/c10/LongWorkloadRequestMessageType] message type is forwarded to the BackEndService.

Listing 10-94. *Message Forwarding*

```
ELSE IF @message_type_name =
  N'http://ssb.csharp.at/SSB_Book/c10/LongWorkloadRequestMessageType'
BEGIN
    -- forward the workload request to the back end service
    EXEC sp_BindingGetBackend @dh, @bind_dh OUTPUT;

    SEND ON CONVERSATION @bind_dh MESSAGE TYPE
        [http://ssb.csharp.at/SSB_Book/c10/LongWorkloadRequestMessageType]
        (@message_body);
END
```

In Listing 10-94, you use the sp_BindingGetBackend stored procedure (described in Listing 10-89) to retrieve the backend conversation from the front-end conversation. If a conversation to the BackEndService isn't available, the sp_BindingGetBackend stored procedure will start a new conversation with the BackEndService through the BEGIN DIALOG CONVERSATION T-SQL statement.

More interesting is how the [http://ssb.csharp.at/SSB_Book/c10/ SetPriorityMessageType] message type is handled inside the sp_FrontendService stored procedure. Listing 10-95 shows the relevant T-SQL code.

Listing 10-95. *Setting the Priority of the Conversation Group*

```
ELSE IF @message_type_name =
  N'http://ssb.csharp.at/SSB_Book/c10/SetPriorityMessageType'
BEGIN
    -- Increase the priority of this conversation.
    -- We need the target-side conversation group
    -- of the backend conversation bound to @dh
    DECLARE @cg UNIQUEIDENTIFIER;

    SELECT @cg = tep.conversation_group_id
    FROM sys.conversation_endpoints tep WITH (NOLOCK)
    JOIN sys.conversation_endpoints iep WITH (NOLOCK) ON
        tep.conversation_id = iep.conversation_id
        AND tep.is_initiator = 0
        AND iep.is_initiator = 1
    JOIN RequestsBindings rb ON
        iep.conversation_handle = rb.BackendConversation
    WHERE rb.FrontendConversation = @dh;

    IF @cg IS NOT NULL
    BEGIN
        -- retrieve the desired priority from the message body
        DECLARE @priority TINYINT;
        SELECT @priority = cast(@message_body as XML).value (N'(/priority)[1]',
            N'TINYINT');

        EXEC sp_EnqueuePriority @cg, @priority;
    END
END
```

In Listing 10-95, you need the target-side conversation group of the back-end conversation of which you want to set the priority. To get the conversation group ID, you use the information available in the sys.conversation_endpoints system catalog view. As soon as you acquire the correct conversation group ID, you set the new priority of the conversation group through the sp_EnqueuePriority stored procedure. The processing of all the other message types (such as EndDialog and Error) is straightforward and easy. Refer to the source code for this chapter in the Source Code/Download area of the Apress website (http://www.apress.com).

Back-end Service Program

Let's now take a look at the service program for the BackEndService. You implement this service program in the sp_BackendService stored procedure. This stored procedure must perform the following steps:

1. Retrieve a conversation group with a priority.

2. Receive all the messages from the retrieved conversation group.

3. Process the messages.

Because the sp_DequeuePriority stored procedure is quite long, I'll show you the code in several steps, as described previously. Listing 10-96 shows the retrieval of a conversation group with a priority. This code uses the sp_DequeuePriority stored procedure from Listing 10-91.

Listing 10-96. *Retrieving a Conversation Group with Priority*

```
CREATE PROCEDURE sp_BackendService
AS
SET NOCOUNT ON
DECLARE @dh UNIQUEIDENTIFIER;
DECLARE @cg UNIQUEIDENTIFIER
DECLARE @message_type_name SYSNAME;
DECLARE @message_body VARBINARY(MAX);

BEGIN TRANSACTION;

-- dequeue a priority conversation_group
-- or wait for an unprioritized one from the queue
EXEC sp_DequeuePriority @cg OUTPUT;

IF (@cg IS NULL)
BEGIN
   WAITFOR
   (
      GET CONVERSATION GROUP @cg
      FROM [BackEndQueue]
   ), TIMEOUT 1000;
END
```

In Listing 10-96, you first try to retrieve a conversation group with a priority through the sp_DequeuePriority stored procedure. This stored procedure returns the conversation group with the highest priority, if available. If no conversation group with an assigned priority is available (such as @cg IS NULL), you just retrieve the next unlocked conversation group with the GET CONVERSATION GROUP T-SQL statement. Finally, the variable @cg stores the conversation group (with a priority or without a priority) that is processed within the next steps. Next, you retrieve the messages for the specified conversation group (variable @cg) for further processing. See Listing 10-97.

Listing 10-97. *Retrieving Messages for Processing*

```
WHILE @cg IS NOT NULL
BEGIN
   RECEIVE TOP (1)
      @dh = conversation_handle,
      @message_type_name = message_type_name,
      @message_body = message_body
   FROM [BackEndQueue]
   WHERE conversation_group_id = @cg;
```

After you store the current message in the @message_body variable and its message type in the @message_type_name variable, you can process the message in the same way as you've already done in all the other service programs. Listing 10-98 shows the processing of the [http://ssb.csharp.at/ SSB_Book/c10/LongWorkloadRequestMessageType] message type.

Listing 10-98. *Message Processing*

```
ELSE IF @message_type_name =
   N'http://ssb.csharp.at/SSB_Book/c10/LongWorkloadRequestMessageType'
BEGIN
   -- simulate a really lengthy workload. sleep for 2 seconds.
   WAITFOR DELAY '00:00:02';

   -- send back the 'result' of the workload
   -- For our sample the result is simply the request wrapped in a <response> tag
   -- decorated with the current time and @@spid attributes
   DECLARE @result XML;
   SELECT @result =
   (
      SELECT
         @@SPID as [@spid],
         GETDATE() as [@time],
         CAST(@message_body AS XML) AS [*]
         FOR XML PATH ('result'), TYPE
   );

   SEND ON CONVERSATION @dh
   MESSAGE TYPE [http://ssb.csharp.at/SSB_Book/c10/LongWorkflowResponseMessageType]
      (@result);
END;
```

In Listing 10-98, the straightforward message-processing logic simply returns XML data with the current @@SPID and the current time as a response.

Using Priority-Based Message Processing

After you set up the priority-based messaging, it's time to use it. The only thing left to do is to configure the sp_FrontendService and sp_BackendService stored procedures for internal activation on the corresponding queues. Listing 10-99 shows the needed T-SQL code.

Listing 10-99. *Configuring Service Broker Activation*

```
ALTER QUEUE [FrontEndQueue]
WITH ACTIVATION
(
   STATUS = ON,
   MAX_QUEUE_READERS = 10,
   PROCEDURE_NAME = [sp_FrontendService],
   EXECUTE AS OWNER
)
GO


ALTER QUEUE [BackEndQueue]
WITH ACTIVATION
(
   STATUS = ON,
   MAX_QUEUE_READERS = 10,
   PROCEDURE_NAME = [sp_BackendService],
   EXECUTE AS OWNER
)
GO
```

Finally, you need to create a simple initiator service that sends messages to the FrontendService (see Listing 10-100).

Listing 10-100. *Creating the Initiator Service*

```
CREATE QUEUE [SampleClientQueue]
GO

CREATE SERVICE [SampleClientService]
ON QUEUE [SampleClientQueue]
GO
```

By now, you're able to send messages to the FrontendService and also set the priority of the conversation groups. To make this sample more realistic, I only set the conversation priority after ten sent messages. Every tenth message will get processed with a higher priority than the other sent messages. Listing 10-101 shows the message-sending code.

Listing 10-101. *Sending Messages with Priority*

```
DECLARE @dh UNIQUEIDENTIFIER;
DECLARE @i INT;
SELECT @i = 0;
WHILE @i < 100
BEGIN
    BEGIN TRANSACTION;
    BEGIN DIALOG CONVERSATION @dh
        FROM SERVICE [SampleClientService]
        TO SERVICE N'FrontEndService'
        ON CONTRACT [http://ssb.csharp.at/SSB_Book/c10/RequestWithPriorityContract]
        WITH ENCRYPTION = OFF;

    DECLARE @request XML;
    SELECT @request =
    (
        SELECT GETDATE() AS [@time],
            @@SPID AS [@spid],
            @i
            FOR XML PATH ('request'), TYPE
    );


    SEND ON CONVERSATION @dh MESSAGE TYPE
        [http://ssb.csharp.at/SSB_Book/c10/LongWorkloadRequestMessageType]
        (@request);
    -- Every 10 requests ask for a priority bump

    IF (@i % 10) = 0
    BEGIN
        DECLARE @priority XML;

        SELECT @priority = (SELECT @i
        FOR XML PATH ('priority'), TYPE);

        SEND ON CONVERSATION @dh MESSAGE TYPE
            [http://ssb.csharp.at/SSB_Book/c10/SetPriorityMessageType]
            (@priority);
    END

    COMMIT;

    SELECT @i = @i + 1;
END
GO
```

In Listing 10-101, after ten messages, you send a priority message of the message type [http:// ssb.csharp.at/SSB_Book/c10/SetPriorityMessageType], so that the current conversation group gets a higher priority than the other conversation groups. Now when you retrieve the response messages from the FrontendService, you can see from the response that the messages with the higher priority are processed earlier than all the other messages. Listing 10-102 shows the receiving code for the response messages.

Listing 10-102. *Receiving the Response Messages*

```
DECLARE @dh UNIQUEIDENTIFIER;
DECLARE @message_body NVARCHAR(4000);
BEGIN TRANSACTION

WAITFOR
(
   RECEIVE
      @dh = conversation_handle,
      @message_body = cast(message_body as NVARCHAR(4000))
   FROM [SampleClientQueue]
), TIMEOUT 10000;

WHILE @dh IS NOT NULL
BEGIN
   END CONVERSATION @dh;
   PRINT @message_body;
   COMMIT;

   SELECT @dh = NULL;
   BEGIN TRANSACTION;

   WAITFOR
   (
      RECEIVE
         @dh = conversation_handle,
         @message_body = cast(message_body as NVARCHAR(4000))
      FROM [SampleClientQueue]
   ), TIMEOUT 10000;
END
COMMIT;
GO
```

In Listing 10-102, the received response messages are printed out through the PRINT T-SQL statement. You can easily inspect the result inside SQL Server Management Studio when you go to the Messages register in the Results window. Figure 10-23 shows the printed response messages.

```
Results    Messages
<result spid="54" time="2007-01-10T22:55:09.013"><request time="2007-01-10T22:55:06.293" spid="56">90</request></result>
<result spid="54" time="2007-01-10T22:55:11.010"><request time="2007-01-10T22:55:06.160" spid="56">80</request></result>
<result spid="54" time="2007-01-10T22:55:13.013"><request time="2007-01-10T22:55:05.933" spid="56">70</request></result>
<result spid="54" time="2007-01-10T22:55:15.020"><request time="2007-01-10T22:55:05.823" spid="56">60</request></result>
<result spid="54" time="2007-01-10T22:55:17.013"><request time="2007-01-10T22:55:05.700" spid="56">50</request></result>
<result spid="54" time="2007-01-10T22:55:19.010"><request time="2007-01-10T22:55:05.573" spid="56">40</request></result>
<result spid="54" time="2007-01-10T22:55:21.013"><request time="2007-01-10T22:55:05.377" spid="56">30</request></result>
<result spid="54" time="2007-01-10T22:55:23.010"><request time="2007-01-10T22:55:05.250" spid="56">20</request></result>
<result spid="54" time="2007-01-10T22:55:25.017"><request time="2007-01-10T22:55:05.080" spid="56">10</request></result>
<result spid="54" time="2007-01-10T22:55:27.037"><request time="2007-01-10T22:55:04.937" spid="56">1</request></result>
<result spid="54" time="2007-01-10T22:55:29.037"><request time="2007-01-10T22:55:04.983" spid="56">2</request></result>
<result spid="54" time="2007-01-10T22:55:31.027"><request time="2007-01-10T22:55:05" spid="56">3</request></result>
<result spid="54" time="2007-01-10T22:55:33.037"><request time="2007-01-10T22:55:05.017" spid="56">4</request></result>
<result spid="54" time="2007-01-10T22:55:35.030"><request time="2007-01-10T22:55:05.017" spid="56">5</request></result>
<result spid="54" time="2007-01-10T22:55:37.033"><request time="2007-01-10T22:55:05.030" spid="56">6</request></result>
<result spid="54" time="2007-01-10T22:55:39.047"><request time="2007-01-10T22:55:05.030" spid="56">7</request></result>
```

Figure 10-23. *The response messages*

In Figure 10-23, the request messages with the higher priority (90, 80, 70, 60, 50, 40, 30, 20, and 10) are returned first, and then the other messages with the normal priorities follow (1, 2, 3, 4, 5, 6, 7, . . .). As you can see from this sample, the BackendService is able to process conversations with an assigned priority easily. You can use this approach for your priority-based messaging infrastructure and plug in the required service code you need for your implementation.

Summary

In this chapter, I showed you several real-world application scenarios in which the Service Broker functionality provides a lot of advantages. In the first section I demonstrated how you can use Service Broker to call ASP.NET 2.0 web services reliably. Then we had a look at the implementation of asynchronous triggers to execute the trigger-processing logic asynchronously. Next, I talked about the implementation of a batch framework on top of Service Broker. As you've seen, the SQLCLR provides a lot of power inside SQL Server 2008.

Next, I introduced a simple publish-subscribe framework built with Service Broker. This framework is useful if you want to distribute messages to several registered subscribers. I also talked about priority-based message processing and how you can achieve priority-based message processing for conversation groups. SQL Server 2008 provides a concept referred to as conversation priorities.

In the next chapter, I'll concentrate on addressing several SQL Server scale-out scenarios with Service Broker. Stay tuned.

Summary

CHAPTER 11

■■■

High Availability and Scalability

This chapter will introduce the high-availability and scalability options you can choose from when you deploy your Service Broker applications. This chapter will cover the following topics in detail:

- *Database mirroring*: Database mirroring is a new high-availability feature in SQL Server 2008. With database mirroring, you can mirror a SQL Server 2008 database between two server instances. One database acts as the *principal*, and the other database acts as the *mirror*. When you use Service Broker, you can also mirror your Service Broker service between two databases, and Service Broker will ensure that your messages are forwarded to the current principal.

- *Load balancing*: Service Broker provides built-in functionality for load balancing. When you provide more than one route at the initiating service for a specific service name, Service Broker randomly picks a route from the available ones and sends the conversation's messages along this route. Therefore, load balancing is easy with Service Broker.

- *Message forwarding*: Message forwarding allows an instance of SQL Server to accept messages from outside the instance and send those messages to a different instance. In this case, the instance acts as a *Service Broker message forwarder*. With message forwarding, you can encapsulate your physical Service Broker infrastructure and use message forwarding to scale things out.

- *Configuration notice service*: An administrator typically configures Service Broker routing information. To provide dynamic routing information for your Service Broker application, you can use a configuration notice service. A configuration notice service exists on the initiating service side and provides dynamic routing information for a target service.

- *Data-dependent routing*: One strategy to achieve scale-out is to load-balance a Service Broker service. Another strategy is data partitioning. While Service Broker naturally provides a mechanism for load balancing, it is also possible to build highly scalable Service Broker applications that use partitioned data using Service Broker. The key to achieving this lies in data-dependent routing, which is the subject of this section.

The great thing about Service Broker is that you can use all the high-availability and scalability features provided by SQL Server 2008. Compared to other messaging technologies, such as MSMQ, this is a huge benefit because you can use the infrastructure already provided by SQL Server 2008.

All the features I'll discuss in this chapter are configurable at deployment of your Service Broker applications. You don't have to concentrate on them during the development phase of Service Broker projects (as you do with distributed Service Broker applications, discussed in Chapters 7 and 8). Your SQL Server administrator controls how much availability and scalability is needed for your Service Broker application. Let's look at the options.

Database Mirroring

Database mirroring is a first-class software solution for providing database availability in SQL Server 2008. The main difference between database clustering and database mirroring is that you apply database clustering to a whole SQL Server instance, whereas you implement database mirroring per database, and it works only with databases that use the full recovery model.

Database mirroring maintains two copies of a single database that must reside on different instances of SQL Server 2008. One server instance, the *principal server*, serves the database to clients, while the other server acts as a hot standby server, called the *mirror server*. Database mirroring is a simple strategy that offers the following benefits:

- *Data protection*: Database mirroring provides complete or nearly complete data redundancy, depending on whether the supported operating mode is in high-safety mode or high-performance mode.

- *Database availability*: In the event of a disaster, failover quickly brings the standby copy of the database online.

Implementation Details

The principal and mirror servers communicate and cooperate as so-called *partners* within a database mirroring session. The two partners perform complementary roles in the session: the principal role and the mirror role. At any given time, one partner performs the principal role, and the other partner performs the mirror role. Each partner is described as "owning" its current role. The partner that owns the principal role is known as the principal server, and its copy of the database is the current principal database. The partner that owns the mirror role is known as the mirror server, and its copy of the database is the current mirror database.

When you deploy database mirroring in a production system, the principal database is the production database. In an alternative configuration, a third SQL Server instance— the so-called *witness*—is involved in a database-mirroring scenario. The witness is necessary for the database mirroring session to support automatic failover in case of emergency, which is the only reason to have a witness. Figure 11-1 illustrates the architecture of database mirroring.

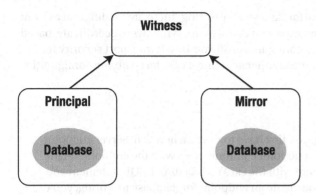

Figure 11-1. *Database mirroring architecture*

Database mirroring involves redoing every insert, delete, and update operation that occurs on the principal database in the mirror database—as quickly as possible. Redoing is accomplished by sending every active transaction log record to the mirror server, and this is done through the reliability features of Service Broker. The mirror server applies the received log records to the mirror database, in sequence. Unlike replication, which works at the logical level, database mirroring works at the level of the physical log record. All database-mirroring sessions support only one principal server and one mirror server.

A database-mirroring session runs either synchronously or asynchronously. In an asynchronous operation, transactions are committed without waiting for the mirror server to write the log to disk, which maximizes the performance between the two mirrored databases. In a synchronous operation, a committed transaction is committed on both mirroring partners, but with the cost of increased transaction latency.

There are two mirroring operation modes. The high-safety mode supports synchronous operation. Under the high-safety mode, when a session begins, the mirror server synchronizes the mirror database with the principal database as quickly as possible. Once the databases are synchronized successfully, a committed transaction is committed on both mirroring partners.

The second operating mode, the high-performance mode, runs asynchronously. The mirror server attempts to keep up with the log records sent by the principal server. The mirror database might lag somewhat behind the principal database. Typically, the gap between the two databases is small. However, the gap can become substantial if the principal server is under a heavy workload or if the system of the mirror server is overloaded.

In high-performance mode, as soon as the principal server sends a log record to the mirror server, the principal server sends a confirmation to the client without waiting for an acknowledgment from the mirror server. This means that transactions commit without waiting for the mirror server to write the log to disk. Such asynchronous operations permit the principal server to run with minimum transaction latency, at the risk of some potential data loss.

Setting Up Database Mirroring

The first thing you need to do when using database mirroring is to configure communication between the principal and the mirror server. Because database mirroring uses Service Broker as the underlying communication technology between both mirrored SQL Server instances, you have to configure transport security between those SQL Server instances.

When you configure transport security for database mirroring, there are no differences from normal distributed Service Broker scenarios. You can also use Windows- or certificate-based transport security. I'll show you how to configure certificate-based transport security for database mirroring, because it's the more complicated one. Let's start with the configuration of the database-mirroring endpoint.

Database-Mirroring Endpoint

When configuring database mirroring, you first have to create a new SQL Server endpoint that supports database mirroring. This endpoint communicates with the endpoint on the mirroring server. You create this endpoint with the CREATE ENDPOINT T-SQL statement you already know from Chapter 7. When you create an endpoint for database mirroring, you can specify a lot of options. Listing 11-1 shows the available options.

Listing 11-1. CREATE ENDPOINT *Options for Database Mirroring*

```
FOR DATABASE MIRRORING
(
    [ AUTHENTICATION = { WINDOWS [ { NTLM | KERBEROS | NEGOTIATE } ]
    | CERTIFICATE certificate_name } ]
    [ [ , ] ENCRYPTION = { DISABLED | SUPPORTED | REQUIRED }
    [ ALGORITHM { RC4 | AES | AES RC4 | RC4 AES } ] ]
    [,] ROLE = { WITNESS | PARTNER | ALL }
)
```

Table 11-1 describes the parameters specific to database mirroring.

Table 11-1. *Parameters Specific for Database Mirroring*

Parameters	Description
ROLE	The database-mirroring role that the endpoint supports
WITNESS	Specifies that the endpoint can perform the witness role
PARTNER	Specifies that the endpoint can perform the partner role
ALL	Specifies that the endpoint can perform both witness and partner roles

Listing 11-2 creates an endpoint for database mirroring. You also have to create a new certificate because you're using certificate-based transport security.

Listing 11-2. *Creating an Endpoint for Database Mirroring*

```
USE master
GO

CREATE CERTIFICATE MirroringCertPrivate
    WITH SUBJECT = 'For database mirroring authentication - MirroringCertPrivate',
    START_DATE = '01/01/2007'
GO
```

```
CREATE ENDPOINT MirroringEndpoint
STATE = STARTED
AS TCP
(
    LISTENER_PORT = 4740
)
FOR DATABASE_MIRRORING
(
    AUTHENTICATION = CERTIFICATE MirroringCertPrivate,
    ROLE = ALL
)
GO

BACKUP CERTIFICATE MirroringCertPrivate
    TO FILE = 'c:\MirroringCertPrincipalPublic.cert'
GO
```

Note in Listing 11-2 that you dump the public key portion of the newly created certificate to the file system, because you must import the public key certificate on the mirror server. You also have to create an endpoint for database mirroring on the mirror server. You can use the same T-SQL as in Listing 11-2.

Security Configuration

Once you create the database-mirroring endpoints on both SQL Server instances and exchange the public key certificates of both endpoints, you can configure security. First, you have to create a new SQL Server login and SQL Server user, and then you map the public key certificate to that user. You have to do this on both the principal and mirror servers. Listing 11-3 shows the relevant T-SQL code.

Listing 11-3. *Security Configuration for Database Mirroring*

```
CREATE LOGIN MirrorLogin WITH PASSWORD = 'password1!'
GO

CREATE USER MirrorUser FOR LOGIN MirrorLogin
GO

CREATE CERTIFICATE MirroringCertPublic
    AUTHORIZATION MirrorUser
    FROM FILE = 'c:\MirroringCertMirrorPublic.cert'
GO

GRANT CONNECT ON ENDPOINT::MirroringEndpoint TO MirrorLogin
GO
```

Listing 11-3 shows how you import the public key certificate from the opposite database mirroring endpoint and grant the CONNECT permission on that endpoint to the previously created MirrorLogin. You have to do this on both SQL Server instances participating in the database-mirroring session.

Database Preparation

Once you configure both SQL Server instances, you must prepare the database to be used for the database-mirroring session. For this sample, I've prepared a database with the OrderService from the previous chapters. I've created all the necessary Service Broker objects (message types, contracts, queues, and routes) as well as the tables needed by the various Service Broker services. Please refer to the T-SQL script included in the source code for the database-mirroring sample in the Source Code/Download area of the Apress website (http://www.apress.com).

Let's take a closer look at how to deploy this database on the principal and the mirror servers, because this is a bit different from other SQL Server scenarios. First, you have to create the whole database on the principal server. You also must make sure that the database uses the *full recovery model*. You can check this through the database properties in SQL Server Management Studio (see Figure 11-2).

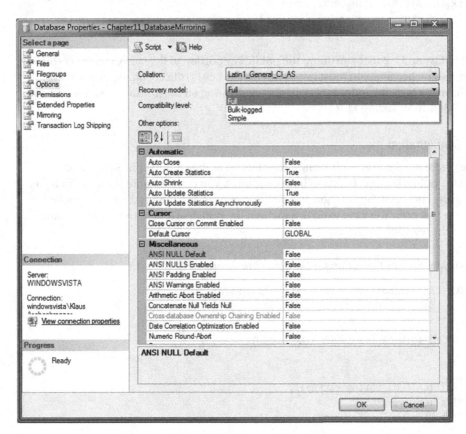

Figure 11-2. *Checking the recovery model of the deployed database*

After you check the recovery model of the database, you have to do a full backup of the database and then a log backup. This is required for database mirroring to work. Listing 11-4 shows the T-SQL to accomplish both tasks.

Listing 11-4. *Database and Log Backup*

```
BACKUP DATABASE [Chapter11_DatabaseMirroring]
    TO DISK = 'd:\Chapter11_DatabaseMirroring.bak'
    WITH NOFORMAT, NOINIT,
    NAME ='Chapter11_DatabaseMirroring-Full Database Backup',
    SKIP, NOREWIND, NOUNLOAD,  STATS = 10
GO

BACKUP LOG Chapter11_DatabaseMirroring
    TO DISK = 'd:\Chapter11_DatabaseMirroringLog.bak'
GO
```

After you back up the database and the log, you have to restore the database and the log on the mirror server. Listing 11-5 shows the necessary T-SQL that you must execute on another SQL Server instance.

Listing 11-5. *Restoring the Database and the Log File on the Mirror Server*

```
RESTORE DATABASE [Chapter11_DatabaseMirroring]
    FROM DISK = 'D:\Chapter11_DatabaseMirroring.bak'
    WITH FILE = 1,
    NOUNLOAD, STATS = 10
GO

RESTORE LOG Chapter11_DatabaseMirroring
    FROM DISK = 'd:\Chapter11_DatabaseMirroringLog.bak'
    WITH FILE = 1,
    NORECOVERY
GO
```

In Listing 11-5, you restore the database on the principal server with the NORECOVERY option. This is a requirement for the database on the mirror server. Now that you've created the database on both the principal and the mirror servers, the only thing left to do is to enable database mirroring on both servers. Execute the T-SQL in Listing 11-6 on the mirror server.

Listing 11-6. *Setting the Partner on the Mirror Server*

```
ALTER DATABASE Chapter11_DatabaseMirroring
SET PARTNER = 'TCP://PrincipalInstance:4740'
GO
```

Then execute the T-SQL in Listing 11-7 on the principal server.

Listing 11-7. *Setting the Partner on the Principal Server*

```
ALTER DATABASE Chapter11_DatabaseMirroring
SET PARTNER = 'TCP://MirrorInstance:4740'
GO
```

■**Caution** Be sure to always set the database-mirroring partner on the mirror server first and then on the principal server. If you do this in the wrong order, database mirroring won't work.

Now database mirroring is completely set up. You can verify that database mirroring is working by using the Database Mirroring Monitor. You start this tool by navigating to the Tasks context menu of the database. See Figure 11-3.

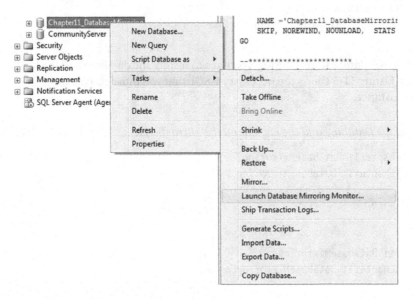

Figure 11-3. *Starting the Database Mirroring Monitor*

You can also now initiate a failover between both partners, so that they change their roles: the principal server becomes the mirror server, and the mirror server becomes the principal server. You can do this with the Failover button in the database properties on the Mirroring page.

Using Service Broker with Database Mirroring

If you've configured the database that implements OrderService for database mirroring, you can use the mirrored service from a Service Broker initiator. The only thing you have to change on the initiator's side is the route to OrderService. When you create the route to OrderService, you also need to specify the mirror server through the MIRRORED ROUTE parameter. See Listing 11-8.

Listing 11-8. *Creating a Route to a Mirrored Service Broker Service*

```
CREATE ROUTE OrderServiceRoute
   WITH SERVICE_NAME = 'OrderService',
   BROKER_INSTANCE = '1F5DB6A9-20FA-4114-BFD9-35FE8B8BE40B',
   ADDRESS = 'TCP://PrincipalInstance:4742',
   MIRROR_ADDRESS = 'TCP://MirrorInstance:4743'
GO
```

Note in Listing 11-8 that you must also specify the broker instance GUID (through the BROKER_INSTANCE argument) of the mirrored database. You can get this GUID through the service_broker_guid column of the sys.databases catalog view. If you've created the route to the mirrored Service Broker service successfully, you can now send a new request message to OrderService. See Listing 11-9.

Listing 11-9. *Sending a Message to a Mirrored Service Broker Service*

```
BEGIN TRANSACTION;
    DECLARE @ch UNIQUEIDENTIFIER
    DECLARE @msg NVARCHAR(MAX);

    BEGIN DIALOG CONVERSATION @ch
        FROM SERVICE [ClientService]
        TO SERVICE 'OrderService'
        ON CONTRACT [http://ssb.csharp.at/SSB_Book/c11/OrderContract]
        WITH ENCRYPTION = OFF;

    SET @msg =
        '<OrderRequest>
            <Customer>
                <CustomerID>4242</CustomerID>
            </Customer>
            <Product>
                <ProductID>123</ProductID>
                <Quantity>5</Quantity>
                <Price>40.99</Price>
            </Product>
            <CreditCard>
                <Holder>Klaus Aschenbrenner</Holder>
                <Number>1234-1234-1234-1234</Number>
                <ValidThrough>2009-10</ValidThrough>
            </CreditCard>
            <Shipping>
                <Name>Klaus Aschenbrenner</Name>
                <Address>Wagramer Strasse 4/803</Address>
                <ZipCode>1220</ZipCode>
                <City>Vienna</City>
                <Country>Austria</Country>
            </Shipping>
        </OrderRequest>';

    SEND ON CONVERSATION @ch MESSAGE TYPE
    [http://ssb.csharp.at/SSB_Book/c11/OrderRequestMessage] (@msg);
COMMIT;
GO
```

As you can see in Listing 11-9, whether or not the Service Broker service is mirrored is completely transparent to the message-sending code. The mirroring is configured through the previously created route. So, you can easily configure mirroring for an existing Service Broker service, because you do everything through configuration and you don't have to change the internal implementation of your Service Broker service.

Load Balancing

Service Broker provides support for load balancing. Load balancing is a technique for spreading tasks among available resources to avoid some resources being idle while others have tasks queued for execution. In the context of SQL Server 2008 and Service Broker, the resource is a Service Broker service that is hosted on different SQL Server instances. In this case, the service is referred to as a *load-balanced Service Broker service*. A load-balanced Service Broker service provides you with the following advantages:

- *High availability*: If one of the SQL Server instances of your Service Broker service is offline (maybe because of maintenance), your Service Broker application will work without any problems, because the other running SQL Server can handle and execute the request.

- *Scale-out*: If you have several thousand concurrent clients communicating with your service, a load-balanced Service Broker service can spread out the Service Broker requests. In this case, each service just has to handle and execute a few hundred requests instead of all several-thousand client requests. This approach helps you scale out your Service Broker application.

Figure 11-4 shows how you can use a load-balanced Service Broker service for a SQL Server 2008 scale-out scenario.

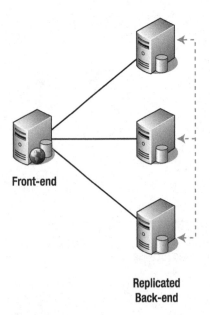

Front-end

**Replicated
Back-end**

Figure 11-4. *A load-balanced Service Broker service*

As you can see in Figure 11-4, the same Service Broker service is deployed on two or more SQL Server instances. Deploying the identical Service Broker service to different SQL Server instances is the one and only requirement when you want to support a load-balancing scenario with Service Broker. Deploying a load-balanced Service Broker application involves the following two steps:

1. *Deploying the service*: You have to deploy the identical Service Broker service to different SQL Server instances. This involves the creation of the used message types, contracts, and associated queue objects.

2. *Configuring the initiator*: Once you deploy your Service Broker service to different SQL Server instances, you must configure the load-balanced scenario. On the initiator's side of the Service Broker conversation, you just have to create a dedicated route for each deployed Service Broker service, and you also have to configure at least transport security between the Service Broker services.

As you can see, it's easy to set up a load-balanced scenario for Service Broker. If you've set up the required routes to the different deployed target services on the initiator's side, Service Broker will randomly pick a route from the sys.routes catalog view and forward the request to the chosen target service. As soon as Service Broker receives an acknowledgment for a message in a conversation, Service Broker uses the Service Broker identifier contained in the acknowledgment message for other messages in the conversation. Once the first acknowledgment message is received, all future messages in the conversation are routed using the Service Broker identifier in the acknowledgment message.

In this way, you can ensure that for each conversation, a target service is randomly picked up from the available services (as configured in the sys.routes catalog view) and the started conversation is completely bound to the originally picked-up SQL Server instance. This makes sense, because as soon as you start to process messages from a conversation on a SQL Server instance, you have an affinity to that instance, because the instance stores the data that was generated through message processing. The instance might also store conversation state information, depending on your service implementation details. Let's have a look at how to set up a load-balanced scenario with Service Broker.

Service Deployment

The first step in setting up a load-balanced scenario with Service Broker is to deploy the load-balanced Service Broker service to two or more different SQL Server instances. You have to deploy the following Service Broker objects:

- Message types

- Contracts

- Queue

- Service

- Service program

As you can see, the deployment of a load-balanced Service Broker service isn't very different from the normal deployment process. The only difference is that the service is deployed to two or more SQL Server instances.

■**Note** From a Service Broker perspective, load balancing would also work between different SQL Server instances hosted on the same machine. As you can probably guess, however, it wouldn't make much sense in this case, because it's not a real load-balancing scenario. Therefore, I refer to a SQL Server instance instead of a different SQL Server machine.

Let's deploy OrderService from Chapter 6 to support a load-balanced scenario. Figure 11-5 shows the load-balanced scenario you want to achieve.

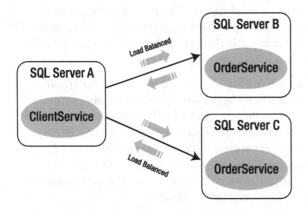

Figure 11-5. OrderService *in a load-balanced scenario*

As you can see in Figure 11-5, the OrderService is deployed to two different SQL Server instances: OrderServiceInstance1 and OrderServiceInstance2. When you deploy OrderService to the two instances, you have to set up at least transport security between ClientService and the two instances of OrderService. When you deploy both instances of OrderService, you'll see that there is no difference between both deployments. You can easily scale out a Service Broker application with load balancing; you just have to deploy an additional instance of the required Service Broker service on another SQL Server instance. You don't have to do anything else on the target side.

Initiator Configuration

As soon as you deploy OrderService, you're ready to deploy ClientService, which communicates with OrderService. The difference here is that you have to configure two routes: one route to OrderInstance1 and the other route to OrderInstance2. Finally, you also have to set up transport security for both deployed OrderServices on the initiator's side. Listing 11-10 shows the T-SQL code to configure OrderService on the initiator's side for load balancing.

Listing 11-10. *Configuration of the* OrderService *for Load Balancing*

```
USE Chapter11_ClientService
GO


CREATE ROUTE OrderServiceRoute1
    WITH SERVICE_NAME = 'OrderService',
    ADDRESS = 'TCP://OrderServiceInstance1:4741'
GO


-- The route to the second load-balanced OrderService
CREATE ROUTE OrderServiceRoute2
    WITH SERVICE_NAME = 'OrderService',
    ADDRESS = 'TCP://OrderServiceInstance2:4742'
GO



USE master
GO


CREATE MASTER KEY ENCRYPTION BY PASSWORD = 'password1!'
GO


CREATE CERTIFICATE ClientServiceCertPrivate
    WITH SUBJECT = 'For Service Broker authentication - ClientServiceCertPrivate',
    START_DATE = '01/01/2007'
GO

CREATE ENDPOINT ClientServiceEndpoint
STATE = STARTED
AS TCP
(
    LISTENER_PORT = 474
)
FOR SERVICE_BROKER
(
    AUTHENTICATION = CERTIFICATE ClientServiceCertPrivate
)
GO


BACKUP CERTIFICATE ClientServiceCertPrivate
    TO FILE = 'c:\ClientServiceCertPublic.cert'
GO


CREATE LOGIN OrderServiceLogin WITH PASSWORD = 'password1!'
GO
```

```
CREATE USER OrderServiceUser FOR LOGIN OrderServiceLogin
GO

CREATE CERTIFICATE OrderServiceCertPublic1
   AUTHORIZATION OrderServiceUser
   FROM FILE = 'c:\OrderServiceCertPublic1.cert'
GO

CREATE CERTIFICATE OrderServiceCertPublic2
   AUTHORIZATION OrderServiceUser
   FROM FILE = 'c:\OrderServiceCertPublic2.cert'
GO

GRANT CONNECT ON ENDPOINT::ClientServiceEndpoint TO OrderServiceLogin
GO
```

As you can see in Listing 11-10, you configure two routes to OrderService:
OrderServiceRoute1 and OrderServiceRoute2. Therefore, Service Broker now has two different options to forward your message to the final destination OrderService. The Service
Broker classifier randomly picks one of the two routes and forwards the message on the
chosen route to the target service.

As soon as you configure the routing information and transport security between the
Service Broker services, you're able to send a request message ([http://ssb.csharp.at/
SSB_Book/c11/ OrderRequestMessage] message type) to OrderService. Refer back to Listing
11-9 for the T-SQL.

As you can see in Listing 11-9, there again is almost no difference in the message-sending
code when you send a message to a load-balanced Service Broker service. The only difference
lies in the configuration of the sys.routes catalog view. As soon as the Service Broker classifier
finds more than one route to a target service, the opened conversations are dispatched randomly between the available Service Broker services. When you connect to each deployed
OrderService, you'll see that the received messages are processed and that the state information for each individual conversation is stored in the ApplicationState table. If you have more
SQL Server instances available, you could add additional OrderService instances to the load-
balancing scenario. Easy, isn't it?

Message Forwarding

Message forwarding is another scale-out technology available inside Service Broker. Service
Broker message forwarding allows an instance of SQL Server to accept messages from outside
the instance and send those messages to a different SQL Server instance. You can use message
forwarding for the following scenarios:

- Abstracting your network topology to other messaging applications

- Simplifying administration by creating a single centralized instance that holds the
  routing information for your domain

- Distributing work among several instances

When you enable message forwarding, the routing table in msdb.sys.routes determines whether a message that arrives from another instance is forwarded. If the address for the matching route is not LOCAL, SQL Server will forward the message to the address specified. Otherwise, the received message will be delivered locally.

Reliable Delivery

An instance that forwards a message doesn't acknowledge the message to the sender. Only the final destination acknowledges the message. If the sender doesn't receive an acknowledgment from the destination after a period of time, the sender will try to resend the message. An instance that performs message forwarding doesn't need to store forwarded messages. Instead, SQL Server holds messages to be forwarded in the memory of the SQL Server instance.

The amount of memory available for message forwarding is specified when message forwarding is configured. This strategy allows efficient, stateless message forwarding. In the event that an instance that performs message forwarding fails, no messages are lost. Each message is always maintained at the sender until the final destination acknowledges the sent message.

Security

Service Broker message forwarding doesn't require a forwarding instance to decrypt the forwarded message. Therefore, only the database that participates in the conversation must have dialog security configured. However, because transport security applies to the connections between SQL Server instances, each SQL Server instance must have transport security correctly configured for the instance that it communicates with.

For example, if instance A and instance B communicate through a forwarding instance, then both instance A and instance B must have transport security configured correctly for the forwarding instance. Because the instances don't exchange messages directly, the instances don't have transport security configured to communicate with each other. Let's take a look at the different scenarios where you can use message forwarding.

Network Topology Abstraction

Service Broker message forwarding allows you to abstract your network topology to other clients who call your Service Broker service. Let's assume a scenario where you want to deploy OrderService from Chapter 6 into your production system, so that other clients can communicate with OrderService. Figure 11-6 shows a possible deployment scenario.

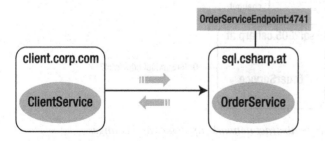

Figure 11-6. *Deploying* OrderService *into production*

As you can see in Figure 11-6, OrderService is deployed on the computer sql.csharp.at. If the administrator of ClientService wants to create a connection to OrderService, he has to create a route for OrderService that specifies tcp://sql.csharp.at:4741 as the target address. This approach will work without any problems. But what if the administrator of the OrderService must move the Service Broker to another machine, such as sql2008.csharp.at? In this case, the administrator of the locally deployed ClientService has to change the route to OrderService. Now imagine that several thousand clients are accessing the OrderService. Figure 11-7 illustrates this problem.

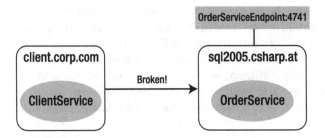

Figure 11-7. *Changing the network address of the* OrderService

As you can see, it's not always practical to reference a target service directly, because in this case, the address is directly associated with the client. Another more suitable approach would be for the administrator of OrderService to deploy a forwarding service. The forwarding service just routes the incoming requests from the clients of the OrderService, which you can deploy everywhere inside the corporate network. If the administrator has to move OrderService from sql.csharp.at to sql2008.csharp.at, he only has to change one route—the route that is configured at the forwarding service. See Figure 11-8.

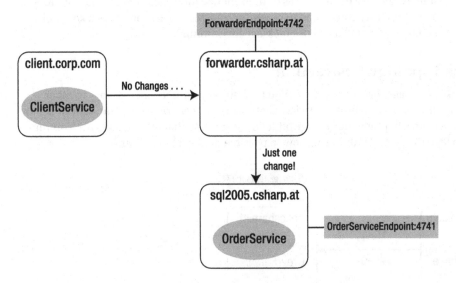

Figure 11-8. *Using a forwarding service to abstract network topologies and changes*

If you deploy this Service Broker scenario in your production system, all your clients will need to know is the address of the Service Broker forwarding service, forwarder.csharp.at. If you change something in your internal network topology, you just have to change the sys.routes catalog view from the forwarding services. None of your clients will have to do anything, because they're just sending messages to the forwarding service, and they have no information about where the real Service Broker services are deployed. As you can see, message forwarding can help you to decouple your clients from your internal network topology and configuration.

Centralized Routing Instance

You can also use this scenario to implement a centralized routing instance. When you implement a centralized routing instance, all clients are sending messages to one Service Broker forwarding service. This forwarding service has all available routes to the different deployed target services. This centralized routing service can also implement things such as load balancing. It would be completely transparent to your clients whether or not one target service is load-balanced. The clients just know the address of the forwarding service, nothing more. It's completely up to the administrator how the target services are deployed in the internal network.

Work Distribution

Another scenario where a Service Broker forwarding service provides a huge benefit is when you want to distribute the workload among several Service Broker instances. Think of a scenario where you have a hundred thousand concurrent users. (I know that this is a very rare scenario, but I want to show you that Service Broker also supports these scenarios.) If a hundred thousand concurrent users are trying to access a single target service, then the SQL Server instance hosting the target service can't possibly accept all client connections because of the maximum available TCP socket connections. The underlying operating system can't handle that number of users.

However, you can spread out all the client connections to several forwarding services and have each forwarding service forward requests to a dedicated deployed target service. Which target service the incoming request is forwarded to is configured through the sys.routes catalog view. Figure 11-9 illustrates this.

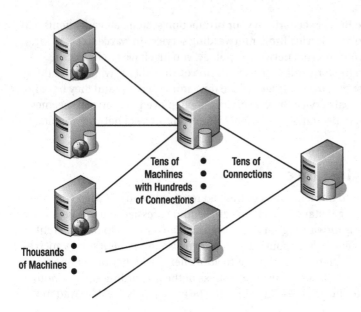

Figure 11-9. *Using forwarding services to implement work distribution*

Using Message Forwarding

I've shown several scenarios where a Service Broker forwarding service would make sense and provide you with greater flexibility. Now I want to show you how to activate and configure message forwarding. It's then completely up to you which scenario you want to support with message forwarding, because the required configuration steps are always the same:

1. Activate message forwarding.

2. Set up transport security.

3. Route configuration.

Let's have a detailed look at each of these three steps.

Activate Message Forwarding

In this message-forwarding example, I want to implement the scenario from Figure 11-6 where ClientService communicates through a forwarding service with OrderService. First, you have to set up the message-forwarding service. In general, you configure message forwarding at a Service Broker endpoint. Because you're hosting the message-forwarding service on a separate instance of SQL Server 2008 (this could even be a SQL Server Express instance), you have to create a new Service Broker endpoint and configure it for message forwarding. Listing 11-11 shows the required T-SQL.

Listing 11-11. *Setting Up Message Forwarding*

```
USE master
GO

CREATE MASTER KEY ENCRYPTION BY PASSWORD = 'password1!'
GO

CREATE CERTIFICATE MessageForwardingServiceCertPrivate
   WITH SUBJECT =
      'For Service Broker authentication - MessageForwardingServiceCertPrivate',
   START_DATE = '01/01/2007'
GO

CREATE ENDPOINT ForwardingServiceEndpoint
STATE = STARTED
AS TCP
(
   LISTENER_PORT = 4740
)
FOR SERVICE_BROKER
(
   AUTHENTICATION = CERTIFICATE MessageForwardingServiceCertPrivate,
   MESSAGE_FORWARDING = ENABLED
)
GO

BACKUP CERTIFICATE MessageForwardingServiceCertPrivate
   TO FILE = 'c:\MessageForwardingServiceCertPublic.cert'
GO
```

As you can see in Listing 11-11, the complete infrastructure needed for message forwarding is configured inside the master database. You don't need to create another database, because you don't have to host a Service Broker service. The only thing needed for message forwarding is a Service Broker endpoint. Message forwarding is activated on the Service Broker endpoint with the MESSAGE_FORWARDING parameter. Table 11-2 describes the parameters available to configure message forwarding for a Service Broker endpoint.

Table 11-2. *Parameters for Message Forwarding*

Parameter	Description
MESSAGE_FORWARDING = { ENABLED | DISABLED }	ENABLED specifies that message forwarding is activated on this Service Broker endpoint.
MESSAGE_FORWARDING_SIZE = forward_size	forward_size specifies the maximum amount of memory (in megabytes) to be used by the endpoint when storing forwarded messages.

Setting Up Transport Security

Because the forwarding endpoint establishes a TCP connection with both the initiator service and the target service, you must also configure at least Service Broker transport security for message forwarding to function. Because of this, the public key portion of the associated certificate of the Service Broker endpoint is dumped to the file system. You must import this public key certificate at both the initiator service and target service, and you must associate it with a SQL Server user, as you saw in Chapters 7 and 8. Listing 11-12 shows how to configure transport security on the initiator's side. You configure the target side in the same way. Please refer to the enclosed T-SQL script in the source code for more information about the target side's configuration.

Listing 11-12. *Security Configuration on the Initiator's Side*

```
USE master
GO

CREATE MASTER KEY ENCRYPTION BY PASSWORD = 'password1!'
GO

CREATE CERTIFICATE ClientServiceCertPrivate
   WITH SUBJECT = 'For Service Broker authentication - ClientServiceCertPrivate',
   START_DATE = '01/01/2007'
GO

BACKUP CERTIFICATE ClientServiceCertPrivate
   TO FILE = 'c:\ClientServiceCertPublic.cert'
GO

CREATE LOGIN MessageForwardingServiceLogin WITH PASSWORD = 'password1!'
GO

CREATE USER MessageForwardingServiceUser FOR LOGIN MessageForwardingServiceLogin
GO

CREATE CERTIFICATE MessageForwardingServiceCertPublic
   AUTHORIZATION MessageForwardingServiceUser
   FROM FILE = 'c:\MessageForwardingServiceCertPublic.cert'
GO

GRANT CONNECT ON ENDPOINT::ClientServiceEndpoint TO MessageForwardingServiceLogin
GO
```

As you can see, you're just creating a new certificate and dumping the public key portion of the certificate to the file system. Also, you're creating a new user and associating the public key certificate of the message-forwarding endpoint to that user. These are just the normal steps needed to set up transport security for Service Broker.

Further, the Service Broker endpoint must also import the public key certificates of the initiator service and the target service, so that transport security will function. Listing 11-13 shows the necessary code to create a trust relationship between the initiator service and the target service at the message forwarder.

Listing 11-13. *Security Configuration at the Message Forwarder*

```
CREATE LOGIN ClientServiceLogin WITH PASSWORD = 'password1!'
GO

CREATE USER ClientServiceUser FOR LOGIN ClientServiceLogin
GO

CREATE CERTIFICATE ClientServiceCertPublic
   AUTHORIZATION ClientServiceUser
   FROM FILE = 'c:\ClientServiceCertPublic.cert'
GO

GRANT CONNECT ON ENDPOINT::ForwardingServiceEndpoint TO ClientServiceLogin
GO

CREATE LOGIN OrderServiceLogin WITH PASSWORD = 'password1!'
GO

CREATE USER OrderServiceUser FOR LOGIN OrderServiceLogin
GO

CREATE CERTIFICATE OrderServiceCertPublic
   AUTHORIZATION OrderServiceUser
   FROM FILE = 'c:\OrderServiceCertPublic.cert'
GO

GRANT CONNECT ON ENDPOINT::ForwardingServiceEndpoint TO OrderServiceLogin
GO
```

As you can see in Listing 11-13, you map each public key certificate to a database user who has a CONNECT permission on the ForwardingServiceEndpoint.

Route Configuration

You're missing the routes on the initiator's side, the target side, and the message-forwarding endpoint. Listing 11-14 shows the code to create the route from the initiator's service to the message forwarder.

Listing 11-14. *The Route from the Initiator's Service to the Message Forwarder*

```
CREATE ROUTE MessageForwardingServiceRoute
   WITH SERVICE_NAME = 'OrderService',
   ADDRESS = 'TCP://MessageForwardingInstance:4740'
GO
```

All messages targeted to OrderService are sent directly through this route to the message forwarder. Additionally, you need a route from OrderService back to the message forwarder. This route is used when OrderService sends a response message or an acknowledgment message back to ClientService. See Listing 11-15.

Listing 11-15. *The Route from the Target Service Back to the Message Forwarder*

```
CREATE ROUTE MessageForwardingServiceRoute
   WITH SERVICE_NAME = 'ClientService',
   ADDRESS = 'TCP://MessageForwardingInstance:4740'
GO
```

All messages dedicated for the ClientService are forwarded through this route to the message-forwarding service at TCP://MessageForwardingInstance:4740. Finally, you have to deploy the necessary routes at the message forwarder. Here you need the following two routes:

- A route from the message forwarder to OrderService

- A route from the message forwarder back to ClientService

Listing 11-16 shows how to create these two routes.

Listing 11-16. *Creating the Routes at the Message Forwarder*

```
CREATE ROUTE OrderServiceRoute
   WITH SERVICE_NAME = 'OrderService',
   ADDRESS = 'TCP://OrderServiceInstance:4742'
GO

CREATE ROUTE ClientServiceRoute
   WITH SERVICE_NAME = 'ClientService',
   ADDRESS = 'TCP://ClientServiceInstance:4741'
GO
```

As soon as you set up all the required routes, you can send a request message from ClientService to OrderService. This message will be sent first to the message forwarder, and after passing this intermediary, it will be forwarded to the final destination, OrderService. Please refer back to Listing 11-9, which shows the necessary T-SQL.

Monitoring Message Forwarding

If you want to monitor the messages that are currently being forwarded to the message forwarder, Service Broker provides this information through the sys.dm_broker_forwarded_messages catalog view. Table 11-3 shows the columns of this view.

Table 11-3. *Columns of the* sys.dm_broker_forwarded_messages *Catalog View*

Column	Data Type	Description
conversation_id	UNIQUEIDENTIFIER	Stores the conversation ID to which the forwarded message belongs.
is_initiator	BIT	Indicates if the message is associated with the initiator of the conversation.
to_service_name	NVARCHAR(512)	The name of the service to which the message is forwarded.
to_broker_instance	NVARCHAR(512)	The instance GUID of the service to which the message is forwarded.
from_service_name	NVARCHAR(512)	The name of the service from which the message is received.
from_broker_instance	NVARCHAR(512)	The instance GUID of the service from which the message is received.
adjacent_broker_address	NVARCHAR(512)	The network address to which the message is forwarded.
message_sequence_number	BIGINT	Stores the sequence number of the message.
message_fragment_number	INT	When the received message is fragmented, this column stores the current fragment number of the message.
hops_remaining	TINYINT	Stores the number of the remaining forwarders until the messages reach their final destination—the target service.
time_to_live	INT	Indicates the amount of time until the message is invalid and discarded. In this case, the message must be resent.
time_consumed	INT	Indicates the amount of time the message is alive. Every time the message is forwarded, this amount of time is increased by the time it has taken to forward the message.
message_id	UNIQUEIDENTIFIER	Stores the ID of the forwarded message.

Configuration Notice Service

In most circumstances, an administrator configures routing information for Service Broker applications through the CREATE ROUTE T-SQL statement, introduced in Chapter 7. However, in some cases, it would be better to retrieve routing information dynamically at runtime. Maybe you want to call another Service Broker service or do a lookup in Active Directory. For these scenarios, Service Broker provides you with the ability to implement a *configuration notice service*.

With a Service Broker configuration notice service, Service Broker provides functionality that allows you to create applications that provide dynamic routing information to the Service Broker application. When Service Broker can't find a route for a conversation, it checks the routing table for a service with the name [SQL/ServiceBroker/BrokerConfiguration]. If an entry exists for that service, Service Broker will create a new conversation with that service and send a message on the opened conversation requesting that a route be created.

When the conversation with the [SQL/ServiceBroker/BrokerConfiguration] service ends, Service Broker again attempts to route the message to the next hop along the route to the final destination. If no route exists at this point, Service Broker will mark all messages for the conversation as DELAYED. After a time-out period, Service Broker will again request a route from the [SQL/ ServiceBroker/BrokerConfiguration] service.

Implementing Dynamic Routing

Most of the work involved in implementing dynamic routing is in determining the address for the requested service name. Which approach you use to determine the address of the requested service is up to you: you can call another Service Broker service, you can call a web service, or you can start an Active Directory lookup through a managed stored procedure. It's completely up to you and depends on your requirements.

The implementation of the configuration notice service is simple. The service program reads the received message from the associated queue. This message follows the [http://schemas.microsoft.com/ SQL/ServiceBroker/BrokerConfigurationNotice/MissingRoute] message type that is part of the [http://schemas.microsoft.com/SQL/ServiceBroker/BrokerConfigurationNotice] contract. The retrieved message contains the service name, and the service program must provide the route to this specified service. If the service program is able to retrieve the requested routing information, the service program will create the route and finally end the conversation. If the service program isn't able to determine the requested route, the service program must end the conversation with an error.

Notice that in each case, the service program that implements the configuration notice service has to end the conversation. Service Broker sends one [http://schemas.microsoft.com/SQL/ ServiceBroker/BrokerConfigurationNotice/MissingRoute] message at a time for a specific service, regardless of the number of conversations to that service. Furthermore, Service Broker uses the largest possible time-out for requests to the configuration notice service. So, if the configuration notice service doesn't end the conversation, Service Broker won't create a new request to the service. If the configuration notice service doesn't create a route, or if the lifetime of the route that the service created expires, a message to the service will remain delayed until the conversation lifetime expires.

Implementing the Configuration Notice Service

Let's implement a configuration notice service. To demonstrate the functionality of a configuration notice service, let's store the routing information for a requested service name in a table called RoutingInformation. Listing 11-17 shows the definition of this table and how to insert some sample data.

Listing 11-17. *Definition of the* RoutingInformation *Table*

```
CREATE TABLE RoutingInformation
(
   ID INT IDENTITY(1, 1) PRIMARY KEY NOT NULL,
   ServiceName NVARCHAR(256) NOT NULL,
   Address NVARCHAR(256) NOT NULL
)
GO

INSERT INTO RoutingInformation (ServiceName, Address)
VALUES
(
   'OrderService',
   'TCP://OrderServiceInstance:4741'
)
GO
```

As you can see in Listing 11-17, the RoutingInformation table stores the service name in the ServiceName column and the routing information for this service in the Address column. You then insert a route for the OrderService. This table is used by the configuration notice service to retrieve the routing information for the OrderService. Next, you have to create the configuration notice service and associate a queue with that service. Listing 11-18 shows the necessary T-SQL.

Listing 11-18. *Creating the Configuration Notice Service*

```
CREATE QUEUE BrokerConfigurationQueue WITH STATUS = ON
GO

CREATE SERVICE [SQL/ServiceBroker/BrokerConfiguration]
ON QUEUE BrokerConfigurationQueue
(
   [http://schemas.microsoft.com/SQL/ServiceBroker/BrokerConfigurationNotice]
)
GO
```

As you can see in Listing 11-18, the [SQL/ServiceBroker/BrokerConfiguration] service supports the [http://schemas.microsoft.com/SQL/ServiceBroker/ BrokerConfigurationNotice] contract. This is a requirement for a configuration notice service. As soon as you create the configuration notice service, you have to implement the required service program for that service. This service program has to do the following steps:

1. Read the received message from the queue.

2. Extract the service name.

3. Retrieve the route for this service.

4. Create the route.

5. End the conversation.

Before learning how to implement the service program, take a look at Listing 11-19, which shows the message that Service Broker sends automatically when a route to a configuration notice service is available.

Listing 11-19. *Message Sent to the Configuration Notice Service*

```
<MissingRoute
   xmlns="http://schemas.microsoft.com/SQL/ServiceBroker/BrokerConfigurationNotice/
   MissingRoute">
   <SERVICE_NAME>
      OrderService
   </SERVICE_NAME>
</MissingRoute>
```

The message shown in Listing 11-19 is created by Service Broker and is forwarded to the configuration notice service. Therefore, it's stored in the BrokerConfigurationQueue for this example. As you can see, the XML <SERVICE_NAME> element contains the service name for which routing information is requested—in this case, for OrderService. With this information, you can now easily implement the ProcessConfigurationNoticeRequestMessages stored procedure that acts as the service program for the configuration notice service. Listing 11-20 shows the whole implementation of this stored procedure.

Listing 11-20. *Implementation of the* ProcessConfigurationNoticeRequestMessages *Stored Procedure*

```
CREATE PROCEDURE ProcessConfigurationNoticeRequestMessages
AS
BEGIN
    DECLARE @ch UNIQUEIDENTIFIER;
    DECLARE @messagetypename NVARCHAR(256);
    DECLARE @messagebody XML;
    DECLARE @responsemessage XML;

    WHILE (1=1)
    BEGIN
      BEGIN TRANSACTION

      WAITFOR (
         RECEIVE TOP(1)
            @ch = conversation_handle,
            @messagetypename = message_type_name,
            @messagebody = CAST(message_body AS XML)
         FROM [BrokerConfigurationQueue]
      ), TIMEOUT 1000

      IF (@@ROWCOUNT = 0)
      BEGIN
         ROLLBACK TRANSACTION
         BREAK
      END
```

```
IF (@messagetypename =
   'http://schemas.microsoft.com/SQL/ServiceBroker/BrokerConfigurationNotice/
    MissingRoute')
BEGIN
   DECLARE @serviceName NVARCHAR(256);
   DECLARE @route NVARCHAR(256);
   DECLARE @sql NVARCHAR(MAX);

   -- Extract the service name from the received message
   WITH XMLNAMESPACES (DEFAULT
      'http://schemas.microsoft.com/SQL/ServiceBroker/
      BrokerConfigurationNotice/MissingRoute')
   SELECT @serviceName = @messagebody.value(
   '/MissingRoute[1]/SERVICE_NAME[1]', 'nvarchar(max)');

   -- Extract the route from the table "RoutingInformation"
   SELECT @route = Address FROM RoutingInformation
   WHERE ServiceName = @serviceName;

   -- Create the dynamic T-SQL statement that inserts the
   -- configured route into the sys.routes catalog view
   SET @sql = 'IF NOT EXISTS (SELECT * FROM sys.routes WHERE name = ' +
      CHAR(39) + 'OrderServiceRoute' + CHAR(39) + ') '
   SET @sql = @sql + 'BEGIN ';


   SET @sql = @sql + 'CREATE ROUTE OrderServiceRoute WITH SERVICE_NAME = ' +
      CHAR(39) + 'OrderService' + CHAR(39) + ', ADDRESS = ' + CHAR(39) +
      @route + CHAR(39);
   SET @sql = @sql + ' END';

   -- Execute the dynamic T-SQL statement
   EXEC sp_executesql @sql;

   -- End the conversation
   END CONVERSATION @ch;
END

IF (@messagetypename =
   'http://schemas.microsoft.com/SQL/ServiceBroker/EndDialog')
BEGIN
   -- End the conversation
   END CONVERSATION @ch;
END
```

```
        IF (@messagetypename =
           'http://schemas.microsoft.com/SQL/ServiceBroker/
           BrokerConfigurationNotice/MissingRemoteServiceBinding')
        BEGIN
           -- End the conversation
           END CONVERSATION @ch;
        END

        COMMIT TRANSACTION
    END
END
GO
```

Let's take a closer look at the ProcessConfigurationNoticeRequestMessages stored procedure. First, you use the RECEIVE T-SQL statement to read the received message from the BrokerConfigurationQueue:

```
WAITFOR (
    RECEIVE TOP(1)
        @ch = conversation_handle,
        @messagetypename = message_type_name,
        @messagebody = CAST(message_body AS XML)
    FROM [BrokerConfigurationQueue]
), TIMEOUT 1000
```

As soon as a new message is retrieved from the BrokerConfigurationQueue, you process the [http://schemas.microsoft.com/SQL/ServiceBroker/BrokerConfigurationNotice/MissingRoute] message type:

```
-- Extract the service name from the received message
WITH XMLNAMESPACES (DEFAULT
    'http://schemas.microsoft.com/SQL/ServiceBroker/
    BrokerConfigurationNotice/MissingRoute')
SELECT @serviceName = @messagebody.value(
'/MissingRoute[1]/SERVICE_NAME[1]', 'nvarchar(max)');
```

As you can see, you extract through the value() XML data type method the requested service name from the received XML message. After this bunch of T-SQL statements, the requested service name is stored in the local @serviceName variable. Next, you use the retrieved service name to retrieve the corresponding service address from the RoutingInformation table:

```
-- Extract the route from the table "RoutingInformation"
SELECT @route = Address FROM RoutingInformation
WHERE ServiceName = @serviceName;
```

Now that you've retrieved the service address, you can create the necessary route to the requested service—in this case, OrderService. You do this by executing a T-SQL statement dynamically:

```
-- Create the dynamic T-SQL statement that inserts the
-- configured route into the sys.routes catalog view
SET @sql = 'IF NOT EXISTS (SELECT * FROM sys.routes WHERE name = ' +
    CHAR(39) + 'OrderServiceRoute' + CHAR(39) + ') '
SET @sql = @sql + 'BEGIN ';

SET @sql = @sql + 'CREATE ROUTE OrderServiceRoute WITH SERVICE_NAME = ' +
    CHAR(39) + 'OrderService' + CHAR(39) + ', ADDRESS = ' + CHAR(39) +
    @route + CHAR(39);
SET @sql = @sql + ' END';

-- Execute the dynamic T-SQL statement
EXEC sp_executesql @sql;
```

You use the CHAR(39) function to put the character ' into the dynamically-built T-SQL statement. You then create the route through the sp_executesql stored procedure. Finally, you end the conversation. This is an explicit requirement of a configuration notice service, because if you don't end the conversation, it won't work.

After the conversation with the configuration notice service ends, the Service Broker classifier tries again to resolve the address of OrderService. The classifier succeeds on the second try, because now you have a configured route to OrderService. Therefore, the sent request message will be delivered successfully to OrderService. The only thing left to do is to create a route in the local database to the configuration notice service and to activate the internal activation mechanism on the BrokerConfigurationQueue. See Listing 11-21 for these two steps.

Listing 11-21. *Configuration of the Configuration Notice Service*

```
CREATE ROUTE ConfigurationNoticeServiceRoute
    WITH SERVICE_NAME = 'SQL/ServiceBroker/BrokerConfiguration',
    ADDRESS = 'LOCAL'
GO

ALTER QUEUE BrokerConfigurationQueue
WITH ACTIVATION
(
    STATUS = ON,
    PROCEDURE_NAME = ProcessConfigurationNoticeRequestMessages,
    MAX_QUEUE_READERS = 1,
    EXECUTE AS SELF
)
GO
```

If you don't activate the internal activation on the BrokerConfigurationQueue, Service Broker will try to retrieve the route to OrderService through the configuration notice service. Figure 11-10 shows the sys.transmission_queue catalog view, where the transmission_status column indicates that a route is located through a configuration notice service.

	conversation_handle	to_service_name	to_broker_instance	from_service_name	transmission_status
1	BFD32B5D-0EB2-DB11-8507-0014C2E615AA	OrderService		ClientService	Locating routes and security information via the Broker Configuration Service.

Figure 11-10. *Locating a route through a configuration notice service*

Further, you can also look at the sys.conversation_endpoints catalog view, where you can see an open conversation with the configuration notice service. See Figure 11-11.

	state	state_desc	far_service	far_broker_instance	principal_id	far_principal_id
1	CO	CONVERSING	SQL/ServiceBroker/BrokerConfiguration	18E00833-2F17-4A05-B074-26983D80EEC3	1	-1
2	CO	CONVERSING	SQL/ServiceBroker/BrokerConfiguration	18E00833-2F17-4A05-B074-26983D80EEC3	1	-1

Figure 11-11. *The open conversation with the configuration notice service*

As you can see, a configuration notice service could be helpful if you must dynamically locate and create routing information in your Service Broker application. It's completely up to you from which source you extract the required routing information. You can call another Service Broker service, a web service, or even a managed stored procedure that does a lookup in the Active Directory.

Data-Dependent Routing

One strategy to achieve scale-out is to load-balance a Service Broker service. Another strategy is data partitioning. While Service Broker naturally provides a mechanism for load balancing, it is also possible to build highly scalable Service Broker applications that use partitioned data using Service Broker. The key to achieving this lies in data-dependent routing.

Before we go into the details of data-dependent routing, let's have a look at how Service Broker supports a load-balancing scenario. When you configure a load-balancing scenario with Service Broker, you have to configure several routes to identical Service Broker services. The main purpose of the routing infrastructure provided by Service Broker is to decouple the target service from its location. When you initiate a new conversation to a target service, the target service is specified using the service name as a string literal and optionally the broker instance (a GUID) of the target broker.

Routes are database objects that help the Service Broker infrastructure determine where to deliver messages. A route maps a service name and optionally the broker instance with the address of a remote SQL Server instance endpoint. Routes enable the database administrator to move Service Broker services from one database to another without requiring the application to be rewritten. A target service may match multiple routes, in which case Service Broker will choose one of them in a round-robin fashion. This functionality can help you to replicate, load-balance, and distribute load across Service Broker services.

But when you have to partition data in your Service Broker application, the Service Broker routing infrastructure will not help you. An example is a customer table partitioned by country across several databases, with a Service Broker service in each database used for updating the customer information. Data-dependent routing can be easily implemented as a Service Broker service that either forwards an incoming conversation or redirects the initiator service to the right destination. In this section, I'll show how you can use both approaches with Service Broker.

DATA PARTITIONING

Data partitioning means that you store your data in several physical locations. In the simplest case, you can store partitioned data in a partitioned table. Partitioned tables were a feature first introduced with SQL Server 2005. But things get more complicated if you have to store partitioned data in different physical locations.

Consider a customer management system that has to store customer data across the whole world. Now imagine that a law enforces you to store customer data only in the origin country. Therefore, you have to create a database in each country in which you store the customer data from this country. With this approach, you have partitioned your data to different physical storage locations. When you now want to update customer data, you could have a dedicated component that forwards or redirects the update request to the correct country database. This is referred to as data-dependent routing or data-dependent forwarding. Both techniques are examined in this chapter.

Data-Dependent Forwarding

In this section, I'll show you how a data-dependent routing service can forward request messages to the correct target service based on information that is stored in the original request message sent from the initiator service. Figure 11-12 illustrates how a data-dependent routing service forwards received messages to the real target service. In this scenario, an initiator service sends out customer update requests.

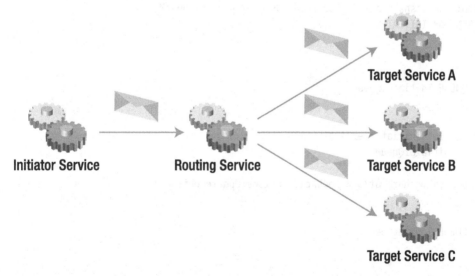

Figure 11-12. *The message flow in a data-dependent forwarding scenario*

In the scenario shown in Figure 11-12, an initiator service sends out customer update requests to the RoutingService. The customer update requests also specify to which data partition the update request will apply. As soon as the RoutingService receives a customer update request, it checks an internal mapping table to determine which target service the request must be forwarded to. If no mapping exists, it will invoke a classifier component with the message body to obtain the name of the real target service. Then the RoutingService begins a new conversation with the retrieved target service name. In this case, it could be the CustomersEuropeService or CustomersUSAService. At the last step, the RoutingService creates a mapping for both the inbound and the outbound conversation and finally forwards the customer update request on the previously created conversation.

If the real target service ends the conversation, the RoutingService receives an EndDialog message. In this case, it checks whether an outbound conversation exists for the current conversation and ends it. In either case, it will also end the inbound conversation. If the RoutingService receives an Error message, it also checks whether an outbound conversation exists for this conversation and ends it with an error. It will also end the inbound conversation. Listing 11-22 shows the definition of the required message type, the required contract, and the needed Service Broker services.

Listing 11-22. *Creating the Service Broker Infrastructure*

```
CREATE MESSAGE TYPE
    [http://ssb.csharp.at/SSB_Book/c10/CustomerUpdateRequestMessage]
    VALIDATION = WELL_FORMED_XML
GO

CREATE CONTRACT [http://ssb.csharp.at/SSB_Book/c10/CustomerUpdateContract]
(
    [http://ssb.csharp.at/SSB_Book/c10/CustomerUpdateRequestMessage]
        SENT BY INITIATOR
)
GO

CREATE QUEUE InitiatorQueue
GO

CREATE SERVICE InitiatorService
ON QUEUE InitiatorQueue
(
    [http://ssb.csharp.at/SSB_Book/c10/CustomerUpdateContract]
)

CREATE QUEUE RoutingQueue
GO

CREATE SERVICE RoutingService
ON QUEUE RoutingQueue
(
    [http://ssb.csharp.at/SSB_Book/c10/CustomerUpdateContract]
)
GO
```

```
CREATE QUEUE CustomersEuropeQueue
GO

CREATE SERVICE CustomersEuropeService
ON QUEUE CustomersEuropeQueue
(
    [http://ssb.csharp.at/SSB_Book/c10/CustomerUpdateContract]
)
GO

CREATE QUEUE CustomersUSAQueue
GO

CREATE SERVICE CustomersUSAService
ON QUEUE CustomersUSAQueue
(
    [http://ssb.csharp.at/SSB_Book/c10/CustomerUpdateContract]
)
GO
```

As you can see in Listing 11-22, this example only uses the CustomerUpdateRequestMessage message type and the CustomerUpdateContract contract. For the CustomersEuropeService and the CustomersUSAService, there are also two tables that store some customer information. See Listing 11-23 for more details on both tables.

Listing 11-23. *The Required Customer Tables*

```
CREATE TABLE CustomersEurope
(
    CustomerID NVARCHAR(256) NOT NULL PRIMARY KEY,
    CustomerName NVARCHAR(256),
    CustomerAddress NVARCHAR(256),
    City NVARCHAR(256)
)
GO

CREATE TABLE CustomersUSA
(
    CustomerID NVARCHAR(256) NOT NULL PRIMARY KEY,
    CustomerName NVARCHAR(256),
    CustomerAddress NVARCHAR(256),
    City NVARCHAR(256)
)
GO
```

```
INSERT INTO CustomersEurope (CustomerID, CustomerName, CustomerAddress, City)
VALUES
(
    'AKS',
    'Klaus Aschenbrenner',
    'Wagramer Straße 4/803',
    'Vienna'
)

INSERT INTO CustomersUSA (CustomerID, CustomerName, CustomerAddress, City)
VALUES
(
    'MSFT',
    'Microsoft Corp.',
    'Two Microsoft Way',
    'Redmond'
)
```

In the next step, you need a table that maps an inbound conversation to an outbound conversation, and vice versa. This table is called ResolvedConversations and its definition is shown in Listing 11-24.

Listing 11-24. *The* ResolvedConversations *Table*

```
CREATE TABLE ResolvedConversations
(
    InboundConversation UNIQUEIDENTIFIER NOT NULL,
    OutboundConversation UNIQUEIDENTIFIER NOT NULL,
    PRIMARY KEY (InboundConversation)
)
GO
```

When there is no mapping present for the current conversation, a classifier component is called that returns the real target service for the incoming request message. All used classifier components are configured through the RoutingServiceConfig table. Listing 11-25 shows the definition of this table.

Listing 11-25. *The* RoutingServiceConfig *Table*

```
CREATE TABLE RoutingServiceConfig
(
    ServiceName SYSNAME NOT NULL,
    Classifier SYSNAME NOT NULL,
    PRIMARY KEY (ServiceName)
)
GO
```

```
INSERT INTO RoutingServiceConfig
VALUES
(
    'RoutingService',
    'MySampleClassifierComponent'
)
GO
```

As you can also see in Listing 11-25, the MySampleClassifierComponent is configured for the RoutingService inside the RoutingServiceConfig table. Listing 11-26 shows the implementation of the classifier component.

Listing 11-26. *The Implementation of the* MySampleClassifierComponent *Stored Procedure*

```
CREATE PROCEDURE MySampleClassifierComponent
(
    @ContractName NVARCHAR(256),
    @MessageTypeName NVARCHAR(256),
    @MessageBody VARBINARY(MAX),
    @ToServiceName NVARCHAR(256) OUTPUT
)
AS
BEGIN
    DECLARE @customerPartition NVARCHAR(256);
    DECLARE @xmlMessage XML;

    -- Retrieve the customer partition from the received request message
    SET @xmlMessage = CONVERT(XML, @MessageBody);
    SET @customerPartition =
      @xmlMessage.value('
      (/CustomerUpdateRequest/CustomerPartition)[1]', 'nvarchar(256)');

    -- Retrieve the service name that processes this customer partition
    SELECT @ToServiceName = ServiceName FROM CustomerPartitions
    WHERE CustomerPartition = @customerPartition
END
GO
```

As you can see in Listing 11-26, the MySampleClassifierComponent uses the CustomerPartition XML element from the customer update request message to retrieve the correct target service from the CustomerPartitions table. Listing 11-27 shows the definition of the CustomerPartitions table.

Listing 11-27. *The* CustomerPartitions *Table*

```
CREATE TABLE CustomerPartitions
(
    CustomerPartition NVARCHAR(50) NOT NULL,
    ServiceName NVARCHAR(50) NOT NULL,
    PRIMARY KEY (CustomerPartition, ServiceName)
)
GO

INSERT INTO CustomerPartitions (CustomerPartition, ServiceName)
VALUES ('European', 'CustomersEuropeService')
GO

INSERT INTO CustomerPartitions (CustomerPartition, ServiceName)
VALUES ('USA', 'CustomersUSAService')
GO
```

As you can see in Listing 11-27, the customer update request message is forwarded to the CustomersEuropeService when the included XML element in the request message contains the string literal European; otherwise, when the XML element contains the string literal USA the customer update request message is forwarded to the CustomersUSAService.

Let's have now a more detailed look at the service program that is hosted at the RoutingService. The service program is implemented in the RouteMessages stored procedure. Listing 11-28 shows the implementation of this stored procedure.

Listing 11-28. *The* RouteMessages *Stored Procedure*

```
CREATE PROCEDURE RouteMessages
AS
BEGIN
    DECLARE @messageTypeName NVARCHAR(256)
    DECLARE @contractName NVARCHAR(256)
    DECLARE @messageBody VARBINARY(MAX)
    DECLARE @inboundConversation UNIQUEIDENTIFIER

    WHILE (1=1)
    BEGIN
        -- Begin a new transaction
        BEGIN TRANSACTION
```

```
    -- Receive a new message from the RoutingQueue
    WAITFOR
    (
        RECEIVE TOP(1)
            @inboundConversation = conversation_handle,
            @contractName = service_contract_name,
            @messageTypeName = message_type_name,
            @messageBody = message_body
        FROM RoutingQueue
    ), TIMEOUT 5000;

    IF (@@ROWCOUNT = 0)
    BEGIN
        -- We got no message from the RoutingQueue
        ROLLBACK TRANSACTION;
        BREAK;
    END

    -- Process the received error message
    IF (@messageTypeName =
        N'http://schemas.microsoft.com/SQL/ServiceBroker/Error')
    BEGIN
        EXEC ProcessErrorMessages @inboundConversation, @messageBody;
    END
    -- Process the received EndDialog message
    ELSE IF (@messageTypeName =
        N'http://schemas.microsoft.com/SQL/ServiceBroker/EndDialog')
    BEGIN
        EXEC ProcessEndDialogMessages @inboundConversation;
    END
    -- Process all other request message
    ELSE
    BEGIN
        EXEC ProcessRequestMessages @inboundConversation, @contractName,
            @messageTypeName, @messageBody;
    END

    -- Commit the transaction
    COMMIT
  END
END;
GO
```

As you can see in Listing 11-28, the real message processing occurs in the stored procedures ProcessErrorMessages, ProcessEndDialogMessages, and ProcessRequestMessages. The most important stored procedure here is ProcessRequestMessages, which processes the customer update request messages from the initiator service. Listing 11-29 shows the implementation of this stored procedure.

Listing 11-29. *The* ProcessRequestMessages *Stored Procedure*

```
CREATE PROCEDURE ProcessRequestMessages
(
    @InboundConversation UNIQUEIDENTIFIER,
    @ContractName NVARCHAR(256),
    @MessageTypeName NVARCHAR(256),
    @MessageBody VARBINARY(MAX))
AS
BEGIN
    DECLARE @outboundConversation UNIQUEIDENTIFIER
    DECLARE @classifier SYSNAME
    DECLARE @toserviceName NVARCHAR(256)

    -- Select the associated outbound conversation
    SELECT @outboundConversation = OutboundConversation
    FROM ResolvedConversations
    WHERE InboundConversation = @InboundConversation;

    -- Check if we already have a associated outbound conversation
    IF (@outboundConversation IS NULL)
    BEGIN;
        -- We have no outbound conversation, therefore we have to call the classifier
        -- component, that returns us the correct target service
        SELECT @classifier = Classifier
        FROM RoutingServiceConfig
        WHERE ServiceName = 'RoutingService';

        -- Execute the classifier component
        EXEC @classifier @contractName, @messageTypeName, @messageBody,
            @toServiceName OUTPUT;

        -- Check if the classifier component returned the name of the
        -- correct target service
        IF (@toServiceName IS NULL)
        BEGIN
            -- We got no target service, therefore we end the conversation
            -- with an error
            END CONVERSATION @InboundConversation
                WITH ERROR = 1
                DESCRIPTION = N'Cannot resolve the message to target service.';
                RETURN;
        END
```

```
    -- Begin a new conversation with the outbound target service
    BEGIN DIALOG @outboundConversation
        FROM SERVICE [RoutingService]
        TO SERVICE @toServiceName
        ON CONTRACT @contractName
        WITH ENCRYPTION = OFF;

    -- Store the association between the inbound and outbound conversation
    INSERT INTO ResolvedConversations
    VALUES
    (
        @InboundConversation,
        @outboundConversation
    )

    -- Store the association between the outbound and inbound conversation
    INSERT INTO ResolvedConversations
    VALUES
    (
        @outboundConversation,
        @InboundConversation
    )
  END;

  -- Send the original message to the target service
  SEND ON CONVERSATION @outboundConversation
      MESSAGE TYPE @messageTypeName (@messageBody);
END
GO
```

As you can see in Listing 11-29, the ProcessRequestMessages stored procedure deals with
the classifier component to retrieve the target service, to which the original request message
should be forwarded:

```
SELECT @classifier = Classifier
FROM RoutingServiceConfig
WHERE ServiceName = 'RoutingService';

-- Execute the classifier component
EXEC @classifier @contractName, @messageTypeName, @messageBody,
    @toServiceName OUTPUT;
```

After the correct target service is retrieved from the classifier component, the
ProcessRequestMessages stored procedure begins a new conversation with that service
and inserts the mapping between the inbound and the outbound conversation into the
ResolvedConversations table:

```
-- Begin a new conversation with the outbound target service
BEGIN DIALOG @outboundConversation
    FROM SERVICE [RoutingService]
    TO SERVICE @toServiceName
    ON CONTRACT @contractName
    WITH ENCRYPTION = OFF;

-- Store the association between the inbound and outbound conversation
INSERT INTO ResolvedConversations
VALUES
(
    @InboundConversation,
    @outboundConversation
)

-- Store the association between the outbound and inbound conversation
INSERT INTO ResolvedConversations
VALUES
(
    @outboundConversation,
    @InboundConversation
)
END;
```

Finally, the original request message is sent to the real target service:

```
SEND ON CONVERSATION @outboundConversation
    MESSAGE TYPE @messageTypeName (@messageBody);
```

The Error and EndDialog message types are processed in the ProcessErrorMessages and the ProcessEndDialogMessages stored procedures. Because both stored procedures are very similar, I just present the ProcessEndDialogMessages stored procedure in Listing 11-30. For the ProcessErrorMessages stored procedure, refer to the source code for this chapter.

Listing 11-30. *The* ProcessEndDialogMessages *Stored Procedure*

```
CREATE PROCEDURE ProcessEndDialogMessages
(
    @InboundConversation UNIQUEIDENTIFIER
)
AS
BEGIN
    DECLARE @outboundConversation UNIQUEIDENTIFIER;

    -- Select the associated outbound conversation
    SELECT @outboundConversation = OutboundConversation
    FROM ResolvedConversations
    WHERE InboundConversation = @InboundConversation;
```

```
-- If we got a outbound conversation, we end it
IF (@outboundConversation IS NOT NULL)
BEGIN
    END CONVERSATION @outboundConversation;
END

-- End the inbound conversation
END CONVERSATION @InboundConversation;

-- Delete the inbound conversation from the association table
DELETE FROM ResolvedConversations
WHERE InboundConversation = @InboundConversation
OR OutboundConversation = @InboundConversation;
END
GO
```

By now you've seen the whole Service Broker functionality of the RoutingService. The only thing that is left is the processing of the forwarded customer update request message at the CustomersEuropeService and the CustomersUSAService. The service programs of both Service Broker services are implemented in the ProcessEuropeanCustomers and ProcessAmericanCustomers stored procedures. Because both stored procedures are very similar, Listing 11-31 only shows the definition of the ProcessEuropeanCustomers stored procedure.

Listing 11-31. *The* ProcessEuropeanCustomers *Stored Procedure*

```
CREATE PROCEDURE ProcessEuropeanCustomers
AS
    WHILE (1=1)
    BEGIN
        DECLARE @conversationHandle UNIQUEIDENTIFIER
        DECLARE @messageTypeName NVARCHAR(256)
        DECLARE @messageBody XML
        DECLARE @customerID NVARCHAR(256)
        DECLARE @customerAddress NVARCHAR(256)

        -- Begin a new transaction
        BEGIN TRANSACTION

        -- Receive a new message from the RoutingQueue
        WAITFOR
        (
            RECEIVE TOP(1)
                @conversationHandle = conversation_handle,
                @messageTypeName = message_type_name,
                @messageBody = message_body
            FROM CustomersEuropeQueue
        ), TIMEOUT 5000;
```

```
        IF (@@ROWCOUNT = 0)
        BEGIN
            -- We got no message from the RoutingQueue
            ROLLBACK TRANSACTION;
            BREAK;
        END

        IF (@messageTypeName =
            N'http://schemas.microsoft.com/SQL/ServiceBroker/EndDialog')
        BEGIN
            END CONVERSATION @conversationhandle
        END
        ELSE IF (@messageTypeName =
            N'http://ssb.csharp.at/SSB_Book/c10/CustomerUpdateRequestMessage')
        BEGIN
            -- Process the CustomerUpdateRequest message
            SET @customerID =
                @messageBody.value('(/CustomerUpdateRequest/CustomerID)[1]',
                'nvarchar(256)');
            SET @customerAddress =
                @messageBody.value('(/CustomerUpdateRequest/CustomerAddress)[1]',
                'nvarchar(256)');

            -- Update the database table
            UPDATE CustomersEurope
                SET CustomerAddress = @customerAddress
            WHERE CustomerID = @CustomerID

            -- End the conversation
            END CONVERSATION @conversationHandle
        END

        COMMIT TRANSACTION
    END
GO
```

As you can see in Listing 11-31, the ProcessEuropeanCustomers stored procedure just retrieves the received message from the CustomersEuropeQueue, extracts the customer ID and the new customer address from the XML message, and finally does a simple UPDATE T-SQL statement on the CustomersEurope table.

Let's now have a look how the initiator service can send a customer update request message to the RoutingService. As I've said in the beginning of this section, the request message must contain the customer partition to which the request should be forwarded. In this example, the customer partition is specified in the XML element node <CustomerPartition> that is part of the customer update request message. Have a look at Listing 11-32.

Listing 11-32. *The Request Message Sent from the Initiator Service to the* RoutingService

```
DECLARE @dialogHandle UNIQUEIDENTIFIER

BEGIN TRANSACTION

-- Begin a new conversation with the RoutingService
BEGIN DIALOG @dialogHandle
   FROM SERVICE InitiatorService
   TO SERVICE 'RoutingService'
   ON CONTRACT [http://ssb.csharp.at/SSB_Book/c10/CustomerUpdateContract]
   WITH ENCRYPTION = OFF;

-- Send a CustomerUpdateRequest with the specified customer partition
--(eg. 'Europe' or 'USA')
SEND ON CONVERSATION @dialogHandle MESSAGE TYPE
   [http://ssb.csharp.at/SSB_Book/c10/CustomerUpdateRequestMessage]
(
N'<CustomerUpdateRequest>
   <CustomerPartition>European</CustomerPartition>
   <CustomerID>AKS</CustomerID>
   <CustomerAddress>Pichlgasse 16/6</CustomerAddress>
</CustomerUpdateRequest>');

-- Commit the transaction
COMMIT TRANSACTION
GO
```

As you can see in Listing 11-32, the sent customer update request message specifies the European customer partition:

```
SEND ON CONVERSATION @dialogHandle MESSAGE TYPE
   [http://ssb.csharp.at/SSB_Book/c10/CustomerUpdateRequestMessage]
(
N'<CustomerUpdateRequest>
   <CustomerPartition>European</CustomerPartition>
   <CustomerID>AKS</CustomerID>
   <CustomerAddress>Pichlgasse 16/6</CustomerAddress>
</CustomerUpdateRequest>');
```

When you now want to forward the request message to the American customer partition, you just have to change the <CustomerPartition> XML element node inside the customer update request message to USA:

```
SEND ON CONVERSATION @dialogHandle MESSAGE TYPE
   [http://ssb.csharp.at/SSB_Book/c10/CustomerUpdateRequestMessage]
(
N'<CustomerUpdateRequest>
   <CustomerPartition>USA</CustomerPartition>
   <CustomerID>MSFT</CustomerID>
   <CustomerAddress>One Microsoft Way</CustomerAddress>
</CustomerUpdateRequest>');
```

When you now look at the CustomersEurope and CustomersUSA tables, you can see that the customer records were changed. See Figure 11-13.

	CustomerID	CustomerName	CustomerAddress	City
1	AKS	Klaus Aschenbrenner	Pichlgasse 16/6	Vienna

	CustomerID	CustomerName	CustomerAddress	City
1	MSFT	Microsoft Corp.	One Microsoft Way	Redmond

Figure 11-13. *The changed customer tables*

Data-Dependent Redirection

In the previous section I showed how you can talk to a data-partitioned Service Broker service through data-dependent forwarding. Instead of data-dependent forwarding, you can use data-dependent redirection. One of the main drawbacks of data-dependent forwarding, as described in the previous section, is that each initiator service has to forward messages through the RoutingService. This results in the following two disadvantages:

- You have to delegate trust to the RoutingService, because the target service can't authenticate the initiator services directly and you lose out on the built-in security model.

- Under heavy load, the RoutingService could become a bottleneck since all conversations are routed through it, and each message in your Service Broker application must pass through this service.

The use of data-dependent redirection instead of data-dependent forwarding solves both of these problems. Figure 11-14 shows how the RoutingService can redirect inbound conversations rather than forwarding the incoming messages.

As you can see in Figure 11-14, the initiator service begins a new conversation and sends a request message to the RoutingService. The RoutingService receives the request message and applies the classifier component to obtain the service name and broker instance of the target service where this conversation must be redirected to. The RoutingService replies in the same conversation with the RedirectMessage containing the service name and the broker instance found through the classifier component, and finally ends the conversation with the initiator service.

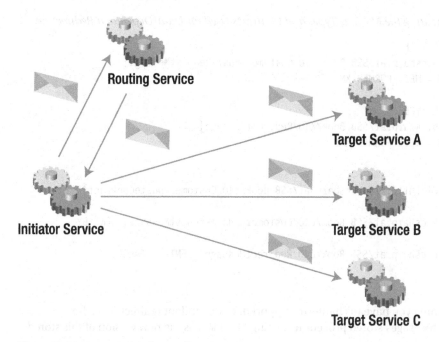

Figure 11-14. *Data-dependent redirection*

When the initiator service receives the RedirectMessage, it will also end the conversation with the RoutingService and begin a new conversation targeting the service name and broker instance as specified by the received RedirectMessage. Finally, the initiator service resends the original request message to the final destination. It is obvious that since the initiator service directly communicates with the target service, the target service can authenticate the initiator service and apply the right level of access control. Also, once the conversation has been bound to the final target service, all subsequent messages will be sent directly to that target service, thus freeing the RoutingService from processing them. This will improve the overall scalability of your Service Broker application.

The only limitations of this approach are that the initiator services must have routes to the target services, and vice versa. Also, the contracts need to be extended to include the new required RedirectMessage message type, and the services should be able to handle them appropriately.

Let's now have a look at how we can change the Service Broker application from the previous section to use data-dependent redirection instead of data-dependent forwarding. In the first step, you have to create the new RedirectMessage message type, and you also have to add this message type to the CustomerUpdateContract. Listing 11-33 shows the needed T-SQL code.

Listing 11-33. *Creating the Message Types and Contracts Used for Data-Dependent Redirection*

```
CREATE MESSAGE TYPE
    [http://ssb.csharp.at/SSB_Book/c10/CustomerUpdateRequestMessage]
    VALIDATION = WELL_FORMED_XML
GO
CREATE MESSAGE TYPE
    [http://ssb.csharp.at/SSB_Book/c10/RedirectMessage]
    VALIDATION = WELL_FORMED_XML
GO

CREATE CONTRACT [http://ssb.csharp.at/SSB_Book/c10/CustomerUpdateContract]
(
    [http://ssb.csharp.at/SSB_Book/c10/CustomerUpdateRequestMessage] SENT BY
INITIATOR,
    [http://ssb.csharp.at/SSB_Book/c10/RedirectMessage] SENT BY TARGET
)
GO
```

The next thing you have to change to support data-dependent redirection is the
ProcessRequestMessages stored procedure. Listing 11-34 shows the new version of this stored
procedure.

Listing 11-34. *The* ProcessRequestMessages *Stored Procedure, Which Now Redirects Incoming
Messages*

```
CREATE PROCEDURE ProcessRequestMessages
(
    @InboundConversation UNIQUEIDENTIFIER,
    @ContractName NVARCHAR(256),
    @MessageTypeName NVARCHAR(256),
    @MessageBody VARBINARY(MAX)
)
AS
BEGIN
    DECLARE @classifier SYSNAME
    DECLARE @toServiceName NVARCHAR(256)
    DECLARE @toBrokerInstance NVARCHAR(256)
    DECLARE @replyMessage NVARCHAR(1000)

    -- Select the correct classifier component
    SELECT @classifier = Classifier
    FROM RoutingServiceConfig
    WHERE ServiceName = 'RoutingService';

    -- Execute the classifier component
    EXEC @classifier @contractName, @messageTypeName, @messageBody,
        @toServiceName OUTPUT, @toBrokerInstance OUTPUT;
```

```
    IF (@toServiceName IS NULL)
    BEGIN
        -- End the conversation if we received no target service name
        END CONVERSATION @inboundConversation
            WITH ERROR = 1
            DESCRIPTION = N'Cannot resolve the message to target service.';
        RETURN;
    END


    -- Construct the redirection message
    SET @replyMessage =
        N'<RedirectTo>' +
            N'<ServiceName>' + @toServiceName + N'</ServiceName>' +
            N'<BrokerInstance>' + @toBrokerInstance + N'</BrokerInstance>' +
        N'</RedirectTo>';

    -- Send the redirection message back to the InitiatorService
    SEND ON CONVERSATION @inboundConversation
        MESSAGE TYPE [http://ssb.csharp.at/SSB_Book/c10/RedirectMessage]
(@replyMessage);

    -- End the conversation between the InitiatorService and the TargetService
    END CONVERSATION @inboundConversation;
END
GO
```

As you can see in Listing 11-34, as soon as the classifier component has returned the correct service name and broker instance, a reply message is constructed and returned to the initiator service. Finally, the conversation with the initiator service is ended:

```
-- Construct the redirection message
SET @replyMessage =
    N'<RedirectTo>' +
        N'<ServiceName>' + @toServiceName + N'</ServiceName>' +
        N'<BrokerInstance>' + @toBrokerInstance + N'</BrokerInstance>' +
    N'</RedirectTo>';

-- Send the redirection message back to the InitiatorService
SEND ON CONVERSATION @inboundConversation
    MESSAGE TYPE [http://ssb.csharp.at/SSB_Book/c10/RedirectMessage] (@replyMessage);

-- End the conversation between the InitiatorService and the TargetService
END CONVERSATION @inboundConversation;
```

At this point, you have to change the implementation of the ProcessInitiatorQueue stored procedure that processes the received messages from the InitiatorQueue. In the new implementation, you also have to handle the RedirectMessage type that is retrieved from the RoutingService. Listing 11-35 shows the new implementation of the ProcessInitiatorQueue stored procedure.

Listing 11-35. *The New Implementation of the* ProcessInitiatorQueue *Stored Procedure*

```
CREATE PROCEDURE ProcessInitiatorQueue
AS
    WHILE (1=1)
    BEGIN
        DECLARE @conversationHandle UNIQUEIDENTIFIER
        DECLARE @messageTypeName NVARCHAR(256)
        DECLARE @messageBody XML

        -- Begin a new transaction
        BEGIN TRANSACTION

        -- Receive a new message from the RoutingQueue
        WAITFOR
        (
            RECEIVE TOP(1)
                @conversationHandle = conversation_handle,
                @messageTypeName = message_type_name,
                @messageBody = message_body
            FROM InitiatorQueue
        ), TIMEOUT 5000;

        IF (@@ROWCOUNT = 0)
        BEGIN
            -- We got no message from the RoutingQueue
            ROLLBACK TRANSACTION;
            BREAK;
        END

        IF (@messageTypeName = 'http://ssb.csharp.at/SSB_Book/c10/RedirectMessage')
        BEGIN
            DECLARE @conversationHandleTargetService UNIQUEIDENTIFIER
            DECLARE @targetService NVARCHAR(256)
            DECLARE @brokerIdentifier NVARCHAR(256)
            DECLARE @originalMessage XML

            -- Retrieve the original sent message through the
            -- RETENTION feature of Service Broker
            SELECT @originalMessage = message_body FROM InitiatorQueue
            WHERE
                conversation_handle = @conversationHandle AND
                message_type_name =
                'http://ssb.csharp.at/SSB_Book/c10/CustomerUpdateRequestMessage'
```

```
        -- Retrieve the redirected TargetService
        SET @targetService =
            @messageBody.value('(/RedirectTo/ServiceName)[1]', 'nvarchar(256)');
        SET @brokerIdentifier =
            @messageBody.value('(/RedirectTo/BrokerInstance)[1]', 'nvarchar(256)');

        -- Begin a new conversation with the redirected TargetService
        BEGIN DIALOG @conversationHandleTargetService
            FROM SERVICE InitiatorService
            TO SERVICE @targetService, @brokerIdentifier
            ON CONTRACT [http://ssb.csharp.at/SSB_Book/c10/CustomerUpdateContract]
            WITH ENCRYPTION = OFF;

        -- Send the original request message to the redirected TargetService
        SEND ON CONVERSATION @conversationHandleTargetService
            MESSAGE TYPE
            [http://ssb.csharp.at/SSB_Book/c10/CustomerUpdateRequestMessage]
            (@originalMessage)

        -- End the conversation with the RoutingService
        END CONVERSATION @conversationhandle
    END
    ELSE IF (@messageTypeName =
        'http://schemas.microsoft.com/SQL/ServiceBroker/EndDialog')
    BEGIN
        END CONVERSATION @conversationHandle
    END

    -- Commit the transaction
    COMMIT TRANSACTION
END
GO
```

The big difference in this version of the ProcessInitiatorQueue stored procedure is that it now also supports the handling of the RedirectMessage. In the first step, the original CustomerUpdateRequestMessage is retrieved from the InitiatorQueue. Please keep in mind that you have to enable the retention support on the InitiatorQueue (as described in Chapter 6) to make this work. The original CustomerUpdateRequestMessage is then redirected to the final target service:

```
-- Retrieve the original sent message through the RETENTION feature of Service
Broker
SELECT @originalMessage = message_body FROM InitiatorQueue
WHERE
    conversation_handle = @conversationHandle AND
    message_type_name =
    'http://ssb.csharp.at/SSB_Book/c10/CustomerUpdateRequestMessage'
```

In the next step, the ProcessInitiatorQueue stored procedure retrieves the target service name and the broker identifier from the RedirectMessage:

```
-- Retrieve the redirected TargetService
SET @targetService =
    @messageBody.value('(/RedirectTo/ServiceName)[1]', 'nvarchar(256)');
SET @brokerIdentifier =
    @messageBody.value('(/RedirectTo/BrokerInstance)[1]', 'nvarchar(256)');
```

As soon as the target service name and the broker identifier are retrieved from the RedirectMessage, the ProcessInitiatorQueue stored procedure opens a new conversation with the final target service and sends the original CustomerUpdateRequestMessage over this opened conversation. Finally, it ends the conversation with the RoutingService:

```
-- Begin a new conversation with the redirected TargetService
BEGIN DIALOG @conversationHandleTargetService
    FROM SERVICE InitiatorService
    TO SERVICE @targetService, @brokerIdentifier
    ON CONTRACT [http://ssb.csharp.at/SSB_Book/c10/CustomerUpdateContract]
    WITH ENCRYPTION = OFF;

-- Send the original request message to the redirected TargetService
SEND ON CONVERSATION @conversationHandleTargetService
    MESSAGE TYPE
    [http://ssb.csharp.at/SSB_Book/c10/CustomerUpdateRequestMessage]
    (@originalMessage)

-- End the conversation with the RoutingService
END CONVERSATION @conversationhandle
```

When you now send a request message to the RoutingService (the same as shown in Listing 11-32), a RedirectMessage is sent back from the RoutingService to the initiator service. As soon as the RedirectMessage is received at the initiator service, it starts a new conversation with the final target service and resends the original CustomerUpdateRequestMessage over this conversation. You can now also change the specified partition in the CustomerUpdateRequestMessage to redirect the submitted request to another Service Broker service, where the request actually gets processed.

Summary

In this chapter, I introduced several high-availability and scale-out scenarios available in SQL Server 2008 and Service Broker. It's a simple configuration option if you want to use database mirroring, a load-balanced Service Broker service, or a message-forwarding service. If you need to retrieve routing information for a Service Broker service dynamically, you can use a configuration notice service. In the last section of this chapter, you saw how you can implement data-dependent routing with Service Broker. Here you have the choice between data-dependent forwarding and data-dependent redirection, as described in the last pages.

As an addition to this chapter, you'll find in the source code a sample that shows how you can scale out the batch job framework from Chapter 10. The sample starts with a distributed scenario, as introduced in Chapters 7 and 8. In the next step, the sample shows how you can integrate a message-forwarding service into the distributed scenario. After the message-forwarding service is integrated into the batch job framework architecture, the target service that does the real batch job processing is configured with an additional target service to support a load-balanced Service Broker service. And finally, the last step shows how you can implement a configuration notice service directly at the message-forwarding service to dynamically retrieve the routing information to the load-balanced target services.

In the next chapter, the final chapter of this book, my coauthor Remus Rusanu shows you how to administer and troubleshoot Service Broker solutions.

CHAPTER 12

■■■

Administration

To administer and configure SQL Service Broker, you can use the tools that come with SQL Server 2008:

- *SQL Server Management Studio (SSMS)*: With SQL Server 2008, a new Broker Statistics Report is introduced. Also, Object Explorer in SSMS shows all of the Service Broker objects in a database as well as the Service Broker endpoint, and allows you to script the creation, deletion, and modification of these objects.

- *SQL Profiler*: With SQL Profiler, you can trace the message flow between various Service Broker services. This tool is handy for debugging Service Broker applications.

- *Performance counters*: SQL Server 2008 provides several performance objects and counters that you can use to monitor the overall performance and throughput of Service Broker applications.

- *SQL Server Management Objects (SMO)*: You can use this managed assembly to programmatically create and retrieve information about Service Broker applications.

- *Service Broker Diagnostics Tool*: ssbdiagnose.exe is a diagnostics tool for Service Broker that is included in the SQL Server Client Tools.

In this chapter we'll cover these administrative tools, show how to use SSMS and SMO to deploy and manage Service Broker objects, and explore how to use the SQL Profiler events to monitor Service Broker activity. We will also show how to use the Service Broker Diagnostics Tool to troubleshoot problems that can be encountered with a Service Broker deployment.

SQL Server Management Studio

SSMS is the one-stop shop for all your SQL Server administrative tasks, and with the enhancements in SQL Server 2008, some of the Service Broker tasks can be accomplished from SSMS directly. You can find SSMS in the Microsoft SQL Server 2008 startup menu after the client tools are installed. For administering Service Broker, there are three main facilities:

- *Object Explorer*: Object Explorer is the tree view that allows you to explore, configure, and create new Service Broker objects in a database.

- *Template Explorer*: Template Explorer contains predefined T-SQL templates for creating, altering, and dropping Service Broker objects.

- *Broker Statistics Report*: The Broker Statistics Report is a built-in report in SSMS that displays which Service Broker objects are deployed, the number of messages in user queues or pending transmission, the number of conversations, and the number of activation-related counters.

Object Explorer

When SQL Server Management Studio is started, by default it shows Object Explorer on the left, connected to the current SQL Server instance. If Object Explorer is not visible from the menu, choose View ➤ Object Explorer or press F8. Under each database node in Object Explorer is a Service Broker node that contains all the Service Broker objects in a database: message types, contracts, queues, services, priority definitions, routes, and remote service bindings.

All the objects shown in the Object Explorer have the option to be scripted into a CREATE, ALTER, or DROP script from the context menu (opened by right-clicking the object), and this applies to Service Broker objects as well. The script can be sent to a new query window in SSMS, to a file, to the clipboard, or to a new SQL Agent job. SQL Server 2008 provides options to create new objects like message types, contracts, services, and so forth. But unlike the similar options for other objects (such as tables), using one of these options does not launch a dialog that helps you define the object to be created. Instead, Object Explorer loads an appropriate template script for the action you selected. You can then replace the template parameters and run the script to create the desired object.

Also under the Server Objects node in Object Explorer is the Service Broker endpoint. Since there can be just one endpoint created for Service Broker in a SQL Server instance, this node only shows the presence of the endpoint. The only option available on the Service Broker endpoint node is to create a script that either creates or drops the endpoint.

Template Explorer

Template Explorer is a tool in SSMS that lets you view, use, and manage the SSMS templates. To open Template Explorer, select View ➤ Template Explorer from the SSMS menu or press Ctrl+Alt+T.

After you install SSMS, a number of templates for Service Broker become available; they cover creating, altering, and dropping all Service Broker objects such as services, queues, and contracts, including endpoints. In addition, some of the templates are more complex, like specific contract templates for one-way contracts and for request-response contracts. The "Service Broker/Application" section in the Template Explorer in SSMS contains templates that provide the skeleton of an internally activated request-response service, including the code for the activated procedure.

MANAGEMENT STUDIO TEMPLATES

Templates are Transact-SQL files that contain parameters that you must replace with actual values before you run the script. The SSMS environment recognizes the special notation of angled brackets used to denote template parameters in a script. Each parameter is in the format `<name, type, value>`, where name is the parameter name, `type` is its type, and `value` is the default value of the parameter. Here's an example of a template in a script:

```
CREATE CONTRACT <contract-name, sysname, test_contract>
(<message-type-name, sysname, to_msg> SENT BY INITIATOR)
```

The Replace Template Parameters dialog box in SSMS lets you easily replace the parameters with actual values. Open this dialog by clicking the Specify Values for Template Parameters button on the SQL Editor toolbar, by choosing Query ➤ Specify Values for Template Parameters from the menu, or by pressing Ctrl+Shift+M. The following graphic shows the Replace Template Parameters dialog box for the previous script.

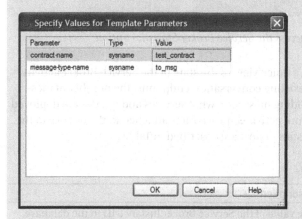

After the parameter values are replaced with meaningful values, SSMS replaces each template parameter with its corresponding value and the template script becomes a valid Transact-SQL script that you can execute. Our example script becomes

```
CREATE CONTRACT test_contract
(to_msg SENT BY INITIATOR)
```

Broker Statistics Report

New in SQL Server 2008 is a predefined statistics report for Service Broker. The report is generated for a database at a time and is accessible from the context menu of the Service Broker node under a database node in Object Explorer. Figure 12-1 shows how to launch the report for Service Broker.

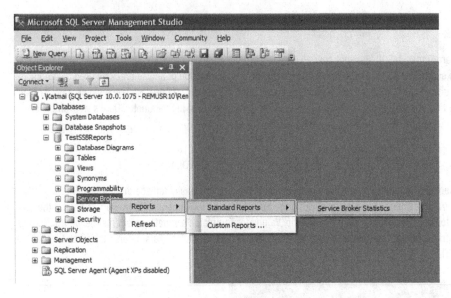

Figure 12-1. *Using the context menu to access the Service Broker Statistics option*

The Broker Statistics Report offers a quick view of the state of the Service Broker activity in a database. It shows the number of existing conversation endpoints, the number of messages in the queues, the number of pending messages, what services and queues are deployed in the database, and some statistics about activated procedures attached to the queues in the database. The fields of the Broker Statistics Report are described in Table 12-1.

Table 12-1. *Broker Statistics Report Fields*

Report Field	Description
Service Broker Instance ID	The value of the Service Broker Instance ID in the database. This value is taken from the sys.databases.service_broker_guid column.
Status	The Enabled or Disabled status of the Service Broker in the database. This value is taken from the sys.databases.is_broker_enabled column.

The charts in the Broker Statistics Report are described in Table 12-2.

Table 12-2. *Broker Statistics Report Charts*

Chart Name	Description
# Messages in Queues	The number of pending messages in the queues in the database. Each queue containing messages is a slice in the pie. Note that the report shows the total number of messages regardless of the actual status of the messages. If the Retention option is turned on, this chart shows the total number of messages, including the retained messages.
# Conversations	The number of conversation endpoints. The pie chart splits the conversations by current status (CONVERSING, ERROR, DISCONNECTED_OUTBOUND, CLOSED, etc.) and thus each status shows as one slice in the pie.

Chart Name	Description
# Messages Pending in Transmission Queue	The number of pending messages in the database sys.transmission_queue. The pie chart is sliced based on the sender service of the message so that each chart slice will show the number of pending messages sent by each service.

The report also contains three tables: Services, Queues, and Tasks Activations. These tables are collapsed and do not appear by default. You need to click the + link to show each table.

The Services table in the Broker Statistics Report is described in Table 12-3.

Table 12-3. *Services Table Columns*

Column	Description
Service Name	The name of the service. You can drill into each service in the report to reveal all conversations to or from that service.
Owner	The owner of the service.
Queue Name	The schema qualified name of the queue to which the service is bound.
# Total Messages (In Service Queue)	The total number of messages in the service queue, regardless of the status of the messages. You can drill into this column by clicking the + link on the column header to reveal the next four additional columns.
# Messages (Ready)	The number of messages in the service queue ready to be received. This column is normally hidden and can be shown by drilling into the # Total Messages column header.
# Messages (Received Retained)	The number of messages in the service queue that were received but are retained because the Retention option is enabled on the queue. This column is normally hidden and can be shown by drilling into the # Total Messages column header.
# Messages (Not Complete)	The number of messages in the service queue that have not yet been completely reassembled. This column is normally hidden and can be shown by drilling into the # Total Messages column header.
# Messages (Sent Retained)	The number of messages in the service queue that have been sent but are retained because the Retention option is enabled on the queue. This column is normally hidden and can be shown by drilling into the # Total Messages column header.
# Messages (Sent Pending)	The number of messages sent from this service that are still pending to be transmitted.

The Services table report contains a child table with all conversations for each service. The child table is shown for each service when you click the + link next to the service name. Table 12-4 shows the columns of this child table.

Table 12-4. *Services Conversation Child Table Columns*

Column	Description
Conversation Group ID	The conversation group ID of the group to which the conversation belongs
Conversation Handle	The conversation handle
State	The conversation state: CONVERSING, ERROR, DISCONNECTED_OUTBOUND, CLOSED, etc.
Type	The conversation role: Initiator or Target
Far Service	The far (remote) service name
Far Broker Instance	The far (remote) service broker instance
# Total Message (In Service Queue)	The number of messages in the service queue belonging to this conversation
# Total Messages (Send Pending)	The number of messages in the sys.transmission_queue belonging to this conversation
Expiration Date	The conversation lifetime expiration date
Transmission Status	The transmission status for this conversation's messages pending to be sent

The Queues table in the Broker Statistics Report is described in Table 12-5.

Table 12-5. *Queues Table Columns*

Column	Description
Name	The schema qualified name of the queue. You can drill into each service to reveal activated tasks running on that queue.
Status	The Enabled/Disabled status of the queue.
Retention	The Enabled/Disabled status of message retention on the queue.
# Total Messages (In Service Queue)	The total number of messages in the queue, regardless of the status of the messages. You can drill into this column by clicking the + link on the column header to show the next four additional columns.
# Messages (Ready)	The number of messages in the queue ready to be received. This column is normally hidden and can be shown by drilling into the # Total Messages column header.
# Messages (Received Retained)	The number of messages in the queue that were received but are retained because the Retention option is enabled on the queue. This column is normally hidden and can be shown by drilling into the # Total Messages column header.
# Messages (Not Complete)	The number of messages in the queue that have not yet been completely reassembled. This column is normally hidden and can be shown by drilling into the # Total Messages column header.
# Messages (Sent Retained)	The number of messages in the queue that have been sent but are retained because the Retention option is enabled on the queue. This column is normally hidden and can be shown by drilling into the # Total Messages column header.

Column	Description
Activation	The Enabled/Disabled state of activation on the queue.
Activation Procedure	The schema qualified name of the activated procedure.
Max. Readers	The maximum number of instances of the activated procedure that the queue starts.
State	The activation queue monitor status. This value and the following values are taken from the sys.dm_broker_queue_monitors view and are empty for queues that do not have configured internal activation or that have an event notification defined on the queue for the QUEUE_ACTIVATION. The value of this column can be one of the following: INACTIVE when the queue is empty and there is no activation occurring. NOTIFIED when the activation procedure was launched or the event notification was notified but no RECEIVE was yet issued on the queue. RECEIVES_OCCURRING when the procedure was launched or the event notification was notified and RECEIVE statements were issued on the queue.
# Tasks waiting	The number of tasks that have issued a WAITFOR(RECEIVE ...) on the queue and are waiting for messages to be available. Note that the number includes any tasks that are waiting for a WAITFOR (RECEIVE ...) on the queue to complete, not only the activated tasks.
Last time the queue was empty	This is the last time when a RECEIVE on the queue has returned an empty result set. Note that this is monitored only if activation or event notification for QUEUE_ACTIVATION is enabled for the queue.
Last time the queue was active	This is the last time an activated procedure for the queue was launched or an event notification for QUEUE_ACTIVATION was sent.

The Queues table contains a child table with all the activated tasks for each queue. This can be accessed by pressing the + link next to each queue name. Table 12-6 shows the activated tasks child table columns.

Table 12-6. *Queue Activated Tasks Child Table Columns*

Column	Description
Procedure Name	The name of the procedure that is being run by the activated task
CPU time (ms)	The time the activated task has been executing, in milliseconds
Memory Usage (KB)	The memory consumed by the activated task, in kilobytes
# Reads	The number of logical reads performed by the task
# Writes	The number of logical writes performed by the task
Execute as	The server principal name under which security credentials the task is running

The Tasks Activations table is described in Table 12-7. This table shows the performance counters for activation events in the database.

Table 12-7. *Tasks Activations Columns*

Column	Description
Performance Counter Name	The name of the performance counter. The activation counters are described in Table 12-10.
Value	The value of the performance counter.

The Broker Statistics Report is a good way to get a quick glimpse at the state of Service Broker–related activity in a database. It shows whether there are active conversations, whether queues have pending messages to be processed, or whether the transmission queue has pending messages to be sent. The report also shows the state of activated procedures in the database. Figure 12-2 shows the Services and Queues portion of a Broker Statistics Report.

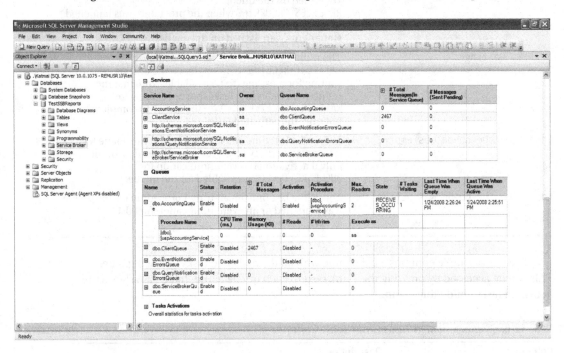

Figure 12-2. *The Broker Statistics Report*

The Broker Statistics Report, like other reports produced by SSMS, can be exported as an Excel workbook or as a PDF file.

Using SQL Profiler

Let's look at the events generated in a distributed scenario and how to read the output of SQL Profiler. I'll use the OrderService example, introduced in Chapter 7. When you want to trace the Service Broker traffic occurring between Service Broker services, you have to select the necessary Service Broker event classes in the first step (refer back to Figure 12-1 and Table 12-1 for the event selection). After you've done the event selection, SQL Profiler starts the tracing process. You can pause and stop the tracing process through the menu items under the Replay menu.

Service Broker SQL Profiler Events

The SQL Profiler events have a fixed schema that was originally suitable for the kind of database events produced by SQL Server. But Service Broker events, like many other events produced by SQL Server, have data fields that don't necessarily map with the schema of the database events. So many columns of the Service Broker events are overloaded and contain information that is not related to the title of the column as shown by SQL Profiler. Table 12-8 shows the columns overloaded by Service Broker events.

Table 12-8. *Service Broker SQL Profiler Events Overloaded Columns*

Event Class	Overloaded Columns
Broker:Conversation	DBUserName contains the near (local) service broker instance ID of the conversation. FileName contains the far (remote) service name of the conversation. GUID contains the conversation ID value. MethodName contains the conversation group ID value. ObjectName contains the conversation handle value. RoleName contains the conversation endpoint role: Initiator or Target. TargetUserName contains the conversation near (local) service name. TargetLoginName contains the conversation's contract name.
Broker:Conversation Group	GUID contains the conversation group ID value.
Broker:Connection	GUID contains the connection transport stream ID value, a Service Broker internal identifier that can be used to correlate the event with the corresponding entry in the sys.dm_broker_connections DMV. ObjectName contains the TCP/IP address of the connection peer host, in the same format as the one used for service routes.
Broker:Message Classify	GUID contains the conversation ID value. LinkedServerName contains the origin of the message: Local or Transport.
Broker:Message Undeliverable	BigIntData1 contains the message sequence number. BigIntData2 contains the message acknowledgment sequence number. DBUserName contains the message sender service broker instance. FileName contains the message sender service name. GUID contains the message conversation ID value. IntegerData contains the message fragment number. IntegerData2 contains the message fragment acknowledgment number. RoleName contains the message sender role: Initiator or Target. TargetUserName contains the message destination service name. TargetLoginName contains the conversation's contract name.
Broker:Remote Message Acknowledgement	BigIntData1 contains the message sequence number. BigIntData2 contains the message acknowledgment sequence number. IntegerData contains the message fragment number. IntegerData2 contains the message fragment acknowledgment number. RoleName contains the message sender role: Initiator or Target.

> **Note** The `Broker:Message Undeliverable` event class is incorrectly documented in MSDN and in Books Online as `Broker:Message Drop`.

The Initiator's Side

Figure 12-3 shows the events displayed by SQL Profiler when `ClientService` sends a request message to `OrderService`.

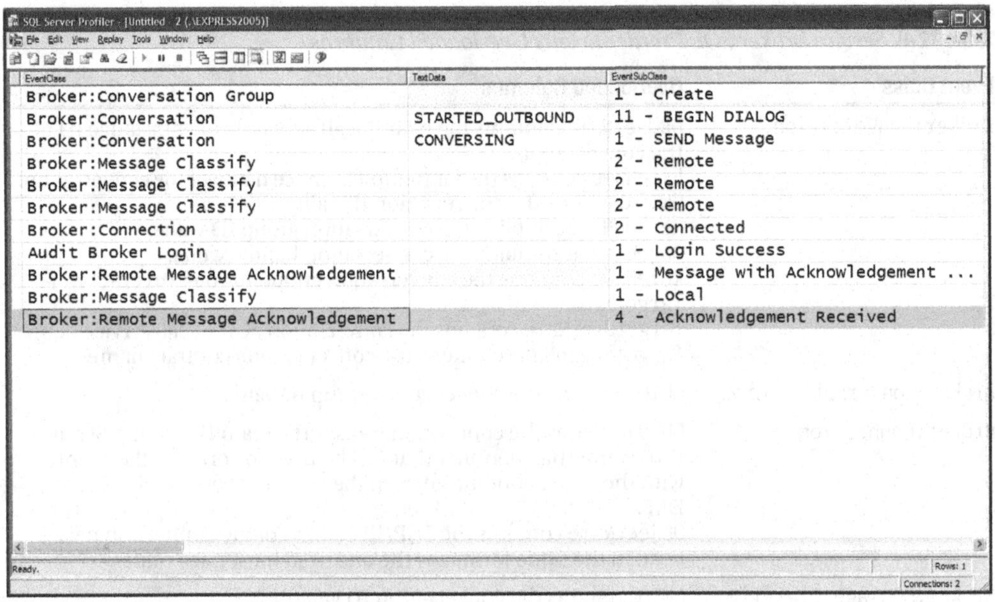

Figure 12-3. *Generated events on the initiator's side*

Listing 12-1 shows the Service Broker code you can use to reproduce the trace events from Figure 12-3.

Listing 12-1. *Sending a Request Message from the* `ClientService` *to the* `OrderService`

```
BEGIN TRANSACTION;
    DECLARE @ch UNIQUEIDENTIFIER
    DECLARE @msg NVARCHAR(MAX);

    BEGIN DIALOG CONVERSATION @ch
        FROM SERVICE [ClientService]
        TO SERVICE 'OrderService'
        ON CONTRACT [http://ssb.csharp.at/SSB_Book/c07/OrderContract]
        WITH ENCRYPTION = OFF;
```

```
SET @msg =
    '<OrderRequest>
     <Customer>
         <CustomerID>4242</CustomerID>
     </Customer>
     <Product>
         <ProductID>123</ProductID>
         <Quantity>5</Quantity>
         <Price>40.99</Price>
     </Product>
     <CreditCard>
         <Holder>Klaus Aschenbrenner</Holder>
         <Number>1234-1234-1234-1234</Number>
         <ValidThrough>2009-10</ValidThrough>
     </CreditCard>
     <Shipping>
         <Name>Klaus Aschenbrenner</Name>
         <Address>Wagramer Strasse 4/803</Address>
         <ZipCode>1220</ZipCode>
         <City>Vienna</City>
         <Country>Austria</Country>
     </Shipping>
    </OrderRequest>';

  SEND ON CONVERSATION @ch
      MESSAGE TYPE [http://ssb.csharp.at/SSB_Book/c07/OrderRequestMessage]
      (@msg);
COMMIT;
GO
```

When the ClientService sends a new message to the OrderService, Service Broker first creates a new conversation group. You can see this in the EventClass column of Figure 12-1. The EventSubClass column provides more information about the event. In this case, a conversation group was created. After the conversation group was created, a new conversation was initialized through the BEGIN DIALOG CONVERSATION T-SQL statement. Then a message was sent through the opened conversation.

After the message-sending transaction is committed, you invoke the Service Broker classifier component to retrieve the routing information for the message. In this case, ClientService communicates with the locally deployed OrderService. The EventSubClass column indicates this with the string Local. This means that the message is routed within the same SQL Server instance.

Next, OrderService sends a request message to CreditCardService, which is indicated through the event class Broker:Conversation and the BEGIN DIALOG event subclass. When the dialog with the CreditCardService is established, the message-sending transaction is committed, and the Service Broker classifier tries to route the committed message. This is indicated through the Broker:Message Classify event class and the Remote event subclass. The event subclass here is Remote, because CreditCardService was deployed on a remote SQL Server instance.

The Broker:Activation event class is generated when a configured stored procedure is activated, so you can easily determine whether a received message is processed. If Service Broker receives an acknowledgment message for a sent message, a Broker:Remote Message Acknowledgement event will be generated. With this event, you can easily determine whether the return route from the target service back to the initiator service works. If you don't get a Broker:Message Acknowledgement event, your return route won't be configured properly, and the initiator service will re-send the message. This also means that the target service will drop the duplicated received message. This is indicated on the target side through the Broker:Message Drop event.

The Target Side

Let's now have a look at the target side, CreditCardService. Figure 12-4 shows the profiler output when a message is received and processed from OrderService.

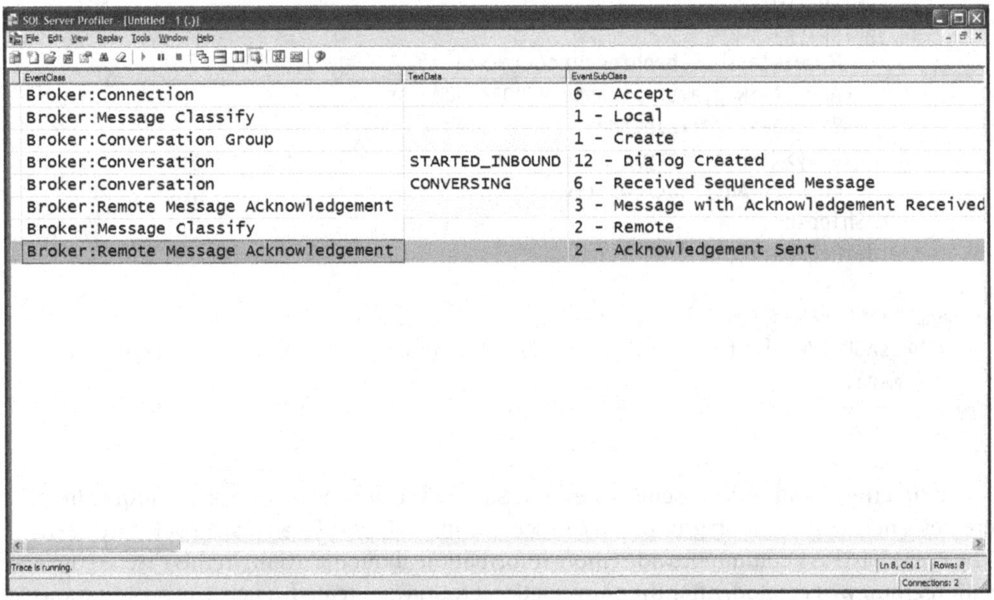

Figure 12-4. *Generated events on the target side*

First, Service Broker tries to log in to the master database. The DatabaseID column indicates in which database the event occurred. In this case, it's the database with the ID 1, which is the master database. The value of the DatabaseID column matches the value of the database_id column in the sys.databases catalog view. This event occurs as soon as another Service Broker application sends a message to this remote Service Broker instance. This is an essential piece of information for troubleshooting a distributed Service Broker application.

After the remote Service Broker application has connected, the classifier tries to route the received message. In this case, the classifier finds and uses the AutoCreatedLocal route that is deployed in the msdb database. When the received message is routed to the correct database (in this case, the database with ID 6), Service Broker creates a conversation group and a dialog on the target side of the conversation.

After the conversation is established, the configured stored procedure for CreditCardService is activated and processes the received message. After the message-sending transaction is committed, the message is handed over to the classifier, which finds a remote route back to OrderService (the Remote event subclass). When all messages are processed by the activated stored procedure, the Broker:Activation event with the event subclass Ended is generated. This means that the running instance of the stored procedure is shut down and taken out of memory.

I hope you see from this short introduction how handy SQL Profiler is for debugging and troubleshooting distributed Service Broker applications. You can easily determine whether messages are routed correctly, whether security is set up correctly, and whether all necessary stored procedures are running and processing incoming messages. If you have to implement or maintain a distributed Service Broker application, and a sent message isn't received on the target side, SQL Profiler should be your first tool for diagnosing issues.

System Monitor

You can use System Monitor to monitor and measure the performance of Service Broker applications. Service Broker provides performance objects and counters available to System Monitor. You can also use the sys.dm_os_performance_counters Dynamic Management View to view the performance counter values of a SQL Server instance. A performance object is used to group a set of performance counters to a logical unit. Table 12-9 describes the available performance objects.

Table 12-9. *Service Broker Performance Objects Available to System Monitor*

Performance Object	Description
SQLServer:Broker Activation	This performance object provides information on stored procedure activation.
SQLServer:Broker Statistics	This performance object provides general Service Broker information.
SQLServer:Broker TO Statistics	This performance object provides information about the Service Broker Transmission Objects.
SQLServer:Broker/DBM Transport	This performance object provides networking information for Service Broker and database mirroring.

The SQLServer:Broker Activation performance object provides a lot of information, as performance counters, for monitoring an activated stored procedure. Table 12-10 lists the performance counters available for SQLServer:Broker Activation.

Table 12-10. *Performance Counters for* SQLServer:Broker Activation

Performance Counter	Description
Stored Procedures Invoked/sec	This performance counter provides the number of all activated stored procedures inside the current SQL Server instance.
Task Limit Reached	This performance counter provides how many tasks (stored procedures) would have started but did not because the maximum number of stored procedures were already running.
Task Limit Reached/sec	This performance counter provides the number of times per second of how many tasks (stored procedures) would have been started but did not because the maximum number of stored procedures were already running.
Tasks Aborted/sec	This performance counter reports the number of activated stored procedures that ended with an error.
Tasks Running	This performance counter reports the current number of activated stored procedures.
Tasks Started/sec	This performance counter reports the average number of stored procedures activated per second.

The SQLServer:Broker Statistics object contains performance counters that report general Service Broker information. It gives you statistical information about how long messages are queued/enqueued, how many messages are forwarded to a Service Broker forwarding service, or how many messages are rejected and dropped. Table 12-11 lists the performance counters available in SQLServer:Broker Statistics.

Table 12-11. *Performance Counters for* SQLServer:Broker Statistics

Performance Counter	Description
Broker Transaction Rollbacks	This performance counter provides the number of transactions rolled back on the context of Service Broker.
Dialog timer event count	This performance counter contains the number of dialog timers currently active in the dialog protocol layer.
Enqueued Local Messages Total	This performance counter provides the number of messages placed in the queues on the monitored SQL Server instance, counting only the messages that didn't arrive through the network.
Enqueued Local Messages/sec	This performance counter provides the number of messages per second placed in the queues on the monitored SQL Server instance, counting only the messages that didn't arrive through the network.
Enqueued Messages Total	This performance counter provides the total number of messages placed in the queues on the monitored SQL Server instance.
Enqueued Messages/sec	This performance counter provides the total number of messages per second placed in the queues on the monitored SQL Server instance.
Enqueued P1…P10 Messages/sec	This performance counter provides the total number of Priority 1 messages per second placed in the queues on the monitored SQL Server instance. There is a separate counter for each priority: P1, P2, … P10.

Performance Counter	Description
Enqueued Transport Msg Frag Tot	This performance counter provides the total number of message fragments placed in the queues on the monitored SQL Server instance.
Enqueued Transport Msg Frags/sec	This performance counter provides the total number of message fragments per second placed in the queues on the monitored SQL Server instance.
Enqueued Transport Msgs Total	This performance counter provides the total number of messages placed in the queues on the monitored SQL Server instance, counting only the messages that arrived through the network.
Enqueued Transport Msgs/sec	This performance counter provides the total number of messages placed in the queues per second on the monitored SQL Server instance, counting only the messages that arrived through the network.
Forwarded Messages Total	This performance counter provides the total number of messages forwarded on this computer.
Forwarded Messages/sec	This performance counter provides the total number of messages forwarded per second on the monitored computer.
Forwarded Msg Byte Total	This performance counter provides the total size (in bytes) of messages forwarded on the monitored computer.
Forwarded Msg Bytes/sec	This performance counter provides the total size (in bytes) of messages forwarded per second on the monitored computer.
Forwarded Msg Discarded Total	This performance counter provides the total number of messages received on the forwarding service but not forwarded successfully.
Forwarded Msg Discarded/sec	This performance counter provides the total number of messages received per second on the forwarding service but not forwarded successfully.
Forwarded Pending Msg Bytes	This performance counter provides the total size (in bytes) of messages pending for forwarding on the monitored SQL Server instance.
Forwarded Pending Msg Count	This performance counter provides the total number of messages pending for forwarding on the monitored SQL Server instance.
SQL RECEIVE Total	This performance counter provides the total number of RECEIVE T-SQL statements processed on the monitored SQL Server instance.
SQL RECEIVEs/sec	This performance counter provides the total number of RECEIVE T-SQL statements processed per second on the monitored SQL Server instance.
SQL SEND Total	This performance counter provides the total number of SEND T-SQL statements processed on the monitored SQL Server instance.
SQL SENDs/sec	This performance counter provides the total number of SEND T-SQL statements processed per second on the monitored SQL Server instance.

The `SQLServer:Broker TO Statistics` performance object gives you more information about the Transmission Objects. Transmission Objects are responsible for the conversation message send, retry, and acknowledgments logic. For every active conversation there is a Transmission Object. Because the number of active conversations can grow very large in the whole SQL Server instance, the Transmission Objects will be saved into `tempdb`. The performance counters measure the rate at which these Transmission Objects are being created, saved, and loaded. Table 12-12 lists the individual performance counters in the `SQLServer:Broker TO Statistics` performance object.

Table 12-12. *Performance Counters for* `Broker TO Statistics`

Performance Counter	Description
`Avg. Length of Batched Writes`	This performance counter provides the average number of Transmission Object saved in a batch.
`Avg. Time Between Batches (ms)`	This performance counter provides the average time between two batches of Transmission Object saves.
`Avg. Time to Write Batch (ms)`	This performance counter provides the average time to save a Transmission Object batch.
`Transmission Object Gets/sec`	This performance counter provides the number of Transmission Objects requested per second.
`Transmission Object Writes/sec`	This performance counter provides the number of Transmission Objects saved per second.
`Transmission Object Dirtied/sec`	This performance counter provides the number of Transmission Objects marked dirty per second.

The `SQLServer:Broker/DBM Transport` performance object gives you more information about the physical transportation of Service Broker messages between distributed deployed Service Broker services. Here you get information about message fragmentation, how many bytes are transferred between different Service Broker services, how many bytes are pending for transfer across the wire, how many bytes are received, and how many bytes are sent. Table 12-13 lists the various performance counters available in the `SQLServer:Broker/DBM Transport` performance object.

Table 12-13. *Performance Counters for* `SQLServer:Broker/DBM Transport`

Performance Counter	Description
`Current Bytes for Recv I/O`	This performance counter provides the number of bytes to be read by the currently running transport receive operation.
`Current Bytes for Send I/O`	This performance counter provides the number of bytes in message fragments that are currently in the process of being sent over the network.
`Current Msg Frags for Send I/O`	This performance counter provides the total number of message fragments that are in the process of being sent over the network.
`Message Fragment Send Size Avg`	This performance counter provides the average size of the message fragments sent over the network.
`Message Fragment Send Total`	This performance counter provides the total number of message fragments sent over the network.

Performance Counter	Description
Message Fragment Sends/sec	This performance counter provides the total number of message fragments sent over the network per second.
Message Fragment P1...P10 Sends/sec	This performance counter provides the total number of Priority 1 message fragments sent over the network per second. There is a separate counter for each priority: P1, P2, ... P10.
Msg Fragment Receive Total	This performance counter provides the total number of message fragments received over the network.
Msg Fragment Receives/sec	This performance counter provides the total number of message fragments received over the network per second.
Msg Fragment Recv Size Avg	This performance counter provides the average size of message fragments received over the network.
Open Connection Count	This performance counter provides the number of network connections that Service Broker currently has open.
Pending Bytes for Recv I/O	This performance counter provides the number of bytes contained in message fragments that have been received from the network but have not yet been placed on a queue or have been discarded.
Pending Bytes for Send I/O	This performance counter provides the number of bytes in message fragments that are ready to be sent over the network.
Pending Msg Frags for Recv I/O	This performance counter provides the number of message fragments that have been received from the network but have not yet been placed on a queue or have been discarded.
Pending Msg Frags for Send I/O	This performance counter provides the total number of message fragments that are ready to be sent over the network.
Receive I/O Bytes Total	This performance counter provides the total number of bytes received over the network by Service Broker endpoints and database-mirroring endpoints.
Receive I/O Bytes/sec	This performance counter provides the total number of bytes received per second over the network by Service Broker endpoints and database-mirroring endpoints.
Receive I/O Len Avg	This performance counter provides the average number of bytes for a transport receive operation.
Receive I/Os/second	This performance counter provides the number of transport receive I/O operations per second that the Service Broker transport layer has completed.
Send I/O Bytes Total	This performance counter provides the total number of bytes sent over the network by Service Broker endpoints and database-mirroring endpoints.
Send I/O Bytes/sec	This performance counter provides the total number of bytes sent over the network per second by Service Broker endpoints and database-mirroring endpoints.
Send I/O Len Avg	This performance counter provides the average size in bytes of each transport send operation.
Send I/Os/sec	This performance counter provides the number of transport send I/O operations per second that have been completed.

SQL Server Management Objects

SQL Server Management Objects (SMO) is a managed .NET assembly for programmatic access to SQL Server 2008. Microsoft SQL Server Management Studio is implemented with SMO to provide all the functionality it has. You can use SMO to build customized SQL Server applications that retrieve information from SQL Server and to create, alter, and drop objects inside SQL Server 2008. You can easily add new message types, new contracts, queues, or even services to your Service Broker application programmatically. Figure 12-5 shows you the relevant SMO classes for the management of Service Broker functionality.

Figure 12-5. *SMO classes for Service Broker*

Table 12-14 describes the most important SMO classes for use with Service Broker.

Table 12-14. *SMO Classes for Service Broker*

SMO Class	Description
MessageType	This class represents a message type that defines the content of a Service Broker message.
ServiceQueue	This class represents a queue object that stores received Service Broker messages.
RemoteServiceBinding	This class represents a remote service binding used for security purposes when communicating with a remote Service Broker service.
ServiceRoute	This class represents a route that contains routing information for a Service Broker service.
ServiceContract	This class represents a contract that specifies the direction and the used message types in a Service Broker conversation.
BrokerService	This class represents a Service Broker service, which can initiate and accept conversations.

All the available SMO classes are implemented in the `Microsoft.SqlServer.Smo` assembly that is placed inside the Global Assembly Cache (GAC) during the installation of SQL Server 2008. Therefore, you must reference this assembly when you want to use the functionality of SMO in your own project. Now let's talk about how to use SMO.

Creating Service Broker Objects

In this section, I'll show you how you can programmatically create a new Service Broker service from scratch with SMO. Create a Console Application project in Visual Studio. From the References node in Solution Explorer, add the required reference to the SMO assemblies: `Microsoft.SqlServer.Smo`, `Microsoft.SqlServer.ConnectionInfo`, `Microsoft.SqlServer.Management.Sdk.Sfc`, and `Microsoft.SqlServer.ServiceBrokerEnum`. In beginning of the `Program.cs` file, declare the `using` directive of the SMO namespace:

```
using Microsoft.SqlServer.Management.Smo;
```

The first SMO object you have to use is a `Server` object to create a connection to a SQL Server instance (see Listing 12-2).

Listing 12-2. *Connecting to SQL Server Through SMO*

```
Server svr = new Server("localhost");

Console.WriteLine("Language: " + svr.Information.Language);
Console.WriteLine("OS version: " + svr.Information.OSVersion);
Console.WriteLine("Edition: " + svr.Information.Edition);
Console.WriteLine("Root directory: " + svr.Information.RootDirectory);
```

As you can see in Listing 12-2, you can retrieve additional information about the SQL Server instance through the `Information` property. Figure 12-6 shows the output of this code fragment.

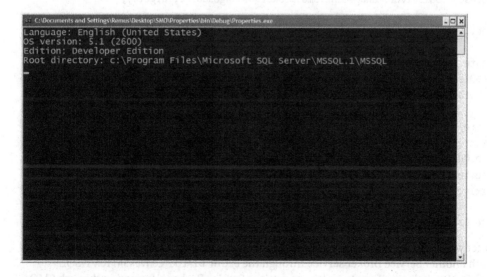

Figure 12-6. *Retrieving connection information*

After you establish a connection to the SQL Server instance, you're able to create a new SQL Server database that hosts your Service Broker service. You can do this through the Database class (see Listing 12-3).

Listing 12-3. *Creating a New Database*

```
Database db = new Database(svr, "Chapter12_SMOSample");
db.Create();
```

Note that you have to call the Create method after you've created the Database object. When you call the Create method, SMO executes the required CREATE DATABASE T-SQL statement against the SQL Server connection. As soon as the new database is prepared, you can create all necessary Service Broker objects. See Listing 12-4 for more information.

Listing 12-4. *Creating the Needed Service Broker Objects*

```
// Create the required message types
MessageType requestMessage = new MessageType(db.ServiceBroker, "RequestMessage");
MessageType responseMessage = new MessageType(db.ServiceBroker, "ResponseMessage");

requestMessage.Create();
responseMessage.Create();

// Create the service contract
ServiceContract contract = new ServiceContract(db.ServiceBroker, "SampleContract");


contract.MessageTypeMappings.Add(new MessageTypeMapping(contract, "RequestMessage",
    Microsoft.SqlServer.Management.Smo.Broker.MessageSource.Initiator));
contract.MessageTypeMappings.Add(new MessageTypeMapping(contract, "ResponseMessage",
    Microsoft.SqlServer.Management.Smo.Broker.MessageSource.Target));

contract.Create();

// Create the queue
ServiceQueue queue = new ServiceQueue(db.ServiceBroker, "SampleQueue");
queue.Create();

// Create the Service Broker service
BrokerService service = new BrokerService(db.ServiceBroker, "SampleService");
service.QueueName = "SampleQueue";
service.ServiceContractMappings.Add(new ServiceContractMapping(
    service, "SampleContract"));

service.Create();
```

After you create all the necessary Service Broker objects, you're able to start a conversation with another Service Broker service through the BEGIN DIALOG CONVERSATION T-SQL statement. Now let's concentrate on how to retrieve Service Broker information through SMO.

Retrieving Information

In this section, I'll show you how to retrieve information about the deployed Service Broker application from the previous section. When you establish a connection to a SQL Server instance, you can use the collection properties MessageTypes, ServiceContracts, Queues, and Services to retrieve information about the deployed Service Broker objects (see Listing 12-5).

Listing 12-5. *Retrieving Service Broker Information*

```
foreach (MessageType messageType in db.ServiceBroker.MessageTypes)
{
    Console.WriteLine(messageType.Name);
}


foreach (ServiceContract serviceContract in db.ServiceBroker.ServiceContracts)
{
    Console.WriteLine(serviceContract.Name);
}


foreach (ServiceQueue serviceQueue in db.ServiceBroker.Queues)
{
    Console.WriteLine(serviceQueue.Name);
    Console.WriteLine("\tActivation enabled:" + serviceQueue.IsActivationEnabled);
    Console.WriteLine("\tMax Queue Readers: " + serviceQueue.MaxReaders);
    Console.WriteLine("\tProcedure name: " + serviceQueue.ProcedureName);
}


foreach (BrokerService brokerService in db.ServiceBroker.Services)
{
    Console.WriteLine(brokerService.Name);
    Console.WriteLine("\tQueue name: " + brokerService.QueueName);
}
```

Figure 12-7 shows part of the output of this simple SMO application.

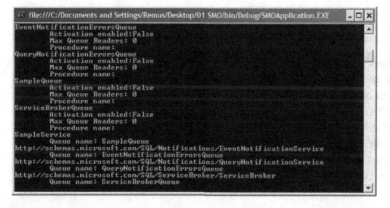

Figure 12-7. *Retrieving Service Broker information*

Troubleshooting

Service Broker applications are not difficult to troubleshoot at all if you follow the right steps. But unlike other database applications, not all problems will manifest as execution errors when you run your T-SQL batches on the server. Because of the asynchronous and distributed nature of Service Broker, most problems are reported by Service Broker through the profiler events. You just need to learn where to look for those error messages and you will be an expert Service Broker troubleshooter in no time!

There are three types of problems that usually need troubleshooting:

- *Conversation problems* appear when Service Broker conversations can't deliver messages to the intended service and are related to service configuration issues like routes and certificates.

- *Connection problems* appear when Service Broker cannot connect two SQL Server instances in order to exchange messages between them.

- *Activation problems* appear when a stored procedure associated with a Service Broker queue is not behaving as expected or has coding errors, but because of the background nature of activation these problems are not evident.

Conversation Problems

The first place to look for an error is your application message queue. A lot of times the conversation experienced an error and the reason is given in an error message enqueued in your application's service queue. But too often the application will simply consume this error message silently. Later when investigating the problem, you find yourself facing a real mystery: the messages sent have vanished without a trace; there is nothing to be investigated. Whenever you're faced with such a scenario, the first place to look is the application code itself—more than likely, it is consuming error messages from the queue silently and not reporting anything.

After you convince yourself that the application itself is not silently consuming error messages, the next place to look is the sys.transmission_queue view on the database from where the messages are sent. This view shows all messages that are pending delivery to their destination services by Service Broker. Every message sent will be kept in sys.transmission_queue until it is acknowledged by the destination service.

TRANSMISSION STATUS

Service Broker keeps a status for every conversation that has a message pending. The status is normally empty, but if the message cannot be transmitted, Service Broker will fill this status with the error information explaining why the message cannot be transmitted. This status information is reset before each attempt to send a message again on the conversation. The sole purpose of this status information is for troubleshooting and debugging, as it is not used internally by Service Broker.

The function GET_TRANSMISSION_STATUS can be used to retrieve the transmission status of any conversation, and the view sys.transmission_queue projects this function result for all pending messages as the transmission_status column.

For troubleshooting, the most important column in this view is `transmission_status`. If Service Broker cannot send a message, this column will contain the reason why. Anything other than a blank `transmission_status` value indicates a problem and your message will not even leave the database until the problem is solved. Here are some of the most common errors:

- `The target service name could not be found. Ensure that the service name is specified correctly and/or the routing information has been supplied.` There is no route for the destination service. Create the necessary route.

- `The session keys for this conversation could not be created or accessed. The database master key is required for this operation.` There is no database master key or it cannot be accessed by Service Broker. Create a database master key and ensure the service master key encryption of the database master key exists.

- `Dialog security is not available for this conversation because there is no remote service binding for the target service. Create a remote service binding, or specify ENCRYPTION = OFF in the BEGIN DIALOG statement.` There is no `REMOTE SERVICE BINDING` for the target service. Create a `REMOTE SERVICE BINDING`.

- `Dialog security is unavailable for this conversation because there is no security certificate bound to the database principal (Id: 1). Either create a certificate for the principal, or specify ENCRYPTION = OFF when beginning the conversation.` A certificate is required for the user with the ID specified in the error message. Create or import the necessary certificate.

Any other error that happens in SQL Server during message delivery can be caught by the Service Broker, including out-of-memory errors, database integrity errors, disk space errors, and operating system errors. A comprehensive list of all errors that can appear in `transmission_status` is not possible.

If the `transmission_status` column of a message is blank, it means the message can be sent. Note that Service Broker may periodically erase the `transmission_status` column before attempting to transmit a message again. Therefore, the status may be blank for a short time but set itself back to an error message shortly. You shouldn't worry that there is a problem with the `transmission_status` column unless it stays blank for a long period of time. Also when you're making configuration changes, Service Broker will not react to all of them immediately. Most configuration changes are detected by Service Broker only on a periodic interval of 15 seconds, so when investigating an issue and making a change, don't be alarmed if the system does not appear to react to your change. It will react to it the next time it checks for configuration changes; for some changes, that may take up to a minute.

To validate that Service Broker is indeed sending the message, use the Profiler application attached to the sending SQL Server instance. Each time a message is sent, an event of class `Broker:Remote Message Acknowledgement` with subclass `1 - Message with Acknowledgement Sent` is fired by Service Broker, and this event will appear in Profiler. To make sure that the profiler event is indeed for the conversation you are investigating, use the `GUID` column of the profiler event to verify that it has the expected conversation ID value, because there might be other Service Broker activity in the system.

Once you've ensured that Service Broker is indeed sending the messages, you should focus on the message recipient instead of the message sender. Attach the SQL Profiler to the receiving SQL Server instance and monitor the Broker category events. Look for the events indicating a successful message delivery:

1. Service Broker will first try to find a destination service for the incoming message. For this, the routing table of the msdb database will be used. Look for the Broker: Message Classify event in the Profiler that will indicate this event occurred. A successful classification will have an event subclass 1 - Local. Since this classification occurs in msdb, the event Database ID column will have the msdb database ID, which is typically 4.

2. The message will be delivered to the appropriate service. If this is the first message, it will create the conversation endpoint, and this will generate two Profiler events, one of class Broker:Conversation Group with the event subclass 1 - Create and one of class Broker:Conversation with the event subclass 12 - Dialog Created.

3. The message is handed to the appropriate conversation. This will generate an event of class Broker:Conversation with the subclass 6 - Received Sequenced Message.

4. The message dispatch sequence is completed and an event of class Broker:Remote Message Acknowledgement with the subclass 3 - Message with Acknowledgement Received is generated.

If you see the events described here, it means the message was successfully delivered to the target conversation. The message is now in the target service queue ready to be processed. Again, to make sure the events you monitor are actually for the conversation you are trying to troubleshoot, use the GUID column of the event to validate they belong to the right conversation; this column contains the conversation ID for each event generated.

After the message is enqueued, an acknowledgment for the message has to be sent to the sender. Service Broker will not send the acknowledgment immediately, but instead wait for up to a second. This is to give the application servicing the destination service a chance to dequeue the message and respond with its own SEND. In that case, Service Broker can piggyback the acknowledgment on the response message, resulting in a considerable network bandwidth saving.

In Service Broker terms, the messages sent by the application are called *sequenced* because they are carrying a conversation message sequence number, while the acknowledgments sent by Service Broker without an underlying application message are called *unsequenced*.

If the acknowledgment is piggybacked on an application response message, then you will have to check the Profiler to see the event for the acknowledgment being sent back—an event of class Broker:Remote Message Acknowledgement with subclass 1 - Message with Acknowledgement Sent. If the application does not respond in one second, a stand-alone acknowledgment is sent back (an unsequenced message). This will also generate a Broker:Remote Message Acknowledgement event but with subclass 2 - Acknowledgement Sent.

After you've validated that the destination Service Broker is indeed receiving the message and sending back an acknowledgment, you must now turn your attention back to the sender and check out how it handles the acknowledgment sent by the message destination. What you are looking for is the event Broker:Remote Message Acknowledgement with a subclass 3 - Message with Acknowledgement Received (if the acknowledgment was sequenced) or subclass 4 - Acknowledgement Received (if the acknowledgment was unsequenced).

After the acknowledgment is received, the message will be deleted from the database transmission queue and will disappear from the sys.transmission_queue view, indicating a successful delivery.

Your troubleshooting investigation will more than likely find something different in the events you see in the Profiler than the sequence I described because, well, you are investigating some problem so something must be different. Here are some of the Profiler events indicating problems and the likely cause of these problems:

- *Broker:Message Classify with subclass 3 - Delayed*: The destination service does not have a route. Check the database ID of the event; if it is 4, then this is the classification of an incoming message and the problem is with the routes in the msdb database.

- *Broker: Message Undeliverable*: A message that was received could not be delivered to a conversation or be forwarded. This event is the best indicator of a problem. Check the event TextData column for details why the message could not be delivered.

- *Broker: Message Undeliverable when the TextData column is This message could not be delivered because it is a duplicate*: A message is being retried by the sender because it did not receive an acknowledgment. Usually this event is repeated about once every minute as the sender is retrying the message. Most likely it is a misconfigured route that prevents acknowledgments from reaching the sender, in which case it is quickly followed by an event of class Broker: Message Classify with subclass 3 - Delayed.

- *Broker: Message Undeliverable when the TextData column is This message could not be delivered because the security context could not be retrieved*: There are two possible causes for this error:

  - There is a time drift between the system clock of the sender and the system clock of the receiver, in which case you will have to align the two system clocks.

  - One of the certificates used by the sender is not recognized by the receiver. In this case, an event of class Audit Broker Conversation will be produced by Service Broker and the details of this event will indicate the certificate with the problem. Look at the event subclass and at the DBUserName column (which will contain the problem certificate issuer name) as well as the TargetLoginName column (which will contain the serial number). If you see Service Broker is not using the certificate you were expecting to secure the message, remember that when faced with multiple valid choices, Service Broker will choose the certificate with the latest expiration date.

Connection Problems

Connection problems troubleshooting is also based on the Profiler events. The events to look for are the Broker:Connection class and Audit Broker Login class in the Security Audit category. The Service Broker will fire the Broker:Connection class event several times during the lifetime of the connection, with different event subclasses: Connected, Connect Failed, Closed, Closing, Closed, Accept, Send IO Error, and Receive IO Error.

The most important for troubleshooting are the Closing and Connect Failed subclasses: the TextData for these events contains the reason for a connection being closed or the reason it could not be established in the first place. When a connection is closing and the generated Profile event contains no error message in the TextData column, it means the connection is simply closing because of idle inactivity and does not indicate a problem.

Connections are shared among conversations: there will be only one connection between two SQL Server instances, and all messages will be sent back and forth using the same connection. This means that a connection is in no way tied to a specific conversation. But it is true that connection opening will be triggered by a specific conversation trying to send a message. Any error that happens during the establishing of the connection will be reported as the transmission_status for the dialog that requested that connection as well as for any other dialog that is trying to reach the same destination. So the first place to look for connection errors is the transmission_status column in the sys.transmission_queue view.

Here are some of the more typical error messages that can be seen in both the transmission_status or in the TextData of the Broker:Connection event when there is a connection problem. Note that since the address that the connection is trying to connect to is given by a route, oftentimes the root of the connection problem is actually a route in a database.

- *Connection attempt failed with error: '10061(No connection could be made because the target machine actively refused it.)'. Can't open a TCP socket with the address specified in the route for the destination service*: Ensure that the hostname and port number in the route address are correct and verify that the port is not blocked by a firewall.

- *DNS lookup failed with error: '11001(No such host is known.)'. The hostname specified in the route address for the destination service cannot be resolved through DNS lookup*: Correct the route to specify the correct hostname.

- *Connection handshake failed. The login '...' does not have CONNECT permission on the endpoint. The peer SQL Server instance is not allowed to connect to this SQL Server instance on the Service Broker endpoint*: Grant the required CONNECT permission on the Service Broker endpoint.

- *An error occurred while receiving data: '64(The specified network name is no longer available.)'*: This error message happens because the other SQL Server instance you are trying to connect to is closing the connection. The most likely cause is an authentication or authorization failure. The proper way to diagnose the issue is to attach the SQL Profiler to the other SQL Server instance and monitor the Broker:Connection events.

Internal Activation Problems

When Service Broker activates a stored procedure on a service queue, the stored procedure runs just as it would be running when invoked from a user connection, except there is no user connection. This introduces a couple of differences:

- The security context of execution is an EXECUTE AS USER context, and such a context is different from an ordinary user connection security context. Because the context is not verified by the SQL Server instance through a login (a server principal) but only through a user (a database principal), the context is only trusted in the context of the database that launched the activated procedure.

- There isn't a connection the procedure can send any output to, so all output produced by the procedure is instead logged by Service Broker in the SQL Server error log. Such output includes any PRINT statements, any error raised by the procedure, and any result sets produced.

The different execution context usually results in the procedure behaving as expected when tested from a user connection like an SSMS query window, but producing unexpected behavior when running under the activation context. Combining this with the fact that any error or output from the activated procedure is apparently lost usually results in a frustrated developer. The simple trick here is to know where to look, and again the SQL Profiler tool is your best friend. Whenever your activated stored procedure appears to have a mind of its own, remember to attach the Profiler and watch for the Broker:Activation event class. This event will be raised, with different subclasses, when an activated procedure is launched into execution, when it terminates execution, when it aborts, and whenever it produces any output. In the last case, the TextData will contain the output text that would normally have been sent to the connection, like the text of a PRINT statement or the message of an error.

To troubleshoot an activated procedure, first turn off activation, using ALTER QUEUE [<queuename>] WITH ACTIVATION (STATUS = OFF). Once activation is turned off, run the activated procedure manually by invoking it from an SSMS query window, but you have to make it run in a security context similar to the one under activation. So before invoking the procedure, first run the statement EXECUTE AS USER = '<procedure_execute_as_user>'. When the procedure executes, it will report any errors back to your SSMS connection and you can troubleshoot it if there is a problem with it.

A different kind of problem is when the activated procedures apparently are not being launched, despite the fact that the queue contains messages to be processed. Here is how I recommend approaching such a problem:

- First, make sure the queue is actually enabled. You can use SSMS Object Explorer to inspect the queue properties, or you can manually check the sys.service_queues view and verify that the is_receive_enabled and is_enqueue_enabled columns have the value 1. If the queue was disabled, you can enable it by running ALTER QUEUE [<queuename>] WITH STATUS = ON;.

- Next verify that activation is configured correctly and enabled. Again, use either the SSMS Object Explorer to inspect the queue properties or the sys.service_queues view and validate that

  - Activation is enabled.

  - A procedure is configured for activation and the procedure exists in the database.

  - The max_queue_readers parameter for activation is greater than 0.

  - The EXECUTE AS principal is configured and correct.

- Check the queue monitors for the queue being investigated. Use either the Broker Statistics Report as described in Table 4 or the sys.dm_broker_queue_monitors DMV. The Queue Monitor should be in the INACTIVE state if there are no messages in the queue or RECEIVES_OCCURRING otherwise. If the Queue Monitor stays in the NOTIFIED state for a long time, it means the activated queue is not issuing RECEIVE statements against this queue. Inspect the procedure code and validate that the procedure issues the RECEIVE statement on the queue that activates the procedure.

- Check the running activated tasks. Use the sys.dm_broker_activated_tasks DMV. If the queue has launched any activated procedure, it will show up as a row in this view and you can see the connection SPID of the activated task. You can then investigate these activated connections to see if they are blocked from making progress.

Service Broker Diagnostics Tool

Knowing how to troubleshoot Service Broker is important if you plan to develop an application that relies on Service Broker facilities or if you administer a SQL Server instance that hosts a Service Broker application. But Microsoft recognized that troubleshooting knowledge is hard to come by. Although all the information needed to troubleshoot issues exists and is accessible, knowing where to look and what to expect is not easy. In SQL Server 2008, a new tool is installed when you select the Client Tools installation: ssbdiagnose.exe, the Service Broker Diagnostics Tool.

Normally this tool is installed in the %ProgramFiles%\Microsoft SQL Server\100\Tools\ Binn folder, together with other client tools like bcp.exe, sqlcmd.exe, or sqldiag.exe. The Service Broker Diagnostics Tool helps you analyze a Service Broker service deployment and investigate problems. While it is true that a knowledgeable administrator can collect all the information the tool collects and draw the same conclusions to diagnose a problem, the tool does this automatically and does not require the advanced Service Broker know-how on the user's part. The Service Broker Diagnostics Tool can run in two modes:

- *Configuration mode*: In this mode the tool is checking whether a pair of services can exchange messages.

- *Runtime mode*: In this mode the tool is connecting to one or more SQL Server instances and is using the Profiler tracing infrastructure to monitor for events indicating a Service Broker problem.

The Service Broker Diagnostics Tool requires sysadmin privileges on the SQL Server instances it investigates.

Configuration Mode

To launch the Service Broker Diagnostics Tool in Configuration mode, specify the CONFIGURATION option. The command-line syntax is as follows:

```
SSBDIAGNOSE [<GeneralOptions>] CONFIGURATION {<FromService> <ToService>}
                    { ON CONTRACT contract_name }
                    [ ENCRYPTION {ON | OFF | ANONYMOUS} ]

<GeneralOptions> ::=
        [-XML]
        [-LEVEL {ERROR | WARNING | INFO}]
        [<ConnectionOptions>]

<FromService> ::=
        FROM SERVICE service_name [<ConnectionOptions>] [<MirrorOptions>]

<ToService> ::=
        TO SERVICE service_name [,broker_id]
        [<ConnectionOptions>] [<MirrorOptions>]

<MirrorOptions> ::=
        MIRROR <ConnectionOptions>

<ConnectionOptions> ::=
        {-E |   {-U login_id [-P password]}}
        [-S server_name[\instance_name]]
        [-d database_name]
        [-l login_timeout]
```

In Configuration mode the diagnostics tool syntax is similar to the syntax of the BEGIN DIALOG statement in Transact-SQL. You specify the 'from' service name, the 'to' service name, the 'on' contract name, and the encryption-required on/off setting. For the two service names ('from' and 'to'), you also need to specify the connection parameters for the tool to connect to the SQL Server instance and database hosting each service. If any of the services are hosted in a mirrored database, you must also specify the connection parameters for the SQL Server instance hosting the mirror. Table 12-15 lists the most important verifications done by the tool when running the Configuration mode checks.

Not all the objects verified by the tool when running in Configuration mode are specified in the command line. This is because once the service names and contract used have been specified, all the other objects involved (queues, message types, endpoints, etc.) can be discovered by the tool itself by inspecting the system metadata catalogs.

Other validations are performed by the tool, mostly to check for some nontrivial problems, as I have discovered from my own experience. An example of such a problem is that the tool validates not only that the service security is configured correctly both from the 'from' service to the 'to' service and the other way, but also that the database principals used in both direction are actually the same. I've seen a deployment where the configuration was using a different pair of database principals when sending replies from the 'to' service to the 'from' service, and this was very counterintuitive to investigate and diagnose the first time.

Table 12-15. *Configuration Mode Verifications*

Object Being Verified	Checks Performed
Service Contract	The contract is deployed on both databases involved. The contract has identical definitions on both databases: the same message types are used, the message types are sent in the same direction, and the message type validation is the same.
Service	The service is deployed in the database specified in the connection arguments. The 'to' service (target) is bound to the contract used.
Queue	The queue is enabled. Activation arguments are consistent: either none is specified, or all are specified and correct. The queue is on a read-write filegroup.
Database	Service Broker is enabled in the database. The database is read-write. The database is not restricted to single-user access mode.
Routes	A route exists from the 'from' to the 'to' service and the other way around. The route address matches the machine name hosting the other service and the Service Broker endpoint listening port. If one of the services is hosted in a mirrored database, then the route to it is verified to be a mirrored route and the mirror_ address of the route is verified to match the machine name and Service Broker endpoint listening port of the mirror host.
Service Security	Certificates are correctly deployed and exchanged. The proper REMOTE SERVICE BINDING was created. The SEND permission was granted on the 'to' service. A database master key is created in each database involved.
Service Broker Endpoints	Endpoints are deployed and started. The authentication and encryption modes of the two endpoints involved are compatible with each other. The authentication principal used by the peer endpoint (Windows or Certificate) has been granted the CONNECT permission on the endpoint.

Runtime Mode

Launching the Service Broker Diagnostics Tool in Runtime mode is done by specifying the RUNTIME option. The command-line syntax of this mode is as follows:

```
SSBDIAGNOSE [<GeneralOptions>] RUNTIME
      [-SHOWEVENTS]
      [<TimeoutOptions>]
      [<DialogOptions>]
      <ConnectToOptions>

<GeneralOptions> ::=
      [-XML]
      [-LEVEL {ERROR | WARNING | INFO}]
      [<ConnectionOptions>]
```

```
<TimeoutOptions> ::=
        -TIMEOUT timeout

<DialogOptions> ::=
        {-NEW | -ID conversationId}

<ConnectToOptions> ::=
        CONNECT TO <ConnectionOptions>
        [<ConnectToOptions>]

<ConnectionOptions> ::=
        {-E |   {-U login_id [-P password]}}
        [-S server_name[\instance_name]]
        [-d database_name]
        [-l login_timeout]
```

When running in Runtime mode, the tool is no longer investigating the configuration of a specific pair of services but instead is monitoring a series of SQL Server instances to which it connects and waits for events indicating a problem. It uses the SQL Profiler infrastructure for that: it starts traces on all SQL Server instances it connects to and then monitors the output of the traces. Some events raised by Service Broker are clear indicators of a problem; for example, the Broker:Connection event with a subclass Closing and the TextData containing an error, Broker:Classify, with a subclass Delayed or the Broker:Message Undeliverable event. When such an event is detected, the tool will use the event information (like the conversation ID of the conversation that raised the event) to find all the information it needs and then, internally, launch the Configuration mode of the tool to investigate the problem. So even when running in Runtime mode the diagnostics will actually come from the Configuration mode of the tool. However, you don't have to specify the service name or contract name arguments since the tool is able to locate them.

Another way to run the Runtime mode diagnostics tool is to specify a conversation ID. In fact, you specify either a conversation ID or a conversation handle; it doesn't matter since the tool is able to distinguish between them by searching the databases it connects to. When you specify a conversation ID, the tool will filter the events only to those related to the conversation you specify. The primary purpose of this filtering is to reduce the quantity of information and diagnostics offered by the tool when running in Runtime mode. If the -NEW option is specified, the tool will filter the events to only events that relate to conversations started after the tool is launched. Since not all events are directly related to a conversation, those events that are not related to a conversation will not be filtered out and will appear even when the -ID or -NEW options are specified.

Normally in Runtime mode the tool never finishes and does not exit until stopped by pressing Ctrl+C. You can specify a timeout with the -TIMEOUT option and the tool will exit after the specified timeout.

Service Broker Diagnostics Tool Output

The Service Broker Diagnostics Tool will produce three types of output messages:

- Diagnostics are configuration problems the tool was able to identify. They are directly actionable by an administrator, and fixing them should result in a correct deployment.

- Events are SQL Profiler events indicating problems that the tool has detected when in Runtime mode. Events are not shown by default, but they can be enabled by specifying the -SHOWEVENTS arguments in the tool command line. After such an event, the tool will try to diagnose the problem internally and produce some additional diagnostic messages, but this is not always guaranteed to succeed.

- Problems are issues the tool has encountered that are preventing the tools from making progress. An example of such an issue is when the tool detects an event in Runtime mode but is unable to investigate because it is not connected to a SQL Server instance involved in the conversation that produced the event.

The normal output of the Service Broker Diagnostics Tool is a list of diagnostic messages in a tabular format that contains the error message number, the SQL Server instance and the database name to which the error refers, and the error message itself. If the SQL Server instance name or the database name is blank, it means the error message does not apply to a specific SQL Server instance and/or database.

When the -XML parameter is specified in the command line, the tool will format the output as an XML document. This way, the tool can be plugged into an automated monitoring system that can run the tool and then automate the processing of the tool output.

To illustrate the use of the Service Broker Diagnostics Tool, I'm going to create a setup similar to the one you had already encountered in Chapters 7 and 8, but I will intentionally change the setup to omit some of the necessary definitions or to configure something incorrectly. You must follow the same steps to exchange the certificates used for Service Broker dialog security as you did for the examples in Chapter 8. Create a folder called C:\SSB Book c12 on your disk to store the exchanged certificates, and prior to running this example, drop any Service Broker endpoint already existing on your SQL Server.

■**Caution** Do not use the following examples for inspiration; they contain intentional errors!

Listing 12-6 contains the script to run at the initiator.

Listing 12-6. *Setup for Initiator*

```
USE MASTER;
GO

CREATE ENDPOINT [ServiceBroker]
    STATE = STARTED
    AS TCP (LISTENER_PORT = 4022)
    FOR SERVICE_BROKER (AUTHENTICATION = WINDOWS, ENCRYPTION = DISABLED);
GO
```

```
CREATE DATABASE [ClientDatabase];
GO


USE [ClientDatabase];
GO


CREATE MASTER KEY ENCRYPTION BY PASSWORD = 'Password!';
GO


CREATE MESSAGE TYPE [http://ssb.csharp.at/SSB_Book/c12/RequestMessage]
      VALIDATION = NONE;
CREATE MESSAGE TYPE [http://ssb.csharp.at/SSB_Book/c12/ResponseMessage]
      VALIDATION = WELL_FORMED_XML;
CREATE CONTRACT [http://ssb.csharp.at/SSB_Book/c12/Contract] (
      [http://ssb.csharp.at/SSB_Book/c12/RequestMessage] SENT BY INITIATOR,
      [http://ssb.csharp.at/SSB_Book/c12/ResponseMessage] SENT BY ANY);
GO


CREATE QUEUE [ClientQueue];
CREATE SERVICE [ClientService] ON QUEUE [ClientQueue];
GO


CREATE CERTIFICATE [ClientService]
      WITH SUBJECT = 'ClientService',
      START_DATE = '01/01/2008';
GO


BACKUP CERTIFICATE [ClientService]
      TO FILE = 'C:\SSB_Book_c12\ClientService.cer';
GO
```

Next, run the script in Listing 12-7 on the target.

Listing 12-7. *Setup for Target*

```
USE MASTER;
GO


CREATE ENDPOINT [ServiceBroker]
      STATE = STARTED
      AS TCP (LISTENER_PORT = 4023)
      FOR SERVICE_BROKER (AUTHENTICATION = WINDOWS, ENCRYPTION = REQUIRED);
GO


CREATE DATABASE [AccountingDatabase];
GO


USE [AccountingDatabase];
GO
```

```
CREATE MASTER KEY ENCRYPTION BY PASSWORD = 'Password!';
GO

CREATE MESSAGE TYPE [http://ssb.csharp.at/SSB_Book/c12/RequestMessage]
      VALIDATION = WELL_FORMED_XML;
CREATE MESSAGE TYPE [http://ssb.csharp.at/SSB_Book/c12/ResponseMessage]
      VALIDATION = WELL_FORMED_XML;
CREATE CONTRACT [http://ssb.csharp.at/SSB_Book/c12/Contract] (
      [http://ssb.csharp.at/SSB_Book/c12/RequestMessage] SENT BY INITIATOR,
      [http://ssb.csharp.at/SSB_Book/c12/ResponseMessage] SENT BY TARGET);
GO

CREATE QUEUE [AccountingQueue];
CREATE SERVICE [AccountingService] ON QUEUE [AccountingQueue]
      ([http://ssb.csharp.at/SSB_Book/c12/Contract]);
GO

CREATE CERTIFICATE [AccountingService]
      WITH SUBJECT = 'AccountingService';
GO

BACKUP CERTIFICATE [AccountingService]
      TO FILE = 'C:\SSB_Book_c12\AccountingService.cer';
GO
```

Now return to the initiator and run the script in Listing 12-8.

Listing 12-8. *Configuring the Initiator Route and Security*

```
USE [ClientDatabase];
GO

CREATE USER [ClientServiceUser] WITHOUT LOGIN;
GO

CREATE CERTIFICATE [ClientService]
      AUTHORIZATION [ClientServiceUser]
      FROM FILE = 'C:\SSB_Book_c12\ClientService.cer';
GO

CREATE ROUTE [ClientServiceRoute] WITH
      SERVICE_NAME = 'clientService',
      ADDRESS = 'tcp://remusr10:4022';
GO
```

Finally, run the script in Listing 12-9 at the target.

Listing 12-9. *Configuring the Target Route and Security*

```
USE [AccountingDatabase];
GO


CREATE USER [AccountingServiceUser] WITHOUT LOGIN;
GO


CREATE CERTIFICATE [AccountingService]
    AUTHORIZATION [AccountingServiceUser]
    FROM FILE = 'C:\SSB_Book_c12\AccountingService.cer';
GO

CREATE REMOTE SERVICE BINDING [AccountingServiceRSB]
    TO SERVICE 'AccountingService'
    WITH USER = [AccountingServiceUser];
GO

CREATE ROUTE [AccountingServiceRoute] WITH
    SERVICE_NAME = 'AccountingService',
    ADDRESS = 'tcp://remusr10:4023';
GO
```

CAN YOU SPOT THE ERRORS?

Listings 12-6, 12-7, 12-8, and 12-9 constitute an example of incorrect deployment scripts. Can you spot the errors before using the Service Broker Diagnostics Tool? Before reading on, try to spot them yourself.

- The message type [http://ssb.csharp.at/SSB_Book/c12/ResponseMessage] is defined as sent by ANY in one listing and sent by TARGET in another.

- The message type [http://ssb.csharp.at/SSB_Book/c12/RequestMessage] is defined as VALIDATION = NONE in one listing and as VALIDATION = WELL_FORMED_XML in another.

- The route [ClientServiceRoute] has a typo in the service name.

- The user [ClientServiceUser] needs to be granted SEND permission on the target service.

Note that none of the errors are syntax errors; the scripts execute correctly without warnings or errors.

To launch the Service Broker Diagnostics Tool, run this command line:

```
ssbdiagnose configuration from service "ClientService" -S . -d ClientDatabase to➡
service "AccountingService" -S .\Katmai -d AccountingDatabase on contract➡
"http://ssb.csharp.at/SSB_Book/c12/Contract"
```

The result of running the tool is shown in Figure 12-8. Let's walk through each of the issues reported by the tool:

- *29925 REMUSR10 ClientDatabase Contract http://ssb.csharp.at/SSB_Book/c12/ Contract does not have the same definition on the initiator and target*: The tool has found that the contract definition is different on the initiator and on the target. Indeed, if we look back at the scripts we've run, the contract is defined with the message type [http://ssb.csharp.at/SSB_Book/c12/ResponseMessage] sent by ANY in Listing 12-6 but the same message type is sent by TARGET in Listing 12-7.

- *29931 REMUSR10\Katmai AccountingDatabase There is no route for service ClientService and broker instance 126A71DA-ABC6-481D-A60C-AB19EBD87540*: The tool is reporting that there is no route back from the target service to the initiator. In Listing 12-8 we did create the route, but the SERVICE_NAME argument has a typo in it: it should be 'ClientService', not 'clientService'. Note that because of how Service Broker routing works, the tool doesn't report that a route has a typo in it, but only that there is no route to the intended service.

- *29926 REMUSR10 ClientDatabase Message type http://ssb.csharp.at/SSB_Book/c12/ RequestMessage does not have the same definition on the initiator and target*: We defined this message type as VALIDATION = NONE in Listing 12-6 but it's defined as VALIDATION = WELL_FORMED_XML in Listing 12-7.

- *29975 AccountingService AccountingDatabase User ClientServiceUser does not have SEND permission on service AccountingService*: Although we created certificates, created a remote service binding, and exchanged the certificates, we omitted one more necessary step: Listing 12-9 should have a GRANT SEND ON SERVICE::[AccountingService] TO [ClientServiceUser];.

- *29958 REMUSR10 There is no compatible encryption requirement between server REMUSR10 and server REMUSR10\Katmai*: Listing 12-6 creates a Service Broker endpoint with ENCRYPTION = DISABLED while Listing 12-7 creates one with ENCRYPTION = REQUIRED. These two settings are incompatible as one disables encryption while the other requires it.

- *29955 REMUSR10\Katmai Could not validate the CONNECT permission of login RUSANU\REMUSR10$ on endpoint ServiceBroker due to exception Could not obtain information about Windows NT group/user 'RUSANU\REMUSR10$', error code 0x534*: The tool has found not a diagnostic but a problem. The tool cannot validate the Windows account RUSANU\REMUSR10$, my laptop domain account, because I am running while disconnected from the network. This is not necessarily something that would prevent your Service Broker application from running correctly, but it is something that prevents the Service Broker Diagnostics Tool itself from succeeding in its analysis.

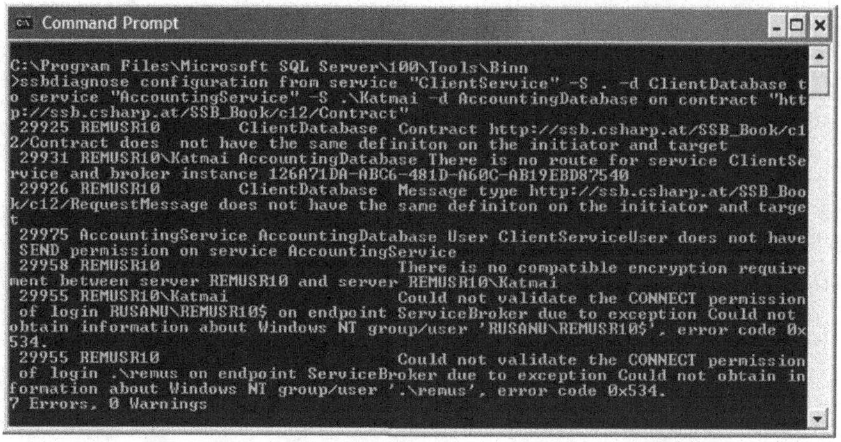

Figure 12-8. *Service Broker Diagnostics Tool*

As you can see, the Service Broker Diagnostics Tool has identified the mistakes in the configuration scripts. The tool does not offer remedies for the issues it reports, because most of the time there are more ways to fix a reported issue and the correct way depends a lot on the specifics of your application or your deployment.

Summary

This chapter covered the administration tools available for Service Broker. Using SSMS, SQL Profiler, or SMO you can deploy new services and modify services, queues, endpoints, and so forth. The Broker Statistics Report offers an overall view of Service Broker objects in a database.

The remainder of the chapter covered troubleshooting Service Broker. Understanding how Service Broker delivers messages is the first step to troubleshooting incidents when the message flow is stopped. Using the new Service Broker Diagnostics Tool takes the guesswork out of troubleshooting.

Index

▪Numbers and symbols

@ch variable, 49

@msg variable, 49

▪A

ABP (adjacent broker protocol), 240

AccountingRecordings table

  creating a new booking record into, 201–202

  definition of, 199–200

AccountingRequestMessage message, sent by OrderService, 199

AccountingRequestMessage message type, processing of, 331–333

AccountingResponse, sending to OrderService, 202

AccountingService, 184

  compensation transactions for, 221

  computer deployed on, 248

  creating returning route to OrderService from, 250

  creation of booking record by, 199–202

  starting a new conversation with, 193–195

AccountingService service

  message types handled by, 331

  processing of AccountingRequestMessage message type, 331–333

AccountingServiceInstance machine, SQL Server objects for, 249–250

acknowledgment message, sending to sender of original message, 241–242

activated procedure, troubleshooting, 539–540

activated stored procedures

  common causes when not running, 125

  ensuring they are correctly started, 125

  implementing with managed assembly, 143–148

strange behavior you can encounter in, 87

  troubleshooting, 124–125

activated tasks child table, columns in Broker Statistics Report, 519–520

activation, troubleshooting, 124–125

ACTIVE FOR BEGIN_DIALOG option, 295

activity data, used to perform a specific activity, 311

Activity Monitor, conversation lock in, 169–170

ADD SIGNATURE statement, 93

Adjacent Broker Protocol (ABP), Service Broker communication protocol, 239

administration,

  SQL Service Broker, 513

  tools provided by Service Broker, 31

ALTER AUTHORIZATION statement, 37

ALTER ENDPOINT T-SQL statement, 317

ALTER MESSAGE TYPE statement, 37

ALTER QUEUE statement, 78–79

ALTER ROUTE command, 246

ALTER SERVICE statement, 45–46

anonymous dialog security

  function of, 277

  setting up, 284–286

anonymous transport security, setting up, 279–280

application state

  updating, 333

  updating and committing transaction, 177

ApplicationState table

  creating, 185

  content of, 177

  inserting new state information into, 190

  retrieving stored state information from, 189

  stored application state in, 183

  structure of, 173, 328

  writing modified information back to, 195–196

Apress Source Code/download area, website address, 331

articles

defined for publish-subscribe scenario, 420

sending, 429–430

ASP.NET web service, implementing, 372

asymmetric keys. *See also* public and private keys (asymmetric keys)

problems associated with, 260

asynchronous message processing, 6–7

asynchronous triggers, 376–385

defining the problem, 376, 409

function of, 351

with Service Broker, 376

audit backend, creating a dummy, 231–234

auditing, using set-based processing for, 231–234

AuditingTrail table, 233-234

authentication. *See also* connection authentication

supported by HTTP endpoints, 317

author, defined for publish-subscribe scenario, 420

AutoCreatedLocal route, 272–273

■B

backend service program, implementing, 454–456

BackEndService, message forwarding to, 452–453

base class constructor, implementing, 131

Base64 formats, manipulating, 373

batch frameworks, 419–420

architecture of, 408

extending, 417

function of, 351, 409

implementing, 410–416

payload for batch job, 409

writing for processing batch jobs, 408–420

batch job

creating new, 418

execution, 414–416

framework, 409

instantiation, 414

request message, 410

batch job type

contained in batch job request, 409

implementing new, 419

registering new, 419–420

request message for new, 418

batched commits, 225–227

<BatchJobData> element, function of, 410

BatchJobFactory class, GetBatchJob method for, 414

BatchJobProcessingService, submitting new batch job to, 416

BatchJobs table, 412

BatchJobType attribute, function of, 410

BatchJobTypeA class, mapping batch job type to, 413

BEGIN CONVERSATION TIMER statement, 367–368

BEGIN DIALOG CONVERSATION statement, 46–48, 379, 523

BEGIN DIALOG statement

creating a new dialog with, 165

options to use ENCRYPTION in, 289

switching to use the new certificate, 295

using with WITH RELATED_CONVERSATION clause, 167

BeginConversationWithAccountingService method, 330–331

BeginDialog method

CallExternalMethodActivity that calls, 402

implementing in ServiceBrokerImpl class, 392–393

BeginTimer method, implementing, 368

binary data, marshaling and unmarshaling, 235–236

binary payload, moving to for audit records, 235

BizTalk Server, 15

<body element>, 356

body of message, 69

BOL topic
   ConfiguringtheHTTPKernel-
     ModeDriver(Http.sys), 319
   Extending Database Impersonation by
     Using EXECUTE AS, 91

boxcarring, 241

Broker: Message Classify with subclass 3 -
   Delayed, 537

Broker: Message Undeliverable event class,
   522

Broker: Message Undeliverable message, 537

Broker category events, monitoring, 535–536

Broker class
   available methods of, 107
   using Receive method of, 109–110

BROKER INSTANCE parameter, 272

Broker Statistics Report, 514–520. *See also*
   Service Broker

BrokerMethodAttribute class, 128

BuildCallbackMap method, 133–134

BuildGcgrCommand method, 179–180

■C

callback problems, with query notifications,
   348–349

CallExternalMethodActivity, that calls
   BeginDialog method, 402

Campbell, David, white paper by, 13

catalog views, getting contract information
   through, 40–41

centralized administration tools, provided by
   Service Broker, 31

centralized routing instance, implementing,
   477

certificate-based authentication
   function of, 254
   in Service Broker security, 27

certificate-based transport security
   function of, 260–267
   how certificates relate to each endpoint,
     260–261
   setting up, 259–267

certificates
   as containers for public-key/private-key
     pairs, 259
   creating a login and granting it
     permissions, 93–95
   removing private key from, 94
   replacing, 294–295
   Service Broker features for replacing
     expired, 271
   switching BEGIN DIALOG statement to
     use new, 295

charts, in Broker Statistics Report, 516–517

classifier component, 272
   for route lookup in Service Broker, 241
   matching routes for Service Broker
     service, 244

client application
   function of in asynchronous message
     processing, 6
   waiting for response messages in, 141–142

client/server and n-tier application
   architectures, problems associated
   with, 305

ClientService
   creating with network address in name,
     274
   sending message to OrderService from,
     186–187
   sending request to the OrderService from,
     522–524
   start of new conversation with
     OrderService by, 184

ClientService and OrderService, creating
   routes between, 274

cmdGetData_Click and Get Data methods,
   implementing, 341–342

code signin, creating a certificate needed for,
   93–94
   to correct poison-message error, 98–99

CodeActivity, that writes message to console,
   402

Codeplex site, website address for, 111

COMMIT, after messages are processed,
   227–228

communication, TCP used by Service Broker
   for, 239–240

communication channel, establishing, 250–253

compensating transactions, if product is not in inventory, 203

compensation logic, with Service Broker, 215–221

compensation messages, 216–217

compensation transactions
defining message types for, 215–216
for AccountingService, 221
for undoing actions executed earlier, 215–221
initiating, 217–220

Configuration mode, troubleshooting diagnostics tool in, 540–541

configuration notice service
configuration of, 489
creating, 485
implementing, 483-484
locating a route through, 489
message sent to, 486
steps for implementing the service program, 485

configuration notice services, function of, 461

<ConfigurationRecord> element, finding and matching, 113–114

ConfiguringtheHTTPKernel-ModeDriver(Http.sys), 319

CONNECT permission, granting to SQL Server login, 257–258

connection authentication, types of offered by Service Broker, 254–267

connection problems, troubleshooting, 537–538

contracts
available through catalog views, 39
between Service Broker services, 24
creating for Service Broker applications, 37–41
deleting existing, 41
getting of defined services, 45
how message types are assembled into, 24
initiator services and, 46
viewing defined, 39

Conversation class, 128–130

conversation endpoints
conversation priorities at, 443
conversation priority levels assigned to, 439
creating, 51

conversation group lock
to ensure messages are processed in order, 164–165
verifying, 169

conversation group locking, 19–20
in Service Broker, 11

conversation groups
acquiring lock on available, 176
and locks provided by Service Broker, 163–221
creating new, 165
example of, 19–20
expanding, 166–167
grouping dialogs into, 165–170
how they travel to target queue, 167–168
initiating multiple conversations in, 166–170
number of conversations in, 19
proving both messages are sent on same, 168–169
setting priority of, 453–454

conversation lock, in Activity Monitor, 169–170

Conversation Priority feature
at TargetQueue, 443
enabling, 438–445
match preference table, 439
of Service Broker, 438–439

conversation priority objects, creating, 438–439

conversation problems, troubleshooting, 534–537

conversations
arguments for reusing, 377
between initiator and target services, 379–380
creating with different assigned priorities, 441
ending one with errors, 69–72
in Service Broker programming, 17
types of in Service Broker architecture, 17
vs. conversation groups, 446

conversation_group_id, 167

   for storing state of conversation group, 171

CREATE ASSEMBLY statement

   arguments for, 145–146

   for deployment of managed assembly, 415–416

   syntax for, 145

   using, 147

CREATE BROKER PRIORITY statement, 438

CREATE CERTIFICATE statement

   ACTIVE FOR BEGIN_DIALOG option on, 295

   EXPIRY_DATE option for, 294

   parameters for, 262–263

   syntax for, 261–262

CREATE CONTRACT statement, 38–39

CREATE ENDPOINT options, for data mirroring, 464

CREATE ENDPOINT statement

   arguments for, 320–322

   for creating implicit namespace reservation, 318

   for creating new endpoint in SQL Server instance, 251–252

   parameters for, 252

   syntax for, 251–252, 319–320

CREATE EVENT NOTIFICATION statement

   arguments for, 67–68, 105

   creating a new event notification with, 104–105

   for subscribing to poison message notification, 66

   syntax for, 104–105

CREATE MESSAGE TYPE statement

   arguments for, 35–36

   syntax for, 34–35

CREATE QUEUE statement

   arguments for, 41–42

   arguments for internal activation, 79

   enabling internal activation on a service queue, 78–79

   syntax for, 41

CREATE REMOTE SERVICE BINDING statement, 283–284

CREATE ROUTE statement, 245–246

CREATE SERVICE statement, 43–44

CREATE TABLE script, for PendingRequest table, 365

CREATE TABLE statement, creating ProcessedMessages table with, 58

CREATE USER statement, for creating new database user, 282

CreateWebRequest method, implementing, 362–363

credit card transaction record, creating new, 198–199

CreditCardQueue, processing messages from, 197–198

CreditCardRequestMessage message, 196

CreditCardService, 184

   computer deployed on, 248

   creating returning route to OrderService from, 250

   implementing, 196–199

   processing compensation messages on, 220–221

   starting new conversation with, 193–195

   XML message sent to, 293

CreditCardServiceInstance machine, SQL Server objects for, 249

CreditCardTransactions table, 196–197

CROSS APPLY operator, unmarshaling binary message data with, 236–237

current row, fetching of cursor into T-SQL variables for, 230–231

cursor-based message processing, 228–231

   measurements for, 231

CursorReceive stored procedure, changes to for batch commit, 230

CustomerInsertedRequestMessage message type, processing, 383–384

CustomerPartitions table, definition of, 495–496

<CustomerPartition> XML element node, changing, 503–504

Customers table, inserting new record into, 384

■D

data access library, provided by SQLCLR, 327

data partitioning, 491

data protection, provided by database mirroring, 462

data retrieval, defining member variables for, 341

data-dependent forwarding, 491–504

data-dependent redirection, 504–510

data-dependent routing, 461, 490

database
  and log backup, 466
  creating to host simple logging functionality, 96–97
  registering Service Broker assembly in, 146–147

database clustering vs. database mirroring, 462

database mirroring
  architecture of, 462
  benefits of, 462
  CREATE ENDPOINT options for, 464
  creating endpoint for, 464
  creating new certificate for, 464
  database availability provided by, 462
  doing full backup and log backup of database, 466
  enabling on both servers, 467
  function of, 461
  implementation details, 462
  initiating a failover between partners, 468
  operation modes, 463
  parameters specific for, 464
  security configuration for, 465
  setting up, 463
  using Service Broker with, 468
  vs. database clustering, 462

Database Mirroring Monitor, for verifying database mirroring is working, 468

database objects, developing with SQLCLR, 326–327

database preparation, for database-mirroring session, 466

database-mirroring endpoint, configuring, 464

[DEFAULT] contract, 41

DECLARE cursorMessages CURSOR statement, 230

deferred message processing, advantages of, 7

deferred messaging service vs. asynchronous message processing, 7

diagnostics tool, Service Broker, 540–549

dialog authentication, certificates required for, 276–277

dialog encryption
  function of, 287
  specifying, 288–289

dialog initiator, summary of KEK actions, 276–277

dialog lifetime, 18–19

dialog protocol (endpoint protocol), 240

dialog security, 26–28
  architecture of, 278
  authentication provided by, 275
  in advanced distributed Service Broker programming, 271
  in Service Broker applications, 275–286
  on initiator service, 282–283
  on target service, 281–282
  replacing certificates for, 295
  setting up on initiator's endpoint, 282
  SQL objects you must create for, 281
  vs. transport security, 27–28, 275

dialog timer
  function of, 365
  instantiation of on current conversation, 379

dialogs, function of, 18

DialogTimer message, function of, 368

DispatchMessage method, implementing, 136–137

DisplayBeginDialog, CodeActivity, 402

DisplayRequestMessageSent, CodeActivity, 402

DisplayResponseMessageReceived, CodeActivity, 402

DisplayWorkflowEnd activity, for TargetService, 395

DisplayWorkflowStart activity, for TargetService, 394

distributed Service Broker applications
  keys required for, 260–261
  overview and creation of, 239–267
distributed Service Broker programming, advanced, 271
distributed systems
  certificates used to establish user identity, 259
  security considerations for, 8–9
distributed transactions, performance problems with, 30
domain user accounts, for various SQL Server machines, 255
DROP CONTRACT T-SQL statement, deleting existing contracts with, 41
DROP MESSAGE TYPE statement, 37
DROP ROUTE command, 246
DROP SERVICE statement, 46
dynamic rerouting, achieving fault tolerance with, 8
dynamic routing, implementing, 484

■ E
email, as example of messaging, 6
email sending requests, sending to TargetQueue, 436–437
encryption
  disabling for endpoints, 287–288
  in advanced distributed Service Broker programming, 271
  of Service Broker messages, 287–290
  recommendation for, 289–290
  remote service binding and, 289
  turning off, 287
  using transport and dialog in combination, 287
ENCRYPTION = ON/OFF clause
  specifying dialog encryption for current conversation, 288–289
  options in BEGIN DIALOG statement, 289
ENCRYPTION attribute, possible values for, 288
END CONVERSATION statement, 58–59
END DIALOG messages, grouped together to conversation group, 169

EndOfMessageStream message type, processing, 384
endpoint protocol. See dialog protocol (endpoint protocol)
endpoints. See also HTTP endpoints
  certificates required for key exchange to succeed, 260
  creating and deploying to SQL Server instances, 251–253
  introducing by exchanging public keys, 266–267
  lack of support for anonymous requests, 317
enterprise application integration (EAI), using messaging technology for, 15
error handling, in Service Broker, 22, 62–72
error messages
  handling, 70–72
  typical, 538
European customer partition, request message specification of, 503
event notification
  using, 104–105
  using of poison messages, 68–69
event-notification message, content of, 106–107
EXECUTE AS clause, troubleshooting activation with, 125
EXECUTE AS context, stored procedure executing in, 91
Execute method
  defined by IBatchJob interface, 412
  implementing a batch job, 414
exist() method, 314–315
explicit reservation, creating, 318
Export Service Listing Wizard, 297–299
Extending Database Impersonation by Using EXECUTE AS, BOL topic for, 91
external activated application, 114–115
external activation, 103–119
  combining with internal activation, 75
  enabling, 105–107
  for several queues, 110
  function of, 75
  Service Broker function in, 76
  setting up for Service Broker queue, 104
  using for parallel activation of internal stored procedures, 120–122

external activators, processing Service Broker messages with, 104

external application, configuration for, 112–113

external console applications
activating, 110–119
architecture of multiple, 116–117
implementing, 107–110
Main method of, 107–108
output of, 109–115, 118–119
several activated, 116–119

ExternalActivator application
command prompt commands, 111–112
configuring, 112–115
installing as Windows service, 119
uninstalling Windows service, 119
when running in the console, 111

ExternalActivatorQueue, checking for event notification message on, 108–109

ExternalDataExchangeService class, registering Local Service in instance of, 396

externally activated applications, configuration of two, 117–118

■F

fault tolerance, for message-based systems, 7–8

FetchNextMessageBatch method, implementing, 135–136, 179

fields, of Broker Statistics Report, 516

first thread, processing messages on, 169

FlightTicketJob class, implementing, 418–419

FlightTickets table, definition of, 417

forwarding service, using to abstract network topologies and changes, 476

FrontEndQueue, message retrieval from, 452

FrontEndService program, implementing, 452–454

full dialog security
configuring, 278–279
function of, 277
setting up, 280–284

full recovery model, checking, 466

■G

GET CONVERSATION GROUP statement
groups returned by, 444
using, 171–172

GetBatchJob method, 414

GetConversation method, 134–135

GetPendingRequest method, 369–370

GetResponse method, 364

GET_TRANSMISSION_STATUS function, 534

■H

<headers element>, defining header information with, 356

hidden tables feature, implementing queues with, 25

high-availability and scalability options, in Service Broker applications, 461

high-performance mode, in database mirroring, 463

high-safety mode, in database mirroring, 463

historical artifacts, as type of reference data, 310

HONOR_BROKER_PRIORITY database option, setting, 439

host process, communication with, 387

hosts file, for assigning NetBIOS names to computer, 249

HTTP endpoints, 316–317
syntax for creating, 323–324

HTTP namespace reservations, verifying, 318–319

http.sys, function of, 316

httpcfg.exe tool, in Windows Support tools, 319

<httpRequest>, attributes and child elements for, 356

HttpRequestSchema XML schema collection, used by request message, 356

HttpWebRequest object, initialization of, 363

hybrid encryption, advantage of, 260

I

IBatchJob interface, 412

immutable data, 309

implicit reservation, creating, 318

initiator

    configuration of, 472

    configuring the route and security, 546

    setup script to run at, 544–545

initiator at target, information needed for, 302

initiator services

    and contracts, 46

    creating a trust relationship with target service, 481

    creating, 456

    dialog security on, 282–283

    request message sent to RoutingService from, 502–503

initiator side, on SQL Profiler, 522

initiator WebClientService, creating, 357

InitiatorQueue, 29

    processing incoming messages on, 82–83

    writing managed stored procedure for message processing on, 149–150

InitiatorService, 29

    implementing, 401–407

    request message sent to TargetService from, 410

    sending message to TargetService from, 47–53

    WF hosting code for, 402–404

    workflow activities, 402

InitiatorService class, implementing, 149–150

InitiatorService1, definition of, 436

InitiatorService2, definition and conversation priorities, 439–441

inner loop, in receive loop, 172

inside data, messages, 310

InstantiateBatchJob method, implementing, 414

internal activated queue, sending message to, 81–82

internal activation

    checking configuration success, 79

    configuration on initiator side, 83–84

    enabling for TargetQueue, 90–91, 436

    enabling on service queue, 78–79

    function of, 74

    handling launch problems, 539–540

    queue monitor activation of new instance in, 76

    setting up, 77

    setting up queue for, 78–79

internal activation problems, troubleshooting, 538–540

inventory

    updating, 206

    calculating new quantity of, 205

inventory application, implementing, 151–160

Inventory table

    creating and populating, 153–154

    updating, 154–157, 202–203

InventoryRequestMessage message, 202

InventoryService, 184

    getting OrderRequestMessage from OrderService, 202–206

    starting a conversation with, 193–195

InventoryTargetQueue, returned response message in, 160

IServiceBrokerMessageExchange interface, 389

IserviceBrokerMethods interface, 388

JK

KEK. *See* key exchange key (KEK)

Kerberos authentication, SPN registration required by, 254–255

key exchange key (KEK), 276–277

L

letters

    as example of messaging, 5–6

    vs. email, 6

Listener, 15

listener method, 346–347

load balanced Service Broker application, deploying, 471

load balanced Service Broker service
    advantages of, 470
    deploying, 471
    objects you have to deploy, 471
    using for SQL Server scale-out scenario, 470

load balancing
    achieving fault tolerance with, 8
    function of, 461
    Service Broker support for, 470

load-balanced Service Broker service
    advantages of, 470
    deployment of, 471

load-balancing scenario, Service Broker support for, 490

LoadApplicationState stored procedure, implementing, 180–182

LoadState method, implementing, 182, 328–329

LOCAL routes, 272–273

Local Services
    implementing, 390–393
    interfaces for, 388–389
    using, 387–390

locking and transaction management, 163–238

logging database, calling stored procedure from, 96–97

LongWorkloadRequestMessageType, 446

LongWorkloadResponseMessageType, 446

■M

Main method, of external console application, 107–108

MainForm class, user interface of, 341

maintenance, in message applications, 12

managed assembly
    architecture and design of, 131–137
    classes in, 128
    deploying, 145–147, 150–151, 415–416
    for Service Broker objects, 128–131
    implementing activated stored procedure with, 143–148
    registration of new, 419

managed Service Broker client
    implementing, 138
    sending new message to, 138

managed service program
    building, 143–151
    registration of, 370–372

managed stored procedure
    development of with SQLCLR, 326
    processing incoming messages on InventoryTargetService, 154
    processing of Service Broker messages by, 148–149
    registering, 147–148, 155–156
    skeleton of, 177–178

Management Studio templates, 515

marshaled messages, processing, 236–237

match preference table, conversation priority, 439

matched subscribers, sending received article to, 428

MatchRequestFilter method, 361–362

MatchResponseFilter method, 364

MAX_QUEUE_READERS
    configuration of, 85–86
    starting all configured at once with, 119–124

MDAC. See Microsoft Data Access Components (MDAC)

message body, 4

Message class
    function of, 128
    methods for, 130–131

message concepts, for message-based programming, 4–6

message correlation, 26
    in messaging systems, 12

message delivery, provided by Service Broker, 18

message envelope, 4

message exchange
    in Service Broker, 28–29
    sequence diagram of, 217

message flow, sequence of, 34

message forwarder, 481–482

message forwarding
   activating and configuring, 478
   function of, 461
   in Service Broker, 474
   monitoring, 482
   network topology abstraction, 475
   parameters available to configure, 479
   scenarios used for, 474
   security, 475
   setting up, 478
message header, 4
message ordering, in Service Broker, 20
message processing
   basic receive loop for, 222–223
   in Service Broker, 28–29
   in Service Broker programming, 17
message queues, retrieving status of, 80–81
message receiving and state handling, in T-SQL batch, 179–180
message retention
   for complex message processing, 208
   using on OrderQueue, 208–209
message sequencing. *See* sequencing
message sequencing and correlation, in message-based systems, 11–12
message sequencing and ordering, 20
message throughput, controlling, 84–87
message type handling, implementing, 145
message types
   associating with method implementations, 132–133
   changing, 37
   creating for request and response messages, 36
   defining, 36–39, 446
   defining for Service Broker application, 34–36
   deleting existing, 37
   implementing methods for, 131–133
   in Service Broker, 23–24, 34–37
   sent from initiator to target service, 381–382
   validations supported in Service Broker, 23–24
   viewing defined, 36

message types and contract, creation of, 357
message validation, in Service Broker programming, 24
message-based applications, performance considerations for, 29–30
message-based processing, fundamentals of, 3–16
message-based solutions, implementing, 6–7
message-based systems
   fault tolerance for, 7–8
   message sequencing and correlation in, 11–12
   transaction management in, 10–11
message-processing logic,
   implementing, 30, 329
   on initiator side, 61–62
MessageLog table
   definition of, 411–412
   processed message in, 416
MessageReceivedEventArgs class, 389–390
messages
   anatomy of, 4
   creating the body of, 50
   fragmentation of when sending, 241
   inside data, 310
   options if not rolling back current transaction, 63
   process of sending, 240–242
   processing and sending a response, 57
   proving both are sent on same conversation group, 168–169
   received in initiating queue, 61
   received in target queue, 53–54
   receiving sent from a queue, 55–56
   reliable delivery of forwarded, 475
   reliable delivery of in Service Broker, 22
   retrieving and processing, 53–62
   rolling back, 62–63
   routes involved in a distributed Service Broker scenario, 242–244
   sending, 47–53, 309
   sending on [DEFAULT] contract, 50–51
   sending out of priority order, 444–445
   sending over created conversation and committing, 50

sending with priority, 456

steps for processing, 57

structure of, 4

T-SQL batch for processing on target side, 59–61

validation of, 50

message_body column, casting to the XML data type, 106–107

messaging

in daily life, 4–6

problems associated with, 9–12

messaging architectures, for messaging solutions, 12–14

messaging sequence, for HelloWorld application, 34

messaging solutions, using on projects, 6–9

messaging technologies, others available, 14–15

Microsoft Data Access Components (MDAC), used by SQL Server clients, 315–316

Microsoft Network Monitor 3.0, website address for, 290

Microsoft SQL Server 2005 Service Broker. *See* Service Broker

mirror server

function of, 462

restoring the database and log file on, 467

mirrored Service Broker service

creating a route to, 468

sending a message to, 469

modify() method, 315

MSDB routes, setting up, 247

MSMQ

as available messaging technology, 14–15

drawbacks to using, 14–15

maintenance in, 12

transaction handling in, 9

multiple queue readers, in Service Broker, 30

MySampleClassifierComponent stored procedure, 495

N

n-tier and client/server application architectures, problems with, 305

namespace reservation, 318

native web services

for communication between client and service, 315–326

support for SODA, 311

.NET Base-Class Library (BCL), for writing high-performance code, 326

.NET service logic, writing, 327

NetBIOS names, 248–249

network topology abstraction, to other clients, 475

nodes() method, 315

notification subscriptions, troubleshooting, 347–348

O

Object Explorer, 513–514

OnChange event handler, for SqlNotification class, 342–343

OnCustomerInserted database trigger, T-SQL code of, 378–380

OnCustomerInsertedRequestMessage method, 384

OnHttpRequest method, 358–359

OnTimer method, 369

operands, using reference data for, 310

order-entry application, building, 183–215

OrderQueue, message-processing logic for, 190

OrderRequestMessage, 193–196

OrderService

ClientService start of conversation with, 184

computer deployed on, 248

creating route to, 468

deploying into production, 475

deploying to support load-balanced scenario, 472

implementing, 329

problem from changing network address of, 476

processing response messages, 206–210

request message sent by, 199

sending new message to, 186–187

sending request from ClientService to, 522–524

Service Listing document, 298–299

setting up routes to other services from, 250

start of conversation with ShippingService, 184

OrderService.sql script, website address for object definitions in, 185

outer loop

in receive loop, 172

that implements state-processing logic, 187–189

outside data, sending, 309–310

P

parallel activation, for starting configured queue readers, 119–124

parameter substitution, creating, 103

partners, principal and mirror servers functioning as, 462

PendingRequest table, CREATE TABLE T-SQL script for, 365

performance, in Service Broker programming, 17

performance counters, in Service Broker 2008, 513

performance measurements

measuring performance of stored procedures, 223–225

with batched commits, 227

with set-based message processing, 234

permission sets, supported in SQLCLR, 147

permissions, nonadministrative, 318

phone calls. *See* telephone calls

Player, for replaying method calls, 15

poison message event notification, subscribing to, 66

poison messages

defined, 62

error message in Service Broker, 67

event notification of, 68–69

handling of, 66–69

support, 97–98

post-event notification, setting up, 124

PreloadQueue stored procedure, 223–224

principal server, function of, 462

priority table, creating, 450–452

priority-based message processing

configuring Service Broker activation, 456

creating the initiator service, 456

function of, 352

handling of messages in, 445

implementing, 445–459

options, 445

receiving response messages, 458–459

sending messages with priority, 456–458

using, 456–459

priority-based messaging, implementing, 446–459

private key, removing after signing stored procedure, 94

ProcessAccountingRequestMessages stored procedure, 200–201

ProcessBatchJob managed stored procedure, 411–412

ProcessBatchJobTasks method, 415

ProcessConfigurationNoticeRequestMessages stored procedure, 486, 488

ProcessCustomerInsertedClientQueue stored procedure, 382–383

ProcessedEmailMessages table

definition of, 434–435

syntax for, 58

ProcessEndDialogMessages stored procedure, 500–501

ProcessEuropeanCustomers stored procedure, 501–502

ProcessInitiatorQueue stored procedure, 507–510

ProcessInsertedCustomer stored procedure, 383–385

ProcessInsertedCustomers stored procedure, 385

ProcessInventoryQueryRequest method, 157–159

ProcessInventoryRequestMessage stored procedure, 203–205

ProcessInventoryUpdate method, 154–155

ProcessMessages method, of TargetService
    class, 108–109

ProcessOrderMessages stored procedure, 177

ProcessOrderRequestMessage method, 330

ProcessOrderRequestMessages stored
    procedure, 190–193
    implementing compensation logic in,
        217–221

ProcessOrderResponseMessages stored
    procedure, 213–215

ProcessRequestMessages stored procedure
    activated that handles multiple queues,
        101–103
    classifier component to retrieve target
        service, 499
    for redirecting incoming messages,
        506–507
    implementing, 432–434, 498
    writing, 432–435

ProcessResponseMessages stored procedure,
    configuring, 83–84

ProcessShippingRequestMessages stored
    procedure, 210–212

ProcessShippingResponseMessage method,
    335–337

ProcessTargetQueue1 stored procedure,
    168–169

ProcessTargetQueue2 stored procedure,
    168–169

ProductID and Quantity, extracting from
    message, 205

Profiler, events indicating problems, 537

public and private keys (asymmetric keys),
    259–260

public key certificate, 283

public keys, 266–267

publication and subscription management,
    stored procedures for, 425

Publications and Subscriptions tables,
    creating, 422–423

publish-subscribe frameworks, 420–430
    function of, 351

publish-subscribe scenario, defining the
    infrastructure, 421–423

publisher, defined for publish-subscribe
    scenario, 420

publisher logic, applying, 423–428

PublisherService
    contracts support for, 421
    requesting information from, 428

Q

query notification objects, in new database,
    339–340

query notification subscriptions, function of,
    337

query notifications
    based on Service Broker, 337
    callback problems with, 348–349
    implementing, 337–339
    needed in SODA, 337
    registration of query and subscriber into,
        337–338
    setting up Service Broker objects for, 344
    to reduce demands on database server,
        337–350
    troubleshooting, 347–348
    using in middle tier or on Smart Client,
        339
    when to use, 349–350
    when cached data has changed, 312

query() method, using, 313–314

queue
    columns available for, 54
    defining for received message, 41–43

queue monitors
    determining if activation is necessary
        with, 75–76
    listing active in SQL Server instance, 75

queue reader, considerations for using, 76

queue reader management, effect on
    performance, 10

Queued Components, 15

queues
    creating sending and receiving, 42
    in Service Broker, 25
    PreloadQueue stored procedure for
        preloading, 223–224
    processing many with single stored
        procedure, 99–103

Queues table
  activated tasks child table columns, 519–520
  columns in Broker Statistics Report, 518–519
QUEUE_ACTIVATION event notification, 104

■R

Read method, 136
real-world application scenarios, 351–459
receive loop
  nested loops in, 172–173
  performance measurement with a basic, 224–225
  with state handling, 172–173, 176-177
RECEIVE statement
  arguments for, 55
  processing pending messages from a queue with, 54
  processing received message with, 114–115
  syntax for, 55
  using, 446
  using with WAITFOR statement, 56–57
  using with WHERE clause, 176–177
RECEIVE T-SQL statement, sequence of messages retrieved by, 443–445
ReceiveMessage method, of ServiceBrokerImpl class, 398
recovery model, checking of the database, 466
reference data, uses for, 309–311
reliable messaging, achieving fault tolerance with, 7–8
remote service binding (RSB)
  contained by host database initiating service, 277
  creating, 283–284
  encryption and, 289
REMOTE SERVICE BINDING, creating on initiator side, 285
Replace Template Parameters dialog box, in SSMS, 515
request and response messages (SOA), 307
request bindings, for priority-based messaging, 448–450

request message
  basic structure of, 371
  information contained in message sent by client, 409
  sent by client application, 207–208
RequestBindings table, creating, 448
RequestFilter table, structure of, 353–354
RequestMessage, 29
ResolvedConversations table, 494
  inserting conversation mapping into, 499–500
resource data, used internally for a service, 311
response messages
  creating and sending back to OrderService, 199
  implementing, 364
  processing, 333
  processing by OrderService, 206–207
  sending that order can't be processed, 205–206
ResponseFilter table, 354–355
ResponseFilterAction.Error enumeration value, 364
ResponseMessage, 29
RETENTION feature
  enabling on a queue, 209
  using on OrderQueue, 208–209
retry mechanism, function of, 364–371
route configuration, creating, 481
RouteMessages stored procedure, 496–498
routes
  defining for distributed application, 247–248
  function of, 26
  in a distributed Service Broker scenario, 242–244
  managing, 244–246
  scale-out scenarios supported through, 8
  setting up between ClientService and OrderService, 274
  setting up for deploying Service Broker instances, 247–250
  understanding function of, 242–244
  used by Service Broker to send messages, 240

routing
　　algorithm, 244
　　for Service Broker services, 239
　　in Service Broker, 242–244
RoutingInformation table, defining and
　　inserting sample data, 484
RoutingServiceConfig table, 494–495
Run method, 357–358
Runtime mode, troubleshooting diagnostics
　　tool in, 542–543
Rusanu, Remus, 511

█S

SAVE TRANSACTION statement, creating
　　savepoint with, 63
SavePendingRequest method, 364, 366–367
savepoint, creating, 63
SaveState method, 182–183, 329
scheduled tasks, 75
security
　　in Service Broker, 26–28, 247
　　in Service Broker programming, 17
　　setting up between Service Broker
　　　services, 253–267
　　types provided by Service Broker, 26
security configuration
　　at message forwarder, 481
　　for database mirroring, 465
　　on initiator's side, 480
security protocol, used by Service Broker,
　　275–277
SELECT*FROM sys.conversation_endpoints
　　query, rows returned from, 53
SEND and RECEIVE commands, 168
SEND ON CONVERSATION statement, 48–49
　　composing and sending response
　　　message through, 58
SendEndDialogMessage activity, for
　　TargetService, 395
SendOrderRequestMessage stored
　　procedure, 323
SendResponse method, 364

SendResponseMessage activity
　　CallExternalMethodActivity, 402
　　for TargetService, 394
SendShippingRequestMessage method, 333
sent request message, 371
sequence numbers, for message sequencing
　　and ordering, 20
sequenced message, 536
sequencing, in messaging systems, 11
[Serializable] attribute, for
　　MessageReceivedEventArgs class,
　　390
Server Objects node, Service Broker endpoint
　　in, 514
service. See also Service Broker service
　　anatomy of in Service Broker
　　　programming, 17
Service base class, 143
Service Broker. See also SQL Service Broker
　　activation, 73–126
　　activation basics, 73–76
　　administration and configuration,
　　　513–549
　　areas performance benefits provided in,
　　　29–30
　　arguments for reusing conversations, 377
　　as messaging bus in SODA architectures,
　　　312
　　automatic creation of conversation group,
　　　165
　　benefit of one API provided by, 31
　　benefits as messaging platform, 31
　　captured message, 291–293
　　centralized administration tools provided
　　　by, 31
　　combining WF and, 387–390
　　compensation logic with, 215–221
　　configuring routes and changing name of
　　　ClientService, 274
　　conversation group locking in, 11
　　conversations in Service Broker
　　　architecture, 17
　　detecting and dealing with poison
　　　messages, 66–69
　　dialog security, 27–28
　　dialogs, 17–18

implementing activation solutions with, 73–126

implementing infrastructure for SMTP server, 431–432

in action, 33–72

introduction to, 17–31

kinds of activation supported by, 74

lack of monologue support in, 17

locking of conversation groups by, 164

message exchange in, 28–29

message forwarding in, 474

message ordering in, 20

message sent acknowledgment to sender, 536

message sequencing and ordering in, 20

message types, 23–24, 34–37

monologue between publisher and subscriber services, 17

objects created for message exchange, 29

option for message encryption, 287–290

performance statistics, 238

priority-based message processing in, 445–459

queue reader management in, 10

reliable delivery of messages in, 22

reliable messaging provided by, 31

reliable web service requests, 352–459

resending and acknowledgment protocol in, 21–22

retrieving message routing information, 523

running a messaging system based on, 7

scale-out scenarios provided by, 31

security, 26–28

security modes, 253–254

security protocol, 275–277

service programs in, 26

setting up certificate-based transport security with, 261–267

setting up security between distributed services, 253–267

SQL Profiler events, 521

SQL Server Management Studio (SSMS), 513

startup strategies, 74–75

transaction management in, 11, 222–238

transmission queue, 21–22

types of dialog security provided by, 277

types of problems for troubleshooting, 534

using Conversation Priority feature of, 438

using for message-based processing, 3–16

using SOA with, 13

using with database mirroring, 468

vs. MSMQ transaction handling, 9

with managed code, 127–161

workflow-driven solutions, 351, 386–408

workload throttling through, 352, 430–445

Service Broker activation

configuring, 148, 456

disabling for service queue, 84–85

issues addressed by, 74

when it is necessary, 75–76

Service Broker applications

defining, 33–34

error handling, 33, 62–72

HelloWorld, 33

implementing, 33–72

implementing with managed code, 151–160

retrieving and processing messages, 33

sending messages between services, 33

troubleshooting, 534

Service Broker assembly, registering in database, 146

Service Broker client, building managed, 137–142

Service Broker communication, setting up endpoints for, 252–253

Service Broker contracts. *See also* contracts

inability to alter, 41

Service Broker conversation timer, function of, 367–369

Service Broker Diagnostics tool, 540–549

errors in configuration scripts, 547–549

in SQL Server Client Tools, 513

launching, 547

launching in Configuration mode, 540–541

output, 544–549

output message types, 544

run modes, 540

troubleshooting in Configuration mode, 540–541

troubleshooting in Runtime mode, 542

Service Broker dialog timer, function of, 365

Service Broker endpoints

creating and deploying to SQL Server instances, 251–253

message forwarding activated on, 479

information needed for settings, 303

Service Broker forwarder, 27

Service Broker forwarding service, work distribution benefit provided by, 477

Service Broker infrastructure

creating, 380–383, 409–410, 447–448, 492–493

defining, 421–423

for reliable web service calls, 352–357

implementing, 446–448

required customer tables for, 493–494

Service Broker managed assembly. *See* managed assembly

Service Broker message, for ordering items from inventory, 159–160

Service Broker message forwarding. *See* message forwarding

Service Broker messages

captured header, 292–293

header format, 292

information contained in header, 291–292

replaying, 294

Service Broker objects

case sensitivity of, 34

created for message exchange, 29

creating, 531–532

for creating infrastructure, 380–382

management of, 33

message types needed, 356

processing received message, 409

required for order-entry application, 184–185

retrieving information about deployed, 533

using, 356–357

Service Broker programming, advanced distributed, 271–304

Service Broker protocols, in Service Broker conversation, 240

Service Broker request message, sending, 374–375

Service Broker response message, to OrderService from CreditCardService, 293

Service Broker services

anatomy of, 22–23

available in Management Studio after created, 44–45

configuration information, 353–356

creating certificates to establish trust relationship between, 263–266

creating for sample application, 44

creating new, 23

creation of, 357

defining, 43–46

establishing connection between, 297

exchanged message types between, 186

implementing, 331–333

outside data, 309–310

processed messages from, 215

processing of messages in, 25

relationship between for order-entry application, 183–184

revoking rights to connect to SQL Server instance, 267

sending directions defined by, 24

starting conversation with distributed deployed, 258–259

using TCP/IP connections to send messages, 239–240

Service Broker transport security, configuring, 480

Service class

function of, 128

implementing base class constructor of, 131

methods for, 128–129

service interaction data, for communicating between services, 311

Service Listing
  exporting, 297–299
  importing, 300–303
Service Listing document
  importing an initiator service at a target
    service, 301–302
  importing target service to an initiator
    service, 302–303
  starting the import of, 300–303
  XML nodes contained in, 299
Service Listing Import Wizard, deployment
    options provided by, 300–301
Service Listing Manager
  function of, 296–303
  startup screen of, 296
  website address for, 296
Service Listing Manager tool, for security
    setup and configuration, 271
Service Principal Name (SPN), registration of,
    254–255
service program
  batched commit in, 225–227
  implementing for configuration notice
    service, 485
service programs, 26, 148–150
  activation in message exchange, 29
  error handling in, 62–66
  writing to process incoming message,
    383–385
Service-Oriented Architecture (SOA), 12–13
  architectures, 307–308
  data in, 305, 308–311
  emergence of as dominant service-centric
    architecture, 306–307
  features in SQL Server 2008, 305, 311–350
  scaling out, 307
Service-Oriented Database Architecture
    (SODA), 305–350
  evolution of, 305–308
  function of, 13–14, 305
  implementing business functionality in,
    14
  white paper by David Campbell, 13

ServiceBrokerImpl class
  app.config file for, 391–392
  default constructor, 391
  implementing BeginDialog method in,
    392–393
  methods implemented through ADO.NET,
    391
ServiceBrokerInterface, in Samples directory,
    128
ServiceBrokerInterface managed assembly,
    for message processing with state
    handling, 177
ServiceBrokerLocalService class, 390–391
ServiceException class, 128
Services conversation child table, columns in
    Broker Statistics Report, 517–518
Services MMC snap-in, for configuring SQL
    Server service account, 255
Services table, columns in Broker Statistics
    Report, 517
SessionConversations table, definition of,
    377
SessionServiceProcedure stored procedure,
    91–95
set-based message processing, table and
    stored procedure for, 231–234
set-based processing, of incoming messages,
    231–234
SetPriorityRequestMessageType, 446
shipping information, accessing in
    <shipping> node, 208-209
ShippingInformation table, DDL script for,
    210
ShippingRequestMessage, construction of,
    407–408
ShippingResponseMessage method,
    OrderService processing of, 335–337
ShippingResponseMessages
  processing, 212–213
  sending back to ClientService, 213–215
ShippingService
  interaction with, 333–337
  sending final request message to, 209–210
ShippingServiceRequest message, received
    from OrderService, 210

Simple Mail Transfer Protocol (SMTP) server
    accessing in a synchronous way, 431
    creating Service Broker objects for,
        431–432
    target service definition, 432
SimpleQueryNotification application
    creating Products table for, 340–341
    defining member variables for data
        retrieval, 341
    for using query notifications in Smart
        Client application, 340–343
    implementing cmdGetData_Click and Get
        Data methods, 341–342
    user interface of MainForm class, 341
SimpleWorkflowTargetService workflow
    class, 399–400
single log writes, in Service Broker, 30
Smart Client, 352–353
    using web proxy in, 371–376
SOA. *See* Service-Oriented Architecture (SOA)
SOA applications, function of, 306–307
SOA principles, application based on, 306
SOAP request, converting to binary Base64
    format, 373
SODA. *See* Service-Oriented Database
    Architecture (SODA)
SODA service provider, 308
source code, website address for, 454
sp_AddOrUpdatePendingRequest stored
    procedure, 365–366
sp_BackendService stored procedure,
    454–456
sp_BindingGetBackend stored procedure
    implementing, 448–450
    retrieving backend conversation with, 453
sp_BindingGetPeer stored procedure,
    448–449
sp_DequeuePriority stored procedure
    implementing, 451
    message processing, 455–456
    retrieving a conversation group with
        Priority, 454–455
sp_EnqueuePriority stored procedure,
    451–452
sp_executesql, calling to execute T-SQL
    statement, 103

sp_FrontEndService stored procedure, 452
sp_MatchRequestFilter stored procedure,
    355
sp_MatchResponseFilter stored procedure,
    364
sp_MatchResponseFilter stored procedure,
    355
sp_ProcessBatchJobSubmissions, 411
sp_ProcessPublicationRequest stored
    procedure, 425–426
sp_ProcessPublicationRequest stored
    procedure, 425–426
sp_PublisherService stored procedure,
    423–428
sp_PublishPublication stored procedure,
    426–427
sp_RemovePublication stored procedure, 428
sp_SendOnPublication stored procedure,
    427–428
SQL Profiler, 513, 521–522
    generated events on target side, 524
    using, 520
SQL Server
    connecting to through SMO, 531
    creating new database, 532
    retrieving connection information, 531
SQL Server 2005, features in, 13–14
SQL Server 2008
    context connections in, 145
    conversation lock in Activity Monitor of,
        169–170
    endpoints used to configure connection
        points, 240
    HTTP endpoints in, 317
    integration of http.sys kernel-mode driver
        in, 316
    limitation of, 33
    namespace reservation in, 318
    native web services support for SODA, 311
    new XML features in, 58
    query notifications when cached data has
        changed, 312
    queue and service objects created in new
        database, 339
    registration of query and subscriber into
        query notifications, 337–338

SODA features in, 305, 311–350

SQLCLR feature for writing .NET code, 312

using HTTP endpoints for native web services, 316–317

XML support for creating SODA architecture, 311

XML support in, 312–315

SQL Server 2008 database, creating managed stored functions in, 373–374

SQL Server 2008 Surface Area Configuration utility, for activating HTTP endpoints, 317

SQL Server Broker Activation, performance counters for, 525–526

SQL Server Broker Statistics, performance counters for, 526–528

SQL Server Broker TO Statistics, performance counters, 528

SQL Server Broker/DBM Transport, performance counters for, 528–530

SQL Server Client Tools, Service Broker Diagnostics tool in, 513

SQL Server databases, 37

SQL Server instances, creating databases for implementation of services, 249–250

SQL Server logins

adding to master database, 256–257

creating for SQL Server that communicates with you, 255–257

granting CONNECT permission to, 257–258

SQL Server machines, domain user accounts for, 255

SQL Server Management Objects (SMO), 513, 530

SQL Server Management Studio (SSMS), 513

created queues in, 42

for message application maintenance, 12

for SQL Server administrative tasks, 513–525

templates, 514–515

SQL Server objects

for AccountingServiceInstance machine, 249–250

for CreditCardServiceInstance machine, 249

SQL Server service account, configuring, 255

SQL Server Surface Area Configuration utility, 253

SQL Server utility, for activating HTTP endpoints, 317

SQL Server web service, browsing the deployed, 324–325

SQL Service Broker, administration and configuration, 513–549

SQLCLR

advantages of using in SODA, 327

data access library provided by, 327

for integrating .NET runtime into database, 312

permission sets supported in, 147

using in SODA, 326–327

sqlcmd, for message application maintenance, 12

SqlDependency class, 340. *See also* System.Data.SqlDependency class

SqlDependency object, creation of by an application, 340

SqlDependency.OnChange event handler, 348

SqlDependency.Start method, T-SQL code produced by, 348

SqlDependency.Stop method, 348

SqlNotification class, OnChange event handler for, 342–343

SqlNotificationEventArgs class, properties for, 343

SqlNotificationRequest class, 344–347

SqlNotificationRequest object, creating, 344–346

ssbdiagnose.exe, for Client Tools installation, 540

StartDialog stored procedure, 29

startup tasks, function of, 75

state handling

for Service Broker conversations, 170–171

implementing, 328–329

receive loop with, 172–177

with managed stored procedure, 177–215

state variables, initializing to initial state, 189–190

state-processing logic, implementing by
    outer loop, 187–189
state_desc column, possible states for
    conversation stored in, 53
statistics report, launching for Service Broker,
    515–516
Stock Keeping Unit (SKU), resource data
    used for, 311
stored procedures
    calling in another database, 95–99
    changing execution context of, 92–93
    creating certificate for signing, 93
    executing with higher privileges, 95
    for internal activation on target side,
        77–78
    for manipulating content of Priority table,
        451
    for processing incoming messages on
        InitiatorQueue, 82–83
    getting associated queue for current,
        100–101
    measuring performance of, 223–225
    signing, 87–95
    using single to process many queues,
        99–103
    with message-sending logic, 322–323
    writing activated to query for messages to
        process, 100–103
subscriptions
    requesting, 428–429
    troubleshooting, 347–348
symmetric error handling, in Service Broker,
    22
symmetric error messaging, for sent
    messages, 24
symmetric keys, disadvantages of, 260
sys service_message_types catalog view,
    36–37
sys.assemblies catalog view, 147–148
sys.conversation_endpoint catalog view,
    165–166, 490
    columns in, 51–53
sys.conversation_groups catalog view,
    165–166
sys.conversation_priorities catalog view, 441

sys.dm_broker_activated_tasks DMV, 82,
    86–87, 100
sys.dm_broker_forwarded_messages catalog
    view, 482
sys.dm_broker_queue_monitors, 79–80
sys.dm_exec_sessions DMV, 87
sys.dm_qn_subscriptions catalog view, 337
sys.routes table, 241
sys.services catalog view, 44–45
sys.service_contracts catalog view, 39
sys.service_contract_message_usage catalog
    view, 39
sys.service_contract_message_usages
    catalog view, 39–40
sys.service_queues, for activated stored
    procedure, 79
sys.service_queues catalog view, 42–43
sys.transmission_queue catalog view, 443
System Monitor, 525–530
System.Data namespace, 31
System.Data.SqlDependency class, 339–343
System.Data.SqlNotificationRequest class,
    339
System.Messaging namespace, 31

▪T

T-SQL batch, stepping through line-by-line,
    49–50
T-SQL statement
    executing dynamically built, 103
    for reenabling the target queue, 67
T-SQL statements. See individual statement
    names, 72
Tabular Data Stream (TDS) protocol, 315
target
    configuring route and security, 546–547
    setup script for, 545–546
target at initiator, settings for, 302–303
target database, enabling .NET Framework
    execution support in, 385
target queue
    generating high message workload for, 85
    reenabling, 67
    unprocessed messages stored in, 85

target service
    route back to message forwarder from, 482
    sending original request message to, 500
    using [Default] contract on, 46
target side, on SQL Profiler, 524
TargetQueue
    configuring internal activation for, 436
    conversation priorities at, 443
    message-processing stored procedure for, 140–141
    retrieving new message from, 398
    sending email sending requests to, 436–437
    setting up external activation on, 105–106
    the sent message on, 140
TargetService, 29
    creating Service Broker objects for, 393–394
    defining in a class derived from Service base class, 143
    implemented as a workflow, 394
    implementing, 393–401
    implementing message loop of, 396–398
    implementing a more complex, 407–408
    implementing entry point for, 143–144
    sending message from InitiatorService to, 47–53
    sending request message to, 81–82, 400–401
    WF hosting code for, 395–396
    workflow activities, 394–395
TargetService class, ProcessMessages method of, 108–109
Tasks Activations table, 520
telephone calls, as example of messaging, 6
Template Explorer, 513–514
TO SERVICE clause, specifying as string literal, 50
TO SERVICE parameter, 241
tracing
    setting up, 290–291
    starting a new capture and adding a filter, 291

transaction management, 163
    in message systems, 10–11
    in message-based applications, 30
    in Service Broker, 11, 30, 222–238
transaction techniques, improving service program performance with, 222–238
Transmission Control Protocol (TCP), used by Service Broker, 239
transmission queue
    in message exchange, 29
    in Service Broker, 21–22
transmission status
    common errors, 535
    in Service Broker, 534
transmission status column, meaning of blank, 535
transport encryption, configuring, 287–288
transport protocol
    function of, 290–294
    in advanced distributed Service Broker programming, 271
    setting up tracing, 290–291
TRANSPORT routes, 273–275
    configuring in distributed scenario, 274
    configuring in Smart Client scenario, 275
    in Service Broker, 272
    using in Smart Client scenario, 273
transport security, 26–27. *See also* Windows-based transport security
    authentication options, 27
    combinations of ENCRYPTION attribute for, 288
    configuring on initiator's side, 480
    creating new certificate for, 294–295
    setting up, 480
    TRANSPORT route and LOCAL route, 271
    vs. dialog security, 27–28, 275
    wildcard routes, 272
triggers. *See also* asynchronous triggers
    implementing, 377–380
    writing in .NET language with SQLCLR, 327

troubleshooting
    activated procedure, 539–540
    activated stored procedures, 124–125
    connection problems, 537–538
    conversation problems, 534–537
    internal activation problems, 538–540
    query notifications, 347–348
    Service Broker applications, 534
    Service Broker Diagnostics tool, 540–542
TRUSTWORTHY flag, activating during development phase, 95
TRY/CATCH statements, handling of message types in, 62–66
TryWebRequest method, 363–364

U

UML (Unified Modeling Language), website address, 134
UML sequence diagram, when new message is received and processed, 134
Unified Modeling Language. *See* UML (Unified Modeling Language)
unsequenced message, 536
UPDATE statement, 195–196
URL namespaces, reserving, 318
user-defined aggregates, development of, 327
user-defined data types, development of, 326
user-defined functions, development of, 326

V

validation, supported by Service Broker, 23–24
value() method, 314
Visual Studio 2008, Service Broker managed assembly inside, 128

W

WAITFOR statement
    fetching messages from TargetQueue to table variable, 230
    using with GET CONVERSATION GROUP statement, 172
    using with RECEIVE statement, 56–57
WaitForResponseMessage, HandleExternalEventActivity, 402
WCF
    as messaging technology, 15
    channel for Service Broker, 240
web methods, defined, 316
web proxy
    implementing, 357–371
    using in a smart client, 371–376
web service call
    architecture for doing reliable, 352
    retrieving SOAP response from, 375–376
web service helper page, displaying, 372
web service requests, reliable, 351–459
web services
    defined, 316
    describing using WSDL format, 317
    execution of, 360–361
    exposing, 319–325
    using, 325–326
WebProxyService
    communicating with, 357
    service program for, 357
WebProxyService class
    sending the Service Broker request to, 374–375
    stored procedure that acts as service program for, 357
website address
    Apress Source Code/Download area, 331, 454
    Codeplex site, 111
    definitions of objects in OrderService.sql script, 185
    downloading code for Chapter 5, 81
    for query notification information, 350
    information about Network Monitor, 290
    information about UML, 134
    Service Listing Manager tool, 296

WF (Windows workflow foundation),
    combining Service Broker and,
    387–390

WF host process, interaction between Local
    Services and, 387

WF hosting code
    for TargetService, 395–396
    for InitiatorService, 402–404

WF programming model, for building
    workflow-driven solutions, 386–387

WHERE clause, using on spid column, 100

WHILE loop, creating, 222–223

Windows authentication, 254–255

Windows Communication Foundation
    (WCF). *See* WCF

Windows workflow foundation. *See* WF
    (Windows workflow foundation)

Windows-based authentication, in Service
    Broker security, 27

Windows-based transport security, setting
    up, 254–259

witness, in database-mirroring scenario, 462

workload distribution, implementing, 477

workload throttling, 430–445

WSDL document, generated for web service,
    324–325

XYZ

XML data type methods, 193
    function of, 312–313

XML format, support for distributed systems,
    307

XML message, sent to CreditCardService
    service, 293

XML schema collection
    assigning to XML message, 35
    associating with a column, parameter, or
        variable, 312

XML schema collections, defining, 356–357

XML support
    for creating SODA architecture, 311
    in SQL Server 2008, 312–315

XML web services, as messaging technology,
    15

XmlSerializer class, using, 359–360

You Need the Companion eBook

Your purchase of this book entitles you to buy the companion PDF-version eBook for only $10. Take the weightless companion with you anywhere.

We believe this Apress title will prove so indispensable that you'll want to carry it with you everywhere, which is why we are offering the companion eBook (in PDF format) for $10 to customers who purchase this book now. Convenient and fully searchable, the PDF version of any content-rich, page-heavy Apress book makes a valuable addition to your programming library. You can easily find and copy code—or perform examples by quickly toggling between instructions and the application. Even simultaneously tackling a donut, diet soda, and complex code becomes simplified with hands-free eBooks!

Once you purchase your book, getting the $10 companion eBook is simple:

❶ Visit **www.apress.com/promo/tendollars/**.

❷ Complete a basic registration form to receive a randomly generated question about this title.

❸ Answer the question correctly in 60 seconds, and you will receive a promotional code to redeem for the $10.00 eBook.

THE EXPERT'S VOICE™

2855 TELEGRAPH AVENUE │ SUITE 600 │ BERKELEY, CA 94705

Offer valid through 12/23/08.

Printed in the United States
By Bookmasters